A TAX GUIDE FOR AMERICAN CITIZENS IN CANADA

Richard Pound and Max Reed

CARSWELL®

A cataloguing record for this publication is available from Library and Archives Canada.

ISBN 978-0-7798-5364-9

The acid free paper used in this publication meets the minimum requirements of the American National Standard for Information Services — Permanence of Paper for Printed Library Materials. ANSI Z39.48-1984.

Composition: Computer Composition of Canada LP

Printed in Canada by Thomson Reuters.

CARSWELL, A DIVISION OF THOMSON REUTERS CANADA LIMITED

One Corporate Plaza
2075 Kennedy Road
Toronto, Ontario
M1T 3V4

Customer Relations
Toronto 1-416-609-3800
Elsewhere in Canada/U.S. 1-800-387-5164
Fax 1-416-298-5082
www.carswell.com
E-mail www.carswell.com/email

Table of Contents

Introduction 1

1. About This Guide 3
2. How to Use This Guide 5
3. The Basics of Filing a US Income Tax Return: How to File, Who Must File, and Deadlines 9

Part 1 **Simple Solutions** 13

4. You Have Salary Income 15

Part 2 **US Federal Income Tax** 29

5. The Form 1040 31

Part 2A **Personal Information and Family Details** 35

6. Overview of Lines 1–6 37

Part 2B **Calculating Your Income** 45

7. Overview of Lines 7–22 47
8. Interest and Dividend Income 53
9. Selling an Asset 61
10. If You Sold Stocks, Bonds, or US Mutual Funds 71
11. If You Sold Your Home 79
12. Retirement Income 91
13. Income from Rental Property 95
14. The Foreign Earned Income Exclusion and the Foreign Housing Exclusion 109

Part 2C **Calculating Your Adjusted Gross Income** 121

15. Overview of Lines 23–27 123
16. Moving Expenses 127
17. Student Loan Interest Deduction – Line 33 131
18. Tuition Fees Deduction 135

Part 2D **Deductions** 139

19. Overview of Lines 38–42 141
20. Medical and Dental Expenses 147
21. Taxes You Paid 153
22. Mortgage Interest Deduction 157
23. Investment Interest 161
24. Charitable Contributions 165
25. Casualty and Theft Losses 169
26. Employee Expenses/Business Deductions 177
27. Miscellaneous Deductions 187

Part 2E **Calculating How Much Tax You Owe** 189

28. Overview Lines 44 and 56–60 191
29. Figuring How Much Your Tax You Owe 197
30. Estimated Tax 209

Part 2F **Reducing Your Tax Credits** 213
31. Overview of Lines 47–77 215
32. The Foreign Tax Credit 221
33. The Child and Dependent Care Expenses Credit 241
34. Child Tax Credit – Line 51 247
35. Tax Credit for Those Who are Elderly or Disabled – Line 51 251
36. Education Tax Credits 257

Part 3 **State and Local Tax** 269
37. Overview of State and Local Tax 271

Part 4 **US Estate and Gift Tax** 277
38. Overview of Estate and Gift Tax 279

Part 5 **Compliance Issues** 281
39. Overview of Compliance Issues 283
40. Filing Overdue Returns 285
41. If You Have a Canadian RRSP 287
42. If You Own Canadian Mutual Funds 291
43. You Have a TFSA, RESP, or RDSP 305
44. If You Have More Than $10,000 in Non-US Bank Accounts 309
45. If You Have More Than $200,000 in Non-US Assets 313

Part 6 **Dealing with the IRS: If You Get Audited** 321
46. What to do if the IRS Asks for More Information 323

Part 7 **Renouncing Your US Citizenship** 325
47. Overview of How to Renounce Your US Citizenship 327

Appendix 1 **Blank Forms** 337
Appendix 2 **2012 Tax Tables** 401
Appendix 3 **Historical IRS Underpayment Rates** 415
Index 417

INTRODUCTION

1

ABOUT THIS GUIDE

US citizens in Canada have been required to file US tax returns for a long time. Recently, however, this obligation became more pressing. As of January 1, 2013, Canadian banks must enter into information sharing agreements with the IRS. Thus, the IRS will have a lot of your financial information already. There are serious and expensive penalties if you don't file a US return. To give just one example, you may be fined $10,000 for simply failing to report your non-US bank accounts. Since your bank is now obligated to tell the IRS about these accounts, there is little chance of evading the IRS's scrutiny.

Many US citizens living outside the US have never filed a US tax return. It can be a daunting task. This book tries to help you make it as easy as possible. We translate tax jargon into ordinary language. We offer step-by-step instructions for every form you will likely have to fill out. Blank copies of those forms are included in Appendix 1 of this guide.

Unfortunately, there is no tax software that offers an easy solution. Canadian tax software is not designed to complete US tax returns. And US tax software does not offer some of the unique wrinkles that apply to US citizens in Canada. Nor does it translate US tax concepts into language familiar to Canadian residents.

We welcome your feedback on this guide. Please send it to:
ustaxesforcanadians@gmail.com

IRS Circular 230 Disclosure

To ensure compliance with requirements imposed by the IRS, we inform you that any US federal tax advice contained in this publication is not intended or written by the authors to be used, and cannot be used by you or any taxpayer for the purpose of avoiding any penalties that may be imposed on you or any other person under the Internal Revenue Code.

Publication does not give legal advice

This publication does not necessarily deal with every important topic or cover every aspect of the topic with which it deals. It provides general information rather than legal advice that is specific to your situation. You should always verify your specific situation with the relevant IRS publication and/or a tax professional.

2

HOW TO USE THIS GUIDE

This chapter explains how to use this guide.

1. WHO IS THIS BOOK FOR?

This book is designed for the US citizen in Canada who is not self-employed. We do not cover self-employment. If you are self-employed, you should have your tax returns prepared by a professional accountant. Equally, this book is not for those who have really complicated tax situations. We do not address such topics as partnerships, trusts, closely held corporations, farming income, business income, or a number of other advanced topics.

We do not provide specific legal advice. Instead, we explain the way things generally work. Your particular situation may be different, so if something here doesn't quite fit right, we encourage you to consult a tax professional such as an accountant or a lawyer. Further, it is impossible to cover everything. There are a lot of topics and sub-topics that this guide omits. You should always check the Internal Revenue Service (IRS) publications or consult a tax professional if you have questions.

2. OVERVIEW OF THIS BOOK

In addition to this introduction, this book has seven parts.

Part 1 offers a simple solution to those who only earn salary income. If you qualify to use it, it will explain from start to finish how to fill out your tax return.

Part 2 is the bulk of the book. It walks you through the Form 1040, the income tax return that all US citizens are required to file, line by line. It has six sub-parts. Each sub-part covers a different portion of Form 1040. The sub-parts are introduced by a line-by-line overview of the different parts of the Form. Once you know what topics apply to you, you should consult the more in-depth chapters that follow the overview. The six sub-parts are as follows:

- Part 2A shows you how to list your personal and family details;
- Part 2B shows how to compute and list your total income;
- Part 2C deals with adjustments to your total income;
- Part 2D concerns deductions you can claim;
- Part 2E tells you how to calculate how much tax you owe;
- Part 2F informs on how to reduce this tax owing using available tax credits.

Part 3 is an overview of US state and local taxes. You will probably not owe these taxes but this chapter instructs you how to ensure that you are not treated as a resident by a US state.

Part 4 introduces US estate and gift tax. You will have to pay estate tax if upon your death your total estate (wherever located) is worth over $5 million.

Part 5 deals with compliance issues. As a holder of non-US bank accounts, you likely have to disclose your accounts and the amounts they contain to the IRS. Plus, if you have one or more common Canadian accounts, such as an RRSP, TFSA, or RESP, these give rise to their own special reporting obligations.

Part 6 surveys what to do if you get audited or if the IRS asks for more information.

Finally, Part 7 instructs you how to renounce your US citizenship.

3. HOW TO START

This is a big book with lots of information. It can be overwhelming. We've tried to make it as digestible as possible. Each part starts with an overview and is then followed by more detailed chapters. The in-depth chapters are designed to walk you through particular topics step-by-step and end with an example. So, you should work through each individual chapter as necessary.

Here is how we suggest you start out.

a. Start tax season by filing your Canadian return first. Convert all of the amounts to US dollars using the instructions in Chapter 2. Or you can do this as you progress through the book.

b. Take out the blank Form 1040 from Appendix 1. You can also use this book in conjunction with www.freefillableforms.com. This website has online versions of all the forms discussed in this book.

c. Read the introduction to Part 1 to see if you can make use of the simple solution.

d. If not, fill out your personal details on the top of the Form 1040 according to the instructions in Chapter 6.

e. You have to report all of your income. Read Chapter 7 to learn what income is.

f. Consult the more in-depth Chapters (8–14) in Part 2(b) to learn how to report that income.

g. Repeat the process of reading the overview and, as necessary, consulting the more in-depth chapters for the rest of Part 2.

h. Consult Part 3 to make sure you don't have to pay state or local taxes.

i. Read the overview to Part 5 to see if you have to file any compliance forms. Fill out and file those compliance forms.

j. File your tax return using the instructions in Chapter 3.

4. TAX SOFTWARE

You may use software like U-File or Turbo Tax to fill out your Canadian taxes. As of the date of writing, there was no software designed for US citizens in Canada. There is software that helps Americans file their tax returns, but we think this makes things more confusing.

There is, however, a great website called Free Fillable Forms which you can access at www.freef-illableforms.com. It has electronic copies of all of the forms discussed in this book. It will also do many of the calculations for you. You can use it in conjunction with the instructions in this book and do your taxes electronically instead of by hand.

5. IMPACT ON CANADIAN RETURN

Many readers will ask what impact meeting their US tax obligations will have on their Canadian tax obligation. The answer is: very little. In fact, you should always start out tax season by preparing your Canadian return first. Most US citizens in Canada will not owe any US tax. As this guide explains, the US offers its citizens abroad very generous exclusions and deductions. If, however, you do owe money to the IRS, you can use the Canadian foreign tax credit to offset this.

6. EVERYTHING MUST BE IN US DOLLARS

All amounts in this book are in US dollars. Likewise, all amounts you put on any form you send to the IRS must be in US dollars. You must convert Canadian dollar amounts into US dollars using the instructions in Chapter 3.

7. IRS PUBLICATIONS AND FORMS

Throughout this guide, we often refer to IRS publications from which we have borrowed many examples, explanations, and lists. We have also examples of the various tax forms you will need to fill out. All forms and publications are available at www.irs.gov. Blank copies of the forms are available in Appendix 1.

8. PROFESSIONAL TAX ADVICE

Occasionally in this guide, we will suggest that if your tax matters are particularly complicated, you seek professional tax advice. At present, we do not have a list of accountants in Canada who professionally prepare US tax returns.

9. CHANGES IN THE LAW

We have done our best to keep this book up to date. As of publication, it is current for tax year 2012. But major tax changes may happen at any time so do not rely on it for tax years after 2012.

10. FEEDBACK

If you have feedback for the authors on how to improve future editions of this book, please send them to ustaxesforcanadians@gmail.com. We may not have time to reply but we really appreciate your feedback.

3

THE BASICS OF FILING A US INCOME TAX RETURN: HOW TO FILE, WHO MUST FILE, AND DEADLINES

This chapter sets out the basics of who must file, how to file, and when to file.

1. ALL US CITIZENS MUST FILE A RETURN

Simply put, all US citizens and US-resident aliens (permanent residents) must file a tax return. You are automatically a US citizen if you were born in the United States or if you became a US citizen by naturalization. Children born to US citizens abroad also usually become US citizens. The following United States Customs and Immigration Service website tells you if your child is eligible for citizenship: http://www.uscis.gov/portal/site/uscis/citizenship. Most people, however, know whether they are US citizens. What they may not know is how to file their tax returns to comply with those obligations.

2. IF YOU DO NOT EARN A LOT OF MONEY YOU MAY NOT HAVE TO FILE A RETURN

People who are normally required to file a US return, but who have low incomes, may be able to avoid filing a return. If you fall into one of the following categories and earn less than the amount listed you will not have to file a return.

Filing Status	Amount (US dollars)
Single	9,500
Single and 65 or older	10,950
Head of household	12,200
Head of Household and 65 or older	13,650
Qualifying widow(er)	15,300
Qualifying widow(er) and 65 or older	16,450
Married filing jointly	19,000
Not living with spouse at end of year	3,700
One spouse 65 or older	20,150
Both spouses 65 or older	21,300
Married filing separately	3,700

The various filing statuses are explained in Chapter 6. Most people, however, earn more money than this and will, therefore, have to file a return.

3. WHEN TO FILE YOUR RETURN

All US tax returns must normally be postmarked by April 15. If you owe money to the IRS, it must be paid by this date. It is always a good idea to try and file your return by this date. However, US citizens in Canada are entitled to an automatic 2 month extension. That means that your return would be due June 15. To qualify for this extension you must attach a statement to your Form 1040 explaining your situation. Normally, this need only be a letter listing your permanent address outside of the United States or Puerto Rico. Be aware, however, if you owe money and use this extension you will have to pay interest from April 15 onwards.

You can also benefit from an automatic additional four-month extension. To take advantage of this, you should either file either an electronic or paper copy of Form 4868 (found in Appendix 1). Again, be aware that if you take advantage of this extension you and you owe money you will have to pay interest from April 15 onwards.

You can request a further two-month extension on top of the two- and four-month ones. Unlike those discussed above, this extra two-month extension is discretionary. That means you have to write to the IRS by October 15 of the tax year in which you are filing and explain why you need it. Letters requesting this additional extension should be sent to the following address:

Department of the Treasury
Internal Revenue Service Center
Austin, TX 73301-0045

You can also get an extension to help you for the "foreign earned income exclusion." This exclusion allows you essentially to exclude US $95,100 of your salary income from tax. It is explained further in Chapter 14, but for now it is sufficient to say that it is probably the most important deduction available to US citizens in Canada. Your filing date can be postponed until 30 days after the time period required to qualify for the extension.

To get the extension you must meet three criteria:

1. You are a US citizen or resident alien.
2. You will qualify for the foreign income exclusion by virtue of the "bona fide residence" test or the "physical presence" residence test but will not satisfy these tests until after the normal filing deadline. For now, don't worry about these two tests. They are explained in Chapter 14.
3. Your tax home (essentially your place of residence) is in a foreign country for the entire period that you wish to use to meet either of these tests.

4. WHAT TO FILE

The basic return for individuals is IRS Form 1040. Depending on your individual circumstances, you will have to attach one or more forms to it. The purpose of this book is to explain what to do and how to do it.

5. HOW TO FILE

The best way to file is to follow the step-by-step instructions in this book and fill out the forms by hand or online at www.freefilefillableforms.com. Traditionally, paper copies of tax returns were filed. Hard copies can still be sent to the IRS at two different addresses.

1) If you are not including a cheque or money order send your return to:

Department of the Treasury
Internal Revenue Service Center
Austin, TX 73301-0215 USA

2) If you are including a cheque or money order send it to:

Internal Revenue Service Center
P.O. Box 1303
Charlotte, NC 28201-1303 USA

Like Canadian tax returns, US returns can also be filed electronically (e-filed). If you use the Free Fillable Forms website it will let you e-file your return.

You can pay any money you owe electronically via the following services.

Service Provider	**Telephone** (English and Spanish)	**Website**	**Convenience Fees** (Credit Card Option)	**Convenience Fees** (ATM/Debit Card Option)	**Customer Service Number**
WorldPay US, Inc.	1-888-9-PAY-TAX™ (1-888-972-9829)	payUSAtax.com	1.89%[3]	$3.49	1-888-877-0450 (live operator) 1-877-517-4881 (automated, 24/7)
	1-855-9-PAY-TAX™ (1-855-972-9829)	ValueTaxPayment.com	2.29%[3]	$3.49	1-888-877-0450 (live operator) 1-877-517-4881 (automated, 24/7)
Official Payments Corporation	1-888-UPAY-TAX™ (1-888-872-9829)	officialpayments.com/fed	2.35%[3]	$3.95[2]	1-877-754-4413
Link2Gov Corporation	1-888-PAY1040™ (1-888-729-1040)	PAY1040.com Businesstaxpayment.com	2.35%[3]	$3.89	1-888-658-5465

Note that only certain payments can be made electronically. No payment in excess of $100,000 may be made online unless the WorldPay service is used in which case the limit is $500,000.

Only payments related to Form 1040, 1040 EZ, or Form 4868 or 5329 may be made online.

6. CURRENCY CONVERSION

Finally, you should note that all dollar amounts discussed in this text are in US dollars. This is because all of the rules regarding US taxes are expressed in US dollars. It will not surprise you to learn that the IRS requires you to list all amounts on any and all forms in US dollars. But if you live and work in Canada much of your income is likely in Canadian dollars. So you will need to convert these amounts.

Fortunately the currency conversion process is fairly straightforward. The IRS has no official exchange rate. As long as you use a posted exchange rate consistently there should be no problems. The IRS suggests, but does not require, that you use an average rate if you receive income throughout the year. The following is the average exchange rates for prior years. The IRS publishes the updated figure on its website. The 2012 figure was not available at the time of publication.

2011	2010	2009	2008	2007	2006
1.029	1.072	1.187	1.109	1.117	1.180

To convert from Canadian to US dollars, divide the Canadian amount by the applicable yearly average exchange rate in the above table. So in 2011 $1,000 Canadian was, on average, worth $970 US.

To convert from US dollars to Canadian multiply the US dollar amount by the applicable yearly average exchange rate in the table above. In 2011 $1,000 US was, on average, worth $1,029 Canadian.

While exchange rates do vary throughout the year, it makes sense to simply use the average rate for something like salary income instead of calculating it on a weekly or bi-weekly basis and computing your own average. This saves a lot of time, even though it may not result in the most favourable outcome. If you have a significant income or expense that occurred on a particular day, you can use the exchange rate from that day instead of the yearly average. The IRS suggests the following websites for daily rates:

www.oanda.com
www.xe.com
www. x-rates.com

PART 1

SIMPLE SOLUTION

YOU HAVE SALARY INCOME

This part identifies a simple solution that will easily allow many US citizens in Canada to meet their filing obligations. You can only use the solution presented here if you meet all of the following criteria:

- Earn less than $95,100 as a single person, or $190,200 as a married couple, in total income that comes from salary, commissions, bonuses, professional fees or tips. In Canada this type of income is reported on a T4 form.
- Do not have any other type of income. This includes pensions, royalties, rental income, capital gains, gambling winnings, alimony, social security benefits or from self-employment. If you have any other type of income than salary income you should not use this solution.
- Live outside of the United States for at least 330 days of the year or can establish that have lived in Canada for more than a year and intend to permanently reside here.
- You can have an RRSP. If you do, you will need to file a special form to have the IRS treat your RRSP like the Canadian government does. Please consult Chapter 41 if you have an RRSP.

We will show you how to fill out Form 1040 and Form 2555-EZ. We explain these forms below and give you an example of how to fill out each one. Be warned that even if you make use of the simple solution presented here, you will still have to consult Part 5 to see if any of the compliance issues apply to you.

1. INTRODUCTION TO THE FORM 1040

All US citizens in Canada are required to file Form 1040 in respect of each tax year. A blank copy of Form 1040 is included in Appendix 1. It is the standard form for all individuals. You should start your tax return by filling out the first part of it. Let's see what that looks like.

Form **1040** Department of the Treasury—Internal Revenue Service (99)
U.S. Individual Income Tax Return **2011** OMB No. 1545-0074 IRS Use Only—Do not write or staple in this space.

For the year Jan. 1–Dec. 31, 2011, or other tax year beginning , 2011, ending , 20 — See separate instructions.

Your first name and initial | Last name | **Your social security number**

If a joint return, spouse's first name and initial | Last name | **Spouse's social security number**

Home address (number and street). If you have a P.O. box, see instructions. | Apt. no. | ▲ Make sure the SSN(s) above and on line 6c are correct.

City, town or post office, state, and ZIP code. If you have a foreign address, also complete spaces below (see instructions).

Foreign country name | Foreign province/county | Foreign postal code

Presidential Election Campaign Check here if you, or your spouse if filing jointly, want $3 to go to this fund. Checking a box below will not change your tax or refund. ☐ **You** ☐ **Spouse**

Filing Status

Check only one box.

1 ☐ Single
2 ☐ Married filing jointly (even if only one had income)
3 ☐ Married filing separately. Enter spouse's SSN above and full name here. ▶
4 ☐ Head of household (with qualifying person). (See instructions.) If the qualifying person is a child but not your dependent, enter this child's name here. ▶
5 ☐ Qualifying widow(er) with dependent child

Exemptions

6a ☐ **Yourself.** If someone can claim you as a dependent, **do not** check box 6a
b ☐ **Spouse**
c **Dependents:**

(1) First name Last name	(2) Dependent's social security number	(3) Dependent's relationship to you	(4) ✓ if child under age 17 qualifying for child tax credit (see instructions)
			☐
			☐
			☐
			☐

If more than four dependents, see instructions and check here ▶ ☐

d Total number of exemptions claimed

Boxes checked on 6a and 6b
No. of children on 6c who:
• lived with you
• did not live with you due to divorce or separation (see instructions)
Dependents on 6c not entered above
Add numbers on lines above ▶

The boxes for name and address are self-explanatory. The two complicated items on this part of the form are the Social Security Number and filing status. Let's take them in turn.

2. SOCIAL SECURITY NUMBER

The Social Security Number is the American equivalent of the Canadian Social Insurance Number (SIN). It identifies a particular taxpayer to the IRS. If you do not have a Social Security Number, you should apply for one. You must provide the Social Security Administration with proof of your US citizenship, your age, and your identity. To get a SSN you should:

1. Gather your proof of citizenship. These include a US passport, Certificate of Naturalization, or Certificate of Citizenship.
2. Present your birth certificate.
3. If you are 12 or older, you have to appear in person for an interview and prove that you did not ever receive a Social Security Number. The following documents are examples of how to do this:
    - o A current or previous passport, school and/or employment records, and any other record that would show long-term residence outside the United States could be used to show you do not have a Social Security number.
4. Gather proof of identity. An acceptable document must be current (not expired) and show your name, identifying information (date of birth or age), and preferably a recent photograph. For example, as proof of identity Social Security must see your:
    - US driver's licence;
    - State-issued non-driver identification card; or
    - US passport;
    - Employee ID card;
    - School ID card;
    - Health insurance card (not a Medicare card); or
    - US military ID card.
5. Once you have assembled this documentation, you should fill out form SS-5Fs (included in Appendix 1) and send it to either the US Embassy in Ottawa or your nearest US consulate. The list of US consulates is below.

Office Location	Region Served	Contact information
Ottawa	Eastern Ontario (Kingston, Lanark, Leeds, Prescott, Renfrew, Russell and Stormont); and those parts of the Québec regions of Outaouais and Abitibi-Témiscamingue near Ottawa.	490 Sussex Drive Ottawa, Ontario Telephone (General): 613-688-5335 Telephone (Emergency): 613-238-5335 E-mail (Consular Section): ottawacons@state.gov
Vancouver	British Columbia and Yukon Territory	1075 West Pender Street Vancouver, British Columbia V6E 2M6 Telephone (General): 604-685-4311 Telephone (Emergency): 604-685-4311 E-mail (Citizen Services): vancouverACS@state.gov

Office Location	Region Served	Contact information
Calgary	Alberta, Saskatchewan, Manitoba and Northwest Territories	615 Macleod Trail, S.E. Suite 1000 Calgary, Alberta T2G 4T8 Phone: (403) 266-8962
Toronto	Ontario (except for areas east of Kingston, which are included in the Ottawa consular district)	360 University Ave. Toronto, Ontario M5G 1S4 Fax (Citizen Services): 416-595-6501 Phone (General): 416.595.1700 E-mail (general US passport, notarial or citizenship inquiries): TorontoPassport@state.gov
Montreal	Greater Montreal and the regions of southern Quebec province (Laurentides, Lanaudiere, Laval, Montreal, Montregie, Estrie, and the southern parts of Centre-du-Quebec); including Drummondville	315 Place d'Youville, Suite 500 Montréal, Québec H2Y 0A4 Phone (General): 514-398-9695 Email: montreal-ACS@state.gov
Quebec City	Those regions of Quebec province to the north and east of the Montreal and Ottawa Districts (indicated above), plus the territory of Nunavut	2 Place Terrasse Dufferin (Vieux Quebec, behind Château Frontenac) Québec, Québec G1R 4T9 Telephone (General): 418-692-2095 E-mail (Citizen Services): quebecniv@state.gov
Halifax	Atlantic Canada (New Brunswick, Newfoundland, Nova Scotia and P.E.I.) and the French islands of St. Pierre & Miquelon.	Suite 904, Purdy's Wharf Tower II 1969 Upper Water Street Halifax, NS B3J 3R7 Phone (General): (902) 429-2480

3. GETTING AN INDIVIDUAL TAXPAYER IDENTIFICATION NUMBER (ITIN)

American citizens must apply for a Social Security Number. Those who aren't citizens, such as a spouse of a US Citizen living in Canada who is not a US citizen, should apply for an Individual Taxpayer Identification Number (ITIN) if you want them to take advantage of the foreign earned income exclusion (explained below).

To get an ITIN you should fill out Form W-7 (in Appendix 1) and send it along with certified copies of:

- Proof of identity (e.g., a driver's licence or passport)
- Proof of foreign nationality (e.g., a birth certificate or passport)
- A letter explaining the reason why an ITIN number is being requested

Mail the completed Form W-7 application together with the certified copies of the documents to:

Internal Revenue Service
ITIN Operation
P.O. Box 149342
Austin, TX 78714-9342

4. FILING STATUS

Filing status describes your current family situation. In general, your filing status, or family situation, will affect how much tax you pay.

There are 5 options presented on Form 1040: single, married filing jointly, married filing separately, head of household, and qualifying widow(er). You should select the status that applies as of December 31 of the year for which you are filing your tax return (December 31, 2012 for a 2012 return).

Let's review each option.

1) *Single*. As it implies, this is for people who have never married or whose divorce is final.

2) *Married filing jointly*. You can select this status if you were married at the end of the year for which you are filing returns (December 2012 for a 2012 return). Or you can select this option if your spouse died during the year for which you are filing and you did not remarry during that year. To be eligible to file joint returns, heterosexual couples may be either legally married or in a common-law relationship. Common-law relationship is defined by the law of the province in which you live. Note that the definition of marriage remains controversial in the United States. As of the date of publication, the IRS only recognizes marriages between a man and a woman. Gay couples, even if they may be legally married in Canada, are not eligible to file joint US returns.

3) *Married filing separately*. This status simply means that you are married but have chosen to file separate US returns.

If both spouses are US citizens, and therefore both are required to file returns, the decision to file jointly or separately is strategic. In general, most married couples file jointly. The reasons are as follows. Your taxable income is calculated based on your entire income as a couple. You will most likely pay a lower tax rate than married couples who file separately. Other benefits of filing jointly include: 1) less time and cost to file a return and 2) certain tax credits are only available to married couples filing jointly. In short, unless you have professional tax advice to the contrary, our experience is that joint filing is likely to be the most beneficial. Concretely, this means that the names of both individuals go on Form 1040 and both their incomes and deductions are reported on the same form.

However, many US citizens in Canada are married to persons who are not US citizens. If this is the case, you can choose to treat your spouse as a US citizen. This will allow you to claim a larger foreign earned income exclusion as a couple. But this choice also means that all of your spouse's income will be exposed to US tax. The choice is discussed more under Section 5 below.

4) *Head of household status*. This status is for unmarried individuals who support dependents such as children or elderly parents. It entitles you to certain deductions normally not available to single people. To qualify for this status you must meet the following criteria:

   - Be unmarried, legally separated, or married to a person who is not a US citizen or permanent resident.

and

- You paid over half the expenses of keeping up a home that was the main home of your parent/grandparent for all of the tax year. Your parent/grandparent does not have to live with you.

or

- You paid half the expenses for a home in which one of your dependent lives. The qualifications for a dependent are explained in Chapter 6.

The cost of keeping a house includes expenses such as rent, mortgage interest, real estate taxes, insurance on the home, repairs, utilities, and food consumed in the home.

Head of household status provides tax advantages to US citizens in Canada who are married to a non-US citizen. If you are married to someone who is not a US citizen, and you do not choose to treat them as a US citizen for tax purposes (described more below), you may be apt to claim the head of household status. All of the details of head of household status are explained in IRS Publication 501. If you have any doubts as to your eligibility to claim the head of household status, you should review publication 501 in detail.

5) *Qualifying widow(er) with dependent child.* To qualify for this status the following conditions apply:

   - Your spouse died in the two years prior to the one for which you are filing a return and you did not remarry before the end of that year. For instance, if you are filing a 2012 return your spouse died in either 2010 or 2011 and you did not remarry before the end of 2012.
   - The child who you claim as a dependent lived with you for the entire tax year for which you are filing a return.
   - You paid for more than half the expenses of keeping a home (explained below).

IRS Publication 501 fully explains all of the nuances of qualifying widow(er) with dependent child. If you have questions about this status you can learn more in that publication.

5. ELECTING TO TREAT YOUR SPOUSE AS A US CITIZEN

If you are married to someone who is not a US citizen, your spouse would not normally have to pay US taxes. But if it is advantageous to you, and your spouse agrees, you can choose to treat your spouse as a US citizen. This choice is called an election. There are some advantages to this.

First, both spouses can claim the foreign earned income exclusion (discussed below) of up to $190,200 of combined income. Second, you will be able to take advantage of the tax advantages available to married couples who file jointly. The big disadvantage is that your spouse's income is subject to US income tax to which it would not otherwise be subject. A simple example illustrates this concept.

Fred is a US citizen who lives in Montreal. Joanne, his wife, was born in Canada and is not a US citizen. Fred has a salary of $100,000 and no other types of income. Joanne earns a salary of $50,000 and also has no other types of income. Normally, Fred is obliged to file a US tax return but Joanne is not. However, both can choose to treat Joanne as a US citizen for tax purposes. That means that they would file a joint return that lists their total income of $150,000. Both can take advantage of the foreign earned income exclusion and exclude up to $190,200 as non-taxable. Had Fred not chosen to file a joint return with Joanne, he would have had to find other deductions to avoid paying tax on the $5,000 not covered by his foreign earned income exclusion. So for Fred and Joanne it would be advantageous to elect to treat Joanne as a US citizen.

As this example shows, the election makes sense if the US citizen spouse earns substantially more than the non-US citizen spouse. That way the US citizen spouse can take advantage of the extra foreign earned income exclusion. If the situation is reversed and the non-US citizen spouse earns much more than the US citizen spouse, it would probably be unwise for the US citizen spouse to make this election. Similarly, it may be unwise if the non-US citizen spouse has significant income from a non-salary source, since this type of income is not covered by the foreign earned income exclusion and would end up being unnecessarily taxed in the US.

Note that if you want to treat your spouse as a US citizen, your spouse must obtain an ITIN using the procedure outlined above in section 3. Alternatively, if you have dependents and you do not elect to treat your spouse as a US citizen, you can claim the head of household status. If you have no dependents, file as a single person.

6. EXEMPTIONS – LINE 6(A) AND 6(B)

If your filing status is single, married filing separately, head of household, or qualified widow(er) with children, you should only check box 6(a). However, you cannot check box 6(a) if someone else (such as a parent, if you are young) claims you on their return as a dependent. If you are married and filing jointly you should check both box 6(a) and 6(b).

7. DEPENDENTS – LINE 6(C)

A dependent is someone, such as children or elderly parents, who relies on you for financial support. Under the solution outlined in this chapter, you do not need to worry about whether your children qualify as dependents. All you need to do is simply list their names on line 6. You do not need to worry about whether you can take the exemption for them or not.

This concludes the discussion of how to complete the first part of Form 1040.

8. THE SECOND PART OF THE FORM 1040 – LISTING YOUR INCOME

We now turn to the second part – where you list your income.

Income				
Attach Form(s) W-2 here. Also attach Forms W-2G and 1099-R if tax was withheld.	7	Wages, salaries, tips, etc. Attach Form(s) W-2	7	
	8a	**Taxable** interest. Attach Schedule B if required	8a	
	b	**Tax-exempt** interest. **Do not** include on line 8a — 8b		
	9a	Ordinary dividends. Attach Schedule B if required	9a	
	b	Qualified dividends — 9b		
	10	Taxable refunds, credits, or offsets of state and local income taxes	10	
	11	Alimony received	11	
	12	Business income or (loss). Attach Schedule C or C-EZ	12	
If you did not get a W-2, see instructions.	13	Capital gain or (loss). Attach Schedule D if required. If not required, check here ▶ ☐	13	
	14	Other gains or (losses). Attach Form 4797	14	
	15a	IRA distributions — 15a — b Taxable amount	15b	
	16a	Pensions and annuities — 16a — b Taxable amount	16b	
	17	Rental real estate, royalties, partnerships, S corporations, trusts, etc. Attach Schedule E	17	
Enclose, but do not attach, any payment. Also, please use **Form 1040-V.**	18	Farm income or (loss). Attach Schedule F	18	
	19	Unemployment compensation	19	
	20a	Social security benefits — 20a — b Taxable amount	20b	
	21	Other income. List type and amount	21	
	22	Combine the amounts in the far right column for lines 7 through 21. This is your **total income** ▶	22	

Since this solution only deals with salary, commissions, bonuses, professional fees or tips what is most important to us is line 7. You will note that line 7 mentions a W-2 form. This is the American equivalent of the T4 form that most Canadians receive from their employer. Most likely you will not receive a W-2 form. Instead, you should take the number from box 14 on your T4, convert it to US dollars (as discussed in Chapter 3) and enter that amount on line 7. Taxable benefits such as travel benefits are included in box 14 of your T4 form, so there is no need to worry about those.

9. THE FOREIGN EARNED INCOME EXCLUSION – EXCLUDING YOUR INCOME FROM US TAX

The US government allows US citizens abroad to take advantage of a significant tax break. The foreign earned income exclusion allows you to shelter a sizeable chunk of your salary from US tax without having to worry about other more complex tax credits.

The amount of the exclusion you can claim is calculated on Form 2555-EZ and then listed on line 21 of Form 1040. The maximum excludable amount increases every year. For 2012 it is $95,100 for a single person and $190,200 for a couple filing jointly.

10. ELIGIBILITY FOR THE FOREIGN EARNED INCOME EXCLUSION

To be eligible for the foreign earned income exclusion you must satisfy all three of the following criteria:

- Your income must come from salaries, wages, commissions, bonuses, professional fees or tips earned in Canada (or any other country than the United States). For our present purposes, this is the only type of income that is excludable.

Note: If you have other types of income, you cannot use the solution presented in this chapter.

- Canada must be your tax home. This generally means that you live in and pay taxes on that income in Canada.
- You meet either the bona fide residence test or the physical presence test (described below).

Type of income

Not all types of income qualify for the foreign earned income exclusion. If you have other types of income, do not attempt to follow the solution presented in this chapter.

Tax home outside of the United States

This stage of the test will not be a problem for most US citizens residing in Canada. To meet it, you must show that you are normally an employee at a place outside the United States (Canada for most people).

Bona fide residence test

Meeting the bona fide residence test is one way to establish your eligibility for the foreign earned income exclusion. Generally, you have to be able to prove that you were a resident of Canada for an uninterrupted period of time that includes at least one entire tax year (January to December). Aside from this, there are few hard and fast rules. Residency is based on intention to reside in a particular place. It is evaluated through words and acts. Each situation is analyzed on its own merits as a question of fact. So, the question you have to be prepared to answer is whether you can demonstrate that your true place of residence, for more than a year, is Canada. For most people who have been in Canada for many years, this will not be a problem. If you have doubts about whether you will meet this test, you should consult a tax professional who can give you advice that is unique to your own situation. Note that, if at any time, you tell the government of Canada that you are not a resident of Canada, then you will not meet this test. Taking a vacation in the US or elsewhere will not change this determination.

The physical presence test

The other way to show that you are eligible for the foreign earned income exclusion is the physical presence test. You can meet the physical presence test if you are outside the United States for 330 days during a 12-month period. It is important to note that it does not matter which country you are in as long as it is not the United States. A day is defined as a full 24-hour period that starts at midnight. The 330-day period does not have to be consecutive. That means you can visit the United States for a week or two and still meet the test.

Try to qualify for both tests

To claim the foreign earned income exclusion, you need to meet only one of the tests set out above. But we suggest filling out both sections of the Form 2555-EZ to ensure that you are able to claim the exemption.

If you are married and filing jointly

We mentioned above that you can elect to treat your spouse as a US citizen in order to claim a larger foreign earned income exclusion. The only wrinkle is that, if you do this, both spouses must meet the test for the foreign earned income exclusion. That means that they must both have their tax home in Canada and qualify under either the bona fide residence test or the physical presence test.

Let's use an example to explain this. Joe is a US citizen who lives in Winnipeg. He has been living there for several years. Maggie, his wife, was born in Canada and is not a US Citizen. Joe has a salary of $100,000 and no other types of income. Maggie earns a salary of $50,000 and also has no other types of income. During 2012, Joe and Maggie spent the entire year in Canada with the exception of a 2 week trip to New York City. Because they both spent at least 330 non-consecutive days outside the US, Joe and Maggie both meet the physical presence test and can take advantage of the foreign earned income exclusion. Also, they both meet the bona fide residency test as they are able to show an intention to reside in Canada.

Forms used to claim the exemption

To take advantage of this solution you need to fill out form 2555-EZ and file it together with Form 1040. We show you how to do this in the next section.

11. HOW TO CLAIM THE EXCLUSION: MODEL FORMS 2555-EZ AND 1040

Now that we have explained the theory behind the exclusion, let's walk through a sample of the solution presented in this chapter. For this example, we'll consider Joe and Maggie Smith, but change some of the details. Joe and Maggie Smith are married and live in Winnipeg. Joe is a US citizen but Maggie is not. Joe has lived in Winnipeg for several years and tends not to visit the United States for more than a few days a year. Joe earns $90,000 in salary as a teacher for the Winnipeg School Division. Maggie is also a teacher but makes $92,000 and owns some stocks which produce dividends. Joe does not have any other sources of income. Fred, their son, is 12 and lives with them.

Joe qualifies for the foreign earned income exclusion because a) his income is salary and it was earned in Canada and b) his tax home is in Canada and c) he meets both the bona fide and physical presence residence tests. It does not make sense for Joe and Maggie to choose to treat Maggie as a US citizen because he does not need the extra foreign earned income tax credit. If they did this, he would expose Maggie's dividend income to US tax.

First, Joe has to fill out Form 2555-EZ for himself. It would look like this.

Form **2555-EZ** Department of the Treasury Internal Revenue Service (99)

Foreign Earned Income Exclusion

▶ See separate instructions. ▶ Attach to Form 1040.

OMB No. 1545-0074 **2011** Attachment Sequence No. **34A**

Name shown on Form 1040: Joe Smith (filing as a single person)

Your social security number: 123-456-789

You May Use This Form If You:
- Are a U.S. citizen or a resident alien.
- Earned wages/salaries in a foreign country.
- Had total foreign earned income of $92,900 or less.
- Are filing a calendar year return that covers a 12-month period.

And You:
- Do not have self-employment income.
- Do not have business/moving expenses.
- Do not claim the foreign housing exclusion or deduction.

The 2012 amount is $ 95100.

Part I **Tests To See If You Can Take the Foreign Earned Income Exclusion**

1 Bona Fide Residence Test

a Were you a bona fide resident of a foreign country or countries for a period that includes an entire tax year (see page 2 of the instructions)? ☑ Yes ☐ No
- If you answered "Yes," you meet this test. Fill in line 1b and then go to line 3.
- If you answered "No," you **do not** meet this test. Go to line 2 to see if you meet the Physical Presence Test.

b Enter the date your bona fide residence began ▶ June 1, 2004, and ended (see instructions) ▶

Joe still lives in Canada

2 Physical Presence Test

a Were you physically present in a foreign country or countries for at least 330 full days during— 2011 **or** any other period of 12 months in a row starting or ending in 2011? ☑ Yes ☐ No
- If you answered "Yes," you meet this test. Fill in line 2b and then go to line 3.
- If you answered "No," you **do not** meet this test. You **cannot** take the exclusion unless you meet the Bona Fide Residence Test above.

b The physical presence test is based on the 12-month period from ▶ 01/01/2012 through ▶ 31/12/2012.

3 Tax Home Test. Was your tax home in a foreign country or countries throughout your period of bona fide residence or physical presence, whichever applies? ☑ Yes ☐ No
- If you answered "Yes," you can take the exclusion. Complete Part II below and then go to page 2.
- If you answered "No," you **cannot** take the exclusion. **Do not** file this form.

Part II **General Information**

4 Your foreign address (including country): 63 Scotia Street Winnipeg Manitoba Canada

5 Your occupation: Teacher

6 Employer's name: Winnipeg School Division

7 Employer's U.S. address (including ZIP code): N/A

8 Employer's foreign address: 1577 Wall St E Winnipeg, MB R3E 2S5

9 Employer is (check any that apply):
a A U.S. business ☐
b A foreign business ☐
c Other (specify) ▶ Government ☐

10a If you filed Form 2555 or 2555-EZ after 1981, enter the last year you filed the form. ▶

b If you did not file Form 2555 or 2555-EZ after 1981, check here ▶ ☑ and go to line 11a now.

c Have you ever revoked the foreign earned income exclusion? ☐ Yes ☐ No

d If you answered "Yes," enter the tax year for which the revocation was effective. ▶

11a List your tax home(s) during 2011 and date(s) established. ▶ Canada, January 1, 2011

b Of what country are you a citizen/national? ▶ Canada

For Paperwork Reduction Act Notice, see the Form 1040 instructions. Here you can simply put January 1 of the tax year in question 2W Form **2555-EZ** (2011)

This represents a one week holiday that Joe took to Florida.

Page 2

Part III **Days Present in the United States—** Complete this part if you were in the United States or its possessions during 2011.

12

(a) Date arrived in U.S.	(b) Date left U.S.	(c) Number of days in U.S. on business	(d) Income earned in U.S. on business (attach computation)
January 4, 2011	January 11, 2011	7	0

Part IV **Figure Your Foreign Earned Income Exclusion**

13	Maximum foreign earned income exclusion	13	$92,900 00
14	Enter the number of days in your qualifying period that fall within 2011 . . . 14 365 **days**		
15	Did you enter 365 on line 14? ☑ **Yes.** Enter "1.000." ☐ **No.** Divide line 14 by 365 and enter the result as a decimal (rounded to at least three places).	15	× 1 . 000
16	Multiply line 13 by line 15	16	92900 00
17	Enter, in U.S. dollars, the total foreign earned income you earned and received in 2011 (see instructions). Be sure to include this amount on Form 1040, line 7	17	$90000 00
18	**Foreign earned income exclusion.** Enter the **smaller** of line 16 or line 17 here and in parentheses on **Form 1040, line 21.** Next to the amount enter "2555-EZ." On Form 1040, subtract this amount from your income to arrive at total income on Form 1040, line 22 . . . ▶	18	90000 00

This amount changes every year so use the most current amount.

Enter 365 if you meet either the bona fide residency test or the physical presence test.

Form **2555-EZ** (2011)

Joe should complete his Form 2555 EZ and attach it to his Form 1040. His Form 1040 would look like this.

Form **1040** Department of the Treasury—Internal Revenue Service (99)
U.S. Individual Income Tax Return **2011** OMB No. 1545-0074 IRS Use Only—Do not write or staple in this space.

For the year Jan. 1–Dec. 31, 2011, or other tax year beginning , 2011, ending , 20 See separate instructions.

Your first name and initial	Last name	Your social security number
Joe	Smith	1 2 3 | 4 5 | 6 7 8 9
If a joint return, spouse's first name and initial	Last name	Spouse's social security number
Home address (number and street). If you have a P.O. box, see instructions. 63 Scotia St.	Apt. no.	▲ Make sure the SSN(s) above and on line 6c are correct.
City, town or post office, state, and ZIP code. If you have a foreign address, also complete spaces below (see instructions). Winnipeg		**Presidential Election Campaign** Check here if you, or your spouse if filing jointly, want $3 to go to this fund. Checking a box below will not change your tax or refund. ☑ You ☐ Spouse
Foreign country name: Canada	Foreign province/county: Manitoba	Foreign postal code: K2P 2K8

Filing Status
Check only one box.
1 ☐ Single
2 ☐ Married filing jointly (even if only one had income)
3 ☑ Married filing separately. Enter spouse's SSN above and full name here. ▶ Maggie Smith - no SSN
4 ☐ Head of household (with qualifying person). (See instructions.) If the qualifying person is a child but not your dependent, enter this child's name here. ▶
5 ☐ Qualifying widow(er) with dependent child

Exemptions
6a ☑ **Yourself.** If someone can claim you as a dependent, **do not** check box 6a — Boxes checked on 6a and 6b: 1
b ☐ **Spouse**
c **Dependents:**

(1) First name Last name	(2) Dependent's social security number	(3) Dependent's relationship to you	(4) ✓ if child under age 17 qualifying for child tax credit (see instructions)
Fred Smith	N / A	Son	☐
			☐
			☐
			☐

If more than four dependents, see instructions and check here ▶ ☐

No. of children on 6c who: • lived with you: 1; • did not live with you due to divorce or separation (see instructions); Dependents on 6c not entered above

d Total number of exemptions claimed — Add numbers on lines above ▶ 2

Joe can ignore the child tax credit.

Income

Attach Form(s) W-2 here. Also attach Forms W-2G and 1099-R if tax was withheld.

If you did not get a W-2, see instructions.

Enclose, but do not attach, any payment. Also, please use Form 1040-V.

7	Wages, salaries, tips, etc. Attach Form(s) W-2	7	90,000 00
8a	**Taxable** interest. Attach Schedule B if required	8a	
b	**Tax-exempt** interest. **Do not** include on line 8a — 8b		
9a	Ordinary dividends. Attach Schedule B if required	9a	
b	Qualified dividends — 9b		
10	Taxable refunds, credits, or offsets of state and local income taxes	10	
11	Alimony received	11	
12	Business income or (loss). Attach Schedule C or C-EZ	12	
13	Capital gain or (loss). Attach Schedule D if required. If not required, check here ▶ ☐	13	
14	Other gains or (losses). Attach Form 4797	14	
15a	IRA distributions 15a — b Taxable amount	15b	
16a	Pensions and annuities 16a — b Taxable amount	16b	
17	Rental real estate, royalties, partnerships, S corporations, trusts, etc. Attach Schedule E	17	
18	Farm income or (loss). Attach Schedule F	18	
19	Unemployment compensation	19	
20a	Social security benefits 20a — b Taxable amount	20b	
21	Other income. List type and amount Form 2555EZ	21	-90,000 00
22	Combine the amounts in the far right column for lines 7 through 21. This is your **total income** ▶	22	0 0

Adjusted Gross Income

23	Educator expenses	23	
24	Certain business expenses of reservists, performing artists, and fee-basis government officials. Attach Form 2106 or 2106-EZ	24	
25	Health savings account deduction. Attach Form 8889	25	
26	Moving expenses. Attach Form 3903	26	
27	Deductible part of self-employment tax. Attach Schedule SE	27	
28	Self-employed SEP, SIMPLE, and qualified plans	28	
29	Self-employed health insurance deduction	29	
30	Penalty on early withdrawal of savings	30	
31a	Alimony paid b Recipient's SSN ▶	31a	
32	IRA deduction	32	
33	Student loan interest deduction	33	
34	Tuition and fees. Attach Form 8917	34	
35	Domestic production activities deduction. Attach Form 8903	35	
36	Add lines 23 through 35	36	
37	Subtract line 36 from line 22. This is your **adjusted gross income** ▶	37	

See the example in Chapter 2 for how to fill out Form 2555EZ.

Joe does not have any other types of income so he does not need to worry about this part of the form.

For Disclosure, Privacy Act, and Paperwork Reduction Act Notice, see separate instructions. Cat. No. 11320B Form **1040** (2011)

Form 1040 (2011) Page **2**

Tax and Credits	38	Amount from line 37 (adjusted gross income)	38	
	39a	Check if: ☐ **You** were born before January 2, 1947, ☐ Blind. ☐ **Spouse** was born before January 2, 1947, ☐ Blind. **Total boxes checked ▶ 39a**		
	b	If your spouse itemizes on a separate return or you were a dual-status alien, check here ▶ 39b☐		
	40	**Itemized deductions** (from Schedule A) **or** your **standard deduction** (see left margin)	40	
	41	Subtract line 40 from line 38	41	
	42	**Exemptions.** Multiply $3,700 by the number on line 6d	42	
	43	**Taxable income.** Subtract line 42 from line 41. If line 42 is more than line 41, enter -0-	43	
	44	**Tax** (see instructions). Check if any from: **a** ☐ Form(s) 8814 **b** ☐ Form 4972 **c** ☐ 962 election	44	
	45	**Alternative minimum tax** (see instructions). Attach Form 6251	45	
	46	Add lines 44 and 45 ▶	46	
	47	Foreign tax credit. Attach Form 1116 if required — 47		
	48	Credit for child and dependent care expenses. Attach Form 2441 — 48		
	49	Education credits from Form 8863, line 23 — 49		
	50	Retirement savings contributions credit. Attach Form 8880 — 50		
	51	Child tax credit (see instructions) — 51		
	52	Residential energy credits. Attach Form 5695 — 52		
	53	Other credits from Form: **a** ☐ 3800 **b** ☐ 8801 **c** ☐ — 53		
	54	Add lines 47 through 53. These are your **total credits**	54	
	55	Subtract line 54 from line 46. If line 54 is more than line 46, enter -0- ▶	55	0
Other Taxes	56	Self-employment tax. Attach Schedule SE	56	
	57	Unreported social security and Medicare tax from Form: **a** ☐ 4137 **b** ☐ 8919	57	
	58	Additional tax on IRAs, other qualified retirement plans, etc. Attach Form 5329 if required	58	
	59a	Household employment taxes from Schedule H	59a	
	b	First-time homebuyer credit repayment. Attach Form 5405 if required	59b	
	60	Other taxes. Enter code(s) from instructions	60	
	61	Add lines 55 through 60. This is your **total tax** ▶	61	0
Payments	62	Federal income tax withheld from Forms W-2 and 1099 — 62 — 0		
	63	2011 estimated tax payments and amount applied from 2010 return — 63		
	64a	**Earned income credit (EIC)** — 64a		
	b	Nontaxable combat pay election — 64b		
	65	Additional child tax credit. Attach Form 8812 — 65		
	66	American opportunity credit from Form 8863, line 14 — 66		
	67	First-time homebuyer credit from Form 5405, line 10 — 67		
	68	Amount paid with request for extension to file — 68		
	69	Excess social security and tier 1 RRTA tax withheld — 69		
	70	Credit for federal tax on fuels. Attach Form 4136 — 70		
	71	Credits from Form: **a** ☐ 2439 **b** ☐ 8839 **c** ☐ 8801 **d** ☐ 8885 — 71		
	72	Add lines 62, 63, 64a, and 65 through 71. These are your **total payments** ▶	72	0
Refund	73	If line 72 is more than line 61, subtract line 61 from line 72. This is the amount you **overpaid**	73	0
	74a	Amount of line 73 you want **refunded to you.** If Form 8888 is attached, check here ▶☐	74a	0
Direct deposit? See instructions.	▶ b	Routing number ▶ c Type: ☐ Checking ☐ Savings		
	▶ d	Account number		
	75	Amount of line 73 you want **applied to your 2012 estimated tax** ▶ — 75 — 0		
Amount You Owe	76	**Amount you owe.** Subtract line 72 from line 61. For details on how to pay, see instructions ▶	76	0
	77	Estimated tax penalty (see instructions) — 77		

Standard Deduction for—
• People who check any box on line 39a or 39b **or** who can be claimed as a dependent, see instructions.
• All others:
Single or Married filing separately, $5,800
Married filing jointly or Qualifying widow(er), $11,600
Head of household, $8,500

If you have a qualifying child, attach Schedule EIC.

Since Joe has zero income it is not necessary for him to worry about other deductions or exemptions.

Joe has paid no US tax on his income because none was withheld by his Canadian employer

Joe cannot claim the earned income credit because he filed Form 2555EZ

Joe has no income so he owes no tax and gets no refund.

Third Party Designee Do you want to allow another person to discuss this return with the IRS (see instructions)? ☐ **Yes.** Complete below. ☑ **No**
Designee's name ▶ Phone no. ▶ Personal identification number (PIN) ▶

Sign Here Under penalties of perjury, I declare that I have examined this return and accompanying schedules and statements, and to the best of my knowledge and belief, they are true, correct, and complete. Declaration of preparer (other than taxpayer) is based on all information of which preparer has any knowledge.
Joint return? See instructions. Keep a copy for your records.
Your signature | Date | Your occupation | Daytime phone number
Spouse's signature. If a joint return, **both** must sign. | Date | Spouse's occupation | If the IRS sent you an Identity Protection PIN, enter it here (see inst.)

Paid Preparer Use Only
Print/Type preparer's name | Preparer's signature | Date | Check ☐ if self-employed | PTIN
Firm's name ▶ | Firm's EIN ▶
Firm's address ▶ | Phone no.

Form **1040** (2011)

You will note that in the above example Joe's use of the foreign earned income exclusion reduces his income to zero. That means he owes no tax. Because he owes no tax, he does not need to worry about what other deductions he may be entitled to and does not need to fill out the rest of the form. This is a relatively straightforward example that should suit most people who have only salary income and earn less than $95,000 (in 2012).

PART 2

US FEDERAL INCOME TAX

5

THE FORM 1040

Form 1040 is the standard tax form that all individuals must fill out. If you can't take advantage of one of the simple solutions previously described, you have to start from scratch. This part helps you do that. It explains the Form 1040 step by step and line by line. For simplicity's sake, we have broken the task of filling out the Form 1040 into six separate sections:

(A) Personal information and family details.

(B) Listing your income.

(C) Calculating your adjusted gross income.

(D) Calculating how much tax you owe.

(E) Subtracting your tax credits from your tax payable.

(F) Figuring out if you can benefit from a refundable tax credit.

Each part starts with an overview that surveys the topics to follow. We suggest the following approach. Take a blank Form 1040 from Appendix 1. Read through the introductory chapters for each section to see what items are applicable to you. Then, as necessary, refer to the more detailed chapters later in the section. That way you will have a good sense of what information you need to report and where to look more in-depth.

In its entirety, the Form 1040 looks like this.

Form **1040** Department of the Treasury—Internal Revenue Service (99)
U.S. Individual Income Tax Return 2011 OMB No. 1545-0074 IRS Use Only—Do not write or staple in this space.

For the year Jan. 1–Dec. 31, 2011, or other tax year beginning , 2011, ending , 20 See separate instructions.

Your first name and initial | Last name | **Your social security number**

If a joint return, spouse's first name and initial | Last name | **Spouse's social security number**

Home address (number and street). If you have a P.O. box, see instructions. | Apt. no. | ▲ Make sure the SSN(s) above and on line 6c are correct.

City, town or post office, state, and ZIP code. If you have a foreign address, also complete spaces below (see instructions).

Presidential Election Campaign
Check here if you, or your spouse if filing jointly, want $3 to go to this fund. Checking a box below will not change your tax or refund. ☐ **You** ☐ **Spouse**

Foreign country name | Foreign province/county | Foreign postal code

Filing Status

Check only one box.

1 ☐ Single
2 ☐ Married filing jointly (even if only one had income)
3 ☐ Married filing separately. Enter spouse's SSN above and full name here. ▶
4 ☐ Head of household (with qualifying person). (See instructions.) If the qualifying person is a child but not your dependent, enter this child's name here. ▶
5 ☐ Qualifying widow(er) with dependent child

Exemptions

6a ☐ **Yourself.** If someone can claim you as a dependent, **do not** check box 6a
b ☐ **Spouse**
c **Dependents:**

(1) First name Last name	(2) Dependent's social security number	(3) Dependent's relationship to you	(4) ✓ if child under age 17 qualifying for child tax credit (see instructions)
			☐
			☐
			☐
			☐

If more than four dependents, see instructions and check here ▶ ☐

d Total number of exemptions claimed

Boxes checked on 6a and 6b
No. of children on 6c who:
• lived with you
• did not live with you due to divorce or separation (see instructions)
Dependents on 6c not entered above
Add numbers on lines above ▶

Income

Attach Form(s) W-2 here. Also attach Forms W-2G and 1099-R if tax was withheld.

If you did not get a W-2, see instructions.

Enclose, but do not attach, any payment. Also, please use **Form 1040-V.**

7 Wages, salaries, tips, etc. Attach Form(s) W-2 — 7
8a **Taxable** interest. Attach Schedule B if required — 8a
b **Tax-exempt** interest. **Do not** include on line 8a — 8b
9a Ordinary dividends. Attach Schedule B if required — 9a
b Qualified dividends — 9b
10 Taxable refunds, credits, or offsets of state and local income taxes — 10
11 Alimony received — 11
12 Business income or (loss). Attach Schedule C or C-EZ — 12
13 Capital gain or (loss). Attach Schedule D if required. If not required, check here ▶ ☐ — 13
14 Other gains or (losses). Attach Form 4797 — 14
15a IRA distributions — 15a — b Taxable amount — 15b
16a Pensions and annuities — 16a — b Taxable amount — 16b
17 Rental real estate, royalties, partnerships, S corporations, trusts, etc. Attach Schedule E — 17
18 Farm income or (loss). Attach Schedule F — 18
19 Unemployment compensation — 19
20a Social security benefits — 20a — b Taxable amount — 20b
21 Other income. List type and amount — 21
22 Combine the amounts in the far right column for lines 7 through 21. This is your **total income** ▶ — 22

Adjusted Gross Income

23 Educator expenses — 23
24 Certain business expenses of reservists, performing artists, and fee-basis government officials. Attach Form 2106 or 2106-EZ — 24
25 Health savings account deduction. Attach Form 8889 — 25
26 Moving expenses. Attach Form 3903 — 26
27 Deductible part of self-employment tax. Attach Schedule SE — 27
28 Self-employed SEP, SIMPLE, and qualified plans — 28
29 Self-employed health insurance deduction — 29
30 Penalty on early withdrawal of savings — 30
31a Alimony paid **b** Recipient's SSN ▶ — 31a
32 IRA deduction — 32
33 Student loan interest deduction — 33
34 Tuition and fees. Attach Form 8917 — 34
35 Domestic production activities deduction. Attach Form 8903 — 35
36 Add lines 23 through 35 — 36
37 Subtract line 36 from line 22. This is your **adjusted gross income** ▶ — 37

For Disclosure, Privacy Act, and Paperwork Reduction Act Notice, see separate instructions. Cat. No. 11320B Form **1040** (2011)

Form 1040 (2011) Page 2

Tax and Credits

38	Amount from line 37 (adjusted gross income)	38	
39a	Check if: ☐ **You** were born before January 2, 1947, ☐ Blind. ☐ **Spouse** was born before January 2, 1947, ☐ Blind. **Total boxes checked ▶ 39a** ☐		
b	If your spouse itemizes on a separate return or you were a dual-status alien, check here ▶ 39b ☐		
40	**Itemized deductions** (from Schedule A) **or** your **standard deduction** (see left margin)	40	
41	Subtract line 40 from line 38	41	
42	**Exemptions.** Multiply $3,700 by the number on line 6d	42	
43	**Taxable income.** Subtract line 42 from line 41. If line 42 is more than line 41, enter -0-	43	
44	**Tax** (see instructions). Check if any from: **a** ☐ Form(s) 8814 **b** ☐ Form 4972 **c** ☐ 962 election	44	
45	**Alternative minimum tax** (see instructions). Attach Form 6251	45	
46	Add lines 44 and 45 ▶	46	
47	Foreign tax credit. Attach Form 1116 if required	47	
48	Credit for child and dependent care expenses. Attach Form 2441	48	
49	Education credits from Form 8863, line 23	49	
50	Retirement savings contributions credit. Attach Form 8880	50	
51	Child tax credit (see instructions)	51	
52	Residential energy credits. Attach Form 5695	52	
53	Other credits from Form: **a** ☐ 3800 **b** ☐ 8801 **c** ☐	53	
54	Add lines 47 through 53. These are your **total credits**	54	
55	Subtract line 54 from line 46. If line 54 is more than line 46, enter -0- ▶	55	

Standard Deduction for—
- People who check any box on line 39a or 39b **or** who can be claimed as a dependent, see instructions.
- All others:

Single or Married filing separately, $5,800

Married filing jointly or Qualifying widow(er), $11,600

Head of household, $8,500

Other Taxes

56	Self-employment tax. Attach Schedule SE	56	
57	Unreported social security and Medicare tax from Form: **a** ☐ 4137 **b** ☐ 8919	57	
58	Additional tax on IRAs, other qualified retirement plans, etc. Attach Form 5329 if required	58	
59a	Household employment taxes from Schedule H	59a	
b	First-time homebuyer credit repayment. Attach Form 5405 if required	59b	
60	Other taxes. Enter code(s) from instructions	60	
61	Add lines 55 through 60. This is your **total tax** ▶	61	

Payments

If you have a qualifying child, attach Schedule EIC.

62	Federal income tax withheld from Forms W-2 and 1099	62	
63	2011 estimated tax payments and amount applied from 2010 return	63	
64a	**Earned income credit (EIC)**	64a	
b	Nontaxable combat pay election 64b		
65	Additional child tax credit. Attach Form 8812	65	
66	American opportunity credit from Form 8863, line 14	66	
67	First-time homebuyer credit from Form 5405, line 10	67	
68	Amount paid with request for extension to file	68	
69	Excess social security and tier 1 RRTA tax withheld	69	
70	Credit for federal tax on fuels. Attach Form 4136	70	
71	Credits from Form: **a** ☐ 2439 **b** ☐ 8839 **c** ☐ 8801 **d** ☐ 8885	71	
72	Add lines 62, 63, 64a, and 65 through 71. These are your **total payments** ▶	72	

Refund

73	If line 72 is more than line 61, subtract line 61 from line 72. This is the amount you **overpaid**	73	
74a	Amount of line 73 you want **refunded to you.** If Form 8888 is attached, check here ▶ ☐	74a	
▶ b	Routing number ▶ c Type: ☐ Checking ☐ Savings		
▶ d	Account number		
75	Amount of line 73 you want **applied to your 2012 estimated tax** ▶ 75		

Direct deposit? See instructions.

Amount You Owe

76	**Amount you owe.** Subtract line 72 from line 61. For details on how to pay, see instructions ▶	76	
77	Estimated tax penalty (see instructions)	77	

Third Party Designee

Do you want to allow another person to discuss this return with the IRS (see instructions)? ☐ **Yes.** Complete below. ☐ **No**

Designee's name ▶ Phone no. ▶ Personal identification number (PIN) ▶

Sign Here

Under penalties of perjury, I declare that I have examined this return and accompanying schedules and statements, and to the best of my knowledge and belief, they are true, correct, and complete. Declaration of preparer (other than taxpayer) is based on all information of which preparer has any knowledge.

Joint return? See instructions. Keep a copy for your records.

Your signature	Date	Your occupation	Daytime phone number
Spouse's signature. If a joint return, **both** must sign.	Date	Spouse's occupation	If the IRS sent you an Identity Protection PIN, enter it here (see inst.)

Paid Preparer Use Only

Print/Type preparer's name	Preparer's signature	Date	Check ☐ if self-employed	PTIN
Firm's name ▶		Firm's EIN ▶		
Firm's address ▶		Phone no.		

Form **1040** (2011)

PART 2A

PERSONAL INFORMATION AND FAMILY DETAILS[1]

[1] This chapter is based on and some of the text is copied from the IRS' instructions to Form 1040. This publication is available on the IRS website.

6

OVERVIEW OF LINES 1–6

This chapter explains the first part of the Form 1040 where you enter your personal information and family details. Since it is relatively straightforward, we have included all of the relevant information in the overview. The first part of the Form 1040 looks like this.

Form **1040** Department of the Treasury—Internal Revenue Service (99)
U.S. Individual Income Tax Return **2011** OMB No. 1545-0074 IRS Use Only—Do not write or staple in this space.

For the year Jan. 1–Dec. 31, 2011, or other tax year beginning , 2011, ending , 20 See separate instructions.

Your first name and initial | Last name | **Your social security number**

If a joint return, spouse's first name and initial | Last name | **Spouse's social security number**

Home address (number and street). If you have a P.O. box, see instructions. | Apt. no. | ▲ Make sure the SSN(s) above and on line 6c are correct.

City, town or post office, state, and ZIP code. If you have a foreign address, also complete spaces below (see instructions).

Foreign country name | Foreign province/county | Foreign postal code

Presidential Election Campaign
Check here if you, or your spouse if filing jointly, want $3 to go to this fund. Checking a box below will not change your tax or refund. ☐ **You** ☐ **Spouse**

Filing Status

Check only one box.

1 ☐ Single
2 ☐ Married filing jointly (even if only one had income)
3 ☐ Married filing separately. Enter spouse's SSN above and full name here. ▶
4 ☐ Head of household (with qualifying person). (See instructions.) If the qualifying person is a child but not your dependent, enter this child's name here. ▶
5 ☐ Qualifying widow(er) with dependent child

Exemptions

6a ☐ **Yourself.** If someone can claim you as a dependent, **do not** check box 6a . . . . . .
b ☐ **Spouse** . . . .

Boxes checked on 6a and 6b

c **Dependents:** (1) First name Last name	(2) Dependent's social security number	(3) Dependent's relationship to you	(4) ✓ if child under age 17 qualifying for child tax credit (see instructions)
			☐
			☐
			☐
			☐

If more than four dependents, see instructions and check here ▶ ☐

No. of children on 6c who:
• lived with you
• did not live with you due to divorce or separation (see instructions)
Dependents on 6c not entered above

d Total number of exemptions claimed . . . . **Add numbers on lines above ▶**

This chapter addresses the following topics:

1. Getting a Social Security Number.
2. Getting an individual taxpayer identification number.
3. Choosing the appropriate filing status.
4. Claiming exemptions.
5. Identifying your dependents.

The boxes about name and address are self-explanatory. The two complicated items on this part of the form are the Social Security Number and filing status. Let's take them in turn.

1. SOCIAL SECURITY NUMBER

The Social Security Number is the American equivalent of the Canadian Social Insurance Number (SIN). It identifies a particular taxpayer to the IRS. If you do not have a Social Security Number, you should apply for one. You must provide the Social Security Administration with proof of your US citizenship, your age, and your identity. To get a SSN you should:

- Gather your proof of citizenship. These include a US passport, Certificate of Naturalization, or Certificate of Citizenship.
- Present your birth certificate.
- If you are 12 or older, you have to appear in person for an interview and prove that you did not ever receive a Social Security Number. The following documents are examples of how to do this:
    - A current or previous passport, school and/or employment records, and any other record that would show long-term residence outside the United States could be used to show you do not have a Social Security Number.
- Gather proof of identity. An acceptable document must be current (not expired) and show your name, identifying information (date of birth or age) and preferably a recent photograph. For example, as proof of identity Social Security must see your:
    - US driver's licence;
    - State-issued non-driver identification card;
    - US passport;
    - Employee ID card;
    - School ID card;
    - Health insurance card (not a Medicare card); or
    - US military ID card.
- Once you have assembled this documentation, you should fill out form SS-5Fs (included in Appendix 1) and send it to either the US Embassy in Ottawa or your nearest US consulate. The list of US consulates is below.

Office Location	Region Served	Contact information
Ottawa	Eastern Ontario (Kingston, Lanark, Leeds, Prescott, Renfrew, Russell and Stormont); and those parts of the Québec regions of Outaouais and Abitibi-Témiscamingue near Ottawa.	490 Sussex Drive Ottawa, Ontario Telephone (General): 613-688-5335 Telephone (Emergency): 613-238-5335 E-mail (Consular Section): ottawacons@state.gov
Vancouver	British Columbia and Yukon Territory	1075 West Pender Street Vancouver, British Columbia V6E 2M6 Telephone (General): 604-685-4311 Telephone (Emergency): 604-685-4311 E-mail (Citizen Services): vancouverACS@state.gov
Calgary	Alberta, Saskatchewan, Manitoba and Northwest Territories	615 Macleod Trail, S.E. Suite 1000 Calgary, Alberta T2G 4T8 Phone: (403) 266-8962

Office Location	Region Served	Contact information
Toronto	Ontario (except for areas east of Kingston, which are included in the Ottawa consular district)	360 University Ave. Toronto, Ontario M5G 1S4 Fax (Citizen Services): 416-595-6501 Phone (General): 416.595.1700 E-mail (general US passport, notarial or citizenship inquiries): TorontoPassport@state.gov
Montreal	Greater Montreal and the regions of southern Quebec province (Laurentides, Lanaudiere, Laval, Montreal, Montregie, Estrie, and the southern parts of Centre-du-Quebec); including Drummondville	315 Place d'Youville, Suite 500 Montréal, Québec H2Y 0A4 Phone (General): 514-398-9695 Email: montreal-ACS@state.gov
Quebec City	Those regions of Quebec province to the north and east of the Montreal and Ottawa Districts (indicated above), plus the territory of Nunavut	2 Place Terrasse Dufferin (Vieux Quebec, behind Château Frontenac) Québec, Québec G1R 4T9 Telephone (General): 418-692-2095 E-mail (Citizen Services): quebecniv@state.gov
Halifax	Atlantic Canada (New Brunswick, Newfoundland, Nova Scotia and P.E.I.) and the French islands of St. Pierre & Miquelon.	Suite 904, Purdy's Wharf Tower II 1969 Upper Water Street Halifax, NS B3J 3R7 Phone (General): (902) 429-2480

2. GETTING AN INDIVIDUAL TAXPAYER IDENTIFICATION NUMBER (ITIN)

American citizens must apply for a Social Security Number. Those who aren't citizens, such as a spouse of a US Citizen living in Canada who is not a US citizen, should apply for an Individual Taxpayer Identification Number (ITIN) if you want them to take advantage of the foreign earned income exclusion (explained below).

To get an ITIN you should fill out Form W-7 (in Appendix 1) and send it along with certified copies of:

- Proof of identity (e.g., a driver's licence or passport);
- Proof of foreign nationality (e.g., a birth certificate or passport);
- A letter explaining the reason why an ITIN number is being requested.

Mail the completed Form W-7 application together with the certified copies of the documents to:

Internal Revenue Service
ITIN Operation
P.O. Box 149342
Austin, TX 78714-9342

3. FILING STATUS

Filing status describes your current family situation. In general, your filing status, or family situation, will affect how much tax you pay. There are five options presented in Form 1040: single, married filing jointly, married filing separately, head of household, and qualifying widow(er). You should select the status that applies as of December 31 of the year for which you are filing your taxes (December 31, 2012 for a 2012 return).

Let's review each option.

- *Single.* Choose this if you are single or if your divorce is final.
- *Married filing jointly.* You can select this status if you were married at the end of the year for which you are filing returns (December 2012 for a 2012 return). Or you can select this option if your spouse died during the year for which you are filing and you did not remarry during that year. Heterosexual couples may be either legally married or in a common law relationship to file joint returns. Common law relationship is defined by the law of the province that you live in. Note that the definition of marriage remains controversial in the United States. As of writing, the IRS only recognized marriages between a man and a woman. Gay couples, while they may be legally married in Canada, are not eligible to file joint US returns.
- *Married filing separately.* This status simply means that you are married but have chosen to file separate US returns. If both spouses are US citizens, and therefore both have to file returns, the decision to file jointly or separately is a strategic one. We recommend that most married couples file jointly. The reasons are as follows. Your taxable income is calculated based on your entire income as a couple. You will most likely pay a lower tax rate than married couples who file separately. Other benefits of filing jointly include: 1) spousal contributions to an Investment Retirement Account 2) less time and cost to file a return and 3) certain tax credits are only available to married couples filing jointly. These include the dependent care credit, the earned income credit, the American Opportunity credit, the lifetime learning credit, and the deduction for interest on education loans. Concretely, this means that the names of both individuals go on the Form 1040 and both their incomes and deductions are reported on the same form.

  However, many US citizens in Canada are married to persons who are not US citizens. If this is the case, you can choose to treat your spouse as a US citizen. This will allow you to claim a larger foreign earned income exclusion as a couple. But the choice also means that all of your spouse's income is exposed to US tax. The choice is discussed further in Chapter 14.
- *Head of household status.* This status covers unmarried individuals who support dependents such as children or elderly parents. It entitles you to certain deductions normally not available to single people. To qualify for this status you meet the following criteria:
  - Be unmarried, legally separated, or married to a person who is not a US citizen or permanent resident.

  and

  - You paid over half the expenses of keeping up a home that was the main home for all of the tax year in question of your parent. Your parent does not have to live with you.

  or

- o You paid half the expenses for a home in which one of your dependents lives. Who qualifies as a dependent is explained below.

The cost of keeping a house includes expenses such as rent, mortgage interest, real estate taxes, home insurance, repairs, utilities, and food eaten in the home. Importantly, head of household status provides tax advantages to US citizens in Canada who are married to a non-US citizen. If you are married to someone who is not a US citizen, and you do not choose to treat them as one for tax purposes (described more below), you can claim the head of household status if you have dependents. All of the details of head of household status are explained in IRS Publication 501. If you have any doubts as to your eligibility to claim the head of household status, you should review that publication in detail.

- *Qualifying widow(er) with dependent child.* To qualify for this status the following conditions apply:
  - o Your spouse died in the two years prior to the one in which you are filing a return (i.e., 2010 or 2011 for a 2012 return) and you did not remarry before the end of 2011.
  - o The child who you claim as a dependent lived with you for the entire tax year for which you are filing a return.
  - o You paid for over half the expenses of keeping your home.

As above, IRS Publication 501 fully explains all of the nuances of qualifying widow(er) with dependent child. If you have questions about this status you can learn more in that publication.

4. EXEMPTIONS – LINE 6(A) AND 6(B)

If your filing status is single, married filing separately, head of household, or qualified widow(er) with children, you should only check box 6(a). However, you cannot check box 6(a) if someone else (such as your parents if you are young) claims you on their return as a dependent. If you are married and filing jointly you should check both box 6(a) and 6(b).

5. DEPENDENTS – LINE 6(C)

A dependent is someone, such as a child or an elderly parent, who relies on you for financial support. You are able to lower your tax burden because you support them. There are a number of different types of dependents.

a. Children

Let's discuss children first. You can list a child as a dependent if you can answer "yes" to one of the questions in each of the following seven criteria. Some of the steps may be satisfied in more than one way.

- Is the child related to you in one of the following ways: Son, daughter, stepchild, foster child, brother, sister, stepbrother, stepsister, half-brother, half-sister, or a descendant of any of them (for example, your grandchild, niece, or nephew)?

And

- You can answer "yes" to one of the following questions:

a) Was the child under 19 and younger than you or your spouse if filing jointly?

or

b) Was the child under 24 at the end of the tax year in question and a student?

or

c) Was the child permanently disabled?

and

- The child did not provide half or more of his or her own support for the tax year for which you are filing a return;

and

- Lived with you for more than half of the tax year for which you are filing a return;

and

- The child was a US citizen or a resident of Canada or Mexico. However, if your child was adopted you may be able to claim him or her as a dependent even if he or she doesn't meet this part of the test. See the *exception to citizenship* test in publication 501 for more details;

and

- The child was not married;

and

- Neither you nor your spouse (if you are filing jointly) can be claimed as a dependent on anyone else's return.

If your child satisfies each of the six criteria above and cannot be claimed as a dependent on anyone else's return, then you can claim him or her as a dependent. Note that if your child was kidnapped, or you shared custody of the child with another person who you are separated or divorced from, see publication 501 for the special circumstances that are applicable to these situations. Similarly, if your child was adopted you may be able to claim adoption expenses for him or her. Publication 501 has more details on adoption expenses.

b. Child tax credit

Note that box 4 on line 6(c) mentions the child tax credit. Eligibility for this credit is very easy to determine. If the child is your dependent, is under 17, and is a US citizen or resident alien, then you can tick box 4 next to that child's name. The amount of tax reduction that you can benefit from is discussed in Chapter 34. That amount is listed on line 51.

c. Relatives

You can also claim a relative as a dependent. As with children, there is a multi-stage test that is used to evaluate whether a relative can be claimed as a dependent. You can list a relative as a dependent if you can answer "yes" to <u>one</u> of the questions in each of the following categories.

- Does the person have one of the following relationships to you:
- Son, daughter, stepchild, foster child, or a descendant of any of them (for example, your grandchild);

  or

  - Brother, sister, half-brother, half-sister, or a son or daughter of any of them (for example, your niece or nephew);

  or

  - Father, mother, or an ancestor or sibling of either of them (for example, your grandmother, grandfather, aunt, or uncle);

  or

  - Stepbrother, stepsister, stepfather, stepmother, son-in-law, daughter-in-law, father-in-law, mother-in-law, brother-in-law, or sister-in-law;

  or

  - Any other person (other than your spouse) who lived with you all year as a member of your household if your relationship did not violate local law. You should be careful about claiming a dependent under this category and consult IRS publication 501 before doing so.

and

- The person was not listed as a dependent child by any (other) taxpayer;

and

- The person had a gross income in the tax year in question of less than $3,700 unless the person was disabled. If the person was disabled please consult the exception to gross income test in publication 501 for more information;

and

- You provided more than half of the support for the relative during the tax year in question;

and

- The person was a US citizen or a resident of Canada or Mexico;

and

- The person was not married. If the person was married please consult publication 501 for the unique circumstances under which you can claim the person as a dependent;

and

- The person cannot be claimed as a dependent on anyone else's return.

Once you have filled out the first section of the Form 1040, it is time to figure out your income.

The next section helps you do this.

PART 2B

CALCULATING YOUR INCOME

7

OVERVIEW OF LINES 7–22[1]

The United States requires that you report all income from all sources no matter where it was earned. So if you have any sort of income or revenue, even if it is not addressed in this guide, you need to report it. Lines 7–22 of the Form 1040 are where you report your income. If you do not know where to report a certain type of income you can do so on line 21. The next section of the Form 1040 looks like this.

Income				
	7	Wages, salaries, tips, etc. Attach Form(s) W-2		7
	8a	**Taxable** interest. Attach Schedule B if required		8a
	b	**Tax-exempt** interest. **Do not** include on line 8a	8b	
Attach Form(s) W-2 here. Also attach Forms W-2G and 1099-R if tax was withheld.	9a	Ordinary dividends. Attach Schedule B if required		9a
	b	Qualified dividends	9b	
	10	Taxable refunds, credits, or offsets of state and local income taxes		10
	11	Alimony received		11
	12	Business income or (loss). Attach Schedule C or C-EZ		12
	13	Capital gain or (loss). Attach Schedule D if required. If not required, check here ▶ ☐		13
If you did not get a W-2, see instructions.	14	Other gains or (losses). Attach Form 4797		14
	15a	IRA distributions 15a	b Taxable amount	15b
	16a	Pensions and annuities 16a	b Taxable amount	16b
	17	Rental real estate, royalties, partnerships, S corporations, trusts, etc. Attach Schedule E		17
Enclose, but do not attach, any payment. Also, please use **Form 1040-V.**	18	Farm income or (loss). Attach Schedule F		18
	19	Unemployment compensation		19
	20a	Social security benefits 20a	b Taxable amount	20b
	21	Other income. List type and amount		21
	22	Combine the amounts in the far right column for lines 7 through 21. This is your **total income** ▶		22

We will go line by line to explain what to put in each box. Where necessary we refer you to a later chapter that explains the topic in more detail.

1. WAGES AND SALARY INCOME – LINE 7

Wages, salaries, tips, commissions and professional fees are the most common form of income. You will note that line 7 mentions a W-2 form. This is the American equivalent of the T4 form that most Canadians receive from their employer. Unless you have a US employer, you will likely not receive a W-2 form. Instead, you should take the number from box 14 on your T4, convert it to US dollars and enter that amount on line 7. Currency conversion is outlined in Chapter 3.

Note, however, that the United States and Canada have different standards of what is a taxable benefit. It may be that your employer reports a benefit as taxable in Canada but that may not be taxable in the United States. If you are concerned about this, you will need to ask your employer for a breakdown of your T4. Then you should take each of these items and check in publication 525 to see if they are taxable. Most people, however, should have access to enough tax credits and reductions to make this extra step unnecessary.

If you have multiple T4 forms from different sources, you should record the total amount of income on line 7.

---

[1] This chapter is based on, and some text is copied from, the IRS' instructions for Form 1040.

If you are a student in a degree granting program and you receive a scholarship that is greater than your tuition expenses, you should report the excess amount on this line. For more information please see IRS Publication 970.

2. TAXABLE INTEREST – LINE 8(A)

Interest is passive income that comes from savings accounts, savings bonds, term deposits, and guaranteed investment certificates. The institution that pays you interest will usually send you a T5 form that states how much interest you received and for what reason. Interest income is discussed further in Chapter 8.

Note that if you have a Tax Free Savings Account (TFSA), you still need to report interest income from the TFSA for US purposes. You will need to contact your financial institution to figure out the amount of interest that has accrued. This is discussed further in Chapter 8 which deals with interest and dividends. There are also separate reporting obligations for your Tax Free Savings Account. If you have a TFSA you should consult Chapter 43.

3. TAX EXEMPT INTEREST – LINE 8(B)

This line is for tax-exempt interest. Note that income sheltered in a Canadian Tax Free Savings Account (TFSA) is not tax-exempt in the United States. This line is reserved for particular sources such as US municipal bonds. Most Canadians probably do not own these. We suggest leaving this line blank unless you receive a Form 1099-INT from an American source that specifies that the interest is tax-exempt.

4. DIVIDEND INCOME – LINE 9(A)

Dividends are payments made from a corporation to shareholders. If you have dividend income, reported in a T5 form, then you will have to report this income on line 9(a). Be careful to report only the amount of the dividend actually received, not the grossed-up amount that you are required to report for Canadian tax purposes. Note that if you have a Tax Free Savings Account, any dividend income earned within that account may be tax free in Canada but it is not in the United States. You need to figure out how much dividend income you have earned and report it as part of Form 1040. All of this is discussed more in Chapter 8.

5. QUALIFIED DIVIDENDS – LINE 9(B)

Typically, dividends simply form part of your normal income. But the IRS has special rules called qualified dividends that are taxed at a lower than normal rate. Qualified dividends are those from stocks or bonds that you have held for a significant period of time and that meet other criteria. They are discussed in Chapter 8.

6. INCOME FROM STATE AND LOCAL TAX REFUNDS – LINE 10

Most US citizens in Canada will not receive refunds because, generally, US state and local tax is not withheld from their paycheques. Further, if you do not itemize your deductions (which is explained in more detail in section 2(d)) then any refund you may receive from your state and or local taxes (see Chapter 38 on whether you have to pay state or local taxes) is not taxable. If you receive a Form 1099-G, then you put the income it reports on line 10.

You may wonder about taxes paid in Canada. These are also deductible. The deduction is discussed further in Chapter 21.

So unless you receive a Form 1099-G or itemized your deductions and deducted US state or local taxes you can ignore this line.

7. ALIMONY – LINE 11

Alimony is another term for spousal support. It is money that one person pays another during or after a divorce. If you pay alimony you can deduct the payments that you make from your taxes. We explore those deductions later in Part 2(d). For now, all we are concerned about is income. If you receive spousal support under a divorce order, that income has to be reported here. Just write the amount you received in the particular tax year on line 11.

Note that spousal support is different from child support. You do not have to report child support as income.

8. BUSINESS INCOME – LINE 12

This is where you report self-employment income that you received from carrying on an unincorporated sole-proprietorship. This guide does not cover self-employment status. If you are self-employed you should consult a tax professional or the instructions for Schedule SE.

9. CAPITAL GAINS OR LOSSES – LINE 13

Capital gains arise when you sell a capital asset that has increased in value. Conversely, capital losses arise when you sell a capital asset that has decreased in value. Capital assets include everything you own and use for personal purposes, pleasure, or investment. Some examples include stocks or bonds held in your personal account, a house owned and used by you and your family, household furnishings, a car used for pleasure or commuting, coin or stamp collections, gems and jewelry, and gold, silver, or any other metal. If you have any doubt whether an item is a capital asset, please consult Chapter 4 of IRS publication 550.

Chapter 9 addresses general sales of goods. Chapter 10 deals with stocks, bonds, mutual funds and other financial instruments. Finally, Chapter 11 explains what to do if you sell your home. Note that if you sold Canadian mutual funds you will need to consult Chapter 42. Mutual funds may pose problems so we have dedicated a special chapter to them.

10. OTHER GAINS OR LOSSES – LINE 14

This line is where you report ordinary (i.e., non-capital) gains and losses. Most things that you own as an individual are capital, so losses or gains from dispositions of them are reported on line 13.

This line is primarily for those who operate a business or who are self-employed. Both of these scenarios are beyond the scope of this guide and are not covered. You should seek professional tax advice or consult IRS Publication 17 to learn more.

11. IRA DISTRIBUTIONS – LINE 15

This line is not relevant for most US citizens in Canada who probably do not have Investment Retirement Account (IRAs). It is where you report income from your (IRA). If you have an IRA and you receive a distribution from it you have to report the income here. You will likely receive a Form 1099-R from the institution that administers the IRA. IRA distributions are shown in boxes 1 and 2a of Form 1099-R. Report fully taxable distributions, including early distributions on Form 1040, line 15b, (no entry is required on Form 1040, line 15a). If only part of the distribution is taxable, enter the total amount on Form 1040, line 15a, and the taxable part on Form 1040, line 15b. If you made non-deductible contributions to your IRA, you do not need to pay tax on them. However, you will need to fill out and file Form 8606. A blank copy of this form and instructions for completing and filing it are on the IRS website. Do not list income from a RRIF here or other Canadian retirement plan here.

12. PENSIONS AND ANNUITIES – LINE 16(A)

Here is where you report income from private pension plans, annuities, and government pension plans. Private pension plans come in a number of different shapes and sizes. An annuity is a form of insurance that entitles the person who paid for it to a series of periodic sums.

Once retired, many Canadians will receive income from the Canada Pension Plan and from Old Age Security. We discuss how to report this income in Chapter 12.

13. INCOME FROM RENTAL REAL ESTATE, ROYALTIES, PARTNERSHIPS, S CORPORATIONS – LINE 17

Income from rental real estate is discussed in Chapter 13. Be aware that this is quite complicated. Partnership income and income from S corporations are outside the scope of this guide. If you have this type of income you should consult a tax professional.

14. FARM INCOME – LINE 18

The US tax treatment of farm income is also quite complicated. If you have farm income you should consult a tax professional.

15. UNEMPLOYMENT BENEFITS – LINE 19

This line is where you report Employment Insurance benefits. If you received these, you will receive a T4E form from the Canada Revenue Agency. Take the amount listed in box 14 of this form, convert it to US dollars, and put it on line 19.

16. SOCIAL SECURITY BENEFITS – LINE 20(A) AND 20(B)

If you receive Social Security Benefits, you will receive a Form SSA-1099 that details the amount of your benefits.

If you are a resident of Canada you do not have to pay US tax on your Social Security Benefits. Report your net benefits (the amount in box 5 of your Form SSA-1099) on line 20a and the taxable part on line 20b. Since you have no taxable portion of them, you should write nil on line 20(b).

17. OTHER INCOME – LINE 21

This line is for income that does not fit in other categories. This includes the foreign earned income exclusion and the foreign housing exclusion. These are the most important tax benefits available to US citizens abroad. They allow you to exclude up to $95,100 if you are single, or $190,200 if you are married and file a joint return, of certain types of income from tax. Additionally, you are allowed to exclude a certain portion of your housing expenses. The foreign earned income exclusion is discussed further in Chapter 14. Once you have computed the amount there, simply enter it on line 21 and subtract it from your total income.

It is also where you report any other income that you can't place in the appropriate box above. This includes:

- *Gambling, including lottery, winnings.* No matter where you win it, income from gambling must be reported to the IRS.
- *Cancelled debts.* If someone forgives a debt, then the money you would otherwise have owed them is treated as income and should be reported on line 21.
- Money received from an insurance contract if it exceeded the sum of the premiums.

Or any other type of income that you have that doesn't fit into other categories. You do not need to report the following types of income:

- child support payments;
- life insurance proceeds;
- gifts and bequests;
- damages for physical injuries and sickness;
- gifts, bequests, and inheritances;
- veteran's benefits;
- welfare benefits;
- workers' compensation.

18. TOTAL INCOME – LINE 22

At line 22 you should add up all of the amounts for lines 7 through 21 but only in the right hand column.

That concludes our review of the income section of the Form 1040.

8

INTEREST AND DIVIDEND INCOME[1]

This chapter outlines how to calculate and report your interest and dividend income from any financial product except for Canadian mutual funds. For interest and dividend income that comes from Canadian mutual funds, you need to consult Chapter 42 first.

Note that any interest or dividend income that you earn inside a Tax Free Savings Account (TFSA), a Registered Education Savings Plan (RESP), or a Registered Disability Savings Plan (RDSP) must be reported on your Form 1040 and tax must be paid on it. If you have one of these accounts, you have to call your financial institution and ask them how much interest and/or dividend income you have earned inside these accounts. Then simply report the income on your Form 1040. Additionally, you should consult Chapter 43 because these accounts have separate compliance issues.

This chapter is organized as follows:

1. Interest income – line 8(a).
2. Tax-exempt interest – line 8(b).
3. Ordinary dividends – line 9(a).
4. Qualified dividends – line 9(b).
5. If you have more than $1500 in interest or dividend income.

1. INTEREST INCOME – LINE 8(A)

a. Identifying sources of interest income

Interest income comes from numerous sources. Common examples include savings accounts, guaranteed investment certificates, money market funds, and other such accounts. The institution that pays you the interest, for instance a bank, will usually issue you a receipt telling you how much you've earned.

If you receive interest from a Canadian source, like a savings account at Royal Bank, you will normally receive a T5 form. Be aware that the Canadian T5 Form also includes dividend income and capital gains dividends. Income from these sources is reported elsewhere on Form 1040. The T5 form looks like this.

---

[1] This chapter is based on, and some text is copied from, IRS Publication 550.

Canada Revenue Agency — Agence du revenu du Canada

T5

Year / Année

STATEMENT OF INVESTMENT INCOME
ÉTAT DES REVENUS DE PLACEMENTS

Dividends from Canadian corporations – Dividendes de sociétés canadiennes | Federal credit – Crédit fédéral

24	Actual amount of eligible dividends / Montant réel des dividendes déterminés
25	Taxable amount of eligible dividends / Montant imposable des dividendes déterminés
26	Dividend tax credit for eligible dividends / Crédit d'impôt pour dividendes déterminés
13	Interest from Canadian sources / Intérêts de source canadienne
18	Capital gains dividends / Dividendes sur gains en capital
10	Actual amount of dividends other than eligible dividends / Montant réel des dividendes autres que des dividendes déterminés
11	Taxable amount of dividends other than eligible dividends / Montant imposable des dividendes autres que des dividendes déterminés
12	Dividend tax credit for dividends other than eligible dividends / Crédit d'impôt pour dividendes autres que des dividendes déterminés
21	Report Code / Code du feuillet
22	Recipient identification number / Numéro d'identification du bénéficiaire
23	Recipient type / Type de bénéficiaire

Other information (see the back) / Autres renseignements (voir au verso): Box / Case — Amount / Montant; Box / Case — Amount / Montant; Box / Case — Amount / Montant

Recipient's name (last name first) and address – Nom, prénom et adresse du bénéficiaire

Payer's name and address – Nom et adresse du payeur

Interest income from non-Canadian sources will be reported here and identified as box 15.

This is where your interest income from Canadian sources is listed

Currency and identification codes / Codes de devise et d'identification: 27 Foreign currency / Devises étrangères; 28 Transit – Succursale; 29 Recipient account / Numéro de compte du bénéficiaire

For information, see the back.
Pour obtenir des renseignements, lisez le verso.

Privacy Act, Personal Information Bank number CRA PPU 150 and CRA PPU 005 / Loi sur la protection des renseignements personnels, Fichiers de renseignements personnels ARC PPU 150 et ARC PPU 005

T5 (11)

If you receive taxable interest from a US source, it will be reported on a Form 1099-INT.

☐ CORRECTED (if checked)

PAYER'S name, street address, city, state, ZIP code, and telephone no.

OMB No. 1545-0110

2012

Form **1099-DIV**

Dividends and Distributions

Copy B
For Recipient

This is where you will find the amount you should report on line 9(a)

Enter this amount on line 9(b).

1a	Total ordinary dividends $
1b	Qualified dividends $
2a	Total capital gain distr. $
2b	Unrecap. Sec. 1250 gain $
2c	Section 1202 gain $
2d	Collectibles (28%) gain $
3	Nondividend distributions $
4	Federal income tax withheld $
5	Investment expenses $
6	Foreign tax paid $
7	Foreign country or U.S. possession
8	Cash liquidation distributions $
9	Noncash liquidation distributions $
10	Exempt-interest dividends $
11	Specified private activity bond interest dividends $
12	State
13	State identification no.
14	State tax withheld $

PAYER'S federal identification number

RECIPIENT'S identification number

RECIPIENT'S name

Street address (including apt. no.)

City, state, and ZIP code

Account number (see instructions)

This is important tax information and is being furnished to the Internal Revenue Service. If you are required to file a return, a negligence penalty or other sanction may be imposed on you if this income is taxable and the IRS determines that it has not been reported.

Form **1099-DIV** (keep for your records) Department of the Treasury - Internal Revenue Service

The following types of income should also be reported as interest income:

- Interest from installment sale payments. These would be outlined in a contract of sale.
- Interest on an annuity contract.
- Interest income from frozen deposits.
- Loans that you make at below fair market value above $10,000. The interest that you do not charge is considered income.
- Interest on US Savings bonds.
- The original issue discount on a debt instrument. This means that you purchased a debt instrument for less than its value at maturity.

These are quite complicated and uncommon, so you can likely ignore them. They are discussed further in Publication 525.

b. Reporting interest income

You should convert the amount listed in box 13 or 15 on form T5 into US dollars and enter the amount on line 8(a). If you receive more than one T5 form, you should add all of the amounts up and enter the total on line 8(a). Add to this any amount reported on a Form 1099-INT that you receive. If your total is more than $1500, you have to fill out Schedule B and attach it to your return. How to do this is discussed below.

2. TAX-EXEMPT INTEREST – LINE 8(B)

This line is for tax-exempt interest. Note that income sheltered in a Tax Free Savings Account (TFSA) is not tax-exempt in the United States. This line is reserved for particular sources such as US municipal bonds. Most Canadians probably do not own these. We suggest leaving this line blank unless you receive a Form 1099-INT from an American source that specifies that the interest is tax-exempt.

3. ORDINARY DIVIDENDS – LINE 9(A)

a. What are ordinary dividends?

Dividends are certain payments made from a corporation to shareholders in their capacity as shareholders, normally as a means of distributing income earned by the corporation. The term “ordinary” refers only to how they are taxed.

b. Identifying ordinary dividend income

You can have dividend income from stock you own directly or through mutual funds or money market funds. No matter where in the world these may be located, you must report the income for US tax purposes. If your brokerage account is with a Canadian financial institution, you will receive a T5 Form except if your dividends were earned inside a TFSA, RESP, or RDSP.

Canada Revenue Agency / Agence du revenu du Canada

T5
STATEMENT OF INVESTMENT INCOME
ÉTAT DES REVENUS DE PLACEMENTS

Year / Année

Total the amounts listed in these two boxes. This is your total dividend income from Canadian sources.

Dividend income from non-Canadian sources will be listed here and identified as box 15.

For information, see the back.
Pour obtenir des renseignements, lisez le verso.

There are two boxes on Form T5 about which you should be concerned in terms of reporting. Boxes 10, 13, and 24 contain the total amount of dividends that you have to report on your Form 1040. For now, do not worry whether the amount of dividends is eligible for a Canadian tax credit or not. You have to report all of the income on your Form 1040.

If you get dividend income from US sources, you will be sent a Form 1099-Div by your financial institution or the company paying the dividend. The form looks like this:

☐ CORRECTED (if checked)

PAYER'S name, street address, city, state, ZIP code, and telephone no.

1a Total ordinary dividends $

1b Qualified dividends $

OMB No. 1545-0110

2012

Form 1099-DIV

Dividends and Distributions

This is where you will find the amount you should report on line 9(a)

2a Total capital gain distr. $

2b Unrecap. Sec. 1250 gain $

Copy B For Recipient

PAYER'S federal identification number

RECIPIENT'S identification number

2c Section 1202 gain $

2d Collectibles (28%) gain $

RECIPIENT'S name

Enter this amount on line 9(b).

3 Nondividend distributions $

4 Federal income tax withheld $

5 Investment expenses $

Street address (including apt. no.)

6 Foreign tax paid $

7 Foreign country or U.S. possession

City, state, and ZIP code

8 Cash liquidation distributions $

9 Noncash liquidation distributions $

This is important tax information and is being furnished to the Internal Revenue Service. If you are required to file a return, a negligence penalty or other sanction may be imposed on you if this income is taxable and the IRS determines that it has not been reported.

Account number (see instructions)

10 Exempt-interest dividends $

11 Specified private activity bond interest dividends $

12 State

13 State identification no.

14 State tax withheld $

Form **1099-DIV** (keep for your records) Department of the Treasury - Internal Revenue Service

Box 1(a) reports your ordinary dividends.

Certain items are not considered dividends. These include:

- Capital gains distributions from American mutual funds. These should be reported as capital gains.
- Exempt interest dividends. These are shown in box 8 of Form-1099 DIV.
- Dividends on veterans' insurance.
- Dividends on insurance policies.

These are all defined and discussed more thoroughly in publication 550. Of import here is that they are not dividend income that needs to be reported.

c. Reporting dividend income

Total up boxes 10, 13, and 24 from any T5. Then add in any amounts from box 1(a) from a Form 1099-Div. If you have multiple sources of dividend income, all you need to do is add them up, convert the total to US dollars, and put the total on line 9a. If you have more than $1,500 in dividend income, you will be required to attach Schedule B to your return. We discuss how to fill out Schedule B below.

4. QUALIFIED DIVIDENDS – LINE 9(B)

a. What are qualified dividends?

Usually, dividends simply form part of your normal income. But special rules apply to "qualified dividends," which are taxed at a lower than normal rate (15% or 0%). Qualified dividends are those from stocks or bonds that you have held for a significant period of time and that meet other criteria. You may receive a Form 1099-DIV that lists your qualified dividends in box 1(b). If so, simply take the amount listed there and insert it on line 9(b). If you do not receive a Form 1099-DIV you have to determine if you have received qualified dividends.

A Canadian financial institution will normally not report when dividend income is "qualified," since that concept does not apply in Canada. So you have to figure it out yourself.

What follows is quite complicated. If you do not want to bother, you can simply enter your dividend income as ordinary income and use a deduction or tax credit to reduce the amount of tax payable on it.

b. Figuring out if your dividend income is qualified

Qualified dividends must meet three criteria:

- You must have held the stock for a certain amount of time.
- The dividends must have been paid by a US corporation or a qualified foreign corporation.
- The dividends must not be the non-qualified type of dividends.

Let's take the three criteria in turn.

i. Holding period

You must have held the stock for more than 60 days during the 121-day period that begins 60 days before the ex-dividend date. The ex-dividend date is the first date following the declaration of a dividend on which the buyer of a stock is not entitled to receive that dividend payment.

When a company declares a dividend, it sets a record date when you must be on the company's books as a shareholder to receive the dividend. The ex-dividend date is normally set for stocks two business days before the record date. To figure out when this date is, you will likely have to look on the website of the company which is paying the dividend.

Here is an example. You bought 5,000 shares of XYZ Corp. common stock on July 8, 2011. XYZ Corp. has declared a cash dividend of 10 cents per share. The ex-dividend date was July 15, 2011. Your Form 1099-DIV from XYZ Corp. shows $500 in box 1a (ordinary dividends) and in box 1b (qualified dividends). However, you sold the 5,000 shares on August 11, 2011. You held your shares of XYZ Corp. for only 34 days of the 121-day period (from July 9, 2011, through August 11, 2011). The 121-day period began on May 16, 2011 (60 days before the ex-dividend date), and ended on September 13, 2011. You have no qualified dividends from XYZ Corp. because you held the XYZ stock for less than 61 days.

ii. Qualified corporation

In order to claim qualified dividends, the corporation issuing them either has to be a US or a qualified foreign corporation. A foreign corporation is a qualified foreign corporation if it meets any of the following conditions:

1. The corporation is incorporated in a US possession.
2. The corporation is eligible for the benefits of a comprehensive income tax treaty with the United States. Note that Canada and most major western countries fulfill this criterion. For a complete list of those treaties, see Table 1-3 of Publication 550.
3. The corporation does not meet (1) or (2) above, but the stock for which the dividend is paid is readily tradable on an established securities market in the United States.

iii. Must not be this type of dividend

Finally, the IRS has established a list of dividends that are not qualified. They are as follows:

- Capital gain distributions.
- Dividends paid on deposits with mutual savings banks, cooperative banks, credit unions, US building and loan associations, US savings and loan associations, federal savings and loan associations, and similar financial institutions. (Report these amounts as interest income.)
- Dividends from a corporation that is a tax-exempt organization or farmer's cooperative during the corporation's tax year in which the dividends were paid or during the corporation's previous tax year.
- Dividends paid by a corporation on employer securities held on the date of record by an employee stock ownership plan (ESOP) maintained by that corporation.

- Dividends on any share of stock to the extent you are obligated (whether under a short sale or otherwise) to make related payments for shares of in substantially similar or related property.
- Payments in lieu of dividends, but only if you know or have reason to know the payments are not qualified dividends.
- Payments shown on Form 1099-DIV, box 1b, from a foreign corporation to the extent you know or have reason to know the payments are not qualified dividends.

c. Reporting qualified dividends

Take the amount from box 1(b) of Form 1099-Div and enter it on line 9(b). Should you have more than one Form-1099 Div, total them and enter the amount on line 9(b). Similarly, take all amounts of dividends that you think are qualified and enter them on line 9(b). If you have more than $1,500 in dividend income you will be required to complete Schedule B.

5. IF YOU HAVE MORE THAN $1,500 IN INTEREST OR DIVIDEND INCOME

If you have more than $1,500 in interest or dividend income you need to fill out Schedule B and attach it to your Form 1040. The form is fairly straightforward. In the first section, you list the name of the payer and the amount of interest you received. Then on line 2 you add the amounts. Unless you own series EE or I US Savings Bonds issued after 1989, you can ignore line 3. If you do own these type of bonds, you should consult publication 550 on how to report income from them. On line 4, enter the total from line 2 and on your Form 1040, line 8a.

For Part II, you do the same with your dividend income. At line 6, add the amounts on line 5. Enter the total and on Form 1040, line 9a.

Part III is more complicated. Since you likely have a Canadian bank account, you have to complete this section. Similarly, if you have any sort of bank account in Canada you have to check "yes" on box 7(a). Box 7(b) relates to the Report of Foreign Bank and Financial Accounts (FBAR).

This is discussed further in Chapter 44. Consult that chapter before deciding what to do with box 7(b). Briefly, if the aggregate of all of your bank accounts is more than $10,000 you will have to fill out the FBAR form.

Line 8 relates to your contributions to or money you received from a trust.

Note that you do not have to attach receipts to the Schedule B form.

Let's take a look at an example of a Schedule B. In this scenario, Dan Langer has savings accounts at Royal Bank and ING Direct that paid him interest, and owns some Apple and Research in Motion stock directly. Because he has more than $1,500 of income, he must complete Part 3. He has a bank account in Canada so he checks "yes" on box 7(a). He also has accounts where the total is more than $10,000. He will have to complete and file the FBAR form.

SCHEDULE B (Form 1040A or 1040)

Department of the Treasury Internal Revenue Service (99)

Interest and Ordinary Dividends

▶ Attach to Form 1040A or 1040. ▶ See instructions on back.

OMB No. 1545-0074

2011

Attachment Sequence No. 08

Name(s) shown on return: Daniel Langer

Your social security number: 123-456-789

Part I Interest

(See instructions on back and the instructions for Form 1040A, or Form 1040, line 8a.)

Note. If you received a Form 1099-INT, Form 1099-OID, or substitute statement from a brokerage firm, list the firm's name as the payer and enter the total interest shown on that form.

			Amount
1	List name of payer. If any interest is from a seller-financed mortgage and the buyer used the property as a personal residence, see instructions on back and list this interest first. Also, show that buyer's social security number and address ▶	1	
	ING Direct Tax Free Savings Account		$1250
	Royal Bank		300
2	Add the amounts on line 1	2	1550
3	Excludable interest on series EE and I U.S. savings bonds issued after 1989. Attach Form 8815	3	
4	Subtract line 3 from line 2. Enter the result here and on Form 1040A, or Form 1040, line 8a ▶	4	1550

Note. If line 4 is over $1,500, you must complete Part III.

Part II Ordinary Dividends

(See instructions on back and the instructions for Form 1040A, or Form 1040, line 9a.)

Note. If you received a Form 1099-DIV or substitute statement from a brokerage firm, list the firm's name as the payer and enter the ordinary dividends shown on that form.

			Amount
5	List name of payer ▶ Apple Inc.	5	1750
	Research in Motion Inc.		250
	Royal Bank of Canada Inc.		500
6	Add the amounts on line 5. Enter the total here and on Form 1040A, or Form 1040, line 9a ▶	6	2500

Note. If line 6 is over $1,500, you must complete Part III.

Part III Foreign Accounts and Trusts

(See instructions on back.)

You must complete this part if you **(a)** had over $1,500 of taxable interest or ordinary dividends; **(b)** had a foreign account; or **(c)** received a distribution from, or were a grantor of, or a transferor to, a foreign trust.

		Yes	No
7a	At any time during 2011, did you have a financial interest in or signature authority over a financial account (such as a bank account, securities account, or brokerage account) located in a foreign country? See instructions	✓	
	If "Yes," are you required to file Form TD F 90-22.1 to report that financial interest or signature authority? See Form TD F 90-22.1 and its instructions for filing requirements and exceptions to those requirements	✓	
b	If you are required to file Form TD F 90-22.1, enter the name of the foreign country where the financial account is located ▶ Canada		
8	During 2011, did you receive a distribution from, or were you the grantor of, or transferor to, a foreign trust? If "Yes," you may have to file Form 3520. See instructions on back	✓	

For Paperwork Reduction Act Notice, see your tax return instructions. Cat. No. 17146N Schedule B (Form 1040A or 1040) 2011

9

SELLING AN ASSET[1]

This chapter helps you determine the US tax implications if you sell something you own. Selling your home or another piece of real estate is discussed in Chapter 11. Likewise, selling stocks or bonds is discussed in Chapter 10. This chapter is focused on selling assets, such as a car or boat, that are not your main home or stocks and bonds. To make use of it, start with section 1 and work through the sections sequentially. They are as follows:

1. Capital gains/loss defined.
2. Ordinary gains/loss defined.
3. Calculating a capital gain or loss.
4. Calculating the adjusted cost basis.
5. Reporting the capital gain or loss.
6. Deducting and carrying over capital losses.

1. CAPITAL GAINS/LOSS DEFINED

Selling any item you own has tax consequences. The tax treatment depends on what kind of asset you sell. Capital assets, those which are subject to capital gains tax, include everything you own and use for personal purposes, pleasure, or investment. Some examples include stocks or bonds held in your personal account, a house owned and used by you and your family, household furnishings, a car used for pleasure or commuting, coin or stamp collections, gems and jewelry, and gold, silver, or any other metal. Chapter 4 of Publication 550 further comments on what are capital assets.

If the capital asset has increased in value when you sell it, you have realized a capital gain. If it has decreased in value upon sale, you have suffered a capital loss and you can deduct this from your income which may be subject to tax.

2. ORDINARY GAIN/LOSS DEFINED

Most personal property is treated as a capital asset. Items which are not capital assets, such as property used in a business, are referred to as "ordinary" assets. Not surprisingly, sales of ordinary assets generate ordinary gains or ordinary losses. These generally arise in a business setting and so are not covered by this guide. See Chapter 3 of Publication 544 for more information on this. Our focus here is on capital gains and losses.

3. CALCULATING A CAPITAL GAIN OR LOSS

Generally, when you sell an asset that is not a stock or bond you will not receive a tax slip that lists your capital gain, no capital, or loss. You have to calculate it yourself. The formula for determining a capital gain or loss is Selling price – selling expenses – adjusted cost basis = capital gain (positive total) or capital loss (negative total). The first two parts of this formula are straightforward. The selling price is the (full) price that someone paid for the item. The selling expenses are any expenses you incurred related to its sale. For example, if you sold your car for $15,000 and it cost you $300 to put up flyers related to its sale, the formula would be $15,000 – $300 ($14,700)

[1] This chapter is based on, and some text is copied from, IRS Publication 544 which is available on the IRS website.

– adjusted cost basis = capital gain or loss. In the next section, we discuss how to calculate adjusted cost basis.

4. CALCULATING THE ADJUSTED COST BASIS

The adjusted cost basis is the original basis (cost) of the asset plus or minus any appropriate adjustments.

a. The basis (cost)

The basis of property you buy is usually its cost. The cost is the amount you paid in cash, debt obligations, other property, or services. Your cost also includes amounts you paid for the following items related to the asset's purchase:

- sales tax;
- freight;
- installation and testing;
- excise taxes;
- legal and accounting fees;
- revenue stamps;
- recording fees;
- real estate taxes.

For instance, if you bought a cottage for $300,000 and paid $10,000 in transfer taxes and legal fees on it, your basis is $310,000.

b. Adjustments to the basis

Adjustments to the basis differ significantly depending on the type of property sold. That's why we've included separate chapters for those assets that people sell most often. There are, however, some general rules that apply.

i. Increasing the basis

Improvements that last longer than a year increase the basis. These must be distinguished from repairs. Repairs merely keep something as it has always been. Improvements, on the other hand, are new and should increase the value of the asset. For instance, if you own a car and you put a new radio in it you can treat this as an improvement. But if you merely have your existing radio fixed then this is a repair rather than an improvement. The following table presents some common examples of things that will increase the basis:

Increases to Basis
Capital improvements: Putting an addition on your home Replacing an entire roof Paving your driveway Installing central air conditioning Rewiring your home

Increases to Basis
Assessments for local improvements: Water connections Sidewalks Roads
Casualty losses: Restoring damaged property
Legal fees: Cost of defending and perfecting a title
Zoning costs

Note that this list is far from exhaustive.

ii. Decreases to the basis

The general rule is that if you receive money or credit towards your property you should deduct that amount from the basis. For instance, if your car is damaged in an accident and your insurance company pays to fix it, you have to deduct the amount of the insurance payment from the basis. The following are some specific items that reduce the basis of property:

- deductions previously allowed (or allowable) for amortization, depreciation, and depletion;
- subsidies for energy conservation measures;
- vehicle credits;
- residential energy credits;
- investment credit (part or all) taken;
- casualty and theft losses and insurance reimbursement;
- certain cancelled debt excluded from income;
- rebates from a manufacturer or seller;
- easements;
- gas-guzzler tax;
- adoption tax benefits;
- credit for employer-provided child care.

Note that this list is far from exhaustive. Nevertheless, it is worth providing a bit more detail on some of these items.

Casualties and thefts. If you have a casualty (basically a loss from a traumatic event) or theft loss, decrease the basis in your property by any insurance or other reimbursement and by any deductible loss not covered by insurance. Casualty losses are further explored in Chapter 25.

Depreciation. You cannot usually depreciate the cost of personal property. So you do not need to worry about this.

Vehicle tax credits. If you receive a tax credit, such as for having an environmentally friendly car, you must reduce your car's basis by the amount of this credit.

5. REPORTING THE CAPITAL GAIN OR LOSS

Once you have figured out the adjusted cost basis, simply subtract it from the total sale price (minus selling expenses). The result is your capital gain (if positive) or loss (if negative). All that remains is to report it. How you report it depends on how long you owned the asset. A long-term asset is one you owned for a year or longer whereas a short-term asset is one that you held for less than a year.

a. Form 8949

Reporting capital gains and losses is a two-step process. First, the gain or loss should be reported on Form 8949. Form 8949 is mostly self-explanatory, but there are a few wrinkles. Second, the results of what gets put on Form 8949 must be reported on Schedule D.

At the very top of the form there is a checkbox that asks whether the transactions were reported on Form-1099 B and reported to the IRS. As explained above, you are not likely to receive a tax slip if you sell your car or other capital assets, so you should check box C. As the instructions indicate, you are only supposed to include transactions of a similar type. So if you have some that were reported on a Form-1099 B and others that were not you must complete two separate Form 8949s.

Now, let's examine the various columns on Form 8949.

Column (a)—Description of Property. Here you enter the description of the item you are selling such as the name or type of asset.

Column (b)—Code. This is a special code that you can use to explain any adjustment to gain or loss in column (g). You can ignore this box unless you sold option premiums, have a loss from a "wash" sale, have gains you would like to rollover, sold qualified small business stock, sold your home, are a nominee for someone else, or there was a mistake on your form 1099-B. If any of these situations apply, see the instructions to Form 8949 that can be found on the IRS website.

Column (c)—Date Acquired. Here you put the date you acquired the asset. If the property was inherited, write "inherited" and the date you inherited it.

Column (d)—Date Sold. Here put the date you sold the property.

Column (e)—Sales Price. Here put the price you received for the item.

Column (f)—Cost or Other Basis. Enter the (basis) or cost of property. The method for calculating this is described above.

Column (g)—Adjustments to Gain or Loss. You can ignore this box unless one of the following scenarios applies:

- sold option premiums;
- have a loss from a "wash" sale;
- have gains you would like to rollover;
- sold qualified small business stock;
- sold your home;
- are a nominee for someone else;
- or there was a mistake on your form 1099-B.

If any of these situations apply, see the instructions to Form 8949 that can be found on the IRS website.

Add the amounts in columns (e) and (f). Enter here and include on Schedule D, line 8 (if box A is checked), line 9 (if box B is checked), or line 10 (if box C is checked). You repeat the same steps for Part II of the form.

b. Example

Let's use an example to explain this. Joe bought his car in 2005 for $30,000 plus taxes of $500. So his basis was $30,500. Over the years, he installed air conditioning because the car did not initially have it. This cost him $2,000. That means that his adjusted cost basis is $32,500. In 2012 he sold the car for $15,000. There were no other relevant factors, such as credits or insurance payments. That means he had a capital loss of $17,500. He would fill out his Form 8949 as follows.

Form **8949**
Department of the Treasury
Internal Revenue Service (99)

Sales and Other Dispositions of Capital Assets
▶ See Instructions for Schedule D (Form 1040).
▶ For more information about Form 8949, see www.irs.gov/form8949
▶ Attach to Schedule D to list your transactions for lines 1, 2, 3, 8, 9, and 10.

OMB No. 1545-0074
2011
Attachment Sequence No. 12A

Name(s) shown on return: Joe Smith
Your social security number: 123-45-6789

Part I **Short-Term Capital Gains and Losses—Assets Held One Year or Less**

Note: You **must** check **one** of the boxes below. Complete a separate Form 8949, page 1, for **each** box that is checked.
***Caution.** Do not complete column (b) or (g) until you have read the instructions for those columns (see the Instructions for Schedule D (Form 1040)). Columns (b) and (g) do not apply for most transactions and should generally be left blank.

☐ **(A)** Short-term transactions reported on Form 1099-B with basis reported to the IRS ☐ **(B)** Short-term transactions reported on Form 1099-B but basis not reported to the IRS ☐ **(C)** Short-term transactions for which you cannot check box A or B

1 (a) Description of property (Example: 100 sh. XYZ Co.)	(b) Code, if any, for column (g)*	(c) Date acquired (Mo., day, yr.)	(d) Date sold (Mo., day, yr.)	(e) Sales price (see instructions)	(f) Cost or other basis (see instructions)	(g) Adjustments to gain or loss, if any*

2 Totals. Add the amounts in columns (e) and (f). Also, combine the amounts in column (g). Enter here and include on Schedule D, **line 1** (if **box A** above is checked), **line 2** (if **box B** above is checked), or **line 3** (if **box C** above is checked) . . . . ▶	2		

For Paperwork Reduction Act Notice, see your tax return instructions. Cat. No. 37768Z Form **8949** (2011)

Form 8949 (2011) Attachment Sequence No. **12A** Page **2**

Name(s) shown on return. Do not enter name and social security number if shown on other side.	**Your social security number**
Joe Smith	123-45-6789

Part II **Long-Term Capital Gains and Losses—Assets Held More Than One Year**

Note: You **must** check **one** of the boxes below. Complete a *separate* Form 8949, page 2, for **each** box that is checked.

***Caution.** Do not complete column (b) or (g) until you have read the instructions for those columns (see the Instructions for Schedule D (Form 1040)). Columns (b) and (g) do not apply for most transactions and should generally be left blank.

☐ **(A)** Long-term transactions reported on Form 1099-B with basis reported to the IRS ☐ **(B)** Long-term transactions reported on Form 1099-B but basis not reported to the IRS ☑ **(C)** Long-term transactions for which you cannot check box A or B

3 (a) Description of property (Example: 100 sh. XYZ Co.)	(b) Code, if any, for column (g)*	(c) Date acquired (Mo., day, yr.)	(d) Date sold (Mo., day, yr.)	(e) Sales price (see instructions)	(f) Cost or other basis (see instructions)	(g) Adjustments to gain or loss, if any*
2005 BMW		2005	2012	15,000	32500	
4 Totals. Add the amounts in columns (e) and (f). Also, combine the amounts in column (g). Enter here and include on Schedule D, **line 8** (if **box A** above is checked), **line 9** (if **box B** above is checked), or **line 10** (if **box C** above is checked) . . . ▶ 4				15,000	32,500	

Form **8949** (2011)

And he would fill out his Schedule D as follows.

SCHEDULE D (Form 1040)
Department of the Treasury Internal Revenue Service (99)

Capital Gains and Losses

▶ Attach to Form 1040 or Form 1040NR. ▶ See Instructions for Schedule D (Form 1040).
▶ Use Form 8949 to list your transactions for lines 1, 2, 3, 8, 9, and 10.

OMB No. 1545-0074
2011
Attachment Sequence No. **12**

Name(s) shown on return: Joe Smith
Your social security number: 123-45-6789

Part I Short-Term Capital Gains and Losses—Assets Held One Year or Less

Complete Form 8949 before completing line 1, 2, or 3. This form may be easier to complete if you round off cents to whole dollars.	(e) Sales price from Form(s) 8949, line 2, column (e)	(f) Cost or other basis from Form(s) 8949, line 2, column (f)	(g) Adjustments to gain or loss from Form(s) 8949, line 2, column (g)	(h) Gain or (loss) Combine columns (e), (f), and (g)
1 Short-term totals from all Forms 8949 with box A checked in Part I		( )		
2 Short-term totals from all Forms 8949 with box B checked in Part I		( )		
3 Short-term totals from all Forms 8949 with box C checked in Part I		( )		

4 Short-term gain from Form 6252 and short-term gain or (loss) from Forms 4684, 6781, and 8824	4	
5 Net short-term gain or (loss) from partnerships, S corporations, estates, and trusts from Schedule(s) K-1	5	
6 Short-term capital loss carryover. Enter the amount, if any, from line 8 of your **Capital Loss Carryover Worksheet** in the instructions	6	( )
7 **Net short-term capital gain or (loss).** Combine lines 1 through 6 in column (h). If you have any long-term capital gains or losses, go to Part II below. Otherwise, go to Part III on the back	7	

Part II Long-Term Capital Gains and Losses—Assets Held More Than One Year

Complete Form 8949 before completing line 8, 9, or 10. This form may be easier to complete if you round off cents to whole dollars.	(e) Sales price from Form(s) 8949, line 4, column (e)	(f) Cost or other basis from Form(s) 8949, line 4, column (f)	(g) Adjustments to gain or loss from Form(s) 8949, line 4, column (g)	(h) Gain or (loss) Combine columns (e), (f), and (g)
8 Long-term totals from all Forms 8949 with box A checked in Part II		( )		
9 Long-term totals from all Forms 8949 with box B checked in Part II		( )		
10 Long-term totals from all Forms 8949 with box C checked in Part II	15000	(32500)		17000

11 Gain from Form 4797, Part I; long-term gain from Forms 2439 and 6252; and long-term gain or (loss) from Forms 4684, 6781, and 8824	11	
12 Net long-term gain or (loss) from partnerships, S corporations, estates, and trusts from Schedule(s) K-1	12	
13 Capital gain distributions. See the instructions	13	
14 Long-term capital loss carryover. Enter the amount, if any, from line 13 of your **Capital Loss Carryover Worksheet** in the instructions	14	( )
15 **Net long-term capital gain or (loss).** Combine lines 8 through 14 in column (h). Then go to Part III on the back	15	(17000)

For Paperwork Reduction Act Notice, see your tax return instructions. Cat. No. 11338H **Schedule D (Form 1040) 2011**

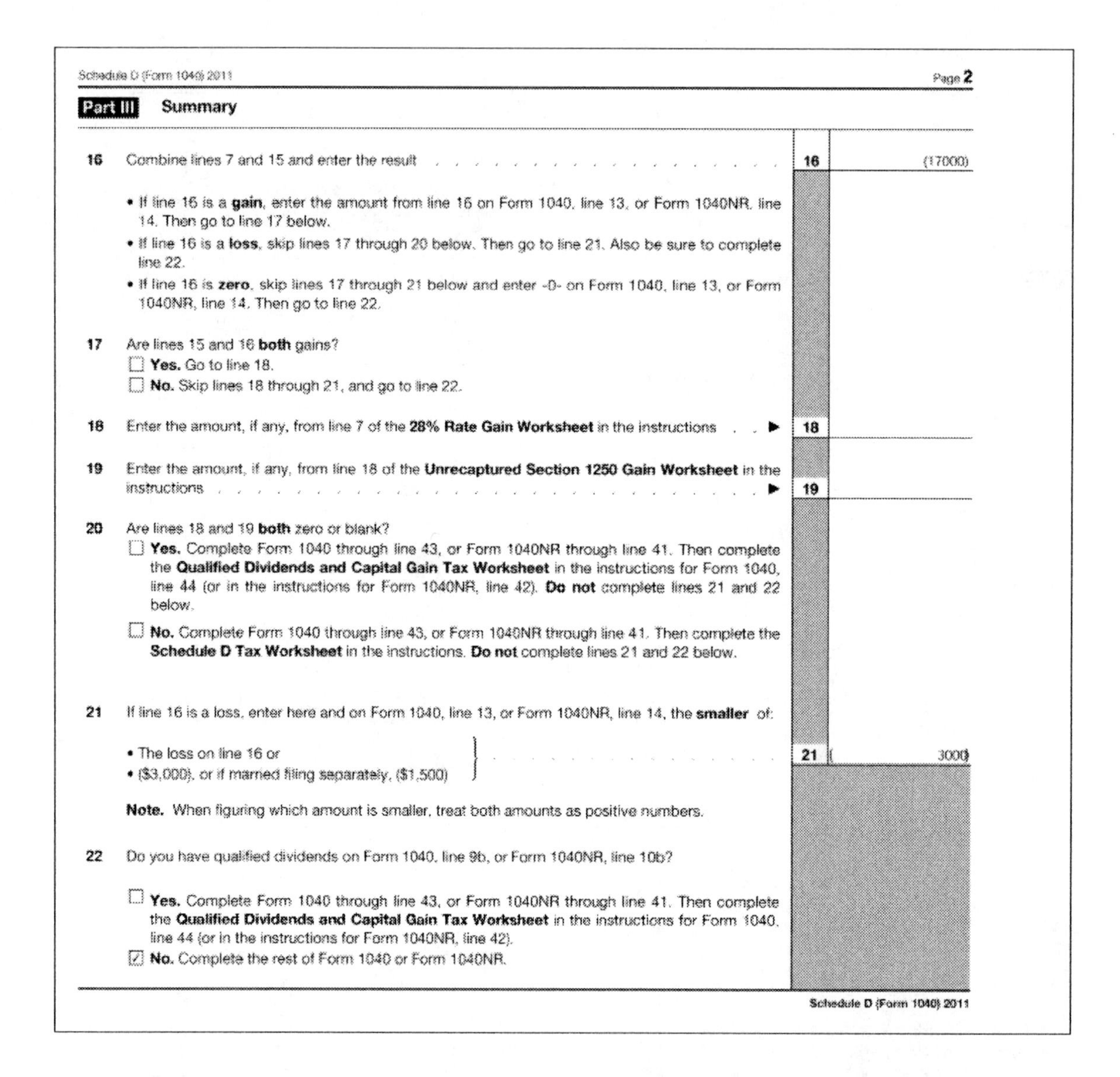

Schedule D (Form 1040) 2011 Page **2**

Part III **Summary**

16 Combine lines 7 and 15 and enter the result **16** (17000)

- If line 16 is a **gain**, enter the amount from line 16 on Form 1040, line 13, or Form 1040NR, line 14. Then go to line 17 below.
- If line 16 is a **loss**, skip lines 17 through 20 below. Then go to line 21. Also be sure to complete line 22.
- If line 16 is **zero**, skip lines 17 through 21 below and enter -0- on Form 1040, line 13, or Form 1040NR, line 14. Then go to line 22.

17 Are lines 15 and 16 **both** gains?
☐ **Yes.** Go to line 18.
☐ **No.** Skip lines 18 through 21, and go to line 22.

18 Enter the amount, if any, from line 7 of the **28% Rate Gain Worksheet** in the instructions . . ▶ **18**

19 Enter the amount, if any, from line 18 of the **Unrecaptured Section 1250 Gain Worksheet** in the instructions . . . . ▶ **19**

20 Are lines 18 and 19 **both** zero or blank?
☐ **Yes.** Complete Form 1040 through line 43, or Form 1040NR through line 41. Then complete the **Qualified Dividends and Capital Gain Tax Worksheet** in the instructions for Form 1040, line 44 (or in the instructions for Form 1040NR, line 42). **Do not** complete lines 21 and 22 below.
☐ **No.** Complete Form 1040 through line 43, or Form 1040NR through line 41. Then complete the **Schedule D Tax Worksheet** in the instructions. **Do not** complete lines 21 and 22 below.

21 If line 16 is a loss, enter here and on Form 1040, line 13, or Form 1040NR, line 14, the **smaller** of:

- The loss on line 16 or
- ($3,000), or if married filing separately, ($1,500) } **21** (3000)

Note. When figuring which amount is smaller, treat both amounts as positive numbers.

22 Do you have qualified dividends on Form 1040, line 9b, or Form 1040NR, line 10b?
☐ **Yes.** Complete Form 1040 through line 43, or Form 1040NR through line 41. Then complete the **Qualified Dividends and Capital Gain Tax Worksheet** in the instructions for Form 1040, line 44 (or in the instructions for Form 1040NR, line 42).
☑ **No.** Complete the rest of Form 1040 or Form 1040NR.

Schedule D (Form 1040) 2011

6. DEDUCTING AND CARRYING OVER CAPITAL LOSSES

Note that Joe can claim up to $3,000 in capital losses to reduce his income. All he needs to do is enter ($3,000) on line 16 of his Form 1040. He can also carry over the losses to use in a future year.

Generally, you have a capital loss carryover if either of the following situations apply to you.

- Your net loss on Schedule D, line 16, is more than the yearly limit.
- Your taxable income without your deduction for exemptions is less than zero.

If you have a total net loss on line 16 of Schedule D that is more than the yearly limit on capital loss deductions, you can carry over the unused part to the next year and treat it as if you had incurred it in that next year. If part of the loss is still unused, you can carry it over to later years until it is completely used up.

When you calculate the amount of any capital loss carryover to the next year, you must take the current year's allowable deduction into account, whether or not you claimed it and whether or not you filed a return for the current year. When you carry over a loss, it remains long term or short term. A long-term capital loss you carry over to the next tax year will reduce that year's long-term capital gains before it reduces that year's short-term capital gains.

The amount of your capital loss carryover is the amount of your total net loss that is more than the lesser of:

1. Your allowable capital loss deduction for the year (maximum $3,000), or

2. Your taxable income increased by your allowable capital loss deduction for the year and your deduction for personal exemptions.

Here is an example that illustrates these rules.

Bob and Gloria sold their car in 2011. The sale resulted in a capital loss of $7,000. They had no other capital transactions. Their taxable income was $26,000. On their joint 2011 return, they can deduct $3,000. The unused part of the loss, $4,000 ($7,000 – $3,000), can be carried over to 2012.

If their capital loss had been $2,000, their capital loss deduction would have been $2,000. They would have no carryover. For more information on capital loss carryovers, please see Chapter 4 of IRS publication 550.

10

IF YOU SOLD STOCKS, BONDS, OR US MUTUAL FUNDS[1]

This chapter explains how to report gains or losses from sales of stocks or bonds and US mutual fund or exchange traded funds. Please consult Chapter 42 if you sell Canadian mutual funds.

Additionally, you should be aware that you have to report gains from the sale of financial products that are held inside a Tax Free Savings Account (TFSA), Registered Education Savings Plan (RESP), or Registered Disability Savings Plan (RDSP). Please see Chapter 43 for more information. This chapter is organized as follows:

1. Recognizing gains and losses from stocks/bonds/mutual funds.
2. Calculating the basis of a stock or bond.
3. Calculating the capital gain or loss.
4. How long did you own the stock, bond or mutual fund.
5. Reporting the capital gain or loss.

1. RECOGNIZING GAINS AND LOSSES FROM STOCKS/BONDS/MUTUAL FUNDS

The simple rule is whenever you sell a stock or bond you will realize either a capital gain or loss. Sometimes you will receive a tax information slip that shows the amount of this gain or loss. Canadian financial institutions may issue you a T3, T4PS, or T5 form. American financial institutions may give you a Form 1099-B. Note that if you receive a form that lists capital gains distributions you should report them in a similar way. If you receive a form for all of your capital gains you can skip down to section 4. All you need to do is determine how long you had owned these and then report them on Schedule D.

In any case, even if you do not receive a tax slip you still must calculate and report the capital gains/losses. The formula is as follows: amount realized from the sale – basis (the cost) = reportable capital gain or loss. A negative total is a capital loss, whereas a positive total is a capital gain. The rest of the chapter walks you through this formula.

2. CALCULATING THE BASIS (COST) OF THE STOCK OR BOND

The first step is to figure out the asset's basis. Basis is a technical tax term for cost. So, you have to figure out what the asset was worth when you bought it. From there, you can figure out the difference between the sale price and the original price. The way to figure the basis depends on what type of asset it is.

---

[1] This chapter is based on, and some text is copied from, IRS Publication 550.

a. Stocks, bonds, and other financial instruments

For stocks (including exchange traded funds), bonds, and other financial instruments it is quite easy to figure out the basis. All you need to do is go back to the date of purchase and look up what price you paid for it. This should be fairly easy to find. Then you just add any fees, such as brokerage commissions, associated with the purchase and divide them per unit. There is not that much that will impact the market price you paid.

Let's take an example. Say you bought 500 shares of Apple Inc. on March 1, 2005 at $75 each. For this transaction you also paid a $30 commission to your brokerage. The basis of each share is $75 plus the fraction of the commission that is attributable to each share ($30 commission /500 (number of shares) = 6 cents per share.)

b. US mutual funds

US mutual funds are slightly more complicated. Recall that Canadian mutual funds are addressed in Chapter 42.

Often, people buy shares of the same mutual fund in small amounts over a long period of time. If you can trace the cost of the particular shares you sold, then you should calculate the basis (cost) in the same way that you do for stocks and bonds. However, if you can't do this, you identify the first shares you acquired as the ones you sold. Let's say you acquired 1000 shares of a mutual fund over the course of 2010 using an automated purchase plan. Now you want to sell 300 of them. The price of the first 300 shares becomes the cost used to calculate the gain.

The other option is to take an average of the price you paid for the mutual fund. Note, however, that this can only be done if you acquired the shares after December 31, 2010 in connection with a dividend reinvestment plan. So, the possibility of using the average is quite limited. Publication 550 describes how to make this choice.

c. Stocks, bonds, and mutual funds received from a spouse

Figuring out the basis of stocks or bonds transferred from your spouse is quite straightforward. You simply take the cost that your spouse paid and consider it your own.

d. Property you inherit

The basis of stocks and bonds you inherit is the fair market value of the property at the date of death of the person from whom you inherited it, unless the estate selects a different valuation date. In that case, you should simply use the fair market value on the valuation date that the person in charge of the estate has chosen. To determine whether the estate has chosen another valuation date, you will have to contact the person responsible for managing the estate. For stocks, bonds, and mutual funds, the fair market value can be easily established by simply looking at the relevant market on which the stock or bond is traded. If you cannot do this, you should seek professional advice as to how to value the stocks and bonds you inherit.

3. CALCULATING THE CAPITAL GAIN OR LOSS

After you have calculated the basis, it is very simple to figure out the actual capital gain or loss. All you have to do is take the price at which the asset was sold (less any expenses incurred) and subtract the basis. If the amount is positive, you have a capital gain to report. If the amount is negative, you have a capital loss.

Here is an example. Let's say that you buy 300 shares of Exxon at $50/share. For this transaction, you pay a fee of $30. Including the commission, the basis of each Exxon share is $50.10. Let's say you sold 150 shares for $60. On each share you have a capital gain of $9.90. Take that amount and multiply it by 150 (the total number of shares) to arrive at your total capital gain of $1,485. From this number, you can subtract any commissions you paid on the sale.

4. HOW LONG DID YOU OWN THE STOCK, BOND, OR MUTUAL FUND?

The length of time you hold the asset determines in part how much tax you will pay on it. The starting date for the calculation is the day after you purchased the stock, bond, or mutual fund. The end date is the day you sold the asset. A long-term asset is one you owned for a year or longer, whereas a short-term asset is one that you held for less than a year.

Let's consider an example to illustrate this relatively simple point. If you bought investment property on February 3, 2010, and sold it on February 3, 2011, your holding period is not more than 1 year and you have a short-term capital gain or loss. If you sold it on February 4, 2011, your holding period is more than 1 year and you have a long-term capital gain or loss.

As above, if you own financial products other than stocks, ETFs, bonds or mutual funds, the rules are more complicated. You should consult Publication 550.

5. REPORTING THE GAIN OR LOSS

There is a two-step process to reporting capital gains and losses. The first is to list them all on Form 8949. The second step is to transfer the information from Form 8949 to Schedule D.

Form 8949 is mostly self-explanatory, but there are a few wrinkles. First, at the very top of the form there is a checkbox that asks whether the transactions were reported on Form-1099 B and reported to the IRS. As explained above, you will only receive a Form-1099 B for those transactions done through an American financial institution. Unless you have received this form, you should check box C. As the instructions indicate, you are only supposed to include transactions of a similar type. So, if you have some that were reported on a Form-1099 B and others that were not, you must fill out two separate Form 8949s.

Now, let's turn our attention to the various columns of the Form 8949.

Column (a)—Description of Property. Here you enter the description of the item you are selling such as the name of the stock or bond.

Column (b)—Code. This is a special code that you can use to explain any adjustment to the gain or loss in column (g). You can ignore this box unless you sold option premiums, have a loss from a wash stale, have gains you would like to rollover, sold qualified small business stock, sold your home, are a nominee for someone else, or there was a mistake on your form 1099-B. If any of these situations apply please see the instructions to Form 8949 that can be found on the IRS website.

Column (c)—Date Acquired. Here you put the date you acquired the stock or bond. If you inherited this, write "inherited" here.

Column (d)—Date Sold. Here you put the date you sold the asset.

Column (e)—Sales Price. Here put the price you received for the item. Report the total sales price for all shares sold.

Column (f)—Cost or Other Basis. Here is where you enter the (basis) or cost of the asset. The method for calculating this is described above.

Column (g)—Adjustments to Gain or Loss. You can ignore this box unless you sold option premiums, have a loss from a wash sale, have gains you would like to rollover, sold qualified small business stock, sold your home, are a nominee for someone else, or there was a mistake on your Form 1099-B. If any of these situations apply please see the instructions to Form 8949 that can be found on the IRS website.

Add the amounts in columns (e) and (f). Enter here and include on Schedule D, line 8 (if box A is checked), line 9 (if box B is checked), or line 10 (if box C is checked). You need to repeat the same steps for Part II of the form.

Let's take the following example. Adam Smith is a very active recreational trader of stocks who lives in Canada. His stock trades are not reported on a Form-1099 B. That means he has to check box C on Form 8949. In 2011, Adam made the following short-term trades.

He purchased 500 shares of Apple Inc. on March 15, 2010 at $75 a piece (total $37,500). He sold them all for $100 on March 1, 2011 (total $50,000). That means he incurred a short term capital gain of $25 a share. On August 1, 2011, he also purchased 250 shares of Google Inc. at $200 each for a total purchase price of $50,000. He sold them a month later on September 1, 2011 for $125 (total $31,250). Thus, he suffered a short-term capital loss of $18,750. Adam totals columns (e) and (f). Adding columns (e) and (f) shows that he has a short-term capital loss of US $6,250.

Adam also has long-term capital gains. On July 1, 2005, he purchased 1000 units of a Bank of America mutual fund located in the United States for $25 each for a total of US$25,000. He then sold them on March 1, 2011 for US$40/share for a total of US$40,000. Adam reports this information on his Form 8949 which looks like this.

Form **8949**

Department of the Treasury
Internal Revenue Service (99)

Sales and Other Dispositions of Capital Assets

► See Instructions for Schedule D (Form 1040).
► For more information about Form 8949, see *www.irs.gov/form8949*
► Attach to Schedule D to list your transactions for lines 1, 2, 3, 8, 9, and 10.

OMB No. 1545-0074
2011
Attachment Sequence No. **12A**

Name(s) shown on return: Adam Smith

Your social security number: 123-456-789

Part I **Short-Term Capital Gains and Losses—Assets Held One Year or Less**

Note: You **must** check **one** of the boxes below. Complete a *separate* Form 8949, page 1, for **each** box that is checked.
***Caution.** Do not complete column (b) or (g) until you have read the instructions for those columns (see the Instructions for Schedule D (Form 1040)). Columns (b) and (g) do not apply for most transactions and should generally be left blank.

☐ **(A)** Short-term transactions reported on Form 1099-B with basis reported to the IRS
☐ **(B)** Short-term transactions reported on Form 1099-B but basis not reported to the IRS
☑ **(C)** Short-term transactions for which you cannot check box A or B

1 (a) Description of property (Example: 100 sh. XYZ Co.)	(b) Code, if any, for column (g)*	(c) Date acquired (Mo., day, yr.)	(d) Date sold (Mo., day, yr.)	(e) Sales price (see instructions)	(f) Cost or other basis (see instructions)	(g) Adjustments to gain or loss, if any*
500 Apple Inc. shares		03/15/2010	03/01/2011	50,000	37,500	
250 Google Inc. Shares		08/01/2011	09/01/2011	31,250	50,000	
2 Totals. Add the amounts in columns (e) and (f). Also, combine the amounts in column (g). Enter here and include on Schedule D, **line 1** (if **box A** above is checked), **line 2** (if **box B** above is checked), or **line 3** (if **box C** above is checked) . . . ► **2**				81,250	87,500	

For Paperwork Reduction Act Notice, see your tax return instructions. Cat. No. 37768Z Form **8949** (2011)

Form 8949 (2011) Attachment Sequence No. **12A** Page **2**

Name(s) shown on return. Do not enter name and social security number if shown on other side.
Adam Smith

Your social security number
123-456-789

Part II Long-Term Capital Gains and Losses—Assets Held More Than One Year

Note: You **must** check **one** of the boxes below. Complete a *separate* Form 8949, page 2, for **each** box that is checked.

***Caution.** Do not complete column (b) or (g) until you have read the instructions for those columns (see the Instructions for Schedule D (Form 1040)). Columns (b) and (g) do not apply for most transactions and should generally be left blank.

☐ **(A)** Long-term transactions reported on Form 1099-B with basis reported to the IRS
☐ **(B)** Long-term transactions reported on Form 1099-B but basis not reported to the IRS
☑ **(C)** Long-term transactions for which you cannot check box A or B

3 (a) Description of property (Example: 100 sh. XYZ Co.)	(b) Code, if any, for column (g)*	(c) Date acquired (Mo., day, yr.)	(d) Date sold (Mo., day, yr.)	(e) Sales price (see instructions)	(f) Cost or other basis (see instructions)	(g) Adjustments to gain or loss, if any*
1000 shares Bank of America mutual fund		07/01/2011	03/01/2011	40,000	25,000	
4 Totals. Add the amounts in columns (e) and (f). Also, combine the amounts in column (g). Enter here and include on Schedule D, **line 8** (if **box A** above is checked), **line 9** (if **box B** above is checked), or **line 10** (if **box C** above is checked) . . . . ▶			4	40,000	25,000	

Form **8949** (2011)

Adam next has to take the information on his Form 8949 and transfer it to Schedule D.

SCHEDULE D (Form 1040)

Department of the Treasury Internal Revenue Service (99)

Capital Gains and Losses

► Attach to Form 1040 or Form 1040NR. ► See Instructions for Schedule D (Form 1040).
► Use Form 8949 to list your transactions for lines 1, 2, 3, 8, 9, and 10.

OMB No. 1545-0074

2011

Attachment Sequence No. 12

Name(s) shown on return	Your social security number
Adam Smith	123-456-789

Part I Short-Term Capital Gains and Losses—Assets Held One Year or Less

Complete Form 8949 before completing line 1, 2, or 3. This form may be easier to complete if you round off cents to whole dollars.	(e) Sales price from Form(s) 8949, line 2, column (e)	(f) Cost or other basis from Form(s) 8949, line 2, column (f)	(g) Adjustments to gain or loss from Form(s) 8949, line 2, column (g)	(h) Gain or (loss) Combine columns (e), (f), and (g)
1 Short-term totals from all Forms 8949 with **box A** checked in **Part I**	0	(0)	0	00
2 Short-term totals from all Forms 8949 with **box B** checked in **Part I**	0	(0)	0	0
3 Short-term totals from all Forms 8949 with **box C** checked in **Part I**	81,250	(87500)		(6250)

4 Short-term gain from Form 6252 and short-term gain or (loss) from Forms 4684, 6781, and 8824	4	0
5 Net short-term gain or (loss) from partnerships, S corporations, estates, and trusts from Schedule(s) K-1	5	0
6 Short-term capital loss carryover. Enter the amount, if any, from line 8 of your **Capital Loss Carryover Worksheet** in the instructions	6	(0)
7 **Net short-term capital gain or (loss).** Combine lines 1 through 6 in column (h). If you have any long-term capital gains or losses, go to Part II below. Otherwise, go to Part III on the back	7	(6250)

Part II Long-Term Capital Gains and Losses—Assets Held More Than One Year

Complete Form 8949 before completing line 8, 9, or 10. This form may be easier to complete if you round off cents to whole dollars.	(e) Sales price from Form(s) 8949, line 4, column (e)	(f) Cost or other basis from Form(s) 8949, line 4, column (f)	(g) Adjustments to gain or loss from Form(s) 8949, line 4, column (g)	(h) Gain or (loss) Combine columns (e), (f), and (g)
8 Long-term totals from all Forms 8949 with **box A** checked in **Part II**	0	(0)	0	0
9 Long-term totals from all Forms 8949 with **box B** checked in **Part II**	0	(0)	0	0
10 Long-term totals from all Forms 8949 with **box C** checked in **Part II**	40,000	(25,000)	0	15,000

11 Gain from Form 4797, Part I; long-term gain from Forms 2439 and 6252; and long-term gain or (loss) from Forms 4684, 6781, and 8824	11	0
12 Net long-term gain or (loss) from partnerships, S corporations, estates, and trusts from Schedule(s) K-1	12	0
13 Capital gain distributions. See the instructions	13	0
14 Long-term capital loss carryover. Enter the amount, if any, from line 13 of your **Capital Loss Carryover Worksheet** in the instructions	14	(0)
15 **Net long-term capital gain or (loss).** Combine lines 8 through 14 in column (h). Then go to Part III on the back	15	15,000

For Paperwork Reduction Act Notice, see your tax return instructions. Cat. No. 11338H **Schedule D (Form 1040) 2011**

Schedule D (Form 1040) 2011 Page 2

Part III **Summary**

16 Combine lines 7 and 15 and enter the result **16** 8750

- If line 16 is a **gain**, enter the amount from line 16 on Form 1040, line 13, or Form 1040NR, line 14. Then go to line 17 below.
- If line 16 is a **loss**, skip lines 17 through 20 below. Then go to line 21. Also be sure to complete line 22.
- If line 16 is **zero**, skip lines 17 through 21 below and enter -0- on Form 1040, line 13, or Form 1040NR, line 14. Then go to line 22.

17 Are lines 15 and 16 **both** gains?
☑ **Yes.** Go to line 18.
☐ **No.** Skip lines 18 through 21, and go to line 22.

18 Enter the amount, if any, from line 7 of the **28% Rate Gain Worksheet** in the instructions . . ▶ **18** 0

19 Enter the amount, if any, from line 18 of the **Unrecaptured Section 1250 Gain Worksheet** in the instructions . . . . ▶ **19** 0

20 Are lines 18 and 19 **both** zero or blank?
☑ **Yes.** Complete Form 1040 through line 43, or Form 1040NR through line 41. Then complete the **Qualified Dividends and Capital Gain Tax Worksheet** in the instructions for Form 1040, line 44 (or in the instructions for Form 1040NR, line 42). **Do not** complete lines 21 and 22 below.

☐ **No.** Complete Form 1040 through line 43, or Form 1040NR through line 41. Then complete the **Schedule D Tax Worksheet** in the instructions. **Do not** complete lines 21 and 22 below.

21 If line 16 is a loss, enter here and on Form 1040, line 13, or Form 1040NR, line 14, the **smaller** of:

- The loss on line 16 or
- ($3,000), or if married filing separately, ($1,500) } . . . . **21** ( )

Note. When figuring which amount is smaller, treat both amounts as positive numbers.

22 Do you have qualified dividends on Form 1040, line 9b, or Form 1040NR, line 10b?

☐ **Yes.** Complete Form 1040 through line 43, or Form 1040NR through line 41. Then complete the **Qualified Dividends and Capital Gain Tax Worksheet** in the instructions for Form 1040, line 44 (or in the instructions for Form 1040NR, line 42).
☐ **No.** Complete the rest of Form 1040 or Form 1040NR.

Schedule D (Form 1040) 2011

Adam takes the amount on line 16 and puts it on line 13 of his Form 1040.

There are a couple of points to note from Schedule D. First, if you are selling stocks, bonds, or US mutual funds that you own directly, you can ignore lines 4, 5, 11, 12, 18, and 19 on Schedule D. Second, unlike the above example, you may have had a capital loss. If this is the case, all you need is to follow the instructions on line 21. If so, you get to deduct up to $3,000 in capital losses from your income. So, you can enter the lesser your loss on line 16 and $3,000 ($1,500 if you are married and filing separately) on line 13 of your return. If you have a larger loss than this, see Chapter 9 or IRS Publication 550 for the rules about carrying forward capital losses.

11

IF YOU SOLD YOUR HOME[1]

Selling real estate can have serious tax consequences. This chapter assists you in computing the income on the sale of your main home or another piece of real estate you own. It is organized as follows:

1. Figure out the basis (the cost) of your home.
2. Figure out the adjusted cost basis.
3. Figure out the amount realized (the sale price).
4. Calculate the capital gain or loss.
5. Reporting the capital gain or loss on your main home.
6. Reporting the capital gains for a sale of real estate that is not your main home.
7. Other issues.

The formula for calculating capital gains is: selling price – sales expenses – adjusted cost basis = capital gain or loss. If the home is your "main home" (principal residence) you can exclude up to $250,000 in capital gains from tax if single or $500,000 if married and filing jointly.

1. FIGURING OUT THE BASIS (THE COST) OF YOUR HOME

To calculate whether you have a capital gain on the sale of your home or other piece of real estate you first need to determine the basis. The basis is a technical tax term for the original cost of something.

a. Real estate you purchased

The purchase price is usually the basis for real estate you own. You can include some of the fees associated with closing the deal in the basis. These include the following:

1. Abstract fees (abstract of title fees);
2. Charges for installing utility services;
3. Legal fees (including fees for the title search and preparing the sales contract and deed);
4. Recording fees;
5. Survey fees;
6. Transfer taxes;
7. Owner's title insurance;

[1] This chapter is based on, and some text is copied from, IRS Publication 523.

8. Any amounts the seller owes that you agree to pay, such as:

    a. Certain real estate taxes;
    b. Back interest;
    c. Recording or mortgage fees;
    d. Charges for improvements or repairs;
    e. Sales commissions.

Some settlement fees and closing costs you cannot include in your basis are:

1. Fire insurance premiums;

2. Rent for occupancy of the house before closing;

3. Charges for utilities or other services related to occupancy of the house before closing;

4. Any fee or cost that you deducted as a moving expense;

5. Charges connected with getting a mortgage loan, such as:

    a. Mortgage insurance premiums;
    b. Loan assumption fees;
    c. Cost of a credit report;
    d. Fee for an appraisal required by a lender.

6. Fees for refinancing a mortgage.

b. Real estate you constructed

If you contracted to have your house built on land you own, your basis is:

1. The cost of the land, plus

2. The amount it cost you to complete the house, including:

    a. The cost of labour and materials;
    b. Any amounts paid to a contractor;
    c. Any architect's fees;
    d. Building permit charges;
    e. Utility meter and connection charges;
    f. Legal fees directly connected with building the house.

c. Real estate that is inherited

Inheritance changes things. If you inherited the real estate before 2010, the basis is the fair market value of the home at the time when its original owner died. Determining this can be complicated. One way is to consult the property tax records. The records should demonstrate how the value of the property has changed over time. Also, you may wish to consult the probate files of the person from whom you inherited the property. If you cannot make a satisfactory determination, you may have to pay to have your home appraised.

Different rules apply to property inherited after 2010. The basis is the lesser of the current fair market value of the property and the basis for the person who owned it previously. For example, if your parents bought their home in 1940 for $50,000 and, when they died in 2010, it was worth

$600,000, the basis you must use is $50,000. More information about this can be found in publication 551.

d. Real estate acquired by gift

If you receive a piece of real estate as a gift, your basis is generally that of the person who gave it to you. So if your uncle purchased a cottage in 1960 for $40,000 and gives it to you in 2012, then the basis is $40,000.

2. FIGURING OUT THE ADJUSTED COST BASIS

Once you have the basis, you need to factor any adjustments into it to arrive at the adjusted cost basis. Adjustments can either increase or lower the original basis. Improvements increase the basis while payments you receive lower it.

a. Improvements

Improvements to your home increase the basis while repairs do not. Improvements add to the value of your home, prolong its useful life, or adapt it to new uses. Repairs, on the other hand, maintain your home in good condition but do not add to its value or prolong its life. The IRS offers the following examples of improvements:

Additions Bedroom Bathroom Deck Garage Porch Patio	**Heating & Air Conditioning** Heating system Central air conditioning Furnace Duct work Central humidifier Filtration system
Lawn & Grounds Landscaping Driveway Walkway Fence Retaining wall Sprinkler system Swimming pool	**Plumbing** Septic system Water heater Soft water system Filtration system
Miscellaneous Storm windows, doors New roof Central vacuum Wiring upgrades Satellite dish Security system	**Interior Improvements** Built-in appliances Kitchen modernization Flooring Wall-to-wall carpeting
	Insulation Attic Walls Floors Pipes and duct work

You may adjust the cost based on other improvements that are not on this list. Adjusting the basis for improvements is easy. Simply take the cost of each improvement made and add it to the original basis (cost).

An example shows how this works. Tim bought a house in Toronto in 1996 for $250,000. To purchase the house, he paid $5,000 in land transfer taxes, $2,500 in legal fees, and $5,000 for title insurance. Tim's basis is therefore $262,500. Over the years, Tim spends $5,000 renovating the bathroom, $2,000 replacing the carpeting, and pays $10,000 for a pool. That means that his adjusted cost basis is the original basis ($262,500) plus the $17,000 in improvements he made for a total of $279,500.

b. Things that reduce the basis

Just as the basis can be increased through improvements, there are certain things that can decrease it. Some examples are as follows:

- Deductible casualty (defined below) losses.
- Insurance payments you received or expect to receive for casualty losses.
- Payments you received for granting an easement or right-of-way.
- Depreciation allowed or allowable if you used your home for business or rental purposes.
- Non-business energy property credit (allowed beginning in 2006 but not for 2008) claimed for making certain energy saving improvements you added to the basis of your home.
- Residential energy efficient property credit (allowed beginning in 2006) claimed for making certain energy saving improvements you added to the basis of your home.
- Adoption credit you claimed for improvements added to the basis of your home.
- Non-taxable payments from an adoption assistance program of your employer you used for improvements you added to the basis of your home.
- Energy conservation subsidy excluded from your gross income because you received it (directly or indirectly) from a public utility after 1992 to buy or install any energy conservation measure. An energy conservation measure is an installation or modification primarily designed either to reduce consumption of electricity or natural gas or to improve the management of energy demand for a home.
- General sales taxes claimed as an itemized deduction on Schedule A (Form 1040) that were imposed on the purchase of personal property, such as a houseboat used as your home or a mobile home.

Many of these are very specific and will not apply to a US citizen in Canada. The one that might cause the most confusion is casualty losses. A casualty loss can result from the damage, destruction or loss of your property from any sudden, unexpected, or unusual event such as a flood, hurricane, tornado, fire, earthquake, or even volcanic eruption. If you receive insurance payments for this type of loss (e.g., a tree fell and damaged your roof) you should subtract them from the basis. Reductions to the basis should be subtracted from the total basis including improvements.

Recall the example from the previous section. Tim bought a house in Toronto in 1996 for $250,000. To purchase the house, he paid $5,000 in land transfer taxes, $2,500 in legal fees and $5,000 for title insurance. Tim's basis is therefore $262,500. Over the years, Tim spends $5,000 renovating the bathroom, $2,000 installing wall-to-wall carpeting, and pays $10,000 for a pool. That means that his adjusted cost basis is the original basis ($262,500) plus the $17,000 in improvements he made for a total of $279,500. Let's say that in 2000 a severe thunderstorm damaged Tim's house and the repairs cost $5,000. He received that amount from the insurance company to cover the cost. He must therefore deduct $5,000 from his basis. So it would become $274,500.

3. FIGURING THE AMOUNT REALIZED (THE SALE PRICE)

Once you have calculated the adjusted cost basis, most of the work is done. Recall that the formula is amount realized – adjusted costs basis = capital gain or loss. The next step is how to figure out the amount realized. It may seem obvious that the sale price is simply the price you sold it for. However, the actual sale price is just the starting point. From it you can subtract the expenses you paid to sell the property. These include the following:

- real estate agent commissions;
- advertising fees;
- legal fees;
- loan charges paid by the seller, such as loan placement fees or "points".

An example will illustrate this. Let's say Tim sold his house for $350,000. But he paid $25,000 in real estate commissions, and $2,500 in legal fees. Even though the sale price is $350,000, the amount that Tim realizes is $322,500.

4. CALCULATING THE CAPITAL GAIN OR LOSS

The formula for determining a capital gain or loss is: Selling price – selling expenses – adjusted cost basis = capital gain or loss. In other words, take the amount realized from section 3 and subtract the adjusted cost basis determined in section 2 from it. The result is the capital gain or loss that you have realized.

To explain this, let's reprise Tim's example from earlier. Tim bought a house in Toronto in 1996 for $250,000. To purchase the house, he paid $5,000 in land transfer taxes, $2,500 for a lawyer to close the deal, and $5,000 for title insurance. Tim's basis is therefore $262,500. Over the years, Tim spends $5,000 renovating the bathroom, $2,000 replacing the carpeting and pays $10,000 for a pool. That means that his adjusted cost basis is the original basis ($262,500) plus the $17,000 in improvements he made for a total of $279,500. In 2000 a severe thunderstorm damaged Tim's house and the repairs cost $5,000. He received that amount from the insurance company to cover the cost. He must therefore deduct $5,000 from his basis. So it would become $274,500. When the improvements and deductions are made, Tim's adjusted cost basis is $274,500.

Recall that Tim sold his house for $350,000 in 2011. But he paid $25,000 in real estate commissions, and $2,500 in legal fees. Even though the sale price is $350,000, the amount that Tim realizes is $322,500.

So to calculate his capital gain Tim needs to subtract his adjusted costs basis ($274,500) from his amount realized ($322,500). Tim's total capital gain is $48,000. In the next section we show you how to report this amount.

5. REPORTING THE CAPITAL GAIN OR CAPITAL LOSS ON YOUR MAIN HOME

If the real estate you are selling is your main home (i.e., your principal residence), you can exclude up to $250,000 in capital gains from tax. This section explains the process for doing this. However, if the real estate is not your main home, please go to section 6 of this chapter.

a. What is your main home?

The term "main home" means where you live most of the time. It does not need to be a house. It can be a house, houseboat, mobile home, cooperative apartment, or condominium. But it must have a construction on it. So that means that it cannot solely be land. Most people will know what their main home is. It is where they live and spend the most time. These factors help determine what your main home is:

1. Where you work.
2. The location of your family members' main home.
3. Your mailing address for bills and correspondence.
4. The address listed on your:
    a. Federal and state tax returns;
    b. Driver's licence;
    c. Car registration;
    d. Voter registration card.
5. The location of the banks you use.
6. The location of recreational clubs and religious organizations of which you are a member.

b. Your capital gain is more than zero and less than $250,000

If the home is your main home (i.e., it meets the test outlined in section a), you may be able to exclude up to $250,000 of the capital gains generated by the sale from tax. To exclude up to $250,000 all of the following things must be true:

- You owned the home for at least 2 years (the ownership test)
- You lived in the home for at least 2 years (the use test)
- During the 2-year period ending on the date of the sale, you did not exclude a gain from the sale of another home.

If these three things are true, and the gain is less than $250,000, you do not have to report the sale to the IRS. In the next section, we further explain the ownership and use tests.

i. The ownership and use tests explained

The required 2 years of ownership and use during the 5-year period ending on the date of the sale do not have to be continuous nor do they have to occur at the same time. You meet the tests if you can show that you owned and lived in the property as your main home for either 24 full months or 730 days (365 × 2) during the 5-year period ending on the date of sale.

Some examples illustrate how the ownership and use tests work. Let's start with one where both the ownership and use tests are met. Mya bought and moved into her main home in September 2008. She sold the home at a gain on September 15, 2011. During the 5-year period ending on the date of sale (September 16, 2006 – September 15, 2011), she owned and lived in the home for more than 2 years.

The following example shows that the ownership and use tests do not have to be consecutive. Naomi bought and moved into a house in July 2007. She lived there for 13 months and then moved in with a friend. She moved back into her own house in 2010 and lived there for 12 months until she sold it in July 2011. Naomi meets the ownership and use tests because, during the 5-year period ending on the date of sale, she owned the house for more than 2 years and lived in it for a total of 25 (13 + 12) months.

ii. Exceptions to the use test

There is an exception to the use test if:

- You become physically or mentally unable to care for yourself, and
- You owned and lived in your home as your main home for a total of at least 1 year during the 5-year period before the sale of your home.

Under this exception, you are considered to live in your home during any time within the 5-year period that you own the home and live in a facility (including a nursing home) to care for persons in your condition. If you meet this exception to the use test, you still have to meet the 2-out-of-5-year ownership test to claim the exclusion.

c. Your capital gain is between $250,000 and $500,000

You can exclude up to $500,000 of the gain in value on the sale of your main home if all of the following are true.

- You are married and file a joint return for the year.
- Either you or your spouse owned the property for two years (ownership test).
- Both you and your spouse lived in the property for two years (use test).
- During the 2-year period ending on the date of the sale, neither you nor your spouse excluded a gain from the sale of another home.

If you do not meet these requirements, then you cannot take the $500,000 exclusion. You may be able to take the $250,000 exclusion if one spouse qualifies under the situation described in section 5(b) above. The following examples illustrate how this rule works.

Example 1—both spouses live in the house

Joanne bought a house on March 1, 2009. She and her husband Jon lived there from April 1, 2009 until July 1, 2011 when they sold it. If they file a joint return, they will be able to exclude up to $500,000 in gains from their income.

Example 2—one spouse sells a home.

Emily sells her home in June 2011. She marries Jamie later in the year. She meets the ownership and use tests, but Jamie does not. Emily can exclude up to $250,000 of gain on a separate or joint return for 2011. The $500,000 maximum exclusion for certain joint returns does not apply because Jamie does not meet the use test.

Example 3—each spouse sells a home.

The facts are the same as in example 2 except that Jamie also sells a home in 2011 before he marries Emily. He meets the ownership and use tests on his home, but Emily does not. Emily and Jamie can each exclude up to $250,000 of gain from the sale of their individual homes. The $500,000 maximum exclusion for certain joint returns does not apply because Emily and Jamie do not jointly meet the use test for the same home.

If you are able to exclude all of your gain, you do not need to report this.

d. You had to sell your home because of special circumstances

If you fail to meet the requirements to qualify for the $250,000 or $500,000 exclusion, you may still qualify for a reduced exclusion. This applies to those who:

- Fail to meet the ownership and use tests, or
- Have used the exclusion within 2 years of selling their current home.

In both cases, to qualify for a reduced exclusion, the sale of your main home must be due to one of the following reasons:

- a change in place of employment;
- health;
- unforeseen circumstances.

Publication 523 describes these situations in more detail.

e. You have a capital loss

A capital loss on your main home is non-deductible. However, you still have to report the loss. To do so you must complete Form 8949. The instructions for filling out Form 8949 are below. All you have to do is follow them, except for a slight adjustment. Enter the letter "L" in column (b) of that form. Enter the amount of the loss as a positive number in column (g) of that form. Then transfer the information on Form 8949 to Schedule D.

f. You have a gain larger than the available exclusion

It may be that the sale of your home generates a capital gain larger than the available exclusion ($250,000 or $500,000). This could be because your home is extremely valuable or the basis was very low. Either way, you must report the gain. Doing so is relatively straightforward. First, you report the gain on Form 8949 and then transfer the information to Schedule D. The text of the forms is self-explanatory, so an example is the best way to show this. Peter and Betty Clark, who are married and file a joint return, bought a home in 1969. They lived in it as their main home until they sold it in February 2011 and moved into a retirement community. Their records show the following.

Original cost	$40,000
Legal fees for title search	250
Improvements (roof)	2,000
Selling price	695,000
Selling expenses, including commission	25,000

The Clarks figure the adjusted basis of the home they sold which is the original cost ($40,000) plus the legal fees ($250) and the roof improvements ($2,000). The selling price is $695,000 minus the selling expenses of $25,000 for a total of $652,750. Since they are married, meet the ownership and use tests, and file a joint return for the year, they qualify to exclude $500,000 of the gain. They report the sale on Form 8949 and Schedule D (Form 1040). On Form 8949, Part II, they report their selling price of $695,000 in column (e), their adjusted basis of $42,250 in column (f), and their exclusion of $500,000 in column (g). They enter "H" in column (b).

Their Form 8949 looks like this.

Form 8949 (2011) Attachment Sequence No. **12A** Page **2**

Name(s) shown on return. Do not enter name and social security number if shown on other side. Peter and Betty CLark

Your social security number 001-00-1111

Part II Long-Term Capital Gains and Losses—Assets Held More Than One Year

Note: You **must** check **one** of the boxes below. Complete a separate Form 8949, page 2, for **each** box that is checked.

***Caution.** Do not complete column (b) or (g) until you have read the instructions for those columns (see the Instructions for Schedule D (Form 1040)). Columns (b) and (g) do not apply for most transactions and should generally be left blank.

☐ **(A)** Long-term transactions reported on Form 1099-B with basis reported to the IRS ☐ **(B)** Long-term transactions reported on Form 1099-B but basis not reported to the IRS ☑ **(C)** Long-term transactions for which you cannot check box A or B

Put in letter H here to represent that you are taking the exclusion

3 (a) Description of property (Example: 100 sh. XYZ Co.)	(b) Code, if any, for column (g)*	(c) Date acquired (Mo., day, yr.)	(d) Date sold (Mo., day, yr.)	(e) Sales price (see instructions)	(f) Cost or other basis (see instructions)	(g) Adjustments to gain or loss, if any*
Main Home	H	3/5/1969	2/5/2011	695,000	42,250	(500,000)
4 Totals. Add the amounts in columns (e) and (f). Also, combine the amounts in column (g). Enter here and include on Schedule D, **line 8** (if **box A** above is checked), **line 9** (if **box B** above is checked), or **line 10** (if **box C** above is checked) ▶ 4				695,000	42,250	(500,000)

Form **8949** (2011)

Then they take this information and transfer it to Schedule D. That form looks like this.

SCHEDULE D (Form 1040)

Department of the Treasury Internal Revenue Service (99)

Capital Gains and Losses

▶ Attach to Form 1040 or Form 1040NR. ▶ See Instructions for Schedule D (Form 1040).
▶ Use Form 8949 to list your transactions for lines 1, 2, 3, 8, 9, and 10.

OMB No. 1545-0074
2011
Attachment Sequence No. 12

Name(s) shown on return	Your social security number
Peter and Betty Clark	001-00-1111

Part I Short-Term Capital Gains and Losses—Assets Held One Year or Less

Complete Form 8949 before completing line 1, 2, or 3. This form may be easier to complete if you round off cents to whole dollars.	**(e)** Sales price from Form(s) 8949, line 2, column (e)	**(f)** Cost or other basis from Form(s) 8949, line 2, column (f)	**(g)** Adjustments to gain or loss from Form(s) 8949, line 2, column (g)	**(h) Gain or (loss)** Combine columns (e), (f), and (g)
1 Short-term totals from all Forms 8949 with **box A** checked in **Part I**		( )		
2 Short-term totals from all Forms 8949 with **box B** checked in **Part I**		( )		
3 Short-term totals from all Forms 8949 with **box C** checked in **Part I**		( )		

4 Short-term gain from Form 6252 and short-term gain or (loss) from Forms 4684, 6781, and 8824	4	
5 Net short-term gain or (loss) from partnerships, S corporations, estates, and trusts from Schedule(s) K-1	5	
6 Short-term capital loss carryover. Enter the amount, if any, from line 8 of your **Capital Loss Carryover Worksheet** in the instructions	6	( )
7 Net short-term capital gain or (loss). Combine lines 1 through 6 in column (h). If you have any long-term capital gains or losses, go to Part II below. Otherwise, go to Part III on the back	7	

Part II Long-Term Capital Gains and Losses—Assets Held More Than One Year

Complete Form 8949 before completing line 8, 9, or 10. This form may be easier to complete if you round off cents to whole dollars.	**(e)** Sales price from Form(s) 8949, line 4, column (e)	**(f)** Cost or other basis from Form(s) 8949, line 4, column (f)	**(g)** Adjustments to gain or loss from Form(s) 8949, line 4, column (g)	**(h) Gain or (loss)** Combine columns (e), (f), and (g)
8 Long-term totals from all Forms 8949 with **box A** checked in **Part II**		( )		
9 Long-term totals from all Forms 8949 with **box B** checked in **Part II**		( )		
10 Long-term totals from all Forms 8949 with **box C** checked in **Part II**	695,000	(42,250)	(500,000)	152,750

11 Gain from Form 4797, Part I; long-term gain from Forms 2439 and 6252; and long-term gain or (loss) from Forms 4684, 6781, and 8824	11	
12 Net long-term gain or (loss) from partnerships, S corporations, estates, and trusts from Schedule(s) K-1	12	
13 Capital gain distributions. See the instructions	13	
14 Long-term capital loss carryover. Enter the amount, if any, from line 13 of your **Capital Loss Carryover Worksheet** in the instructions	14	( )
15 Net long-term capital gain or (loss). Combine lines 8 through 14 in column (h). Then go to Part III on the back	15	152,750

For Paperwork Reduction Act Notice, see your tax return instructions. Cat. No. 11338H **Schedule D (Form 1040) 2011**

Take the amount on line 15 and put it on line 13 of your Form 1040.

6. REPORTING THE CAPITAL GAINS FOR A SALE OF REAL ESTATE THAT IS NOT YOUR MAIN HOME

If you sell real estate that is not your main home, but that you use for personal use and rent out less than 14 days a year, you must do the following.

a) Use section 1 to calculate the basis.

b) Look at section 2 to figure out the adjusted cost basis.

c) Calculate the amount realized using section 3.

d) Subtract the adjusted cost basis from the amount realized. The total is your capital gain or loss.

e) Since the real estate sold is not your main home, you are not eligible to claim a capital gains exclusion.

f) Report the gain in the same manner as described in section 5, without taking the exclusion. List the relevant information on Form 8949 (omitting letter H in column (a) and leaving column (g) blank) and then transfer it to Schedule D. Take the amount on line 15 and put it on line 13 of your Form 1040.

g) If the total is a loss, you still have to fill out Form 8949 and Schedule D, but you cannot deduct the loss from your income.

7. OTHER ISSUES

Please see publication 523 if any of the following issues apply to you:

- You acquired your home in a like-kind exchange.
- You are selling real estate that is not your main home (i.e., a cottage or an investment property that you rent out for more than 14 days).
- You are a member of the American armed forces.
- You have renounced your US citizenship.
- You had a US federal mortgage subsidy.
- At some point you claimed the US first-time homebuyer credit on this property.
- Your situation does not fit perfectly into what is described above.

12

RETIREMENT INCOME

This chapter explores how to report "retirement income," which is shorthand for the various income sources on which retirees rely such as pension income, CPP payments, RRSP withdrawals etc. This chapter is laid out as follows:

1. Identifying retirement income.
2. Reporting the income.
3. Non-taxable pension income.
4. Social Security benefits.

1. IDENTIFYING RETIREMENT INCOME

Retirement income is varied. Identifying it can be somewhat complicated. Below, we go through a number of the different sources of income. As elsewhere, if you have multiple sources, you need to total them and report them on line 16(b) of Form 1040.

a. Canada Pension Plan income

Canada Pension Plan income received by US citizens in Canada is not taxable. You do not need to report it.

b. Old Age Security

Old Age Security income received by US citizens in Canada is not taxable. You do not need to report it.

c. Registered Retirement Income Fund (RRIF)

Once you turn 71, or earlier if you choose to, you may convert your RRSP into a RRIF which means that it can produce income for you. This income must be reported for US purposes. If you receive income from a RRIF, you will also receive a T4RIF. It looks like this.

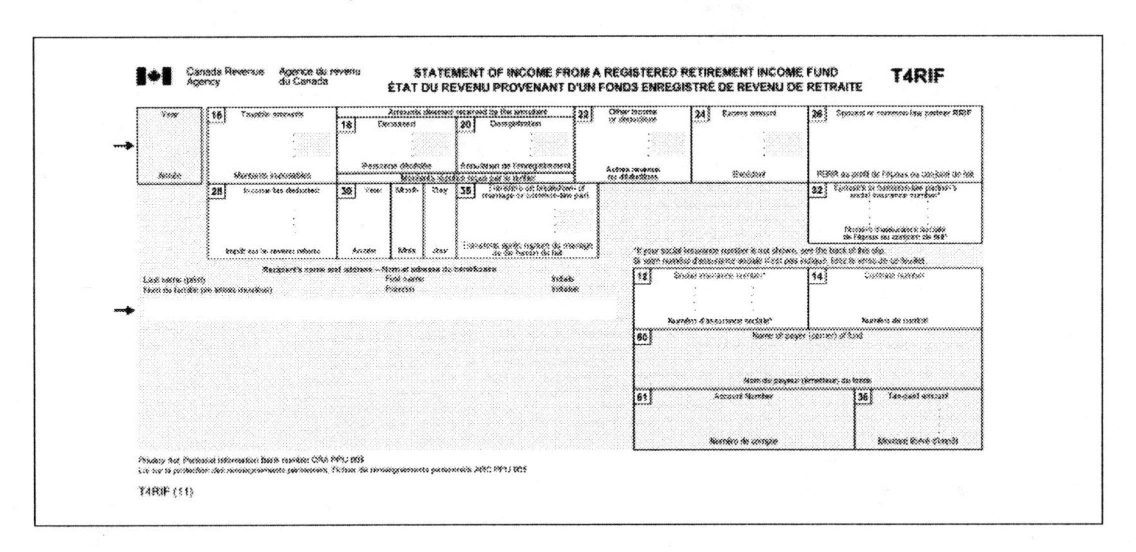

Canada Revenue Agency / Agence du revenu du Canada

STATEMENT OF INCOME FROM A REGISTERED RETIREMENT INCOME FUND
ÉTAT DU REVENU PROVENANT D'UN FONDS ENREGISTRÉ DE REVENU DE RETRAITE

T4RIF

Take the amount in box 16 and enter it on line 16(b) of Form 1040 (after converting it to US dollars as referred to earlier). Remember that all amounts on this slip are expressed in Canadian dollars and so must be converted to US dollars.

d. RRSP withdrawal

Occasionally, you may withdraw money from your RRSP. If you do, you will receive a T4RSP. It looks like this.

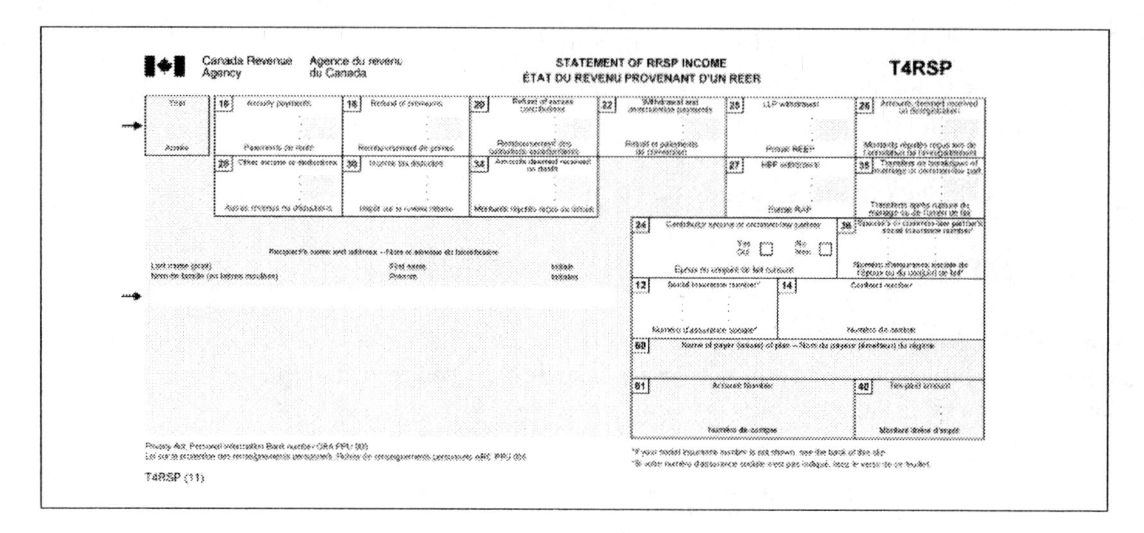
Canada Revenue Agency / Agence du revenu du Canada

STATEMENT OF RRSP INCOME
ÉTAT DU REVENU PROVENANT D'UN REER

T4RSP

16 | 18 | 20 | 22 | 25 | 26
28 | 30 | 34 | 27 | 35
24 | 36
12 | 14
60
61 | 40

T4RSP (11)

Take the amounts listed in box 16, box 22, box 25, and/or box 27 and report them on line 16(b) of your Form 1040. Again, you will need to convert any amount from Canadian dollars to US dollars.

e. Other pension income (annuity or employer-provided pension)

If you have a private pension, or an annuity, you will get a T4A from the institution that administers it. This form can be used for several purposes. The form looks like this.

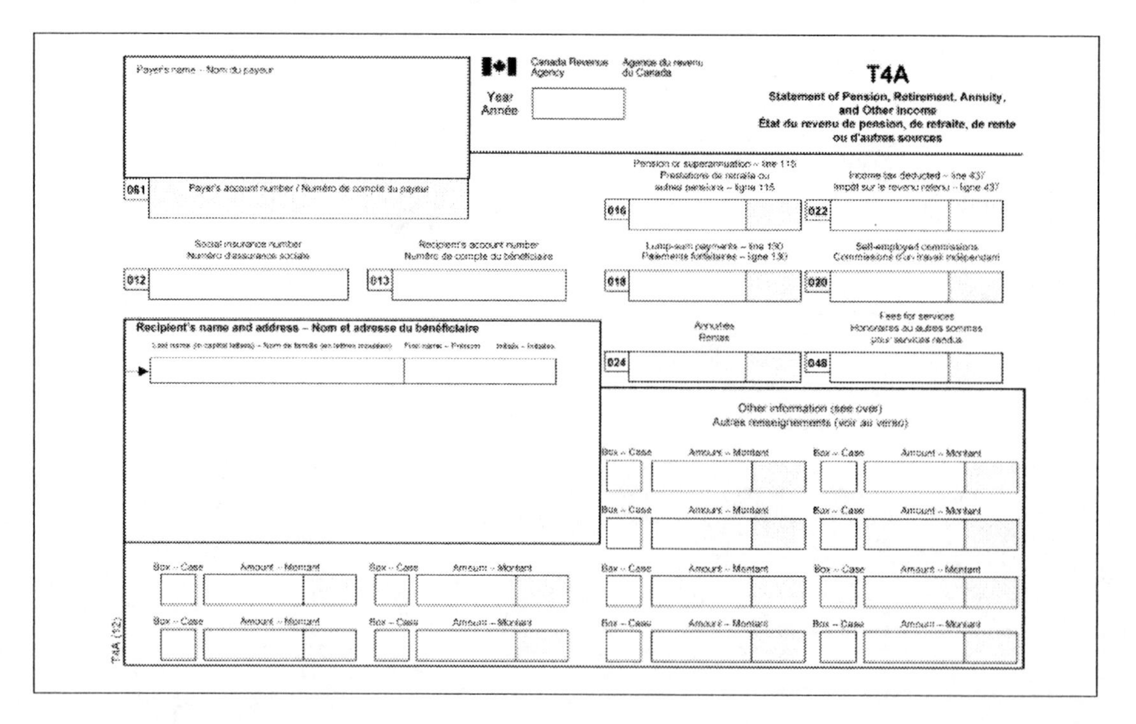
Payer's name – Nom du payeur

Canada Revenue Agency / Agence du revenu du Canada

Year / Année

T4A

Statement of Pension, Retirement, Annuity, and Other Income
État du revenu de pension, de retraite, de rente ou d'autres sources

061 Payer's account number / Numéro de compte du payeur

016 Pension or superannuation – line 115 / Prestations de retraite ou autres pensions – ligne 115

022 Income tax deducted – line 437 / Impôt sur le revenu retenu – ligne 437

012 Social insurance number / Numéro d'assurance sociale

013 Recipient's account number / Numéro de compte du bénéficiaire

018 Lump-sum payments – line 130 / Paiements forfaitaires – ligne 130

020 Self-employed commissions / Commissions d'un travail indépendant

Recipient's name and address – Nom et adresse du bénéficiaire

024 Annuities / Rentes

048 Fees for services / Honoraires ou autres sommes pour services rendus

Other information (see over)
Autres renseignements (voir au verso)

Box – Case	Amount – Montant	Box – Case	Amount – Montant

T4A (12)

f. Pension income from American or other sources

Depending on your personal circumstances, you may have pension income from American or other foreign sources. You must report all such income on line 16(b). If you have American pension income, you may receive a Form 1099-R. Here is a blank example.

☐ CORRECTED (if checked)

PAYER'S name, street address, city, state, and ZIP code		1 Gross distribution $ 2a Taxable amount $	OMB No. 1545-0119 2012 Form 1099-R	Distributions From Pensions, Annuities, Retirement or Profit-Sharing Plans, IRAs, Insurance Contracts, etc.
		2b Taxable amount not determined ☐	Total distribution ☐	Copy B Report this income on your federal tax return. If this form shows federal income tax withheld in box 4, attach this copy to your return.
PAYER'S federal identification number	RECIPIENT'S identification number	3 Capital gain (included in box 2a) $	4 Federal income tax withheld $	
RECIPIENT'S name		5 Employee contributions /Designated Roth contributions or insurance premiums $	6 Net unrealized appreciation in employer's securities $	
Street address (including apt. no.)		7 Distribution code(s) IRA/ SEP/ SIMPLE ☐	8 Other $ %	This information is being furnished to the Internal Revenue Service.
City, state, and ZIP code		9a Your percentage of total distribution %	9b Total employee contributions $	
10 Amount allocable to IRR within 5 years $	11 1st year of desig. Roth contrib.	12 State tax withheld $ $	13 State/Payer's state no.	14 State distribution $ $
Account number (see instructions)		15 Local tax withheld $ $	16 Name of locality	17 Local distribution $ $

Form 1099-R www.irs.gov/form1099r Department of the Treasury - Internal Revenue Service

If the Form 1099-R is from an Individual Retirement Account (IRA) do not report it on this line. If not, you should just take the amount listed in box 2(a) and report it on line 16(b). Foreign (non-American) pension plans may report their income in a variety of ways. The key is that you must report all such income for US tax purposes.

2. REPORTING THE INCOME

Generally, payments from pension plans and annuities are fully taxable, particularly if you paid for the pension or annuity using tax-deferred amounts. The whole point behind RRSPs and many pension plans is to simply delay the income you are paid until you are in a lower tax bracket.

Income tax is deferred on contributions to an RRSP. Eventually an RRSP is converted into an RRIF. The income produced by the RRIF is taxable.

Your annual contribution to most employer provided pension plans is tax deductible. So the income generated by those plans, once you retire, is taxable. It may be, however, that your pension contributions were not tax deferred or would not have been considered tax-deferred under US rules. If you believe this may be the case, we suggest you seek professional tax advice. Otherwise, our suggestion is to report *all* (subject to the exception below) income you receive by way of a pension or annuity.

Once you have determined the income you must report, the reporting of it is very easy. Simply add up all of the pension income that you have from different sources, convert it to US dollars, and include it on line 16(b). Unless you have non-taxable retirement income (discussed below) you can leave line 16(a) blank.

3. NON-TAXABLE PENSION INCOME

The general rule is that most retirement income is taxable in the year that it is distributed to you.

There is one major exception to this. If you contributed after-tax dollars to your pension or annuity, your pension payments are only partially taxable. Contribution of after-tax dollars means that you paid tax on the income used to make the contributions when you received it (i.e., you did not deduct it) and then contributed the particular amounts to a pension plan or annuity. This is relatively uncommon. For instance, you cannot over-contribute to your Canadian RRSP without paying a penalty in Canada regarding the over-contribution. After-tax contributions frequently arise when you purchase a non-registered annuity from an insurance company with after-tax income. You will not pay tax on the part of the payment that represents a return of the after-tax amount you paid. Expressed another way, an annuity payment reflects both a return of capital and an income component. Only the income portion is taxable; the capital portion is not.

Figuring out the tax-free part of an annuity is complicated. To make matters worse, the IRS's rules governing annuities are designed for particular annuity products available in the United States or provided by employers. There may or may not be equivalent products in Canada. For these reasons, if you think you have an annuity or pension to which you have made a non-deductible contribution, you should seek professional tax assistance. At the very least, you should read publication 575.

4. SOCIAL SECURITY BENEFITS

If you receive Social Security benefits, you will receive a Form SSA-1099 that indicates the amount of your benefits. As noted above, if you are a resident of Canada, you do not have to pay US tax on your Social Security benefits. Report your net benefits (the amount in box 5 of your Form SSA-1099) on line 20a. Since there is no taxable portion of them, you can leave line 20(b) blank.

13

INCOME FROM RENTAL PROPERTY[1]

This chapter discusses how to report income from rental property that you own. This can be complicated. Start with section 1 to classify your rental property and then go to either section 2 or section 3 to figure out how to calculate and report your income. This chapter is organized as follows:

1. Classifying rental property.
2. Purely for profit rental property.
3. Rental property that you make use of.
4. Selling property that you rent out.
5. Other issues and further information.

1. CLASSIFYING RENTAL PROPERTY

There are two categories of rental property: that owned purely for profit and that which is for partly personal use. Making this distinction is key to properly reporting your income and expenses.

You use property as a home during the tax year if you use it for personal purposes more than the greater of:

- 14 days, and
- 10% of the total days it is rented to others at a fair rental price.

A day of personal use is a day during which the property is used by:

- You or any other person who owns an interest in it.
- A member of your family or a member of the family of any other person who owns an interest in it.
- Anyone under an arrangement that lets you use some other dwelling unit (e.g., a house swap).
- Anyone at less than a fair rental price.

A fair rental price for your property generally is the amount of rent that a person who is not related to you would be willing to pay.

An example shows this distinction in action. You own a condominium apartment in a resort area. You rented it at a fair rental price for a total of 170 days during the year. For 12 of these days, the tenant was not able to use the apartment and allowed you to use it even though you did not refund any of the rent. Your family actually used the apartment for 10 of those days. Therefore, the apartment is treated as having been rented for 160 (170 – 10) days. You calculated that 10% of the total days rented to others at a fair rental price is 16 days. Your family also used the apartment for 7 other days during the

[1] This chapter is based on, and some text is copied from, IRS Publication 527.

year. You used the apartment as a home because you used it for personal purposes for 17 days. That is more than the greater of 14 days or 10% of the 160 days it was rented (16 days). This means that you have to go to section 3 to figure out how to pay tax on the income from it.

2. PURELY FOR PROFIT RENTAL PROPERTY

This section addresses purely for profit rental property. Basically, you report your income, subtract your expenses, and come up with the total on Schedule E. You report this total on line 17 of the Form 1040.

Let's start with how to figure out what to put on Schedule E. As usual, we explain the concepts first and then show you how to fill out the form, using an example.

a. Calculating out your rental income

Rent, including rent paid in advance, is the principal income generated from a rental property. However, if your tenant pays any of your expenses these payments are also considered income. Calculate the total amount of rent you collected, add in any tenant-paid expenses, and that's your total income.

b. Calculating your expenses

Expenses related to renting your property can be deducted from your rental income. You should deduct any expenses in the year you pay them. The following are common expenses:

- advertising;
- auto and travel expenses necessary to collect rent;
- cleaning and maintenance;
- commissions;
- credit check fees regarding tenants;
- depreciation;
- insurance;
- mortgage interest you pay on your property;
- janitorial services;
- legal and other professional fees relating to paying taxes for the property or resolving disputes with tenants;
- local transportation expenses necessary to collect rent;
- management fees;
- mortgage interest paid to banks, etc.;
- points (prepaid mortgage interest);
- repairs;

- taxes; and
- utilities.

Most of these are quite straightforward. Some, however, are worthy of further exploration.

Depreciation. Depreciation means the long-term decrease in the value of assets. Often, this is due to natural wear and tear. The deductions are taken over the expected life of the property. Calculating depreciation is discussed in the next section.

Repairs. Repairs are incurred to help keep the property in good operating condition, but do not add to the value of the property. Examples of repairs include repainting your property inside or out, fixing gutters or floors, fixing leaks, plastering, and replacing broken windows. Items that add value to the property are called improvements. The following table gives examples of improvements:

Additions	**Miscellaneous**	**Plumbing**
Bedroom	Storm windows, doors	Septic system
Bathroom	New roof	Water heater
Deck	Central vacuum	Soft water system
Garage	Wiring upgrades	Filtration system
Porch	Satellite dish	
Patio	Security system	**Interior Improvements**
		Built-in appliances
Lawn & Grounds	**Heating & Air Conditioning**	Kitchen modernization
Landscaping		Flooring
Driveway	Heating system	Wall-to-wall carpeting
Walkway	Central air conditioning	
Fence	Furnace	**Insulation**
Retaining wall	Duct work	Attic
Sprinkler system	Central humidifier	Walls, floor
Swimming pool	Filtration system	Pipes, duct work

Distinguishing between a repair and an improvement is not always easy. Remember that the key difference is whether a piece of work merely kept the property in good operating condition (a repair) or increased the property's value (an improvement).

If you own a condominium, you also own a share of the common elements, such as land, lobbies, elevators, and service areas. You and the other condominium owners may pay dues or assessments to a special corporation that is organized to take care of the common elements. Special rules apply if you rent your condominium to others. You can deduct as rental expenses all the expenses discussed in this section. In addition, you can deduct any dues or assessments paid for maintenance of the common elements. You cannot deduct special assessments you pay to a condominium management corporation for improvements. Improvements are added to the cost or basis rather than being currently deductible. However, you may be able to recover your share of the cost of any improvement by claiming depreciation.

c. Depreciation

i. What is depreciation?

Depreciation is meant to be an estimation of the probable long-term decrease in the value of capital property that is due to use. For example, if you rent out a house, it will likely be in worse shape after a few years of tenant use than it was at the start. Depreciation is designed to compensate for this.

You are able to claim depreciation expenses for a property if all of the following are true:

- You own the property.
- You rent out the property.
- The property has a determinable useful life. This means that it must be something that wears out.
- The property is expected to last more than one year.

Note that you cannot claim depreciation costs on land.

You begin to depreciate your rental property when you place it in service for the production of income. You stop depreciating it either when you have fully recovered your cost or other basis, or when you retire it from service, whichever happens first.

ii. Methods of calculating depreciation

If you started renting your property before 1987, IRS Publication 527 explains what method of depreciation you should use. Otherwise, simply follow the explanation below. There are a few steps to figuring out how to calculate depreciation:

1. Calculate the basis (cost).
2. Determine adjustments to the basis.
3. Determine how much depreciation you can claim using the percentage tables.

Let's take each of these criteria in order.

1. Calculating out the basis (cost) of the property

The first step is to figure out the basis of the property. Basis means the amount you purchased it for. To this you can also add other costs of purchasing such as:

1. abstract fees (abstract of title fees);
2. charges for installing utility services;
3. legal fees (including fees for the title search and preparing the sales contract and deed);
4. recording fees;
5. survey fees;

6. transfer taxes;

7. owner's title insurance;

8. any amounts the seller owes that you agree to pay, such as:

   a. certain real estate taxes (discussed later);
   b. back interest;
   c. recording or mortgage fees;
   d. charges for improvements or repairs;
   e. sales commissions.

2.(a) Things that increase the basis

After you have figured out the basis (cost) you need to adjust it for any improvements that you've made to the property. The adjusted cost basis means the basis (cost), as determined in section iii, plus the cost of any improvements made since you acquired the property and minus any payments received.

Let's discuss improvements first. The basis of your property can increase over time as you make improvements to it. The general rule is that improvements to your home can increase the basis while repairs cannot. Improvements add to the value of your property, prolong its useful life, or adapt it to new uses. The IRS offers the following examples of improvements:

Additions Bedroom Bathroom Deck Garage Porch Patio	**Heating & Air Conditioning** Heating system Central air conditioning Furnace Duct work Central humidifier Filtration system
Lawn & Grounds Landscaping Driveway Walkway Fence Retaining wall Sprinkler system Swimming pool **Miscellaneous** Storm windows, doors New roof Central vacuum Wiring upgrades Satellite dish Security system	**Plumbing** Septic system Water heater Soft water system Filtration system **Interior Improvements** Built-in appliances Kitchen modernization Flooring Wall-to-wall carpeting **Insulation** Attic Walls Floors Pipes and duct work

You may also adjust the cost based on other improvements that are not on this list. Adjusting the basis for improvements is easy. Simply take the cost of each improvement made and add it to the original basis (cost).

An example shows how this work. Tim bought a house in Toronto in 1996 for $250,000. To purchase the house, he paid $5,000 in land transfer taxes, $2,500 in legal fees and $5,000 for title insurance. Tim's basis is therefore $262,500. Over the years, Tim spends $5,000 renovating the bathroom, $2,000 installing wall-to-wall carpeting, and pays $10,000 for a pool. That means that his adjusted cost basis is the original basis ($262,500) plus the $17,000 in improvements he made for a total of $279,500.

2.(b) Things that reduce the basis

Just as the basis can be increased through improvements, there are certain things that can decrease it. Some examples are as follows:

- Insurance or other payments you receive as the result of a casualty or theft loss.
- Casualty loss not covered by insurance for which you took a deduction.
- Amount(s) you receive for granting an easement.
- Residential energy credits you were allowed before 1986, or after 2005, if you added the cost of the energy items to the basis of your rental property.
- Subsidies for energy conservation measures.
- Special depreciation allowance claimed on qualified property.
- Depreciation you deducted on your tax returns. If you did not deduct the maximum amount of depreciation possible, you have to see *Depreciation* under *Decreases to Basis* in Publication 551.

Many of these are very specific and will not apply to a US citizen in Canada. The one that might cause the most confusion is casualty losses. A casualty loss can result from the damage, destruction, or loss of your property from any sudden, unexpected, or unusual event such as a flood, hurricane, tornado, fire, earthquake, or even volcanic eruption. If you receive insurance payments for this type of loss (e.g., a tree fell and damaged your roof) you should subtract them from the basis. Reductions to the basis should simply be subtracted from the total basis including improvements.

Recall the example from the previous section. Tim bought a house in Toronto in 1996 for $250,000. To purchase the house, he paid $5,000 in land transfer taxes, $2,500 in legal fees and $5,000 for title insurance. Tim's basis is therefore $262,500. Over the years, Tim spends $5,000 renovating the bathroom, $2,000 replacing the carpeting and pays $10,000 for a pool. That means that his adjusted cost basis is the original basis ($262,500) plus the $17,000 in improvements he made for a total of $279,500. Let's say that in 2000 a severe thunderstorm damaged Tim's house and the repairs cost $5,000. He received that amount from the insurance company to cover the cost. He must therefore deduct $5,000 from his basis. So it would become $274,500.

3. How much depreciation deduction can you take for residential property?

Depreciation is a complex topic. The following explanation is a simple introduction. It may not result in the absolute best outcome for you. We have included it so that you understand the topic at hand. If you need more information please seek professional advice or read IRS publication 527.

Once you have figured out what your adjusted cost basis is (step B), you need to figure out what percentage of the property's value you are entitled to deduct each year. The IRS has concluded that the depreciation of your property will take place over 27.5 years. The following chart helps you find the percentage. To use it, go to the month that the property was placed in service and the number of years that it has been since that property was placed in service.

Year	Month property placed in service											
	1	2	3	4	5	6	7	8	9	10	11	12
1	3.485%	3.182%	2.879%	2.576%	2.273%	1.970%	1.667%	1.364%	1.061%	0.758%	0.455%	0.152%
2-9	3.636	3.636	3.636	3.636	3.636	3.636	3.636	3.636	3.636	3.636	3.636	3.636
10	3.637	3.637	3.637	3.637	3.637	3.637	3.636	3.636	3.636	3.636	3.636	3.636
11	3.636	3.636	3.636	3.636	3.636	3.636	3.637	3.637	3.637	3.637	3.637	3.637
12	3.637	3.637	3.637	3.637	3.637	3.637	3.636	3.636	3.636	3.636	3.636	3.636
13	3.636	3.636	3.636	3.636	3.636	3.636	3.637	3.637	3.637	3.637	3.637	3.637
14	3.637	3.637	3.637	3.637	3.637	3.637	3.636	3.636	3.636	3.636	3.636	3.636
15	3.636	3.636	3.636	3.636	3.636	3.636	3.637	3.637	3.637	3.637	3.637	3.637
16	3.637	3.637	3.637	3.637	3.637	3.637	3.636	3.636	3.636	3.636	3.636	3.636
17	3.636	3.636	3.636	3.636	3.636	3.636	3.637	3.637	3.637	3.637	3.637	3.637
18	3.637	3.637	3.637	3.637	3.637	3.637	3.636	3.636	3.636	3.636	3.636	3.636
19	3.636	3.636	3.636	3.636	3.636	3.636	3.637	3.637	3.637	3.637	3.637	3.637
20	3.637	3.637	3.637	3.637	3.637	3.637	3.636	3.636	3.636	3.636	3.636	3.636
21	3.636	3.636	3.636	3.636	3.636	3.636	3.637	3.637	3.637	3.637	3.637	3.637
22	3.637	3.637	3.637	3.637	3.637	3.637	3.636	3.636	3.636	3.636	3.636	3.636
23	3.636	3.636	3.636	3.636	3.636	3.636	3.637	3.637	3.637	3.637	3.637	3.637
24	3.637	3.637	3.637	3.637	3.637	3.637	3.636	3.636	3.636	3.636	3.636	3.636
25	3.636	3.636	3.636	3.636	3.636	3.636	3.637	3.637	3.637	3.637	3.637	3.637
26	3.637	3.637	3.637	3.637	3.637	3.637	3.636	3.636	3.636	3.636	3.636	3.636
27	3.636	3.636	3.636	3.636	3.636	3.636	3.637	3.637	3.637	3.637	3.637	3.637
28	1.97	2.273	2.576	2.879	3.182	3.485	3.636	3.636	3.636	3.636	3.636	3.636
29							0.152	0.455	0.758	1.061	1.364	1.667

This looks complicated, but is quite easy. Let's say that you started renting a property with an adjusted cost basis of $250,000 in February 2010. The current date is August 2012. That means that we are in year 3. So you go to the line of February (month 2) of Year 3. The appropriate percentage is 3.636%. The amount you can deduct is the percentage x the adjusted cost basis or 0.03636 × 250,000 = $9,090. So you can deduct depreciation of $9,090.

Let's take another date just to make sure this is clear. Again, you started renting out a condo you own in February 2010. The current date is April 2014. That means we are in year 4. The percentage under February Year 4 is also 3.636. This becomes .03636 × $250,000 for a total depreciation deduction of $9,090.

You will notice that with the exception of the first year, the depreciation amounts do not vary that much. As stated above, you are entitled to continue taking depreciation deductions on rental residential property for 27 years.

vii. Other depreciation amounts

You may be able to claim depreciation deductions for other items that you purchased for the residential real property such as a fridge, stove, fences, shrubbery etc. IRS Publication 527 describes how to calculate the depreciation on these items.

d. If I lose money, can I deduct the loss?

Losses from rental real estate activities are passive activities—meaning that you did not work for the income. Deductions for losses from passive activities are limited. You generally cannot offset income, other than passive income, with losses from passive activities. Like all rules, this has exceptions.

If you are a real estate professional, you may be able to deduct some of this income. See IRS publication 527 for more information.

More commonly, if you or your spouse actively participated in a passive rental real estate activity, you can deduct up to $25,000 of loss from the activity from your non-passive income (e.g., income from wages). You are considered to have actively participated in a rental real estate activity if you (and your spouse) owned at least 10% of the rental property and you made management decisions (such as selecting tenants, spending money, or setting rental terms) or arranged for others to provide services (such as repairs). Put simply, if you are the landlord, in addition to being the owner, you may be able to deduct your losses. An example shows how this works.

Mike is single and had the following income and losses during the tax year:

Salary	$42,300
Dividends	300
Interest	1,400
Rental loss	(4,000)

The rental loss was from the rental of a house Mike owned. Mike had, himself, advertised and rented the house to the current tenant. He also collected the rents, which usually came by mail. All repairs were either made or contracted out by Mike. Although the rental loss is from a passive activity, because Mike actively participated in the rental property management he can use the entire $4,000 loss to offset his other income.

As we've said, there is a maximum loss deduction of $25,000. However, if your modified adjusted gross income (line 38 of Form 1040) is more than $100,000 there are restrictions on the deductions you can take. If this is the case, please see IRS publication 527.

Generally, if your modified adjusted gross income (line 38 of the Form 1040) is $150,000 or more ($75,000 or more if you are married filing separately), you are not able to take the deduction. In short, if you earn less than $100,000 you can deduct up to $25,000 in losses from your income. Losses are limited for those who earn more than $100,000.

e. Reporting this information

Now that we have explained briefly how to calculate your expenses, your income, and your depreciation, let's examine how to report. You must complete and attach Form 4562 for rental activities only if you are claiming the following:

- depreciation, including the special depreciation allowance, for property you started renting out in the tax year for which you are filing;
- depreciation on listed property (such as a car or stove), regardless of when it was placed in service; or
- any other car expenses, including the standard mileage rate or lease expenses.

IRS publication 946 has more information on Form 4562.

If you are in business of renting out property, or you provide substantial services to your tenants (such as maid service or regular cleaning) you may have to fill out Schedule C. IRS Publication 527 discusses this in more detail. However, if you simply use rental property income as an investment, and it is not your primary occupation you must complete Schedule E.

In February 2006, Marie Pfister bought a rental house for $135,000 (house $120,000 and land $15,000) and immediately began renting it out. In 2011, she rented it all 12 months for a monthly rental of $1,125. In addition to her rental income of $13,500 (12 x $1,125), Marie had the following expenses.

Mortgage interest	$8,000
Fire insurance (1-year policy)	250
Miscellaneous repairs	400
Real estate taxes imposed and paid	500
Maintenance	200

Marie uses the following table (the same one reproduced above) to calculate her depreciation deductible.

Year	Month property placed in service											
	1	2	3	4	5	6	7	8	9	10	11	12
1	3.485%	3.182%	2.879%	2.576%	2.273%	1.970%	1.667%	1.364%	1.061%	0.758%	0.455%	0.152%
2-9	3.636	3.636	3.636	3.636	3.636	3.636	3.636	3.636	3.636	3.636	3.636	3.636
10	3.637	3.637	3.637	3.637	3.637	3.637	3.636	3.636	3.636	3.636	3.636	3.636
11	3.636	3.636	3.636	3.636	3.636	3.636	3.637	3.637	3.637	3.637	3.637	3.637
12	3.637	3.637	3.637	3.637	3.637	3.637	3.636	3.636	3.636	3.636	3.636	3.636
13	3.636	3.636	3.636	3.636	3.636	3.636	3.637	3.637	3.637	3.637	3.637	3.637
14	3.637	3.637	3.637	3.637	3.637	3.637	3.636	3.636	3.636	3.636	3.636	3.636
15	3.636	3.636	3.636	3.636	3.636	3.636	3.637	3.637	3.637	3.637	3.637	3.637
16	3.637	3.637	3.637	3.637	3.637	3.637	3.636	3.636	3.636	3.636	3.636	3.636
17	3.636	3.636	3.636	3.636	3.636	3.636	3.637	3.637	3.637	3.637	3.637	3.637
18	3.637	3.637	3.637	3.637	3.637	3.637	3.636	3.636	3.636	3.636	3.636	3.636
19	3.636	3.636	3.636	3.636	3.636	3.636	3.637	3.637	3.637	3.637	3.637	3.637
20	3.637	3.637	3.637	3.637	3.637	3.637	3.636	3.636	3.636	3.636	3.636	3.636
21	3.636	3.636	3.636	3.636	3.636	3.636	3.637	3.637	3.637	3.637	3.637	3.637
22	3.637	3.637	3.637	3.637	3.637	3.637	3.636	3.636	3.636	3.636	3.636	3.636
23	3.636	3.636	3.636	3.636	3.636	3.636	3.637	3.637	3.637	3.637	3.637	3.637
24	3.637	3.637	3.637	3.637	3.637	3.637	3.636	3.636	3.636	3.636	3.636	3.636
25	3.636	3.636	3.636	3.636	3.636	3.636	3.637	3.637	3.637	3.637	3.637	3.637
26	3.637	3.637	3.637	3.637	3.637	3.637	3.636	3.636	3.636	3.636	3.636	3.636
27	3.636	3.636	3.636	3.636	3.636	3.636	3.637	3.637	3.637	3.637	3.637	3.637
28	1.97	2.273	2.576	2.879	3.182	3.485	3.636	3.636	3.636	3.636	3.636	3.636
29							0.152	0.455	0.758	1.061	1.364	1.667

She is currently in year 6. So she selects February of Year 6 from the table. The percentage is 3.636%. Land is not subject to depreciation. So Marie multiplies 0.0363 × $120,000 (the basis of the house and not the land) to calculate the amount of depreciation she can deduct. The result is $4,363. With this, Marie figures her net rental income or loss for the house as follows:

Total rental income received ($1,125 × 12)	$13,500
Minus: Expenses	
Mortgage interest	$8,000
Fire insurance	250
Miscellaneous repairs	400

Real estate taxes	500
Maintenance	200
Total expenses	–9,350
Balance	4,150
Minus: Depreciation ($120,000 × 3.636%)	–4,363
Net rental loss for house	**$213**

Marie had a net loss for the year. Because she actively participated in her passive rental real estate activity, earned less than $100,000 and her loss was less than $25,000, she can deduct the full amount of the loss. She uses Schedule E, Part I, to report her rental income and expenses. She enters her income, expenses, and depreciation for the house in the column for Property A and enters her loss on line 22. Marie's Schedule E is shown next.

SCHEDULE E (Form 1040)
Department of the Treasury
Internal Revenue Service (99)

Supplemental Income and Loss
(From rental real estate, royalties, partnerships, S corporations, estates, trusts, REMICs, etc.)
▶ Attach to Form 1040, 1040NR, or Form 1041. ▶ See separate instructions.

OMB No. 1545-0074
2011
Attachment Sequence No. **13**

Name(s) shown on return: Marie Pfister
Your social security number: 444-00-8888

A Did you make any payments in 2011 that would require you to file Form(s) 1099? (see instructions) ☐ Yes ☑ No
B If "Yes," did you or will you file all required Forms 1099? ☐ Yes ☑ No

Part I **Income or Loss From Rental Real Estate and Royalties** **Note.** If you are in the business of renting personal property, use **Schedule C** or **C-EZ** (see instructions). If you are an individual, report farm rental income or loss from **Form 4835** on page 2, line 40.

Caution. For each rental property listed on line 1, check the box in the last column only if you owned that property as a member of a qualified joint venture (QJV) reporting income not subject to self-employment tax.

1	Physical address of each property–street, city, state, zip	Type–from list below	2 For each rental real estate property listed, report the number of days rented at fair rental value and days with personal use. See instructions.		Fair Rental Days	Personal Use Days	QJV
A	444 Yonge St. Toronto Ontario	1		A	365	0	
B				B			
C				C			

Type of Property:
1 Single Family Residence 3 Vacation/Short-Term Rental 5 Land 7 Self-Rental
2 Multi-Family Residence 4 Commercial 6 Royalties 8 Other (describe)

			Properties A	Properties B	Properties C
Income:					
3a	Merchant card and third party payments. For 2011, enter -0-	3a			
b	Payments not reported to you on line 3a	3b	13,500		
4	Total not including amounts on line 3a that are not income (see instructions)	4	13,500		
Expenses:					
5	Advertising	5			
6	Auto and travel (see instructions)	6			
7	Cleaning and maintenance	7	200		
8	Commissions	8			
9	Insurance	9	250		
10	Legal and other professional fees	10			
11	Management fees	11			
12	Mortgage interest paid to banks, etc. (see instructions)	12	8000		
13	Other interest	13			
14	Repairs	14	400		
15	Supplies	15			
16	Taxes	16	500		
17	Utilities	17			
18	Depreciation expense or depletion	18	4363		
19	Other (list) ▶	19			
20	Total expenses. Add lines 5 through 19	20	13713		
21	Subtract line 20 from line 4. If result is a (loss), see instructions to find out if you must file **Form 6198**	21	(213)		
22	Deductible rental real estate loss after limitation, if any, on **Form 8582** (see instructions)	22	(213)	( )	( )

23a	Total of all amounts reported on line 3a for all rental properties	23a	
b	Total of all amounts reported on line 3a for all royalty properties	23b	
c	Total of all amounts reported on line 4 for all rental properties	23c	13,500
d	Total of all amounts reported on line 4 for all royalty properties	23d	
e	Total of all amounts reported on line 12 for all properties	23e	8000
f	Total of all amounts reported on line 18 for all properties	23f	4363
g	Total of all amounts reported on line 20 for all properties	23g	13713
24	**Income.** Add positive amounts shown on line 21. **Do not** include any losses	24	
25	**Losses.** Add royalty losses from line 21 and rental real estate losses from line 22. Enter total losses here	25	(213)
26	**Total rental real estate and royalty income or (loss).** Combine lines 24 and 25. Enter the result here. If Parts II, III, IV, and line 40 on page 2 do not apply to you, also enter this amount on Form 1040, line 17, or Form 1040NR, line 18. Otherwise, include this amount in the total on line 41 on page 2	26	(213)

For Paperwork Reduction Act Notice, see your tax return instructions. Cat. No. 11344L **Schedule E (Form 1040) 2011**

3. RENTAL PROPERTY THAT YOU MAKE USE OF

If you rent out property that you also use, the way that you report this income is different. Recall that the threshold for what constitutes personal use is calculated by the day. Your property falls into this category if use you it for personal purposes more than the greater of 14 days a year or 10% of the total days it is rented to others at a fair rental price.

a. Figuring your income

Rent, including that paid in advance, is the principal income generated by a rental property. However, if your tenant pays any of your expenses these are also considered income. So your total income is the total rent you received during a particular tax year, plus any such expenses paid by the tenant. You are not required to report any income if your property is rented for less than 15 days.

b. Calculating your expenses

The same types of expenses are deductible for personal use rental property and non-personal use rental property. So the list under section 2(b) above applies equally here. The difference is that you need to divide your expenses between the personal use of your home and the rental use. When dividing your expenses, follow these rules:

- Any day that the unit is rented at a fair rental price is a day of rental use even if you used the unit for personal purposes that day.
- Any day that the unit is available for rent but not actually rented is not a day of rental use.

Here is an example. Your cottage was available for rent from June 1 through August 31 (92 days). Your family used the cottage during the last 2 weeks in May (14 days). You were unable to find a renter for the first week in August (7 days). The person who rented the cottage for July allowed you to use it over a weekend (2 days) without any reduction in or refund of rent. The cottage was not used at all before May 17 or after August 31.

You calculate the part of the cottage expenses to treat as rental expenses as follows.

- The cottage was used for rental a total of 85 days (92 − 7). The days it was available for rent, but not rented (7 days), are not days of rental use. The July weekend (2 days) you used it is rental use because you received a fair rental price for the weekend.
- You used the cottage for personal purposes for 14 days (the last 2 weeks in May).
- The total use of the cottage was 99 days (14 days personal use + 85 days rental use).
- Your rental expenses are 85/99 (86%) of the cottage expenses.

c. Depreciation

Personal use property can give rise to depreciation expenses. Use the same method outlined in section 2(c) above.

d. Reporting income and expenses

If a property is rented fewer than 15 days, its primary function is not considered to be rental and it need not be reported on Schedule E (Form 1040). You are not required to report the rental income and rental expenses from this activity in such circumstances. The expenses, including qualified mortgage interest, property taxes, and any qualified casualty loss will be reported as normally allowed on Schedule A (Form 1040). See the instructions for Schedule A for more information on deducting these expenses.

If your property is rented for at least 15 days, you must report your rental income and expenses (including depreciation) on Schedule E. However, the personal portion of expenses, including qualified mortgage interest, property taxes, and qualified casualty loss (if any), will be reported as normally allowed on Schedule A (Form 1040). Again, you will have to allocate your expenses on Schedule E according to the number of days the property was rented out. The rental portion of the expenses will be reported on Schedule E (Form 1040) in the following order:

1. advertising and other fees directly related to obtaining tenants for the rental property;
2. the rental portion of qualified home mortgage interest, property taxes, and qualified casualty loss (if any);
3. rental operating expenses for the property up to the amount of the rental income for the property (minus 1 and 2);
4. depreciation for the property up to the amount of the rental income for the property.

If you have excess expenses (so you incur a loss), you cannot deduct this against other income (passive or otherwise). Instead, you must carry over the losses until you have sufficient *rental* income to use them.

An example may clarify the matter. On June 1, Tim and Emily Donovan bought a vacation condominium to use as rental property. They began advertising in June that the property would be available for rent beginning July 1. The Donovans used the property for 10 days during June. They didn't have any tenants in July, so family and friends used it for the 15 days they weren't using the property themselves. On August 3, they began renting it for $300 per week (a fair rental price) and rented it continuously through December 20 (20 weeks). They had no tenants for the rest of December, so the Donovans used the property for the rest of the year. In short, they rented it for 142 days and used it personally for 52 days for a total of 194 days. Rental use of the property accounted for 73% of its total use, so they can allocate 73% of their expenses to offset the rental income.

The property went on the rental market on July 1. It is this date therefore that is used to calculate the depreciation. Based on the table above, they calculate $1,200 depreciation for the 6 months it was available for rent.

They had the following costs associated with the vacation property for the seven months they owned it.

Mortgage interest	$7,714	× .73 =5,631
Real estate taxes	300	× .73 = 219
Repairs	400	× .73 = 292
Fire insurance	120	× .73 = 87.60
Advertising	150	150
Depreciation	1200	× .73 = 876

Total after reduction: $7,255.60 in expenses. Note that the advertising expense can be entirely offset against the rental income.

The Donovans received $6,000 (20 weeks × $300 per week), in total rent. Even when their expenses are discounted to reflect their use of the property, they have more expenses than income. This means that they can carry over $1255.60 in expenses to next year. Again, they cannot deduct the loss.

The Donovans' Schedule E looks like this.

SCHEDULE E (Form 1040) Department of the Treasury Internal Revenue Service (99)

Supplemental Income and Loss

(From rental real estate, royalties, partnerships, S corporations, estates, trusts, REMICs, etc.)

▶ Attach to Form 1040, 1040NR, or Form 1041. ▶ See separate instructions.

OMB No. 1545-0074 **2011** Attachment Sequence No. **13**

Name(s) shown on return: Tim and Emily Donavan — Your social security number: 666-00-7777

A Did you make any payments in 2011 that would require you to file Form(s) 1099? (see instructions) ☐ Yes ☑ No

B If "Yes," did you or will you file all required Forms 1099? ☐ Yes ☑ No

Part I Income or Loss From Rental Real Estate and Royalties **Note.** If you are in the business of renting personal property, use **Schedule C** or **C-EZ** (see instructions). If you are an individual, report farm rental income or loss from **Form 4835** on page 2, line 40.

Caution. For each rental property listed on line 1, check the box in the last column only if you owned that property as a member of a qualified joint venture (QJV) reporting income not subject to self-employment tax.

1	Physical address of each property–street, city, state, zip	Type–from list below	2 For each rental real estate property listed, report the number of days rented at fair rental value and days with personal use. See instructions.		Fair Rental Days	Personal Use Days	QJV
A	75 Fulton ave. # 2 Wassaga Beach Ontario			A	142	52	
B				B			
C				C			

Type of Property:
1 Single Family Residence 3 Vacation/Short-Term Rental 5 Land 7 Self-Rental
2 Multi-Family Residence 4 Commercial 6 Royalties 8 Other (describe)

		Line	Properties A	Properties B	Properties C
Income:					
3a	Merchant card and third party payments. For 2011, enter -0-	3a			
b	Payments not reported to you on line 3a	3b	6000		
4	Total not including amounts on line 3a that are not income (see instructions)	4	6000		
Expenses:					
5	Advertising	5	150		
6	Auto and travel (see instructions)	6			
7	Cleaning and maintenance	7			
8	Commissions	8			
9	Insurance	9			
10	Legal and other professional fees	10			
11	Management fees	11			
12	Mortgage interest paid to banks, etc. (see instructions)	12	5,631		
13	Other interest	13			
14	Repairs	14			
15	Supplies	15			
16	Taxes	16	219		
17	Utilities	17			
18	Depreciation expense or depletion	18			
19	Other (list) ▶	19			
20	Total expenses. Add lines 5 through 19	20	6000		
21	Subtract line 20 from line 4. If result is a (loss), see instructions to find out if you must file **Form 6198**	21			
22	Deductible rental real estate loss after limitation, if any, on **Form 8582** (see instructions)	22	(6000)	( )	( )

Note that there is no need to report the non-used expenses (depreciation). Simply keep a record and report them next year.

23a	Total of all amounts reported on line 3a for all rental properties	23a	
b	Total of all amounts reported on line 3a for all royalty properties	23b	
c	Total of all amounts reported on line 4 for all rental properties	23c	6000
d	Total of all amounts reported on line 4 for all royalty properties	23d	
e	Total of all amounts reported on line 12 for all properties	23e	5631
f	Total of all amounts reported on line 18 for all properties	23f	
g	Total of all amounts reported on line 20 for all properties	23g	6000
24	**Income.** Add positive amounts shown on line 21. **Do not** include any losses	24	
25	**Losses.** Add royalty losses from line 21 and rental real estate losses from line 22. Enter total losses here	25	( )
26	**Total rental real estate and royalty income or (loss).** Combine lines 24 and 25. Enter the result here. If Parts II, III, IV, and line 40 on page 2 do not apply to you, also enter this amount on Form 1040, line 17, or Form 1040NR, line 18. Otherwise, include this amount in the total on line 41 on page 2	26	0

For Paperwork Reduction Act Notice, see your tax return instructions. Cat. No. 11344L **Schedule E (Form 1040) 2011**

4. SELLING RENTAL PROPERTY

If you sell rental property that is not your main home, it will likely not be treated as a capital gain. Instead, it is an ordinary gain. IRS Publication 544 has more details about how to report the income from such a sale.

5. OTHER ISSUES AND FURTHER INFORMATION

If you live in a cooperative, the rules outlined in this chapter are modified. Please consult IRS publication 527 for an explanation of how to figure your income/expenses.

If you change your home or other property (or a part of it) to rental use at any time other than at the beginning of your tax year, you must allocate yearly expenses, such as taxes and insurance, between rental use and personal use. Again, please see IRS publication 527 for instructions on how this functions.

If you rent part of your property, you must allocate certain expenses between the part of the property used for rental purposes and the part of the property used for personal purposes, notionally as though you had two separate pieces of property. IRS Publication 527 has more details.

14

THE FOREIGN EARNED INCOME EXCLUSION AND THE FOREIGN HOUSING EXCLUSION[1]

There are two very important exclusions from the calculation of income that are available to US citizens who live outside of the United States: the foreign earned income exclusion and the foreign housing exclusion.

The first allows you to exclude up to $95,100 income from taxes if you are single or $190,200 if you are married and file a joint return.

The foreign housing exclusion allows you to exclude about $15,000 in income to compensate for money you spent on housing.

An exclusion is different than a deduction. It means you are not required to include such income in calculating your total income subject to tax. So you can still use whatever deductions and credits you have to reduce tax on income not covered by the exclusions.

Here, we explain how to claim these exclusions. This chapter is organized as follows:

1. Types of income that you can exclude.
2. Qualifying for the foreign earned income exclusion.
3. Amount you can exclude.
4. Reporting the foreign earned income exclusion.
5. Qualifying for the foreign housing exclusion.
6. Reporting the foreign housing exclusion.
7. Consequences of taking the foreign earned income and/or housing exclusion.

1. TYPES OF INCOME THAT YOU CAN EXCLUDE

The foreign earned income exclusion and the foreign housing exclusion apply only to certain types of income. First, it only applies to income received for working outside of the United States. Second, only "earned income" can be excluded. Earned income is defined as pay for personal services performed. The following chart fleshes out this definition:

Earned Income	Unearned Income	Variable Income
Salaries and wages	Dividends	Business profits
Commissions	Interest	Royalties
Bonuses	Capital gains	Rents
Professional fees	Gambling Winnings	Scholarships and fellowships
Tips	Alimony	

[1] This chapter is based on, and some text is copied from, IRS Publication 54. It is available on the IRS website.

Earned Income	Unearned Income	Variable Income
	Social security benefits	
	Pensions	
	Annuities	

The first two categories are clear enough. The third category may be a source of confusion. Let's explore some of these distinctions.

Professional fees. If you are engaged in a professional occupation (such as a doctor or lawyer), all fees received in the performance of these services are earned income.

Income of an artist. Income you receive from the sale of paintings you created is earned income.

Business profits. If you receive profits from a business you own, the distinction can be quite complicated. We suggest you consult a tax professional.

Royalties. Royalties received by a writer are earned income:

- when you transfer copyright to someone else; and
- when they are received under a contract to write a book or series of articles.

Rental income. Generally, rental income is unearned income. If you perform personal services (such as choosing the tenants or hiring the repair people) in connection with the production of rent, up to 30% of your net rental income can be considered earned income.

Scholarships and fellowships. Any portion of a scholarship or fellowship grant that is paid to you for teaching, research, or other services is considered earned income and you must report it.

2. QUALIFYING FOR THE FOREIGN EARNED INCOME EXCLUSION

We will explain the theory behind the exemption before walking you through the specifics of how to fill out Form 2555-EZ or Form 2555. To be eligible for the foreign earned income exclusion you must satisfy either of these two tests:

- Your tax home must be outside the United States.
- You must meet the bona fide residence test or the physical presence test.

Let's take these criteria in turn.

a. Tax home outside of the United States

The concept of tax home outside of the United States is a bit vague. Generally, it means that your residence or domicile is not in the United States. If you live and work in Canada this will not likely be a problem for you. However, if your situation is more complicated, for example you work in one country and live in the other, you should get professional tax advice to figure out how to report your income.

b. Bona fide residence test

The next criterion you have to meet is satisfying one of the residency tests. Meeting the bona fide residence test is one way to establish your eligibility for the foreign earned income exclusion. Generally, you have to prove that you were a resident of Canada for an uninterrupted period of time that includes at least one entire tax year (January to December). Aside from this there are few hard and fast rules. The bona fide residence test is based on intention to reside in a particular place. It is evaluated through words and acts. Each situation is analyzed on its own merits. When determining whether a taxpayer was a bona fide resident of a foreign country, courts ask a number of questions including:

(1) Did the taxpayer intend to reside outside of the United States?

(2) Did the taxpayer establish his or her home outside the United States for a temporary or indefinite period?

(3) Did the taxpayer participate in social and cultural activities and assimilate into the foreign environment?

(4) Did the taxpayer maintain a physical presence in the foreign country consistent with his or her employment?

(5) What was the nature of the taxpayer's employment outside of the United States?

(6) Did the taxpayer pay taxes outside of the United States?

(7) Did the taxpayer demonstrate the status of a resident or a sojourner (someone only in or out of the US for a temporary amount of time)?

(8) How did the taxpayer's employer consider the taxpayer?

(9) Where did the taxpayer's family, if any, live?

(10) What was the nature and duration of the taxpayer's employment?

(11) Did the taxpayer demonstrate good faith in living outside the USA?

These questions are only important if you feel that the situation is ambiguous. It is more important to show that you have resided in Canada for over a year and intend to make it your home. For most people who have been in Canada for a few years, this will not be a problem. If you have doubts about whether you will meet this test, consult a tax professional who can give you advice that is unique to your own situation. Note that if at any time you tell the government of Canada that you are not a resident of Canada then you will not meet this test.

c. The physical presence test

The other way to show that you are eligible for the foreign earned income exclusion is the physical presence test. You can meet the physical presence test if you are outside the United States for 330 days during a 12-month period. It is important to note that it does not matter which country you are in as long as it is not the United States. A day is defined as a full 24-hour period that starts at midnight. For calculation of presence in the US, however, if you arrive in the US at 23:59 on day one and leave at 00:01 on day 3, you are considered to have been present in the US for 3 days.

The 330-day period does not have to be consecutive. That means you can visit the United States for up to 35 days a year and still meet the test.

d. Qualifying for both tests

To claim the foreign earned income exclusion and the foreign housing exclusion, you need to meet only one of the tests set out above. But we suggest filling out both sections of the Form 2555-EZ (explained below) to ensure that you are able to claim the exemption.

3. AMOUNT YOU CAN EXCLUDE

You can exclude up to $95,100 as a single person, or $190,200 as a married couple, using the foreign earned income exclusion.

a. Increasing the exclusion by treating your spouse as a US citizen

A married couple who file a joint return is eligible for a larger foreign income exclusion than a single person. Many US citizens in Canada are married to non-Americans. If you are married to someone who is not a US citizen, he or she would not normally have to pay US taxes. But if it is advantageous, and your spouse consents, you can choose to treat your spouse as an American. This choice is called an election. It could allow you and your spouse to double the foreign earned income exclusion you and your spouse are entitled to.

The big disadvantage is that you and your spouse are subjecting your spouse's income to US income tax to which it would not otherwise be subject. A simple example illustrates this concept nicely.

Fred is a US citizen who lives in Montreal. Joanne his wife was born in Canada and is not a US citizen. Fred has a salary of $100,000 and no other types of income. Joanne earns a salary of $50,000 and also has no other types of income. Normally, Fred is obliged to file a US tax return but Joanne is not. However, Fred and Joanne can choose to treat Joanne as a US citizen for tax purposes. That means that they would file a join return that lists their total income of $150,000. Both can take advantage of the foreign earned income exclusion and exclude up to $190,200 as non-taxable. Had Fred and Joanne not chosen to file a joint return, he would have had to find other deductions to avoid paying tax on the $5,000 not covered by his foreign earned income exclusion. So for Fred and Joanne it would be advantageous to choose to treat Joanne as a US citizen.

As this example shows, the election makes sense if the US citizen spouse earns substantially more than the non-US citizen spouse. That way the US citizen spouse can take advantage of the extra foreign earned income exclusion. If the situation is reversed and the non-US citizen spouse earns much more than the US citizen spouse, it would probably be unwise for the US citizen spouse to make this election. Similarly, it may be unwise if the non-US citizen spouse has significant income from a non-salary source since this income is not covered by the foreign earned income exclusion. It would therefore be subject to US tax.

Note if you and your spouse decide to treat your spouse as a US citizen, your spouse must obtain an ITIN using the procedure outlined in Chapter 3.

4. REPORTING THE FOREIGN EARNED INCOME EXCLUSION

To claim the foreign earned income exclusion, you must file either Form 2555 or Form 2555-EZ. The forms are similar, but Form 2555-EZ is more straightforward. As long as you have no self-employment income, business expenses, or moving expenses, and are not going to claim the foreign housing exclusion (discussed below) you can file Form 2555-EZ. Here, we will show you how to file Form 2555 EZ using the following example.

For this example, we'll consider Joe and Maggie Smith. Joe and Maggie Smith are married and live in Winnipeg. Joe is a US citizen but Maggie is not. Joe has lived in Winnipeg for several years and tends not to visit the United States for more than a few days a year. Joe earns $90,000 in salary as a teacher for the Winnipeg School Division. Maggie is also a teacher but makes $92,000 and owns some stocks which produce dividends. Joe does not have any other sources of income. Fred, their son, is 12 and lives with them.

Joe qualifies for the foreign earned income exclusion because a) his income is salary and it was earned in Canada and b) his tax home is in Canada and c) he meets both the bona fide and physical presence residence tests. It does not make sense for Joe and Maggie to treat Maggie as a US citizen because he does not need the extra foreign earned income tax credit. If they did this, they would expose Maggie's income to US tax.

First, Joe has to fill out Form 2555-EZ for himself. It would look like this.

Form **2555-EZ** — **Foreign Earned Income Exclusion** — OMB No. 1545-0074 — **2011**

Department of the Treasury
Internal Revenue Service (99)

▶ See separate instructions. ▶ Attach to Form 1040.

Attachment Sequence No. **34A**

Name shown on Form 1040: Joe Smith (filing as a single person)
Your social security number: 123-456-789

You May Use This Form If You:
- Are a U.S. citizen or a resident alien.
- Earned wages/salaries in a foreign country.
- Had total foreign earned income of $92,900 or less.
- Are filing a calendar year return that covers a 12-month period.

And You:
- Do not have self-employment income.
- Do not have business/moving expenses.
- Do not claim the foreign housing exclusion or deduction.

The 2012 amount is $ 95100.

Part I Tests To See If You Can Take the Foreign Earned Income Exclusion

1 Bona Fide Residence Test

a Were you a bona fide resident of a foreign country or countries for a period that includes an entire tax year (see page 2 of the instructions)? ☑ Yes ☐ No
- If you answered "Yes," you meet this test. Fill in line 1b and then go to line 3.
- If you answered "No," you **do not** meet this test. Go to line 2 to see if you meet the Physical Presence Test.

b Enter the date your bona fide residence began ▶ June 1, 2004, and ended (see instructions) ▶

Joe still lives in Canada

2 Physical Presence Test

a Were you physically present in a foreign country or countries for at least 330 full days during— 2011 **or** any other period of 12 months in a row starting or ending in 2011? ☑ Yes ☐ No
- If you answered "Yes," you meet this test. Fill in line 2b and then go to line 3.
- If you answered "No," you **do not** meet this test. You **cannot** take the exclusion unless you meet the Bona Fide Residence Test above.

b The physical presence test is based on the 12-month period from ▶ 01/01/2012 through ▶ 31/12/2012.

3 Tax Home Test. Was your tax home in a foreign country or countries throughout your period of bona fide residence or physical presence, whichever applies? ☑ Yes ☐ No
- If you answered "Yes," you can take the exclusion. Complete Part II below and then go to page 2.
- If you answered "No," you **cannot** take the exclusion. **Do not** file this form.

Part II General Information

4 Your foreign address (including country): 63 Scotia Street Winnipeg Manitoba Canada

5 Your occupation: Teacher

6 Employer's name: Winnipeg School Division

7 Employer's U.S. address (including ZIP code): N/A

8 Employer's foreign address: 1577 Wall St E Winnipeg, MB R3E 2S5

9 Employer is (check any that apply):
a A U.S. business ☐
b A foreign business ☐
c Other (specify) ▶ Government ☐

10a If you filed Form 2555 or 2555-EZ after 1981, enter the last year you filed the form. ▶
b If you did not file Form 2555 or 2555-EZ after 1981, check here ▶ ☑ and go to line 11a now.
c Have you ever revoked the foreign earned income exclusion? ☐ Yes ☐ No
d If you answered "Yes," enter the tax year for which the revocation was effective. ▶

11a List your tax home(s) during 2011 and date(s) established. ▶ Canada, January 1, 2011
b Of what country are you a citizen/national? ▶ Canada

For Paperwork Reduction Act Notice, see the Form 1040 instructions. Form **2555-EZ** (2011)

Here you can simply put January 1 of the tax year in question

This represents a one week holiday that Joe took to Florida.

Page **2**

Part III **Days Present in the United States—** Complete this part if you were in the United States or its possessions during 2011.

12 (a) Date arrived in U.S.	(b) Date left U.S.	(c) Number of days in U.S. on business	(d) Income earned in U.S. on business (attach computation)
January 4, 2011	January 11, 2011	7	0

Part IV **Figure Your Foreign Earned Income Exclusion**

13	Maximum foreign earned income exclusion	13	$92,900 00
14	Enter the number of days in your qualifying period that fall within 2011 — 14: 365 **days**		
15	Did you enter 365 on line 14? ☑ **Yes.** Enter "1.000." ☐ **No.** Divide line 14 by 365 and enter the result as a decimal (rounded to at least three places).	15	× 1 . 000
16	Multiply line 13 by line 15	16	92900 00
17	Enter, in U.S. dollars, the total foreign earned income you earned and received in 2011 (see instructions). Be sure to include this amount on Form 1040, line 7	17	$90000 00
18	**Foreign earned income exclusion.** Enter the **smaller** of line 16 or line 17 here and in parentheses on **Form 1040, line 21.** Next to the amount enter "2555-EZ." On Form 1040, subtract this amount from your income to arrive at total income on Form 1040, line 22 ▶	18	90000 00

This amount changes every year so use the most current amount.

Enter 365 if you meet either the bona fide residency test or the physical presence test.

Form **2555-EZ** (2011)

Joe has to take the amount from line 18 on this form and put it on Form 1040 line 21 and mark Form 2555-EZ next to it.

5. QUALIFYING FOR THE FOREIGN HOUSING EXCLUSION

The foreign earned income exclusion is not the only tax benefit extended to US citizens abroad. You can also exclude income from tax based on your housing expenses. As long as you qualify for the foreign earned income exclusion, you can also take the foreign housing exclusion.

Do not confuse the foreign housing exclusion with the foreign housing deduction. The latter is for those people who have self-employment income only.

The foreign housing exclusion is allowed in addition to the foreign earned income exclusion, but only if you have more foreign earned income than you can exclude using the foreign earned income exclusion—in other words, if you earn more than $95,100 (2012 figure). If you are married (including common law) and live together and are filing a joint return, you must calculate your expenses together. If you are married, live together, but are filing separate returns, only one spouse can claim the foreign housing exclusion.

a. How to calculate the foreign housing exclusion

Calculating the housing exclusion is somewhat complicated. The amount you are allowed to exclude is computed as follows: your total housing expenses – the base amount = the eligible deduction. There is a maximum exclusion that is determined based on where you live.

i. Your housing expenses

Let's take each step of the equation in turn. First, you have to calculate your housing expenses. The rule is that these expenses must be reasonable and relate to your housing. They include rent, repairs, utility bills, property taxes not deductible elsewhere (do not include your property taxes here as you can deduct them elsewhere), parking, or anything else that is related to the cost of operating your home. Admittedly, this is a bit of a vague description, but that reflects the nature of the test. You should not include interest related to a mortgage here as that is a separate deduction that we will explore elsewhere.

The following expenses have been deemed unreasonable: lavish home improvements, taxes that are otherwise deductible (Canadian property taxes are deductible elsewhere), the cost of buying property, the cost of domestic labour, pay television subscriptions, furniture or other accessories, or improvements that increase the value of the property.

ii. The base amount

Second, you have to figure out the base amount to subtract from your housing expenses. The IRS assumes that you would pay certain housing expenses anyway if you lived in the US, so you are not allowed to claim the full amount of your expenses. The base amount, the part which you are not allowed to claim, is 16% of the maximum foreign earned income exclusion, but it is calculated on a per day basis. In 2012 the maximum foreign earned income exclusion is $95,100. 16% of that is $15,216 per year or $41.68 per day that you lived outside the United States. Put simply, if you were a resident of Canada (or anywhere outside the United States) for 365 days the base amount of expenses you are not allowed to claim is $15,216.

Note that being a resident does not mean you cannot travel elsewhere. It simply means that your home base was in a particular place. Subtract the base amount from your housing expenses to figure out how much income you can exclude from tax.

iii. The maximum exclusion

Third, you need to make sure that your exclusion is less than the allowable maximum.

Unless you live in a particular city that is considered particularly expensive, you may not deduct more than 30% of the value of the foreign earned income exclusion. For 2012, this means that you cannot deduct more than $28,530 in housing expenses. However, if you live in one of the following cities your limit is as follows (all amounts in US dollars):

Calgary	42,500
Dartmouth	35,500
Edmonton	36,900
Halifax	35,500
London	31,500
Montreal	60,100
Ottawa	52,400
Quebec	28,200
Toronto	51,100
Vancouver	48,900
Victoria	34,800
Winnipeg	34,300

If your city is not on this list, the maximum of the expenses you can deduct in 2012 is $28,530.

6. REPORTING THE FOREIGN HOUSING EXCLUSION

To claim the foreign housing exclusion you must complete Form 2555.

Let's review the above using an example. Dave Jones is a single US citizen who lives in Toronto and works as a lawyer. His annual salary is $100,000 and he has $15,000 in dividend and interest income. He can exclude $95,100 of his salary income (but none of his other income) based on the foreign earned income exclusion. Dave pays $1,500 a month in rent and during 2012 spent $4,000 to rent a parking space. His total housing expenses are $22,000. Dave cannot exclude $15,216 of these expenses because that is the base amount. But he can exclude $6,784 in income because he has those living expenses.

Dave's Form 2555 looks like this:

Form **2555** — Department of the Treasury, Internal Revenue Service

Foreign Earned Income

▶ See separate instructions. ▶ Attach to Form 1040.

OMB No. 1545-0074 — **2011** — Attachment Sequence No. **34**

For Use by U.S. Citizens and Resident Aliens Only

Name shown on Form 1040: David Jones — Your social security number: 123-456-789

Part I General Information

[Note on form: Check with your employer regarding this answer.]

1 Your foreign address (including country): 23 Spadina Avenue, Toronto Ontario M5V 2M5
2 Your occupation: Lawyer
3 Employer's name ▶ Stikeman Elliot LLP
4a Employer's U.S. address ▶ N/A
b Employer's foreign address ▶ 199 Bay St. #5300 Toronto, Ontario M5L 1G4
5 Employer is (check any that apply): a ☑ A foreign entity b ☐ A U.S. company c ☐ Self d ☐ A foreign affiliate of a U.S. company e ☐ Other (specify) ▶
6a If, after 1981, you filed Form 2555 or Form 2555-EZ, enter the last year you filed the form. ▶
b If you did not file Form 2555 or 2555-EZ after 1981 to claim either of the exclusions, check here ▶ ☐ and go to line 7.
c Have you ever revoked either of the exclusions? ☐ Yes ☐ No
d If you answered "Yes," enter the type of exclusion and the tax year for which the revocation was effective. ▶
7 Of what country are you a citizen/national? ▶ United States, Canada
8a Did you maintain a separate foreign residence for your family because of adverse living conditions at your tax home? See **Second foreign household** in the instructions ☐ Yes ☑ No
b If "Yes," enter city and country of the separate foreign residence. Also, enter the number of days during your tax year that you maintained a second household at that address. ▶
9 List your tax home(s) during your tax year and date(s) established. ▶ Toronto Canada, January 1, 1984

Next, complete either Part II or Part III. If an item does not apply, enter "NA." If you do not give the information asked for, any exclusion or deduction you claim may be disallowed.

[Note on form: when you started living in the city you now live in.]

Part II Taxpayers Qualifying Under Bona Fide Residence Test (see instructions)

10 Date bona fide residence began ▶ January 1, 1996, and ended ▶ ongoing
11 Kind of living quarters in foreign country ▶ a ☐ Purchased house b ☑ Rented house or apartment c ☐ Rented room d ☐ Quarters furnished by employer
12a Did any of your family live with you abroad during any part of the tax year? ☐ Yes ☑ No
b If "Yes," who and for what period? ▶
13a Have you submitted a statement to the authorities of the foreign country where you claim bona fide residence that you are not a resident of that country? See instructions ☐ Yes ☑ No
b Are you required to pay income tax to the country where you claim bona fide residence? See instructions ☑ Yes ☐ No
If you answered "Yes" to 13a and "No" to 13b, you do not qualify as a bona fide resident. Do not complete the rest of this part.
14 If you were present in the United States or its possessions during the tax year, complete columns **(a)–(d)** below. **Do not** include the income from column **(d)** in Part IV, but report it on Form 1040.

(a) Date arrived in U.S.	(b) Date left U.S.	(c) Number of days in U.S. on business	(d) Income earned in U.S. on business (attach computation)	(a) Date arrived in U.S.	(b) Date left U.S.	(c) Number of days in U.S. on business	(d) Income earned in U.S. on business (attach computation)

15a List any contractual terms or other conditions relating to the length of your employment abroad. ▶ -
b Enter the type of visa under which you entered the foreign country. ▶ N/A - I am a Canadian citizen
c Did your visa limit the length of your stay or employment in a foreign country? If "Yes," attach explanation ☐ Yes ☑ No
d Did you maintain a home in the United States while living abroad? ☐ Yes ☑ No
e If "Yes," enter address of your home, whether it was rented, the names of the occupants, and their relationship to you. ▶

For Paperwork Reduction Act Notice, see the Form 1040 instructions. Cat. No. 11900P Form **2555** (2011)

Form 2555 (2011) | You do not need to fill out both part II & part III but it does not hurt to do so. | Page **2**

Part III **Taxpayers Qualifying Under Physical Presence Test** (see instructions)

16 The physical presence test is based on the 12-month period from ▶ January 1 2012 through ▶ December 31 2012

17 Enter your principal country of employment during your tax year. ▶ Canada

18 If you traveled abroad during the 12-month period entered on line 16, complete columns **(a)–(f)** below. Exclude travel between foreign countries that did not involve travel on or over international waters, or in or over the United States, for 24 hours or more. If you have no travel to report during the period, enter "Physically present in a foreign country or countries for the entire 12-month period." **Do not** include the income from column **(f)** below in Part IV, but report it on Form 1040.

(a) Name of country (including U.S.)	**(b)** Date arrived	**(c)** Date left	**(d)** Full days present in country	**(e)** Number of days in U.S. on business	**(f)** Income earned in U.S. on business (attach computation)
Barbados	January 15	January 22	7	0	0

Part IV **All Taxpayers**

Note: *Enter on lines 19 through 23 all income, including noncash income, you earned and actually or constructively received during your 2011 tax year for services you performed in a foreign country. If any of the foreign earned income received this tax year was earned in a prior tax year, or will be earned in a later tax year (such as a bonus), see the instructions.* ***Do not*** *include income from line 14, column* ***(d)****, or line 18, column* ***(f)****. Report amounts in U.S. dollars, using the exchange rates in effect when you actually or constructively received the income.*

If you are a cash basis taxpayer, report on Form 1040 all income you received in 2011, no matter when you performed the service.

	2011 Foreign Earned Income			Line	**Amount (in U.S. dollars)**
19	Total wages, salaries, bonuses, commissions, etc.			**19**	100,000
20	Allowable share of income for personal services performed (see instructions):				
a	In a business (including farming) or profession			**20a**	
b	In a partnership. List partnership's name and address and type of income. ▶			**20b**	
21	Noncash income (market value of property or facilities furnished by employer—attach statement showing how it was determined):				
a	Home (lodging)			**21a**	
b	Meals			**21b**	
c	Car			**21c**	
d	Other property or facilities. List type and amount. ▶			**21d**	
22	Allowances, reimbursements, or expenses paid on your behalf for services you performed:				
a	Cost of living and overseas differential	**22a**			
b	Family	**22b**			
c	Education	**22c**			
d	Home leave	**22d**			
e	Quarters	**22e**			
f	For any other purpose. List type and amount. ▶	**22f**			
g	Add lines 22a through 22f			**22g**	
23	Other foreign earned income. List type and amount. ▶			**23**	
24	Add lines 19 through 21d, line 22g, and line 23			**24**	
25	Total amount of meals and lodging included on line 24 that is excludable (see instructions)			**25**	
26	Subtract line 25 from line 24. Enter the result here and on line 27 on page 3. This is your **2011 foreign earned income** ▶			**26**	100,000

Form **2555** (2011)

Form 2555 (2011) Page 3

Part V All Taxpayers

27	Enter the amount from line 26	27	100,000
	Are you claiming the housing exclusion or housing deduction? ☑ **Yes.** Complete Part VI. ☐ **No.** Go to Part VII.		

Part VI Taxpayers Claiming the Housing Exclusion and/or Deduction

This is the 2011 amount. The 2012 is $15,216. This number changes every year.

28	Qualified housing expenses for the tax year (see instructions)	28	22000
29a	Enter location where housing expenses incurred (see instructions) ▶ Toronto		
b	Enter limit on housing expenses (see instructions)	29b	51,100
30	Enter the **smaller** of line 28 or line 29b	30	22000
31	Number of days in your qualifying period that fall within your 2011 tax year (see instructions) — 31: 365 days		
32	Multiply $40.72 by the number of days on line 31. If 365 is entered on line 31, enter $14,864.00 here	32	14804
33	Subtract line 32 from line 30. If the result is zero or less, do not complete the rest of this part or any of Part IX	33	7196
34	Enter employer-provided amounts (see instructions) — 34: 0		
35	Divide line 34 by line 27. Enter the result as a decimal (rounded to at least three places), but do not enter more than "1.000"	35	× .
36	**Housing exclusion.** Multiply line 33 by line 35. Enter the result but do not enter more than the amount on line 34. Also, complete Part VIII ▶	36	7196

Note: *The housing deduction is figured in Part IX. If you choose to claim the foreign earned income exclusion, complete Parts VII and VIII before Part IX.*

Fill this in if your employer contributes to your housing expenses.

Part VII Taxpayers Claiming the Foreign Earned Income Exclusion

37	Maximum foreign earned income exclusion	37	$92,900 00
38	• If you completed Part VI, enter the number from line 31. • All others, enter the number of days in your qualifying period that fall within your 2011 tax year (see the instructions for line 31). — 38: 365 days		
39	• If line 38 and the number of days in your 2011 tax year (usually 365) are the same, enter "1.000." • Otherwise, divide line 38 by the number of days in your 2011 tax year and enter the result as a decimal (rounded to at least three places).	39	× 1 . 00
40	Multiply line 37 by line 39	40	92900
41	Subtract line 36 from line 27	41	92804
42	**Foreign earned income exclusion.** Enter the **smaller** of line 40 or line 41. Also, complete Part VIII ▶	42	92804

The 2012 amount is 95100.

Part VIII Taxpayers Claiming the Housing Exclusion, Foreign Earned Income Exclusion, or Both

43	Add lines 36 and 42	43	100000
44	Deductions allowed in figuring your adjusted gross income (Form 1040, line 37) that are allocable to the excluded income. See instructions and attach computation	44	0
45	Subtract line 44 from line 43. Enter the result here and in parentheses on **Form 1040, line 21.** Next to the amount enter "Form 2555." On Form 1040, subtract this amount from your income to arrive at total income on Form 1040, line 22	45	100000

Part IX Taxpayers Claiming the Housing Deduction— Complete this part only if **(a)** line 33 is more than line 36 and **(b)** line 27 is more than line 43.

46	Subtract line 36 from line 33	46	
47	Subtract line 43 from line 27	47	
48	Enter the **smaller** of line 46 or line 47	48	
	Note: *If line 47 is* ***more than*** *line 48 and you could not deduct all of your 2010 housing deduction because of the 2010 limit, use the worksheet on page 4 of the instructions to figure the amount to enter on line 49. Otherwise, go to line 50.*		
49	Housing deduction carryover from 2010 (from worksheet on page 4 of the instructions)	49	
50	**Housing deduction.** Add lines 48 and 49. Enter the total here and on Form 1040 to the left of line 36. Next to the amount on Form 1040, enter "Form 2555." Add it to the total adjustments reported on that line ▶	50	

Form **2555** (2011)

Take the amount on line 45 and enter it on Form 1040 line 21. Then on Form 1040 subtract this amount to arrive at your total income on line 22 of Form 1040.

7. CONSEQUENCES OF TAKING THE FOREIGN EARNED INCOME AND/OR HOUSING EXCLUSION

There are several consequences to taking these exclusions. For much of this book, we assume that you will take the exclusion(s). So we repeat these effects in other places. For now, though, you should simply be aware that if you take the exclusions you cannot:

- Take the earned income credit.
- Claim a foreign tax credit on taxes paid on income you exclude. The foreign tax credit is discussed more in Chapter 32.
- Take a deduction for moving expenses paid for with income that you excluded.

Taking the exclusions will also change the way you compute tax payable on income that you cannot exclude (either because it is in excess of the exclusion or it is the wrong type). Nevertheless, it is clearly a benefit to take one or both exclusions.

PART 2C

CALCULATING YOUR ADJUSTED GROSS INCOME

15

OVERVIEW OF LINES 23–27

Adjusted gross income means your gross income (the total which was entered on line 22) minus certain expenses. In this next section, we explain certain deductions that you can claim that will reduce your gross income. The next section of Form 1040 looks like this.

Adjusted Gross Income	23	Educator expenses	23		
	24	Certain business expenses of reservists, performing artists, and fee-basis government officials. Attach Form 2106 or 2106-EZ	24		
	25	Health savings account deduction. Attach Form 8889	25		
	26	Moving expenses. Attach Form 3903	26		
	27	Deductible part of self-employment tax. Attach Schedule SE	27		
	28	Self-employed SEP, SIMPLE, and qualified plans	28		
	29	Self-employed health insurance deduction	29		
	30	Penalty on early withdrawal of savings	30		
	31a	Alimony paid **b** Recipient's SSN ▶	31a		
	32	IRA deduction	32		
	33	Student loan interest deduction	33		
	34	Tuition and fees. Attach Form 8917	34		
	35	Domestic production activities deduction. Attach Form 8903	35		
	36	Add lines 23 through 35		36	
	37	Subtract line 36 from line 22. This is your **adjusted gross income** ▶		37	

For Disclosure, Privacy Act, and Paperwork Reduction Act Notice, see separate instructions. Cat. No. 11320B Form **1040** (2011)

This chapter surveys lines 23–37 of Form 1040. Where necessary, it directs you to other chapters that provide a more in-depth explanation of how to calculate the amounts on particular lines.

1. EDUCATOR EXPENSES – LINE 23

If you were a kindergarten–grade 12 teacher, instructor, counsellor, or principal for at least 900 hours during the tax year for which you are filing, you can take advantage of this deduction. On this line, you can deduct up to $250 (or $500 if you are married and filing jointly and both qualify for the deduction) in expenses related to what you purchase for use in your classroom. You must have paid these expenses yourself and they cannot have been reimbursed. Publication 529 gives more information on this deduction.

2. BUSINESS EXPENSES FOR CERTAIN CATEGORIES OF EMPLOYEES – LINE 24

This line is for the following deductions:

- certain business expenses of National Guard and reserve members who travelled more than 100 miles from home to perform services as a National Guard or reserve member;
- business expenses of fee-basis state or local government officials;
- performing-arts-related expenses as a qualified performing artist.

The first two categories won't apply to most readers of this book. If they apply to you, please see the instructions to Form 2106 for more details. The last category is a bit broader. You are considered a qualified performing artist if you:

1. Performed services in the performing arts as an employee for at least two employers during the tax year;
2. Received from at least two of those employers wages of $200 or more per employer;
3. Had allowable business expenses attributable to the performing arts of more than 10% of gross income from the performing arts; and
4. Had adjusted gross income of $16,000 or less before deducting expenses as a performing artist.

If you meet these criteria, you can deduct your employee expenses on line 24 as opposed to on Schedule A. Please see Chapter 26 to learn more about employee business expenses.

3. HEALTH SAVINGS ACCOUNT DEDUCTION – LINE 25

These types of accounts are not generally available in Canada, so this deduction is of little interest to US citizens in Canada. If, however, you have a US Health Savings Account, you can find more information on how to claim this deduction in the instructions to Form 8889 which is available on the IRS website.

4. MOVING EXPENSES – LINE 26

Moving expenses are only deductible if they are in connection with a move of more than 80 km for a new job. Note that if you have taken the foreign earned income exclusion, which we recommend you always do, you cannot deduct moving expenses related to income that you excluded. Therefore your moving expense deduction may be less robust than it otherwise would be. Consult Chapter 16 to learn more about moving expenses.

5. DEDUCTION FOR PAYING SELF-EMPLOYMENT TAX – LINE 27

This line is where you deduct any self-employment tax you have paid. Taxes for those who are self-employed are complicated and, as such, not covered in this guide. We recommend that you have them prepared by a tax professional. Please consult the following IRS website or a tax professional for more assistance:

http://www.irs.gov/businesses/small/selfemployed/index.html

If you are not self-employed you can ignore this line.

6. SELF-EMPLOYED RETIREMENT DEDUCTIONS – LINE 28

This line relates to retirement plans for those who are self-employed. Taxes for those who are self-employed are complicated and outside the scope of this guide. Nevertheless, Publication 560 has more information on these plans. If you are not self-employed you can ignore this line.

7. SELF-EMPLOYED HEALTH INSURANCE DEDUCTION – LINE 29

This line also relates to self-employment issues. Those who are not self-employed can ignore it.

8. PENALTY ON EARLY WITHDRAWAL OF SAVINGS – LINE 30

If you withdrew money from a certificate of deposit or other time-deposit savings account prior to your certificate maturing, you may have incurred a penalty for early withdrawal. This penalty is charged by the bank and withheld directly from your proceeds from the certificate. This is reported in on a Form 1099-INT. If you receive this form, deduct the entire penalty. Most readers of this guide will probably not receive this form and can ignore this line.

9. IRA DEDUCTION – LINE 32

Line 32 deals with deductions for IRA contributions only. Do not report RRSP contributions here (these are discussed in Chapter 41). So far as we are aware, no Canadian financial institution offers an IRA to Canadians. Therefore, it is unlikely that you will have made contributions to an IRA in the tax year for which you are filing. If you have moved from the United States to Canada, we suggest consulting a professional tax advisor about your retirement accounts. There are significant US tax issues with contributing to an IRA from Canada. In short, most people can ignore line 32 and leave it blank.

10. STUDENT LOAN INTEREST DEDUCTION – LINE 33

This is the line where you can deduct up to $2,500 of interest you paid on a student loan. This is discussed more in Chapter 17.

11. TUITION AND FEES DEDUCTION – LINE 34

This deduction allows you to reduce your income by up to $4,000 resulting from tuition fees that you pay for either yourself, your spouse, or your dependent. It is discussed more in Chapter 18.

12. DOMESTIC PRODUCTION ACTIVITIES DEDUCTION – LINE 35

This line relates to oil production activities and other manufacturing activities in the United States. It is outside the scope of this guide.

13. CONCLUSION: ADJUSTED GROSS INCOME

After you fill out the above lines, you need to total lines 23–35 and subtract that amount from your total income that you listed on line 22. This results in what is called your adjusted gross income. It is the amount of money, prior to certain deductions, on which your tax payable will be calculated. Enter this amount on line 37.

16

MOVING EXPENSES[1]

This chapter explains how to deduct moving expenses. Before explaining the deduction, you should note that if you exclude all or part of your income using the foreign earned income exclusion or the foreign housing exclusion, you cannot deduct the part of your moving expense that is allocable to the excluded income. This reduces the value of the moving expenses deduction and increases its complexity. This chapter is organized as follows:

1. Computing your moving expenses.
2. Reporting your moving expenses.
3. Moving expenses and the foreign earned income exclusion.

1. COMPUTING YOUR MOVING EXPENSES

a. Can you claim moving expenses?

To qualify for moving expenses, your move must be related to the start of a new job. Generally, the rule is that your move has to be within one year of starting a new job. Your new workplace must generally be more than 50 miles (80 km) farther from your old home than your old workplace was. Also, you must work at least 39 weeks during the first 12 months after you move. The following diagram illustrates this rule.

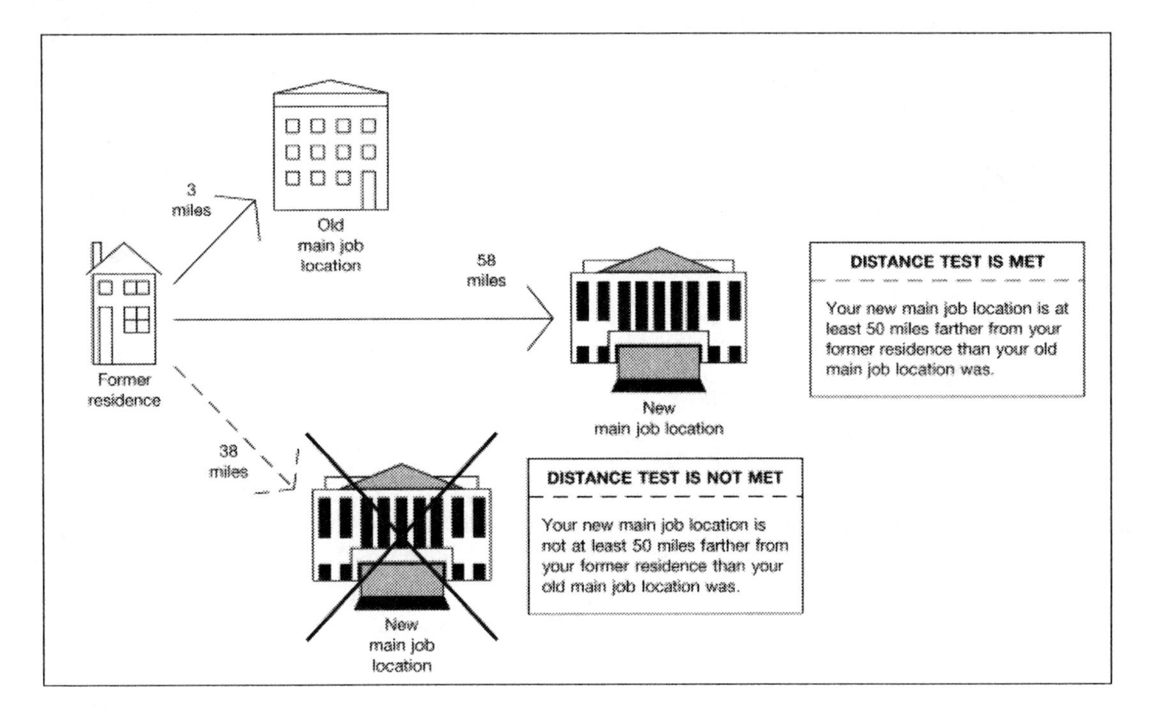

[1] This chapter is based on, and some of the text is copied from, IRS publication 521.

b. What expenses can you deduct

Once you have established that your moving expenses are eligible for a deduction, the next task is to figure out what kind of expenses you can deduct. If you are moving to a location outside of the United States (i.e., a move within Canada) you can deduct the following expenses:

- The cost of moving household goods and personal effects from your former home to your new home.
- The cost of travelling (including lodging) from your former home to your new home.
- The cost of moving household goods and personal effects to and from storage.
- The cost of storing household goods and personal effects while you are at the new job location.

Generally, moving expenses must be deducted in the year in which they were incurred. If you are moving to or from the United States, publication 521 explains how to calculate your moving expenses.

c. Non-deductible expenses

The following expenses are non-deductible:

- any part of the purchase price of your new home;
- vehicle registration plate;
- driver's licence;
- expenses of buying or selling a home (including closing costs, mortgage fees, and pre-paid interest);
- expenses of entering into or breaking a lease;
- home improvements to help sell your home;
- loss on the sale of your home;
- losses from disposing of memberships in clubs;
- mortgage penalties;
- pre-move house hunting expenses;
- real estate taxes;
- refitting of carpet and draperies;
- return trips to your former residence;
- security deposits (including any given up due to the move).

d. Employer reimburses your expenses

When you start a new job, many employers may pay your moving expenses. As a general rule, you are not allowed to deduct moving expenses for which someone reimburses you. A moving allowance may be treated as income depending on the arrangement with your employer. There are generally two possible arrangements. If your employer paid your eligible moving expenses directly, or reimbursed you for the exact amount you spent, then the reimbursement is not income. Sometimes, however, an employer will just give you a stipend to spend as you see fit. In this case, you have to fill out Form 3903 below. Any excess of the stipend over your actual expenses should be reported as income on line 7.

2. REPORTING YOUR MOVING EXPENSES

You have to report moving expenses on Form 3903. Let's walk through this form. At line 1, you should record the transportation and storage of household goods. On line 2 you can deduct the travel and lodging it cost to get from your old residence to your new residence. You can either enter the actual amount of money you spent or mileage of 23.5 cents a mile (1.6 km). On line 4, you must list how much, if any, of these moving expenses were paid for by your employer.

Let's use an example to explain this concept. Troy McClure is a US citizen who moved from Winnipeg to Toronto in August 2012 to take a job in the film industry that started in November 2012. He did not make use of the foreign earned income or housing exclusion in 2011. This move was more than 50 miles (80 km). It was also within a year of his employment in the new city. Troy spent $10,000 moving his belongings and $800 on a plane ticket and a hotel room. The film gave Troy $2,500 to pay for his moving expenses. Troy would fill out Form 3903 as follows.

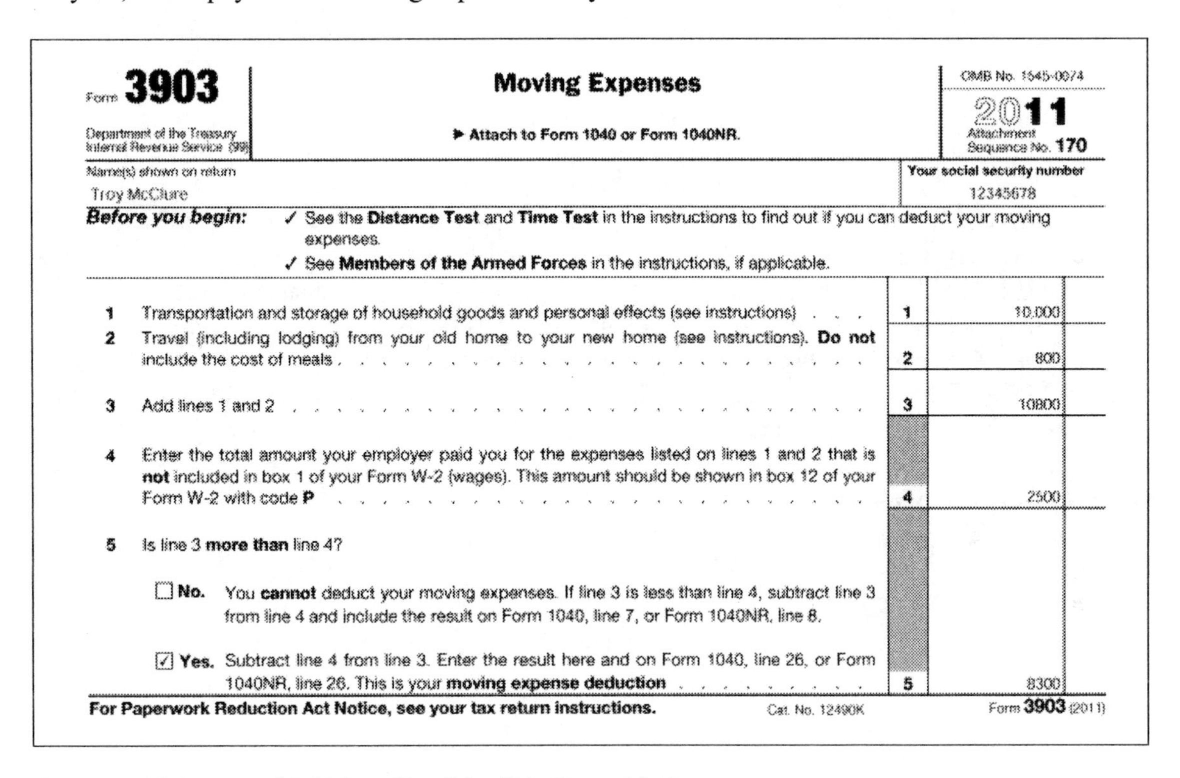

Form **3903** Department of the Treasury Internal Revenue Service (99)

Moving Expenses

▶ Attach to Form 1040 or Form 1040NR.

OMB No. 1545-0074 **2011** Attachment Sequence No. **170**

Name(s) shown on return: Troy McClure — **Your social security number:** 12345678

Before you begin: ✓ See the **Distance Test** and **Time Test** in the instructions to find out if you can deduct your moving expenses.
✓ See **Members of the Armed Forces** in the instructions, if applicable.

1	Transportation and storage of household goods and personal effects (see instructions)	1	10,000
2	Travel (including lodging) from your old home to your new home (see instructions). **Do not** include the cost of meals	2	800
3	Add lines 1 and 2	3	10800
4	Enter the total amount your employer paid you for the expenses listed on lines 1 and 2 that is **not** included in box 1 of your Form W-2 (wages). This amount should be shown in box 12 of your Form W-2 with code **P**	4	2500
5	Is line 3 **more than** line 4? ☐ **No.** You **cannot** deduct your moving expenses. If line 3 is less than line 4, subtract line 3 from line 4 and include the result on Form 1040, line 7, or Form 1040NR, line 8. ☑ **Yes.** Subtract line 4 from line 3. Enter the result here and on Form 1040, line 26, or Form 1040NR, line 26. This is your **moving expense deduction**	5	8300

For Paperwork Reduction Act Notice, see your tax return instructions. Cat. No. 12490K Form **3903** (2011)

Troy would then put $8,300 on line 26 of his Form 1040.

3. MOVING EXPENSES AND THE FOREIGN EARNED INCOME EXCLUSION

Moving expenses present challenges if you take the foreign earned income exclusion. The easiest route is to simply not deduct your moving expenses. Unlike income, there is no legal requirement to report all of the deductions for which you may be eligible. However, even if you benefit from the foreign earned income exclusion, you may be able to deduct some moving expenses. The rule is that those moving expenses related to income excluded by the foreign earned income or housing exclusion may not be deducted. So, if you make use of these exclusions and still wish to deduct your moving expenses, you must have excess foreign earned income that you could not exclude. The following explanation assumes that you were not a resident of the United States at any point during the tax year in question.

There are a number of steps in figuring out what portion of your moving expenses you can actually deduct:

1. Divide the amount of foreign earned income that you excluded using the foreign earned income and/or housing exclusions by your total foreign earned income. Remember that foreign earned income is a specific subset of your total income. It does not include income from passive sources such as interest or capital gains. This is explained more in Chapter 14. The result from the above division should be a decimal less than 1.
2. Take the decimal from step 1 and multiply it by the total moving expense deduction listed on line 5 of Form 3903.
3. The total is the amount of moving expenses that are allocable to foreign earned income and thus not deductible.
4. Subtract the total in step 3 from your total moving expenses. If the result is positive, you can enter this amount on line 26 of your Form 1040.

Let's use an example to illustrate this. Jeanine moved from Toronto to Montreal to take a new job. This move was more than 50 miles (80 km). She paid movers $6,000 and spent $150 to take the train. She received no reimbursement for these expenses. So her total deductible moving expenses were $6,150. However, in tax year 2012 Jeanine earned $150,000 in salary. She excluded $100,000 in income using the foreign earned income and housing exclusions. Following the instructions above, to figure out the amount of moving expenses she can deduct she has to do the following. First, she divides $100,000 (amount excluded) by $150,000 (total foreign earned income). The result is .66. Second, she takes the result and multiplies it by her total moving expenses (.66 × 6,150 = 4,059). Therefore, $4,059 is the portion of her moving expenses that she cannot deduct as a result of claiming the foreign earned income exclusion. Third, she subtracts $4,059 from her total moving expenses ($6,150 – $4,059 = $2,091). This means that she can deduct $2,091 in moving expenses from her taxes. She enters this amount on line 26 of her Form 1040.

17

STUDENT LOAN INTEREST DEDUCTION – LINE 33[1]

This chapter outlines the student loan interest deduction. It is only available if your modified adjusted gross income is less than $75,000 as an individual or $150,000 if you are married and filing jointly. If you meet the criteria outlined below, you may be able to reduce your income subject to tax by up to $2,500. To claim a student loan interest deduction you must:

1. Pay interest on a qualified student loan.
2. Have appropriate education expenses.
3. Pay those expenses to an eligible educational institution.
4. Have an adjusted gross income of less than $75,000, or $150,000 if you are married and filing jointly.

Let's take each criterion in turn. After doing so, we will explain how to calculate the deduction.

1. A QUALIFIED STUDENT LOAN

Student loan interest is interest you paid during the year on a qualified student loan. It includes both required and voluntary interest payments. A qualified student loan is one taken out to pay appropriate educational expenses (defined in the next section).

- For you, your spouse, or a person who was your dependent when you took out the loan;
- Paid or incurred within a reasonable period of time before or after you took out the loan; and
- For education provided during an academic period for an eligible student.

Remember that the definition of dependent is very broad. It includes both children and relatives whom you support. It is further discussed in Chapter 6. Also note that there is no limitation on the source of the loan.

2. QUALIFIED HIGHER EDUCATION EXPENSES

For purposes of the student loan interest deduction, these expenses are the total costs of attending an eligible educational institution, including graduate school. They include amounts paid for the following items:

- tuition and fees;
- room and board;
- books, supplies, and equipment;
- other necessary expenses (such as transportation).

---

[1] This chapter is based on, and some text is copied from, IRS Publication 17.

The cost of room and board qualifies only to the extent that it is not more than the greater of:

- the allowance for room and board, as determined by the eligible educational institution, that was included in the cost of attendance for a particular academic period and living arrangement of the student; and
- the actual amount charged if the student is residing in housing owned or operated by the eligible educational institution.

3. THE EXPENSES MUST BE INCURRED AT AN ELIGIBLE EDUCATION INSTITUTION

An eligible educational institution is any college, university, vocational school, or other postsecondary educational institution eligible to participate in a student aid program administered by the Department of Education. It includes virtually all accredited public, non-profit, and proprietary (privately owned profit-making) postsecondary institutions in the United States. Most Canadian institutions are also considered eligible educational institutions. To qualify, the school must participate in the US Department of Education's Federal Student Aid (FSA) programs. You can search on the following website to see if your school is eligible (www.fafsa.ed.gov/index.htm). Once there, click on "Federal School Code Search" to bring up the search engine. You can also ask your educational institution whether they participate in US Federal Student Aid programs.

4. ADJUSTED GROSS INCOME OF LESS THAN $75,000, OR $150,000 IF FILING JOINTLY

The foreign earned income and housing exclusions complicate the calculation of your adjusted gross income. You cannot simply take the amount that is found on line 38 of your Form 1040. To claim the student loan interest deduction, your gross income includes any amount excluded under the foreign earned income or housing exclusions. So as long as all of your income, including that excluded under the foreign earned income and housing exclusion, is less than $75,000, or $150,000 if married and filing jointly, you can claim the student loan interest deduction.

Let's use an example to explain this. Take the case of Jenny Jones. She is a US citizen who lives in Fredericton and just finished at the University of New Brunswick. She earns $35,000 working in a bank and had $2,500 in interest income. In 2011 she paid $2,500 in interest payments on her student loan. She took the foreign earned income exclusion to exclude her salary. However, she could not exclude her interest income because it is not covered by the foreign earned income exclusion. To avoid paying tax on this she wants to claim a deduction based on her student loan payments. Because she used the foreign earned income exclusion, Jenny's salary income is not taxable. However, her interest income is. She should attach Form 2555-EZ to her form 1040. Jenny should use the following worksheet to determine if she is eligible to use the student loan tax deduction.

1.	Enter the total interest you paid in 2012 on qualified student loans. **Do not enter more than $2,500.**	**1. $2,500**	
2.	Enter the amount from Form 1040, line 22	**2.** $2,500	
3.	Enter the total of the amounts from Form 1040, lines 23 through 32	**3.** 0	
4.	Enter the total of any amounts entered on the dotted line next to Form 1040, line 36	**4.**	
5.	Add lines 3 and 4	**5.**	
6.	Subtract line 5 from line 2	**6.**	
7.	Enter any foreign earned income exclusion and/or housing exclusion (Form 2555, line 45, or Form 2555-EZ, line 18)	**7. 35,000**	
8.	Enter any foreign housing deduction (Form 2555, line 50)	**8. 0**	
9.	Enter the amount of income from Puerto Rico you are excluding	**9. 0**	
10.	Enter the amount of income from American Samoa you are excluding (Form 4563, line 15)	**10. 0**	
11.	Add lines 6 through 10. This is your **modified adjusted gross income**		**11. 37,500**
12.	Enter the amount shown below for your filing status • Single, head of household, or qualifying widow(er) — $60,000 • Married filing jointly — $120,000		**12. $60,000**
13.	Is the amount on line 11 more than the amount on line 12? 0 **No.** Skip lines 13 and 14, enter -0- on line 15, and go to line 16. 0 **Yes.** Subtract line 12 from line 11		**13.**
14.	Divide line 13 by $15,000 ($30,000 if married filing jointly). Enter the result as a decimal		**14.**
15.	Multiply line 1 by line 14		**15. 0**
16.	**Student loan interest deduction.** Subtract line 15 from line 1. Enter the result here and on Form 1040, line 33. **Do not** include this amount in figuring any other deduction on your return (such as on Schedule A, C, E, etc.).		**16. 2,500**

The trick here is that Jenny's salary income, even though it is excluded for the calculation of tax purposes, must be included to determine her eligibility for the student loan interest deduction. Jenny would then put $2,500 on line 33 of her Form 1040.

5. REPORTING THE DEDUCTION

Assuming you meet the above criteria, it is quite easy to actually report the deduction. First, calculate the total amount of interest on a student loan that you paid in the tax year for which you are filing. Then take this amount and enter it on line 33. If the amount exceeds $2,500, simply enter $2,500 on line 33. You cannot deduct more than $2,500 of student loan interest in a given tax year.

18

TUITION FEES DEDUCTION[1]

The tuition fees deduction allows you to reduce your income by up to $4,000 if you pay tuition expenses. Claiming this deduction may, however, preclude you from taking advantage of other tax credits such as the lifetime learning credit or the American Opportunity Credit. These are discussed more in Chapter 36. Based on your own situation, you will need to decide whether taking the credit or the deduction is more favourable. In this chapter, we explain how to take the deduction. It is organized as follows:

1. Who can take the deduction.
2. Who cannot claim the deduction.
3. What expenses qualify?
4. Who is an eligible student?
5. What is an eligible education institution?
6. Income cut off – $80,000 if single and $160,000 if married filing jointly.
7. Reporting the deduction.

1. WHO CAN TAKE THE DEDUCTION

Generally, you can claim the tuition and fees deduction if all three of the following requirements are met:

1. You paid qualified education expenses of higher education.
2. You paid the education expenses for an eligible student.
3. The eligible student is yourself, your spouse, or your dependent for whom you claim an exemption on your tax return.

Qualified education expenses are defined in section 3. Eligible students are defined in section 4. Recall that the definition of a dependent is broad and includes children as well as relatives who you support. Dependents are discussed in Chapter 6. Also note that the first requirement means that if your child paid his/her expenses his/herself, you cannot take the deduction on their behalf.

2. WHO CANNOT CLAIM THE DEDUCTION

You cannot claim the tuition and fees deduction if any of the following apply:

- Your filing status is married filing separately.
- Another person can claim an exemption for you as a dependent on his or her tax return. You cannot take the deduction even if the other person does not actually claim that exemption.

---

[1] This chapter is based on, and some text is copied from, IRS Publication 970.

- Your modified adjusted gross income (MAGI) is more than $80,000 ($160,000 if filing a joint return). This is discussed in section 6 of this chapter.
- You (or your spouse) were a non-resident alien for any part of 2011 and the non-resident alien did not elect to be treated as a resident alien for tax purposes.
- You or anyone else claims an American opportunity or lifetime learning credit (discussed more in Chapter 36) in 2011 with respect to expenses of the student for whom the qualified education expenses were paid.

3. WHAT EXPENSES QUALIFY: ELIGIBLE EXPENSES

Eligible expenses include university tuition and fees that are a condition of enrollment in the university, such as mandatory equipment rental fees. Generally, the cost of textbooks is not deductible unless the education institution requires their purchase as a condition of attendance. As most institutions do not require this, you should not deduct the costs of textbooks. Similarly, you cannot deduct the cost of rent, insurance, medical expenses, transportation, or similar personal living or family expenses.

Most Canadian institutions will provide you with a T220A form that lists the amount of tuition that you paid. In most circumstances you can just take the number that is in the tuition box on the T220A you receive from the institution and use that as the amount for the purposes of the tuition deduction (after converting the amount to US currency).

The one exception to this is that if you received a scholarship or fellowship, for which the income was tax free (most scholarship income is tax free), then you must reduce the amount of the expenses by the amount of the scholarship. Consult publication 970 for further information.

4. WHO IS AN ELIGIBLE STUDENT?

An eligible student is one enrolled at least half-time in a program leading to a degree, certificate, or other recognized educational credential.

5. WHAT IS AN ELIGIBLE EDUCATION INSTITUTION?

The next question is whether the institution is an eligible institution. The tuition deduction can be claimed at virtually all educational institutions in the United States.

Most Canadian institutions are also considered eligible educational institutions for the purpose. To qualify, the school must participate in the US Department of Education's Federal Student Aid (FSA) programs. You can search on the following website to see if your school is eligible: www.fafsa.ed.gov/index.htm.

6. INCOME CUT OFF – $80,000 IF SINGLE AND $160,000 IF MARRIED FILING JOINTLY

The amount of your modified annual gross income (MAGI) affects the maximum tuition fees deduction. You must include income that you excluded from tax using the foreign earned income and housing exclusions in your MAGI. To figure your MAGI, follow these steps:

1. Enter the amount from Form 1040, line 22 ______________

2. Enter the total from Form 1040, lines 23 through 33 ______________

3. Enter the total of any amounts entered on the dotted line next to Form 1040, line 36 ______________

4. Add steps 2 and 3 and enter the total here ______________

5. Subtract the total on line 4 from step 1 ______________

6. Enter your foreign earned income exclusion and/or housing ______________ exclusion (Form 2555, line 45, or Form 2555-EZ, line 18) ______________

7. Enter your foreign housing deduction (Form 2555, line 50) ______________

8. Add step 5 through 7 and enter the total here ______________

The total on step 8 is your modified adjusted gross income. Take it and use the following chart to calculate your maximum deduction:

If your filing status is...	AND your MAGI is...	THEN your maximum tuition and fees deduction is...
single, head of household, or qualifying widow(er)	not more than $65,000	$4,000.
	more than $65,000 but not more than $80,000	$2,000.
	more than $80,000	$0.
married filing joint return	not more than $130,000	$4,000.
	more than $130,000 but not more than $160,000	$2,000.
	more than $160,000	$0.

7. REPORTING THE DEDUCTION

Once you have determined your eligibility for the deduction, calculated your expenses, and figured out the maximum deduction you can take, you should list this information on Form 8917 and attach that form to your Form 1040. Take the amount on line 6 of Form 8917 and list it on line 34 of the Form 1040.

Let's use an example to illustrate what we've discussed to date. Jim's daughter Mary got into Memorial University. The tuition was $4,000. Her first year textbooks cost another $1,000 and residence cost an additional $2,500. Mary got a $1,000 scholarship that covered part of her tuition. Jim paid all of this. Jim listed Mary as a dependent on his return. We know that Mary's residence fees and textbook expenses cannot be deducted. Jim has to reduce the amount of Mary's tuition expenses by $1,000 because of her scholarship. How does Jim claim this deduction on his return?

1. Jim or Mary will receive a Form T220A from Memorial University.

2. Jim must figure out his modified adjusted gross income (meaning total income without the foreign earned income exclusion). Let's say that Jim's income is $75,000. He completely excludes this using the foreign earned income exception.

It is the figure in line 10 that Jim has to use to calculate the tuition deduction that he is eligible for. He needs to take this figure and use it to fill out Form 8917 which he then attaches to his main Form 1040. Here is an example of what his Form 8917 would look like.

Form **8917**
Department of the Treasury
Internal Revenue Service

Tuition and Fees Deduction

See Instructions.
Attach to Form 1040 or Form 1040A.

OMB No. 1545-0074
2011
Attachment Sequence No. **60**

Name(s) shown on return: Jim Jones
Your social security number: 123456789

CAUTION *You **cannot** take both an education credit from Form 8863 and the tuition and fees deduction from this form for the **same student** for the same tax year.*

Before you begin:
- ✔ To see if you qualify for this deduction, see *Who Can Take the Deduction* in the instructions below.
- ✔ If you file Form 1040, figure any write-in adjustments to be entered on the dotted line next to Form 1040, line 36. See the 2011 Form 1040 instructions for line 36.

1	**(a)** Student's name (as shown on page 1 of your tax return) First name / Last name	**(b)** Student's social security number (as shown on page 1 of your tax return)	**(c)** Qualified expenses (see instructions)
	Mary Jones	987654321	3000

2	Add the amounts on line 1, column (c), and enter the total	2	3000
3	Enter the amount from Form 1040, line 22, or Form 1040A, line 15	3	
4	Enter the total from either: • Form 1040, lines 23 through 33, plus any write-in adjustments entered on the dotted line next to Form 1040, line 36, **or** • Form 1040A, lines 16 through 18.	4	
5	Subtract line 4 from line 3.* If the result is more than $80,000 ($160,000 if married filing jointly), **stop**; you cannot take the deduction for tuition and fees	5	75000
6	**Tuition and fees deduction.** Is the amount on line 5 more than $65,000 ($130,000 if married filing jointly)? ☑ **Yes.** Enter the smaller of line 2, or $2,000. ☐ **No.** Enter the smaller of line 2, or $4,000. **Also enter** this amount on Form 1040, line 34, or Form 1040A, line 19.	6	2000

*If you are filing Form 2555, 2555-EZ, or 4563, or you are excluding income from Puerto Rico, see *Effect of the Amount of Your Income on the Amount of Your Deduction* in Pub. 970, chapter 6, to figure the amount to enter on line 5.

The amount on line 5 is Jim's income including what he excluded using the foreign earned income exclusion.

This chart is replicated in the above text

Section references are to the Internal Revenue Code unless otherwise noted.

What's New

Future developments. The IRS has created a page on IRS.gov for information about Form 8917, at *www.irs.gov/form8917*. Information about any future developments affecting Form 8917 (such as legislation enacted after we release it) will be posted on that page.

General Instructions

Purpose of Form

Use Form 8917 to figure and take the deduction for tuition and fees expenses **paid in 2011.**

This deduction is based on qualified education expenses paid to an eligible postsecondary educational institution. See *What Expenses Qualify*, later, for more information.

TIP *You may be able to take the American opportunity credit or lifetime learning credit for your education expenses instead of the tuition and fees deduction. See Form 8863, Education Credits, and Pub. 970, Tax Benefits for Education, for more information about these credits.*

Who Can Take the Deduction

You may be able to take the deduction if you, your spouse, or a dependent you claim on your tax return was a student enrolled at or attending an eligible educational institution. The deduction is based on the amount of qualified education expenses you paid for the student in 2011 for academic periods beginning in 2011 and those beginning in the first 3 months of 2012.

CAUTION *Qualified education expenses must be reduced by any expenses paid directly or indirectly using tax-free educational assistance. See* Adjusted qualified education expenses, *later.*

Generally, in order to claim the deduction for qualified education expenses for a dependent, you must have paid the expenses in 2011 and must claim an exemption for the student as a dependent on your 2011 tax return (line 6c of Form 1040 or 1040A). For additional information, see chapter 6 of Pub. 970.

You **cannot** claim the tuition and fees deduction if any of the following apply.

- Your filing status is married filing separately.
- Another person can claim an exemption for you as a dependent on his or her tax return. You cannot take the deduction even if the other person does not actually claim that exemption.
- Your modified adjusted gross income (MAGI), as figured on line 5, is more than $80,000 ($160,000 if filing a joint return).
- You were a nonresident alien for any part of the year and did not elect to be treated as a resident alien for tax purposes. More information on nonresident aliens can be found in Pub. 519, U.S. Tax Guide for Aliens.
- You or anyone else claims an American opportunity or lifetime learning credit (Form 8863) in 2011 with respect to expenses of the student for whom the qualified education expenses were paid. However, a state tax credit will not disqualify you from claiming a tuition and fees deduction.

For Paperwork Reduction Act Notice, see your tax return instructions. Cat. No. 37728P Form **8917** (2011)

Jim must attach Form 8917 to his Form 1040. He should then take the amount on line 6 of Form 8917 and put it on line 34 of Form 1040.

PART 2D

DEDUCTIONS

19

OVERVIEW OF LINES 38–42[1]

Next, we introduce the deductions section of Form 1040. While this section only covers three lines on the Form 1040, it is nevertheless important. Line 40 is where you claim most of your deductions. Here you have to choose between deducting a standard amount and computing each individual deduction. The section of the Form 1040 looks like this.

Form 1040 (2011) Page **2**

Tax and Credits	38	Amount from line 37 (adjusted gross income)	38	
	39a	Check if: ☐ **You** were born before January 2, 1947, ☐ Blind. ☐ **Spouse** was born before January 2, 1947, ☐ Blind. } **Total boxes checked ▶ 39a** ☐		
Standard Deduction for—	b	If your spouse itemizes on a separate return or you were a dual-status alien, check here ▶ **39b** ☐		
• People who check any box on line 39a or 39b **or** who can be claimed as a dependent, see instructions.	40	**Itemized deductions** (from Schedule A) **or** your **standard deduction** (see left margin)	40	
	41	Subtract line 40 from line 38	41	
	42	**Exemptions.** Multiply $3,700 by the number on line 6d	42	
	43	**Taxable income.** Subtract line 42 from line 41. If line 42 is more than line 41, enter -0-	43	
	44	**Tax** (see instructions). Check if any from: **a** ☐ Form(s) 8814 **b** ☐ Form 4972 **c** ☐ 962 election	44	
	45	**Alternative minimum tax** (see instructions). Attach Form 6251	45	
	46	Add lines 44 and 45 ▶	46	

The first step is to transfer the amount you entered on line 37 to line 38.

On line 39(a) you should check the box if you or your spouse (if applicable) were born before January 2, 1947. Similarly, check the box if either you or your spouse is blind. The IRS defines blindness as not having more than 20/200 vision in your better eye with glasses or your field of vision is 20 degrees or less. You must have a certified statement from your eye doctor to this effect. Enter the total number of boxes checked on line 39(a) in the large text box immediately to the right of the line.

If your filing status is married filing separately (meaning you have checked box 3), and your spouse itemized deductions (discussed below) on his or her return then you should check line 39(b). You must also check line 39(b) if you were a dual status alien. This is a technical term that means that you were both a non-resident alien (non-resident of the United States) and a resident alien (resident of the United States) in the same year. Because you are a US citizen, you should ignore this box. Lines 39(a) and (b) affect your standard and itemized deductions.

1. ITEMIZED OR STANDARD DEDUCTIONS – LINE 40

You must choose between taking a standard deduction (a set amount) or itemizing (essentially listing individually) your deductions. As a general rule, you will want to take the standard deduction if you do not have many of these expenses or if you do not have the proper receipts. On the other hand, if you have lots of these expenses, you should itemize your deductions. A rule of thumb is that renters do better with the standard deduction while homeowners will benefit more from itemizing. Obviously, to make this choice, you need to know about the various deductions that are available and the amount of the standard deduction.

[1] This chapter is based on, and some text is copied from, the IRS' instructions to Form 1040.

2. AMOUNT OF THE STANDARD DEDUCTION

The amount of the standard deduction depends on your filing status. It increases every year. In 2012 the amounts are as follows:

- Single–$5,950
- Head of Household–$8,700
- Married filing jointly–$11,900
- Married filing separately–$5,950
- Qualifying widower/widower–$11,900

The standard deduction increases if you are blind or over 65. The following table sets out the 2012 amounts.

Table 19-2. Standard Deduction Chart for People Born Before January 2, 1947, or Who are Blind*

Check the correct number of boxes below. Then go to the chart.		
You:	Born before January 2, 1947□	Blind □
Your spouse, if claiming spouse's exemption:	Born before January 2, 1947 □	Blind □
Total number of boxes checked □		
IF your filing status is...	**AND the number in box above is...**	**THEN your standard deduction is...**
Single	1	$7,400
	2	8,850
Married filing jointly	1	$13,050
or Qualifying	2	14,200
widow(er) with	3	15,350
dependent child	4	16,500
Married filing	1	$7,100
separately	2	8,250
	3	9,400
	4	10,550
Head of household	1	$10,150
	2	11,600

If you are claimed as a dependent on someone else's return, you need to perform a different calculation. The following worksheet tells you how much of a standard deduction you can claim if you are listed as a dependent.

Use this worksheet only if someone else can claim you (or your spouse if filing jointly) as a dependent.

Check the correct number of boxes below. Then go to the worksheet.				
You:			Born before January 2, 1947 □	Blind □
Your spouse, if claiming spouse's exemption:			Born before January 2, 1947 □	Blind □
Total number of boxes checked □				
1.	Enter your earned income (defined below). If none, enter -0-.		1.	
2.	Additional amount.		2.	$300
3.	Add lines 1 and 2.		3.	
4.	Minimum standard deduction.		4.	$950
5.	Enter the larger of line 3 or line 4.		5.	
6.	Enter the amount shown below for your filing status. Single or Married filing separately—$5,950 Married filing jointly—$11,900 Head of household—$8,700		6.	
7.	Standard deduction.			
	a.	Enter the smaller of line 5 or line 6. If born after January 1, 1947, and not blind, stop here. This is your standard deduction. Otherwise, go on to line 7b.	7a.	
	b.	If born before January 2, 1947, or blind, multiply $1,450 ($1,150 if married) by the number in the box above.	7b.	
	c.	Add lines 7a and 7b. This is your standard deduction for 2011.	7c.	

Earned income includes wages, salaries, tips, professional fees, and other compensation received for personal services you performed. It also includes any amount received as a scholarship that you must include in your income. Through these charts you should be able to determine your standard deduction.

3. ITEMIZED DEDUCTIONS

If you take the standard deduction, you cannot claim each individual deduction for which you have receipts. The standard deduction saves you time in calculating your taxes, but it may or may not maximize your deduction. Itemized deductions cover the following areas:

- medical and dental expenses not covered by insurance;
- taxes you paid;
- mortgage interest you paid;
- interest on money borrowed for investment purposes;
- charitable donations;
- casualty and theft losses;
- job expenses.

Each of these is explored in more detail in the following sections and in the related chapters. They are all reported on Schedule A to Form 1040.

4. REPORTING YOUR ITEMIZED DEDUCTIONS

All itemized deductions must be reported on Schedule A. Some deductions require using another form before the particular amount is reported on Schedule A. Those instructions are outlined in the particular chapter. Schedule A itself looks like this.

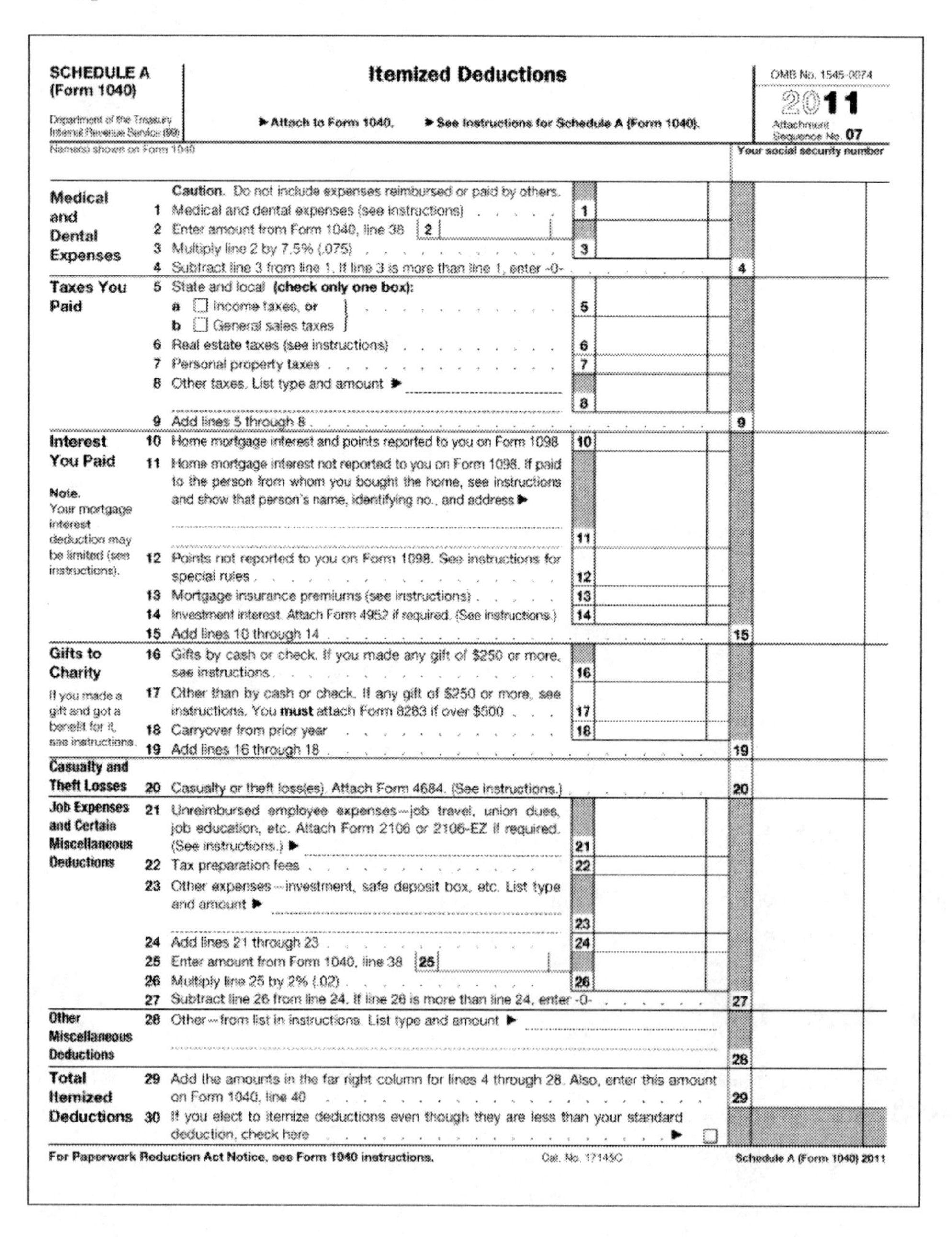

SCHEDULE A (Form 1040)
Department of the Treasury Internal Revenue Service (99)

Itemized Deductions

▶ Attach to Form 1040. ▶ See Instructions for Schedule A (Form 1040).

OMB No. 1545-0074
2011
Attachment Sequence No. 07

Name(s) shown on Form 1040 | Your social security number

Medical and Dental Expenses
Caution. Do not include expenses reimbursed or paid by others.
1 Medical and dental expenses (see instructions) 1
2 Enter amount from Form 1040, line 38 2
3 Multiply line 2 by 7.5% (.075) 3
4 Subtract line 3 from line 1. If line 3 is more than line 1, enter -0- 4

Taxes You Paid
5 State and local (**check only one box**):
a ☐ Income taxes, or
b ☐ General sales taxes 5
6 Real estate taxes (see instructions) 6
7 Personal property taxes 7
8 Other taxes. List type and amount ▶ 8
9 Add lines 5 through 8 9

Interest You Paid
Note. Your mortgage interest deduction may be limited (see instructions).
10 Home mortgage interest and points reported to you on Form 1098 10
11 Home mortgage interest not reported to you on Form 1098. If paid to the person from whom you bought the home, see instructions and show that person's name, identifying no., and address ▶ 11
12 Points not reported to you on Form 1098. See instructions for special rules 12
13 Mortgage insurance premiums (see instructions) 13
14 Investment interest. Attach Form 4952 if required. (See instructions.) 14
15 Add lines 10 through 14 15

Gifts to Charity
If you made a gift and got a benefit for it, see instructions.
16 Gifts by cash or check. If you made any gift of $250 or more, see instructions 16
17 Other than by cash or check. If any gift of $250 or more, see instructions. You **must** attach Form 8283 if over $500 . . . 17
18 Carryover from prior year 18
19 Add lines 16 through 18 19

Casualty and Theft Losses
20 Casualty or theft loss(es). Attach Form 4684. (See instructions.) 20

Job Expenses and Certain Miscellaneous Deductions
21 Unreimbursed employee expenses—job travel, union dues, job education, etc. Attach Form 2106 or 2106-EZ if required. (See instructions.) ▶ 21
22 Tax preparation fees 22
23 Other expenses—investment, safe deposit box, etc. List type and amount ▶ 23
24 Add lines 21 through 23 24
25 Enter amount from Form 1040, line 38 25
26 Multiply line 25 by 2% (.02) 26
27 Subtract line 26 from line 24. If line 26 is more than line 24, enter -0- 27

Other Miscellaneous Deductions
28 Other—from list in instructions. List type and amount ▶ 28

Total Itemized Deductions
29 Add the amounts in the far right column for lines 4 through 28. Also, enter this amount on Form 1040, line 40 29
30 If you elect to itemize deductions even though they are less than your standard deduction, check here . . . . . ▶ ☐

For Paperwork Reduction Act Notice, see Form 1040 instructions. Cat. No. 17145C Schedule A (Form 1040) 2011

Once you have gone through each applicable chapter and filled out Schedule A as required, you should add all of the amounts in the right hand columns and enter the total on line 29. Take this amount and put it on line 40 of your Form 1040. Check the box at line 30 if your total of itemized deductions is less than your standard deduction, and you still claimed an itemized deduction.

5. OTHER DEDUCTIONS THAT CAN BE ITEMIZED

Chapter 27 briefly explores what other deductions can be claimed on lines 23 and 28.

6. LIMITS ON ITEMIZED DEDUCTIONS

For tax year 2012, there is no limit on the amount of itemized deductions you can claim. However, this is scheduled to change for tax year 2013 unless the US Congress changes the current law. Consult the IRS website for a list of changes.

20

MEDICAL AND DENTAL EXPENSES[1]

This chapter explains how to claim a deduction for medical expenses. Medical expenses are the costs of diagnosis, cure, mitigation, treatment, or prevention of disease, and the costs for treatments affecting any part or function of the body. You can only deduct medical expenses that you paid yourself and for which you were not reimbursed. You can deduct on Schedule A (Form 1040) only the amount of your medical and dental expenses that exceed 7.5% of your adjusted gross income (this is listed on Form 1040, line 38). Note that, unlike other topics (such as student loan interest), there is no need to adjust your income on line 38 to take into account income you excluded using the foreign earned income exclusion. This chapter is organized as follows:

1. Whose medical expenses can you deduct.
2. What kinds of medical expenses can you deduct.
3. Non-deductible medical expenses.
4. Reimbursements.
5. Deduction limits.
6. Reporting your deduction.

1. WHOSE MEDICAL EXPENSES CAN YOU DEDUCT

You can generally include medical expenses you pay for yourself, as well as those you pay for someone who was your spouse or your dependent either when the services were provided or when you paid for them. Recall that dependent is a very broad term that encompasses both children and relatives you support. It is discussed more in Chapter 6. The person must have been your dependent either at the time the medical services were provided or at the time you paid the expenses.

2. WHAT KINDS OF MEDICAL EXPENSES CAN YOU DEDUCT

Generally, you can deduct any eligible medical expense. Medical expenses are the costs of diagnosis, cure, mitigation, treatment, or prevention of disease, and the costs for treatments affecting any part or function of the body. These expenses include payments for medical services rendered by physicians, surgeons, dentists, and other medical practitioners. They include the costs of equipment, supplies, and diagnostic devices needed for these purposes.

The following chart is a non-exhaustive list of medical expenses that you can deduct. Publication 502 has more detail on each individual item listed. Note that there may be other deductible expenses that are not included in the chart. As long as they meet the general definition set out above, then you can deduct them.

[1] This chapter is based on and includes text copied from IRS publication 502.

Abortion	Eye Exam
Acupuncture	Eyeglasses
Alcoholism	Eye Surgery
Ambulance	Fertility Enhancement
Annual Physical Examination	Guide Dog or Other Service Animal
Artificial Limb	Health Institute
Artificial Teeth	Health Maintenance Organization (HMO)
Bandages	Hearing Aids
Birth Control Pills	Home Care
Body Scan	Home Improvements
Braille Books and Magazines	Hospital Services
Breast Pumps and Supplies	Insurance Premiums
Breast Reconstruction Surgery	Intellectually and Developmentally Disabled
Capital Expenses	Laboratory Fees
Car	Lactation Expenses
Chiropractor	Lead-Based Paint Removal
Christian Science Practitioner	Learning Disability
Contact Lenses	Legal Fees
Crutches	Lifetime Care—Advance Payments
Dental Treatment	Lodging
Diagnostic Devices	Long-Term Care
Disabled Dependent Care Expenses	Meals
Drug Addiction	Medical Conferences
Drugs	Medical Information Plan
Medicines	Stop-Smoking Programs
Nursing Home	Surgery
Nursing Services	Telephone
Operations	Therapy
Optometrist	Transplants
Organ Donation Expenses	Transportation
Osteopath	Medical-related travel
Oxygen	Vasectomy
Physical Examination	Vision Correction Surgery
Pregnancy Test Kit	Weight-Loss Program
Prosthesis	Wheelchair
Psychiatric Care	Wig
Psychoanalysis	X-ray
Psychologist	
Special Education	
Sterilization	

Most of the above are pretty straightforward. A few of them need explanation.

Capital expenses

Capital expenses mean the amount of money you pay for improvements to your home that enables medical care. Publication 502 offers examples and instructs on how to calculate this deduction.

Insurance premiums

You can include in medical expenses insurance premiums you pay for policies that cover medical care. However, if your employer pays for this plan (even in part) you cannot deduct this expense. Nor can you deduct expenses for life insurance or insurance that provides an income supplement.

Legal fees

You can include in medical expenses legal fees you paid that are necessary to authorize treatment for mental illness.

Transportation

You can include in medical expenses amounts paid for transportation primarily for, and essential to, medical care.

3. NON-DEDUCTIBLE MEDICAL EXPENSES

Publication 502 provides a list of common expenses that you cannot deduct as medical expenses. They are set out in the following chart.

Baby Sitting, Childcare,	Illegal Operations and Treatments
Nursing Services for a Normal, Healthy Baby	Maternity Clothes
Controlled Substances	Medical Savings Account (MSA)
Cosmetic Surgery	Medicines and Drugs from Other Countries
Dancing Lessons	Non-prescription Drugs and Medicines
Diaper Service	Nutritional Supplements
Electrolysis or Hair Removal	Personal Use Items
Flexible Spending Account	Swimming Lessons
Funeral Expenses	Teeth Whitening
Future Medical Care	Veterinary Fees
Hair Transplant	Weight-Loss Program
Health Club Dues	
Health Coverage Tax Credit	
Health Savings Accounts	
Household Help	

Medicines and drugs from other countries

This category only includes drugs that were imported into the United States from another country. Drugs that you purchase in Canada for use in Canada are acceptable deductions.

4. REIMBURSEMENTS

If your expenses are reimbursed by anyone, be it insurance or your employer, you may not deduct them. However, you should not reduce your deductions based on payments for loss of use of a function of the body or loss of earnings. Damages from personal injury awards only reduce your deduction if they specifically reimburse your medical expenses. It may be that your reimbursement exceeds your expenses. If so, the excess is income that you may need to report. The following chart explains whether the excess is taxable.

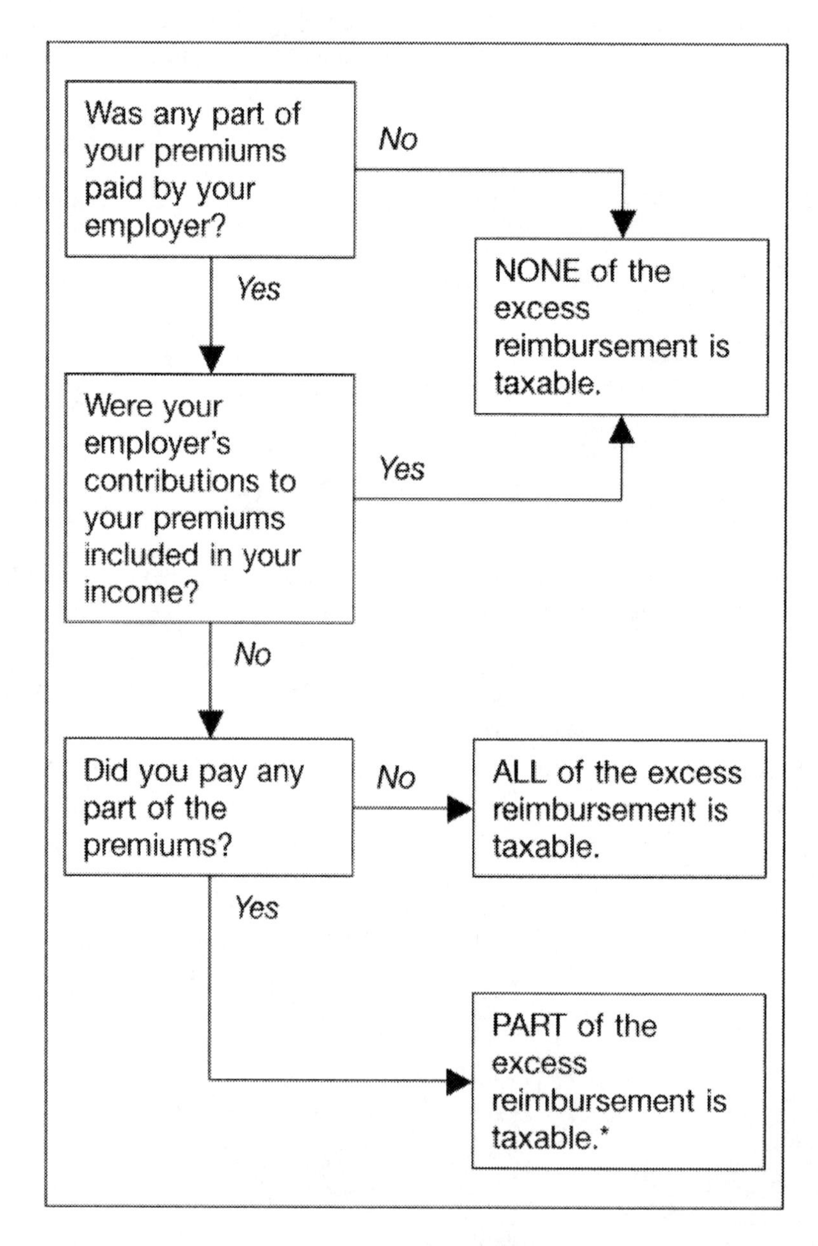

If both you and your employer contribute to your medical insurance plan and your employer's contributions are not included in your gross income, you must include in your gross income the part of your excess reimbursement that is from your employer's contribution.

5. DEDUCTION LIMITATIONS

You can deduct on Schedule A (Form 1040) only the amount of your medical and dental expenses that exceeds 7.5% of your annual gross income (AGI). Your AGI is the amount listed on line 38 of Form 1040. You do not need to adjust this to take into account any income excluded using the foreign earned income or housing exclusion. Here is an example. Your AGI is $40,000, 7.5% of which is $3,000. You paid medical expenses of $2,500. You cannot deduct any of your medical expenses because they are not more than 7.5% of your AGI. This limit is applied as you fill out Schedule A.

6. REPORTING YOUR DEDUCTION

You must use Schedule A to Form 1040 to claim your deductions. The first four lines of Schedule A are where you report your expenses. The instructions for them are as follows:

Line 1. Enter the amount you paid for medical expenses after reducing the amount by payments you received from insurance and other sources.

Line 2. Enter your adjusted gross income on line 38 of the Form 1040

Line 3. Multiply the amount on line 2 (AGI) by 7.5% (.075) and enter the result.

Line 4. If line 3 is more than line 1, enter -0-. Otherwise, subtract the amount on line 3 from the amount on line 1. This is your deduction for medical and dental expenses.

An example illustrates this nicely. Bill and Helen Jones belong to a group medical plan and part of their insurance is paid by Bill's employer. They file a joint return, and their adjusted gross income as shown on line 38 is $33,004. The following list shows the net amounts, after insurance reimbursements, that Bill and Helen paid this year for medical expenses.

1. For themselves, Bill and Helen paid $375 for prescription medicines and drugs, $337 for hospital bills, $439 for doctor bills, $295 for hospitalization insurance, $380 for medical and surgical insurance, and $33 for transportation for medical treatment, which totals $1,859.

2. For Grace Taylor (Helen's dependent mother), they paid $300 for doctors, $300 for insulin, and $175 for eyeglasses, which totals $775.

3. For Betty Jones (Bill's dependent sister), they paid $450 for doctors and $350 for prescription medicines and drugs, which totals $800.

Bill and Helen add all their medical and dental expenses together ($1,859 + $775 + $800 = $3,434). Their adjusted gross income is $33,004. They need to find out what 7.5% of this amount is. So they multiply $33,004 by .075. The result is $2,475. They have to subtract this amount from their total medical expenses ($3,434). The result ($959) is the amount of medical expenses that they can deduct. They calculate their deduction on the medical and dental expenses part of Schedule A, Form 1040, as follows.

SCHEDULE A (Form 1040)

Department of the Treasury Internal Revenue Service (99)

Itemized Deductions

► Attach to Form 1040. ► See Instructions for Schedule A (Form 1040).

OMB No. 1545-0074

2011

Attachment Sequence No. 07

Name(s) shown on Form 1040: Bill and Helen Jones

Your social security number: 000-00-0000

Medical and Dental Expenses		**Caution.** Do not include expenses reimbursed or paid by others.				
	1	Medical and dental expenses (see instructions)	1	3,434		
	2	Enter amount from Form 1040, line 38 [2] 33,004				
	3	Multiply line 2 by 7.5% (.075)	3	2,475		
	4	Subtract line 3 from line 1. If line 3 is more than line 1, enter -0-			4	
Taxes You Paid	5	State and local **(check only one box):** a ☐ Income taxes, **or** b ☐ General sales taxes	5			
	6	Real estate taxes (see instructions)	6			
	7	Personal property taxes	7			
	8	Other taxes. List type and amount ►	8			
	9	Add lines 5 through 8			9	
Interest You Paid	10	Home mortgage interest and points reported to you on Form 1098	10			
Note. Your mortgage interest deduction may be limited (see instructions).	11	Home mortgage interest not reported to you on Form 1098. If paid to the person from whom you bought the home, see instructions and show that person's name, identifying no., and address ►	11			
	12	Points not reported to you on Form 1098. See instructions for special rules	12			
	13	Mortgage insurance premiums (see instructions)	13			
	14	Investment interest. Attach Form 4952 if required. (See instructions.)	14			
	15	Add lines 10 through 14			15	
Gifts to Charity	16	Gifts by cash or check. If you made any gift of $250 or more, see instructions	16			
If you made a gift and got a benefit for it, see instructions.	17	Other than by cash or check. If any gift of $250 or more, see instructions. You **must** attach Form 8283 if over $500	17			
	18	Carryover from prior year	18			
	19	Add lines 16 through 18			19	
Casualty and Theft Losses	20	Casualty or theft loss(es). Attach Form 4684. (See instructions.)			20	
Job Expenses and Certain Miscellaneous Deductions	21	Unreimbursed employee expenses—job travel, union dues, job education, etc. Attach Form 2106 or 2106-EZ if required. (See instructions.) ►	21			
	22	Tax preparation fees	22			
	23	Other expenses—investment, safe deposit box, etc. List type and amount ►	23			
	24	Add lines 21 through 23	24			
	25	Enter amount from Form 1040, line 38 [25]				
	26	Multiply line 25 by 2% (.02)	26			
	27	Subtract line 26 from line 24. If line 26 is more than line 24, enter -0-			27	
Other Miscellaneous Deductions	28	Other—from list in instructions. List type and amount ►			28	
Total Itemized Deductions	29	Add the amounts in the far right column for lines 4 through 28. Also, enter this amount on Form 1040, line 40			29	
	30	If you elect to itemize deductions even though they are less than your standard deduction, check here ► ☐				

For Paperwork Reduction Act Notice, see Form 1040 instructions. Cat. No. 17145C **Schedule A (Form 1040) 2011**

21

TAXES YOU PAID[1]

The IRS allows you to deduct certain taxes from your income. Canadian federal and provincial income taxes as well as municipal property taxes are included in this, as are US state and local taxes. Note that if you exclude income using the foreign earned income or housing exclusion, you cannot deduct taxes paid on that income.

In addition, if you deduct your taxes here you will not be able to take the foreign tax credit for Canadian income tax. The foreign tax credit reduces your US tax payable by one dollar for each dollar of foreign income tax paid. By contrast, the deduction only reduces the income on which your tax is calculated, generally making the foreign tax credit more advantageous.

The downside of the foreign tax credit is that it is *much* more complicated to figure out. The foreign tax credit is explained in detail in Chapter 32.

Note that deducting Canadian property taxes does not affect your use of the foreign tax credit because the foreign tax credit can only be used for income tax. Further, the foreign earned income exclusion does not affect how much of your property taxes you can deduct.

You cannot claim the foreign tax credit on taxes paid in the United States, so you have no choice but to deduct those amounts. Any refunds for US taxes deducted need to be included in income. This chapter is organized as follows:

1. Taxes you can deduct.
2. Taxes you cannot deduct.
3. Deducting taxes and the foreign earned income and/or housing exclusions.
4. Declaring your refund if you deduct US state and local taxes.
5. Reporting your deduction.

1. TAXES YOU CAN DEDUCT

You can deduct the following types of taxes if you paid them in the year for which you are filing.

- Canadian federal income tax. Take the amount from box 22 of your T4 slip. Note you may have paid additional federal or provincial tax so always double check your Canadian return.
- Canadian provincial income tax. Unless you live in Quebec, this amount is included in box 22 of your T4 slip. If you do live in Quebec, you will receive a RL-1 slip and you should look to Box E of that slip to find the amount of provincial tax you paid.
- Canadian property taxes. This amount will be found on the bill(s) sent to you by the municipality in which you own property.

[1] This chapter is based on, and some text is copied from, IRS Publication 17.

- US state and local income taxes. Chapter 37 outlines whether you have to pay or file American state or local income taxes.
- US real-estate taxes.
- US state sales taxes. This includes goods purchased in the United States and brought back across the border. Note that you can only deduct sales taxes if you choose not to deduct US state or local income taxes.

2. TAXES YOU CANNOT DEDUCT

You may not deduct the following types of taxes.

- US Federal income taxes;
- employee contributions to private or voluntary disability plans;
- US Federal excise taxes, such as tax on gasoline, that are not expenses of your trade or business or of producing income;
- Canadian sales tax;
- contributions to Canadian Employment Insurance or Canada Pension Plan;
- land transfer taxes;
- estate taxes;
- American Social Security or Medicare tax;
- gift tax.

3. DEDUCTING TAXES AND THE FOREIGN EARNED INCOME AND/OR HOUSING EXCLUSIONS

The foreign earned income and/or housing exclusions make it more complicated to deduct income taxes; however, the exclusions have no impact on property taxes.

You may not deduct income taxes that you paid on income you excluded using the foreign earned income and/or housing exclusions. However, if you have more foreign earned income than you were able to exclude, you can make use of some of your deductions. To calculate how much of the deduction you can use follow these steps:

1. Divide the amount of foreign earned income that you excluded using the foreign earned income and/or housing exclusions by your total foreign earned income. Remember that foreign earned income is a specific subset of your total income. It does not include income from passive sources such as interest or capital gains. This is explained more in Chapter 14. The result from the above division should be a decimal less than 1.
2. Take the decimal from step 1 and multiply it by the total amount of tax you would like to deduct.
3. The total is the amount of deductible taxes that are allocable to foreign earned income and thus not deductible.

4. Subtract the total in line 3 from your total deductible taxes. If it is positive, you can deduct this amount of tax.

Attach a statement to your return showing how you figured the deductible amount.

This can be confusing. So let's walk through an example. As with all examples in this book, assume that the amounts in question have been converted to US dollars. George is a US citizen living in Canada who works as an accountant. In 2012, he earned $110,000 in salary income and $15,000 in capital gains from selling some stocks. Because capital gains income is not considered foreign earned income (see Chapter 14 for more details on what is foreign earned income), George's total foreign earned income is $110,000. He is able to exclude $95,100 from tax using the foreign earned income exclusion. George paid $2,500 in property taxes for the year and $30,000 in Canadian income taxes. He is able to fully deduct his property taxes. However, he cannot deduct the portion of his income taxes that is related to the portion of the income he excluded using the foreign earned income exclusion.

George follows the steps above to figure out how much of his Canadian income tax he can deduct. First, he divides $95,100 (total earned income excluded) by $110,000 (total earned income). The result is 0.864. Second, he multiplies 0.864 by the amount of Canadian income tax he wants to deduct ($30,000). The result is $25,920 (0.864 x $30,000 = $25,920). This is the amount that is related to foreign earned income and thus non-deductible. Third, he subtracts $25,920 from the total tax he wants to deduct ($30,000) because $25,920 is the amount that relates to the foreign earned income exclusion. The result ($30,000 – $25,920 = $4,080) is the amount of his Canadian income tax that he can deduct.

4. DECLARING YOUR REFUND IF YOU DEDUCT US STATE AND LOCAL TAXES

If you deduct US state and local taxes, and get a refund, you must treat this refund as income and include all or part of it on Form 1040, line 10 in the year you receive the refund.

5. REPORTING YOUR DEDUCTION

There are 5 lines on the second section of Schedule A. As usual, we go through each one and then use an example to illustrate how to fill it out.

a. US state and local taxes – line 5

Line 5 involves US state and local taxes. Here you must make a choice. You can either deduct state and local income taxes or state and local sales taxes. Once you have decided which one, you should check either box (a) for income taxes or box (b) for sales taxes.

If you are going to deduct US state and local income taxes, you should simply write in the total amount of state and local tax you paid on line 5.

If you choose state and local general sales taxes, you can either deduct the total tax you actually paid or use the optional sales tax tables. To figure your state and local general sales tax deduction using the tables, use the Sales Tax Deduction Calculator on the IRS website.

b. Real estate taxes – line 6

Here, simply list the total real estate (often referred to as property) taxes that you paid on property that was not used for business.

c. Personal property taxes – line 7

Do not be confused here. In Canada, property taxes are paid on real estate. This line is for US state and local taxes on personal (not real) property that you own. For instance, if you paid a US local or state tax on your car you would list the amount here.

d. Other taxes – line 8

If you had any deductible tax not listed on line 5, 6, or 7, list the type and amount of tax. Enter only one total on line 8. Include on this line any Canadian (or other foreign) income tax you paid. Again, we generally recommend taking the foreign tax credit instead of the deduction.

e. Example

Let's reprise the example of George from above to illustrate this. Recall that George is a US citizen living in Canada who works as an accountant (all of the following amounts are in US dollars). In 2012, he earned $110,000 in salary income and $15,000 in capital gains from selling some stocks. He is able to exclude $95,100 from tax using the foreign earned income exclusion. George paid $2,500 in property taxes for the year and $30,000 in Canadian income taxes. He is able to fully deduct his property taxes. However, he cannot deduct the portion of his income taxes that is related to the income he excluded using the foreign earned income exclusion. After doing the math, George figures that he can deduct $4,080 in Canadian income tax and $2,500 in property taxes. He then fills out Schedule A as follows.

SCHEDULE A (Form 1040) — **Itemized Deductions** — OMB No. 1545-0074 — **2011**

Department of the Treasury Internal Revenue Service (99) — ▶ Attach to Form 1040. ▶ See Instructions for Schedule A (Form 1040). — Attachment Sequence No. **07**

Name(s) shown on Form 1040: George Smity — Your social security number: 000-00-0000

Medical and Dental Expenses		**Caution.** Do not include expenses reimbursed or paid by others.				
	1	Medical and dental expenses (see instructions)	1			
	2	Enter amount from Form 1040, line 38 [2]				
	3	Multiply line 2 by 7.5% (.075)	3			
	4	Subtract line 3 from line 1. If line 3 is more than line 1, enter -0-			4	
Taxes You Paid	5	State and local **(check only one box):** a ☐ Income taxes, or b ☐ General sales taxes	5	2500		
	6	Real estate taxes (see instructions)	6			
	7	Personal property taxes	7			
	8	Other taxes. List type and amount ▶ Canadian Income Tax	8	4080		
	9	Add lines 5 through 8			9	

22

MORTGAGE INTEREST DEDUCTION[1]

This chapter outlines the mortgage interest deduction. Note that in this chapter we refer to mortgage interest. This means that you must calculate the part of your mortgage payments that are in addition to the principal. These, and only these, are tax deductible. In order to deduct home mortgage interest, you have to itemize deductions and the mortgage must be a secured debt on a home in which you have an ownership interest. Once these criteria are met, the only remaining question is how much of the mortgage interest you can deduct. In answering this question, this chapter is organized as follows:

1. Fully deductible mortgage interest.
2. Partially deductible mortgage interest.
3. How to report this deduction.
4. More information.

Taking the foreign earned interest and/or housing exclusion has no impact on the mortgage interest deduction.

1. FULLY DEDUCTIBLE MORTGAGE INTEREST

Most people will be able to deduct all of their home mortgage interest. How much you can deduct depends on the date of the mortgage, the amount of the mortgage, and how you use the mortgage proceeds. If your mortgage(s) fit into any of the following three categories you can deduct all of the interest:

1. Mortgages you took out on or before October 13, 1987. This kind of debt is referred to as grandfathered debt.
2. Mortgages you took out after October 13, 1987, to buy, build, or improve your home, but only if throughout the tax year in question these mortgages plus any grandfathered debt totaled $1 million or less ($500,000 or less if married filing separately). This kind of debt is referred to as home acquisition debt.
3. Mortgages you took out after October 13, 1987, other than to buy, build, or improve your home, but only if throughout the tax year in question these mortgages totalled $100,000 or less ($50,000 or less if married filing separately) and totalled no more than the fair market value of your home reduced by points 1 and 2. The technical name for this type of debt is home equity debt.

[1] This chapter is based on, and some of the text is copied from, IRS Publication 536.

The following IRS flowchart illustrates these concepts nicely.

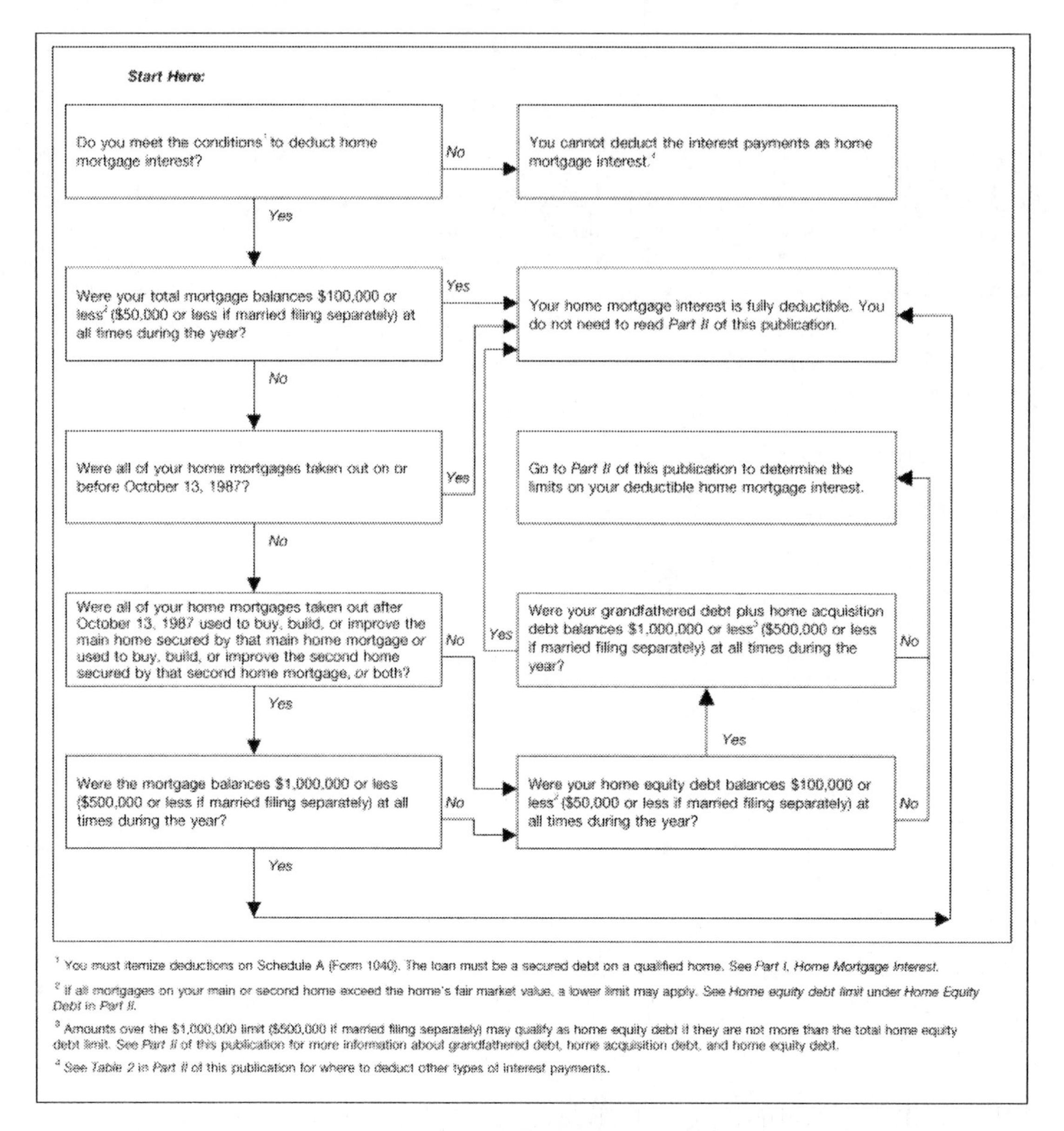

Publication 936 describes how to calculate your mortgage interest deduction if you do not fall into one of these three categories.

2. PARTIALLY DEDUCTIBLE MORTGAGE INTEREST

This section describes certain items that can be included as home mortgage interest and others that cannot.

Late payment charge on mortgage payment. You can deduct as home mortgage interest a late payment charge if it was not for a specific service performed in connection with your mortgage loan.

Mortgage prepayment penalty. If you pay off your home mortgage early, you may have to pay a penalty. You can deduct that penalty as home mortgage interest provided the penalty is not for a specific service performed or cost incurred in connection with your mortgage loan.

Sale of home. If you sell your home, you can deduct your home mortgage interest (subject to any limits that apply) paid up to, but not including, the date of sale.

Loan origination fees, maximum loan charges, loan discount, and discount points. You generally cannot deduct the full amount of these fees in the year paid. They are prepaid interest. So you should deduct them equally over future years. Publication 936 has more information on this.

Mortgage insurance premiums. You can deduct mortgage insurance premiums as mortgage interest in the tax year that you paid them. If your adjusted gross income on Form 1040, line 38, is more than $100,000 ($50,000 if your filing status is married filing separately), the amount of your mortgage insurance premiums that are otherwise deductible is reduced and may be eliminated. See *Line 13* in the instructions for Schedule A (Form 1040) and complete the *Mortgage Insurance Premiums Deduction Worksheet* to figure the amount you can deduct. If your adjusted gross income is more than $109,000 ($54,500 if married filing separately), you cannot deduct your mortgage insurance premiums.

3. HOW TO REPORT THIS DEDUCTION

If you have a mortgage from an American financial institution, you will receive a Form 1098 listing the amount of interest you have paid. Simply take that amount and enter it on line 10 of Schedule A. However, most Canadian financial institutions will not issue Form 1098s. Therefore, you have to calculate the amount of mortgage interest yourself or specifically ask your financial institution to give you the total. Once you know the total enter it on Schedule A line 11.

Line 12 is for loan origination fees, maximum loan charges, and loan discounts.

If you have mortgage insurance premiums, these are deductible as well. Enter the total amount on line 13.

The following brief example will illustrate this. Jen and Ian are a married couple living in Toronto. In 1997, they bought a house. To pay for it, they took out a mortgage of the equivalent of US $500,000. Since this is less than $1 million, they are able to deduct the full amount of their mortgage interest. In 2012, they paid the equivalent of US $15,000 in interest payments. Their financial institution did not issue them a Form 1098, so they had to phone and ask the bank for the amount of interest paid. Then they entered $15,000 on line 11 of Schedule A and the total of the interest expenses ($15,000) on line 15. It looks like this.

SCHEDULE A (Form 1040) | **Itemized Deductions** | OMB No. 1545-0074 | **2011**

Department of the Treasury Internal Revenue Service (99) | ▶ Attach to Form 1040. ▶ See Instructions for Schedule A (Form 1040). | Attachment Sequence No. 07

Name(s) shown on Form 1040: Jen and Ian Richards | Your social security number: 000-00-0000

Medical and Dental Expenses		**Caution.** Do not include expenses reimbursed or paid by others.				
	1	Medical and dental expenses (see instructions)	1			
	2	Enter amount from Form 1040, line 38 [2]				
	3	Multiply line 2 by 7.5% (.075)	3			
	4	Subtract line 3 from line 1. If line 3 is more than line 1, enter -0-			4	
Taxes You Paid	5	State and local **(check only one box):** a ☐ Income taxes, **or** b ☐ General sales taxes	5			
	6	Real estate taxes (see instructions)	6			
	7	Personal property taxes	7			
	8	Other taxes. List type and amount ▶	8			
	9	Add lines 5 through 8			9	
Interest You Paid	10	Home mortgage interest and points reported to you on Form 1098	10	0		
Note. Your mortgage interest deduction may be limited (see instructions).	11	Home mortgage interest not reported to you on Form 1098. If paid to the person from whom you bought the home, see instructions and show that person's name, identifying no., and address ▶	11	15000		
	12	Points not reported to you on Form 1098. See instructions for special rules	12	0		
	13	Mortgage insurance premiums (see instructions)	13	0		
	14	Investment interest. Attach Form 4952 if required. (See instructions.)	14	0		
	15	Add lines 10 through 14			15	15,000

4. MORE INFORMATION

More information on mortgage interest can be found in Publication 936 which is availible on the IRS website.

23

INVESTMENT INTEREST[1]

If you borrow money to buy non-real property you hold for investment, the interest you pay is investment interest. You can deduct investment interest subject to the limit discussed later. However, you cannot deduct interest you incurred to produce tax-exempt income. This chapter explains how to take this deduction. It is organized as follows:

1. Deductible interest.
2. Non-deductible interest.
3. When to deduct investment interest.
4. Limits on the deduction.
5. How to report the deduction.
6. More information.

There is no need to worry about the impact of the foreign earned income exclusion on the investment interest deduction.

1. DEDUCTIBLE INTEREST

It is important to define investment property. Property held for investment includes stocks, bonds, mutual funds and other financial products that produce interest, dividends, annuities, or royalties not associated with business.

Note that only interest expenses used for investment, as opposed to personal, purposes may be deducted.

2. NON-DEDUCTIBLE INTEREST

Some interest payments are not deductible. Certain expenses similar to interest also are not deductible. Non-deductible expenses include the following items:

- personal interest: this includes interest on car loans, interest on taxes, finance charges on credit cards, and late utility payments;
- service charges;
- annual fees for credit cards;
- loan fees;
- credit investigation fees;

[1] This chapter is based on, and some text is copied from, chapter 3 of IRS Publication 550 and the IRS' instructions for Schedule A.

- interest to purchase or carry tax-exempt securities.

You cannot deduct any interest related to a passive activity. A passive activity generally is any activity involving the conduct of any trade or business in which you do not significantly participate and any rental activity. However, if you are involved in renting real estate, the activity is not a passive activity if both of the following are true.

- More than one-half of the personal services you provide during the year in all trades or businesses are performed in real property trades or businesses in which you materially participate.

- You provide more than 750 hours of services during the year in real property trades or businesses in which you materially participate.

3. WHEN TO DEDUCT INVESTMENT INTEREST

You should deduct investment interest in the tax year that you pay it.

4. LIMITS ON THE DEDUCTION

Your deduction for investment interest expense is limited to your net investment income. Investment income is the total interest, dividends, annuities, and royalties from investment properties. Normally, you do not include qualified dividends or capital gains in your discussion of investment income. However, you can choose to do so if you wish. Making this choice increases the amount of income you have and thus the amount of interest expenses you can deduct. The instructions to Form 4952, which are available on the IRS website, indicate how to make this choice.

Your net investment income is this total minus any investment expenses you incurred. Investment expenses are your allowed deductions (other than interest expense) directly connected with the production of investment income. Investment expenses that are included as a miscellaneous itemized deduction on Schedule A (Form 1040) are allowable deductions after applying the 2% limit that applies to miscellaneous itemized deductions. They are explained further in Chapter 27 that deals with miscellaneous itemized deductions or in Publication 550. Use the lesser of:

- the investment expenses included on Schedule A (Form 1040), line 23, and

- the amount on Schedule A, line 27.

You can carry over the amount of investment interest you could not deduct because of this limit to the next tax year. The interest carried over is treated as investment interest paid in that next year.

You can carry over investment interest to the next tax year even if it is more than your taxable income in the year the interest was paid.

5. HOW TO REPORT THE DEDUCTION

Deductible investment interest is reported on line 14. The amount on line 14 is calculated by using Form 4952. However, you do not have to file Form 4952 if all three of the following apply:

1. Your investment interest expense is not more than your investment income from interest and ordinary dividends minus any qualified dividends.

2. You have no other deductible investment expenses.

3. You have no investment interest expense to carryover from a prior tax year.

If you do not need to use and file Form 4952, simply calculate the total interest and mark it on line 14 of Schedule A. But if you do need to file Form 4952 it is slightly more complicated. The following example explains how to fill out the form.

Jane Smith is single. Her 2011 income includes $3,000 in dividends (other than qualified dividends) and a net capital gain of $9,000 from the sale of investment property. She also has a gain of $1,000 from the sale of a painting. She incurred $12,500 of investment interest expense. Her other investment expenses total $980.

For 2011, Jane chooses to include all of her net capital gain in investment income. Her total investment income is $13,000 ($3,000 dividends + $9,000 net capital gain + $1,000 from the sale of the painting). Her net investment income is $12,020 ($13,000 total investment income − $980 other investment expenses).

Her investment interest expense deduction is limited to $12,020, the amount of her net investment income. The $480 disallowed investment interest expense is carried forward to 2012. Jane's illustrated Form 4952 is shown below.

Form **4952** — **Investment Interest Expense Deduction** — OMB No. 1545-0191 — **2011**

Department of the Treasury Internal Revenue Service (99) — ▶ Attach to your tax return. — Attachment Sequence No. **51**

Name(s) shown on return: Jane Smith — Identifying number: 111-00-111

Part I	**Total Investment Interest Expense**				
1	Investment interest expense paid or accrued in 2011 (see instructions)			1	12,500
2	Disallowed investment interest expense from 2010 Form 4952, line 7			2	0
3	**Total investment interest expense.** Add lines 1 and 2			3	12,500
Part II	**Net Investment Income**				
4a	Gross income from property held for investment (excluding any net gain from the disposition of property held for investment)	4a	3000		
b	Qualified dividends included on line 4a	4b			
c	Subtract line 4b from line 4a			4c	3000
d	Net gain from the disposition of property held for investment	4d	10,000		
e	Enter the **smaller** of line 4d or your net capital gain from the disposition of property held for investment (see instructions)	4e	9,000		
f	Subtract line 4e from line 4d			4f	1,000
g	Enter the amount from lines 4b and 4e that you elect to include in investment income (see instructions)			4g	9,000
h	Investment income. Add lines 4c, 4f, and 4g			4h	13,000
5	Investment expenses (see instructions)			5	980
6	**Net investment income.** Subtract line 5 from line 4h. If zero or less, enter -0-			6	12,020
Part III	**Investment Interest Expense Deduction**				
7	Disallowed investment interest expense to be carried forward to 2012. Subtract line 6 from line 3. If zero or less, enter -0-			7	480
8	**Investment interest expense deduction.** Enter the **smaller** of line 3 or 6. See instructions			8	12,020

6. MORE INFORMATION

Chapter 3 of Publication 550 contains more information about investment expenses. It is available on the IRS website.

24

CHARITABLE CONTRIBUTIONS[1]

This chapter explains how to deduct charitable donations. Publication 526 explains how to clacu-late the deduction for property or other non-monetary gifts. You can deduct gifts to both Canadian and American charities on your US tax return. The charity you give to must qualify under the American rules. This may require contacting them. There are limits to the amount of charitable gifts you can deduct. This chapter is organized as follows:

1. Eligible institutions.
2. Eligible contributions.
3. When to deduct.
4. Deduction limits.
5. How to report the deduction.
6. Other issues and further information.

1. ELIGIBLE INSTITUTIONS

Donations to any Canadian or American organization that meets any of the following criteria are deductible:

- The organization's purpose is religious, charitable, educational, scientific, literary, or the prevention of cruelty to children or animals.
- The organization fosters national or international sports competition.
- The organization is devoted to helping war veterans.
- The organization is a fraternal society, order, or association operating under the lodge system.
- The organization is a non-profit cemetery company.
- The United States government or a US state, city, or Indian tribe.

The following list gives some examples of qualified organizations.

- Churches, a convention or association of churches, temples, synagogues, mosques, and other religious organizations.
- Most non-profit charitable organizations such as the Red Cross and the United Way.
- Most non-profit educational organizations, including the Boy (and Girl) Scouts, colleges, museums, and daycare centres if substantially all the childcare provided is to enable individuals (the parents) to be gainfully employed and the services are available to the general public.

[1] This chapter is based on, and some text is copied from, IRS Publication 526.

- Non-profit hospitals and medical research organizations.
- Non-profit volunteer fire companies.
- Public parks and recreation facilities.
- Civil defense organizations.

Note that country clubs, homeowners' associations, political organizations and candidates, and labour unions are not qualified organizations.

2. ELIGIBLE CONTRIBUTIONS

You can deduct your contributions of money or property that you make to, or for the use of, a qualified organization. Publication 526 discusses contributions of property or those that are "for the use of" a qualified organization. If you receive a benefit as a result of making a contribution to a qualified organization, you can deduct only the amount of your contribution that is more than the value of the benefit you receive. Put differently, you cannot deduct the following as a charitable contribution:

- a contribution to a specific individual;
- a contribution to a non-qualified organization;
- the part of a contribution from which you receive or expect to receive a benefit;
- the value of your time or services;
- your personal expenses;
- a qualified charitable distribution from an individual retirement arrangement (IRA);
- appraisal fees.

You do not need to worry about how the foreign earned income and/or housing exclusion applies to charitable deductions.

3. WHEN TO DEDUCT

You deduct a charitable contribution in the year in which the contribution was unconditionally delivered. This means that if you pay by credit card or cheque you should deduct the contribution in the same year that you paid the donation. So if in 2012 you donated $100 to the Red Cross by VISA, then you are eligible to deduct this amount. If you make a conditional gift or give other types of property please see Publication 526.

4. DEDUCTIONS LIMITS

If your total charitable contributions for the year are 20% or less of your adjusted gross income (which is listed on line 38 of your Form 1040), you do not need to read this section. However, if they are more than 20%, you should pay attention to the following discussion about limits.

There are three types of limits. The applicable limit depends on the types of charitable contributions you have made. For instance, most organizations, other than veterans' organizations, fraternal societies, and non-profit cemeteries, are 50% limit organizations. Most charities should be able to tell you if they qualify for the 50% limit. The full set of criteria is found in Publication 526. That means that your deduction to them cannot be more than 50% of your adjusted gross income for the year. Recall that your adjusted gross income is found on line 38 of your Form 1040. For instance, if your adjusted gross income on line 38 of your Form 1040 is $50,000, and you gave $30,000 to a local hospital, you could only deduct $25,000 of that amount.

Those organizations that do not qualify as 50% organizations are 30% organizations. Not surprisingly, you can only deduct up to 30% of your adjusted gross income to them.

You can carry over your contributions that you are not able to deduct in the current year because they exceed your adjusted-gross-income limits. You can deduct the excess in each of the next 5 years until it is used up, but not beyond that time. Your total contributions deduction for the year to which you carry your contributions cannot exceed 50% of your adjusted gross income for that year.

5. HOW TO REPORT THE DEDUCTION

If you make a cash contribution to a charitable organization, you should receive a receipt in the amount of the contribution. Simply total these receipts and enter the total on line 16. You should keep your receipts of any donation over $250. However, you do not need to include them with your return.

Line 17 is for non-cash contributions. Publication 526 has more details on this.

Line 18 is for unused contributions from prior years that you could not use due to the limits discussed in section 4 of this chapter.

Let's illustrate this with an example. Rob Graffin had an adjusted gross income (line 38) of $100,000 in 2012. That year he donated $60,000 to his local hospital by cheque. The hospital is a qualified organization. Rob's deduction limit is 50% of his adjusted gross income ($50,000). He should therefore enter $50,000 on line 16. On line 19, he enters the total.

His Schedule A would look like this.

SCHEDULE A (Form 1040)

Department of the Treasury
Internal Revenue Service (99)

Itemized Deductions

▶ Attach to Form 1040. ▶ See Instructions for Schedule A (Form 1040).

OMB No. 1545-0074
2011
Attachment Sequence No. 07

Name(s) shown on Form 1040 | Your social security number

Medical and Dental Expenses		**Caution.** Do not include expenses reimbursed or paid by others.				
	1	Medical and dental expenses (see instructions)	1			
	2	Enter amount from Form 1040, line 38 [2]				
	3	Multiply line 2 by 7.5% (.075)	3			
	4	Subtract line 3 from line 1. If line 3 is more than line 1, enter -0-			4	
Taxes You Paid	5	State and local **(check only one box):**				
		a ☐ Income taxes, **or** / **b** ☐ General sales taxes	5			
	6	Real estate taxes (see instructions)	6			
	7	Personal property taxes	7			
	8	Other taxes. List type and amount ▶	8			
	9	Add lines 5 through 8			9	
Interest You Paid	10	Home mortgage interest and points reported to you on Form 1098	10			
Note. Your mortgage interest deduction may be limited (see instructions).	11	Home mortgage interest not reported to you on Form 1098. If paid to the person from whom you bought the home, see instructions and show that person's name, identifying no., and address ▶	11			
	12	Points not reported to you on Form 1098. See instructions for special rules	12			
	13	Mortgage insurance premiums (see instructions)	13			
	14	Investment interest. Attach Form 4952 if required. (See instructions.)	14			
	15	Add lines 10 through 14			15	
Gifts to Charity	16	Gifts by cash or check. If you made any gift of $250 or more, see instructions	16	50,000		
If you made a gift and got a benefit for it, see instructions.	17	Other than by cash or check. If any gift of $250 or more, see instructions. You **must** attach Form 8283 if over $500	17	0		
	18	Carryover from prior year	18	0		
	19	Add lines 16 through 18			19	0
Casualty and Theft Losses	20	Casualty or theft loss(es). Attach Form 4684. (See instructions.)			20	50,000

6. OTHER ISSUES AND FURTHER INFORMATION

Publication 526 has information on the following additional topics:

- limits for donations of capital gain property;
- donations of non-cash property such as stock options and promissory notes;
- how to report donations over $500,000;
- tax treatment of donations of borrowed money and conditional gifts;
- full set of criteria on what organizations are eligible and in the 50% limit category.

It also has other information not contained in the above list. Please consult it if your questions are not addressed in this chapter.

25

CASUALTY AND THEFT LOSSES[1]

Casualty and theft deductions allow you to take a tax deduction for property that is lost or destroyed as a result of an unforeseen event. As with all deductions, there is a limit to the amount of casualty and theft losses you can claim.

This chapter is organized as follows:

1. Casualty loss defined.
2. Definition of theft.
3. Proving a loss.
4. Computing the value of your loss.
5. Deduction limits.
6. Reporting the deduction.
7. More information.

1. WHAT IS A CASUALTY LOSS

A casualty is the damage, destruction, or loss of property resulting from an identifiable event that is sudden, unexpected, or unusual. A sudden event is one that is swift, not gradual or progressive. An unexpected event is one that is ordinarily unanticipated and unintended. An unusual event is one that is not a day-to-day occurrence and that is not typical of the activity in which you were engaged.

Examples of casualty losses include, but are not limited to, the following:

- car accidents;
- earthquakes;
- fires;
- floods;
- mine cave-ins;
- shipwrecks;
- sonic booms;
- storms, including hurricanes and tornadoes;
- terrorist attacks;
- vandalism;
- volcanic eruptions.

If the damage was willfully caused by you, such as a fire you set or a car accident you caused, then the losses are not deductible. If the accident was caused by you, but it was not willful, you may be able to deduct the damage. Similarly, damage caused by the family pet is non-deductible. Damage

[1] This chapter is based on, and some text is copied from, IRS Publication 547.

due to progressive deterioration of a property, such as termite or moth damage, is not deductible as a casualty loss. Damage from corrosive drywall is discussed in publication 547.

2. DEFINITION OF THEFT

A theft is the taking and removing of money or property with the intent to deprive the owner of it. The exact nature of the theft is defined under the Criminal Code of Canada. However, you do not need to show a conviction to deduct losses. The following are some examples of theft:

- blackmail;
- burglary;
- embezzlement;
- extortion;
- kidnapping for ransom;
- larceny;
- robbery.

3. PROVING A LOSS

Now that you know what losses you can deduct, you need to know how to prove them.

Unlike other areas, you will not receive a tax slip for goods that were lost or stolen. This means that you need to be able to prove the damage you suffered. Here we explain how to prove this. For a casualty loss, you should be able to show all of the following:

- The type of casualty (car accident, fire, storm, etc.) and when it occurred and that the loss was a direct result of the casualty.
- That you were the owner of the property, or if you leased the property from someone else, that you were contractually liable to the owner for the damage.
- Whether a claim for reimbursement exists for which there is a reasonable expectation of recovery.

For a theft loss, you should be able to show all of the following:

- When you discovered that your property was missing.
- That your property was stolen.
- That you were the owner of the property, or if you leased the property from someone else, that you were contractually liable to the owner for the damage.
- Whether a claim for reimbursement exists for which there is a reasonable expectation of recovery.

The above represents what you need to prove. How you prove it, meaning what documents you need, will depend on the item(s) that was lost or stolen.

4. COMPUTING THE VALUE OF YOUR LOSS

Once you have proven your loss, the next step is to determine the value of the item lost. We give these instructions assuming that you have lost only one item. If you have lost multiple items, simply repeat the instructions for each item. There are three steps to calculating the amount of loss you have suffered. They are as follows:

a. Determine your adjusted basis in the property before the casualty or theft.

b. Determine the decrease in fair market value (FMV) of the property as a result of the casualty or theft.

c. From the smaller of the amounts you determined in (1) and (2), subtract any insurance or other reimbursement you received or expect to receive.

Let's walk through each of these steps in more detail.

a. Establish the adjusted cost basis

The adjusted basis basically means what you paid for the property. Calculating it can be somewhat challenging. The adjusted cost basis is the original basis (cost) of the asset plus or minus any appropriate adjustments. Below are instructions to figure out the basis if you purchased the property. However, if you received it as inheritance or as a gift please consult IRS Publication 551 which is available on the IRS website.

i. The basis (cost)

The basis of property you buy is usually its cost. The cost is the amount you paid in cash, debt obligations, other property, or services. Your cost also includes amounts you paid for the following items related to the asset's purchase:

- sales tax;
- freight;
- installation and testing;
- excise taxes;
- legal and accounting fees;
- revenue stamps;
- recording fees;
- real estate taxes.

For instance, if you bought a cottage for $300,000 and paid $10,000 in transfer taxes and legal fees on it, your basis is $310,000.

b. Adjustments to the basis

Adjustments to the basis differ significantly depending on the type of property sold. That's why we've included separate chapters for those assets that people sell most often. There are, however, some general rules that apply.

i. Increasing the basis

Improvements that last longer than a year increase the basis. These must be distinguished from repairs. Repairs merely keep something as it has always been. Improvements, on the other hand, are new and should increase the value of the asset. For instance, if you own a car and you put a new radio in it you can treat this as an improvement. But if you merely have your existing radio fixed then this is a repair rather than an improvement. The following table presents some common examples of things that will increase the basis:

Increases to Basis
Capital improvements: Putting an addition on your home Replacing an entire roof Paving your driveway Installing central air conditioning Rewiring your home
Assessments for local improvements: Water connections Sidewalks Roads
Casualty losses: Restoring damaged property
Legal fees: Cost of defending and perfecting a title
Zoning costs

Note that this list is far from exhaustive.

ii. Decreases to the basis

The general rule is that if you receive money or credit towards your property you should deduct that amount from the basis. For instance, if your car is damaged in an accident and the insurance company pays to fix it, you have to deduct the amount of the insurance payment from the basis. The following are some specific items that reduce the basis of property:

- non-taxable corporate distributions;
- deductions previously allowed (or allowable) for amortization, depreciation, and depletion;
- exclusion of subsidies for energy conservation measures;
- vehicle credits;
- residential energy credits;
- postponed gain from sale of home;
- investment credit (part or all) taken;
- certain cancelled debt excluded from income;
- rebates from a manufacturer or seller;
- easements;
- gas-guzzler tax;
- adoption tax benefits;
- credit for employer-provided child care.

Note that this list is far from exhaustive. Nevertheless, it is worth providing a bit more detail on some of these items.

Depreciation. You cannot usually depreciate the cost of personal property, so you do not need to worry about this.

Vehicle tax credits. If you receive a tax credit, such as for having an environmentally friendly car, you must reduce your car's basis by the amount of this credit.

b. Calculate the decrease in fair market value

The fair market value (FMV) is the market price of the item. The FMV of stolen property may be exactly the same as the FMV prior to the theft.

Not surprisingly, the FMV of property (as far as the owner of the property is concerned) after a theft is zero. So calculating the decrease in fair market value for a theft is very easy. The decrease is simply the value of the property before it was stolen.

Calculating the decrease in fair market value for a casualty loss is more difficult. A casualty loss may not entirely destroy the property. You should hire a professional appraiser to calculate the difference for you.

c. Insurance reimbursements

Once you know the adjusted basis from section (a) and the decrease in FMV from section (b) you need to figure out which of these two is smaller. From the smaller one, you must deduct any reimbursement from insurance. Once you have made this calculation, you know the loss that you can deduct (subject to the limits discussed in the next section). Here is an example. In 2005, you bought a car worth $30,000. In 2011, you were in an accident that was not your fault. You receive $17,000 in insurance payments. The adjusted cost basis of the car is its purchase price ($30,000). Before the accident, your insurance company tells you the car was worth $20,000. After the accident, it is worth $200. Therefore the decrease in fair market value is $19,800. The decrease in fair market value ($19,800) is smaller than the adjusted cost basis ($30,000). So you have to subtract the insurance payments ($17,000) from the decrease in fair market value ($19,800). The result ($19,800 – $17,000 = $2,800) is the amount of casualty losses that you can deduct, subject to the limits discussed in the next section.

If you receive an insurance payment greater than the adjusted cost basis, you have a gain to report. Consult IRS Publication 547 on how to do this.

5. DEDUCTION LIMITS

Once you know the amount of your theft or loss, you must apply the following deduction limits to figure out how much of it you can actually deduct. If your casualty or theft loss is related to property that you use as an employee, you must reduce your loss by 2% of your adjusted gross income. Please consult publication 547 for more information.

For personal use property that you do not make use of as an employee, there are two separate steps to apply to calculate the deduction. First, you must reduce the loss by $100. This reduction applies to each total casualty or theft loss. It does not matter how many pieces of property are involved in an event. Only a single $100 reduction applies. Second, after you have subtracted the $100, you must reduce the total of all casualty and theft losses by 10% of your adjusted gross income. Recall that your adjusted gross income is found on line 38 of your Form 1040.

The following example illustrates how this works. In June, you discovered that your house had been burglarized. Your loss after insurance reimbursement was $2,000. Your adjusted gross income for the year you discovered the theft is $29,500. Your theft loss is calculated as follows.

1.	Loss after insurance	$2,000
2.	Subtract $100	100
3.	Loss after $100 rule	$1,900
4.	Subtract 10% of $29,500 AGI	$2,950
5.	**Theft loss deduction**	**$-0-**

You do not have a theft loss deduction because your loss ($1,900) is less than 10% of your adjusted gross income ($2,950).

6. REPORTING THE DEDUCTION

Once you have applied the deduction limits to your post-insurance loss, you are ready to report the deduction. You should report the deduction in the tax year during which the loss occurred or the theft was discovered.

There are two steps to reporting a loss from either a casualty or a theft. First, you need to fill out the first page of Form 4684. Second, you need to take the amount from line 18 of Form 4684 and enter it on line 20 of Schedule A. We explain the different lines of Form 4684 and then go through an example.

a. Filling out Form 4684

Since this chapter only covers personal property, you only need to worry about section A of the form.

Line 1 – Describe the type of property (for example, furniture, jewelry, car, etc.).

Line 2 – Cost or other basis usually means original cost plus improvements. This is explained in section 3(a) above.

Line 3 – Enter on this line the amount of insurance or other reimbursement you received or expect to receive for each property.

Unless you have gains from an excess insurance payment, in which case you should consult publication 547, you can skip line 4.

Line 5 – Enter the fair market value before the casualty or theft.

Line 6 – Enter the fair market value after the casualty or theft.

You can skip lines 13, 14, 15 unless you have multiple Forms 4684.

The rest of the form is self-explanatory.

b. Example

Jane Adams is a US citizen living in Canada. She has converted all of the following amounts to US dollars using the instructions in section 1. Jane's adjusted gross income on line 38 of her Form 1040 is $24,000. In 2005, she bought a car worth $30,000. In 2011, she was in an accident that was not her fault. Jane receives $17,000 in insurance payments. The adjust cost basis of the car is its purchase price ($30,000). Before the accident, Jane's insurance company tells her the car was worth $20,000. After the accident, it is worth $200. Therefore the decrease in fair market value is $19,800. The decrease in fair market value ($19,800) is smaller than the adjusted cost basis ($30,000). So Jane has to subtract the insurance payments ($17,000) from the decrease in fair market value ($19,800). The result ($19,800 – $17,000 = $2,800) is the amount that Jane has to subject to the deduction limits. First, she subtracts $100 leaving the total as $2,700. Then she subtracts 10% of her adjusted gross income ($2,400). That means that she can deduct $300 in casualty losses ($2,700 – $2,400 = $300). She fills out form 4864 as follows.

Form **4684**
Department of the Treasury
Internal Revenue Service

Casualties and Thefts
► See separate instructions.
► Attach to your tax return.
► Use a separate Form 4684 for each casualty or theft.

OMB No. 1545-0177
2011
Attachment Sequence No. 26

Name(s) shown on tax return: Jane Adams
Identifying number: 001-230-456

SECTION A—Personal Use Property (Use this section to report casualties and thefts of property **not** used in a trade or business or for income-producing purposes.)

1 Description of properties (show type, location, and date acquired for each property). Use a separate line for each property lost or damaged from the same casualty or theft.
Property **A** Car
Property **B**
Property **C**
Property **D**

		Properties A	Properties B	Properties C	Properties D
2 Cost or other basis of each property	2	30,000			
3 Insurance or other reimbursement (whether or not you filed a claim) (see instructions)	3	17,000			
Note: *If line 2 is **more** than line 3, skip line 4.*					
4 Gain from casualty or theft. If line 3 is **more** than line 2, enter the difference here and skip lines 5 through 9 for that column. See instructions if line 3 includes insurance or other reimbursement you did not claim, or you received payment for your loss in a later tax year	4	0			
5 Fair market value **before** casualty or theft	5	20,000			
6 Fair market value **after** casualty or theft	6	200			
7 Subtract line 6 from line 5	7	19800			
8 Enter the **smaller** of line 2 or line 7	8	19800			
9 Subtract line 3 from line 8. If zero or less, enter -0-	9	2800			

10 Casualty or theft loss. Add the amounts on line 9 in columns A through D	10	2800
11 Enter the **smaller** of line 10 or $100	11	100
12 Subtract line 11 from line 10	12	2700
Caution: *Use only one Form 4684 for lines 13 through 18.*		
13 Add the amounts on line 12 of all Forms 4684	13	2700
14 Add the amounts on line 4 of all Forms 4684	14	0
15 • If line 14 is **more** than line 13, enter the difference here and on Schedule D. **Do not** complete the rest of this section (see instructions). • If line 14 is **less** than line 13, enter -0- here and go to line 16. • If line 14 is **equal** to line 13, enter -0- here. **Do not** complete the rest of this section.	15	0
16 If line 14 is **less** than line 13, enter the difference	16	2700
17 Enter 10% of your adjusted gross income from Form 1040, line 38, or Form 1040NR, line 37. Estates and trusts, see instructions	17	2400
18 Subtract line 17 from line 16. If zero or less, enter -0-. Also enter the result on Schedule A (Form 1040), line 20, or Form 1040NR, Schedule A, line 6. Estates and trusts, enter the result on the "Other deductions" line of your tax return	18	300

For Paperwork Reduction Act Notice, see instructions. Cat. No. 12997O Form **4684** (2011)

Jane then takes the amount on line 18 and enters it on line 20 of Schedule A.

7. MORE INFORMATION

If your situation is not described here, please consult IRS publication 547 which is available on the IRS website.

26

EMPLOYEE EXPENSES/BUSINESS DEDUCTIONS[1]

This chapter addresses unreimbursed employee business expenses.

If your employer reimbursed exactly the amount of expenses you incurred, you do not need to consult this chapter. Similarly, if you are self-employed your expenses are reported differently. Please consult a tax professional if this is the case.

Generally, you can deduct all ordinary and necessary expenses. An ordinary expense is one that is common and accepted in your field of trade, business, or profession. A necessary expense is one that is helpful and appropriate for your business. An expense does not have to be required to be considered necessary. Specifically, we discuss the following common expenses: travel, entertainment, gift, transportation, and car expenses. We explain each of them in turn and then we instruct you how to prove and report these expenses.

1. TRAVEL EXPENSES

Travel expenses are those incurred for business travel away from your tax home. Generally, your tax home is your regular place of business or post of duty, regardless of where you maintain your family home. It includes the entire city or general area in which your business or work is located. Once you have determined that you are travelling away from your tax home, you can determine what travel expenses are deductible. You can deduct ordinary and necessary expenses you have when you travel away from home on business.

The following chart gives examples of the kinds of travel expenses you can deduct.

IF you have expenses for...	THEN you can deduct the cost of...
transportation	travel by airplane, train, bus, or car between your home and your business destination. If you were provided with a ticket or you are riding free as a result of a frequent traveller or similar program, your cost is zero.
taxi, commuter bus, and airport limousine	fares for these and other types of transportation that take you between • the airport or station and your hotel, and • the hotel and the work location of your customers or clients, your business meeting place, or your temporary work location.
baggage and shipping	sending baggage and sample or display material between your regular and temporary work locations.
car	operating and maintaining your car when travelling away from home on business. You can deduct actual expenses or the standard mileage rate as well as business-related tolls and parking. If you rent a car while away from home on business, you can deduct only the business-use portion of the expenses.

[1] This chapter is based on, and some text is copied from, Chapter 26 of IRS Publication 17.

lodging and meals	your lodging and meals if your business trip is overnight or long enough that you need to stop for sleep or rest to properly perform your duties. Meals include amounts spent for food, beverages, taxes, and related tips.
cleaning	dry cleaning and laundry
telephone	business calls while on your business trip. This includes business communication by fax machine or other communication devices.
tips	tips you pay for any expenses in this chart
other	other similar ordinary and necessary expenses related to your business travel. These expenses might include transportation to or from a business meal, public stenographer's fees, computer rental fees, and operating and maintaining .

Some of these items need more explanation.

Meals–You can deduct the cost of meals if it is necessary for you to stop for substantial sleep or rest to properly perform your duties while travelling away from home on business. Meals as entertainment expenses are discussed later. You may not deduct unreasonably lavish or extravagant meals. Business-related entertainment is discussed under the section below entitled Entertainment expenses. Meal expenses can be calculated using one of the following two methods:

- actual cost
- the standard meal allowance

The first requires you to keep receipts of every dollar you spend. The second is a standard per diem rate that is detailed in Publication 1542 which is available on the IRS website. Lastly, if part of your travel expenses are deducted or you pay the expenses of a business associate on the trip, see Chapter 26 of IRS publication 17.

2. ENTERTAINMENT EXPENSES

a. What entertainment expenses are deductible

Entertainment includes any activity generally considered to provide entertainment, amusement, or recreation. Examples include entertaining guests at nightclubs; at social, athletic and sporting clubs; at theatres; at sporting events; on yachts; or on hunting, fishing, vacation, and similar trips. Entertainment also may include meeting personal, living, or family needs of individuals, such as providing meals, a hotel suite, or a car to customers or their families. Further, entertainment includes the cost of a meal you provide to a customer or client, whether the meal is a part of other entertainment or by itself. A meal expense includes the cost of food, beverages, taxes, and tips for the meal.

You cannot deduct dues for membership in a country club, golf and athletic club, airline or hotel club. Similarly, you cannot deduct expenses for use of an entertainment facility that you own.

Expenses for your spouse or the customer's spouse are non-deductible unless they had a clear business purpose.

b. When are entertainment expenses deductible

You can deduct entertainment expenses for entertaining a client, customer, or employee. This deduction may only be taken if the expenses are ordinary and necessary. Further, the expenses must meet the directly-related test or the associated test. The following chart lays out the requirements for an expense to be deductible.

General rule	You can deduct ordinary and necessary expenses to entertain a client, customer, or employee if the expenses meet the directly-related test or the associated test.
Definitions	• Entertainment includes any activity generally considered to provide entertainment, amusement, or recreation, and includes meals provided to a customer or client. • An ordinary expense is one that is common and accepted in your trade or business. • A necessary expense is one that is helpful and appropriate.
Tests to be met	Directly-related test • Entertainment took place in a clear business setting, or • Main purpose of entertainment was the active conduct of business, and you did engage in business with the person during the entertainment period, and • You had more than a general expectation of getting income or some other specific business benefit. **OR** Associated test • Entertainment is associated with your trade or business, and • Entertainment is directly before or after a substantial business discussion.
Other rules	• You cannot deduct the cost of your meal as an entertainment expense if you are claiming the meal as a travel expense. • You cannot deduct expenses that are lavish or extravagant under the circumstances.

c. The 50% rule

You generally can deduct only 50% of your unreimbursed entertainment expenses. This rule applies to expenses incurred while travelling, at home, or at a convention. To calculate the deductible portion of the expense, simply take the price you paid and divide it by half. If your business is the sale of meals or entertainment or the expenses relate to a charitable sports event, please consult publication 463 to see if the expenses are exempt from the 50% limit.

3. GIFT EXPENSES

You can deduct no more than $25 for business gifts you give directly or indirectly to each person during your tax year. Incidental costs, such as engraving on jewelry, or packaging, insuring, and mailing, are generally not included in determining the cost of a gift for purposes of the $25 limit.

4. TRANSPORTATION EXPENSES

a. General transportation expenses

Transportation expenses are different from travel expenses because they do not involve travel away from your home. These expenses include the cost of transportation by air, rail, bus, taxi, etc.

Transportation expenses include the ordinary and necessary costs of all of the following:

- Getting from one workplace to another in the course of your business or profession when you are travelling within the area of your tax home.
- Visiting clients or customers.
- Going to a business meeting away from your regular workplace.
- Getting from your home to a temporary workplace when you have one or more regular places of work. These temporary workplaces can be either within the area of your tax home or outside that area.

They do not, however, include the cost of commuting between your home and your main job. The following graphic illustrates when transportation expenses are deductible and when they are not.

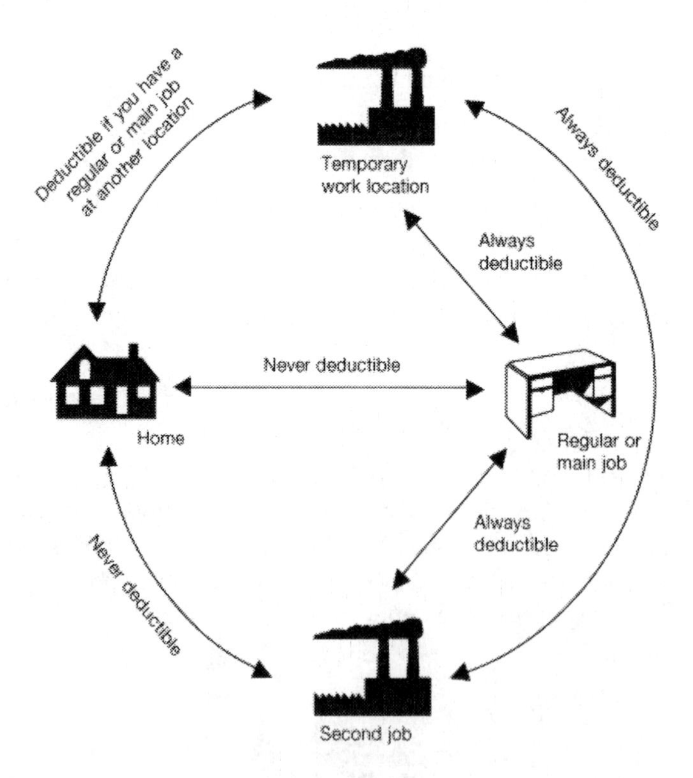

It is worth explaining the terms used on this graphic.

Home – the place where you reside. Transportation expenses between your home and your main job are personal commuting expenses.

Regular or main job – This is your principal place of business. If you have more than one job, you must determine which one is your regular or main job.

Temporary work location – A place where you are assigned to work for one year or less.

Second job – If you regularly work at two or more places in one day, whether or not for the same employer, you can deduct your transportation expenses of getting from one workplace to another. You cannot deduct your transportation costs between your home and a second job on a day off from your main job.

To calculate your transportation expenses, simply total all of your eligible expenses. Car expenses are calculated differently.

b. Car expenses

The rules for when car expenses are deductible are the same as above. However, the procedure for figuring out what your expenses are is different. You can choose to deduct the actual cost of your car or take the standard mileage rate. The standard mileage rate is easier to compute. All you have to do is keep track of how many kilometers are eligible transportation expenses. Then convert this to miles by dividing the total kilometers by 1.6. The total miles should be multiplied by 55.5 cents per mile. Note that this is the 2012 rate. The rate changes every year.

If you do not use the standard mileage rate, you may be able to deduct your actual car expenses. Actual car expenses include:

Depreciation	Lease payments	Registration fees
Gas	Insurance	Repairs
Oil	Garage rent	Tires
Tolls	Parking fees	Licence fees

Simply take the total of all of these expenses. Depreciation expenses are discussed in more detail in Chapter 4 of IRS Publication 463. We recommend that you use the standard mileage rate, as it is much easier to keep track of miles driven than all of the associated expenses. However, it may be that your actual car expenses allow for a larger deduction. Note that if you deduct the actual amount of your car expenses you must file Form 2106 and may not file Form 2106EZ.

5. RECORD KEEPING

You must keep records of your unreimbursed expenses. Generally, you should keep them for three years after you file your tax return. The following chart outlines what kinds of records you should keep for the different types of expenses discussed in this chapter.

<table>
<tr><th rowspan="2">IF you have expenses for...</th><th colspan="4">THEN you must keep records that show details of the following elements.</th></tr>
<tr><th>Amount</th><th>Time</th><th>Place or Description</th><th>Business Purpose and Business Relationship</th></tr>
<tr><td>Travel</td><td>Cost of each separate expense for travel, lodging, and meals. Incidental expenses may be totalled in reasonable categories such as taxis, fees and tips, etc.</td><td>Dates you left and returned for each trip and number of days spent on business.</td><td>Destination or area of your travel (name of city, town, or other designation).</td><td>Purpose: Business purpose for the expense or the business benefit gained or expected to be gained.

Relationship: N/A</td></tr>
<tr><td>Entertainment</td><td>Cost of each separate expense. Incidental expenses such as taxis, telephones, etc., may be totaled on a daily basis.</td><td>Date of entertainment.</td><td>Name and address or location of place of entertainment. Type of entertainment if not otherwise apparent.</td><td rowspan="2">Purpose: Business purpose for the expense or the business benefit gained or expected to be gained. For entertainment, the nature of the business discussion or activity. If the entertainment was directly before or after a business discussion: the date, place, nature, and duration of the business discussion, and the identities of the persons who took part in both the business discussion and the entertainment activity.

Relationship: Occupations or other information (such as names, titles, or other designations) about the recipients that shows their business relationship to you. For entertainment, you must also prove that you or your employee was present if the entertainment was a business meal.</td></tr>
<tr><td>Gifts</td><td>Cost of the gift.</td><td>Date of the gift.</td><td>Description of the gift.</td></tr>
</table>

IF you have expenses for...	THEN you must keep records that show details of the following elements.			
	Amount	Time	Place or Description	Business Purpose and Business Relationship
Transportation	Cost of each separate expense. For car expenses, the cost of the car and any improvements, the date you started using it for business, the mileage for each business use, and the total miles for the year.	Date of the expense. For car expenses, the date of the use of the car.	Your business destination.	Purpose: Business purpose for the expense. Relationship: N/A

6. REPORTING YOUR DEDUCTIONS

Unreimbursed employee business expenses must be reported on Form 2106-EZ. Once you have finished filling out Form 2106-EZ, you enter your total business expenses on line 21 of Schedule A. The text of the Form is self-explanatory. Let's use an example to show you how to fill it out.

Bill Wilson is an employee of Fashion Clothing Co. in Ottawa, Ontario. In a typical travel week, Bill leaves his home in Ottawa on Monday morning and drives to Kingston to exhibit the Fashion line for three days to prospective customers. Then he drives to Cornwall to show Fashion's new line of merchandise to Town Department Store, an old customer. While in Cornwall, he talks with Tom Brown, purchasing agent for Town Department Store, to discuss the new line. He later takes John Smith of Attire Co. out to dinner to discuss Attire Co.'s buying Fashion's new line of clothing.

Bill purchased his car on January 3, 2008. He uses the standard mileage rate for car expense purposes. He records his total mileage, business mileage, parking fees, and tolls for the year. Bill records his expenses and other pertinent information in a travel expense log (not shown). He obtains receipts for his expenses for lodging and for any other expenses of $75 or more.

During the year, Bill drove a total of 40,000 KM (25,000 miles) of which 32,000 KM (20,000 miles) were for business. He answers all the questions in Part II of Form 2106-EZ and figures his car expense to be $11,100 (20,000 miles x 55.5 c/mile = $11,100).

His total employee business expenses are shown in the following table.

Type of Expense	Amount
Parking fees and tolls	$520
Car expenses	11,100
Meals	3,861
Lodging, laundry, dry cleaning	18,318
Entertainment	3,250
Gifts, education, etc.	650
Total	**$37,699**

Bill fills out Form 2106 EZ as follows.

Form **2106-EZ** Department of the Treasury Internal Revenue Service (99)

Unreimbursed Employee Business Expenses

▶ Attach to Form 1040 or Form 1040NR.

OMB No. 1545-0074 **2011** Attachment Sequence No. **129A**

Your name	Occupation in which you incurred expenses	Social security number
Bill Wilson	Sales	555 ¦ 00 ¦ 5555

You Can Use This Form Only if All of the Following Apply.

• You are an employee deducting ordinary and necessary expenses attributable to your job. An ordinary expense is one that is common and accepted in your field of trade, business, or profession. A necessary expense is one that is helpful and appropriate for your business. An expense does not have to be required to be considered necessary.

• You **do not** get reimbursed by your employer for any expenses (amounts your employer included in box 1 of your Form W-2 are not considered reimbursements for this purpose).

• If you are claiming vehicle expense, you are using the standard mileage rate for 2011.

Caution: *You can use the standard mileage rate for 2011 **only if: (a)** you owned the vehicle and used the standard mileage rate for the first year you placed the vehicle in service, **or (b)** you leased the vehicle and used the standard mileage rate for the portion of the lease period after 1997.*

Part I **Figure Your Expenses**

1	Complete Part II. Multiply line 8a by 51¢ (.51) for miles driven **before** July 1, 2011, and by 55.5¢ (.555) for miles driven **after** June 30, 2011. Add the amounts, then enter the result here	1	11,100
2	Parking fees, tolls, and transportation, including train, bus, etc., that **did not** involve overnight travel or commuting to and from work	2	520
3	Travel expense while away from home overnight, including lodging, airplane, car rental, etc. **Do not** include meals and entertainment	3	18,318
4	Business expenses not included on lines 1 through 3. **Do not** include meals and entertainment	4	650
5	Meals and entertainment expenses: $ 7,111 × 50% (.50). (Employees subject to Department of Transportation (DOT) hours of service limits: Multiply meal expenses incurred while away from home on business by 80% (.80) instead of 50%. For details, see instructions.)	5	3556
6	**Total expenses.** Add lines 1 through 5. Enter here and on **Schedule A (Form 1040), line 21** (or on **Schedule A (Form 1040NR), line 7**). (Armed Forces reservists, fee-basis state or local government officials, qualified performing artists, and individuals with disabilities: See the instructions for special rules on where to enter this amount.)	6	34144

Part II **Information on Your Vehicle.** Complete this part **only** if you are claiming vehicle expense on line 1.

7 When did you place your vehicle in service for business use? (month, day, year) ▶ 01 / 03 / 08

8 Of the total number of miles you drove your vehicle during 2011, enter the number of miles you used your vehicle for:

a Business 20,000 b Commuting (see instructions) 2,600 c Other 2,400

9 Was your vehicle available for personal use during off-duty hours? ☑ Yes ☐ No

10 Do you (or your spouse) have another vehicle available for personal use? ☑ Yes ☐ No

11a Do you have evidence to support your deduction? ☑ Yes ☐ No

b If "Yes," is the evidence written? ☑ Yes ☐ No

For Paperwork Reduction Act Notice, see your tax return instructions. Cat. No. 20604Q Form **2106-EZ** (2011)

Bill then enters $34,144 on line 21 of Schedule A.

7. DEDUCTION LIMITS

On Schedule A, you will notice that line 21 is subject to a limit. Basically, you must reduce the total of your unreimbursed employment expenses by 2% of your adjusted gross income. Recall that your adjusted gross income is found on line 38 of your Form 1040. Let's reprise Bill's example to demonstrate how to adjust your employment expenses deduction by this limit. Recall that

Bill entered $34,144 on line 21 of Schedule A. Let's say his adjusted gross income from line 38 of Form 1040 was $50,000. His Schedule A would look like this.

SCHEDULE A (Form 1040) — **Itemized Deductions** — OMB No. 1545-0074 — **2011**

Department of the Treasury Internal Revenue Service (99) ▶ Attach to Form 1040. ▶ See Instructions for Schedule A (Form 1040). Attachment Sequence No. 07

Name(s) shown on Form 1040: Bill Wilson — Your social security number: 50550055

Medical and Dental Expenses		**Caution.** Do not include expenses reimbursed or paid by others.				
	1	Medical and dental expenses (see instructions)	1			
	2	Enter amount from Form 1040, line 38 [2]				
	3	Multiply line 2 by 7.5% (.075)	3			
	4	Subtract line 3 from line 1. If line 3 is more than line 1, enter -0-			4	
Taxes You Paid	5	State and local **(check only one box):** a ☐ Income taxes, **or** b ☐ General sales taxes	5			
	6	Real estate taxes (see instructions)	6			
	7	Personal property taxes	7			
	8	Other taxes. List type and amount ▶	8			
	9	Add lines 5 through 8			9	
Interest You Paid	10	Home mortgage interest and points reported to you on Form 1098	10			
Note. Your mortgage interest deduction may be limited (see instructions).	11	Home mortgage interest not reported to you on Form 1098. If paid to the person from whom you bought the home, see instructions and show that person's name, identifying no., and address ▶	11			
	12	Points not reported to you on Form 1098. See instructions for special rules	12			
	13	Mortgage insurance premiums (see instructions)	13			
	14	Investment interest. Attach Form 4952 if required. (See instructions.)	14			
	15	Add lines 10 through 14			15	
Gifts to Charity	16	Gifts by cash or check. If you made any gift of $250 or more, see instructions	16			
If you made a gift and got a benefit for it, see instructions.	17	Other than by cash or check. If any gift of $250 or more, see instructions. You **must** attach Form 8283 if over $500	17			
	18	Carryover from prior year	18			
	19	Add lines 16 through 18			19	
Casualty and Theft Losses	20	Casualty or theft loss(es). Attach Form 4684. (See instructions.)			20	
Job Expenses and Certain Miscellaneous Deductions	21	Unreimbursed employee expenses—job travel, union dues, job education, etc. Attach Form 2106 or 2106-EZ if required. (See instructions.) ▶	21	34,144		
	22	Tax preparation fees	22	0		
	23	Other expenses—investment, safe deposit box, etc. List type and amount ▶	23	0		
	24	Add lines 21 through 23	24	34,144		
	25	Enter amount from Form 1040, line 38 [25] 50,000				
	26	Multiply line 25 by 2% (.02)	26	1000		
	27	Subtract line 26 from line 24. If line 26 is more than line 24, enter -0-			27	33,144
Other Miscellaneous Deductions	28	Other—from list in instructions. List type and amount ▶			28	
Total Itemized Deductions	29	Add the amounts in the far right column for lines 4 through 28. Also, enter this amount on Form 1040, line 40			29	34,144
	30	If you elect to itemize deductions even though they are less than your standard deduction, check here ▶ ☐				

For Paperwork Reduction Act Notice, see Form 1040 instructions. Cat. No. 17145C **Schedule A (Form 1040) 2011**

Note that after reducing his expenses by 2% of his adjusted gross income ($50,000 x 0.02 = $1,000) Bill's unreimbursed employment expenses are $33,144. He takes this amount and enters it on line 40 of his Form 1040.

8. OTHER ISSUES AND FURTHER INFORMATION

Publication 463 provides more information on travel, entertainment, gift, and car expenses. Publication 1542 provides per diem rates. Finally, Chapter 26 of Publication 17 provides a general overview of the topic. Chapter 28 of Publication 17 discusses additional, albeit less common, employee expenses. All of these publications are available on the IRS website.

27

MISCELLANEOUS DEDUCTIONS[1]

This chapter surveys miscellaneous deductions that you can take. Many of them will not apply to you. But we have listed them here nevertheless. Lines 22 and 23 of Schedule A specifically allow for deductions of tax preparation fees and other expenses. Similarly, line 28 allows for other miscellaneous deductions. The differences between lines 22–23 and line 23 are twofold. First, deductions entered on lines 22–23 are reduced by 2% of your adjusted gross income that is located on line 38 of Form 104. Second, different deductions are allowed on line 23 than on line 28. Here we discuss how to figure the amounts on lines 22–28.

1. LINE 22 – TAX PREPARATION FEES

Enter the fees you paid for preparation of your tax return, including fees paid for filing your return electronically.

2. LINE 23 – OTHER EXPENSES

Schedule A (Form 1040), line 23, you can deduct expenses that you pay:

- to produce or collect income that must be included in your gross income;
- to manage, conserve, or maintain property held for producing such income; or
- to determine, contest, pay, or claim a refund of any tax.

But do not include any personal expenses. Examples of expenses to include on line 23 are as follows:

- appraisal fees;
- certain legal and accounting fees;
- clerical help and office rent;
- custodial (for example, trust account) fees;
- your share of the investment expenses of a regulated investment company;
- certain losses on non-federally insured deposits in an insolvent or bankrupt financial institution. For details, including limits that apply, see Pub. 529;
- casualty and theft losses of property used in performing services as an employee from Form 4684, lines 32 and 38b, or Form 4797, line 18a;
- deduction for repayment of amounts under a claim of right if $3,000 or less;

---

[1] This chapter is based on, and some text is copied from, Chapter 28 of IRS Publication 17 and the IRS' instructions to Schedule A.

- convenience fee charged by the card processor for paying your income tax (including estimated tax payments) by credit or debit card. The deduction is claimed for the year in which the fee was charged to your card;

- safe deposit box rent.

These examples, as well as others, are discussed further in Chapter 28 of Publication 17. For our purposes, it is worth briefly discussing a few of them.

Legal Expenses

You can usually deduct legal expenses that you incur in attempting to produce or collect taxable income or that you pay in connection with the determination, collection, or refund of any tax.

You can also deduct legal expenses that are:

- related to either doing or keeping your job, such as those you paid to defend yourself against criminal charges arising out of your trade or business;

- for tax advice related to a divorce, if the bill specifies how much is for tax advice and it is determined in a reasonable way; or

- to collect taxable alimony.

3. LINE 28 – OTHER EXPENSES

The following other expenses can be itemized and deducted on line 28:

- gambling losses (gambling losses include, but are not limited to, the cost of non-winning bingo, lottery, and raffle tickets), but only offsetting gambling winnings reported on Form 1040, line 21.

- casualty and theft losses of income-producing property from Form 4684, lines 32 and 38b, or Form 4797, line 18a

- loss from other activities from Schedule K-1 (Form 1065-B), box 2

- federal estate tax on income in respect of a decedent

- amortizable bond premium on bonds acquired before October 23, 1986

- deduction for repayment of amounts under a claim of right if over $3,000. See Pub. 525 for details.

- certain unrecovered investment in a pension

- impairment-related work expenses of a disabled person. For more details, see Pub. 529.

More information about any of these deductions can be found in Chapter 28 of Publication 17.

PART 2E

CALCULATING HOW MUCH TAX YOU OWE

OVERVIEW LINES 44 AND 56–60[1]

This chapter provides an overview of how to calculate the tax you owe. It surveys Form 1040 lines 42–46 and 50–56. As usual, first we briefly review the different lines of the return and then direct you to the more in-depth chapters to figure out how to fill in the lines that apply to you. Let's start with a look at lines 42–46. The relevant section of the Form 1040 looks like this.

Form 1040 (2011) Page **2**

Tax and Credits	38	Amount from line 37 (adjusted gross income)	38	
	39a	Check if: { ☐ **You** were born before January 2, 1947, ☐ Blind. ☐ **Spouse** was born before January 2, 1947, ☐ Blind. } **Total boxes checked ▶ 39a** ☐		
Standard Deduction for—	b	If your spouse itemizes on a separate return or you were a dual-status alien, check here ▶ 39b ☐		
• People who check any box on line 39a or 39b **or** who can be claimed as a dependent, see instructions.	40	**Itemized deductions** (from Schedule A) **or** your **standard deduction** (see left margin)	40	
	41	Subtract line 40 from line 38	41	
	42	**Exemptions.** Multiply $3,700 by the number on line 6d	42	
	43	**Taxable income.** Subtract line 42 from line 41. If line 42 is more than line 41, enter -0-	43	
	44	**Tax** (see instructions). Check if any from: **a** ☐ Form(s) 8814 **b** ☐ Form 4972 **c** ☐ 962 election	44	
	45	**Alternative minimum tax** (see instructions). Attach Form 6251	45	
	46	Add lines 44 and 45 ▶	46	

1. EXEMPTIONS – LINE 42

This is where you take a deduction depending on the number of people you financially support. Go back to box 6D above and take the number entered there and multiply that number by $3,800. Enter the total on line 42.

2. TAXABLE INCOME – LINE 43

This is where you compute your total taxable income. To do so, you should take the amount on line 42 and subtract it from the amount on line 41. You should enter the total on line 43. That is your taxable income.

3. TAX OWED – LINE 44

Here is where you calculate your tax liability. The method used to calculate the amount of tax you owe differs based on the type of income you have. The process to calculate the amount of tax you owe is fully explained in Chapter 29. Once you have consulted that chapter, enter the total amount on line 44 of your return.

You can likely disregard the three boxes next to line 44. Form 8814 concerns income tax you pay on interest and dividends received by your children. If your children do not have any assets, you can ignore this. If they do, we recommend seeking professional tax advice on how to fill it out.

Form 4972 is tax on a qualified lump-sum distribution (essentially a large payment) from a pension, profit sharing, or stock bonus plan for persons who are 75 or older. You should receive a Form 1099-R or other tax slip that shows the amounts needed to fill out this form. If you are 75 or older and think you have this type of large, lump-sum distribution, please get professional tax help.

---

[1] This chapter is based on, and some text is copied from, the IRS' instructions for Form 1040.

Box (c) addresses the section 962 election. This is complicated. Basically, it allows you to choose, if you meet a long list of criteria, to be subject to corporate rates. It is very likely that this is not applicable. So you can leave this box blank.

4. ALTERNATIVE MINIMUM TAX – LINE 45

a. You can likely ignore line 45

Alternative minimum tax (AMT) is a separate method of calculating tax for those who pay an unusually low tax rate. It establishes another system to calculate this rate. The calculations are extremely technical and difficult. Most US citizens in Canada do not have to worry about the alternative minimum tax if they have taken advantage of the foreign earned income exclusion unless they

- take advantage of accelerated depreciation.
- have tax exempt interest from private activity bonds.
- deduct drilling, circulation, research, experimental, or mining costs.
- have income (or loss) from tax-shelter farm activities or passive activities.
- have income from long-term contracts not calculated using the percentage-of-completion method of calculating income.
- deduct interest paid on a home mortgage NOT used to buy, build, or substantially improve their home.
- deduct investment interest expense reported on Form 4952.
- use a section 1202 exclusion (small business stock gain exclusion).
- claim any general business credit in Part I on Form 3800.
- claim empowerment zone and renewal community employment credit.
- take the qualified electric vehicle credit.
- use the alternative fuel vehicle refueling property credit.
- take the credit for prior year minimum tax.

If none of these situations apply to you, you do not have to worry about the alternative minimum tax. In the past, few taxpayers have been affected. For instance, in 2010 only 1.3% of all returns paid the alternative minimum tax. Three quarters of these tax filers earned more than $200,000.

Nevertheless, if you want to be extra certain, there is a handy tool on the IRS's website at http://www.irs.gov/businesses/small/article/0,,id=150703,00.html that will tell you if you need to worry about the alternative minimum tax. It may be that after filing your return the IRS sends you a notice saying that you owe alternative minimum tax. Should this occur, please seek professional tax advice.

In short, you can ignore the alternative minimum tax if you take the foreign earned income exclusion and do not fall into one of the above categories. However, below we give you a technical explanation of why we think this. Feel free to read it or just skip to the next section.

b. Technical justification

Here is a cursory technical justification of the above conclusion. The alternative minimum tax is based on your adjusted gross income. Recall that the foreign earned income exclusion allows you to exclude up to $95,100 (single) or $190,200 (married filing jointly) of your income from your adjusted gross income. On top of this, the foreign housing exclusion allows you to exclude your reasonable housing expenses. Thus, once these two exclusions are factored in, most people's adjusted gross income will not be that high but may include some types of income that are not excludable (dividend, interest, capital gains, etc.).

To add to this, there are alternative minimum tax exemptions. These allow people whose total income on line 28 of Form 6251 is below a certain amount to exclude a certain amount from tax. For 2012, the amounts are as follows:

- $50,600 for single and head of household filers;
- $78,750 for married people filing jointly and for qualifying widows or widowers; and
- $39,375 for married people filing separately.

Line 28 of Form 6251 is your adjusted gross income plus several potential sources of income that most people will not have. Our view is that once these exemptions and the foreign earned income and/or housing are factored in most people will not have any exposure to the AMT. If you do have exposure, you can use the foreign tax credit and other credits to reduce it. Thus, you have to have a significant total income to even be subject to the AMT. So, it's probably safe to ignore this line if you claim the foreign earned income exclusion.

5. CONCLUSION: LINES 42–46

After you have calculated all the tax you owe, you should enter the total on line 46.

6. OTHER TAXES: LINES 56–61

a) Most people can ignore lines 56-61

Lines 44–46 are not the only places where you have to calculate the tax you owe. Lines 56–61 also involve taxes you might owe. Unless you fall into one of the very specific situations described below you can ignore these lines. The next section of the Form 1040 looks like this.

b) Specific situations covered by lines 56-61

Other Taxes	56	Self-employment tax. Attach Schedule SE	56	
	57	Unreported social security and Medicare tax from Form: a ☐ 4137 b ☐ 8919	57	
	58	Additional tax on IRAs, other qualified retirement plans, etc. Attach Form 5329 if required	58	
	59a	Household employment taxes from Schedule H	59a	
	b	First-time homebuyer credit repayment. Attach Form 5405 if required	59b	
	60	Other taxes. Enter code(s) from instructions	60	
	61	Add lines 55 through 60. This is your **total tax** ▶	61	

Most people can ignore lines 56–61. They deal with the following situations:

- *People who are self-employed.* You may owe tax on your self-employment income (line 56) and you may have to pay Social Security and Medicare tax. Because self-employment is not covered by this guide, you should consult a tax professional if this situation applies to you.
- *People who contributed too much to an IRA.* If you contributed more than you were allowed to an IRA or other US retirement plan, you may have to pay tax. Line 58 is where you report this. As stated elsewhere, it is rare for Canadians to have IRAs, since they are not available at most Canadian financial institutions. If you do have an IRA and made contributions to it during the year, please get professional tax help as it is complicated to figure out the process.
- *People who employed household help in the United States* (line 59(a)). If you employed domestic help in the United States, please seek professional tax advice.
- *People who took advantage of the first-time homebuyer credit* (line 59(b)). Consult the instructions to Form 5405 for more details.
- *People who fall into one of the following other unique and rare situations* (line 60). On line 60 you list what other taxes you may owe. Most people can safely ignore this line. It deals with very complicated and specific additional taxes. If you do not understand an item on the following list, it probably does not apply to you. As always, if you have doubts, consult a tax professional. The list is as follows:

    1. Additional tax on health savings account (HSA) distributions (see Form 8889, Part II). Identify as "HSA."
    2. Additional tax on an HSA because you did not remain an eligible individual during the testing period (see Form 8889, Part III). Identify as "HDHP."
    3. Additional tax on Archer MSA distributions (see Form 8853). Identify as "MSA."
    4. Additional tax on Medicare Advantage MSA distributions (see Form 8853). Identify as "Med MSA."
    5. Recapture of the following credits.

        a) Investment credit (see Form 4255). Identify as "ICR."

        b) Low-income housing credit (see Form 8611). Identify as "LIHCR."

        c) Qualified plug-in electric vehicle credit (see Form 8834, Part I). Identify as "8834."

        d) Indian employment credit (see Form 8845). Identify as "IECR."

        e) New markets credit (see Form 8874). Identify as "NMCR."

        f) Credit for employer-provided child care facilities (see Form 8882). Identify as "ECCFR."

g) Alternative motor vehicle credit (see Form 8910). Identify as "AMVCR."

h) Alternative fuel vehicle refueling property credit (see Form 8911). Identify as "ARPCR."

i) Qualified plug-in electric drive motor vehicle credit (see Form 8936). Identify as "8936."

6. Recapture of federal mortgage subsidy. If you sold your home in 2011 and it was financed (in whole or in part) from the proceeds of any tax-exempt qualified mortgage bond or you claimed the mortgage interest credit, see Form 8828. Identify as "FMSR."

7. Recapture of COBRA (a type of health insurance) premium assistance. If you received premium assistance under COBRA continuation coverage that covered you, your spouse, or any of your dependents, and your modified adjusted gross income is more than $125,000 ($250,000 if married filing jointly), see Pub. 502. Identify as "COBRA."

8. Section 72(m)(5) excess benefits tax (see Pub. 560). Identify as "Sec. 72(m)(5)."

9. Uncollected social security and Medicare or RRTA tax on tips or group-term life insurance. This tax should be shown in box 12 of Form W-2 with codes A and B or M and N. Identify as "UT."

10. Golden parachute payments. If you received an excess parachute payment (EPP), you must pay a 20% tax on it. This tax should be shown in box 12 of Form W-2 with code K. If you received a Form 1099-MISC, the tax is 20% of the EPP shown in box 13. Identify as "EPP."

11. Tax on accumulation distribution of trusts (see Form 4970). Identify as "ADT."

12. Excise tax on insider stock compensation from an expatriated corporation. You may owe a 15% excise tax on the value of non-statutory stock options and certain other stock-based compensation held by you or a member of your family from an expatriated corporation or its expanded affiliated group in which you were an officer, director, or more-than-10% owner. See section 4985. Identify as "ISC."

13. Interest on the tax due on installment income from the sale of certain residential lots and timeshares. Identify as "453(l)(3)."

14. Interest on the deferred tax on gain from certain installment sales with a sales price over $150,000. Identify as "453A(c)."

15. Additional tax on recapture of a charitable contribution deduction relating to a fractional interest in tangible personal property. See Pub. 526. Identify as "FITPP."

16. Look-back interest under section 167(g) or 460(b). See Form 8697 or 8866. Identify as "From Form 8697" or "From Form 8866."

17. Any negative amount on Form 8885, line 7, because of advance payments of the health coverage tax credit you received for months you were not eligible. Enter this additional tax as a positive amount. Identify as "HCTC."

18. Additional tax on income you received from a non-qualified deferred compensation plan that fails to meet the requirements of section 409A. This income should be shown in box 12 of Form W-2 with code Z, or in box 15b of Form 1099-MISC. The tax is 20% of the amount required to be included in income plus an interest amount determined under section 409A(a)(1)(B)(ii). See section 409A(a)(1)(B) for details. Identify as "NQDC."

19. Additional tax on compensation you received from a non-qualified deferred compensation plan described in section 457A if the compensation would have been includible in your income in an earlier year except that the amount was not determinable until the tax year in question. The tax is 20% of the amount required to be included in income plus an interest amount determined under section 457A(c)(2). See section 457A for details. Identify as "457A."

29

FIGURING HOW MUCH YOUR TAX YOU OWE[1]

Once you have figured out what your taxable income on line 43 is, you need to compute how much tax you owe on that income. This chapter explains that process. Your method to calculate how much tax you owe depends on whether you took the foreign earned income exclusion. This chapter is organized as follows:

1. You did not take the foreign earned income exclusion.
    a. No foreign earned income exclusion and no capital gains or qualified dividends.
        i. You earned less than $100,000.
        ii. You earned more than $100,000.
    b. No foreign earned income exclusion but some capital gains.

or

2. You did take the foreign earned income exclusion.
    a. The worksheet to use.
    b. Example of no capital gains or qualified dividend income.
    c. If you took the foreign earned income exclusion and had capital gains income.
    d. Example of foreign earned income exclusion and capital gains income.

1. YOU DID NOT TAKE THE FOREIGN EARNED INCOME EXCLUSION

There are a few questions to answer in the process of determining which approach to take.

A. Do you have any capital gains income or qualified dividend income? Put differently, is there an amount listed on either line 9(b) or 13 of your Form 1040?

If no, follow the approach outlined in section (a) below. If yes, answer question B.

B. Did you list an amount on line 18 or 19 of Schedule D? Put differently, did you use the section 1250 gain worksheet or the 28% rate gain worksheet?

The answer to question B for most readers of this book will be no. However, if the answer is yes you should get professional tax advice.

If no, follow the approach in section (b) below to figure your tax. If yes, follow the approach in section (c) below.

---

[1] This chapter is based on, and some text is copied from, the IRS' instructions to Form 1040.

a. Figuring tax if you have no qualified dividends or capital gains.

In this case, figuring your tax is quite straightforward. However, the correct approach depends on whether you earn more or less than $100,000.

i. Your total income is under $100,000.

If the amount on line 43 is less than $100,000, simply take the amount on line 43 and use the tax tables in Appendix 2 to find the amount of tax due.

For example, say you are single and line 43 of your Form 1040 reads $56,000. Then you go to the column marked $56,000 in the tax tables and find the following entry.

If line 43 (taxable income) is —		**And you are —**			
At least	but less than	Single	Married filing jointly	Married filing separately	Head of a household
		Your tax is —			
56,000					
56,000	**56,050**	10,131	7,554	10,131	8,774
56,050	**56,100**	10,144	7,561	10,144	8,786
56,100	**56,150**	10,156	7,569	10,156	8,799
56,150	**56,200**	10,169	7,576	10,169	8,811
56,200	**56,250**	10,181	7,584	10,181	8,824
56,250	**56,300**	10,194	7,591	10,194	8,836
56,300	**56,350**	10,206	7,599	10,206	8,849
56,350	**56,400**	10,219	7,606	10,219	8,861
56,400	**56,450**	10,231	7,614	10,231	8,874
56,450	**56,500**	10,244	7,621	10,244	8,886
56,500	**56,550**	10,256	7,629	10,256	8,899
56,550	**56,600**	10,269	7,636	10,269	8,911
56,600	**56,650**	10,281	7,644	10,281	8,924
56,650	**56,700**	10,294	7,651	10,294	8,936
56,700	**56,750**	10,306	7,659	10,306	8,949
56,750	**56,800**	10,319	7,666	10,319	8,961
56,800	**56,850**	10,331	7,674	10,331	8,974
56,850	**56,900**	10,344	7,681	10,344	8,986
56,900	**56,950**	10,356	7,689	10,356	8,999
56,950	**57,000**	10,369	7,696	10,369	9,011

Since your taxable income is more than $56,000 and less than $56,050 and you are single your tax payable is $10,131. That's what you enter on line 44. Note that the above table is from 2011. We have only included it as an example. The 2012 tax tables are included in Appendix 2. Alternatively, you can always find the tax tables for the year for which you are filing in the instructions to Form 1040 which are available on the IRS website.

ii. Your income is over $100,000

If you earn more than $100,000 the process is slightly different. You should use the chart below to calculate your tax. You have to use the version of the chart which applies for the year in respect of which you are filing. The most up-to-date version can be found in the instructions to Form 1040 which are on the IRS website. While the numbers and percentages will change year over year, the layout of the chart remains the same.

The directions on the chart below are fairly self-explanatory. Find the section that matches your filing status and the row that contains your income. Perform the calculations as indicated and enter the result on line 44 of the Form 1040.

Section A — Use if your filing status is **Single.** Complete the row below that applies to you.

Taxable income. If line 43 is —	**(a) Enter the amount from line 43**	**(b) Multiplication amount**	**(c) Multiply (a) by (b)**	**(d) Subtraction amount**	**Tax. Subtract (d) from (c). Enter the result here and on Form 1040, line 44**
At least $100,000 but not over $178,650	$	× 28% (.28)	$	$ 6,539.50	$
Over $178,650 but not over $388,350	$	× 33% (.33)	$	$15,472.00	$
Over $388,350	$	× 35% (.35)	$	$23,239.00	$

Section B — Use if your filing status is **Married filing jointly** or **Qualifying widow(er).** Complete the row below that applies to you.

Taxable income. If line 43 is —	**(a) Enter the amount from line 43**	**(b) Multiplication amount**	**(c) Multiply (a) by (b)**	**(d) Subtraction amount**	**Tax. Subtract (d) from (c). Enter the result here and on Form 1040, line 44**
At least $100,000 but not over $142,700	$	× 25% (.25)	$	$ 7,940.00	$
Over $142,700 but not over $217,450	$	× 28% (.28)	$	$12,221.00	$
Over $217,450 but not over $388,450	$	× 33% (.33)	$	$23,093.50	$
Over $388,450	$	× 35% (.35)	$	$30,860.50	$

Section C — Use if your filing status is **Married filing separately.** Complete the row below that applies to you.

Taxable income. If line 43 is —	(a) Enter the amount from line 43	(b) Multiplication amount	(c) Multiply (a) by (b)	(d) Subtraction amount	Tax. Subtract (d) from (c). Enter the result here and on Form 1040, line 44
At least $100,000 but not over $108,725	$	× 28% (.28)	$	$ 6,110.50	$
Over $108,725 but not over $194,175	$	× 33% (.33)	$	$11,546.75	$
Over $194,175	$	× 35% (.35)	$	$ 15,430.25	$

Section D — Use if your filing status is **Head of a household.** Complete the row below that applies to you.

Taxable income. If line 43 is —	(a) Enter the amount from line 43	(b) Multiplication amount	(c) Multiply (a) by (b)	(d) Subtraction amount	Tax. Subtract (d) from (c). Enter the result here and on Form 1040, line 44
At least $100,000 but not over $122,300	$	× 25% (.25)	$	$ 5,355.00	$
Over $122,300 but not over $198,050	$	× 28% (.28)	$	$9,024.00	$
Over $198,050 but not over $388,350	$	× 33% (.33)	$	18,926.50	$
Over $388,350	$	× 35% (.35)	$	$26,693.50	$

b. You had capital gains or qualified dividend income

If you have either qualified dividend income (line 9(b) of the Form 1040) or capital gains income (line 13 on Form 1040) you should use the approach below to calculate how much tax you owe on all of your income. The worksheet below sets this out.

Most of the instructions on this worksheet are self-explanatory. However, there are a few points to note. Line 16 directs you to use the tax tables if your income is less than $100,000. For an explanation of how to do this please refer to section 1(a)(i) above. Really it is quite easy. Just take the amount you need to calculate and use the tax tables in Appendix 2 to find the amount of tax you owe.

Let's use an example to show you how to fill out this worksheet. Jimmy Jones is a US citizen living in Canada. For 2011, he had $25,000 in taxable income (listed on line 43 of his form 1040), which he did not exclude using the foreign earned income exclusion, $5,000 in qualified dividend income, and $2,000 in long-term capital gains income from selling his stocks. He would figure the amount of tax he owed using the worksheet as follows:

1.	Enter the amount from Form 1040, line 43.	**1.**	25,000
2.	Enter the amount from Form 1040, line 9b*	**2.**	5,000
3.	Are you filing Schedule D?*		
	☐ **Yes.** Enter the **smaller** of line 15 or 16 of Schedule D. If either line 15 or line 16 is blank or a loss, enter -0-	**3.**	2,000
	☐ **No.** Enter the amount from Form 1040, line 13	**3.**	0
4.	Add lines 2 and 3	**4.**	7,000
5.	If filing Form 4952 (used to figure investment interest expense deduction), enter any amount from line 4g of that form. Otherwise, enter -0-	**5.**	0
6.	Subtract line 5 from line 4. If zero or less, enter -0-	**6.**	7,000
7.	Subtract line 6 from line 1. If zero or less, enter -0-	**7.**	18,000
8.	Enter: $34,500 if single or married filing separately, $69,000 if married filing jointly or qualifying widow(er), $46,250 if head of household.	**8.**	34,500
9.	Enter the smaller of line 1 or line 8	**9.**	25,000
10.	Enter the smaller of line 7 or line 9	**10.**	18,000
11.	Subtract line 10 from line 9. This amount is taxed at 0%	**11.**	7,000
12.	Enter the smaller of line 1 or line 6	**12.**	7,000
13.	Enter the amount from line 11	**13.**	7,000
14.	Subtract line 13 from line 12	**14.**	0
15.	Multiply line 14 by 15% (.15)	**15.**	0
16.	Figure the tax on the amount on line 7. If the amount on line 7 is less than $100,000, use the Tax Table to figure this tax. If the amount on line 7 is $100,000 or more, use the Tax Computation Worksheet	**16.**	2,279
17.	Add lines 15 and 16	**17.**	2,279
18.	Figure the tax on the amount on line 1. If the amount on line 1 is less than $100,000, use the Tax Table (section 1(a)(i)) to figure this tax. If the amount on line 1 is $100,000 or more, use the Tax Computation Worksheet section 1(a)(ii)	**18.**	3,329
19.	**Tax on all taxable income**. Enter the **smaller** of line 17 or line 18. Also include this amount on Form 1040, line 44.	**19.**	2,279

The amount on line 16 was figured by going to Appendix 2 and finding the tax payable on $18,000 for a single person. The amount on line 18 was figured by using the tax tables in Appendix 2 to find the tax payable on $25,000. What this worksheet shows is that because of Jimmy's low income, he will not have to pay any tax on his qualified dividends or capital gains.

2. YOU DID TAKE THE FOREIGN EARNED INCOME EXCLUSION

If you exclude income using the foreign earned income and/or housing exclusion, you need to follow a slightly different approach than the one set out above.

a. Foreign earned income exclusion worksheet

Whether or not you have capital gains income, you should use the following worksheet. Note that it refers back to several many of the steps set out above. The worksheet is as follows:

Foreign earned income exclusion worksheet.			
1.	Enter the amount from Form 1040, line 43. If the amount on line 43 is zero, you do not have to pay any tax and thus you do not have to fill out this worksheet.	**1.**	
2.	Enter the amount from your (and your spouse's, if filing jointly) Form 2555, lines 45 and 50, or Form 2555-EZ, line 18. These forms are used to claim the foreign earned income exclusion.	**2.**	
3.	Add lines 1 and 2	**3.**	
4.	**Tax on the amount on line 3.** If you have no capital gains or qualified dividends, follow the instructions in section 1(a) of this chapter to compute this line. That means that if your total income is less than $100,000 you should use the tax tables as described in section 1(a)(i) above. However, if your income is greater than $100,000, you should use the instructions in section 1(a)(ii) above to figure the amount for this line. However, if you do have qualified dividends or capital gains income you should use the chart in section 2(c) to figure out this line.\	**4.**	
5.	**Tax on the amount on line 2.** If the amount on line 2 is less than $100,000, use the tax table approach described in section 1(a)(i) above. If the amount on line 2 is $100,000 or more, use the Tax Computation Worksheet that is explained in section 1(a)(ii) above.	**5.**	
6.	Subtract line 5 from line 4. Enter the result. If zero or less, enter -0-. Also include this amount on Form 1040, line 44.	**6.**	

As line 4 of the worksheet indicates, if you have capital gains or qualified dividend income you will have to use the chart in section 2(c) to figure out what to put on line 4 of the worksheet. The next section provides an example of how to fill out the worksheet if you have no capital gains or qualified dividend income.

b. Example if you have no capital gain or qualified dividend income

If you have no qualified dividend or capital gains income, you can just use the above chart. Here is an example of how to fill it out.

Jane is single and earns $90,000 from her job at a bank in Montreal. She also had $4,000 in interest income. She was able to exclude her salary from tax ($90,000) using the foreign earned income exclusion. She must therefore report this on line 2 of the following worksheet. After deductions and adjustments, her total taxable income on line 43 of her Form 1040 was $2,000. She starts by filling out the foreign earned income exclusion chart. When she gets to line 3, she has to use the tax tables in Appendix 2 to figure out how much tax she owes. The tables reveal that she owes $19,384 in tax. So this is the amount that gets entered on line 4 of the chart below. Then on line 5 she has to look up the tax in the same tables for $90,000. The amount that gets entered on line 4 is $18,824. Line 5, the total tax she must pay, is $19,384 – $18,824. This equals $2,240. So Jane enters 560 on line 5 of the chart and on line 44 of her Form 1040. In short, she has to pay $560 tax on the $2,000 of interest income that she excluded.

Foreign earned income exclusion worksheet.			
1.	Enter the amount from Form 1040, line 43. If the amount on line 43 is zero, you do not have to pay any tax and thus you do not have to fill out this worksheet.	**1.**	2,000
2.	Enter the amount from your (and your spouse's, if filing jointly) Form 2555, lines 45 and 50, or Form 2555-EZ, line 18. These forms are used to claim the foreign earned income exclusion.	**2.**	90,000
3.	Add lines 1 and 2	**3.**	92,000
4.	**Tax on the amount on line 3.** If you have no capital gains or qualified dividends, follow the instructions in section 1(a) of this chapter to compute this line. That means that if your total income is less than $100,000 you should use the tax tables as described in section 1(a)(i) above. However, if your income is greater than $100,000, you should use the instructions in section 1(a)(ii) above to figure the amount for this line. However, if you do have qualified dividends or capital gains income you should use the chart in the next section to figure out what to enter on this line.	**4.**	19,384
5.	**Tax on the amount on line 2.** If the amount on line 2 is less than $100,000, use the tax table approach described in section 1(a)(i) above. If the amount on line 2 is $100,000 or more, use the Tax Computation Worksheet that is explained in section 1(a)(ii) above.	**5.**	18,824
6.	Subtract line 5 from line 4. Enter the result. If zero or less, enter -0-. Also include this amount on Form 1040, line 44 6.	**6.**	560

c. Foreign income exclusion and capital gains income

As line 4 of the chart suggests, if you have capital gains or qualified dividend income, you have to use the chart below.

Do not use the chart in section 1(b) as it will cause you to pay too much tax. Instead, use the following chart.

Note that if the amount on line 9 of the worksheet is greater than zero, you should restart the worksheet but use the instructions from section c.

1.	Enter the amount from line 3 of the foreign earned income exclusion chart in section 2(a)	**1.**	
2.	Enter the amount from Form 1040, line 9b*	**2.**	
3.	Are you filing Schedule D?*		
	☐ **Yes.** Enter the **smaller** of line 15 or 16 of Schedule D. If either line 15 or line 16 is blank or a loss, enter -0-	**3.**	
	☐ **No.** Enter the amount from Form 1040, line 13	**3.**	
4.	Add lines 2 and 3	**4.**	
5.	If filing Form 4952 (used to figure investment interest expense deduction), enter any amount from line 4g of that form. Otherwise, enter -0-	**5.**	
6.	Subtract line 5 from line 4. If zero or less, enter -0-	**6.**	
7.	Enter the amount on line 43 of Form 1040	**7.**	
8.	Subtract the amount on line 7 from the amount on line 6. Do not enter an amount below zero.	**8.**	
9.	If the amount on line 8 is zero, continue filling out the chart. If the line is greater than zero, consult the instructions immediately below the chart and stop filling out the chart.	**9.**	
10.	Subtract line 6 from line 1. If zero or less, enter -0-	**10.**	
11.	Enter: $34,500 if single or married filing separately, $69,000 if married filing jointly or qualifying widow(er), $46,250 if head of household.	**11.**	
12.	Enter the smaller of line 1 or line 11	**12.**	
13.	Enter the smaller of line 10 or line 12	**13.**	
14.	Subtract line 13 from line 12. This amount is taxed at 0%	**14.**	
15.	Enter the smaller of line 1 or line 6	**15.**	
16.	Enter the amount from line 14	**16.**	
17.	Subtract line 16 from line 15	**17.**	
18.	Multiply line 17 by 15% (.15)	**18.**	

19.	Figure the tax on the amount on line 10. If the amount on line 10 is less than $100,000, use the Tax Table (section 1(a)(i)) to figure this tax. If the amount on line 10 is $100,000 or more, use the Tax Computation Worksheet (section 1(a)(ii))	**19.**	
20.	Add lines 18 and 19	**20.**	
21.	Figure the tax on the amount on line 1. If the amount on line 1 is less than $100,000, use the Tax Table ((section 1(a)(i)) to figure this tax. If the amount on line 1 is $100,000 or more, use the Tax Computation Worksheet (section 1(a)(ii))	**21.**	
22.	**Tax on all taxable income.** Enter the **smaller** of line 20 or line 21. Include this amount on line 4 of the foreign earned income exclusion worksheet.	**22.**	

After you finish filling out the chart you should enter the amount on line 22 on the foreign earned income exclusion worksheet that you started.

i. Instructions if line 9 on the above chart is positive.

If the amount on line 9 is positive, things become more complicated. This means that you have what the IRS calls "capital gains excess." The IRS doesn't want you to have to pay extra capital gains tax simply because you took the foreign earned income exclusion. You have two choices. You can either continue to fill out the chart as if line 8 was zero. This is easier, but it will result in you paying more tax than you otherwise would have had to pay. Or you can redo the above worksheet following these instructions:

1. Take the amount you put on line 3 the first time you did the chart and subtract it by the amount on line 8. If the result is negative, enter zero and take the negative number and proceed to step two. Let's say line 3 was $5,000 the first time you did the chart. But line 8 is $8,000. You subtract $8,000 from $5,000 ($5,000 – $8,000 = -$3,000). Enter 0 on the new line three but take the -$3,000 and go to step two.

2. Subtract the remainder from the first step from the amount you entered on line 2 of the chart the first time. This serves to reduce the amount of qualified dividend income you pay tax on. To reprise our example, take the -$3,000 and use it to reduce (but not below zero) the amount that you put on line 2 the first time you did the chart.

3. Take any remainder from step two and use it to reduce the amount you entered on line 18 of Schedule D.

4. Proceed to complete the rest of the chart, but skip over lines 7, 8, and 9.

d. Example if you use the foreign earned income exclusion and have capital gains or qualified dividends

This example shows how to use the foreign income exclusion worksheet in conjunction with the capital gains table.

Jon and Laura are a married couple who live in Winnipeg. Together, they earned $95,000 in salary income and $5,000 in capital gains income from selling some stocks. They excluded all of their salary income using the foreign earned income exclusion but could not benefit from other tax credits to offset their capital gains. So the amount on line 43 of their Form 1040 is $2,000 and their total foreign earned income exclusion is $90,000.

Like everyone who takes the foreign earned income exclusion, Jon and Laura start off with the foreign earned income exclusion worksheet. They fill it out as follows. But when the reach line 4, they have to switch tracks and fill out the capital gains worksheet.

Foreign earned income exclusion worksheet.			
1.	Enter the amount from Form 1040, line 43. If the amount on line 43 is zero, you do not have to pay any tax and thus you do not have to fill out this worksheet.	**1.**	2,000
2.	Enter the amount from your (and your spouse's, if filing jointly) Form 2555, lines 45 and 50, or Form 2555-EZ, line 18. These forms are used to claim the foreign earned income exclusion.	**2.**	90,000
3.	Add lines 1 and 2	**3.**	92,000
4.	**Tax on the amount on line 3**. If you have no capital gains or qualified dividends, follow the instructions in section 1(a) of this chapter to compute this line. That means that if your total income is less than $100,000 you should use the tax tables as described in section 1(a)(i) above. However, if your income is greater than $100,000, you should use the instructions in section 1(a)(ii) above to figure the amount for this line. However, if you do have qualified dividends or capital gains income you should use the chart in section 2(c) to figure out this line.	**4.**	19,124
5.	**Tax on the amount on line 2**. If the amount on line 2 is less than $100,000, use the tax table approach described in section 1(a)(i) above. If the amount on line 2 is $100,000 or more, use the Tax Computation Worksheet that is explained in section 1(a)(ii) above.	**5.**	18,824
6.	Subtract line 5 from line 4. Enter the result. If zero or less, enter -0-. Also include this amount on Form 1040, line 44	**6.**	300

Jon and Laura need to fill out the capital gains and qualified dividends worksheet. They do so as follows: They determine that the amount for line 4 of their foreign earned income exclusion worksheet is $19,124.

1.	Enter the amount from line 3 of the foreign earned income exclusion chart in section 2(a)		**1.**	92,000
2.	Enter the amount from Form 1040, line 9b* (qualified dividends)		**2.**	0
3.	Are you filing Schedule D?*			
	☐ **Yes.**	Enter the **smaller** of line 15 or 16 of Schedule D. If either line 15 or line 16 is blank or a loss, enter -0-	**3.**	
	☐ **No.**	Enter the amount from Form 1040, line 13	**3.**	2,000
4.	Add lines 2 and 3		**4.**	2,000

5.	If filing Form 4952 (used to figure investment interest expense deduction), enter any amount from line 4g of that form. Otherwise, enter -0-	**5.**	0
6.	Subtract line 5 from line 4. If zero or less, enter -0-	**6.**	2,000
7.	Enter the amount on line 43 of Form 1040	**7.**	2,000
8.	Subtract the amount on line 7 from the amount on line 6. Do not enter an amount below zero.	**8.**	
9.	If the amount on line 8 is zero, continue filling out the chart. If the line is greater than zero, consult the instructions immediately below the chart and stop filling out the chart.	**9.**	0
10.	Subtract line 6 from line 1. If zero or less, enter -0-	**10.**	90,000
11.	Enter: $34,500 if single or married filing separately, $69,000 if married filing jointly or qualifying widow(er), $46,250 if head of household.	**11.**	
12.	Enter the smaller of line 1 or line 11	**12.**	69,000
13.	Enter the smaller of line 10 or line 12	**13.**	69,000
14.	Subtract line 13 from line 12. This amount is taxed at 0%	**14.**	0
15.	Enter the smaller of line 1 or line 6	**15.**	2,000
16.	Enter the amount from line 14	**16.**	0
17.	Subtract line 16 from line 15	**17.**	2,000
18.	Multiply line 17 by 15% (.15)	**18.**	300
19.	Figure the tax on the amount on line 10. If the amount on line 10 is less than $100,000, use the Tax Table (section 1(a)(i)) to figure this tax. If the amount on line 10 is $100,000 or more, use the Tax Computation Worksheet (section 1(a)(ii))	**19.**	18,824
20.	Add lines 18 and 19	**20.**	19,124
21.	Figure the tax on the amount on line 1. If the amount on line 1 is less than $100,000, use the Tax Table ((section 1(a)(i)) to figure this tax. If the amount on line 1 is $100,000 or more, use the Tax Computation Worksheet (section 1(a)(ii))	**21.**	19,384
22.	**Tax on all taxable income.** Enter the **smaller** of line 20 or line 21. Include this amount on line 4 of the foreign earned income exclusion worksheet.	**22.**	19,124

So Jon and Laura's total tax due is $300. They enter this on line 44 of their Form 1040.

3. IF YOU OWE THE IRS MONEY

Since most US citizens in Canada will not have had their tax withheld by their employers, you may owe the IRS money. If you owe lots of money to the IRS you may have to pay your estimated tax for future years in advance. The next chapter discusses this and explains how to make these payments.

30

ESTIMATED TAX[1]

Estimated tax is a future payment that you make to the IRS before your tax is actually due. Generally, you owe it if you owe the IRS a significant amount of money. Many (indeed most) US citizens in Canada will not have US tax withheld from their paycheques. So it may very well be that you owe the IRS money in advance. This chapter explains whether you owe this tax and if so, how to pay it.

1. DO YOU OWE ESTIMATED TAX?

Normally, you file a tax return to report your situation in the April following the end of the tax year. However, if you owe the IRS a significant sum of money you may have to pay the tax in advance. The exact dates are discussed below. First, you need to figure out whether you actually owe tax. In most cases, you must pay estimated tax for 2013 if both of the following apply.

1. You expect to owe at least $1,000 in tax for 2013, after subtracting your withholding and refundable credits.
2. You expect the amount withheld by your employer plus your refundable credits to be less than the smaller of
    a. 90% of the tax to be shown on your 2013, or
    b. 100% of the tax shown on your 2012 return.

Let's explain this using an example. Let's say that that the date is April 15, 2013. You have just filed your 2012 tax return. Because your employer did not withhold any US tax from your paycheque, you owe the IRS $2,000. You expect this to be the same for 2013. That means that you meet branch one of the above test. Since your employer does not withhold US tax, you will probably meet the second branch as well.

a. Estimated tax and married couples

Estimated tax applies equally to all different filing statuses. There are, however, some complications for those who chose to file jointly as opposed to separately. If you plan to file a joint return with your spouse for 2013, but you filed separate returns for 2012, your 2012 tax is the total of the tax shown on your separate returns. Conversely, if you plan to file a separate return for 2013 but you filed a joint return for 2012, your 2012 tax is your share of the tax on the joint return. You filed a separate return if you filed as single, head of household, or married filing separately.

To calculate your share of the tax on the joint return, first figure the tax both you and your spouse would have paid had you filed separate returns for 2011 using the same filing status as for 2012.

Then multiply the tax on the joint return by the following fraction.

[1] Much of the text of this chapter is taken from Chapter 4, of IRS Publication 17. It is available on the IRS website.

The tax you would have paid had you filed a separate return
The total tax you and your spouse would have paid had you filed separate returns

An example makes this clearer. Joe and Heather filed a joint return for 2011 showing taxable income of $48,500 and tax payable of $6,429. Of the $48,500 taxable income, $40,100 was Joe's and the rest was Heather's. For 2012, they plan to file married filing separately. Joe figures his share of the tax on the 2011 joint return as follows:

Tax on $40,100 based on a separate return	$6,156
Tax on $8,400 based on a separate return	$843
Total	$6,999
Joe's percentage of total ($6,156 ÷ $6,999)	87.96%
Joe's share of tax on joint return ($6,429 × 87.96%)	$5,655

2. HOW TO CALCULATE YOUR ESTIMATED TAX

To figure your estimated tax, you must calculate your expected adjusted gross income (AGI), taxable income, taxes, deductions, and credits for the year. When computing your 2013 estimated tax, it may be helpful to use your income, deductions, and credits for 2012 as a starting point. Use your 2012 tax return as a guide. To figure your estimated tax for a future year, use exactly the same method you would use to calculate a normal tax return for a past year. However, instead of using actual amounts, you simply use estimated amounts.

3. WHEN TO PAY ESTIMATED TAX

For estimated tax purposes, the tax year is divided into four payment periods. Each period has a specific payment due date. If you do not pay enough tax by the due date of each payment period, you may be charged a penalty even if you are due a refund when you file your income tax return. The payment periods and due dates for estimated tax payments are shown next.

For the period:	Due date:
Jan. 1 – March 31	April 15
April 1 – May 31	June 15
June 1 – August 31	Sept. 15
Sept. 1 – Dec. 31	Jan. 15, next year

If the due date for an estimated tax payment falls on a Saturday, Sunday, or US statutory holiday, the payment will be on time if you make it on the next day that is not a Saturday, Sunday, or US statutory holiday.

4. HOW TO FIGURE OUT EACH PAYMENT

To figure out how much you owe for each period, just take the amount of tax you owe and divide it by 4. For example, early in 2012, Mira Roberts figures that her estimated tax due is $1,800. She makes estimated tax payments on April 15 and June 15 of $450 each ($1,800 ÷ 4).

However, if a significant tax event occurs during one period, you may need to adjust accordingly. For instance, Mira sells investment property at a gain on July 10. Her recalculated estimated tax is $4,100. This would mean that normally her tax owed would be $1,025/period instead of $450 before the sale. Her required estimated tax payment for the third payment period is $2,175. Basically, she has to make up the additional tax owed for the first two payment periods in the third period [$1,025 + additional tax for first period ($1,025 – $450) + additional tax for second period ($1,025 – $450) = $2,175].

If you do not receive your income evenly throughout the year (for example, your income from a repair shop you operate is much larger in the summer than it is during the rest of the year), your required estimated tax payment for one or more periods may be less than the amount figured using the regular installment method.

The annualized income installment method annualizes your tax at the end of each period based on a reasonable estimate of your income, deductions, and other items relating to events that occurred from the beginning of the tax year through the end of the period. Publication 505 describes how to calculate the annualized method.

Note that if you underpay your estimated tax in a given period you may be subject to a penalty.

5. HOW TO PAY ESTIMATED TAX

Payment mechanisms are discussed generally in Chapter 1. Nevertheless, there are five ways to pay estimated tax.

- Credit an overpayment on your 2011 return to your 2012 estimated tax.
- Send in your payment (check or money order) with a payment voucher from Form 1040-ES. An example of this voucher is found below.
- Pay electronically at www.irs.gov/e-pay.
- Pay by electronic funds withdrawal if you are filing Form 1040 or Form 1040A electronically.
- Pay by credit or debit card using a pay-by-phone system or the Internet.

6. WHEN YOU FILE THE RETURN FOR THE YEAR IN WHICH YOU PAID ESTIMATED TAX

Let's say because of your 2012 return you are obliged to pay estimated tax in 2013. In April 2014, you will file your return for tax year 2013. On line 63 of Form 1040, of your 2013 return, you should make sure to take a credit for all of the estimated tax you have already paid. If you ended up paying too much, it might result in a refund. In any case, you do not want to pay the tax you owe twice.

7. PENALTIES

If you did not pay enough tax, either through withholding or by making timely estimated tax payments, you will have an underpayment of estimated tax and you may have to pay a penalty.

Generally, you will not have to pay a penalty for 2011 if any of the following apply:

- The total of your withholding and estimated tax payments was at least as much as your 2010 tax (or 110% of your 2010 tax if your AGI was more than $150,000, $75,000 if your 2011 filing status is married filing separately) and you paid all required estimated tax payments on time.
- The tax balance due on your 2011 return is no more than 10% of your total 2011 tax, and you paid all required estimated tax payments on time.
- Your total 2011 tax minus your withholding and refundable credits is less than $1,000.
- You did not have a tax liability for 2010 and your 2010 tax year was 12 months.
- You did not have any withholding taxes and your current year's tax less any household employment taxes is less than $1,000.

Note that this information is for tax year 2011. The same rules are likely to apply to tax year 2012 and beyond.

PART 2F

REDUCING YOUR TAX CREDITS

31

OVERVIEW OF LINES 47–77

This section introduces tax credits. Once you know the amount of tax you owe, you can use tax credits to reduce it. For instance, if you owe $2,000 and you can apply a tax credit of $1,000, your tax bill will be cut in half. There are two types of tax credits: refundable and non-refundable. Both reduce your tax payable. However, if you end up owing zero tax, the IRS will actually pay you the excess amount of your refundable credits. Here, we survey lines 47–54 of Form 1040 and direct you to the chapter which explains how to compute the amount for each line.

The applicable section of Form 1040 looks like this:

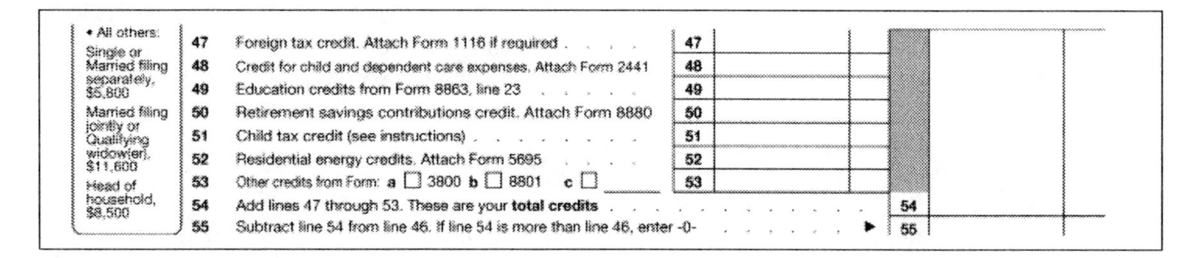

• All others:
Single or Married filing separately, $5,800
Married filing jointly or Qualifying widow(er), $11,600
Head of household, $8,500

47	Foreign tax credit. Attach Form 1116 if required	47	
48	Credit for child and dependent care expenses. Attach Form 2441	48	
49	Education credits from Form 8863, line 23	49	
50	Retirement savings contributions credit. Attach Form 8880	50	
51	Child tax credit (see instructions)	51	
52	Residential energy credits. Attach Form 5695	52	
53	Other credits from Form: a ☐ 3800 b ☐ 8801 c ☐ ______	53	
54	Add lines 47 through 53. These are your **total credits**	54	
55	Subtract line 54 from line 46. If line 54 is more than line 46, enter -0- . . . . . . ▶	55	

1. FOREIGN TAX CREDIT

The foreign tax credit allows you to reduce the amount of tax you pay to the US based on the amount of tax you paid to Canada (or another country) on non-US income. The foreign tax credit is different from the foreign earned income exclusion. The credit reduces the amount of tax you owe, as opposed to the exclusion, which excludes certain income from being subject to tax. As a general rule, you can't take the foreign tax credit on income that you excluded using the foreign earned income exclusion or on tax paid that was later refunded by Canada. Nor can you take advantage of the foreign tax credit if you took the foreign tax deduction described in Chapter 21.

The foreign tax credit is quite complicated. It is discussed further in Chapter 32. Once you have used that chapter to determine how much of the credit you can take, enter the amount on line 47.

2. CREDIT FOR CHILD AND DEPENDENT CARE EXPENSES – LINE 48

This tax credit is available to those who have expenses for child or dependent (i.e., parents) care that enables them to work. The credit may be up to $1,050 if you have one qualifying individual or $2,100 if you have more than one. Remember, this reduces the amount of tax you owe on a dollar for dollar basis. How to calculate the child and dependent care credit is explained in Chapter 33. Once you have used that chapter to calculate the amount, enter it on line 48.

3. EDUCATION CREDITS – LINE 49

Line 49 allows you to take the American Opportunity Credit or the lifetime learning credit. Both credits are for post-secondary education expenses. The American Opportunity Credit can be up to $2,500 and the lifetime learning credit is up to $2,000. The credits overlap and are mutually exclusive. Using them may mean that you cannot use the tuition deduction or the student loan interest deduction. This is all explained in Chapter 36. Consult that chapter and then enter the appropriate amount on line 49.

4. RETIREMENT SAVINGS CONTRIBUTION CREDITS – LINE 50

This line is where you can take a credit if you contribute to an Individual Retirement Account (IRA). An IRA is the American version of an RRSP. IRAs are generally not available in Canada so most US citizens in Canada probably do not contribute to such a plan. You should not enter your RRSP information on this line.

5. CHILD TAX CREDIT – LINE 51

The child tax credit is based on information that you entered on line 6. It can be used to reduce your tax payable by up to $1,000 for each of your qualifying children. The child tax credit is explained in Chapter 34. Once you have used that chapter to compute this amount, enter it on line 51.

6. RESIDENTIAL ENERGY CREDITS – LINE 52

This tax credit is available if you improved the energy efficiency of your home that is located in the United States. If this applies to you please consult Form 5695 and the instructions for that form.

7. OTHER CREDITS – LINE 53

Line 53 allows you to enter other non-refundable tax credits. You will notice that this line gives you three options: Form 3800, Form 8801, and a blank one. Form 3800 involves credits for small businesses and is outside the scope of this guide. Form 8801 deals with credits for minimum tax paid in prior years. The minimum tax is a very complicated topic. If you have paid it, you should get professional tax advice. The blank line can be used for the following other tax credits: (For the credits discussed below, you need to check box C next to line 53 and write in the type of credit used.)

- *General business tax credit.* If you have an interest in a small business or partnership consult publication 324 to see if you can take this credit.
- *The credit for the elderly or the disabled.* This is explained further in Chapter 35.
- *The mortgage interest credit.* You cannot take this credit if you receive a mortgage credit certificate from a US state or local government. Most US citizens in Canada will not receive such a certificate. So you should probably ignore this option. Nevertheless, Chapter 36 of IRS Publication 17 has more information.
- *Tax credits for the purchase of environmentally friendly cars.* If you purchased an electric car, see the instructions to forms 8859, 8936 and 8834 or if you purchased a fuel cell car you should see Forms 8910 and 8911.

8. CONCLUSION: LINES 47 – 54

On line 54 you should add up the totals from lines 47–53. You should then take the amount on line 54 and subtract it from the amount on line 46. This result becomes your total tax payable.

9. OTHER TAXES – LINES 56 – 61

This section of Form 1040 can generally be ignored by most US citizens in Canada. The next section of Form 1040 looks like this.

Other Taxes	56	Self-employment tax. Attach Schedule SE	56	
	57	Unreported social security and Medicare tax from Form: a ☐ 4137 b ☐ 8919	57	
	58	Additional tax on IRAs, other qualified retirement plans, etc. Attach Form 5329 if required	58	
	59a	Household employment taxes from Schedule H	59a	
	b	First-time homebuyer credit repayment. Attach Form 5405 if required	59b	
	60	Other taxes. Enter code(s) from instructions	60	
	61	Add lines 55 through 60. This is your **total tax** ▶	61	

Most people can ignore lines 56 – 61. The section is further explained in Chapter 28 which deals with taxes payable.

10. PAYMENTS AND MORE CREDITS – LINES 62–77

The final section of Form 1040 offers more tax credits. It looks like this:

Payments	62	Federal income tax withheld from Forms W-2 and 1099	62			
	63	2011 estimated tax payments and amount applied from 2010 return	63			
If you have a qualifying child, attach Schedule EIC.	64a	**Earned income credit (EIC)**	64a			
	b	Nontaxable combat pay election 64b				
	65	Additional child tax credit. Attach Form 8812	65			
	66	American opportunity credit from Form 8863, line 14	66			
	67	First-time homebuyer credit from Form 5405, line 10	67			
	68	Amount paid with request for extension to file	68			
	69	Excess social security and tier 1 RRTA tax withheld	69			
	70	Credit for federal tax on fuels. Attach Form 4136	70			
	71	Credits from Form: a ☐ 2439 b ☐ 8839 c ☐ 8801 d ☐ 8885	71			
	72	Add lines 62, 63, 64a, and 65 through 71. These are your **total payments** ▶			72	
Refund	73	If line 72 is more than line 61, subtract line 61 from line 72. This is the amount you **overpaid**			73	
	74a	Amount of line 73 you want **refunded to you.** If Form 8888 is attached, check here ▶ ☐			74a	
Direct deposit? See instructions.	▶ b	Routing number ▶ c Type: ☐ Checking ☐ Savings				
	▶ d	Account number				
	75	Amount of line 73 you want **applied to your 2012 estimated tax** ▶	75			
Amount You Owe	76	**Amount you owe.** Subtract line 72 from line 61. For details on how to pay, see instructions ▶			76	
	77	Estimated tax penalty (see instructions)	77			

Most US citizens in Canada will not have had any tax withheld so you can probably ignore line 62. If, however, your employer did withhold tax and issued you a W-2, you should enter the amount here.

11. ESTIMATED TAX PAYMENTS – LINE 63

If you frequently owe tax, you may have to pay estimated tax. Estimated tax is basically paying the amount you owe in advance. Normally, you would file a return and then pay the tax due as listed on that return. But if you owe money each year you may have to pay some of it in advance. Estimated tax is discussed in Chapter 30. Line 63 is where you enter estimated tax payments that you have already made for the current tax year.

12. EARNED INCOME CREDIT – LINES 64(A) AND 64(B)

This credit reduces the tax of people with low taxable incomes. It is also refundable. This means that if it reduces your tax below zero, the IRS will pay you the difference. Two rules make it unlikely that most US citizens in Canada can benefit from this credit. First, if you take the foreign earned income and/or housing exclusion you cannot claim the credit. Second, even if you did not take the foreign earned income exclusion, you must have lived in the United States for at least half the year.

Please consult IRS publication 596 to see if you can benefit from the earned income credit. In the unlikely event you are eligible, enter the amount on line 64(a). Unless you are a member of the US armed forces you can ignore line 64(b).

13. ADDITIONAL CHILD TAX CREDIT – LINE 65

For certain people who qualify for the child tax credit (see above) a portion of it may be refundable. That means that even if you pay no tax, you will get a refund. This credit is described in Chapter 34 which deals with the child tax credit. Once you have consulted this chapter and computed the amount, if any, you can enter it on line 65.

14. AMERICAN OPPORTUNITY CREDIT – LINE 66

The American Opportunity Credit is a refundable credit for post-secondary education expenses. It is discussed in Chapter 36 which deals with education credits. Once you have consulted this chapter and computed the amount, if any, you can enter it on line 66.

15. FIRST-TIME HOMEBUYER CREDIT – LINE 67

This credit is available to those who bought their first house or condo located in the United States in 2008, 2009, or 2010. It is no longer available. If this situation applies to you please consult Form 5405 and the accompanying instructions. You can then enter the amount on line 67.

16. EXCESS SOCIAL SECURITY TAX WITHHELD – LINE 69

This line applies only to those who had Social Security withheld on their paycheques. This will not apply to most US citizens in Canada. In 2011, the maximum wages that were subject to Social Security tax was $106,800. On that amount you would have had to pay $4485.60. If your employer withheld more than this, you are entitled to a rebate. Use Form 843 and the accompanying instructions to determine if this was the case.

17. CREDIT FOR FEDERAL TAX ON FUELS – LINE 70

This credit is for those who used a specific type of fuel such as kerosene used in aviation or one of the following: biodiesel mixtures, renewable diesel mixtures, alternative fuels (except liquefied hydrogen), alternative fuel mixtures (except liquefied hydrogen). This will not apply to most people. Please consult the instructions to Form 4136 if you think it applies to your situation. Otherwise, most people can simply ignore this line.

18. OTHER CREDITS – LINE 71

Line 71 is for other refundable tax credits. On this line there are four checkboxes. Each is associated with a different refundable credit. They are as follows:

- *Box a 2439 – Credit for undistributed long term capital gains.* This tax credit allows you to offset tax paid on capital gain distributions from a mutual fund that you did not actually receive. The mutual fund will send you a Form 2439 showing the amount of gains. If you receive this tax slip, or you think you have undistributed capital gains, consult Publication 550.
- *Box B 8839 – Adoption expenses.* If you adopt a child, the IRS will refund some of your expenses. Please see the instructions to Form 8839 for more information.
- *Box C 8801 – Credit for prior year minimum tax.* This credit is for those who have paid the alternative minimum tax in prior years. It is quite complicated. We recommend you seek professional tax help if this applies to you or consult Form 8801.
- *Box D Form 8885 – Health coverage tax credit.* This line allows for a tax credit for those who receive a payment from various specific health benefit plans that are not available in Canada including:
    - eligible trade adjustment assistance (TAA) recipient,
    - alternative TAA (ATAA) recipient,
    - reemployment TAA (RTAA) recipient, or
    - Pension Benefit Guaranty Corporation (PBGC) pension payee.

If you are covered under one of these benefit plans, please see Form 8885. Most people, however, can ignore this line.

19. CONCLUSION: REFUNDABLE TAX CREDITS

At this point you should add up lines 62, 63, 64a, and 65 through 71 and enter the total in box 72.

Paying your tax or claiming your refund

If line 72 is more than line 61, subtract line 61 from line 72. This is the amount you overpaid. Enter that amount on line 73. That will be your refund. You can ignore line 74(a) unless you have an American bank account. This does not include a US dollars account at a Canadian bank. The IRS will not issue direct deposit refunds to people who have accounts outside of the United States.

If the amount on line 72 is less than the amount on line 61 follow these instructions. Subtract line 72 from line 61 and enter the total on line 76. The instructions on how to pay any amount owed can be found in Chapter 1. Finally, you sign and date the return, list your occupation and send it off to the IRS. The addresses to use and the due dates can be found in Chapter 3.

32

THE FOREIGN TAX CREDIT[1]

The foreign tax credit allows you to reduce your US tax payable by the amount of Canadian income tax you paid on non-US income. Before plunging into the foreign tax credit you have to make a choice regarding how best to take advantage of your Canadian taxes.

You may either deduct your Canadian tax as an itemized deduction (see Chapter 21) or use it as the basis for the foreign tax credit. The foreign tax credit has certain advantages over the foreign tax deduction. It reduces the amount of tax you owe rather than just your income which is subject to tax. Also, if you use the foreign tax credit you can also claim the standard deduction, because you do not have to itemize your deductions. But the foreign tax credit is much more complicated than the foreign tax deduction, so you have to factor the complexity into your choice.

Should you choose to use the foreign tax credit, this chapter will explain how to calculate it.

This chapter is organized to follow the steps you should take:

1. What taxes are eligible for the credit.
2. Divide your income by source.
3. Divide your income into categories.
4. Fill out a separate Form 1116 for each income category.
5. Form 1116 – Part I – figuring out your total foreign taxable income.
6. Form 1116 – Part II – the amount of Canadian income tax paid.
7. Form 1116 – Part III – computing the credit.
8. Example of the foreign tax credit.

Before getting to the details, we suggest that you seek professional advice if you:

- have Canadian capital losses/gains or qualified dividends that are not reduced using other tax credits.
- have paid taxes to foreign regimes which have been under sanction by the American government, such as Libya, etc.
- took the investment interest deduction and want to take the foreign tax credit.
- have a large amount of US-source income. It may be that you will be able to use the Canada-US Tax Treaty to claim the foreign tax credit for some of this income.

---

[1] The text in this chapter is based on IRS Publication 514. Some of it is copied directly from that publication.

1. WHAT TYPES OF TAXES ARE ELIGIBLE FOR THE CREDIT?

All Canadian federal and provincial income taxes on non-US income are eligible for the foreign tax credit. However, sales taxes, such as the GST or HST, or real property taxes are not. Neither are US federal or state taxes, since those governments are not foreign entities for the purposes of US taxes. Income tax paid to other governments (i.e., not the US or Canada) may also be eligible. Please consult Publication 514 to determine whether they meet the criteria set out there.

You can only claim a US credit on the amount of tax you actually owe to Canada that you paid on Canadian income (or other foreign income). So, if you received a refund on your Canadian taxes, because your employer withheld too much, you are not entitled to report that refund as tax you owe.

2. DIVIDE UP YOUR INCOME BY SOURCE

Generally, you can only claim the foreign tax credit for foreign tax you paid on income sources from outside the United States. Before explaining how to fill out Form 1116 and claim the foreign tax credit, here's how to figure out the source of your income.

The source of your income is where it comes from. Knowing this is essential to figuring out whether you can take the foreign tax credit for that income. The following chart sets out how to do this.

Type of income	Factor Determining Source
Salaries, wages, other compensation	Where services performed
Interest	Residence of payer
Dividends	Where the corporation is located
Rents	Location of property
Royalties:	
Natural resources	Location of property
Patent, copyrights, etc.	Where property is used
Sale of real property	Location of property
Sale of personal property	Seller's tax home
Pension distributions attributable to contributions	Where services were performed that earned the pension

Most of these are pretty straightforward. If you work for a salary in Canada, then the source of that salary is Canada. Interest received from a Canadian bank is income from a Canadian source. The one complicated piece is dividend income. Dividend income from US corporations is treated as US income. Dividend income from foreign corporations is considered foreign. A good rule of thumb for figuring out whether a corporation is foreign or American is to look at what stock exchange it is listed on. If it is listed on multiple stock exchanges, look at where its headquarters are. Any doubts should be resolved by contacting the corporation.

a. Foreign tax credit for US-source income

There is an exception to the above rule. Under the Canada-US Income Tax Treaty, the foreign tax credit may be available for some US-source income. This treaty is designed to help you avoid paying tax twice on the same income. However, because this is extremely complicated, if you have a lot of US-source income, we suggest that you consult a tax professional.

3. DIVIDE YOUR INCOME INTO CATEGORIES

Once you know the source of your income, you divide your income into the following five categories: passive income, general income, income re-sourced by a tax treaty, section 901(j) income (taxes paid to sanctioned countries), and a lump sum distribution from an employer benefit plan. Let's examine each category.

a. Passive income

Passive income generally includes the following:

- dividends;
- interest;
- rents;
- royalties;
- annuities;
- capital gains.
  - Note if you have a lot of Canadian capital gains and you want to reduce them using the foreign tax credit you should consult a professional tax preparer. The rules are very complicated.

b. General income

General income is a residual category for foreign income that does not fall into one of the other categories. It includes wages, salaries, and employee benefits.

c. Income re-sourced by a tax treaty

This category allows you to claim the foreign tax credit for some of your US source income. However, this is quite complicated and should be handled by a tax professional.

d. Section 901(j) income

This category represents income tax paid to certain countries under sanction by the US government, including Cuba, Iran, Libya, North Korea, Sudan, and Syria. Most readers of this guide will not have paid taxes to these countries and can therefore ignore this category.

e. Lump sum distributions from a retirement plan

Should you receive a lump sum distribution from a Canadian retirement plan, you should consult publication 514 or a tax professional regarding any claim for a foreign tax credit on this income.

4. FILL OUT A SEPARATE FORM 1116 FOR EACH INCOME CATEGORY

The foreign tax credit is claimed using Form 1116. The first section asks you to divide your foreign source income into five different categories. It looks like this:

Form **1116** — Department of the Treasury, Internal Revenue Service (99)

Foreign Tax Credit
(Individual, Estate, or Trust)
▶ Attach to Form 1040, 1040NR, 1041, or 990-T.
▶ See separate instructions.

OMB No. 1545-0121 — **2011** — Attachment Sequence No. **19**

Name | **Identifying number** as shown on page 1 of your tax return

Use a separate Form 1116 for each category of income listed below. See **Categories of Income** in the instructions. Check only one box on each Form 1116. Report all amounts in U.S. dollars except where specified in Part II below.

a ☐ Passive category income
b ☐ General category income
c ☐ Section 901(j) income
d ☐ Certain income re-sourced by treaty
e ☐ Lump-sum distributions

f Resident of (name of country) ▶

Note: *If you paid taxes to only one foreign country or U.S. possession, use column A in Part I and line A in Part II. If you paid taxes to* ***more than one*** *foreign country or U.S. possession, use a separate column and line for each country or possession.*

As the form says, you will need to file a separate Form 1116 for each income category. Start by checking the appropriate box. After this, you will need to establish your total foreign taxable income.

5. FORM 1166 PART I – FIGURING OUT YOUR TOTAL FOREIGN TAXABLE INCOME

This section explains how to fill out Part 1 of the Form 1116. It looks like this:

Part I — Taxable Income or Loss From Sources Outside the United States (for Category Checked Above)

		Foreign Country or U.S. Possession			Total
		A	B	C	(Add cols. A, B, and C.)
g	**Enter the name of the foreign country or U.S. possession** ▶				
1a	Gross income from sources within country shown above and of the type checked above (see instructions):				1a
b	Check if line 1a is compensation for personal services as an employee, your total compensation from all sources is $250,000 or more, and you used an alternative basis to determine its source (see instructions) ▶ ☐				
	Deductions and losses (*Caution: See instructions*):				
2	Expenses **definitely related** to the income on line 1a (attach statement)				
3	Pro rata share of other deductions **not definitely related:**				
a	Certain itemized deductions or standard deduction (see instructions)				
b	Other deductions (attach statement)				
c	Add lines 3a and 3b				
d	Gross foreign source income (see instructions)				
e	Gross income from all sources (see instructions)				
f	Divide line 3d by line 3e (see instructions)				
g	Multiply line 3c by line 3f				
4	Pro rata share of interest expense (see instructions):				
a	Home mortgage interest (use worksheet on page 14 of the instructions)				
b	Other interest expense				
5	Losses from foreign sources				
6	Add lines 2, 3g, 4a, 4b, and 5				6
7	Subtract line 6 from line 1a. Enter the result here and on line 15, page 2 ▶				7

a. Establishing your total income – line 1.

On line g, under column A, you should enter "Canada." You can leave the other columns blank unless you have income from other foreign (i.e., non-US) countries.

On line 1a you enter the total income of the particular type that this Form 1116 reports. For instance, if you checked the box for passive income you should enter your total passive income from Canadian sources on line 1a under column A.

Most people can ignore line 1b. However, check the box on line 1b if all of the following criteria apply:

- The income on line 1a is compensation for services you performed as an employee.
- Your total employee compensation from both US and foreign sources was $250,000 or more.
- You used an alternative basis (discussed in Publication 514) to determine the source of the compensation entered on line 1a.

b. Deductions and losses

Once you have figured out your total foreign gross income, you can reduce it based on the amount of US deductions that definitely relate to that foreign income. A deduction is definitely related to a specific class of gross income if it is incurred either:

- as a result of, or coincident to, an activity from which that income is derived; or
- in connection with property from which that income is derived.

For example, employee business deductions are almost always definitely related to foreign income, since the only reason that you have employee business deductions is because you are paid a salary. A complete list will vary depending on your personal situation.

Do not include deductions and losses related to income that you have excluded using the foreign earned income and/or housing exclusion or the deduction for personal exemptions (line 42 of the Form 1040). Let's go through this section line-by-line.

Line 2

Enter your deductions that definitely relate to the gross income from foreign sources shown on line 1a. For example, if you are an employee reporting foreign earned income on line 1a, include on line 2 expenses, such as those incurred to move to a new principal place of work outside the United States or supplies you bought for your job outside the United States.

Do not include any interest expense on line 2. See lines 4a and 4b for special rules for interest expense.

Lines 3a and 3b

Some deductions do not definitely relate to either your foreign-source income or your US-source income. Enter on lines 3a and 3b any deductions (other than interest expense) that:

- are not shown on line 2; and
- are not definitely related to your US source income.

Line 3a. Enter the following itemized deductions (from Schedule A to Form 1040) on line 3a.

- medical expenses (line 4);
- general sales taxes (line 5);
- real estate taxes (line 6).

If you do not itemize deductions, enter your standard deduction on line 3a.

Line 3b. Enter on line 3b any other deductions that do not definitely relate to any specific type of income (for example, the deduction for alimony paid – Form 1040, line 31a).

Line 3d. Enter your gross foreign source income from the category you checked above Part I of this Form 1116. Include any foreign earned income you have excluded on Form 2555 or Form 2555-EZ but do not include any other exempt income.

Line 3e. Enter on line 3e in each column your gross income from all sources and all categories, both US and foreign. Include any foreign earned income you have excluded on Form 2555 or Form 2555-EZ. This means that you should enter your total income from line 37 of your Form 1040 plus the amount of income you excluded on line 21 on that same form.

Line 3f. Divide line 3d by line 3e and round off the result to at least four decimal places (for example, if your result is 0.8756782, round off to 0.8757, not to 0.876 or 0.88). Enter the result, but do not enter more than "1."

Line 4a. If your gross income from foreign sources is over $5,000 and you have deducted home mortgage interest, use the following worksheet to figure out the value of line 4(a).

1.	Enter gross foreign source income of the type shown on Form 1116. **Do not** enter income excluded on Form 2555 or Form 2555-EZ.	**1.**
2.	Enter gross income from all sources. **Do not** enter income excluded on Form 2555 or Form 2555-EZ.	**2.**
3.	Divide line 1 by line 2 and enter the result as a decimal (rounded to at least four places).	**3.**
4.	Enter deductible home mortgage interest (from lines 10 through 13 of Schedule A (Form 1040)).	**4.**
5.	Multiply line 4 by line 3. Enter the result here and on the appropriate Form 1116, line 4a.	**5.**

Line 4b – This line includes investment interest, interest incurred in a trade or business, and passive activity interest. If you deduct these expenses, you need to apportion them amongst your different types of income using the asset method. The asset method is very complicated so you should consult a tax professional if you are using it.

Line 5 – This line is where you enter capital losses from foreign sources. If you have any capital losses from non-US sources, you should consult a professional tax adviser.

Line 6 – This line is the total of the lines above.

6. FORM 1116 PART II – THE AMOUNT OF CANADIAN INCOME TAX PAID

The second part of the Form 1116 requires you to figure out how much Canadian tax you paid on each type of income. Part II looks like this:

Part II Foreign Taxes Paid or Accrued (see instructions)

Country	Credit is claimed for taxes (you must check one) (h) ☐ Paid (i) ☐ Accrued	Foreign taxes paid or accrued								
		In foreign currency				In U.S. dollars				
		Taxes withheld at source on:			(n) Other foreign taxes paid or accrued	Taxes withheld at source on:			(r) Other foreign taxes paid or accrued	(s) Total foreign taxes paid or accrued (add cols. (o) through (r))
	(j) Date paid or accrued	(k) Dividends	(l) Rents and royalties	(m) Interest		(o) Dividends	(p) Rents and royalties	(q) Interest		
A										
B										
C										
8	Add lines A through C, column (s). Enter the total here and on line 9, page 2 . . . . ▶								8	

For Paperwork Reduction Act Notice, see instructions. Cat. No. 11440U Form **1116** (2011)

You should check box H that says that you are claiming the credit for taxes that you have paid rather than taxes you have accrued.

Next, in the row for Country A you have to enter the date that you paid the taxes. Normally it is April 30 of the tax year in question unless the taxes were deducted at source. The challenging part about Part II is figuring out what Canadian taxes you paid on which Canadian income. This may be easy. For example, if you had only salary income and you paid $5,000 in total tax, then all of that tax was paid on the income in the general category.

It may, however, be more complicated if you have multiple types of income. For instance, let's say you have $60,000 in salary income, $15,000 in capital gains income, and $400 in interest income all from Canadian sources. On this income, you paid the Canadian government a total of $10,000 in taxes. Your general category income would be $60,000 and your passive category income would be $15,400. But you may not know what fraction of the $10,000 in tax was paid on the general category income and what was paid on the passive category income.

To solve this problem, the IRS allows you to divide one category's share of income by the share of total taxes you paid. Follow these steps:

1. Figure out what your total income is in each category (i.e., passive or general).
2. For each category, subtract Canadian deductions that are definitely related to that income. A deduction is definitely related if it arises solely as a result of the income earned. A clear example is employment expenses. If you earn a salary, your employment expenses only arose because of that salary. So they are definitely related. This is only one example. It is impossible to provide a full list because everyone's tax situation is different.
3. Most Canadian deductions will not be definitely related to one category. For instance, if you have Canadian medical expenses they aren't related to salary or interest income. That means that you have to allocate them across different categories. To do this, first total all deductions that do not relate to one particular category of income. Then find the net income of each category. Divide the income of one category by your total income and multiply the result by the total deductions (e.g., (total wage income/total income) x total deductions that are not related to one income stream.) Perform this step for all categories.

4. Then for each category calculate what share of your total tax paid belongs to that category. Take the net income from one category and divide it by your total income. Multiply the total by the amount of Canadian tax paid. The result is the amount of Canadian tax that belongs to a particular category.

a. Example of how to fill out Part II.

An example may help.

You paid income taxes of $3,200 to Canada on wages of $80,000 and interest income of $3,000. These were the only items of income on your Canadian return. You also have deductions of $4,400 that are not definitely related to either the wages or interest income. Your total net income is $78,600 ($83,000 – $4,400).

Because the foreign tax is general and not specifically for either item of income, you must allocate the tax between the wages and the interest.

Using the steps above, you should do the following.

1. Figure which amounts fall into the general category and which fall into the passive category. Your total general category income is $80,000 and your total passive category income is $3,000.

2. There are no definitely related expenses. So you can ignore step II.

3. Figure the net income in each category by allocating those expenses that are not definitely related to either category of income. This is done as follows.

   You figure the expenses which are related to wages (general category income) as follows.

$80,000 (wages) / $83,000 (total income)	×	$4,400	=	$4,241
The net wages are $75,759 ($80,000 – $4,241).				

   You figure the expenses allocable to interest (passive category income) as follows.

$3,000 (interest) / $83,000 (total income)	×	$4,400	=	$159
The net interest is $2,841 ($3,000 – $159).				

4. Next you need to figure what share of the tax you paid belongs to each category. To do this, you multiply the total foreign income tax by the following fraction.

$75,759 (net wages) / $78,600 (total net income)	×	$3,200(tax paid)	=	$3,084

You figure the foreign tax on the interest income as follows.

$\frac{\$2,841 \text{ (net interest)}}{\$78,600 \text{ (total net income)}}$	×	\$3,200 (total tax paid)	=	\$116

So the total tax paid that belongs to the general category is \$3,084 and that which belongs to the interest category is \$116. This information is necessary to fill out PartII of the Form 1116.

7. FORM 1116 – PART III

Part III of Form 1116 is where you actually figure the credit. It looks like this:

Form 1116 (2011) Page **2**

Part III Figuring the Credit

Line	Description	Box	Amount	Box	Amount
9	Enter the amount from line 8. These are your total foreign taxes paid or accrued for the category of income checked above Part I	9			
10	Carryback or carryover (attach detailed computation)	10			
11	Add lines 9 and 10	11			
12	Reduction in foreign taxes (see instructions)	12	( )		
13	Taxes reclassified under high tax kickout (see instructions)	13			
14	Combine lines 11, 12, and 13. This is the total amount of foreign taxes available for credit			14	
15	Enter the amount from line 7. This is your taxable income or (loss) from sources outside the United States (before adjustments) for the category of income checked above Part I (see instructions)	15			
16	Adjustments to line 15 (see instructions)	16			
17	Combine the amounts on lines 15 and 16. This is your net foreign source taxable income. (If the result is zero or less, you have no foreign tax credit for the category of income you checked above Part I. Skip lines 18 through 22. However, if you are filing more than one Form 1116, you must complete line 20.)	17			
18	**Individuals:** Enter the amount from Form 1040, line 41, or Form 1040NR, line 39. **Estates and trusts:** Enter your taxable income without the deduction for your exemption	18			
	Caution: *If you figured your tax using the lower rates on qualified dividends or capital gains, see instructions.*				
19	Divide line 17 by line 18. If line 17 is more than line 18, enter "1"			19	
20	**Individuals:** Enter the amount from Form 1040, line 44. If you are a nonresident alien, enter the amount from Form 1040NR, line 42. **Estates and trusts:** Enter the amount from Form 1041, Schedule G, line 1a, or the total of Form 990-T, lines 36 and 37			20	
	Caution: *If you are completing line 20 for separate category* ***e*** *(lump-sum distributions), see instructions.*				
21	Multiply line 20 by line 19 (maximum amount of credit)			21	
22	Enter the **smaller** of line 14 or line 21. If this is the only Form 1116 you are filing, skip lines 23 through 27 and enter this amount on line 28. Otherwise, complete the appropriate line in Part IV (see instructions) ▶			22	

Let's walk through this part of the form line by line.

Line 10 – Enter the unused foreign taxes in the separate category from another tax year that are eligible to be carried forward to or back to the tax year in question. You can carry back one year and then carry forward 10 years any unapplied foreign tax you paid or accrued to any foreign country or US possession (reduced as described under *Line 12,* later) on income in a separate category which exceeds the limitation.

Line 12 – Here is where you reduce your tax payable by the amount of income you excluded using the foreign earned income exclusion. To do so, use the following steps:

a. Take the total amount of income you excluded using the foreign earned income/housing exclusion. Recall that this amount can be found on line 21 of Form 1040.

b. Subtract from it any deductible expenses that you were not able to deduct because they were allocable to that income. For instance, if you claim moving expenses a certain part of the deduction is not allowed because you took the foreign earned income exclusion. Subtract the part that was not allowed here.

c. Take your total foreign earned income. This can be found on line 7 of your Form 1040.

d. Subtract from the amount on step c deductions related to income that you did not exclude. Every time you claim the foreign earned income exclusion there are some deductions that are related to income that are not covered by the exclusion. For instance, to reprise the example of moving expenses: A share of those expenses may not be claimed because they relate to excluded income. However, a share of the expenses relate to non-excluded income. It is this latter share that you subtract here.

e. Finally, divide the amount on line b by the amount on line d.

f. Multiply the result from line f by the foreign taxes you paid on this income.

Line 13 – you can ignore line 13.

Line 16 – you can ignore this line unless you have capital losses. If you do have capital losses and want to claim the foreign tax credit, you should consult a professional tax advisor.

Line 18 – If you have qualified dividends and/or capital gains from a Canadian source and want to rely on the foreign tax credit, you should consult a professional tax advisor. Qualified dividends are discussed in Chapter 8.

Line 20 – you can ignore this line.

The rest of the form is self-explanatory.

8. EXAMPLE OF THE FOREIGN TAX CREDIT[2]

Let's use an example to illustrate how the foreign tax credit works.

a. Setting out Robert's income

Robert Smith, a US citizen, is a salesman who lived and worked in Canada for all of 2011, except for one week he spent in the United States on business. He is single and under 65.

During the year, Robert received income from sources in Canada and the United States.

Income from United States. Robert received wages of $2,400 for services performed during the one week in the United States. He also received dividend income of $3,000 from sources within the United States. None of the dividends are qualified dividends.

Income from Canada. Robert received the following income in Canada during the year and paid tax on the income to Canada over the course of the year through withholdings from his paycheque.

[2] This example is taken from IRS Publication 514. Some of the details have been modified.

In summary, Robert has the following income on which he paid the following taxes. All of the following amounts are in US dollars.

Income	Tax
$130,100 wages	$32,400
$4,000 dividend income	$450
$1,000 interest income	$50

Foreign earned income. Robert is a bona fide resident of Canada. He also meets the physical presence test. He fills out form 2555-EZ (not shown) and excludes $92,900 of the wages he earned in Canada.

Itemized deductions. Robert was entitled to the following itemized deductions.

Interest on home mortgage	$5,900
Real estate tax	1,500
Charitable contribution to a US charity	461
Employee business expenses (See the following discussion for computation.)	734
Total	$8,595

Employee business expenses. Robert paid $3,400 of unreimbursed business expenses, of which $1,000 were definitely related to the wages earned in the United States and $2,400 were definitely related to wages earned in Canada.

Robert must prorate the business expenses related to the wages earned in Canada between the wages he includes on his US tax return and the amount he excludes as foreign earned income. He cannot deduct the part of the expenses related to the income that he excludes. He figures his allowable expenses (related to the wages earned in Canada) as follows:

$$\frac{\$37,200}{\$130,100} \times \$2,400 = \$686$$

His employee business expense deduction is $734. This is the difference between his business expenses of $1,686 ($686 + $1,000 from US business trip) and the 2%-of-adjusted- gross-income limit ($952).

b. Forms 1116

Robert must use two Forms 1116 to figure his allowable foreign tax credit. On one Form 1116, he will mark the block to the left of *General category income,* and figure his foreign tax credit on the wages of $37,200 (Canadian wages minus excluded wages). On the other Form 1116, he will mark the block to the left of *Passive category income,* and figure his foreign tax credit on his interest income of $1,000 and dividend income of $4,000. Robert could also seek professional tax advice to try to re-categorize some of the dividend income as Canadian under the Canada-US Tax Treaty.

Robert's computations are explained for each Form 1116 that must be completed. Both Forms 1116 are illustrated at the end of this chapter.

c. Computation of Taxable Income

Before making any entries on Form 1116, Robert must figure his taxable income on Form 1040.

His taxable income is $35,305 figured as follows:

Gross Income	
Wages (Canada)	$130,100
Less: Foreign earned income exclusion	92,900
	$37,200
Wages (US)	2,400
Interest income (Canada)	1,000
Dividend income (US)	3,000
Dividend income (Canada)	4,000
Total (Adjusted gross income)	$47,600
Less: Total Itemized Deductions	8,595
Taxable income before the personal exemption	$39,005
Less: Personal Exemption	3,700
Taxable Income	$35,305

On each Form 1116, Robert enters $39,005 (his taxable income before the personal exemption) on line 18 of Part III.

d. Part I — Taxable Income or Loss From Sources Outside the United States (for Category Checked Above)

In figuring the limit on both Forms 1116, Robert must separately determine his taxable income from Canada (Form 1116, line 7).

i. Form 1116—General category income.

On this Form 1116, Robert figures his taxable income in Canada for general category income only. He does not include his passive category income of interest and dividends.

Line 1a. Robert enters the foreign wages after exclusion of $37,200 on line 1a.

Line 2. The unreimbursed employee business expenses related to these foreign source wages included in income are $686, as shown earlier. Robert must determine which part of the 2%-of-adjusted-gross-income limit ($952) is allocable to these employee business expenses. He figures this as follows:

$$\frac{\$686}{\$1,686} \times \$952 = \$387$$

The denominator ($1,686) is the total allowable unreimbursed business expenses ($1,000 + $686). The amount of deductible expenses definitely related to $37,200 of taxable foreign wages is $299 ($686 − $387). He enters $299 on line 2. He attaches this explanation to his Form 1116 that he files with his tax return.

Line 3a–g. Robert enters $1,500 on line 3a. This is his real estate tax, which is not definitely related to income from any source. Robert must prorate this itemized deduction by using the ratio of gross income from Canada in general category income (line 3d) to his gross income from all sources (line 3e). For this purpose, gross income from Canada and gross income from all sources include the $92,900 of wages that qualify for the foreign earned income exclusion. He figures the ratable part of deductions, $1,389, as follows and enters it on line 3g.

$\frac{\$130,100}{\$140,500}$	×	$1,500	=	$1,389

Line 4a. Robert apportions his qualified home mortgage interest, $5,900, to general category income as follows:

1.	Enter gross foreign source income of the type shown on Form 1116. Do not enter income excluded on Form 2555.	$37,200
2.	Enter gross income from all sources. Do not enter income excluded on Form 2555.	$47,600
3.	Divide line 1 by line 2 and enter the result as a decimal.	.7815
4.	Enter deductible home mortgage interest (from lines 10 through 13 of Schedule A (Form 1040)).	$5,900
5.	Multiply line 4 by line 3. Enter the result here and on Form 1116, line 4a.	$4,611

Robert enters this amount, $4,611, on line 4a.

Line 6 – Robert adds the amounts on lines 2, 3g, and 4a, and enters that total ($6,299) on line 6.

Line 7 – He subtracts the amount on line 6 from the amount on line 1a to arrive at foreign source taxable income of $30,901 in this category. Robert enters this amount on line 7.

ii. Form 1116 – Passive category income

On this Form 1116, Robert determines his taxable income earned in Canada from passive interest and dividend income.

Line 1a – He adds the $1,000 interest income and the $4,000 dividend income ($5,000) from Canada and enters the total ($5,000) on line 1a. None of the dividends are qualified dividends. If they were qualified dividends, Robert should seek professional tax help.

Line 3a–g. Robert figures the part of his itemized deduction (property tax) allocable to passive category income as follows and enters the amount on line 3g.

$\frac{\$5,000}{\$140,500}$	×	$1,500	=	$53

Line 4a – Robert apportions the qualified home mortgage interest to passive category income as follows:

1.	Enter gross foreign source income of the type shown on Form 1116. Do not enter income excluded on Form 2555.	$5,000
2.	Enter gross income from all sources. Do not enter income excluded on Form 2555.	$47,600
3.	Divide line 1 by line 2 and enter the result as a decimal.	.1050
4.	Enter deductible home mortgage interest (from lines 10 through 13 of Schedule A (Form 1040)).	$5,900
5.	Multiply line 4 by line 3. Enter the result here and on Form 1116, line 4a.	$620

He enters this amount, $620, on line 4a.

Line 6 – Robert adds the amounts on lines 3g and 4a and enters that total ($673) on line 6.

Line 7 – He subtracts the amount on line 6 from the amount on line 1a to arrive at foreign source taxable income of $4,327 in this category. Robert enters this amount on line 7.

e. Part II – Foreign Taxes Paid or Accrued

Robert uses Part II, Form 1116, to report the foreign tax paid or accrued on income from foreign sources.

Form 1116—General category income. On this Form 1116, Robert enters the amount of foreign taxes paid (withheld at source), in foreign currency and in US dollars, on the wages from Canada.

Form 1116—Passive category income. On this Form 1116, Robert enters the amount of foreign taxes paid, in foreign currency and in US dollars, on the interest and dividend income.

f. Part III – Figuring the Credit

Robert figures the amount of foreign tax credit in Part III on each Form 1116.

Form 1116—General category income. On this Form 1116, Robert figures the amount of foreign tax credit allowable for the foreign taxes paid on his wages from Canada.

Line 10 – He has a carryover of $200 for unused foreign taxes paid in 2010 and enters that amount on line 10. He attaches a schedule showing how he figured his $200 carryover to 2011 after carrying back the unused $350 tax paid in 2010 to 2009. The unused foreign tax in 2010 and the excess limit in 2009 are general category income. The unused foreign tax of $200 is carried over to general category income in 2011.

Line 12 – On line 12, Robert must reduce the total foreign taxes paid by the amount related to the wages he excludes as foreign earned income. To do this, he multiplies the $32,400 foreign tax he paid on his foreign wages by a fraction. The numerator of the fraction is his foreign earned income exclusion ($92,900) minus a proportionate part of his definitely related business expenses ($2,400 – $686 = $1,714). The denominator of the fraction is his total foreign wages ($130,100) minus his total definitely related business expenses ($2,400).

$32,400	×	$\frac{\$92,900-\$1,714}{\$130,100-\$2,400}$	=	$23,136

He enters the result, $23,136 on line 12.

Line 14 – His total foreign taxes available for credit are $9,464 ($200 carryover from 2010 + $9,264 paid in 2011 ($32,400 – $23,136)).

Line 20 – Robert calculated his tax using the Foreign Earned Income Tax Worksheet in the Form 1040 instructions.

Line 21 – By completing the rest of Part III, Robert finds that his maximum credit is $7,825.

Line 22 – The foreign tax credit on the general category income is the lesser of the foreign tax available for credit, $9,464, and the maximum credit on line 21, $7,825.

g. Sample Forms 1116

Robert's Forms 1116 look like this.

h. Robert Smith – Form 1116 – general category

Form **1116**

Department of the Treasury
Internal Revenue Service (99)

Foreign Tax Credit

(Individual, Estate, or Trust)

▶ Attach to Form 1040, 1040NR, 1041, or 990-T.

▶ See separate instructions.

OMB No. 1545-0121

2011

Attachment Sequence No. 19

Name: Robert Smith

Identifying number as shown on page 1 of your tax return: 000-00-0000

Use a separate Form 1116 for each category of income listed below. See **Categories of Income** in the instructions. Check only one box on each Form 1116. Report all amounts in U.S. dollars except where specified in Part II below.

a ☐ Passive category income
b ☑ General category income
c ☐ Section 901(j) income
d ☐ Certain income re-sourced by treaty
e ☐ Lump-sum distributions

f Resident of (name of country) ▶ Canada

Note: *If you paid taxes to only one foreign country or U.S. possession, use column A in Part I and line A in Part II. If you paid taxes to* ***more than one*** *foreign country or U.S. possession, use a separate column and line for each country or possession.*

Part I Taxable Income or Loss From Sources Outside the United States (for Category Checked Above)

		Foreign Country or U.S. Possession A	B	C		Total (Add cols. A, B, and C.)
g	**Enter the name of the foreign country or U.S. possession** ▶	Canada				
1a	Gross income from sources within country shown above and of the type checked above (see instructions):	37,200			1a	37,200
b	Check if line 1a is compensation for personal services as an employee, your total compensation from all sources is $250,000 or more, and you used an alternative basis to determine its source (see instructions) ▶ ☐					
	Deductions and losses (*Caution: See instructions*):					
2	Expenses **definitely related** to the income on line 1a (attach statement)	299				
3	Pro rata share of other deductions **not definitely related:**					
a	Certain itemized deductions or standard deduction (see instructions)	1500				
b	Other deductions (attach statement)					
c	Add lines 3a and 3b	1500				
d	Gross foreign source income (see instructions)	130,100				
e	Gross income from all sources (see instructions)	140,500				
f	Divide line 3d by line 3e (see instructions)	.9260				
g	Multiply line 3c by line 3f	1389				
4	Pro rata share of interest expense (see instructions):					
a	Home mortgage interest (use worksheet on page 14 of the instructions)	4611				
b	Other interest expense					
5	Losses from foreign sources					
6	Add lines 2, 3g, 4a, 4b, and 5	6,299			6	6,299
7	Subtract line 6 from line 1a. Enter the result here and on line 15, page 2 ▶				7	30,901

Part II Foreign Taxes Paid or Accrued (see instructions)

Country	Credit is claimed for taxes (you must check one) (h) ☑ Paid (i) ☐ Accrued	Foreign taxes paid or accrued								
		In foreign currency				In U.S. dollars				
		Taxes withheld at source on:			(n) Other foreign taxes paid or accrued	Taxes withheld at source on:			(r) Other foreign taxes paid or accrued	(s) Total foreign taxes paid or accrued (add cols. (o) through (r))
	(j) Date paid or accrued	(k) Dividends	(l) Rents and royalties	(m) Interest		(o) Dividends	(p) Rents and royalties	(q) Interest		
A	12/31/11				32,400				32,400	32,400
B										
C										

8 **Add lines A through C, column (s). Enter the total here and on line 9, page 2** ▶ 8 32,400

For Paperwork Reduction Act Notice, see instructions. Cat. No. 11440U Form **1116** (2011)

Form 1116 (2011) Page **2**

Part III Figuring the Credit

9	Enter the amount from line 8. These are your total foreign taxes paid or accrued for the category of income checked above Part I	9	32,400		
10	Carryback or carryover (attach detailed computation)	10	200		
11	Add lines 9 and 10	11	32,600		
12	Reduction in foreign taxes (see instructions)	12	(23,136)		
13	Taxes reclassified under high tax kickout (see instructions)	13	0		
14	Combine lines 11, 12, and 13. This is the total amount of foreign taxes available for credit			14	9,464
15	Enter the amount from line 7. This is your taxable income or (loss) from sources outside the United States (before adjustments) for the category of income checked above Part I (see instructions)	15	30,901		
16	Adjustments to line 15 (see instructions)	16	0		
17	Combine the amounts on lines 15 and 16. This is your net foreign source taxable income. (If the result is zero or less, you have no foreign tax credit for the category of income you checked above Part I. Skip lines 18 through 22. However, if you are filing more than one Form 1116, you must complete line 20.)	17	30,901		
18	**Individuals:** Enter the amount from Form 1040, line 41, or Form 1040NR, line 39. **Estates and trusts:** Enter your taxable income without the deduction for your exemption	18	39,005		
	Caution: *If you figured your tax using the lower rates on qualified dividends or capital gains, see instructions.*				
19	Divide line 17 by line 18. If line 17 is more than line 18, enter "1"			19	.7922
20	**Individuals:** Enter the amount from Form 1040, line 44. If you are a nonresident alien, enter the amount from Form 1040NR, line 42. **Estates and trusts:** Enter the amount from Form 1041, Schedule G, line 1a, or the total of Form 990-T, lines 36 and 37			20	9,878
	Caution: *If you are completing line 20 for separate category* ***e*** *(lump-sum distributions), see instructions.*				
21	Multiply line 20 by line 19 (maximum amount of credit)			21	7,825
22	Enter the **smaller** of line 14 or line 21. If this is the only Form 1116 you are filing, skip lines 23 through 27 and enter this amount on line 28. Otherwise, complete the appropriate line in Part IV (see instructions) ▶			22	7,825

Part IV Summary of Credits From Separate Parts III (see instructions)

23	Credit for taxes on passive category income	23	500		
24	Credit for taxes on general category income	24	7,825		
25	Credit for taxes on certain income re-sourced by treaty	25			
26	Credit for taxes on lump-sum distributions	26			
27	Add lines 23 through 26			27	8,325
28	Enter the **smaller** of line 20 or line 27			28	8,325
29	Reduction of credit for international boycott operations. See instructions for line 12			29	
30	Subtract line 29 from line 28. This is your **foreign tax credit.** Enter here and on Form 1040, line 47; Form 1040NR, line 45; Form 1041, Schedule G, line 2a; or Form 990-T, line 40a ▶			30	8,325

Form **1116** (2011)

i. Robert Smith- Forms 1116 – passive income

Form **1116**

Department of the Treasury Internal Revenue Service (99)

Foreign Tax Credit

(Individual, Estate, or Trust)

▶ Attach to Form 1040, 1040NR, 1041, or 990-T.

▶ See separate instructions.

OMB No. 1545-0121

2011

Attachment Sequence No. 19

Name: Robert Smith

Identifying number as shown on page 1 of your tax return: 000-00-0000

Use a separate Form 1116 for each category of income listed below. See **Categories of Income** in the instructions. Check only one box on each Form 1116. Report all amounts in U.S. dollars except where specified in Part II below.

a ☑ Passive category income
b ☐ General category income
c ☐ Section 901(j) income
d ☐ Certain income re-sourced by treaty
e ☐ Lump-sum distributions

f Resident of (name of country) ▶ Canada

Note: *If you paid taxes to only one foreign country or U.S. possession, use column A in Part I and line A in Part II. If you paid taxes to* ***more than one*** *foreign country or U.S. possession, use a separate column and line for each country or possession.*

Part I Taxable Income or Loss From Sources Outside the United States (for Category Checked Above)

		A	B	C		Total (Add cols. A, B, and C.)
g	**Enter the name of the foreign country or U.S. possession** ▶	Canada				
1a	Gross income from sources within country shown above and of the type checked above (see instructions): Dividends, Interest	5,000			1a	5000
b	Check if line 1a is compensation for personal services as an employee, your total compensation from all sources is $250,000 or more, and you used an alternative basis to determine its source (see instructions) ▶ ☐					
	Deductions and losses (*Caution: See instructions*):					
2	Expenses **definitely related** to the income on line 1a (attach statement)					
3	Pro rata share of other deductions **not definitely related:**					
a	Certain itemized deductions or standard deduction (see instructions)	1500				
b	Other deductions (attach statement)					
c	Add lines 3a and 3b	1500				
d	Gross foreign source income (see instructions)	5000				
e	Gross income from all sources (see instructions)	140,500				
f	Divide line 3d by line 3e (see instructions)	.0356				
g	Multiply line 3c by line 3f	53				
4	Pro rata share of interest expense (see instructions):					
a	Home mortgage interest (use worksheet on page 14 of the instructions)	620				
b	Other interest expense					
5	Losses from foreign sources					
6	Add lines 2, 3g, 4a, 4b, and 5	673			6	673
7	Subtract line 6 from line 1a. Enter the result here and on line 15, page 2 ▶				7	

Part II Foreign Taxes Paid or Accrued (see instructions)

Credit is claimed for taxes (you must check one): (h) ☑ Paid (i) ☐ Accrued

Country	(j) Date paid or accrued	In foreign currency: Taxes withheld at source on: (k) Dividends	(l) Rents and royalties	(m) Interest	(n) Other foreign taxes paid or accrued	In U.S. dollars: Taxes withheld at source on: (o) Dividends	(p) Rents and royalties	(q) Interest	(r) Other foreign taxes paid or accrued	(s) Total foreign taxes paid or accrued (add cols. (o) through (r))
A	12-31-11	450		50		450		50		
B										
C										

8 **Add lines A through C, column (s). Enter the total here and on line 9, page 2** ▶ 8 500

For Paperwork Reduction Act Notice, see instructions. Cat. No. 11440U Form **1116** (2011)

Form 1116 (2011) Page 2

Part III Figuring the Credit

Line	Description		Amount		Amount
9	Enter the amount from line 8. These are your total foreign taxes paid or accrued for the category of income checked above Part I	9	500		
10	Carryback or carryover (attach detailed computation)	10	0		
11	Add lines 9 and 10	11	500		
12	Reduction in foreign taxes (see instructions)	12	(0)		
13	Taxes reclassified under high tax kickout (see instructions)	13	0		
14	Combine lines 11, 12, and 13. This is the total amount of foreign taxes available for credit			14	500
15	Enter the amount from line 7. This is your taxable income or (loss) from sources outside the United States (before adjustments) for the category of income checked above Part I (see instructions)	15	4327		
16	Adjustments to line 15 (see instructions)	16	0		
17	Combine the amounts on lines 15 and 16. This is your net foreign source taxable income. (If the result is zero or less, you have no foreign tax credit for the category of income you checked above Part I. Skip lines 18 through 22. However, if you are filing more than one Form 1116, you must complete line 20.)	17	4327		
18	**Individuals:** Enter the amount from Form 1040, line 41, or Form 1040NR, line 39. **Estates and trusts:** Enter your taxable income without the deduction for your exemption	18	39,005		
	Caution: *If you figured your tax using the lower rates on qualified dividends or capital gains, see instructions.*				
19	Divide line 17 by line 18. If line 17 is more than line 18, enter "1"			19	.1109
20	**Individuals:** Enter the amount from Form 1040, line 44. If you are a nonresident alien, enter the amount from Form 1040NR, line 42. **Estates and trusts:** Enter the amount from Form 1041, Schedule G, line 1a, or the total of Form 990-T, lines 36 and 37			20	9878
	Caution: *If you are completing line 20 for separate category* **e** *(lump-sum distributions), see instructions.*				
21	Multiply line 20 by line 19 (maximum amount of credit)			21	1,095
22	Enter the **smaller** of line 14 or line 21. If this is the only Form 1116 you are filing, skip lines 23 through 27 and enter this amount on line 28. Otherwise, complete the appropriate line in Part IV (see instructions) ▶			22	500

Part IV Summary of Credits From Separate Parts III (see instructions)

Line	Description		Amount		Amount
23	Credit for taxes on passive category income	23			
24	Credit for taxes on general category income	24			
25	Credit for taxes on certain income re-sourced by treaty	25			
26	Credit for taxes on lump-sum distributions	26			
27	Add lines 23 through 26			27	
28	Enter the **smaller** of line 20 or line 27			28	
29	Reduction of credit for international boycott operations. See instructions for line 12			29	
30	Subtract line 29 from line 28. This is your **foreign tax credit.** Enter here and on Form 1040, line 47; Form 1040NR, line 45; Form 1041, Schedule G, line 2a; or Form 990-T, line 40a ▶			30	

Form **1116** (2011)

Robert put the totals on his other Form 1116. He does not need to do this twice.

Printed on recycled paper

33

THE CHILD AND DEPENDENT CARE EXPENSES CREDIT[1]

This chapter explains the child and dependent care tax credit which allows you to reduce your tax based on expenses you paid to care for a child or a dependent. The term dependent is explained more fully in Chapter 6. You list your dependents on line 6(c) of your Form 1040. Note that the child and dependent care tax credit is non-refundable. It will only reduce your tax to zero and there will be no refund of any unused credit.

This chapter is organized in the following manner:

1. Eligibility for the credit.
2. Eligible expenses.
3. Limits.
4. Amount of the credit.
5. Claiming the credit.
6. Other issues and further information.

1. ELIGIBILITY FOR THE CREDIT

You must meet all of the following seven criteria to claim the credit.

1. The care must be for one or more of the following qualified people:
   a. A child who is your dependent who was younger than 13 when the care was provided.
   b. Your spouse who was not physically or mentally able to care for himself or herself and lived with you for more than half the year.
   c. A person who was not physically or mentally able to care for himself or herself, lived with you for more than half the year, and was your dependent.
2. You or your spouse must have earned income from salary, wages, or professional fees or tips during the year.
3. You must have paid child and dependent care expenses so you (and your spouse if filing jointly) can work or look for work.
4. You must have made payments for child and dependent care to someone you (and your spouse) cannot claim as a dependent. If you are paying your relative, please see Publication 503 for more information.

---

[1] The text for this chapter was taken from Chapter 31 of Publication 17.

5. Your filing status may be single, head of household, or qualifying widow(er) with dependent child. If you are married, you must file a joint return.

6. You must identify the care provider on your tax return.

7. If your employer provides you with an insurance plan that pays for some of your dependent care expenses, you must look at publication 503 to ensure that you can still claim the credit.

These rules are straightforward. If you meet them all, you should continue working through this chapter.

2. ELIGIBLE EXPENSES

You have to start by figuring out what expenses are eligible for the credit. The credit is a percentage of your work-related expenses for child or dependent care expenses. Eligible expenses are those incurred to provide care for a dependent person. You do not have to choose the least expensive way of providing care. The cost of a paid care provider may be an expense for the care of a qualifying person even if another care provider is available at no cost. Expenses are for the care of a qualifying person only if their main purpose is the person's well-being and protection. Expenses for household services qualify if part of the services is for the care of qualifying persons.

Two examples clarify this. The cost of a babysitter while you and your spouse go out to eat is not normally a work-related expense.

3. LIMITS ON EXPENSES

Your expenses are subject to the earned income limit and the dollar limit. The percentage is based on your adjusted gross income. Only include work-related expenses that you paid in the tax year for which you are filing.

a. Earned income limit

The amount of work-related expenses you use to figure your credit cannot be more than:

1. If you are single at the end of the year your earned income for the year; or

2. If you are married at the end of the year the smaller of your and your spouse's earned income for the year.

Earned income includes wages, salaries, tips, other taxable employee compensation, and net earnings from self-employment. It is normally found on line 7 of your Form 1040.

b. Dollar limit

There is a dollar limit on the amount of the work-related expenses you can use to figure the credit. This limit is $3,000 for one qualifying person, or $6,000 for two or more qualifying persons. The dollar limit is a yearly limit. The amount of the dollar limit remains the same no matter how long, during the year, you have eligible expenses.

4. AMOUNT OF THE CREDIT

To determine the amount of your credit, multiply your work-related expenses (after applying the earned income and dollar limits) by a percentage. This percentage depends on your adjusted gross income shown on Form 1040, line 38. The following table shows the percentage to use based on adjusted gross income.

IF your adjusted gross income is:		THEN the percentage is:
Over	But not over	
$0	$15,000	35%
15,000	17,000	34%
17,000	19,000	33%
19,000	21,000	32%
21,000	23,000	31%
23,000	25,000	30%
25,000	27,000	29%
27,000	29,000	28%
29,000	31,000	27%
31,000	33,000	26%
33,000	35,000	25%
35,000	37,000	24%
37,000	39,000	23%
39,000	41,000	22%
41,000	43,000	21%
43,000	No limit	20%

5. HOW TO CLAIM THE CREDIT

To claim the credit, you must fill out Form 2441 and attach it to your Form 1040. As usual, we first explain the different lines of the form before using an example to illustrate how to fill it out.

Line 1

Complete columns (a) through (d) for each person or organization that provided the care. If you do not give correct or complete information, your credit may be disallowed unless you can show you used due diligence in trying to get the required information.

Columns (a) and (b)

Enter the care provider's name and address.

Column (c)

US citizens in Canada should enter "LAFCP" (Living Abroad Foreign Care Provider) in the space for the care provider's taxpayer identification number.

Column (d)

Enter the total amount you actually paid in 2011 to the care provider.

Line 2

Complete columns (a) through (c) for each qualifying person. If you have more than two qualifying persons, attach a statement to your return with the required information. Be sure to put your name and Social Security Number (SSN) on the statement.

Line 4

If filing jointly, figure your and your spouse's earned income separately. Enter your earned income on line 4 and your spouse's earned income on line 5. Earned income includes the amount shown on line 7 of Form 1040.

Line 5 – Spouse who was a student or disabled

Your spouse was a full-time student if he or she was enrolled as a full-time student at a school during any five months of 2011. Your spouse was disabled if he or she was not physically or mentally capable of self-care. Figure your spouse's earned income on a monthly basis.

For each month or part of a month your spouse was a student or was disabled, he or she is deemed to have worked and earned income. His or her earned income for each month is considered to be at least $250 ($500 if more than one qualifying person was cared for in 2011). If your spouse also worked during that month, use the higher of $250 (or $500) or his or her actual earned income for that month. If, in the same month, both you and your spouse were either students or disabled, only one of you can be treated as having earned income in that month.

For any month that your spouse was not a student or disabled, use your spouse's actual earned income if he or she worked during the month.

Line 9 – Credit for Prior Year's Expenses

If you had qualified expenses for 2011 that you did not pay until 2012, you may be able to increase the amount of credit you can claim in 2012. To figure the credit, see the worksheet under *Amount of Credit* in Publication 503.

Line 10 – Credit Limit

Complete this worksheet to figure the amount to enter on line 10.

1.	Enter the amount from Form 1040, line 46;	1.
2.	Enter the amount from Form 1040, line 47;	2.
3.	Subtract line 2 from line 1. Also enter this amount on Form 2441, line 10. But if zero or less, Stop; you cannot take the credit.	3.

Here is an example: Joan Thomas is divorced and has a child who is nine. She works at ACME Computers. Her adjusted gross income (AGI) is $29,000 USD (after she converts it from Canadian dollars), and the entire amount is earned income. A neighbour cares for Joan's child (Seth) after school, on holidays, and during the summer. Joan pays her neighbour $2,400 for this care. Joan fills out her Form 2441 as follows.

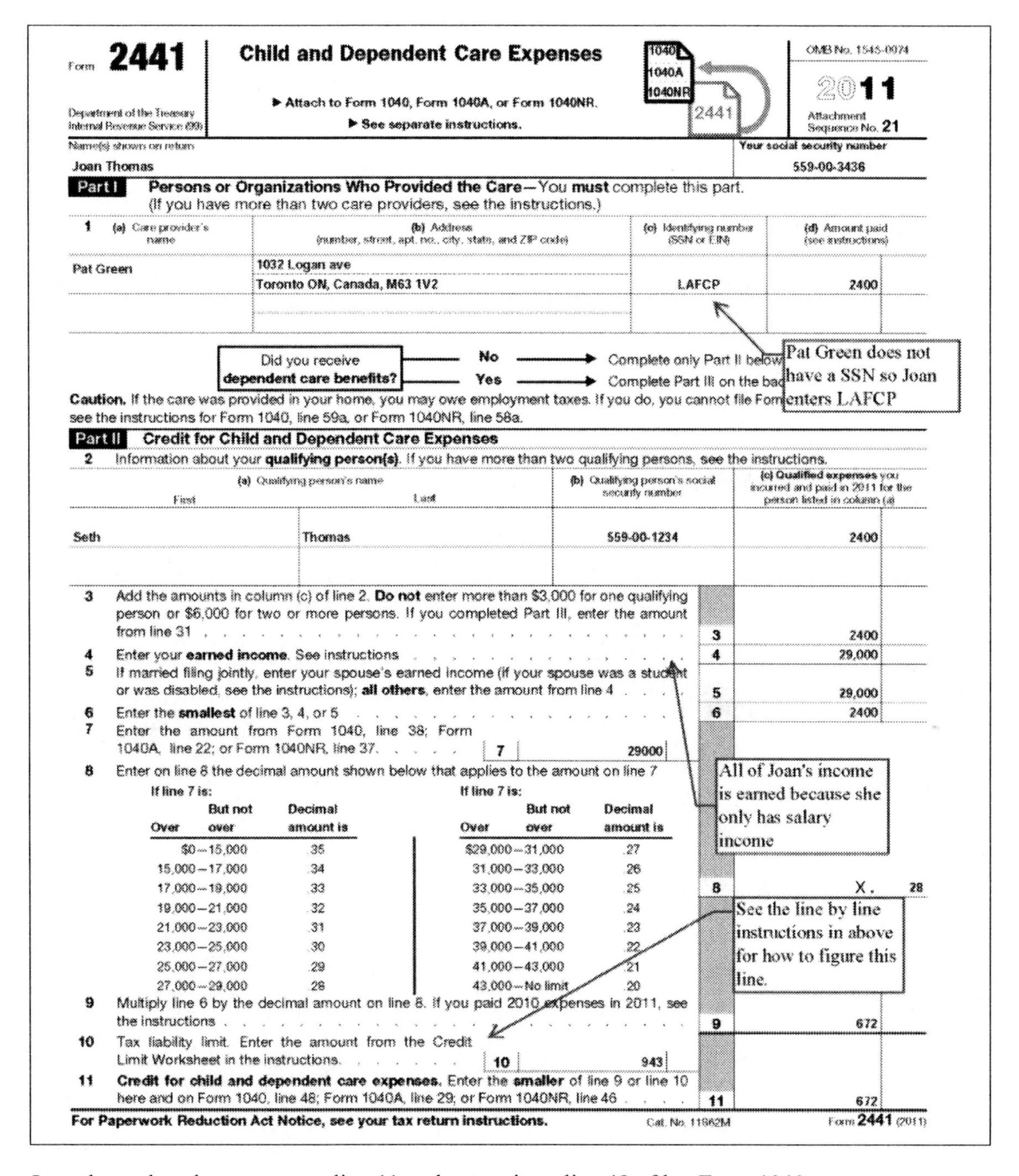

Form **2441** — **Child and Dependent Care Expenses**

Department of the Treasury Internal Revenue Service (99)

▶ Attach to Form 1040, Form 1040A, or Form 1040NR.
▶ See separate instructions.

OMB No. 1545-0074 — 2011 — Attachment Sequence No. 21

Name(s) shown on return: Joan Thomas — Your social security number: 559-00-3436

Part I **Persons or Organizations Who Provided the Care**—You **must** complete this part. (If you have more than two care providers, see the instructions.)

1 (a) Care provider's name	(b) Address (number, street, apt. no., city, state, and ZIP code)	(c) Identifying number (SSN or EIN)	(d) Amount paid (see instructions)
Pat Green	1032 Logan ave Toronto ON, Canada, M63 1V2	LAFCP	2400

Did you receive **dependent care benefits?** No ▶ Complete only Part II below. Yes ▶ Complete Part III on the back

Caution. If the care was provided in your home, you may owe employment taxes. If you do, you cannot file Form ... see the instructions for Form 1040, line 59a, or Form 1040NR, line 58a.

Part II **Credit for Child and Dependent Care Expenses**

2 Information about your **qualifying person(s)**. If you have more than two qualifying persons, see the instructions.

(a) Qualifying person's name — First	Last	(b) Qualifying person's social security number	(c) **Qualified expenses** you incurred and paid in 2011 for the person listed in column (a)
Seth	Thomas	559-00-1234	2400

3 Add the amounts in column (c) of line 2. **Do not** enter more than $3,000 for one qualifying person or $6,000 for two or more persons. If you completed Part III, enter the amount from line 31 . . . . **3** 2400

4 Enter your **earned income**. See instructions **4** 29,000

5 If married filing jointly, enter your spouse's earned income (if your spouse was a student or was disabled, see the instructions); **all others**, enter the amount from line 4 . . . **5** 29,000

6 Enter the **smallest** of line 3, 4, or 5 . . . . **6** 2400

7 Enter the amount from Form 1040, line 38; Form 1040A, line 22; or Form 1040NR, line 37. . . . . **7** 29000

8 Enter on line 8 the decimal amount shown below that applies to the amount on line 7

If line 7 is: Over	But not over	Decimal amount is	If line 7 is: Over	But not over	Decimal amount is
$0	15,000	.35	$29,000	31,000	.27
15,000	17,000	.34	31,000	33,000	.26
17,000	19,000	.33	33,000	35,000	.25
19,000	21,000	.32	35,000	37,000	.24
21,000	23,000	.31	37,000	39,000	.23
23,000	25,000	.30	39,000	41,000	.22
25,000	27,000	.29	41,000	43,000	.21
27,000	29,000	.28	43,000	No limit	.20

8 X. 28

9 Multiply line 6 by the decimal amount on line 8. If you paid 2010 expenses in 2011, see the instructions **9** 672

10 Tax liability limit. Enter the amount from the Credit Limit Worksheet in the instructions. **10** 943

11 **Credit for child and dependent care expenses.** Enter the **smaller** of line 9 or line 10 here and on Form 1040, line 48; Form 1040A, line 29; or Form 1040NR, line 46 . . . **11** 672

For Paperwork Reduction Act Notice, see your tax return instructions. Cat. No. 11862M Form **2441** (2011)

Joan then takes the amount on line 11 and enters it on line 48 of her Form 1040.

6. OTHER ISSUES AND INFORMATION

If your employer gives you a subsidy for your child or elder care expense or provides child or elder care directly, please consult publication 503. This publication and the instructions to form 2441 provide more information on this topic.

34

CHILD TAX CREDIT – LINE 51[1]

The child tax credit allows you to reduce your taxes by as much as $1,000 for each of your qualifying children. If you cannot fully benefit from the child tax credit, you may be able to take the additional tax credit which is explained here as well. Like the child and dependent care tax credit, the child tax credit is non-refundable. That means that it cannot reduce your tax below zero. This chapter explains the following:

1. Who is a qualifying child.
2. The amount of the credit.

1. WHO IS A QUALIFYING CHILD

A qualifying child for purposes of the child tax credit is a child who

- is your son, daughter, stepchild, foster child, brother, sister, stepbrother, stepsister, or a descendant of any of them (for example, your grandchild, niece, or nephew);
- was under the age of 17 at the end the tax year for which you are filing;
- did not provide over half of his or her own support at the end the tax year for which you are filing;
- lived with you for more than half of the year for which you are filing;
- is claimed as a dependent on your return;
- does not file a joint return for the year (or files it only as a claim for refund); and
- was a US citizen, a US national, or a resident of the United States unless you adopted the child in which case his or her nationality does not matter.

For each qualifying child you must check the box on Form 1040 or Form 1040A, line 6c, column (4).

The following example illustrates these rules in action. Your son turned 17 on December 30, 2011. He is a citizen of the United States and you claimed him as a dependent on your return. He does not qualify for the child tax credit because he was not under age 17 at the end of 2011. You would therefore not click the box on column 4, line 6(c) of the Form 1040.

a. Children of divorced or separated parents who live apart

Usually, children of divorced or separated parents are treated for tax purposes as the child of the parent who has custody. If the parent who has custody signs a written statement saying that he or she will not claim the child as a dependent, it may be different. More details on this can be found in IRS Publication 972.

[1] The text of this chapter was taken from chapter 33 of Publication 17 which is available on the IRS website.

2. AMOUNT OF THE CREDIT

The maximum amount you can claim for the credit is $1,000 for each qualifying child. However, you cannot claim if you owe no tax (i.e., the amount on line 46 of your Form 1040 is zero).

a. Child tax credit and the foreign earned income exclusion

If you take the foreign earned income exclusion, you need to use the following worksheet to see if you can claim the credit and figure the amount of the credit.

Child Tax Credit Worksheet *Keep for Your Records*

Before you begin: √ Figure the amount of any credits you are claiming on Form 5695, Part I; Form 8834, Part I; Form 8910; Form 8936; or Schedule R.

CAUTION
- *To be a qualifying child for the child tax credit, the child must be* **under age 17** *at the end of 2011 and meet the other requirements listed earlier, under* Qualifying Child.
- *If you do not have a qualifying child, you cannot claim the child tax credit.*

Part 1

1. Number of qualifying children: ________ × $1,000. Enter the result. **1** ______

2. Enter the amount from Form 1040, line 38; Form 1040A, line 22; or Form 1040NR, line 37. **2** ______

3. **1040 Filers.** Enter the total of any—
   - Exclusion of income from Puerto Rico, and
   - Amounts from Form 2555, lines 45 and 50; Form 2555-EZ, line 18; and Form 4563, line 15.

   1040A and 1040NR Filers. Enter -0-. **3** ______

4. Add lines 2 and 3. Enter the total. **4** ______

5. Enter the amount shown below for your filing status.
   - Married filing jointly - $110,000
   - Single, head of household, or qualifying widow(er) - $75,000
   - Married filing separately - $55,000

   5 ______

6. Is the amount on line 4 more than the amount on line 5?

   ☐ **No.** Leave line 6 blank. Enter -0- on line 7.

   ☐ **Yes.** Subtract line 5 from line 4. **6** ______
   If the result is not a multiple of $1,000, increase it to the next multiple of $1,000. For example, increase $425 to $1,000, increase $1,025 to $2,000, etc.

7. Multiply the amount on line 6 by 5% (.05). Enter the result. **7** ______

8. Is the amount on line 1 more than the amount on line 7?

   ☐ **No.** STOP
   You cannot take the child tax credit on Form 1040, line 51; Form 1040A, line 33; or Form 1040NR, line 48. You also cannot take the additional child tax credit on Form 1040, line 65; Form 1040A, line 39; or Form 1040NR, line 63. Complete the rest of your Form 1040, Form 1040A, or Form 1040NR.

   ☐ **Yes.** Subtract line 7 from line 1. Enter the result. **8** ______
   Go to Part 2 on the next page.

Page 4 **Publication 972 (2011)**

Child Tax Credit Worksheet-*Continued* *Keep for Your Records*

Part 2

9. Enter the amount from Form 1040, line 46; Form 1040A, line 28; or Form 1040NR, line 44. [9]

10. Add the following amounts from:

Form 1040	or Form 1040A	or Form 1040NR	
Line 47	....	Line 45	+
Line 48	Line 29	Line 46	+
Line 49	Line 31	....	+
Line 50	Line 32	Line 47	+

Use only the Form 1040

Form 5695, line 14 . . . . +
Form 8834, line 23 . . . . +
Form 8910, line 22 . . . . +
Form 8936, line 15 . . . . +
Schedule R, line 22 . . . . +

You can ignore this part of the worksheet

Enter the total. [10]

11. Are you claiming any of the following credits?

- Mortgage interest credit, Form 8396.
- Residential energy efficient property credit, Form 5695, Part II.
- District of Columbia first-time homebuyer credit, Form 8859.

Unless you take the mortgage interest credit, ignore this part.

☐ **No.** Enter the amount from line 10.

☐ **Yes.** Complete the Line 11 Worksheet, later, to figure the amount to enter here. [11]

The line 11 worksheet is found in Publication 972

12. Subtract line 11 from line 9. Enter the result. [12]

13. Is the amount on line 8 of this worksheet more than the amount on line 12?

☐ **No.** Enter the amount from line 8.

☐ **Yes.** Enter the amount from line 12. See the **TIP** below.

This is your child tax credit. [13]

Enter this amount on Form 1040, line 51; Form 1040A, line 33; or Form 1040NR, line 48.

1040 1040A 1040NR

TIP You may be able to take the **additional child tax credit** on Form 1040, line 65; Form 1040A, line 39; **or** Form 1040NR, line 63, only if you answered "Yes" on line 13.

- First, complete your Form 1040 through line 64a (also complete line 69), Form 1040A through line 38a, or Form 1040NR through line 62 (also complete line 65).
- Then, use Form 8812 to figure any additional child tax credit.

Publication 972 (2011) **Page 5**

The above worksheet is quite long but mostly straightforward. The annotations on it show what lines you ignore. Once you have calculated the amount, enter it on line 51 of the Form 1040.

35

TAX CREDIT FOR THOSE WHO ARE ELDERLY OR DISABLED – LINE 51[1]

This chapter explains the tax credit for the elderly or the disabled. The credit can be used to reduce the amount of tax you owe. However, it is non-refundable—meaning that it cannot reduce your tax below zero. To claim it you must be 65 or older at the end of the tax year for which you are filing or under 65 and disabled, have taxable disability income, and not of mandatory retirement age. This chapter is organized as follows:

1. Qualifying for the credit.
2. Limits on the credit.
3. Claiming the credit.
4. Other issues and further information.

1. QUALIFYING FOR THE CREDIT

You qualify for this credit if you are a US citizen or resident alien, and either of the following applies.

- You were age 65 or older at the end of the tax year for which you are filing.
- You were under age 65 at the end of the tax year in question and all three of the following statements are true:
  - You retired on disability benefits. You must get a note from your doctor to this effect.
  - You received a payment under your employer's accident or health plan that is included in your income as wages.
  - On January 1 of the tax year in question, you had not reached the mandatory retirement age set by your employer.

If you are married, you and your spouse must file a joint return to claim the credit. The following chart summarizes these rules.

[1] Much of the text of this chapter is taken from IRS Publication 524

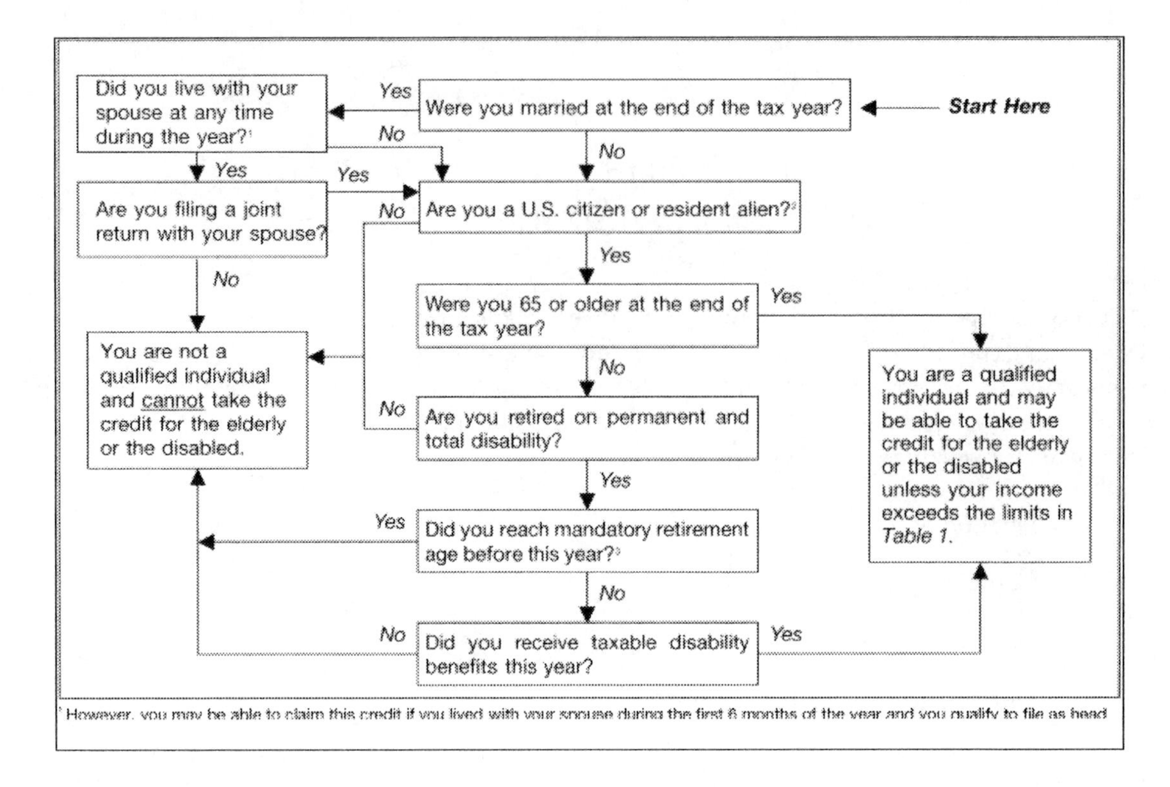

2. LIMITS ON THE CREDIT

As with most tax credits, there are maximum income limits that you cannot exceed. The following chart sets out these limits.

If your filing status is	And your adjusted gross income (line 38 of your Form 1040) is equal to or more than…	OR the total of your nontaxable pension, social security, or disability income is equal to or more than…
Single, head of household or qualifying widower with dependent child	$17,500	$5,000
Married filing jointly and only one spouse qualifies	$20,000	$5,000
Married filing jointly and both spouses qualify	$25,000	$3,750
Married filing separately and you lived apart from your spouse for all of 2011.	$12,500	$3,750

3. CLAIMING THE CREDIT

To claim the credit you have to file Schedule R. A blank copy of the form is available in Appendix 1. In Part 1, simply check the box that reflects your situation.

For Part 2, you will need to attach a physician's statement and check the box on line 2.

Part 3 is slightly more complicated. Most of the lines are explained on the form. There are three worth discussing in more detail.

Line 11

If you checked box 2, 4, 5, 6, or 9 in Part I, use the following chart to complete line 11.

IF you checked . . .	**THEN enter on line 11 . . .**
Box 6	The total of $5,000 plus the disability income you reported on Form 1040A or 1040 for the spouse who was under age 65.
Box 2, 4, or 9	The total amount of disability income you reported on Form 1040A or 1040.
Box 5	The total amount of disability income you reported on Form 1040A or 1040 for both you and your spouse.

Example 1. Bill, aged 63, retired disability benefits in 2011. He received $4,000 of taxable disability income that he reports on Form 1040, line 7. He is filing jointly with his wife who was 67 in 2011, and he checked box 6 in Part I. On line 11, Bill enters $9,000 ($5,000 plus the $4,000 of disability income he reports on Form 1040, line 7).

Example 2. John checked box 2 in Part I and enters $5,000 on line 10. He received $3,000 of taxable disability income, which he enters on line 11. John also enters $3,000 on line 12 (the smaller of line 10 or line 11). The largest amount he can use to figure the credit is $3,000.

Line 13

Line 13a. Enter all Social Security benefits you (and your spouse if filing jointly) received for the tax year in question.

Line 13b. Note that even though Canada Pension Plan and Old Age Security are exempt from US tax they do not count toward the non-taxable pension income category. Do not enter those amounts on this line. Only the following types of pension income fall into that category:

- Non-taxable Social Security payments.
- Non-taxable railroad retirement pension payments treated as Social Security.
- Any other US pension income that is excluded from US tax by federal law that is not the Internal Revenue Code. This category does not apply to most Canadian pension income. Nor does it apply to Canadian Old Age Security and Canada Pension Plan benefits.

Line 21 – Credit Limit Worksheet

You should fill out line 21 according to the following chart.

1.	Enter the amount from Form 1040, line 46.	1.
2.	Enter the amount from Form 1040, lines 47 and 48.	2.
3.	Subtract line 2 from line 1. Enter this amount on Schedule R (Form 1040), line 21. But if zero or less, **STOP**, you cannot take this credit.	3.

Let's use an example to show how this is done. Harriet Yap and her husband Bob are both US citizens living in Canada. Their adjusted gross income from line 38 of their Form 1040 is $20,000. Since this is less than $25,000, they can take the credit. On this income they owe $2,154 in tax so that is the amount they enter on line 46 of their Form 1040. They have taken the foreign tax credit in the amount of $300. So they list that amount on line 47 of their Form 1040. Then they need to fill out Schedule R. They are both 66 and want to claim the credit for the elderly or disabled. They check box 3 because they are married filing jointly. They leave part two of the Schedule R blank because they do not need to file a physician's statement and can ignore line 11. Similarly, as they do not receive Social Security benefits or other non-taxable pension income, they can leave line 13(a) blank.

Before filling out Schedule R, they need to use the chart for line 21 to see if they can take the credit.

1.	Enter the amount from Form 1040, line 46.	1. 2,154
2.	Enter the amount from Form 1040, lines 47 and 48.	2. 300
3.	Subtract line 2 from line 1. Enter this amount on Schedule R (Form 1040), line 21. But if zero or less, **STOP**, you cannot take this credit.	3. 1,854

They then enter $1,854 on line 21. Their completed Schedule R looks like this.

Schedule R (Form 1040A or 1040)
Department of the Treasury
Internal Revenue Service (99)

Credit for the Elderly or the Disabled

Complete and attach to Form 1040A or 1040.

OMB No. 1545-0074
2011
Attachment Sequence No. 16

Name(s) shown on Form 1040A or 1040: Harriet & Bob Yap
Your social security number: 555-00-1234

You may be able to take this credit and reduce your tax if by the end of 2011:
- You were age 65 or older **or** • You were under age 65, you retired on **permanent and total** disability, and you received taxable disability income.

But you must also meet other tests. See instructions.

TIP In most cases, the IRS can figure the credit for you. See instructions.

Part I Check the Box for Your Filing Status and Age

If your filing status is:	And by the end of 2011:	Check only one box:
Single, Head of household, or Qualifying widow(er)	1 You were 65 or older	1 ☐
	2 You were under 65 and you retired on permanent and total disability	2 ☐
Married filing jointly	3 Both spouses were 65 or older	3 ☑
	4 Both spouses were under 65, but only one spouse retired on permanent and total disability	4 ☐
	5 Both spouses were under 65, and both retired on permanent and total disability	5 ☐
	6 One spouse was 65 or older, and the other spouse was under 65 and retired on permanent and total disability	6 ☐
	7 One spouse was 65 or older, and the other spouse was under 65 and **not** retired on permanent and total disability	7 ☐
Married filing separately	8 You were 65 or older and you lived apart from your spouse for all of 2011	8 ☐
	9 You were under 65, you retired on permanent and total disability, and you lived apart from your spouse for all of 2011	9 ☐

Did you check box 1, 3, 7, or 8?
Yes ▶ Skip Part II and complete Part III on the back.
No ▶ Complete Parts II and III.

Part II Statement of Permanent and Total Disability (Complete **only** if you checked box 2, 4, 5, 6, or 9 above.)

If: 1 You filed a physician's statement for this disability for 1983 or an earlier year, or you filed or got a statement for tax years after 1983 and your physician signed line B on the statement, **and**

2 Due to your continued disabled condition, you were unable to engage in any substantial gainful activity in 2011, check this box ▶ ☐

- If you checked this box, you do not have to get another statement for 2011.
- If you **did not** check this box, have your physician complete the statement in the instructions. You **must** keep the statement for your records.

For Paperwork Reduction Act Notice, see your tax return instructions. Cat. No. 11359K **Schedule R (Form 1040A or 1040) 2011**

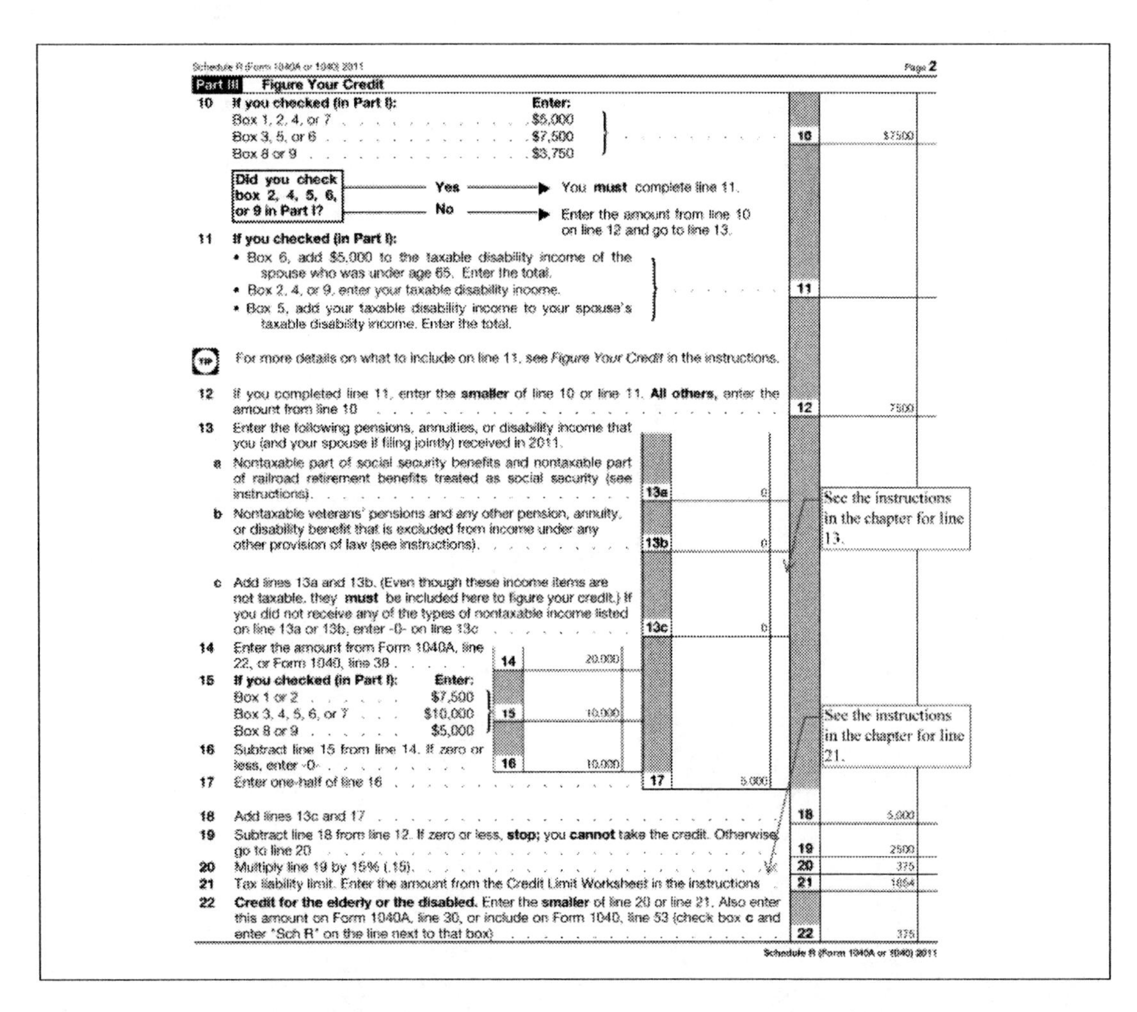

Schedule R (Form 1040A or 1040) 2011 Page 2

Part III Figure Your Credit

10 **If you checked (in Part I):** **Enter:**
Box 1, 2, 4, or 7 . . . . $5,000
Box 3, 5, or 6 . . . . $7,500
Box 8 or 9 . . . . $3,750
} **10** $7500

Did you check box 2, 4, 5, 6, or 9 in Part I?
Yes ▶ You **must** complete line 11.
No ▶ Enter the amount from line 10 on line 12 and go to line 13.

11 **If you checked (in Part I):**
- Box 6, add $5,000 to the taxable disability income of the spouse who was under age 65. Enter the total.
- Box 2, 4, or 9, enter your taxable disability income.
- Box 5, add your taxable disability income to your spouse's taxable disability income. Enter the total.

} **11**

TIP For more details on what to include on line 11, see *Figure Your Credit* in the instructions.

12 If you completed line 11, enter the **smaller** of line 10 or line 11. **All others,** enter the amount from line 10 . . . . **12** 7500

13 Enter the following pensions, annuities, or disability income that you (and your spouse if filing jointly) received in 2011.

a Nontaxable part of social security benefits and nontaxable part of railroad retirement benefits treated as social security (see instructions). **13a** 0

b Nontaxable veterans' pensions and any other pension, annuity, or disability benefit that is excluded from income under any other provision of law (see instructions). **13b** 0

See the instructions in the chapter for line 13.

c Add lines 13a and 13b. (Even though these income items are not taxable, they **must** be included here to figure your credit.) If you did not receive any of the types of nontaxable income listed on line 13a or 13b, enter -0- on line 13c **13c** 0

14 Enter the amount from Form 1040A, line 22, or Form 1040, line 38 . . . . . . **14** 20,000

15 **If you checked (in Part I):** **Enter:**
Box 1 or 2 . . . . $7,500
Box 3, 4, 5, 6, or 7 . . . . $10,000
Box 8 or 9 . . . . $5,000
} **15** 10,000

16 Subtract line 15 from line 14. If zero or less, enter -0- **16** 10,000

17 Enter one-half of line 16 . . . . **17** 5,000

See the instructions in the chapter for line 21.

18 Add lines 13c and 17 . . . . **18** 5,000

19 Subtract line 18 from line 12. If zero or less, **stop;** you **cannot** take the credit. Otherwise, go to line 20 . . . . **19** 2500

20 Multiply line 19 by 15% (.15). **20** 375

21 Tax liability limit. Enter the amount from the Credit Limit Worksheet in the instructions . **21** 1854

22 **Credit for the elderly or the disabled.** Enter the **smaller** of line 20 or line 21. Also enter this amount on Form 1040A, line 30, or include on Form 1040, line 53 (check box **c** and enter "Sch R" on the line next to that box) **22** 375

Schedule R (Form 1040A or 1040) 2011

Then they would enter $375 on line 53 of their Form 1040. They would check box c and enter Schedule R on the line next to that box.

4. OTHER ISSUES AND FURTHER INFORMATION

If you have questions which are not addressed in this chapter, please consult IRS Publication 524 which is available on the IRS website.

36

EDUCATION TAX CREDITS[1]

This chapter outlines tax credits which you can claim if you have post-secondary education expenses. There are two credits available: the American Opportunity Credit and the Lifetime Learning Credit. You have to choose between them for each particular student's expenses. Taking either of them may impact your chance to take the tuition fees deduction that is explained in Chapter 18. You will have to decide if either the credit or the deduction is more advantageous.

This chapter is organized as follows:

1. Overview of the two credits.
2. Ineligibility to claim an education credit.
3. The American Opportunity Credit.
4. The Lifetime Learning Credit.
5. Other issues and further information.

1. OVERVIEW OF THE TWO CREDITS

Since you have to choose between the two competing credits, it makes sense to start with an overview of each. Generally, the American Opportunity Credit is more generous. So if you can take it, you should. The following chart outlines the various criteria for the two credits.

Caution. You can claim both the American Opportunity Credit and the Lifetime Learning Credit on the same return—but not for the same student.

	American Opportunity Credit	**Lifetime Learning Credit**
Maximum credit	Up to $2,500 credit per **eligible student**	Up to $2,000 credit per **return**
Limit on modified adjusted gross income (MAGI)	$180,000 if married filing jointly; $90,000 if single, head of household, or qualifying widow(er).	$122,000 if married filing jointly; $61,000 if single, head of household, or qualifying widow(er).
Refundable or non-refundable	40% of credit may be refundable	Credit limited to the amount of tax you must pay on your taxable income
Number of years of postsecondary education	Available **ONLY** for the first **4** years of postsecondary education	Available for all years of postsecondary education and for courses to acquire or improve job skills
Number of tax years credit available	Available **ONLY** for **4** tax years per eligible student	Available for an unlimited number of years

[1] Much of the content of this chapter is taken from IRS Publication 970 which is available on the IRS website.

Type of degree required	Student must be pursuing a degree or other recognized education credential	Student does not need to be pursuing a degree or other recognized education credential
Number of courses	Student must be enrolled at least half time for at least one academic period beginning during the tax year.	Available for one or more courses
Felony drug conviction	No felony drug convictions as of the end of the tax year	Felony drug convictions are permitted
Qualified expenses	Tuition, fees, and course materials required for enrollment. Course-related books, supplies, and equipment **do not** need to be purchased from the institution in order to qualify.	Tuition and fees required for enrollment or attendance (including amounts required to be paid to the institution for course-related books, supplies, and equipment).
Payments for academic periods	Payments made in 2012 for academic periods beginning in 2012 and in the first 3 months of 2013	

Don't worry if you do not understand all of the details on this chart at this point. It is presented as a simple overview of the two credits. Now, we turn to discussing the credits themselves in more detail.

2. INELIGIBILITY TO CLAIM AN EDUCATION CREDIT

You cannot take an education credit if any of the following apply.

- You are claimed as a dependent on another person's tax return, such as your parent's return.
- Your filing status is married filing separately.
- Your modified adjusted gross income is one of the following:
    a. American Opportunity Credit: $180,000 or more if married filing jointly, or $90,000 or more if single, head of household, or qualifying widow(er).
    b. Lifetime Learning Credit: $122,000 or more if married filing jointly, or $61,000 or more if single, head of household, or qualifying widow(er).
- You took the tuition and fees deduction for the same student.

Your modified adjusted gross income is your adjusted gross income (line 38 from Form 1040) plus any income that you excluded using the foreign earned income exclusion.

Having established a general overview of the rules that apply to the two credits, let's discuss each one in turn. As long as the foregoing does not bar you from taking the credit, you should not have a problem claiming either one. Let's now examine the details of both credits.

3. THE AMERICAN OPPORTUNITY CREDIT

For the tax year, you may be able to claim an American Opportunity Credit of up to $2,500 for qualified education expenses paid for each eligible student. A tax credit reduces the amount of income tax you may have to pay. Unlike a deduction, which reduces the amount of income subject to tax, a credit directly reduces the tax itself. Forty percent of the American Opportunity Credit may be refundable. This means that if the refundable portion of your credit is more than your tax, the excess will be refunded to you. Your allowable American Opportunity Credit may be limited by the amount of your income. Also, the non-refundable part of the credit may be limited by the amount of your tax.

a. Who can claim the credit

Generally, you can claim the American Opportunity Credit as long as you pay qualified education expenses to an eligible educational institution for an eligible student who is either yourself, your spouse, or a dependent for whom you claim an exemption on your tax return.

Let's discuss what we mean by qualified education expenses, eligible educational institution, and eligible student.

i. Qualified education expenses

For purposes of the American Opportunity Credit, qualified education expenses are tuition and certain related expenses required for enrollment or attendance at an eligible educational institution. Student-activity fees are included in qualified education expenses only if the fees must be paid to the institution as a condition of enrollment or attendance. However, expenses for books, supplies, and equipment needed for a course of study are included in qualified education expenses whether or not the materials are purchased from the educational institution.

Qualified education expenses do not include:

- insurance;
- medical expenses (including student health fees);
- room and board;
- transportation;
- similar personal, living, or family expenses.

This is true even if the amount must be paid to the institution as a condition of enrollment or attendance.

ii. Adjustments to education expenses

If you pay qualified education expenses with certain tax-free funds, you cannot claim a credit for those amounts. You must reduce the qualified education expenses by the amount of any tax-free educational assistance and refund(s) you received. These amounts include:

- the tax-free parts of scholarships and fellowships;
- Pell grants received from the US government;

- employer-provided educational assistance;
- veterans' educational assistance;
- any other non-taxable (tax-free) payments (other than gifts or inheritances) received as educational assistance.

So once you have totalled your expenses, you should reduce them by any of the above amounts you received.

iii. Eligible educational institution

An eligible educational institution is any college, university, vocational school, or other postsecondary educational institution eligible to participate in a student aid program administered by the Department of Education. It includes virtually all accredited public, non-profit, and proprietary (privately owned profit-making) postsecondary institutions in the United States. Most Canadian institutions are also considered eligible educational institutions. To qualify the school must participate in the US Department of Education's Federal Student Aid (FSA) programs. You can search on the following website to see if your school is eligible at www.fafsa.ed.gov/index.htm. Once there, click on "Federal School Code Search" to bring up the search engine. You can also ask your educational institution whether they participate in US Federal Student Aid programs.

iv. Eligible student

To claim the American Opportunity Credit, the student for whom you pay qualified education expenses must be an eligible student. This is a student who meets all of the following requirements:

- The student did not have expenses that were used to figure an American Opportunity Credit in any four earlier tax years. This includes any tax year(s) in which you claimed the Hope credit for the same student.
- The student had not completed the first four years of postsecondary education (generally, the freshman, sophomore, junior, and senior years of college) before 2012.
- For at least one academic period beginning in 2012, the student was enrolled at least half time in a program leading to a degree, certificate, or other recognized educational credential.
- The student has not been convicted of any US federal or state felony for possessing or distributing a controlled substance as of the end of 2012.

The following examples illustrate these rules. Mack graduated from high school in June 2011. In September, he enrolled in an undergraduate degree program at College U, and attended full time for both the 2011 fall and 2012 spring semesters. For the 2012 fall semester, Mack was enrolled less than half-time. Because Mack was enrolled in an undergraduate degree program on at least a half-time basis for at least one academic period that began during 2011 and at least one academic period that began during 2012, he is an eligible student for tax years 2011 and 2012 (including the 2012 fall semester when he enrolled at College U on less than a half-time basis).

Dee graduated from high school in June 2011. In January 2012, she enrolled in a one-year postsecondary certificate program on a full-time basis to obtain a certificate as a travel agent. Dee completed the program in December 2012, and was awarded a certificate. In January 2013, she enrolled in a one-year postsecondary certificate program on a full-time basis to obtain a certificate as a computer programmer. Dee is an eligible student for both tax years 2012 and 2013 because she meets the degree requirement, the work load requirement, and the year of study requirement for those years.

b. Figuring the credit

The amount of the American Opportunity Credit (per eligible student) is the sum of:

1. 100% of the first $2,000 of qualified education expenses you paid for the eligible student, and
2. 25% of the next $2,000 of qualified education expenses you paid for that student.

The maximum amount of American Opportunity Credit you can claim in 2012 is $2,500 times the number of eligible students. You can claim the full $2,500 for each eligible student for whom you paid at least $4,000 of qualified education expenses. However, as we discuss in the next section, the amount of the credit you can claim may be reduced by your modified adjusted gross income.

c. Reducing the credit based on your income

Your modified adjusted gross income (MAGI) affects the amount of the American Opportunity Credit that you can claim. Recall that your modified adjusted gross income is your adjusted gross income (listed on line 38 of your Form 1040) plus any income you excluded using the foreign earned income exclusion. To calculate it, take the amount on line 38 and add to it the amount you excluded using the foreign earned income and/or housing exclusion on line 22 of your Form 1040.

The amount of your American Opportunity Credit is phased out (gradually reduced) if your MAGI is between $80,000 and $90,000 ($160,000 and $180,000 if you file a joint return). You cannot claim an American Opportunity Credit if your MAGI is $90,000 or more ($180,000 or more if you file a joint return). If your MAGI is within the range of incomes where the credit must be reduced, you will figure your reduced credit using lines 7–13 of Form 8863. We discuss how to calculate this below when we show you how to fill out Form 8863.

d. Refundable portion of the American Opportunity Credit

Forty percent of the American Opportunity Credit is refundable for most taxpayers. That means that if your tax owed is zero the IRS will actually pay you 40% of the credit. Figuring out the refundable portion is done on Form 8863.

e. Claiming the credit

You claim the American Opportunity Credit by completing Parts I, III, and IV of Form 8863 and submitting it with your Form 1040. Enter the non-refundable part of the credit on Form 1040, line 49 and the refundable part of the credit on Form 1040, line 66. Form 8863 is mostly self-explanatory. There are, however, a few lines on the form which merit explanation.

Line 13

There are certain circumstances that render you ineligible to qualify for a refund. You do **not** qualify for a refund if items 1 (a, b, or c), 2, and 3 below apply to you.

1. You were:

   a. under age 18 at the end of 2012, **or**

   b. age 18 at the end of 2012 **and** your earned income (defined below) was less than one-half of your support (defined below), **or**

   c. over age 18 and under age 24 at the end of 2012 **and** a full-time student **and** your salary income was less than one-half of the money others spent to support you. You were a full-time student if you attended an eligible educational institution full time during any part of five months of the year.

2. At least one of your parents was alive at the end of 2012.

3. You are filing a return as single, head of household, qualifying widow(er), or married filing separately for 2012.

Line 23

Line 23 ensures that you do not take more tax credits than you have tax payable. If you have a lot of tax credits, and little tax, you can use the worksheet below to calculate line 23. Otherwise, you can just enter the total tax credit that you can claim on line 22.

1.	Enter the amount from Form 8863, line 15.	1.
2.	Enter the amount from Form 1040, line 46.	2.
3.	Enter the total, if any of your credits from: • Form 1040, lines 47, 48, and the amount from Schedule R entered on line 53, and the amount from line 5 above.	3.
4.	Subtract line 3 from line 2.	4.
5.	**Non-refundable American Opportunity Credit.** Enter the **smaller** of line 6 or line 9. Enter this amount on Form 8863, line 23.	5.

Let's use an example to illustrate this. Bill Pass, aged 28, and a single taxpayer, is a US citizen living in Calgary. During 2012, he enrolled full time at a local college to earn a degree in law enforcement. This is the first year of his postsecondary education. He paid $5,600 in tuition. He and the college meet all of the requirements for the American Opportunity Credit. Bill's MAGI is $57,000. His income tax liability (line 46 of his Form 1040), before credits, is $8,106. Bill claims no credits other than the American Opportunity Credit.

He fills out his Form 8863 as follows.

Form **8863**

Department of the Treasury
Internal Revenue Service (99)

Education Credits (American Opportunity and Lifetime Learning Credits)

▶ See separate instructions to find out if you are eligible to take the credits.
▶ Attach to Form 1040 or Form 1040A.

OMB No. 1545-0074
2011
Attachment Sequence No. 50

Name(s) shown on return: Bill Pass
Your social security number: 135-00-2468

CAUTION: ***You cannot** take both an education credit and the tuition and fees deduction (see Form 8917) for the **same student** for the same year.*

Part I American Opportunity Credit

Caution: *You **cannot** take the American opportunity credit for more than **4** tax years for the **same student**.*

1	(a) Student's name (as shown on page 1 of your tax return) First name / Last name	(b) Student's social security number (as shown on page 1 of your tax return)	(c) Qualified expenses (see instructions). Do not enter more than $4,000 for each student.	(d) Subtract $2,000 from the amount in column (c). If zero or less, enter -0-.	(e) Multiply the amount in column (d) by 25% (.25)	(f) If column (d) is zero, enter the amount from column (c). Otherwise, add $2,000 to the amount in column (e).
	Bill Pass	135-00-2468	4000	2000	500	2500

2 **Tentative American opportunity credit.** Add the amounts on line 1, column (f). If you are taking the lifetime learning credit for a different student, go to Part II; otherwise, go to Part III . . . . . . ▶ 2 2500

Part II Lifetime Learning Credit

Caution: *You **cannot** take the American opportunity credit and the lifetime learning credit for the **same student** in the same year.*

3	(a) Student's name (as shown on page 1 of your tax return) First name	Last name	(b) Student's social security number (as shown on page 1 of your tax return)	(c) Qualified expenses (see instructions)

4	Add the amounts on line 3, column (c), and enter the total	4	
5	Enter the **smaller** of line 4 or $10,000	5	
6	**Tentative lifetime learning credit.** Multiply line 5 by 20% (.20). If you have an entry on line 2, go to Part III; otherwise go to Part IV	6	

For Paperwork Reduction Act Notice, see your tax return instructions. Cat. No. 25379M Form **8863** (2011)

Because Bill has chosen to take the American oppurtunity credit, he cannot take the lifetime learning credit even though he may be eligible for it.

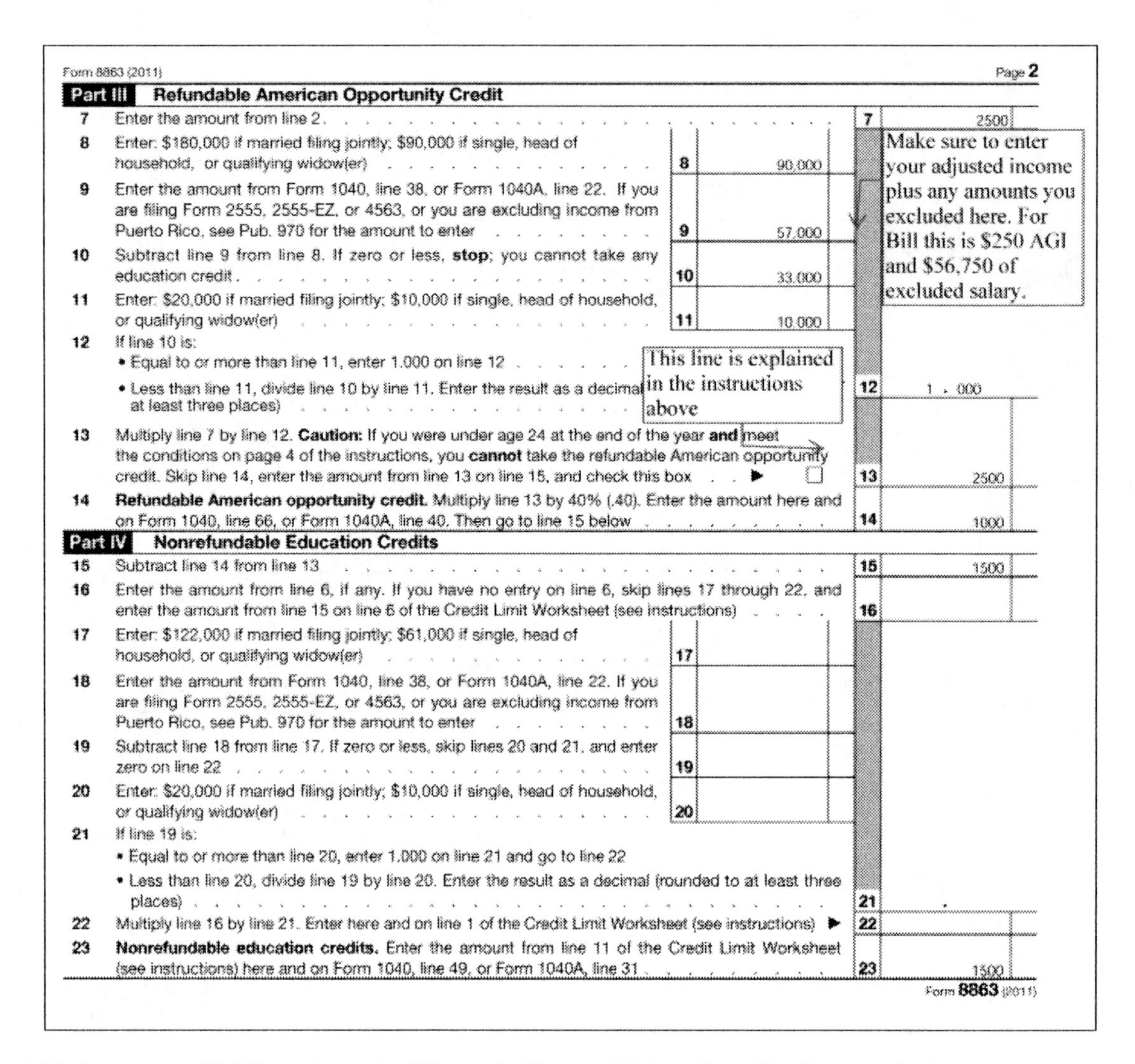

Form 8863 (2011) Page **2**

Part III Refundable American Opportunity Credit

7	Enter the amount from line 2			7	2500
8	Enter: $180,000 if married filing jointly; $90,000 if single, head of household, or qualifying widow(er)	8	90,000		
9	Enter the amount from Form 1040, line 38, or Form 1040A, line 22. If you are filing Form 2555, 2555-EZ, or 4563, or you are excluding income from Puerto Rico, see Pub. 970 for the amount to enter	9	57,000		
10	Subtract line 9 from line 8. If zero or less, **stop**; you cannot take any education credit	10	33,000		
11	Enter: $20,000 if married filing jointly; $10,000 if single, head of household, or qualifying widow(er)	11	10,000		
12	If line 10 is: • Equal to or more than line 11, enter 1.000 on line 12 • Less than line 11, divide line 10 by line 11. Enter the result as a decimal (rounded to at least three places)			12	1 . 000
13	Multiply line 7 by line 12. **Caution:** If you were under age 24 at the end of the year **and** meet the conditions on page 4 of the instructions, you **cannot** take the refundable American opportunity credit. Skip line 14, enter the amount from line 13 on line 15, and check this box ▶ ☐			13	2500
14	**Refundable American opportunity credit.** Multiply line 13 by 40% (.40). Enter the amount here and on Form 1040, line 66, or Form 1040A, line 40. Then go to line 15 below			14	1000

Part IV Nonrefundable Education Credits

15	Subtract line 14 from line 13			15	1500
16	Enter the amount from line 6, if any. If you have no entry on line 6, skip lines 17 through 22, and enter the amount from line 15 on line 6 of the Credit Limit Worksheet (see instructions)			16	
17	Enter: $122,000 if married filing jointly; $61,000 if single, head of household, or qualifying widow(er)	17			
18	Enter the amount from Form 1040, line 38, or Form 1040A, line 22. If you are filing Form 2555, 2555-EZ, or 4563, or you are excluding income from Puerto Rico, see Pub. 970 for the amount to enter	18			
19	Subtract line 18 from line 17. If zero or less, skip lines 20 and 21, and enter zero on line 22	19			
20	Enter: $20,000 if married filing jointly; $10,000 if single, head of household, or qualifying widow(er)	20			
21	If line 19 is: • Equal to or more than line 20, enter 1.000 on line 21 and go to line 22 • Less than line 20, divide line 19 by line 20. Enter the result as a decimal (rounded to at least three places)			21	.
22	Multiply line 16 by line 21. Enter here and on line 1 of the Credit Limit Worksheet (see instructions) ▶			22	
23	**Nonrefundable education credits.** Enter the amount from line 11 of the Credit Limit Worksheet (see instructions) here and on Form 1040, line 49, or Form 1040A, line 31			23	1500

Form **8863** (2011)

Bill then enters $1500 on line 49 of Form 1040 and 1000 on line 66 of Form 1040.

4. THE LIFETIME LEARNING CREDIT

The Lifetime Learning Credit is the second possible way to get a tax break for your education expenses. It is in many respects similar to the American Opportunity Credits, but there are some slight differences. So to explain it we will go through it thoroughly. You may be able to claim a Lifetime Learning Credit of up to $2,000 for qualified education expenses paid for all eligible students. There is no limit on the number of years the Lifetime Learning Credit can be claimed for each student. The Lifetime Learning Credit is non-refundable and is limited by the amount of your income and the amount of your tax.

a. What expenses qualify

The Lifetime Learning Credit is based on qualified education expenses you pay for yourself, your spouse, or a dependent for whom you claim an exemption on your tax return. Generally, the credit is allowed for qualified education expenses paid in 2012 for an academic period beginning in 2012 or in the first 3 months of 2013. For purposes of the Lifetime Learning Credit, qualified education expenses are tuition and certain related expenses required for enrollment in a course at an eligible educational institution. Student-activity fees and expenses for course-related books, supplies, and equipment are included in qualified education expenses only if the fees and expenses must be paid to the institution for the enrollment or attendance.

Qualified education expenses do not include amounts paid for:

- insurance;
- medical expenses (including student health fees);
- room and board
- transportation;
- similar personal, living, or family expenses.

This is true even if the amount must be paid to the institution as a condition of enrollment or attendance.

b. Adjustment to education expenses

If you pay qualified education expenses with certain tax-free funds, you cannot claim a credit for those amounts. You must reduce the qualified education expenses by the amount of any tax-free educational assistance and refund(s) you received. These amounts include:

- the tax-free parts of scholarships and fellowships;
- Pell grants received from the US government;
- employer-provided educational assistance;
- veterans' educational assistance;
- any other nontaxable (tax-free) payments (other than gifts or inheritances) received as educational assistance.

So once you have totalled your expenses, you should reduce them by any of the above amounts you received.

c. Eligible student

For purposes of the Lifetime Learning Credit, an eligible student is a student who is enrolled in one or more courses at an eligible educational institution.

d. Eligible educational institution

An eligible educational institution is any college, university, vocational school, or other postsecondary educational institution eligible to participate in a student aid program administered by the Department of Education. It includes virtually all accredited public, non-profit, and proprietary (privately owned profit-making) postsecondary institutions in the United States. Most Canadian institutions are also considered eligible educational institutions. To qualify the school must participate in the US Department of Education's Federal Student Aid (FSA) programs. You can search on the following website to see if your school is eligible at www.fafsa.ed.gov/index.htm. Once there, click on "Federal School Code Search" to bring up the search engine. You can also ask your educational institution whether they participate in US Federal Student Aid programs.

e. Figuring the credit

The amount of the lifetime learning credit is 20% of the first $10,000 of qualified education expenses you paid for all eligible students. The maximum amount of lifetime learning credit you can claim for 2012 is $2,000 (20% × $10,000). However, that amount may be reduced based on your MAGI. Recall that your MAGI is your adjusted gross income as listed on line 38 of Form 1040 plus any amounts you exclude from tax using the foreign earned income and/or housing exclusion. The amount of your lifetime learning credit is phased out (gradually reduced) if your MAGI is between $51,000 and $61,000 ($102,000 and $122,000 if you file a joint return). You cannot claim a lifetime learning credit if your MAGI is $61,000 or more ($122,000 or more if you file a joint return).

f. Claiming the credit

You claim the lifetime learning credit by completing Parts II and IV of Form 8863 and submitting it with your Form 1040. Enter the credit on Form 1040, line 49. Except for line 23, Form 8863 is relatively self-explanatory.

Line 23 ensures that you do not take more tax credits than you have tax payable. If you have a lot of tax credits, and little tax, you can use the worksheet below to calculate line 23. Otherwise, you can just enter the total tax credit that you can claim on line 22.

1.	Enter the amount from Form 8863, line 22	1.	
2.	Enter the amount from Form 1040, line 46,	2.	
3.	Enter the total, if any, of your credits from: • Form 1040, lines 47, 48, and the amount from Schedule R entered on line 53	3.	
4.	Subtract line 3 from line 2	4.	
5.	**Nonrefundable Lifetime Learning Credit.** Enter the **smaller** of line 1 or line 4	**5.**	

Let's use an example to illustrate how to claim the Lifetime Learning Credit.

Judy Green, a single taxpayer, is taking courses at a community college to be recertified to teach in public schools. Her Modified Adjusted Gross Income (MAGI) is $27,000. Her tax, before credits, is $2,234. She claims no credits other than the lifetime learning credit. In July 2012 she paid $700 for the summer 2011 semester; in August 2011 she paid $1,900 for the fall 2011 semester; and in December 2011 she paid another $1,900 for the spring semester beginning January 2012. Judy and the college meet all the requirements for the Lifetime Learning Credit. She can use all of the $4,500 tuition she paid in 2011 when figuring her credit for her 2011 tax return. She figures her credit as shown on the filled-in Form 8863.

Form **8863**

Department of the Treasury
Internal Revenue Service (99)

Education Credits (American Opportunity and Lifetime Learning Credits)

▶ See separate instructions to find out if you are eligible to take the credits.
▶ Attach to Form 1040 or Form 1040A.

OMB No. 1545-0074
2011
Attachment Sequence No. **50**

Name(s) shown on return: Judy Green
Your social security number: 000-00-7777

You cannot take both an education credit and the tuition and fees deduction (see Form 8917) for the same student for the same year.

Part I American Opportunity Credit

Caution: *You cannot take the American opportunity credit for more than 4 tax years for the same student.*

1	(a) Student's name (as shown on page 1 of your tax return) First name Last name	(b) Student's social security number (as shown on page 1 of your tax return)	(c) Qualified expenses (see instructions). Do not enter more than $4,000 for each student.	(d) Subtract $2,000 from the amount in column (c). If zero or less, enter -0-.	(e) Multiply the amount in column (d) by 25% (.25)	(f) If column (d) is zero, enter the amount from column (c). Otherwise, add $2,000 to the amount in column (e).

2 **Tentative American opportunity credit.** Add the amounts on line 1, column (f). If you are taking the lifetime learning credit for a different student, go to Part II; otherwise, go to Part III . . . . ▶ | 2 |

Part II Lifetime Learning Credit

Caution: *You cannot take the American opportunity credit and the lifetime learning credit for the same student in the same year.*

3	(a) Student's name (as shown on page 1 of your tax return) First name	Last name	(b) Student's social security number (as shown on page 1 of your tax return)	(c) Qualified expenses (see instructions)
	Judy	Green	000-00-7777	4,500

4	Add the amounts on line 3, column (c), and enter the total	4	4500
5	Enter the **smaller** of line 4 or $10,000	5	4500
6	**Tentative lifetime learning credit.** Multiply line 5 by 20% (.20). If you have an entry on line 2, go to Part III; otherwise go to Part IV	6	900

For Paperwork Reduction Act Notice, see your tax return instructions. Cat. No. 25379M Form **8863** (2011)

Form 8863 (2011) Page **2**

Part III Refundable American Opportunity Credit

7	Enter the amount from line 2			7	
8	Enter: $180,000 if married filing jointly; $90,000 if single, head of household, or qualifying widow(er)	8			
9	Enter the amount from Form 1040, line 38, or Form 1040A, line 22. If you are filing Form 2555, 2555-EZ, or 4563, or you are excluding income from Puerto Rico, see Pub. 970 for the amount to enter	9			
10	Subtract line 9 from line 8. If zero or less, **stop**; you cannot take any education credit	10			
11	Enter: $20,000 if married filing jointly; $10,000 if single, head of household, or qualifying widow(er)	11			
12	If line 10 is: • Equal to or more than line 11, enter 1.000 on line 12 . . . . • Less than line 11, divide line 10 by line 11. Enter the result as a decimal (rounded to at least three places)			12	.
13	Multiply line 7 by line 12. **Caution:** If you were under age 24 at the end of the year **and** meet the conditions on page 4 of the instructions, you **cannot** take the refundable American opportunity credit. Skip line 14, enter the amount from line 13 on line 15, and check this box . . ▶ ☐			13	
14	**Refundable American opportunity credit.** Multiply line 13 by 40% (.40). Enter the amount here and on Form 1040, line 66, or Form 1040A, line 40. Then go to line 15 below			14	

Part IV Nonrefundable Education Credits

15	Subtract line 14 from line 13			15	
16	Enter the amount from line 6, if any. If you have no entry on line 6, skip lines 17 through 22, and enter the amount from line 15 on line 6 of the Credit Limit Worksheet (see instructions)			16	900
17	Enter: $122,000 if married filing jointly; $61,000 if single, head of household, or qualifying widow(er)	17	61000		
18	Enter the amount from Form 1040, line 38, or Form 1040A, line 22. If you are filing Form 2555, 2555-EZ, or 4563, or you are excluding income from Puerto Rico, see Pub. 970 for the amount to enter	18	27,000		
19	Subtract line 18 from line 17. If zero or less, skip lines 20 and 21, and enter zero on line 22	19	34,000		
20	Enter: $20,000 if married filing jointly; $10,000 if single, head of household, or qualifying widow(er)	20	10,000		
21	If line 19 is: • Equal to or more than line 20, enter 1.000 on line 21 and go to line 22 • Less than line 20, divide line 19 by line 20. Enter the result as a decimal (rounded to at least three places)			21	1 . 00
22	Multiply line 16 by line 21. Enter here and on line 1 of the Credit Limit Worksheet (see instructions) ▶			22	900
23	**Nonrefundable education credits.** Enter the amount from line 11 of the Credit Limit Worksheet (see instructions) here and on Form 1040, line 49, or Form 1040A, line 31			23	900

Form **8863** (2011)

Judy then enters 900 on line 49 of her Form 1040.

5. OTHER ISSUES AND FURTHER INFORMATION

If your situation is not addressed here, or you need more information, please consult Publication 970 which is available on the IRS website.

PART 3

STATE AND LOCAL TAX

37

OVERVIEW OF STATE AND LOCAL TAX

US Federal taxes aren't the only US taxes you have to worry about. You may have a connection to a US state or city that also imposes income tax. For instance, if you recently moved to Canada from New York City, you may be responsible for filing returns for New York State and New York City, as well as your federal returns. The US federal return is always mandatory. However, the obligation to file tax returns for states, cities, and even counties is determined based on your connection to that state, city and/or county. Each state or city uses different rules to evaluate your connection to it.

This chapter generally explains those rules and summarizes the approaches of various states. We do not address city or county (local) taxes as these are often collected by the state tax authorities. If you can establish that you are not a resident of a state, it is unlikely that you will be considered a resident of a city or county within that state. Finally, should you have to file a state tax return, you will need to get local advice, since each state has its own tax laws. This chapter is organized as follows:

1. States without income tax.
2. How residency is evaluated.
3. What does domicile mean?
4. Factors that indicate domicile.
5. Procedure for changing your domicile.
6. Summary chart of rules for each state.

1. STATES WITHOUT INCOME TAX

There are seven states that do not collect income tax from their residents: Alaska, Florida, Nevada, South Dakota, Texas, Washington, and Wyoming. If you have moved from one of these states, you will not have to worry about your former state imposing income tax.

2. HOW RESIDENCY IS EVALUATED

The basic rule is that if you are a resident of a state, you must file a return there.

Because each state uses its own rules, it is hard to generalize. To find out the exact rules for a state where you had a past connection, you should consult the chart in section 5. This said, there are two common methods of determining residency: the number of days test and domicile.

a. Number of days test

The first method is based on the number of days spent within the state during the taxable year. This is often referred to as the "183 day rule" because many states will treat any individual who spends 183 days or more in the state to be a resident for that year.

New York is an example of a state that uses the 183-day rule to determine non-domiciliary residency. Any individual, who maintains a permanent home in New York State for over 11 months of the year or more and who spends 183 days or more in New York, will be considered a resident of the state for that year. Many states have their own variation of the 183-day rule. For example, New Mexico considers anyone who is physically present in the state for 185 days or more of the taxable year to be a resident, whether or not they maintain a home there. Severing a connection with these types of states is quite easy. Simply do not be present in that state for more than the number of days threshold.

b. Domicile

The second, and most common method, of determining tax liability is through domicile. Of the 43 states that collect income tax, 35 consider any individual domiciled within the state to be a resident, regardless of how much time they actually spend within the state. The remaining 8 states determine residency through the domicile test, but identify certain situations in which individuals may retain their domicile without being taxed. Each of these 8 states use different criteria, so if you have moved from one of these states, it is important to review the relevant section in the Appendix.

3. WHAT DOES DOMICILE MEAN?

Your domicile is your permanent home. It is the place where you intend to return, even when absent for extended periods of time. Unlike residency, you can only be domiciled in one location. Changing your domicile is not simply a matter of moving to a new city or country. Each state requires different forms of evidence before accepting a change of domicile. Generally speaking, a change of domicile requires all of the following:

a. abandonment of your prior domicile;

b. intent to remain in the new locality permanently or indefinitely;

c. physically moving to and residing in the new locality.

The crucial element is your intent. Because intent is subjective, it is determined by examining your actions and associations. The next section discusses some of the more important factors.

4. FACTORS THAT INDICATE DOMICILE

The following list sets out actions which establish your intention. It is not a comprehensive list. It is not necessary for each of these conditions to be met, nor will meeting them all guarantee a change of domicile.

- Where your driver's licence was issued;
- Where your bank accounts are held;
- Where you vote;
- Where you receive your tax returns;
- Where you receive financial mail (e.g., bank statements);
- Where your vehicle is registered;

- Where you have memberships in local or religious organizations;
- Location of your medical professionals.

5. PROCEDURE FOR CHANGING YOUR DOMICILE

Some states have very specific procedures for changing your domicile. For instance, in Michigan, a specific form is required. It is available on the Michigan tax authority website.

Others have no formal procedure. Still, full disclosure is always best. We suggest you write a letter to the appropriate state tax authority saying that you are no longer domiciled in a particular state. In this letter you may wish to refer to some of the above factors to prove your change in domicile. For instance, let's say that you recently moved from New Jersey to Canada. You now work and live in Canada as well as having a Canadian driver's licence. You should write a letter to the tax authority in New Jersey explaining that you moved from there and are now domiciled in Canada and have a Canadian licence etc. You should also stress your intention to reside in Canada indefinitely.

Such a letter does not change your domicile in and of itself. Recall that domicile is established through intention. The act of sending the letter does not demonstrate your intention. It merely informs the state tax authority of other factors which do demonstrate your intention. That's why it is important to explain the factors in the letter.

6. SUMMARY CHART OF RULES FOR EACH STATE

Now that you are familiar with the general rules, you should consult the rules applicable to your particular state. The following chart summarizes these rules.

50 States (A-Z)	Income Tax	Domicile	183-day rule	Contact Info
Alabama	Yes	Yes	Yes	Alabama Department of Revenue, Individual and Corporate Tax Division, P.O. Box 327460, Montgomery, AL 36132-7460; www.revenue.alabama.gov/incometax; (334) 242-1170 (Tax Information)
Alaska	No	N/A	N/A	N/A
Arizona	Yes	Yes	Yes	Arizona Department of Revenue, P.O. Box 29002, Phoenix, AZ 85038-9002; www.revenue.state.az.us; (602) 542-4260 (Form Orders), (602) 255-3381 (Tax Information).
Arkansas	Yes	Yes	Yes	Dept. of Finance and Administration, Income Tax Forms Division, P.O. Box 3628, Little Rock, AK 72203-3628; www.state.ar.us/dfa; (501) 682-1100 (Tax Information)
California	Yes	No	No	State of California, Franchise Tax Board, P.O. Box 942840, Sacramento, CA 94240-0070; www.ftb.ca.gov; (800) 852-5711 or (916) 845-6600 (Outside US)
Colorado	Yes	Yes	No	Colorado Department of Revenue, 1375 Sherman Street, Denver, CO 80261; www.revenue.state.co.us; (303) 238-7378 (Tax Assistance)
Connecticut	Yes	No	Yes	Department of Revenue Services, Taxpayer Services Division, 25 Sigourney Street, Hartford, CT 06106-5032; www.ct.gov/drs; (860) 297-5962 (Taxpayer Assistance) or (800) 382-9463.

50 States (A-Z)	Income Tax	Domicile	183-day rule	Contact Info
Delaware	Yes	No	Yes	Division of Revenue, State Office Building, 9th & French Streets, Wilmington, DE 19801; www.revenue.delaware.gov; (302) 577-8200
Florida	No	N/A	N/A	N/A
Georgia	Yes	Yes	No	State of Georgia, Department of Revenue, Income Tax Division, 1800 Century CenterBlvd, NE, Atlanta, GA 30345; www.etax.dor.ga.gov; (404) 417-2300 or (877) 602-8477
Hawaii	Yes	Yes	Yes	State of Hawaii, Dept. of Taxation, P.O. Box 3559, Honolulu, HI 96811-3559; www.state.hi.us/tax; (808) 587-4242 (Taxpayer Services), (808) 587-1488 (Forms by FAX)
Idaho	Yes	No	Yes	Idaho State Tax Commission, P. O. Box 36, Boise, ID 83722-0410; www.tax.idaho.gov; (208) 334-7660 (Tax Information) or (800) 972-7660.
Illinois	Yes	No	No	Illinois Department of Revenue, P.O. Box 19044, Springfield, IL 62794-9044; www.revenue.state.il.us; (217) 782-3336 (Tax Assistance) or (800) 732-8866
Indiana	Yes	Yes	Yes	Indiana Department of Revenue, 100 N. Senate Ave., Indianapolis, IN 46204-2253; www.in.gov/dor/; (317) 232-2240
Iowa	Yes	Yes	Yes	State of Iowa, Department of Revenue and Finance, Hoover State Office Building, Des Moines, IA 50319; www.state.ia.us/tax; (515) 281-7239 (Forms), (515) 281-3114 (Tax Specialists).
Kansas	Yes	Yes	No	Kansas Taxpayer Assistance Bureau, 915 S.W. Harrison, Topeka, KS 66625-0001; www.ksrevenue.org; (785) 368-8222 (Tax Assistance) or (785) 296-4937 (Tax Forms)
Kentucky	Yes	Yes	Yes	Kentucky Revenue Cabinet, P.O. Box 181, Frankfort, KY 40602; www.revenue.ky.gov; (502) 564-4581.
Louisiana	Yes	Yes	No	Dept. of Revenue and Taxation, Forms Division, P.O. Box 201, Baton Rouge, LA 70821-0201; www.rev.state.la.us; (225) 219-0102
Maine	Yes	Yes	Yes	Maine Revenue Services, 24 State House Station, Augusta, ME 04333-0024; www.maine.gov/revenue/; (207) 626-8475 (Tax Assistance), (207) 624-7894 (Forms Orders)
Maryland	Yes	Yes	Yes	Revenue Administration, Income Tax Division, Annapolis, MD 21411; www.marylandtaxes.com; (410) 260-7980 (Tax Assistance).
Massachusetts	Yes	Yes	Yes	Department of Revenue, 100 Cambridge Street, Boston, MA 02204; www.dor.state.ma.us; (617) 887-MDOR (Tax Information).
Michigan	Yes	Yes	No	Michigan Department of Treasury, Treasury Building, Lansing, MI 48922; www.michigan.gov/treasury; (800) 827-4000 (Tax Assistance), (800) 827-4000 (select option 2 for Forms)
Minnesota	Yes	Yes	No	Minnesota Dept. of Revenue, Mail Station 5510, St. Paul, MN 55146-2220; www.taxes.state.mn.us; (651) 296-3781 or (800) 652-9094 (Tax Information)

50 States (A-Z)	Income Tax	Domicile	183-day rule	Contact Info
Mississippi	Yes	Yes	No	Bureau of Revenue, P.O. Box 23050, Jackson, MS 39255-3050; www.mstc.state.ms.us/; (601) 923-7000 (Tax Assistance).
Missouri	Yes	No	Yes	Missouri Department of Revenue, Jefferson City, MO 65105-2200; www.mo.gov; (800) 877-6881 (Forms), (573) 751-4800 (Forms by FAX), (573) 751-7191 (Taxpayer Assistance)
Montana	Yes	Yes	No	Income Tax Division, Montana Department of Revenue, P.O. Box 5805, Helena, MT 59604-5805; www.mt.gov/revenue; (406) 444-6900
Nebraska	Yes	Yes	Yes	Nebraska Department of Revenue, Nebraska State Office Building, 301 Centennial Mall South, Lincoln, NE 68509-4818; www.revenue.state.ne.us; (402) 471-5729.
Nevada	No	N/A	N/A	N/A
New Hampshire	No*	No	Yes	NH DRA, PO Box 637, Concord, NH 03302-0637, or www.state.nh.gov
New Jersey	Yes	No	Yes	Department of the Treasury, Division of Taxation, PO Box 266, Trenton, NJ 08625-0269; www.state.nj.us/treasury/taxation/; (609) 292-6400 (Tax Assistance).
New Mexico	Yes	Yes	Yes	Taxpayer Information Unit, Taxation and Revenue Department, P.O. Box 630, Santa Fe, NM 87504-0630; www.state.nm.us/tax/; (505) 827-0700.
New York	Yes	No	Yes	NYS Tax Department, Taxpayer Assistance Bureau, W.A. Harriman Campus, Albany, NY 12227; www.tax.state.ny.us; (518) 457-5181 or (518) 485-6800 (Outside US)
North Carolina	Yes	Yes	Yes	Dept. of Revenue, Taxpayer Services Dept., Revenue Building, Raleigh, NC 27640; www.dor.state.nc.us; (877) 252-4052 (Tax Assistance), (877) 252-3052 (Forms), (252) 467-9000 (international callers).
North Dakota	Yes	Yes	Yes	Office of State Tax Commissioner, State Capitol, 16th floor, 600 E. Boulevard Ave., Bismarck, ND 58505-0599; www.nd.gov/tax/; (701) 328-2770.
Ohio	Yes	Yes	Yes	Ohio Department of Taxation, Taxpayer Services, 800 Freeway Drive, N., Columbus, OH 43329; www.tax.ohio.gov; (614) 466-2166 or (800) 282-1780 (Tax Information).
Oklahoma	Yes	Yes	No	Oklahoma Tax Commission, 2501 North Lincoln Blvd., Oklahoma City, OK 73194; www.oktax.state.ok.us; (405) 521-3160 (Tax Assistance).
Oregon	Yes	No	Yes	Oregon Department of Revenue, 955 Center Street, NE, Salem, OR 97310-2551; www.oregon.gov/DOR/; (503) 378-4988 (Taxpayer Assistance) or (800) 356-4222.
Pennsylvania	Yes	No	Yes	Commonwealth of Pennsylvania, Department of Revenue, Taxpayer Services, Harrisburg, PA 17128-1061; www.revenue.state.pa.us; (717) 787-8201.
Rhode Island	Yes	Yes	Yes	State of Rhode Island, Division of Taxation, One Capitol Hill, Providence, RI 02908-5801; www.tax.state.ri.us; (401) 222-1040.

50 States (A-Z)	Income Tax	Domicile	183-day rule	Contact Info
South Carolina	Yes	Yes	No	Department of Revenue, 301 Gervais Street, P.O. Box 125, Columbia, SC 29214; www.sctax.org; (803) 898-5040 (Tax Information).
South Dakota	No	N/A	N/A	N/A
Tennessee	No*	Yes	No	Department of Revenue, Andrew Jackson Bldg., 500 Deaderick St., Nashville, TN 37242, or www.state.tn.us, or telephone: (615) 253-0600
Texas	No	N/A	N/A	N/A
Utah	Yes	Yes	Yes	Utah State Tax Commission, 210 North 1950 West, Salt Lake City, UT 84134; www.utah.gov/residents/taxes.html; (801) 297-2200 (Tax Assistance).
Vermont	Yes	Yes	Yes	Vermont Dept. of Taxes, Taxpayer Services, Pavilion Office Bldg., Montpelier, VT 05609-1401; www.state.vt.us/tax; (802) 828-2865 (Taxpayer Assistance)
Virginia	Yes	Yes	Yes	Virginia Department of Taxation, Taxpayer Services Division, P.O. Box 1115, Richmond, VA 23218; www.tax.virginia.gov; (804) 367-8031 (Tax Assistance) or (804) 440-2541 (Tax Forms).
Washington	No	N/A	N/A	N/A
West Virginia	Yes	No	Yes	The Department of Tax and Revenue, Taxpayer Services Division, P.O. Box 3784, Charleston, WV 25337-3784; www.state.wv.us/taxdiv; (304) 558-3333 or (800) 982-8297
Wisconsin	Yes	Yes	No	Wisconsin Dept. of Revenue, P.O. Box 8903, Madison, WI 53708-8903; www.dor.state.wi.us; (608) 266-2772 (Tax Information).
Wyoming	No	N/A	N/A	N/A

PART 4

US ESTATE AND GIFT TAX

38

OVERVIEW OF ESTATE AND GIFT TAX

US citizens in Canada need to worry about the estate tax and gift tax as well as income tax. The estate tax is payable on death if the estate is worth more than $5 million. Gift tax is payable when you give someone else more than $13,000 in a year. This chapter briefly introduces both taxes so that you know whether or not they apply to you.

1. ESTATE TAX

The estate tax is payable on the value of the total estate at death. There is, however, a large exclusion which may eliminate the need to file an estate tax return. The following chart sets out the value of this exclusion which depends on the year in which the person died.

Year of Death:	File return if estate's value is more than:
2002 and 2003	$1,000,000
2004 and 2005	$1,500,000
2006, 2007, and 2008	$2,000,000
2009	$3,500,000
2010 and 2011	$5,000,000
2012	$5,120,000

As the chart suggests, if the value of an estate was under US $5,120,000 in 2012 then no estate tax return need be filed. That ends the matter. If, however, a return needs to be filed, then professional tax advice should be sought.

Next, we discuss how to calculate the value of an estate.

a. How to calculate the value of an estate

Calculating the value of an estate is somewhat complicated. First, start with the gross estate. A person's *gross estate* includes the value of all property owned partially or outright at the time of death. The gross estate also includes the following:

- Life insurance proceeds payable to the estate or, if the estate owned the policy, to the heirs;
- The value of certain annuities payable to an estate or the heirs; and
- The value of certain property transferred to an estate in the three years prior to death.

The estate tax exemption is calculated on your "taxable estate." That means that you can subtract the following items from the value of the gross estate:

- funeral expenses paid out of the estate;
- debts owed at the time of death;

- the marital deduction (generally, the value of the property that passes from an estate to a surviving spouse);
- the charitable deduction (generally, the value of the property that passes from an estate to a qualifying charity for exclusively charitable purposes); and
- the state death tax deduction (generally any estate, inheritance, legacy, or succession taxes paid as the result of the decedent's death to any state or the District of Columbia).

Let's take an example. Let's say that Jim died in 2012. At the time of death Jim had gross assets of US$5,500,000. He left his house worth $1 million to his wife and gave $400,000 in stocks to charity. While Jim's gross estate was more than $5,120,000, his taxable estate (after deduction of the $1 million and $400,000) was less. Therefore Jim's estate does not need to file an estate tax return.

b. Strategies to minimize estate tax

There are several tax planning strategies available to reduce estate tax. You should consult a tax professional if your estate is sufficiently large that you will be liable for estate tax upon death.

2. GIFT TAX

The second type of tax you have to worry about is gift tax. To discourage people from simply giving their wealth to their heirs before they die, the US taxes gifts. The gift tax applies to transfers of property by gift.

You make a gift if you give property (including money), the use of property, or the right to receive income from property without expecting to receive something of at least equal value in return.

There is an exclusion from gift tax in respect of each person to whom you made a gift. It is as follows:

Gift Tax Annual Exclusion	
Year(s)	**Annual Exclusion**
1998 – 2001	$10,000
2002 – 2005	$11,000
2006 – 2008	$12,000
2009 – 2012	$13,000

So in 2012, if you gave US$13,000 each to your spouse and to your daughter you do not have to pay any gift tax. In addition, the following types of gifts are not taxable:

- tuition or medical expenses paid directly to an educational or medical institution for someone else;
- gifts to your spouse;
- gifts to a political organization for its use; and
- gifts to charities.

Should you have taxable gifts, please consult a professional tax advisor.

PART 5
COMPLIANCE ISSUES

39

OVERVIEW OF COMPLIANCE ISSUES

The IRS has recently increased efforts to crack down on foreign tax fraud. Not only are you responsible for filing a Form 1040 every year and paying any tax due, but you must also report all foreign bank accounts and trusts. We refer to these as compliance issues.

Unfortunately, many common Canadian financial products are regarded by the US as mechanisms for tax avoidance. We first briefly survey and summarize the various compliance issues. Then, we refer you to later chapters for more information.

1. CATCHING UP ON PAST RETURNS

Many US citizens in Canada may have been unaware for a long time that, by reason of their citizenship, they were required to file US tax returns. The IRS recently introduced a program to allow a taxpayer to catch up on past returns with no penalty. You are eligible for this procedure if you have lived outside of the United States since January 1, 2009 and have not filed a US tax return during the same period. To take advantage of this procedure, you need to file three years of past tax returns and six years of Report of Foreign Bank and Financial Accounts (FBAR) reports. You can also take advantage of this procedure to make past elections for past RRSP contributions. This procedure, and how to use it, is discussed further in Chapter 40.

2. YOU HAVE A CANADIAN RRSP

RRSPs are the one Canadian registered plan that the IRS acknowledges. With a bit of paperwork, you can defer US tax on income that builds up inside your Canadian RRSP until you withdraw it. You can also deduct RRSP contributions from your US income. These topics are explained more in Chapter 41.

3. YOU OWN CANADIAN MUTUAL FUNDS

If you own Canadian mutual funds, outside of an RRSP, you may have very demanding reporting requirements. In 2010, the IRS issued a ruling that classified Canadian mutual funds as corporations. Corporations that hold mostly passive income (such as interest or dividends) are considered passive foreign investment corporations by the US government. If you own shares in such a deemed corporation, or receive income from it, then you have to file a form describing the exact nature of your interest. Consult Chapter 42 for more information.

4. YOU HAVE A CANADIAN TFSA, RDSP, OR RESP

Certain registered Canadian government savings plans, in particular the Tax Free Savings Account (TFSA), the Registered Disability Savings Plan (RDSP), or the Registered Education Savings Plan (RESP), present difficulties for the US tax system. You will have to report all income that builds up inside one of these accounts. Also, we suggest that you write to the IRS and inform them that you hold these accounts, the amounts they contain, and request instructions on how to disclose them in the future. Consult Chapter 43 for more information.

5. YOU HAVE BANK ACCOUNTS WITH OVER $10,000

If you have signing authority or ownership interest in bank account(s) that cumulatively total more than $10,000, you will need to file Form TD F 90-22.1 (the Report of Foreign Bank and Financial Accounts (FBAR)) to report where these accounts are held and how much money is in them. In Chapter 44, we explain these requirements and how to file this form. Failure to file this form could result in a $10,000 penalty.

6. YOUR NON-US FINANCIAL ASSETS TOTAL MORE THAN $200,000

Should your non-US financial assets total more than $200,000 you must file Form 8938 to report these assets. Financial assets include stocks, bonds, deferred compensation, interests in a trust, interests in a foreign financial entity, or pensions. We further explore this definition and explain how to report it in Chapter 45.

40

FILING OVERDUE RETURNS

In June 2012, the IRS announced a policy to let certain US citizens abroad catch up on overdue tax returns and information reports without a penalty. The procedure also allows you to file past Forms 8891 which defer tax due on your RRSP (see Chapter 41 for more information). Of course, you will still owe tax and interest, but any fines for failure to file a return or an information form will be waived. This chapter explains how to take advantage of that procedure.

1. ELIGIBILITY

To take advantage of the amnesty, you must have lived outside of the United States since January 1, 2009 and not have filed a tax return during that time.

You must also be what the IRS calls a low-risk taxpayer, meaning that the returns you file show little (less than $1,500) or no tax due. However, you may not be eligible if you have US source income, have been previously audited by the IRS, or you have financial interests outside Canada and the United States.

2. HOW TO USE IT

To take advantage of this amnesty, you have to follow these steps:

1. Submit accurate tax returns for the last three years. These returns should be filled out in the same manner as a current return.
2. Write "streamlined" on the top of each tax return.
3. Pay all back taxes and interest owed. Currently the IRS interest rate is 4% although this may change. Consult the IRS website for the current interest rate.
4. Submit past FBAR reports (Form TD F 90-22.1) for the last six years. Instructions on how to fill out the FBAR report can be found in Chapter 44.
5. Complete and sign the questionnaire included in Appendix 1.
6. If necessary, file a Form 8891 for each past tax year to defer paying tax on income inside your RRSP. The instructions on how to complete this form are found in Chapter 41.
7. Along with the form 8891, you will have to send a letter requesting an extension of time to file you Form 8891. You should indicate that Article XVIII(7) of the Canada-US Tax Treaty allows you to defer tax due on your RRSP. In this letter, which you should sign and date, you should also explain:
    - Why you delayed sending in Form 8891.
    - When you realized you had to file Form 8891.
    - If you relied on a professional advisor, what advice that advisor gave to you.

Note that any statement you sign is done under the penalty of perjury. Do not submit incorrect information.

8. Send the above documents to:

Internal Revenue Service
3651 South I-H 35
Stop 6063 AUSC
Attn: Streamlined
Austin, TX 78741

41

IF YOU HAVE A CANADIAN RRSP

Registered Retirement Savings Plans (RRSPs) are among the most common financial products held by Canadians. They offer two benefits: 1) your contributions can be deducted from your income (up to specified limits) and 2) tax is deferred on any income, including capital gains, accrued inside the RRSP. Thanks to the Canada-US Tax Treaty, US citizens in Canada can take advantage of both benefits on their US tax returns. This chapter explains how to do this.

1. HOW TO DEFER TAX PAYABLE ON YOUR RRSP

Under Article XVIII(7) of the Canada-US Tax Treaty, you have the right to defer US income tax on income that accrues inside an RRSP. To claim this benefit, you must file Form 8891 every year. The form is fairly self-explanatory and looks like this.

Form **8891**
(Rev. July 2008)
Department of the Treasury
Internal Revenue Service

U.S. Information Return for Beneficiaries of Certain Canadian Registered Retirement Plans

► **Attach to Form 1040.** ► **See instructions on back of form.**

OMB No. 1545-0074
Attachment Sequence No. **139**

Name shown on Form 1040 | **Identifying number** (see instructions)

1 Name of plan custodian

2 Account number of plan

3 Address of plan custodian

4 Type of plan (check one box):
☐ Registered Retirement Savings Plan (RRSP)
☐ Registered Retirement Income Fund (RRIF)

5 Check the applicable box for your status in the plan (see *Definitions* in the instructions):
☐ Beneficiary
☐ Annuitant (Complete only lines 7a, 7b, and 8.)

6a Have you previously made an election under Article XVIII(7) of the U.S.-Canada income tax treaty to defer U.S. income tax on the undistributed earnings of the plan? . . . . ► ☐ **Yes** ☐ **No**

b If "Yes," enter the first year the election came into effect ________ and go to line 7a. If "No," go to line 6c.

c If you have not previously made the election described on line 6a above, you can make an irrevocable election for this year and subsequent years by checking this box . . . . ► ☐

7a Distributions received from the plan during the year. Enter here and include on Form 1040, line 16a	**7a**	
b Taxable distributions received from the plan during the year. Enter here and include on Form 1040, line 16b	**7b**	
8 Plan balance at the end of the year. If you checked the "Annuitant" box on line 5, the "Yes" box on line 6a, or the box on line 6c, **stop here. Do not** complete the rest of the form	**8**	
9 Contributions to the plan during the year	**9**	
10 Undistributed earnings of the plan during the year:		
a Interest income. Enter here and include on Form 1040, line 8a	**10a**	
b Total ordinary dividends. Enter here and include on Form 1040, line 9a	**10b**	
c Qualified dividends. Enter here and include on Form 1040, line 9b	**10c**	
d Capital gains. Enter here and include on Form 1040, line 13	**10d**	
e Other income. Enter here and include on Form 1040, line 21. List type and amount ►	**10e**	

For Paperwork Reduction Act Notice, see page 2. Cat. No. 37699X Form **8891** (Rev. 7-2008)

Line 5 is the first part of the form that is not self-explanatory. Unless you are designated as an annuitant under the particular RRSP in question, you should check the box for beneficiary. Beneficiaries are those who are subject to US taxation (US citizens) and would have to pay tax on the income inside the RRSP were it not for the tax treaty.

Line 6 requires you to declare whether you have filed Form 8891 previously. If so, check the yes box and enter the year that you first made this choice on line 6(b). Line 6(c) allows you to make this choice irrevocable.

On line 7, simply enter any distributions that you received from the plan during the year.

If you have elected to defer the tax, you do not need to fill out the form past line 8.

2. DEDUCT YOUR RRSP CONTRIBUTIONS ON YOUR US TAX

It may be possible to deduct your RRSP contributions from your US income under Article XVIII 13 of the Canada-US Tax Treaty. The treaty imposes a few requirements:

1) You must perform services as an employee in Canada for an employer who is a resident of Canada.
2) You can only claim RRSP deductions during a period in which you meet the first criterion.
3) You can only deduct RRSP contributions that are deductible in Canada.

The first two requirements should not be a problem for most US citizens in Canada as long as they are residents of Canada and employed here. Nor should the deduction limit be a problem. After all, you should not be contributing more to your RRSP than you can deduct in Canada, since there are Canadian tax penalties which apply to over-contributions.

To compute the deduction, simply take the amount of your RRSP deductions that you made in the tax year in question. Your financial institution should validate this amount on the slip it sends you confirming your RRSP contributions.

a. Claiming the deduction

Claiming the deduction is a bit more complicated. You must fill out Form 8833 and subtract the amount on line 21 of Form 1040. On the dotted line next to line 21 write, “see attached 8833”.

Filling out Form 8833 has a bit more legalese than some of the other forms we have explained in this book.

The first choice you must make is which box to check. Since you are a US citizen, you should check the first box (required by section 6114). The second box is reserved for those who are considered “aliens” by the United States. Citizens are never considered “aliens.”

You should, however, check the box that indicates that you are a US citizen or resident.

On line 1(a) you should enter “Canada.” On line 1(b) you should enter “par. 13 of Article XVIII.” You can ignore box 2. There is little doubt that you are allowed to claim this deduction. Box 3 will not apply since no income is being paid from the United States. Line 4 does not apply either.

On line 5, you need to write a brief explanation of why you are entitled to this deduction. First, start out by listing the requirements. Here is a suggested first sentence.

> Paragraph 13 of Article XVIII of the Canada-US Tax Treaty allows a US citizen who is a resident of Canada to deduct contributions to a registered retirement savings plan from US tax as long as he/she was employed by a Canadian employer, and had income that was taxable in Canada.

Then simply go on to describe how long you have lived in Canada, where you work, and that you did indeed have taxable income. You should also describe how much you contributed to your Canadian RRSP and that you are only deducting this amount on your US taxes.

Here is an example. Judith MacDonald is employed by *The Globe and Mail* as a writer in Toronto. She is a US citizen and has lived in Canada since 1980. She contributed US$8,000 to her RRSP in 2012. She would fill out her Form 8833 as follows.

Form **8833**
(Rev. August 2006)
Department of the Treasury
Internal Revenue Service

Treaty-Based Return Position Disclosure
Under Section 6114 or 7701(b)

OMB No. 1545-1354

▶ **Attach to your tax return.**

Attach a separate Form 8833 for each treaty-based return position taken. Failure to disclose a treaty-based return position may result in a penalty of $1,000 ($10,000 in the case of a C corporation) (see section 6712).

Name
Judith MacDonald

U.S. taxpayer identifying number
000-1223-45

Address in country of residence
197 Fulton Ave.
Toronto Ontario
Canada, M4L 1B7

Address in the United States
N/A

Check one or both of the following boxes as applicable:

- The taxpayer is disclosing a treaty-based return position as required by section 6114 . . . . ▶ ☑
- The taxpayer is a dual-resident taxpayer and is disclosing a treaty-based return position as required by Regulations section 301.7701(b)-7 . . . . ▶ ☐

Check this box if the taxpayer is a U.S. citizen or resident or is incorporated in the United States . . . . ▶ ☑

1 Enter the specific treaty position relied on:
a Treaty country **Canada**
b Article(s) **Paragraph 13 of Article XVIII**

2 List the Internal Revenue Code provision(s) overruled or modified by the treaty-based return position

3 Name, identifying number (if available to the taxpayer), and address in the United States of the payor of the income (if fixed or determinable annual or periodical). See instructions.

4 List the provision(s) of the limitation on benefits article (if any) in the treaty that the taxpayer relies on to prevent application of that article ▶

5 Explain the treaty-based return position taken. Include a brief summary of the facts on which it is based. Also, list the nature and amount (or a reasonable estimate) of gross receipts, each separate gross payment, each separate gross income item, or other item (as applicable) for which the treaty benefit is claimed
Paragraph 13 of Article XVIII allows a US citizen who is a resident of Canada to deduct contributions to a registered retirement savings plan from US tax as long as he/she was employed by a Canadian employer and had income that was taxable in Canada. I have lived in Canada since 1985. I am a writer employed by the Globe and Mail in Toronto Canada. In 2012, I contributed $8000 to my registered retirement savings plan. I deducted this amount from my Canadian tax.

For Paperwork Reduction Act Notice, see page 3. Cat. No. 14895L Form **8833** (Rev. 8-2006)

On line 21 of her Form 1040, Judith would enter -$8,000 and write "see attached form 8833" next to it.

42

IF YOU OWN CANADIAN MUTUAL FUNDS

US citizens residing in Canada should be aware that if they own shares in Canadian mutual funds, this might become problematic from a US tax perspective. The IRS has recently issued a directive stating that it considered Canadian mutual funds to be corporations.[1] This may have had the consequence of characterizing Canadian mutual funds as passive foreign investment corporations. The ruling did not explicitly say this, but our view is that this may well be the proper legal conclusion. The problem results from the fact that the IRS imposes strict reporting requirements and a punitive tax regime on the owners of shares in passive foreign investment corporations (Canadian mutual funds in the scenario just described). We have written to the IRS seeking clarification, but as of the publication date, we had not received a reply.

Many US citizens in Canada own mutual funds, so we hope the IRS will clarify this point. Absent a clarification, the following methods of reporting exist:

1. Mutual funds held inside of an RRSP should still benefit from the protections of the Canada-US Tax Treaty. As explained in Chapter 41, the treaty allows US citizens in Canada to defer tax income that accrues inside their RRSP until they make a withdrawal. You must follow the instructions in that chapter in order to take advantage of the tax deferral.

2. Even if your mutual funds are held in an RRSP, you still have an obligation to disclose them. We suggest that you write a letter to the IRS and attach it to your tax return (Form 1040) indicating the type of mutual fund you own, where it is located, its value, and request instructions on how to make the disclosure in future years and pay the tax once you withdraw the money from an RRSP.

3. Mutual funds held outside of an RRSP are more complicated. We think that likely the most compliant manner of reporting mutual fund income is to follow the steps outlined in this chapter. However, some tax professionals simply report the income and gains as if the mutual fund were located in the United States (as is explained in Chapters 8 and 10). Then they prepare a letter disclosing the type of funds, their value, and stating that the income from the funds was reported on Form 1040. How to report income from and disclose your mutual funds is your decision. At the very least, you should report all income and gains on your Form 1040 and write a letter disclosing the funds' type, value, location, and request instructions on how to report the income and disclose the funds in future years. Attach this letter to your tax return. The downside of this approach is that it may expose you to higher tax liability in the future because you are not making one of the elections on the Form 8621 (this is described below).

4. Our practical (but not investment) advice is to avoid the potentially punitive US tax rules by holding as few Canadian mutual funds as possible. Instead, buy mutual funds listed in the United States.

Please share your experience and any feedback you receive from the IRS with us via email at ustaxesforcanadians@gmail.com

---

[1] Chief Counsel Advice 201003013

The rest of this chapter outlines what is, in our view, likely the most compliant way of reporting Canadian mutual funds.

1. Is your mutual fund a passive foreign investment corporation?
2. Form 8621.
3. Part 1 – Elections.
4. The QEF Election.
5. The mark-to-market election.
6. Section 1291 Fund.

1. IS YOUR MUTUAL FUND A PASSIVE FOREIGN INVESTMENT CORPORATION?

Canadian mutual funds are treated as corporations. Because they are outside of the United States, they are foreign corporations. A foreign corporation is a passive foreign investment corporation if it meets either the income or asset test described below.

1. *Income test:* 75% or more of the corporation's gross income for its taxable year is passive income. Passive income means dividends, interest, royalties, rents, or annuities.

   OR

2. *Asset test:* At least 50% of the average percentage of assets held by the foreign corporation during the taxable year are assets that produce passive income or that are held for the production of passive income.

The best way to figure out whether your mutual fund meets either the income test or the asset test is to contact the financial institution that administers the mutual fund and ask. Or you can look at the prospectus (the document that describes the mutual fund) or the mutual fund's financial statements to see what its assets are.

If you receive a gain on a direct or indirect sale of a share of, or a distribution from, a mutual fund that meets either the income or the asset test you must file Form 8621. Most Canadian mutual funds will meet either the income or the asset test. However, to be sure, you can always contact your mutual fund provider and ask or look at their financial statements. You must also file the form if you wish to make one of the elections discussed below.

Once you know that you have an interest in a mutual fund that meets the passive foreign investment company definition, you must file Form 8621. You should complete one of these forms for each interest in a mutual fund that you possess. We now turn to helping you fill out this form.

2. FORM 8621

Form 8621 has four parts to it. The first part of Form 8621 is self-explanatory. Fill out your personal details and check the box marked individual if that reflects your status. On the line marked identifying number, enter your US Social Security Number. Where the form asks for the name of the PFIC, simply enter the name and address of the mutual fund company.

3. FORM 8621 PART 1 – ELECTIONS

Part I is where you decide what kind of tax treatment you want to apply to your foreign mutual fund. Although there are nine choices presented in Part1 of the Form 8621, we only discuss the three main options here:

1. *Take the QEF election.* This means that you will be subject to tax on your share of the fund's capital gains and ordinary income. You have to check with your mutual fund to see if it can provide you with the necessary information.

2. *Use the mark-to-market election.* Under this option, you report the annual gain in value as income (even if you did not realize it). If you have previously reported gains, you can report your losses. You can only take the market to market election if your mutual fund is traded on a stock exchange or meets other criteria.

3. *Do nothing.* This means that you will pay tax on the amount you receive or gain at the top marginal rate plus interest payments. If you take neither election, your mutual fund is referred to as a section 1291 fund.

The other boxes are very complicated variants of the three options. We suggest that unless you receive professional advice to the contrary, you stick with the options described above. That means you should only be checking box A for the QEF election, box F for the mark-to-market election or leaving Part 1 blank (to treat it as a section 1291 fund).

Both elections must be made by the due date, including extensions, of your tax return for the tax year in which you are filing.

Box A is the standard QEF election. It requires you to fill out lines 1(a) through 2(c) of Part II.

Box F should be checked if you wish to take the mark-to-market election. You will then need to fill out Part III.

Having briefly introduced the three of them, let's take a look at each in more detail.

4. THE QEF ELECTION

The first option is the QEF election. For it check box A, and fill out lines 1(a) through 2(c) of Part II of the form.

a. Eligibility to take the election

To take this election your mutual fund needs to provide you with an information slip that reports your share of the earnings of the fund are and your share of any capital gains earned. Your mutual fund may also be required to get IRS permission to allow you to take the QEF election.

To our knowledge, only a few Canadian mutual funds provide this slip. Do not utilize the QEF election without first contacting the company that runs your mutual fund to ensure that it has provided you with the correct slip and that it has received the appropriate permissions from the IRS.

b. Effects of the election

The election allows you to pay tax on your share of income and capital gains earned by the mutual fund. In essence, your foreign mutual fund is treated like an American mutual fund. For example, if you own .001% of a mutual fund that earned $10,000,000 in revenue and $5,000,000 in capital gains you would report $100 of income and $50 of capital gains income.

c. When to take the election

You should take the election in the tax year for which you are filing a return and as soon as possible after purchasing a mutual fund. If you owned a share in your mutual fund before you made this election, the IRS considers that you sold your share at fair market value right before you made the election. That means that you have to use the rules in section 6 to figure out the gain. Let's use an example. Say it is 2012 and you have owned your TD mutual fund since 2002. In 2012, the mutual fund company tells you that you can make the QEF election and gives you an information slip. You are assumed to have sold that mutual fund at its fair market value at the moment before you took the election. This means that you have a gain and you have to use the rules from section 6 to calculate it, pay the deferred tax, and interest.

d. How to make the election

There are three steps to taking the election:

1. Check box A on Part 1 of Form 8621.
2. Complete lines 1(a) to 2(c) of Part II of Form 8621 and attach it to your Form 1040.
3. Attach the information form that you get from the IRS to your return.

Let's go through Part II of Form 8621 line by line. That part of the Form looks like this.

Part II **Income From a Qualified Electing Fund (QEF).** All QEF shareholders complete lines 1a through 2c. If you are making Election D, also complete lines 3a through 4c. (See instructions.)

1a	Enter your pro rata share of the ordinary earnings of the QEF	1a			
b	Enter the portion of line 1a that is included in income under section 951 or that may be excluded under section 1293(g)	1b			
c	Subtract line 1b from line 1a. Enter this amount on your tax return as ordinary income			1c	
2a	Enter your pro rata share of the total net capital gain of the QEF	2a			
b	Enter the portion of line 2a that is included in income under section 951 or that may be excluded under section 1293(g)	2b			
c	Subtract line 2b from line 2a. This amount is a net long-term capital gain. Enter this amount in Part II of the Schedule D used for your income tax return. (See instructions.)			2c	
3a	Add lines 1c and 2c			3a	
b	Enter the total amount of cash and the fair market value of other property distributed or deemed distributed to you during the tax year of the QEF. (See instructions.)	3b			
c	Enter the portion of line 3a not already included in line 3b that is attributable to shares in the QEF that you disposed of, pledged, or otherwise transferred during the tax year	3c			
d	Add lines 3b and 3c			3d	
e	Subtract line 3d from line 3a, and enter the difference (if zero or less, enter amount in brackets)			3e	
	Important: *If line 3e is greater than zero, and no portion of line 1a or 2a is includible in income under section 951, you may make Election D with respect to the amount on line 3e.*				
4a	Enter the total tax for the tax year (See instructions.)	4a			
b	Enter the total tax for the tax year determined without regard to the amount entered on line 3e	4b			
c	Subtract line 4b from line 4a. **This is the deferred tax, the time for payment of which is extended by making Election D. See instructions**			4c	

For Disclosure, Privacy Act, and Paperwork Reduction Act Notice, see separate instructions. Cat. No. 64174H Form **8621** (Rev. 12-2011)

Line 1(a) – Enter on line 1(a) your share of the ordinary earnings of the QEF. This amount will be found on the QEF information slip that your mutual fund provider should give you. Recall that if the mutual fund cannot provide this information you cannot take the QEF election.

Line 1(b) – Unless you have a controlled foreign corporation, which most normal taxpayers do not, you can ignore this line.

Line 1(c) – The total on line c is treated as ordinary income and should be reflected on your tax return. Include this amount on line 21 of your Form 1040.

Line 2(a) – Enter here your pro rata share of net capital gains of the QEF. This amount will be found on the QEF information that your mutual fund provider should give you. Recall that if the mutual fund cannot provide this information you cannot take the QEF election.

Line 2(b) – Unless you have a controlled foreign corporation, which most normal taxpayers do not, you can ignore this line.

Line 2(c) – This amount goes on Schedule D of your tax return.

e. Example

Let's use an example to illustrate. Mark owns shares in a TD Bank mutual fund. He is filing for tax year 2012. He contacts TD Bank to see if they can issue him an appropriate information slip and to see if he can take the QEF election. The information slip he receives indicates that his share of the earnings of the fund is $250 and that his share of the capital gains income is $100. He fills out Form 8621 as follows.

Form **8621** (Rev. December 2011) Department of the Treasury Internal Revenue Service

Information Return by a Shareholder of a Passive Foreign Investment Company or Qualified Electing Fund

▶ **See separate instructions.**

OMB No. 1545-1002 Attachment Sequence No. **69**

Name of shareholder	**Identifying number** (see instructions)
Mark Jones	123-456-789
Number, street, and room or suite no. (If a P.O. box, see instructions.)	Shareholder tax year: calendar year 20 12 or other tax year beginning , 20 and ending , 20 .
2329 West Mall	
City or town, state, and ZIP code or country	
Vancouver, BC Canada V6T 1Z4	

Check type of shareholder filing the return: ☑ Individual ☐ Corporation ☐ Partnership ☐ S Corporation ☐ Nongrantor Trust ☐ Estate

Name of passive foreign investment company (PFIC) or qualified electing fund (QEF)	**Employer identification number** (if any)
TD Bank Canadian Index Fund	
Address (Enter number, street, city or town, and country.)	Tax year of company or fund: calendar year 20 or other tax year beginning , 20 and ending , 20 .

Part I Elections (See instructions.)

A ☑ **Election To Treat the PFIC as a QEF.** I, a shareholder of a PFIC, elect to treat the PFIC as a QEF. *Complete lines 1a through 2c of Part II.*

B ☐ **Deemed Sale Election.** I, a shareholder on the first day of a PFIC's first tax year as a QEF, elect to recognize gain on the deemed sale of my interest in the PFIC. *Enter gain or loss on line 10f of Part IV.*

C ☐ **Deemed Dividend Election.** I, a shareholder on the first day of a PFIC's first tax year as a QEF that is a controlled foreign corporation (CFC), elect to treat an amount equal to my share of the post-1986 earnings and profits of the CFC as an excess distribution. *Enter this amount on line 10e of Part IV.*

D ☐ **Election To Extend Time For Payment of Tax.** I, a shareholder of a QEF, elect to extend the time for payment of tax on the undistributed earnings and profits of the QEF until this election is terminated. *Complete lines 3a through 4c of Part II to calculate the tax that may be deferred.*

Note: *If any portion of line 1a or line 2a of Part II is includible under section 951, you may* **not** *make this election. Also, see sections 1294(c) and 1294(f) and the related regulations for events that terminate this election.*

E ☐ **Election To Recognize Gain on Deemed Sale of PFIC.** I, a shareholder of a former PFIC or a PFIC to which section 1297(d) applies, elect to treat as an excess distribution the gain recognized on the deemed sale of my interest in the PFIC, or, if I qualify, my share of the PFIC's post-1986 earnings and profits deemed distributed, on the last day of its last tax year as a PFIC under section 1297(a). *Enter gain on line 10f of Part IV.*

F ☐ **Election To Mark-to-Market PFIC Stock.** I, a shareholder of a PFIC, elect to mark-to-market the PFIC stock that is marketable within the meaning of section 1296(e). *Complete Part III.*

G ☐ **Deemed Dividend Election With Respect to a Section 1297(e) PFIC.** I, a shareholder of a section 1297(e) PFIC, within the meaning of Regulations section 1.1291-9(j)(2)(iv), elect to make a deemed dividend election with respect to the Section 1297(e) PFIC. My holding period in the stock of the Section 1297(e) PFIC includes the CFC qualification date, as defined in Regulations section 1.1297-3(d).

H ☐ **Deemed Dividend Election With Respect to a Former PFIC.** I, a shareholder of a former PFIC, within the meaning of Regulations section 1.1291-9(j)(2)(iv), elect to make a deemed dividend election with respect to the former PFIC. My holding period in the stock of the former PFIC includes the termination date, as defined in Regulations section 1.1298-3(d).

Part II Income From a Qualified Electing Fund (QEF). All QEF shareholders complete lines 1a through 2c. If you are making Election D, also complete lines 3a through 4c. (See instructions.)

1a	Enter your pro rata share of the ordinary earnings of the QEF	1a	250		
b	Enter the portion of line 1a that is included in income under section 951 or that may be excluded under section 1293(g)	1b	0		
c	Subtract line 1b from line 1a. Enter this amount on your tax return as ordinary income			1c	250
2a	Enter your pro rata share of the total net capital gain of the QEF	2a	100		
b	Enter the portion of line 2a that is included in income under section 951 or that may be excluded under section 1293(g)	2b	0		
c	Subtract line 2b from line 2a. This amount is a net long-term capital gain. Enter this amount in Part II of the Schedule D used for your income tax return. (See instructions.)			2c	100
3a	Add lines 1c and 2c			3a	
b	Enter the total amount of cash and the fair market value of other property distributed or deemed distributed to you during the tax year of the QEF. (See instructions.)	3b			
c	Enter the portion of line 3a not already included in line 3b that is attributable to shares in the QEF that you disposed of, pledged, or otherwise transferred during the tax year	3c			
d	Add lines 3b and 3c			3d	
e	Subtract line 3d from line 3a, and enter the difference (if zero or less, enter amount in brackets)			3e	
	Important: *If line 3e is greater than zero, and no portion of line 1a or 2a is includible in income under section 951, you may make Election D with respect to the amount on line 3e.*				
4a	Enter the total tax for the tax year (See instructions.)	4a			
b	Enter the total tax for the tax year determined without regard to the amount entered on line 3e	4b			
c	Subtract line 4b from line 4a. **This is the deferred tax, the time for payment of which is extended by making Election D. See instructions**			4c	

For Disclosure, Privacy Act, and Paperwork Reduction Act Notice, see separate instructions. Cat. No. 64174H Form **8621** (Rev. 12-2011)

Mark then includes $250 on line 21 of his Form 1040 and $100 on his Schedule D. You should see Chapters 9 and 10 for how to fill out your Schedule D.

5. THE MARK-TO-MARKET ELECTION

The mark-to-market election is another option for reporting income from funds that meet the definition of a PFIC.

a. Eligibility

The mark-to-market election is available for mutual funds that are traded on a non-US stock exchange. Exchange traded funds (ETFs) are generally traded on a stock exchange. Thus, there is likely little problem with using the mark-to-market election for your exchange traded funds.

You might also be able to use the mark-to-market election for your mutual funds, if they meet all of the following criteria as established by Regulation 1.1296 – 2(d):

- The mutual fund has more than 100 shareholders;
- The shares of the mutual fund are purchasable by the general public;
- The market quotations of a class of shares are published at least weekly;
- Independent auditors certify financial statements on an annual basis;
- The mutual fund is supervised by a government agency (like a provincial regulator);
- The mutual fund has no debt outstanding;
- 90% of the mutual fund's income is passive (interest, dividends, gains);
- 90% of the mutual fund's assets produce passive income.

Because these criteria are so specific, it is impossible to generalize whether your mutual fund meets them. You will need to contact the mutual fund or your investment advisor and ask these questions.

b. Effects of the election

Under this election, each year you report what your mutual fund was worth, even if you did not sell it. From this, you subtract the cost you paid for it. If the result is a gain, you report this as ordinary income. The result of a loss is deductible only to the extent that gains have previously been reported. How to calculate and report this is described below. It does have an advantage over the default situation in that you do not have to pay interest.

c. Reporting and calculating the mark-to-market election

To make the election:

1. Check box F in Part I,
2. Complete Part III to report the gain or loss, and
3. Consult the section below to determine if you need to fill out Part IV.

i. Do I need to fill out Part IV also?

You also need to fill out Part IV of Form 8621 if this is the first year that you made the mark-to-market election, but you owned the mutual fund for years before the one in which you made the election. Put differently, if the tax year for which you are filing is the first one for which the mark-to-market election has been made, then the section 1291 rules (so Part IV of the form and section 6 of this chapter) apply to the previous years. The section 1291 rules would not apply to the current year. If section 1291 does apply, go to section 6 and make the calculations for past years but do not include the current tax year.

Let's use an example to illustrate. The year is 2013. You have owned an exchange-traded fund which qualified as a passive foreign investment corporation since 2008. In 2013, you take the mark-to-market election on the exchange traded fund for the first time. The rules section 1291 (outlined in section 6) apply to all the years you owned the fund before 2013.

d. Figuring out Part III

Part III of Form 8621 looks like this.

Form 8621 (Rev. 12-2011) Page **2**

Part III **Gain or (Loss) From Mark-to-Market Election** (See instructions.)

5a	Enter the fair market value of your PFIC stock at the end of the tax year	**5a**	
b	Enter your adjusted basis in the stock at the end of the tax year	**5b**	
c	Subtract line 5b from line 5a. If a gain, do not complete lines 6 and 7. Include this amount as ordinary income on your tax return. If a loss, go to line 6	**5c**	
6	Enter any unreversed inclusions (as defined in section 1296(d))	**6**	
7	Enter the loss from line 5c, but only to the extent of unreversed inclusions on line 6. Include this amount as an ordinary loss on your tax return	**7**	
8	**If you sold or otherwise disposed of any section 1296 stock (see instructions) during the tax year:**		
a	Enter the fair market value of the stock on the date of sale or disposition	**8a**	
b	Enter the adjusted basis of the stock on the date of sale or disposition	**8b**	
c	Subtract line 8b from line 8a. If a gain, do not complete line 9. Include this amount as ordinary income on your tax return. If a loss, go to line 9	**8c**	
9a	Enter any unreversed inclusions (as defined in section 1296(d))	**9a**	
b	Enter the loss from line 8c, but only to the extent of unreversed inclusions on line 9a. Include this amount as an ordinary loss on your tax return. If the loss on line 8c exceeds unreversed inclusions on line 9a, complete line 9c	**9b**	
c	Enter the amount by which the loss on line 8c exceeds unreversed inclusions on line 9a. Include this amount on your tax return according to the rules generally applicable for losses provided elsewhere in the Code and regulations	**9c**	

Note. See instructions in case of multiple dispositions.

Line 5(a) asks you for the fair market value of your stake in the PFIC at the end of the tax year. To calculate this amount, just report what your interest in the mutual fund was worth at the end of the tax year in question.

Line 5(b) seeks the adjusted basis for the stock. The adjusted basis is your cost of the stock and must be increased by the amount included in income in previous years. The adjusted basis must be decreased by the amount allowed as a deduction in previous years. If this is your first year making the mark-to-market election, you can ignore this line. However, if you made the election in prior years to take the mark-to-market election, you will need to keep records of how much income you reported and/or how much of a deduction you took and adjust your original basis accordingly.

On line 5(c), you are asked to subtract line 5(b) from line 5(a). If the amount is positive, you have a gain and should include the amount as ordinary income on line 21 of your Form 1040.

Line 6 concerns unreversed inclusions. Unreversed inclusions are the excess of the amounts that were included in income under the mark-to-market rules for prior tax years over the amounts allowed as a deduction under the mark-to-market rules for prior tax years. This means that for each prior year in which you take the mark-to-market election you have to note somewhere the amount of income that you include on section 5(c). That will limit the amount of your allowable deductions for future years. Put differently, you will only be able to deduct in the current tax year up to the amount that you included in income (and thus paid tax on) in prior tax years. Keep these records and include the information every year on line 6 of Form 8621.

On line 7, enter the total loss from line 5(c), but only to the extent that you had an unreversed inclusion on line 6. If you did not have any unreversed inclusions, leave line 7 blank. If you did, enter the amount from line 6.

Line 8 concerns shares in a mutual fund that you sold for which you had previously used the mark-to-market election.

On line 8(a) enter the fair market value of the units on the date they were sold.

Line 8(b) asks for the adjusted basis at the date of sale or disposition. Recall that the adjusted basis includes the amount of income included in prior years (net of any deductions claimed in respect of losses).

Line 8(c) asks for the total of line 8(b) subtracted from line 8(a). If line 8(c) is positive, the result is a gain and should be entered on line 21 of your Form 1040. If line 8(c) is negative, then you must fill out line 9.

On line 9(a) enter any unreversed inclusions. This should be the same amount that is included on line 6.

Line 9(b) – Enter the loss from line 8(c), but only to the extent of unreversed inclusions on line 9(a). This loss is treated as ordinary loss.

Line 9(c) – Enter the amount by which the loss on line 8(c) exceeds the unreversed inclusions. Find this amount by subtracting line 9(b) from line 9(a).

All losses are treated as ordinary losses. Enter the negative amount on line 21 of your Form 1040.

Multiple dispositions. In the case of multiple dispositions, attach a statement for each disposition using the same format shown on lines 8 through 9(c). Then

- Enter “multiple” on lines 8(a), 8(b), and 9(a).
- Enter your net ordinary gains on line 8(c) (do not enter any net losses on line 8(c).
- Enter your net ordinary losses on line 9(b).
- Enter your net “other” losses on line 9(c).

e. Example

George Smith bought some Vanguard exchange traded funds in 2012. Vanguard units are traded on the Toronto Stock Exchange and so therefore he can use the mark-to-market election. He bought 45 shares for which he paid US $15 each. So in total his shares were worth $675 at the time of purchase. At the end of 2012, his shares were worth $20 each. So the total value of these shares was $900. The difference is $225 (value at end of tax year ($900) – original price ($675) = $225). Because this is George’s first year owning the shares, he does not have any past unreversed inclusions. He would check box F of his Form 8621. He would then include $225 on line 21 of his Form 1040.

6. SECTION 1291 FUND

If you are not able to make either the QEF election or the mark-to-market election, your stake in a mutual fund is called a section 1291 fund. The name simply refers to the section of the Internal Revenue Code in which the rules are found. Should this section apply, you will pay tax on your normal distributions (money you receive from the mutual fund).

You will also have to pay extra tax on your excess distributions. An excess distribution is the part of the distribution received from a section 1291 fund in the current tax year that is greater than 125% of the average distributions received in respect to such stock by the shareholder during the three preceding tax years (or, if shorter, the portion of the unit holder's holding period before the current tax year). No part of a distribution received or deemed received during the first tax year of the shareholder's holding period of the stock will be treated as an excess distribution. The excess distribution is determined on a per share basis and is allocated to each day in the shareholder's holding period of the stock.

Here is an illustrative example. Let's say you purchased $10,000 of Canadian mutual funds on January 1, 2007. You didn't receive any income from the fund. On December 31, 2011, you sold the fund for $15,000 for a gain of $5,000 (sale price of $15,000 – cost of $10,000.). You would pay the following taxes and interest on this gain.[2]

Year	Gain allocated	Tax at 35%	Interest at 6%
2007	1,000	350	84
2008	1,000	350	63
2009	1,000	350	42
2010	1,000	350	21
2011	1,000	350	0
Totals	5,000	1750	210

Note that any gain from a section 1291 fund is an "excess" distribution. How to determine whether you have an excess distribution is discussed in the next section.

a. Reporting a distribution or a gain from a section 1291 fund

Part IV of Form 8621 is where you report any gain or distribution from a section 1291 fund. It looks like this.

[2] This example is taken from the following presentation by Price Waterhouse Cooper http://www.pwc.com/ca/en/tax/human-resource-service/webcast/publications/us-citizens-irs-reporting-rules-2011-10-en.pdf

Part IV **Distributions From and Dispositions of Stock of a Section 1291 Fund** (See instructions.)
*Complete a **separate** Part IV for each excess distribution (see instructions).*

10a	Enter your total distributions from the section 1291 fund during the current tax year with respect to the applicable stock. If the holding period of the stock began in the current tax year, see instructions	**10a**	
b	Enter the total distributions (reduced by the portions of such distributions that were excess distributions but not included in income under section 1291(a)(1)(B)) made by the fund with respect to the applicable stock for each of the 3 years preceding the current tax year (or if shorter, the portion of the shareholder's holding period before the current tax year)	**10b**	
c	Divide line 10b by 3. (See instructions if the number of preceding tax years is less than 3.)	**10c**	
d	Multiply line 10c by 125% (1.25)	**10d**	
e	Subtract line 10d from line 10a. This amount, if more than zero, is the excess distribution with respect to the applicable stock. If zero or less and you did not dispose of stock during the tax year, **do not** complete the rest of Part IV. See instructions if you received more than one distribution during the current tax year. Also, see instructions for rules for reporting a nonexcess distribution on your income tax return	**10e**	
f	Enter gain or loss from the disposition of stock of a section 1291 fund or former section 1291 fund. If a gain, complete line 11. If a loss, show it in brackets and **do not** complete line 11.	**10f**	
11a	Attach a statement for each distribution and disposition. Show your holding period for each share of stock or block of shares held. Allocate the excess distribution to each day in your holding period. Add all amounts that are allocated to days in each tax year.		
b	Enter the total of the amounts determined in line 11a that are allocable to the current tax year and tax years before the foreign corporation became a PFIC (pre-PFIC tax years). Enter these amounts on your income tax return as other income	**11b**	
c	Enter the aggregate increases in tax (before credits) for each tax year in your holding period (other than the current tax year and pre-PFIC years). (See instructions.)	**11c**	
d	Foreign tax credit. (See instructions.)	**11d**	
e	Subtract line 11d from line 11c. Enter this amount on your income tax return as "additional tax." (See instructions.)	**11e**	
f	Determine interest on each net increase in tax determined on line 11e using the rates and methods of section 6621. Enter the aggregate amount of interest here. (See instructions.)	**11f**	

Form **8621** (Rev. 12-2011)

The amount that you enter on line 10(a) is determined by whether this is or is not the first year you owned the mutual fund.

i. If this is your first year owning the mutual fund

If the year in which you are filing is the first year that you owned the mutual fund, there is no excess distribution and Part IV should be completed as follows.

a) Enter the total distribution on line 10(a) of Form 8621.

b) Include this amount on line 9(a) of your Form 1040 as ordinary dividend income.

If you did not sell or otherwise dispose of the mutual fund during the tax year, do not complete the rest of Part IV. If you did dispose of that stock during the tax year, skip lines 10(b) through 10(e) and complete lines 10(f) and 11.

ii. If you have owned the mutual fund for more than one tax year

More complicated steps are required if you have owned the fund for more than one year.

On line 10(a) you should enter your total distributions during the current tax year.

Subtract from this amount any excess distribution that is related to this amount. You will calculate this later on line 11(b). So you will have to circle back once you complete line 10(a).

Line 10(b) – Here you should enter the total distributions made by the fund for each of the three years preceding the current tax year (or if fewer than 3 years, the number of years that you held the mutual fund before the current tax year).

Line 10(c) – Divide the amount on line 10(b) by 3. If the number of tax years in your holding period prior to the current tax year is less than 3, divide the amount on line 10(b) by that number.

Line 10(d) – Multiply line 10(c) by 125% (1.25)

Line 10(e) – Subtract line 10(d) from line 10(a). This amount, if more than zero, is the excess distribution with respect to the applicable stock. If zero or less and you did not dispose of the mutual fund shares during the tax year, **do not** complete the rest of Part IV.

Line 10(f) – Enter the gain or loss from the disposition of stock of a section 1291 fund. If a gain, complete line 11. If a loss, show it in brackets and **do not** complete line 11. Note that a gain from the sale of a mutual fund is always an excess distribution.

If there is no excess distribution, meaning that lines 10(e) and 10(f) are either at zero or are negative, simply enter the amount from line 10(a) on line 9(a) of your Form 1040.

iii. If you have an excess distribution

You know that you have an excess distribution if either line 10(e) or line 10(f) is positive. As noted above, all capital gains from the sale of mutual funds are considered excess distributions.

You will have to pay tax on the excess distribution at the highest marginal rate in effect at the time. Plus, you will have to pay interest on the underpayment of taxes. This may be expensive, so it will be worth having your taxes professionally prepared to make sure that the amount of interest is calculated properly and that you have maximized your other tax deductions/credits to reduce it. We have explained the process below. But again, we suggest not doing this yourself.

Line 11(a) – Determine the taxation of the excess distribution on a separate sheet and attach it to Form 8621. Divide the amount on line 10(e) or 10(f), whichever applies, by the number of days during which you held the mutual fund. This is referred to as the "holding period." The holding period of the unit is treated as ending on the date of the distribution or disposition. Your financial institution should be able to tell you for how many days you held the mutual fund.

For instance, let's say that the amount on line 10(e) is $5,000 and you have owned the share of the mutual fund for 5 years prior to the distribution. You would calculate $5,000 (total distribution) /1,825 (365 days/year x 5 years) = 2.73.

Line 11(b) – Enter the amount that is related to the current tax year.

Line 11(c) – Determine the tax for each tax year during which you have owned the mutual fund (other than the current year) by multiplying the part of the excess distribution allocated that year (as determined on line 11(a) by the highest rate of tax in effect for that tax year. For 2003–2012 it was 35%. A historical chart of the top rates is included at the end of the chapter. Add tax computed for all years. Enter this amount on line 11(c).

Line 11(d) – Here is where you can take a foreign tax credit for Canadian taxes that you paid on distributions from a mutual fund. To figure the amount on line 11(d) you need to do the following:

a. Find out how much Canadian tax you paid on the mutual fund income.

b. Apportion that tax between the excess part of the distribution and the non-excess part.

c. Report the amount of foreign tax paid on the excess distribution.

First, let's discuss how to figure out how much Canadian tax you paid on the income.

Canadian mutual fund providers may or may not withhold tax on distributions they make. So you are on your own in figuring out how much Canadian tax you paid. The IRS does not have a specific formula for this. Here is a rough way of doing it:

1. Divide the total distribution by your total income.
2. Multiply the result of step 1 by the total amount of tax you paid.
3. The result of the multiplication is the amount of tax that is creditable to your mutual fund distribution.

Let's take an example. As always, you start by converting all of the relevant amounts to US dollars. Say you received a US $500 dividend from your TD Bank mutual fund. You earned US $50,000 in total income and on which you paid US $15,000 in taxes. Following the steps above:

1. Divide the total distribution ($500) by your total income ($50,000). The result is .01.
2. You then multiply .01 by $15,000 (the total amount of tax you paid).
3. The total, $150, is the amount of Canadian tax that is creditable to your TD bank mutual fund income.

You then take this $150 figure and move on to the next step.

Second, the foreign tax credit has to be apportioned between the part of the distribution that is excess and the part that is not. Do the following:

1. Divide the amount on line 10(e) by the amount on line 10(a).
2. Take the result and multiply it by the total amount of tax you have paid.
3. The total is the amount of foreign tax that you can use to reduce the excess distribution.

To reprise the example, your total Canadian tax is $150 and your total distribution is $500. The excess part of the distribution is $200. So you divide $200 by 500 and the result is .4. Then you multiply .4 by $150 and the result is $60. Under this example you could enter $60 on line 11(d).

If you sell your stake in your mutual fund you cannot make use of the foreign tax credit to reduce the amount of your gain.

Line 11(e) – This amount is the aggregate excess distribution tax and is included on your tax return as additional taxes.

Enter this amount on Form 1040 to the left of the line 44 entry space. Enter "Sec. 1291" next to the amount and include the amount as part of the total for line 44.

Line 11(f) – Interest is charged on the additional tax for the period beginning on the due date of your income tax return for the tax year to which the additional tax is attributable and ending with the due date of your income tax return for the tax year of the excess distribution.

Calculating this interest is complicated. The amount of interest charged changes every quarter. It is calculated according to the rules that govern an underpayment of tax. What this means is that for each three month period in which you have an excess distribution you have to go back and research what the interest rate was. Then you have to compound it daily.

We have included a chart with the historical interest rates in Appendix 3. For example, if you have $500 in excess distributions in 2011, you would have to go to the chart and find the interest rate for the different quarters of 2011 and compound this daily.

Enter the interest at the bottom right margin of Form 1040, page 1 and label it as "Sec. 1291 interest." Include this amount in your check or money order payable to the United States Treasury. If you would otherwise receive a refund, reduce the refund by the interest due.

Historical Highest Marginal Income Tax Rates

Year	Top Marginal Rate	Year	Top Marginal Rate	Year	Top Marginal Rate
1913	7.0%	1947	86.45%	1981	69.13%
1914	7.0%	1948	82.13%	1982	50.00%
1915	7.0%	1949	82.13%	1983	50.00%
1916	15.0%	1950	91.00%	1984	50.00%
1917	67.0%	1951	91.00%	1985	50.00%
1918	77.0%	1952	92.00%	1986	50.00%
1919	73.0%	1953	92.00%	1987	38.50%
1920	73.0%	1954	91.00%	1988	28.00%
1921	73.0%	1955	91.00%	1989	28.00%
1922	56.0%	1956	91.00%	1990	31.00%
1923	56.0%	1957	91.00%	1991	31.00%
1924	46.0%	1958	91.00%	1992	31.00%
1925	25.0%	1959	91.00%	1993	39.60%
1926	25.0%	1960	91.00%	1994	39.60%
1927	25.0%	1961	91.00%	1995	39.60%
1928	25.0%	1962	91.00%	1996	39.60%
1929	24.0%	1963	91.00%	1997	39.60%
1930	25.0%	1964	77.00%	1998	39.60%
1931	25.0%	1965	70.00%	1999	39.60%
1932	63.0%	1966	70.00%	2000	39.60%
1933	63.0%	1967	70.00%	2001	38.60%
1934	63.0%	1968	75.25%	2002	38.60%
1935	63.0%	1969	77.00%	2003	35.00%
1936	79.0%	1970	71.75%	2004	35.00%
1937	79.0%	1971	70.00%	2005	35.00%
1938	79.0%	1972	70.00%	2006	35.00%
1939	79.0%	1973	70.00%	2007	35.00%
1940	81.10%	1974	70.00%	2008	35.00%
1941	81.00%	1975	70.00%	2009	35.00%
1942	88.00%	1976	70.00%	2010	35.00%
1943	88.00%	1977	70.00%	2011	35.00%
1944	94.00%	1978	70.00%	2012	35.00%
1945	94.00%	1979	70.00%		
1946	86.45%	1980	70.00%		

43

YOU HAVE A TFSA, RESP, OR RDSP

Unfortunately, there is a great deal of confusion surrounding how the IRS views common Canadian tax-driven savings plans such as the Tax Free Savings Account (TFSA), the Registered Education Savings Plan (RESP), and the Registered Disability Savings Plan (RDSP). Despite the requirement that US citizens in Canada must file US tax returns, the US and the IRS have provided no guidance regarding such common Canadian investment arrangements. One thing that is clear, however, is that they provide no shelter whatsoever from US tax. This means that for each taxation year, you must report all interest, gains, dividends, or any other income that are earned within any such accounts. For US tax purposes, these accounts do not function the way they are designed to function in Canada.

To make matters more complicated, many accountants suggest that these accounts are foreign trusts (a type of legal arrangement). If this is the case, then a US citizen in Canada holding any of these products would be required to file Forms 3520 and 3520-A every year. These forms are onerous and complicated. Additionally, there may be interest charged on withdrawals from your accounts. Be aware that this is not merely a question of filling out extra forms. It could cost you money as well.

Despite the fact that the US is aware of these Canadian investment products, the IRS has never made its views clear on the appropriate US treatment of them. We have written to the IRS seeking clarification, but no reply had been received by the time this book went to press.

Note, that regardless of their legal classification you must report all TFSA/RESP/RDSP accounts on Form 8938 and/or your FBAR form. This chapter outlines how to deal with your TFSA/RESP/RDSP for US tax purposes. It is organized as follows:

1. Option 1 – avoid the TFSA/RESP/RDSP.
2. Option 2 – have your non-US spouse hold them.
3. Option 3 – keep your TFSA/RESP/RDSP.
    a. Report all income they generate.
    b. Write to the IRS and ask for its views on how to report.

1. OPTION 1 – AVOID THE TFSA/RESP/RDSP

The simplest way to avoid problems is to avoid holding a TFSA/RESP or RDSP altogether. This is not investment advice—it is merely a way of making your US tax obligations simpler to discharge.

2. OPTION 2 – NON-US SPOUSE HOLDS THE ACCOUNT(S)

If you are married to a non-US spouse, another option is to have your spouse hold the TFSA, RESP, or RDSP. As long as you do not elect to treat your spouse as a US resident alien, and you have no signing authority over the account, you will not be required to report these accounts to the IRS.

3. OPTION 3 – KEEP YOUR TFSA, RESP, RDSP

If you have a TFSA, RESP, or a RDSP and want to continue to keep the account(s), we suggest following two steps: a) report all income that the accounts generate and b) advise the IRS of their existence. We discuss these steps in turn.

a. Report and pay tax on all income in a TFSA/RESP/RDSP

Unlike an RRSP, there is no way to defer paying tax on income that accumulates in a TFSA, RESP, or RDSP. Thus, every year you will have to report all income (including gains, dividends, and interest) that builds up inside one of these accounts. Your financial institution will generally not issue you a tax slip with this information on it. Instead, you will have to call them and ask for it or use the financial statements they provide to identify the amounts.

b. Write to the IRS and advise them

The IRS has not made its position clear. In cases where the rules are ambiguous, full disclosure is best. You will likely have to report the accounts on your FBAR form. Nevertheless, we suggest that you write to the IRS (as discussed below) and inform them that you hold a TFSA, RESP, or RDSP and seek its directions on how to report this in the future. It may spur them to clarify their position. It will also demonstrate that while you are unsure of the rules, you have attempted to comply with them as best you can. Such a letter should contain the following information:

- A list of all of your TFSA, RESP, or RDSP accounts, where they are held and the total value of each.
- That you have reported all income contained in those accounts on your Form 1040.
- A description of the purpose of the account. The following should suffice:
  - *TFSA* – A Tax Free Savings Account is a Canadian government-registered account held with a financial institution. It is a Canadian government program designed to encourage saving. Contributions to a Tax Free Savings Account are not deductible in computing income for Canadian tax purposes. However, income earned on those contributions is not taxed—even when withdrawn.
  - *RESP* – A Registered Education Savings Plan (RESP) is a Canadian government-registered account held with a financial institution. It is a Canadian government program which encourages families to save for the eventual costs of children's post-secondary education. Contributions to the account by the parents are not tax deductible. Some contributions are matched by the Canadian government. Tax on any income earned inside the account is deferred until the beneficiary withdraws the amount, at which time it is fully taxable as ordinary income.
  - *RDSP* – A registered disability savings plan (RDSP) is a Canadian government-registered savings plan established to help parents and others save for the long-term financial security of a person who is disabled. RDSPs are usually held with a financial institution. Contributions to the account are not tax deductible. Some contributions are matched by the Canadian government. Tax on any income earned inside the account is deferred until the beneficiary withdraws the amount, at which time it is fully taxable as ordinary income.

- A request that the IRS clarify how to disclose these accounts in the future and how to treat any withdrawals.
- Your signature and the date of the letter. You should attach a copy of the letter to your tax return and keep a copy for your records.

Please share any feedback you receive from the IRS with us at ustaxesforcanadians@gmail.com so we can update the information in subsequent editions.

44

IF YOU HAVE MORE THAN $10,000 IN NON-US BANK ACCOUNTS[1]

The United States has recently imposed very strict disclosure requirements on its citizens. If the total value of your non-US financial accounts exceeds US $10,000 you have to file Form TD-F 90-22.1. The form is otherwise known as Report of the Foreign Bank and Financial Accounts ("FBAR").

1. WHO HAS TO FILE A FBAR

The rule is quite simple. US citizens whose financial accounts cumulatively exceed US $10,000 at any point in the year are required to file a FBAR form.

What financial accounts must be reported? The definition is expansive. A financial account includes, but is not limited to, securities, brokerage, savings, demand, checking, deposit, time deposit, or other accounts maintained with a financial institution. It also includes insurance policies and mutual funds that may be held outside an account. All accounts located outside of the United States must be reported.

In practice, this means that most accounts that most readers of this guide have will have to be reported. Since this is merely a reporting requirement, meaning you do not have to pay tax for simply having these accounts, it is best to err on the side of caution.

As of January 1, 2013, most Canadian financial institutions will also be required to report this information. Problems can arise if your bank reports an account that you do not.

Your spouse is not required to file a separate FBAR report if your FBAR report covers joint accounts.

2. HOW AND WHEN TO FILE

The FBAR is not filed with a filer's federal income tax return. Instead, it must be sent separately to the US treasury at the following address:

United States Department of the Treasury
P.O. Box 32621
Detroit, MI 48232-0621

Regardless of when your taxes are due, you must file the FBAR by June 30 of the year following the calendar year being reported. It is also possible to fill out and file your FBAR online. The following website can be used for this http://bsaefiling.fincen.treas.gov/Enroll_Individual.html.

[1] This chapter is based on, and some text is copied from, the instructions for Form TD-F 90-22.1

3. FILLING OUT THE FBAR FORM

Once you have met the threshold, you must report all of your foreign financial accounts. Let's walk you through the various sections of the form before using an example.

a. Part I – Filer information

This section is where you put in your biographical information. It is mostly self-explanatory. On line 2, you will likely check individual. On line 4, you should enter your Social Security Number.

b. Part II – Information on financial accounts owned separately

In this section, you report financial accounts of which you are the sole owner. Each sub part of the section is identical. That is because each account must be reported separately, but in an identical manner. Aside from line 15, the form is self-explanatory.

Line 15 asks you to determine the maximum account value. The maximum value of an account is a reasonable approximation of the greatest value of currency or non-monetary assets in the account during the calendar year. In the case of non-United States currency, convert the maximum account value for each account into United States dollars. Convert foreign currency by using the Treasury's Financial Management Service rate (this rate may be found at www.fms.treas.gov) from the last day of the calendar year.

c. Part III – Information on financial accounts owned jointly

Here is where you enter information on accounts you hold or own jointly with other people (such as your spouse). As with the previous section, this one is largely self-explanatory.

Line 15 asks for the maximum value of the account. Follow the same instructions as above.

Line 24 seeks the number of joint owners. If, for example, the account is a mutual fund, then the number of owners may not be known. You should just write "unknown."

For lines 25–33, leave blank items for which no information is available. If the filer's spouse has an interest in a jointly owned account, the filer's spouse is the principal joint owner. Enter "(spouse)" on line 26 after the last name of the joint spousal owner.

d. Part IV – Signature authority but no financial interest

This section is for those accounts over which you have a signature authority but not a financial interest. With a few exceptions, this will likely not apply to most individuals. For instance, though, if you have a power of attorney over someone else's bank account and that gives you a signature authority, you must fill out this section.

e. Part V – Consolidated FBAR

You can ignore this section. It is for a United States person that owns directly or indirectly a greater than 50 percent interest in another entity that is required to file an FBAR is permitted to file a consolidated FBAR on behalf of itself and such other entity.

4. PENALTIES

The penalties for failing to file your FBAR are severe. If there is reasonable cause for the failure and the balance in the account is properly reported, no penalty will be imposed. A person who willfully fails to report an account or account identifying information may be subject to a civil monetary penalty equal to the greater of $100,000 or 50 percent of the balance in the account at the time of the violation. As noted above, come January 1, 2013, Canadian banks will start reporting financial information to the IRS.

45

IF YOU HAVE MORE THAN $200,000 IN NON-US ASSETS[1]

US citizens who own foreign financial assets are required to report them. The nature of these reporting obligations depends on where you live. If you are a bona fide resident of a country outside the United States or live outside of the United States for more than 330 days during a 12-month period, you must report any interest in more than $200,000 of financial interest.

The $200,000 level is what the IRS calls a reporting threshold. Cross it and you must file Form 8938. This chapter explains what the threshold is, how to calculate it, and how to file Form 8938 if you meet it. It is organized as follows:

1. Do you have to report your foreign financial interests?
2. What assets are counted toward the reporting threshold?
3. How to value assets that count toward the threshold.
4. If you cross the threshold- filing form 8938.
5. Example.
6. Penalties for failing to file.
7. Further information.

1. DO YOU HAVE TO REPORT YOUR FOREIGN FINANCIAL INTERESTS?

Whether you need to report your assets depends on whether you cross the reporting threshold. If you spend more than 330 days outside the United States or are a bona fide resident of a country outside of the United States for an entire tax year, you are obliged to report your foreign financial assets if they are more than $200,000 on the last day of the tax year or more than $300,000 at any time during the tax year. For those who are married and file a joint return, you must file form 8938 if the total value of all specified foreign financial assets you or your spouse owns is more than $400,000 on the last day of the tax year or more than $600,000 at any time during the tax year. In order to determine if you meet the threshold to file, you need to know how to value those assets.

2. WHAT ASSETS ARE COUNTED TOWARD THE REPORTING THRESHOLD

Having established the general rule, the next question to address is what constitutes foreign financial assets for the purposes of the total. Specified foreign financial assets include the following assets:

- Financial accounts maintained by a non-US financial institution. This includes Canadian pension plans.

---

[1] This chapter is based on, and borrows text from, the instructions to Form 8938.

- The following foreign financial assets if they are held for investment and not held in an account maintained by a financial institution:

  a. stock issued by a foreign corporation;

  b. a capital or profits interest in a non-US partnership;

  c. an interest in a foreign trust or foreign estate.

You have an interest in a specified foreign financial asset if any income, gains, losses, deductions, credits, gross proceeds, or distributions from holding or disposing of the asset are or would be required to be reported, included, or otherwise reflected on your income tax return.

3. HOW TO VALUE ASSETS THAT COUNT TOWARD THE THRESHOLD

Now that you know what type of asset you need to count toward the threshold, the next step is to figure out how to compute the value of those assets. The value of a specified foreign financial asset is the asset's fair market value. The value of a specified foreign financial asset must be first determined in the foreign currency (Canadian dollars) and then converted to US dollars. Use the currency exchange rate on the last day of the tax year to figure the maximum value of a specified foreign financial asset or the value of a specified foreign financial asset for the purpose of determining the total value of your specified foreign financial assets to see whether you have met the reporting threshold.

4. IF YOU CROSS THE THRESHOLD

If you cross the threshold, you are required to file Form 8938. Here we show you how to do this.

a. Assets that need not be reported

You do not have to report a specified foreign financial asset on Form 8938 if you report it on one or more of the following forms that you file timely with the IRS for the same tax year.

- Form 3520 – to report interests in foreign trusts.
- Form 5471 – Information Return of US Persons with Respect to Certain Foreign Corporations.
- Form 8621 – to report interests in mutual funds.
- Form 8891 – to report your RRSP.

Instead, you must identify on Form 8938 the form(s) on which you report the specified foreign financial assets and how many of these forms you file. Items reported on these forms still count towards your threshold. Therefore if you have an RRSP with $400,000 in assets, you have exceeded your threshold and must file a Form 8938 even though that RRSP does not have to be reported on the form 8938 itself.

If you report all of your specified foreign financial assets on other forms, you do not have to report them on Form 8938. Instead, enter your name, identifying number, and address at the top of the form, and complete Part IV only. Complete Part IV in addition to reporting your other specified foreign financial assets if you report only a part of your specified foreign financial assets on one or more of these forms.

b. Identifying information

Enter your name(s), identifying number, address, and tax year as shown on the annual return you are filing with Form 8938.

Identifying number. Enter the first Social Security Number (SSN) or individual taxpayer identification number (ITIN) on your income tax return.

Type of filer. Check the box that shows the type of filer you are. If you are not a married individual filing a joint income tax return, check the "Other individual" box.

Form 8938 for previously filed annual return. Check this box if this Form 8938 is an original, amended, or supplemental Form 8938 that relates to a previously filed return.

c. Part 1 – Foreign deposit and custodial accounts

Use Part I to report information for foreign deposit and custodial accounts. A depositary account is a commercial checking, savings or other bank account and any amount held by an insurance company under an agreement to pay interest. A custodial account is an account you hold which benefits another person (such as your child).

Line 1 – Check the box to indicate if this is a depositary or a custodial account.

Line 2 – Enter the account number of the account or other specific identifying information for the account if there is no account number.

Line 3 – Check one or more boxes to indicate if any of the following applies.

- The account was opened during the tax year.
- The account was closed during the tax year.
- The account was jointly owned with your spouse.
- You did not report any tax item in Part III for this asset.

Line 4 – Enter the maximum value of the account for the tax year. The maximum value is the highest fair market value of an asset over the tax year.

If you used a foreign currency exchange rate to convert the value of the account into US dollars, check the "Yes" box on line 5 and go to line 6. Otherwise, check the "No" box and go to line 7.

Line 6.

If you answered "Yes" on line 5, enter the following information.

1. The foreign currency in which the account is denominated.
2. The foreign currency exchange rate used to convert the value of the account into US dollars.
3. If the US Treasury Financial Management Service did not provide an exchange rate, the source of the foreign currency exchange rate that you used.

You must use the foreign currency exchange rate on the last day of the tax year, even if you closed or disposed of the account before the last day of the tax year.

Lines 7 through 9 – Enter the name and mailing address of the financial institution in which you maintain this account.

d. Part II – Other foreign assets

Use Part II to report information for specified foreign financial assets not held in a non-US financial account. These include stocks, bonds, an interest in a foreign trust, or other assets held outside an account in a financial institution.

Line 1 – Enter a description of the asset. If the asset is stock or securities, include the class or issue of the stock or securities.

Line 2 – Enter the identifying number or other information identifying the asset.

Line 3 – Enter the following information about the asset, if required.

1. If the asset was acquired or disposed of during the year, enter the date of acquisition and/or disposition.
2. If you own the asset jointly with your spouse, check the box on line 3c.
3. If you did not report any income, gain, loss, deduction, or credit for this asset on your tax return or any schedule or form attached to your income tax return filed for the tax year, check the box on line 3d.

Check the box for the value range that represents the maximum value of the asset during the tax year. If the maximum value is more than $200,000, enter the maximum value on line 4e.

Line 4 – Check the box for the value range that represents the maximum value of the asset during the tax year. If the maximum value is more than $200,000, enter the maximum value on line 4e.

Lines 5 and 6 – If you used a foreign currency exchange rate to convert the value of the asset into US dollars, check the "Yes" box on line 5 and go to line 6. Otherwise, check the "No" box and go to line 7.

Line 6

If you answered "Yes" to line 5, enter the following information.

1. The foreign currency in which the asset is denominated.
2. The foreign currency exchange rate used to convert the value of the asset into US dollars.
3. If the US Treasury Financial Management Service did not provide an exchange rate, the source of the foreign currency exchange rate that you used.

Lines 7a through 7e – If the asset you reported on line 1 is stock of a foreign entity or an interest in a foreign entity, complete lines 7a through 7e.

Line 7a – Enter the name of the foreign entity.

Line 7b – Check the box on line 7b to indicate the type of foreign entity.

Line 7c – If the foreign entity is a passive foreign investment company, check the box on line 7c.

Lines 7d and 7e – Enter the mailing address of the foreign entity.

Lines 8a through 8e – If the asset you reported on line 1 is not stock of a foreign entity or an interest in a foreign entity, complete lines 8a through 8e.

Line 8a – Enter the name of the issuer or counterparty and check the appropriate box to indicate if you are reporting for an issuer or a counterparty.

Line 8b – Check the appropriate box to indicate the type of issuer or counterparty.

Line 8c – Check the box to indicate if the issuer or counterparty is a US person or a foreign person.

Lines 8d and 8e – Enter the mailing address of the issuer or counterparty. If the issuer or counterparty has a mailing address in the United States, you can enter the US mailing address.

e. Part III – connecting the taxes paid to the assets reported

Enter the following items for your total assets reported in Part I or Part II and the schedule, form, or return on which you reported the items.

- interest;
- dividends;
- royalties;
- gains or (losses);
- deductions;
- credits.

If you did not report any tax item for a specified foreign financial asset on any form or schedule for the tax year, check the box in line 3d of Part I or Part II for the account or asset.

Take the following example. You own 100 shares of Bombardier – a Canadian company. You report these shares along with your other foreign financial assets in Part II. These shares paid you US$200 in dividends which you reported on line 9(a) of your Form 1040. In Part III you need to list these shares and then indicate where you reported this deduction.

f. Part IV – Excepted foreign financial assets

If you reported a specified foreign financial asset on certain other forms listed on Form 8938 for the same tax year, you may not have to report it on Form 8938. However, you must identify the form where you reported the asset and indicate how many forms you filed.

g. When and how to file

Attach Form 8938 to your Form 1040. You must meet the same deadline that you had for filing Form 1040.

5. EXAMPLE

Marie and Pierre Savoie are US citizens who live in Montreal. They are married and file a joint return. They have the following assets (all amounts in US dollars after using the conversion rate on the IRS website):

- $400,000 in mutual funds and bonds inside an RRSP for which they filed Form 8991. They do not need to report this as it was already reported on the Form 8991.
- 100 shares of Research in Motion Inc. which were worth $8,500 and on which they paid $300 tax for dividends received. They reported the tax paid on this on line 8(b) of their Form 1040.
- $10,000 cash in a joint chequeing account with TD bank which generated $200 of interest which they reported on line 8(a) of their Form 1040.

They fill out the Form 8938 as follows.

Form **8938** (November 2011) Department of the Treasury Internal Revenue Service

Statement of Specified Foreign Financial Assets

▶ See separate instructions ▶ Attach to your tax return

OMB No. 1545-2195 Attachment Sequence No. 175

If you have attached additional sheets, check here ☐

Name(s) shown on return: **Marie and Pierre Savoie** | Identifying number: **1092-299-11**

Number, street, and room or suite no. (if a P.O. box, see instructions): **3025 Sherbooke St. West apt 304**

City or town, province or state, and country (including postal code): **Montreal Quebec**

For tax year beginning , 20 12 , and ending , 20 12

Note. All information must be in English. Show all amounts in U.S. dollars. Show currency conversion rates in Part I, line 6(2), or Part II, line 6(2).

Type of filer

a Specified individual (1) ☑ Married filing a joint return (2) ☐ Other individual

b Specified domestic entity (1) ☐ Partnership (2) ☐ Corporation (3) ☐ Trust (4) ☐ Estate

Check this box if this is an original, amended, or supplemental Form 8938 for attachment to a previously filed return ☐

Part I Foreign Deposit and Custodial Accounts (see instructions)

If you have more than one account to report, attach a continuation sheet with the same information for each additional account (see instructions).

1 Type of account ☑ Deposit ☐ Custodial | 2 Account number or other designation: **123-4556-789**

3 Check all that apply a ☐ Account opened during tax year b ☐ Account closed during tax year c ☑ Account jointly owned with spouse d ☐ No tax item reported in Part III with respect to this asset

4 Maximum value of account during tax year . . . $ **10,000**

5 Did you use a foreign currency exchange rate to convert the value of the account into U.S. dollars? ☑ Yes ☐ No

6 If you answered "Yes" to line 5, complete all that apply.

(1) Foreign currency in which account is maintained	(2) Foreign currency exchange rate used to convert to U.S. dollars	(3) Source of exchange rate used if not from U.S. Treasury Financial Management Service
Canadian dollars	1.029	

7 Name of financial institution in which account is maintained: **TD Bank**

8 Mailing address of financial institution in which account is maintained. Number, street, and room or suite no.: **300 Peel St.**

9 City or town, province or state, and country (including postal code): **Montreal Quebec, Canada, K29 2V1**

Part II Other Foreign Assets (see instructions)

Note. *If you reported specified foreign financial assets on Forms 3520, 3520-A, 5471, 8621, or 8865, you do not have to include the assets on Form 8938. You must complete Part IV. See instructions.*

If you have more than one asset to report, attach a continuation sheet with the same information for each additional asset (see instructions).

1 Description of asset: **100 shares of Research in Motion** | 2 Identifying number or other designation

3 Complete all that apply

a Date asset acquired during tax year, if applicable . . .

b Date asset disposed of during tax year, if applicable . . .

c ☑ Check if asset jointly owned with spouse d ☐ Check if no tax item reported in Part III with respect to this asset

4 Maximum value of asset during tax year (check box that applies)

a ☑ $0 - $50,000 b ☐ $50,001 - $100,000 c ☐ $100,001 - $150,000 d ☐ $150,001 - $200,000

e If more than $200,000, list value . . . $

5 Did you use a foreign currency exchange rate to convert the value of the asset into U.S. dollars? ☑ Yes ☐ No

For Paperwork Reduction Act Notice, see the separate instructions. Cat. No. 37753A Form **8938** (11-2011)

Form 8938 (11-2011) Page **2**

Part II **Other Foreign Assets** *(continued)*

6 If you answered "Yes" to line 5, complete all that apply.

(1) Foreign currency in which asset is denominated	(2) Foreign currency exchange rate used to convert to U.S. dollars	(3) Source of exchange rate used if not from U.S. Treasury Financial Management Service
Canadian dollars	1.029	

7 If asset reported in Part II, line 1, is stock of a foreign entity or an interest in a foreign entity, report the following information.

a Name of foreign entity

b Type of foreign entity (1) ☐ Partnership (2) ☑ Corporation (3) ☐ Trust (4) ☐ Estate

c ☐ Check if foreign entity is a PFIC

d Mailing address of foreign entity. Number, street, and room or suite no.

176 Columbia Street West

e City or town, province or state, and country (including postal code)

Waterloo, Ontario Canada,

8 If asset reported in Part II, line 1, is not stock of a foreign entity or an interest in a foreign entity, enter the following information for the asset.

Note. If this asset has more than one issuer or counterparty, attach a continuation sheet with the same information for each additional issuer or counterparty (see instructions).

a Name of issuer or counterparty

Check if information is for ☐ Issuer ☐ Counterparty

b Type of issuer or counterparty

(1) ☐ Individual (2) ☐ Partnership (3) ☐ Corporation (4) ☐ Trust (5) ☐ Estate

c Check if issuer or counterparty is a ☐ U.S. person ☐ Foreign person

d Mailing address of issuer or counterparty. Number, street, and room or suite no.

e City or town, province or state, and country (including postal code)

Part III **Summary of Tax Items Attributable to Specified Foreign Financial Assets** (see instructions)

Asset Category	Tax item	Amount reported on form or schedule	Where reported: Form and line	Where reported: Schedule and line
I. Foreign Deposit and Custodial Accounts	a Interest	$ 200	Form 1040 line 8(a)	
	b Dividends	$		
	c Royalties	$		
	d Other income	$		
	e Gains (losses)	$		
	f Deductions	$		
	g Credits	$		
II. Other Foreign Assets	a Interest	$		
	b Dividends	$ 300	Form 1040 line 9(a)	
	c Royalties	$		
	d Other income	$		
	e Gains (losses)	$		
	f Deductions	$		
	g Credits	$		

Part IV **Excepted Specified Foreign Financial Assets** (see instructions)

If you reported specified foreign financial assets on the following forms, check the appropriate box(es). Indicate number of forms filed. You do not need to include these assets on Form 8938 for the tax year.

☐ 3520 Number of forms ☐ 3520-A Number of forms ☐ 5471 Number of forms

☐ 8621 Number of forms ☐ 8865 Number of forms

Form **8938** (11-2011)

We filed a Form 8891 for our Canadian RRSP and so we have not reported the assets it contains on this Form 8939.

6. PENALTIES FOR FAILING TO FILE

If you are required to file Form 8938 but do not file a complete and correct Form 8938 by the due date (including extensions), you may be subject to a penalty of $10,000. If you do not file a correct and complete Form 8938 within 90 days after the IRS mails you a notice of the failure to file, you may be subject to an additional penalty of $10,000 for each 30-day period (or part of a period) during which you continue to fail to file Form 8938 after the 90-day period has expired. The maximum additional penalty for a continuing failure to file Form 8938 is $50,000.

No penalty will be imposed if you fail to file Form 8938 or to disclose one or more specified foreign financial assets on Form 8938 and the failure is due to reasonable cause and not to willful neglect. You must affirmatively show the facts that support a reasonable cause claim.

In addition to the penalties already discussed, if you fail to file Form 8938, fail to report an asset, or have an underpayment of tax, you may be subject to criminal penalties.

7. FURTHER INFORMATION

More information can be found in the instructions to form 8938.

PART 6

DEALING WITH THE IRS: IF YOU GET AUDITED

46

WHAT TO DO IF THE IRS ASKS FOR MORE INFORMATION[1]

This chapter overviews what happens after you file your return. Occasionally, the IRS takes an interest in your tax return and asks for more information. Only about 1% of all tax returns are audited.

The process of selecting a return for examination usually begins in one of two ways. First, the IRS uses computer programs to identify returns that may have incorrect amounts. These programs may be based on information returns, such as Forms 1099 and W-2, on studies of past examinations, or on certain issues identified by compliance projects. Second, the IRS uses information from outside sources that indicates that a return may have incorrect amounts. These sources may include newspapers, public records, and private individuals. If the IRS determines that such information is accurate and reliable, it may use it to select a return for examination.

Publication 556 explains the rules and procedures that the IRS follows in examinations. The following sections give an overview of how the IRS conducts examinations.

By mail. Many examinations and inquiries are handled by mail. The IRS will send you a letter with either a request for more information or a reason why it believes a change to your return may be needed. You can respond by mail or you can request a personal interview with an examiner. If you mail the requested information or provide an explanation, the IRS may or may not agree and will explain the reasons for any changes.

By interview. If the IRS notifies you that it will conduct your examination through a personal interview, or you request such an interview, you have the right to ask that the examination take place at a reasonable time and place that is convenient for both you and the IRS. If the examiner proposes any changes to your return, he or she will explain the reasons for the changes. If you do not agree with these changes, you can meet with the examiner's supervisor.

Repeat examinations. If the IRS examined your return for the same items in either of the two previous years and proposed no change to your tax liability, contact the IRS to see if the examination should be discontinued.

Appeals

If you do not agree with the examiner's proposed changes, you can appeal them to the Appeals Office of IRS. Your appeal rights are explained in detail in both Publication 5 (Your Appeal Rights and How To Prepare a Protest If You Don't Agree) and Publication 556.

If you do not wish to use the Appeals Office or disagree with its findings, you may be able to take your case to the US Tax Court, US Court of Federal Claims, or the US District Court. If you take your case to court, the IRS will have the burden of proving certain facts including if you kept adequate records to show your tax liability, cooperated with the IRS, and meet certain other conditions. If the court agrees with you on most issues in your case and finds that the IRS' position was

[1] The text in this chapter is largely taken from IRS Publication 17.

largely unjustified, you may be able to recover some of your administrative and litigation costs. You will not be eligible to recover these costs unless you tried to resolve your case administratively, including going through the appeals system, and you had provided the information necessary to resolve the case.

Collections

Publication 594, The IRS Collection Process, explains your rights and responsibilities regarding payment of federal taxes. It describes:

- What to do when you owe taxes, what to do if you get a tax bill, and what to do if you think your bill is wrong. It also covers making installment payments, delaying collection action, and submitting an offer in compromise.
- IRS collection actions. It also covers liens, releasing a lien, levies, releasing a levy, seizures and sales, and release of property.

Your collection appeal rights are explained in detail in Publication 1660, Collection Appeal Rights.

PART 7

RENOUNCING YOUR US CITIZENSHIP

47

OVERVIEW OF HOW TO RENOUNCE YOUR US CITIZENSHIP[1]

After reading this guide and filing your taxes, it may be that you consider renouncing your US citizenship. This will relieve your yearly tax and disclosure obligation. There may be other non-tax reasons for maintaining your US citizenship. Indeed, you should know that there section 212(a)(10)(E) of the *Immigration and Nationality Act* allows the United States government to bar those who have renounced their citizenship for tax reasons from entering the United States. To our knowledge, this provision has been rarely enforced. Still, this provision exists and you should factor it into your decision. In this chapter, we explain how to do this. The process is called expatriation and may have significant tax consequences.

There are five steps:

1. Become a citizen of another country and get a passport.
2. Call the nearest US consulate and make an appointment.
3. Fill out the State Department form DS-4079.
4. Attend your appointment.
5. File your final US tax return.
6. Part V – financial statements.

Let's review all of these steps in detail.

1. BECOME A CITIZEN OF ANOTHER COUNTRY AND GET A PASSPORT

It is not advisable, and in fact it may not be possible, to renounce your US citizenship unless you are a citizen of another country. Many US citizens in Canada will also be Canadian citizens. If so, your first step is to make sure your Canadian passport is up to date and current.

2. CALL THE NEAREST US CONSULATE AND MAKE AN APPOINTMENT

To formally renounce your citizenship, you have to pay a $450 fee and book an appointment with a consular officer. The following chart sets out the location and contact information of the various US diplomatic offices in Canada.

[1] This chapter is based on, and some text is copied from, the IRS' instructions to Form 8854.

Office Location	Region Served	Contact information
Ottawa	Eastern Ontario (Kingston, Lanark, Leeds, Prescott, Renfrew, Russell and Stormont); and those parts of the Québec regions of Outaouais and Abitibi-Témiscamingue near Ottawa.	490 Sussex Drive Ottawa, Ontario Telephone (General): 613-688-5335 Telephone (Emergency): 613-238-5335 E-mail (Consular Section): ottawacons@state.gov
Vancouver	British Columbia and Yukon Territory	1075 West Pender Street Vancouver, British Columbia V6E 2M6 Telephone (General): 604-685-4311 Telephone (Emergency): 604-685-4311 E-mail (Citizen Services): vancouverACS@state.gov
Calgary	Alberta, Saskatchewan, Manitoba and Northwest Territories	615 Macleod Trail, S.E. Suite 1000 Calgary, Alberta T2G 4T8 Phone: (403) 266-8962
Winnipeg	Emergency Services Only. For Visa and other services contact the Calgary office	N/A
Toronto	Ontario (except for areas east of Kingston, which are included in the Ottawa consular district)	360 University Ave. Toronto, Ontario M5G 1S4 Fax (Citizen Services): 416-595-6501 Phone (General): 416.595.1700 E-mail (general US passport, notarial or citizenship inquiries): TorontoPassport@state.gov
Montreal	Greater Montreal and the regions of southern Quebec province (Laurentides, Lanaudiere, Laval, Montreal, Montregie, Estrie, and the southern parts of Centre-du-Quebec); including Drummondville	315 Place d'Youville, Suite 500 Montréal, Québec H2Y 0A4 Phone (General): 514-398-9695 Email: montreal-ACS@state.gov
Quebec City	Those regions of Quebec province to the north and east of the Montreal and Ottawa Districts (indicated above), plus the territory of Nunavut	2 Place Terrasse Dufferin (Vieux Quebec, behind Château Frontenac) Québec, Québec G1R 4T9 Telephone (General): 418-692-2095 E-mail (Citizen Services): quebecniv@state.gov
Halifax	Atlantic Canada (New Brunswick, Newfoundland + Labrador, Nova Scotia and P.E.I.) and the French islands of St. Pierre & Miquelon.	Suite 904, Purdy's Wharf Tower II 1969 Upper Water Street Halifax, NS B3J 3R7 Phone (General): (902) 429-2480

3. FILL OUT THE STATE DEPARTMENT FORM DS-4079

You must fill out Form DS-4079 before your appointment. You can find a copy in Appendix 1. The content of the form is largely self-explanatory. You do not need to write long answers. The purpose of the form is to demonstrate that you are voluntarily and intentionally giving up your US citizenship. So your answers on the form should show that you understand the irrevocable consequences and are acting free of duress.

Note that you do not have to convince the consular officer that you have no ties to the United States.

Fill out the form but do not sign it. Bring it to your appointment for signing there.

4. ATTEND YOUR APPOINTMENT

At this appointment, you will have to take an oath saying that you have renounced your citizenship. You will also have to sign a statement saying that you accept the consequences of your renunciation. Bring your Canadian passport to your appointment and the form DS-4079 that you filled out but did not sign. At the end of your appointment, you should receive a certificate that officially states that you are no longer a US citizen.

5. FILL OUT YOUR FINAL US TAX RETURN

Formally renouncing your citizenship is fairly easy. But you still have to settle with the IRS. This means filing one last return and filling out form 8854. The method which you use to fill out the form depends on when you expatriated. For our purposes, we are assuming that you renounced your citizenship following the steps above. That means that you will fill out Part IV and V of the form. Section A of Part IV is mandatory. Section B only matters if you are a covered expatriate (explained below). If you are a covered expatriate, we recommend you get professional tax advice.

a. When and where to file your Form 8854

File your initial Form 8854 as soon as possible after the date you relinquish US citizenship or terminate your long-term residence. You remain subject to tax as a US citizen or resident until you both file your initial Form 8854. You should file your Form 8854 by the same date by which you file your Form 1040 (so April 15 unless you take one of the extensions).

You should send your Form 8854 to the following IRS address:

Department of the Treasury
Internal Revenue Service
Philadelphia, PA 19255-0549

b. Part I – general information

This is where you give the IRS your general information. With the exception of line 5, it is self-explanatory.

Line 5 asks for the date that you expatriated. You are considered to have relinquished your US citizenship on the earliest of the following dates.

1. The date you renounced your US citizenship before a diplomatic or consular officer of the United States (provided that the voluntary renouncement was later confirmed by the issuance of a certificate of loss of nationality).

2. The date you furnished to the State Department a signed statement of your voluntary relinquishment of US nationality confirming the performance of an expatriating act (provided that the voluntary relinquishment was later confirmed by the issuance of a certificate of loss of nationality).

3. The date the State Department issued a certificate of loss of nationality.

c. Part IV section A – Are you a covered expatriate

Section A inquires whether you meet the criteria of a covered expatriate. This is something you want to avoid. Covered expatriates will have to pay expatriation tax which means that even after you renounce your citizenship you will still have tax obligations to the IRS.

Before showing you how to fill out section A, let's discuss who is a covered expatriate. There are three scenarios under which you can be considered a covered expatriate.

1. Your average annual net income tax liability for the five tax years ending before the date of expatriation was higher than $147,000.
2. Your net worth was $2 million or more on the date of your expatriation.
3. You fail to certify on Form 8854 that you have complied with all federal tax obligations for the five tax years preceding the date of your expatriation.

Item 1 should be determined by reference to past US tax returns. Item 2 is determined by filling out Part V of Form 8544. Filling out Part V is described in section c. Item 3 is a declaration that you make on Form 8544. Of course, you should only make this declaration if it is true.

i. Exemption for certain dual citizens

However, even if you meet items 1 or 2 above you can exempt yourself if you meet the following requirements:

- You became at birth a US citizen and a citizen of another country and you continue to be a citizen of, and are taxed as a resident of, that other country.
- You were a resident of the United States for not more than 10 years during the 15-tax-year period ending with the tax year during which the expatriation occurred. For the purpose of determining US residency, use the substantial presence test for each of the past 10 years. This test essentially classifies you as a resident of the United States if you have spent a significant amount of time there. You are considered a resident if you spent 31 days in the United States for the current tax year and 183 days during the three-year period that includes the current year and the two years immediately before that, counting:
    - all the days you were present in the current year, and
    - 1/3 of the days you were present in the first year before the current year, and
    - 1/6 of the days you were present in the second year before the current year.

  Here is a useful example from the IRS. Dan was physically present in the United States on 120 days in each of the years 2007, 2008, and 2009. To determine if Dan meets the substantial presence test for 2009, count the full 120 days of presence in 2009, 40 days in 2008 (1/3 of 120), and 20 days in 2007 (1/6 of 120). Since the total for the three-year period is 180 days, Dan is not considered a resident alien under the substantial presence test for 2009.

In short, if you were a dual citizen at birth and you have not spent much time in the United States, you can expatriate as long as you have complied with your tax obligations for the past five years.

ii. Exception for minors

You may qualify for the exception described above if you meet the following requirements.

- You expatriated before you were 18½.
- You were a resident of the United States for not more than 10 tax years before the expatriation occurs.

iii. Filling out Part IV – Section A

Once you know the general rules, filling out the actual form is straightforward. There are only a few lines that need explaining.

Line 2 – You can use the balance sheet in Part V (Schedule A) to arrive at your net worth.

Lines 3 and 4 – This is where you claim the dual citizen exemption discussed above.

Line 6 – Check the "Yes" box if you have complied with your tax obligations for the five tax years ending before the date on which you expatriated, including but not limited to, your obligations to file income tax, employment tax, gift tax, and information returns, if applicable, and your obligation to pay all relevant tax liabilities, interest, and penalties.

6. PART V – FINANCIAL STATEMENT

You are obliged to fill out both Schedule A and Schedule B of this form.

a. Schedule A – balance sheet

The categories on the left side are relatively self-explanatory and many of them will not apply to most people. However, there are a few items that should be discussed.

Marketable stock and securities are those which trade on a public stock exchange or are easily exchanged. Most mutual funds, stocks, bonds and other securities fall into this category.

Non-marketable stock, by contrast is that which is difficult to buy or sell because it does not trade on a normal market or exchange or it is not easy to exchange. Examples of this include government savings bonds which cannot be re-sold to another party.

Line 5(a) is for stock from small corporations of which you own a significant portion.

Line 10 involves non-grantor trusts. These are trusts over which you have no control.

Lines 11 and 12 include any of the following items:

- patent, invention, formula, process, design, pattern, or know-how;
- copyright, literary, musical, or artistic composition;
- trademark, trade name, or brand name;
- franchise, licence, or contract;

- method, program, system, procedure, campaign, survey, study, forecast, estimate, customer list, or technical data;
- any similar item.

Line 19 is where you list any other assets that are not discussed elsewhere on the form.

The columns too are relatively self-explanatory.

Column (a) asks for the fair market value of the asset. There are a number of ways to determine the fair market value of a particular asset. If it is a stock or bond or other financial instrument, you can simply take the price for which it currently trades. The value of your real estate may be on file with your municipality. For other assets, you may need to get an appraiser.

Column (b) asks for the adjusted basis. We have discussed this concept a number of times in this book. Please refer to Chapter 10 for a detailed discussing on how to calculate the adjusted basis of financial products. Similarly, Chapter 11 has instructions for calculating the adjusted basis of real estate.

Column (c) asks for the total of subtracting column (b) from column (a). US citizens in Canada can ignore column (d).

Line 20 refers to installment obligations which arise if you owe money on an installment sale. Most people can ignore this line.

Line 23 is for any other liabilities that you have.

On line 25, simply subtract line 24 from line 20 to determine your net worth.

b. Schedule B – income statement

Here, you have to list your income for the partial tax year leading up to your expatriation date. It only asks you for income from US sources.

On line 1 you should enter all US source income in the various categories. Recall that US source income means income that originates in the United States. This is discussed more in Chapter 32 which deals with the foreign tax credit.

Enter 0 on lines 5, 6, and 7. These do not apply to you.

c. Illustrated example

Benjamin Lowy is a US citizen living in Toronto. On March 15, 2012 he renounced his US citizenship before a consular at the office in Toronto. In the previous five years, Benjamin paid the following amounts of US tax:

- 2006 – $40,210
- 2007 – $45,414
- 2008 – $50,014
- 2009 – $48,589
- 2010 – $42,013

As this is well below an average of $147,000, Ben does not qualify as a covered expatriate. Ben's next task is to calculate his total assets. He needs to use the balance sheet in Part V to do this and enter the total on line 2 of Part IV section A. Ben has the following assets (all of which have been converted to US dollars):

- $50,000 of Canadian mutual funds inside his RRSP. After consulting his financial institution, he determines that he purchased these funds for $30,000.
- A house in Toronto worth $700,000. Using Chapter xxx, he figures that his house has an adjusted cost basis of $450,000. On this house, he has a mortgage of $200,000.
- $15,000 in cash in a savings account.
- A Canadian pension evaluated to be worth $150,000.

After filling out Part V of Form 8854, Ben enters $235,000 on line 2 of Part IV. Ben has no US-source income so he does not have to fill out Schedule B of Part V. The pages of Ben's Form 8854 which he had to fill out look like this.

Form **8854** Department of the Treasury Internal Revenue Service

Initial and Annual Expatriation Statement

For calendar year 2011 or other tax year beginning ...., 2011, and ending ...., 20 ....

▶ See separate instructions. ▶ Please print or type.

OMB No. 1545-0074 **2011** Attachment Sequence No. **112**

Name: Benjamin Lowy | Identifying number (see instructions)

Part I General Information. For all filers.

1 Mailing address and telephone number where you can be reached after expatriation
1030 Logan ave. Toronto Ontario Canada M4K 1V8

2 Address of principal foreign residence (if different from line 1)

3 Country of tax residence (if different from line 2) Canada

4 **Expatriation date.** Check the box that applies (see instructions).

☐ June 4, 2004 – June 16, 2008. Complete Parts II and V

☐ June 17, 2008 – December 31, 2010. Complete Part III if:
- You made an election to defer the payment of tax in 2008, 2009, or 2010,
- You have an item of eligible deferred compensation, or
- You have an interest in a nongrantor trust.

Otherwise, you do not need to file Form 8854.

☑ January 1, 2011 – December 31, 2011. Complete Parts IV and V

5 Date of notification of expatriating act, termination of residency, or claim of treaty benefits (see instructions).

☑ Citizen. Date notification given to Department of State

☐ Long-term resident. Date notification given to Department of Homeland Security

☐ Long-term resident with dual residency in a treaty country. Date commencing to be treated, for tax purposes, as a resident of the treaty country

6 Number of days you were physically present in the United States in the current year

7 List all countries (other than the United States) of which you are a citizen.

a Name of country Canada

b Date you became a citizen of each country listed in line 7a September 1, 1975

8 How you became a U.S. citizen ☑ By birth ☐ By naturalization

Part II For Persons Who Expatriated After June 3, 2004, and Before June 17, 2008

1 Did you complete Form 8854 for any period after June 3, 2004, and before June 17, 2008?

☐ **No. STOP.** You must complete Form 8854 for the year in which you expatriated for immigration purposes before filing this form (see instructions).

☐ **Yes.** Tax year for which Form 8854 first filed .... Go to line 2.

2 Were you physically present in the United States for more than 30 days but not more than 60 days during the tax year? ☐ **Yes** ☐ **No**

a If you checked "**Yes**" to line 2, were you performing services for an unrelated employer? ☐ **Yes** ☐ **No**

b If you checked "**Yes**" to line 2a, are you a citizen or resident, fully liable for income tax, in the country in which you were born, your spouse was born, or either of your parents was born? ☐ **Yes** ☐ **No**

Next: Go to Part V.

For Paperwork Reduction Act Notice, see the separate instructions. Cat. No. 24126N Form **8854** (2011)

Form 8854 (2011) Page **2**

Part III For Persons Who Expatriated After June 16, 2008, and Before January 1, 2011

- If you made an election to defer the payment of tax, complete line 1.
- If you have an item of eligible deferred compensation, complete line 2.
- If you have an interest in a nongrantor trust, complete line 3.

1 Complete columns (a), (b), and (c) for all property on which you deferred tax on your 2008, 2009, or 2010 Form 8854. Complete column (d) for any property you disposed of in 2011 and see the instructions for Part III.

(a) Description of property	(b) Amount of mark-to-market gain or (loss) reported in 2008, 2009, or 2010	(c) Amount of tax deferred in 2008, 2009, or 2010	(d) Date of disposition (if any)

2 Did you receive any distributions of eligible deferred compensation items for 2011? ☐ **Yes** ☐ **No**
If "Yes," Amount of distribution: ______ Amount withheld at source, if any: ______

3 Did you receive any distributions from a nongrantor trust for 2011? ☐ **Yes** ☐ **No**
If "Yes," Amount of distribution: ______ Amount withheld at source, if any: ______

Part IV For Persons Who Expatriated During 2011

Section A Expatriation Information

1 Enter your U.S. income tax liability (after foreign tax credits) for the 5 tax years ending before the date of expatriation.

1st Year Before Expatriation	2nd Year Before Expatriation	3rd Year Before Expatriation	4th Year Before Expatriation	5th Year Before Expatriation
$ 40210	$ 45414	$ 50014	$ 48589	$ 42013

2 Enter your net worth on the date of your expatriation for tax purposes . . . . $ 235,000

3 Did you become at birth a U.S. citizen and a citizen of another country, and do you continue to be a citizen of, and taxed as a resident of, that other country? . . . . ☑ **Yes** ☐ **No**

4 If you answered "Yes" to question 3, have you been a resident of the United States for not more than 10 of the last 15 tax years? . . . . ☐ **Yes** ☑ **No**

5 Were you under age 18½ on the date you expatriated and have you been a U.S. resident for not more than 10 years? . . . . ☐ **Yes** ☑ **No**

6 Do you certify under penalties of perjury that you have complied with all of your tax obligations for the 5 preceding tax years (see instructions)? . . . . ☑ **Yes** ☐ **No**

Form **8854** (2011)

Form 8854 (2011) Page 5

Part V Balance Sheet and Income Statement

Schedule A Balance Sheet

List in U.S. dollars the fair market value (column (a)) and the U.S. adjusted basis (column (b)) of your assets and liabilities as of the following date.

- Part II filers - the end of the tax year for which you are filing the form
- Part IV filers - your expatriation date

For more details, see the separate instructions.

	Assets	(a) Fair market value (FMV)	(b) U.S. adjusted basis	(c) Gain or (loss). Subtract column (b) from column (a)	(d) FMV on beginning date of U.S. residency (optional, for long-term residents only)
1	Cash, including bank deposits	15,000	N/A	15,000	
2	Marketable stock and securities issued by U.S. companies				
3	Marketable stock and securities issued by foreign companies				
4	Nonmarketable stock and securities issued by U.S. companies				
5	Nonmarketable stock and securities issued by foreign companies	50,000	30,000	20,000	
a	Separately state stock issued by foreign companies that would be controlled foreign corporations if you were still a U.S. citizen or permanent resident (see instructions)				
b	Provide the name, address, and EIN, if any, of any such company				
6	Pensions from services performed in the United States				
7	Pensions from services performed outside the United States	150,000	N/A	150,000	
8	Partnership interests (see instructions)				
9	Assets held by trusts you own under sections 671 through 679 (see instructions)				
10	Beneficial interests in nongrantor trusts (see instructions)				
11	Intangibles used in the United States				
12	Intangibles used outside the United States				
13	Loans to U.S. persons				
14	Loans to foreign persons				
15	Real property located in the United States				
16	Real property located outside the United States	700,000	450,000	250,000	
17	Business property located in the United States				
18	Business property located outside the United States				
19	Other assets (see instructions)				
20	Total assets. Add lines 1 through 5 and lines 6 through 19. Do not include amounts on line 5a in this total	915,000	480,000	435000	
	Liabilities	**Amount**			
21	Installment obligations				
22	Mortgages, etc.	200,000			
23	Other liabilities (see instructions)				
24	Total liabilities. Add lines 21 through 23	200,000			
25	**Net worth.** Subtract line 24 from line 20, column (a)	235,000			

Form **8854** (2011)

Appendix 1

BLANK FORMS

This Appendix contains blank versions of the following forms:

Form 1040 338
Form SS-5F 340
Form W-7 341
Schedule A 342
Schedule B 343
Schedule D 344
Schedule E 346
Schedule R 348
Form 8949 349
Form 4868 351
Form 4562 352
Form 2555 354
Form 2555-EZ 357
Form 3903 359
Form 8917 361
Form 4952 363
Form 4684 365
Form 2106 367
Form 2106-EZ 369
Form 1116 371
Form 2441 373
Form 8863 375
Form 8854 377
Form 8891 383
Form 8833 385
Form 8621 387
Form 8938 390
TD F 90-22.1 392
Tax Amnesty questionnaire 393
DS-4079 395

Form **1040** Department of the Treasury—Internal Revenue Service (99)
U.S. Individual Income Tax Return **2012** OMB No. 1545-0074 IRS Use Only—Do not write or staple in this space.

For the year Jan. 1–Dec. 31, 2012, or other tax year beginning , 2012, ending , 20 See separate instructions.

Your first name and initial	Last name		Your social security number
If a joint return, spouse's first name and initial	Last name		Spouse's social security number
Home address (number and street). If you have a P.O. box, see instructions.		Apt. no.	▲ Make sure the SSN(s) above and on line 6c are correct.
City, town or post office, state, and ZIP code. If you have a foreign address, also complete spaces below (see instructions).			**Presidential Election Campaign** Check here if you, or your spouse if filing jointly, want $3 to go to this fund. Checking a box below will not change your tax or refund. ☐ You ☐ Spouse
Foreign country name	Foreign province/state/county	Foreign postal code	

Filing Status

Check only one box.

1 ☐ Single
2 ☐ Married filing jointly (even if only one had income)
3 ☐ Married filing separately. Enter spouse's SSN above and full name here. ▶
4 ☐ Head of household (with qualifying person). (See instructions.) If the qualifying person is a child but not your dependent, enter this child's name here. ▶
5 ☐ Qualifying widow(er) with dependent child

Exemptions

6a ☐ **Yourself.** If someone can claim you as a dependent, **do not** check box 6a . . . . . .
b ☐ **Spouse** . . . .

Boxes checked on 6a and 6b

c **Dependents:** (1) First name Last name	(2) Dependent's social security number	(3) Dependent's relationship to you	(4) ✓ if child under age 17 qualifying for child tax credit (see instructions)
			☐
			☐
			☐
			☐

If more than four dependents, see instructions and check here ▶ ☐

No. of children on 6c who:
• lived with you
• did not live with you due to divorce or separation (see instructions)
Dependents on 6c not entered above

d Total number of exemptions claimed . . . .
Add numbers on lines above ▶

Income

Attach Form(s) W-2 here. Also attach Forms W-2G and 1099-R if tax was withheld.

If you did not get a W-2, see instructions.

Enclose, but do not attach, any payment. Also, please use **Form 1040-V.**

7	Wages, salaries, tips, etc. Attach Form(s) W-2		7
8a	**Taxable** interest. Attach Schedule B if required		8a
b	**Tax-exempt** interest. **Do not** include on line 8a	8b	
9a	Ordinary dividends. Attach Schedule B if required		9a
b	Qualified dividends	9b	
10	Taxable refunds, credits, or offsets of state and local income taxes		10
11	Alimony received		11
12	Business income or (loss). Attach Schedule C or C-EZ		12
13	Capital gain or (loss). Attach Schedule D if required. If not required, check here ▶ ☐		13
14	Other gains or (losses). Attach Form 4797		14
15a	IRA distributions 15a	b Taxable amount	15b
16a	Pensions and annuities 16a	b Taxable amount	16b
17	Rental real estate, royalties, partnerships, S corporations, trusts, etc. Attach Schedule E		17
18	Farm income or (loss). Attach Schedule F		18
19	Unemployment compensation		19
20a	Social security benefits 20a	b Taxable amount	20b
21	Other income. List type and amount		21
22	Combine the amounts in the far right column for lines 7 through 21. This is your **total income** ▶		22

Adjusted Gross Income

23	Reserved	23	
24	Certain business expenses of reservists, performing artists, and fee-basis government officials. Attach Form 2106 or 2106-EZ	24	
25	Health savings account deduction. Attach Form 8889	25	
26	Moving expenses. Attach Form 3903	26	
27	Deductible part of self-employment tax. Attach Schedule SE	27	
28	Self-employed SEP, SIMPLE, and qualified plans	28	
29	Self-employed health insurance deduction	29	
30	Penalty on early withdrawal of savings	30	
31a	Alimony paid b Recipient's SSN ▶	31a	
32	IRA deduction	32	
33	Student loan interest deduction	33	
34	Reserved	34	
35	Domestic production activities deduction. Attach Form 8903	35	
36	Add lines 23 through 35		36
37	Subtract line 36 from line 22. This is your **adjusted gross income** ▶		37

For Disclosure, Privacy Act, and Paperwork Reduction Act Notice, see separate instructions. Cat. No. 11320B Form **1040** (2012)

Form 1040 (2012) Page 2

Tax and Credits

38	Amount from line 37 (adjusted gross income)	38
39a	Check if: ☐ You were born before January 2, 1948, ☐ Blind. ☐ Spouse was born before January 2, 1948, ☐ Blind. Total boxes checked ▶ 39a ☐	
b	If your spouse itemizes on a separate return or you were a dual-status alien, check here ▶ 39b☐	
40	**Itemized deductions** (from Schedule A) **or** your **standard deduction** (see left margin)	40
41	Subtract line 40 from line 38	41
42	**Exemptions.** Multiply $3,800 by the number on line 6d	42
43	**Taxable income.** Subtract line 42 from line 41. If line 42 is more than line 41, enter -0-	43
44	**Tax** (see instructions). Check if any from: **a** ☐ Form(s) 8814 **b** ☐ Form 4972 **c** ☐ 962 election	44
45	**Alternative minimum tax** (see instructions). Attach Form 6251	45
46	Add lines 44 and 45 ▶	46
47	Foreign tax credit. Attach Form 1116 if required — 47	
48	Credit for child and dependent care expenses. Attach Form 2441 — 48	
49	Education credits from Form 8863, line 19 — 49	
50	Retirement savings contributions credit. Attach Form 8880 — 50	
51	Child tax credit. Attach Schedule 8812, if required — 51	
52	Residential energy credit. Attach Form 5695 — 52	
53	Other credits from Form: **a** ☐ 3800 **b** ☐ 8801 **c** ☐ — 53	
54	Add lines 47 through 53. These are your **total credits**	54
55	Subtract line 54 from line 46. If line 54 is more than line 46, enter -0- ▶	55

Standard Deduction for—
- People who check any box on line 39a or 39b **or** who can be claimed as a dependent, see instructions.
- All others:

Single or Married filing separately, $5,950

Married filing jointly or Qualifying widow(er), $11,900

Head of household, $8,700

Other Taxes

56	Self-employment tax. Attach Schedule SE	56
57	Unreported social security and Medicare tax from Form: **a** ☐ 4137 **b** ☐ 8919	57
58	Additional tax on IRAs, other qualified retirement plans, etc. Attach Form 5329 if required	58
59a	Household employment taxes from Schedule H	59a
b	First-time homebuyer credit repayment. Attach Form 5405 if required	59b
60	Other taxes. Enter code(s) from instructions	60
61	Add lines 55 through 60. This is your **total tax** ▶	61

Payments

62	Federal income tax withheld from Forms W-2 and 1099 — 62	
63	2012 estimated tax payments and amount applied from 2011 return — 63	
64a	**Earned income credit (EIC)** — 64a	
b	Nontaxable combat pay election — 64b	
65	Additional child tax credit. Attach Schedule 8812 — 65	
66	American opportunity credit from Form 8863, line 8 — 66	
67	Reserved — 67	
68	Amount paid with request for extension to file — 68	
69	Excess social security and tier 1 RRTA tax withheld — 69	
70	Credit for federal tax on fuels. Attach Form 4136 — 70	
71	Credits from Form: **a** ☐ 2439 **b** ☐ Reserved **c** ☐ 8801 **d** ☐ 8885 — 71	
72	Add lines 62, 63, 64a, and 65 through 71. These are your **total payments** ▶	72

If you have a qualifying child, attach Schedule EIC.

Refund

73	If line 72 is more than line 61, subtract line 61 from line 72. This is the amount you **overpaid**	73
74a	Amount of line 73 you want **refunded to you.** If Form 8888 is attached, check here ▶ ☐	74a
▶ b	Routing number ▶ **c** Type: ☐ Checking ☐ Savings	
▶ d	Account number	
75	Amount of line 73 you want **applied to your 2013 estimated tax** ▶ 75	

Direct deposit? See instructions.

Amount You Owe

76	**Amount you owe.** Subtract line 72 from line 61. For details on how to pay, see instructions ▶	76
77	Estimated tax penalty (see instructions) — 77	

Third Party Designee

Do you want to allow another person to discuss this return with the IRS (see instructions)? ☐ **Yes.** Complete below. ☐ **No**

Designee's name ▶ Phone no. ▶ Personal identification number (PIN) ▶

Sign Here

Under penalties of perjury, I declare that I have examined this return and accompanying schedules and statements, and to the best of my knowledge and belief, they are true, correct, and complete. Declaration of preparer (other than taxpayer) is based on all information of which preparer has any knowledge.

Joint return? See instructions. Keep a copy for your records.

Your signature	Date	Your occupation	Daytime phone number
Spouse's signature. If a joint return, **both** must sign.	Date	Spouse's occupation	If the IRS sent you an Identity Protection PIN, enter it here (see inst.)

Paid Preparer Use Only

Print/Type preparer's name	Preparer's signature	Date	Check ☐ if self-employed	PTIN
Firm's name ▶		Firm's EIN ▶		
Firm's address ▶		Phone no.		

Form **1040** (2012)

SOCIAL SECURITY ADMINISTRATION
Application for a Social Security Card

Form Approved
OMB No. 0960-0066

1 **NAME** TO BE SHOWN ON CARD — First | Full Middle Name | Last

FULL NAME AT BIRTH IF OTHER THAN ABOVE — First | Full Middle Name | Last

OTHER NAMES USED

2 Social Security number previously assigned to the person listed in item 1 ☐☐☐-☐☐-☐☐☐☐

3 **PLACE OF BIRTH** (Do Not Abbreviate) City State or Foreign Country Office Use Only FCI

4 **DATE OF BIRTH** MM/DD/YYYY

5 **CITIZENSHIP** (Check One) ☐ U.S. Citizen ☐ Legal Alien Allowed To Work ☐ Legal Alien **Not** AllowedToWork(See Instructions On Page 3) ☐ Other (See Instructions On Page 3)

6 **ETHNICITY** Are You Hispanic or Latino? (Your Response is Voluntary) ☐ Yes ☐ No

7 **RACE** Select One or More (Your Response is Voluntary) ☐ Native Hawaiian ☐ Alaska Native ☐ Asian ☐ American Indian ☐ Black/African American ☐ Other Pacific Islander ☐ White

8 **SEX** ☐ Male ☐ Female

9 **A. PARENT/ MOTHER'S NAME AT HER BIRTH** First | Full Middle Name | Last

B. PARENT/ MOTHER'S SOCIAL SECURITY NUMBER (See instructions for 9 B on Page 3) ☐☐☐-☐☐-☐☐☐☐ ☐ Unknown

10 **A. PARENT/ FATHER'S NAME** First | Full Middle Name | Last

B. PARENT/ FATHER'S SOCIAL SECURITY NUMBER (See instructions for 10B on Page 3) ☐☐☐-☐☐-☐☐☐☐ ☐ Unknown

11 Has the person listed in item 1 or anyone acting on his/her behalf ever filed for or received a Social Security number card before?
☐ Yes (If "yes" answer questions 12-13) ☐ No ☐ Don't Know (If "don't know," skip to question 14.)

12 Name shown on the most recent Social Security card issued for the person listed in item 1 — First | Full Middle Name | Last

13 Enter any different date of birth if used on an earlier application for a card — MM/DD/YYYY

14 **TODAY'S DATE** MM/DD/YYYY

15 **DAYTIME PHONE NUMBER** ( ) - Area Code Number

16 **MAILING ADDRESS** (Do Not Abbreviate) — Street Address, Apt. No., PO Box, Rural Route No. | City | State/Foreign Country | ZIP Code

I declare under penalty of perjury that I have examined all the information on this form, and on any accompanying statements or forms, and it is true and correct to the best of my knowledge.

17 **YOUR SIGNATURE**

18 **YOUR RELATIONSHIP TO THE PERSON IN ITEM 1 IS:** ☐ Self ☐ Natural Or Adoptive Parent ☐ Legal Guardian ☐ Other (Specify)

DO NOT WRITE BELOW THIS LINE (FOR SSA USE ONLY)

NPN		DOC	NTI	CAN		ITV
PBC	EVI	EVA	EVC	PRA	NWR	DNR	UNIT

EVIDENCE SUBMITTED

SIGNATURE AND TITLE OF EMPLOYEE(S) REVIEWING EVIDENCE AND/OR CONDUCTING INTERVIEW

DATE

DCL DATE

Form **SS-5-FS** (08-2011) ef (08-2011) Destroy Prior Editions Page 5

Form **W-7** (Rev. January 2012)
Department of the Treasury
Internal Revenue Service

Application for IRS Individual Taxpayer Identification Number

▶ **For use by individuals who are not U.S. citizens or permanent residents.**
▶ **See instructions.**

OMB No. 1545-0074

FOR IRS USE ONLY

An IRS individual taxpayer identification number (ITIN) is for federal tax purposes only.

Before you begin:

- ***Do not submit*** *this form if you have, or are eligible to get, a U.S. social security number (SSN).*
- *Getting an ITIN does not change your immigration status or your right to work in the United States and does not make you eligible for the earned income credit.*

Reason you are submitting Form W-7. Read the instructions for the box you check. **Caution:** If you check box **b, c, d, e, f,** or **g, you must file a tax return with Form W-7 unless you meet one of the exceptions** (see instructions).

a ☐ Nonresident alien required to get ITIN to claim tax treaty benefit
b ☐ Nonresident alien filing a U.S. tax return
c ☐ U.S. resident alien **(based on days present in the United States)** filing a U.S. tax return
d ☐ Dependent of U.S. citizen/resident alien } Enter name and SSN/ITIN of U.S. citizen/resident alien (see instructions) ▶
e ☐ Spouse of U.S. citizen/resident alien
f ☐ Nonresident alien student, professor, or researcher filing a U.S. tax return or claiming an exception
g ☐ Dependent/spouse of a nonresident alien holding a U.S. visa
h ☐ Other (see instructions) ▶

Additional information for **a** and **f**: Enter treaty country ▶ and treaty article number ▶

Name (see instructions)
1a First name | Middle name | Last name

Name at birth if different ▶
1b First name | Middle name | Last name

Applicant's mailing address
2 Street address, apartment number, or rural route number. **If you have a P.O. box, see separate instructions.**
City or town, state or province, and country. Include ZIP code or postal code where appropriate.

Foreign (non-U.S.) address (if different from above) (see instructions)
3 Street address, apartment number, or rural route number. **Do not use a P.O. box number.**
City or town, state or province, and country. Include ZIP code or postal code where appropriate.

Birth information
4 Date of birth (month / day / year) | Country of birth | City and state or province (optional) | **5** ☐ Male ☐ Female

Other information
6a Country(ies) of citizenship | **6b** Foreign tax I.D. number (if any) | **6c** Type of U.S. visa (if any), number, and expiration date

6d Identification document(s) submitted (see instructions) ☐ Passport ☐ Driver's license/State I.D. ☐ USCIS documentation ☐ Other
Issued by: No.: Exp. date: / / Date of entry into the United States (MM/DD/YYYY) / /

6e Have you previously received a U.S. temporary taxpayer identification number (TIN) or employer identification number (EIN)?
☐ **No/Do not know.** Skip line 6f.
☐ **Yes.** Complete line 6f. If more than one, list on a sheet and attach to this form (see instructions).

6f Enter: TIN or EIN ▶ and
Name under which it was issued ▶

6g Name of college/university or company (see instructions)
City and state Length of stay

Sign Here

Under penalties of perjury, I (applicant/delegate/acceptance agent) declare that I have examined this application, including accompanying documentation and statements, and to the best of my knowledge and belief, it is true, correct, and complete. I authorize the IRS to disclose to my acceptance agent returns or return information necessary to resolve matters regarding the assignment of my IRS individual taxpayer identification number (ITIN), including any previously assigned taxpayer identifying number.

Signature of applicant (if delegate, see instructions) | Date (month / day / year) / / | Phone number

Keep a copy for your records.

Name of delegate, if applicable (type or print) | Delegate's relationship to applicant ▶ ☐ Parent ☐ Court-appointed guardian ☐ Power of Attorney

Acceptance Agent's Use ONLY
Signature | Date (month / day / year) / / | Phone | Fax
Name and title (type or print) | Name of company | EIN | Office Code

For Paperwork Reduction Act Notice, see separate instructions. Cat. No. 10229L Form **W-7** (Rev. 1-2012)

SCHEDULE A (Form 1040)

Department of the Treasury Internal Revenue Service (99)

Itemized Deductions

▶ Information about Schedule A and its separate instructions is at *www.irs.gov/form1040*.

▶ Attach to Form 1040.

OMB No. 1545-0074

2012

Attachment Sequence No. 07

Name(s) shown on Form 1040 | Your social security number

Section	Line	Description	Box	Amount	Box	Amount
Medical and Dental Expenses		**Caution.** Do not include expenses reimbursed or paid by others.				
	1	Medical and dental expenses (see instructions)	1			
	2	Enter amount from Form 1040, line 38 [2]				
	3	Multiply line 2 by 7.5% (.075)	3			
	4	Subtract line 3 from line 1. If line 3 is more than line 1, enter -0-			4	
Taxes You Paid	5	State and local				
		a ☐ Income taxes b ☐ Reserved	5			
	6	Real estate taxes (see instructions)	6			
	7	Personal property taxes	7			
	8	Other taxes. List type and amount ▶	8			
	9	Add lines 5 through 8			9	
Interest You Paid **Note.** Your mortgage interest deduction may be limited (see instructions).	10	Home mortgage interest and points reported to you on Form 1098	10			
	11	Home mortgage interest not reported to you on Form 1098. If paid to the person from whom you bought the home, see instructions and show that person's name, identifying no., and address ▶	11			
	12	Points not reported to you on Form 1098. See instructions for special rules	12			
	13	Reserved	13			
	14	Investment interest. Attach Form 4952 if required. (See instructions.)	14			
	15	Add lines 10 through 14			15	
Gifts to Charity If you made a gift and got a benefit for it, see instructions.	16	Gifts by cash or check. If you made any gift of $250 or more, see instructions	16			
	17	Other than by cash or check. If any gift of $250 or more, see instructions. You **must** attach Form 8283 if over $500	17			
	18	Carryover from prior year	18			
	19	Add lines 16 through 18			19	
Casualty and Theft Losses	20	Casualty or theft loss(es). Attach Form 4684. (See instructions.)			20	
Job Expenses and Certain Miscellaneous Deductions	21	Unreimbursed employee expenses—job travel, union dues, job education, etc. Attach Form 2106 or 2106-EZ if required. (See instructions.) ▶	21			
	22	Tax preparation fees	22			
	23	Other expenses—investment, safe deposit box, etc. List type and amount ▶	23			
	24	Add lines 21 through 23	24			
	25	Enter amount from Form 1040, line 38 [25]				
	26	Multiply line 25 by 2% (.02)	26			
	27	Subtract line 26 from line 24. If line 26 is more than line 24, enter -0-			27	
Other Miscellaneous Deductions	28	Other—from list in instructions. List type and amount ▶			28	
Total Itemized Deductions	29	Add the amounts in the far right column for lines 4 through 28. Also, enter this amount on Form 1040, line 40			29	
	30	If you elect to itemize deductions even though they are less than your standard deduction, check here ▶ ☐				

For Paperwork Reduction Act Notice, see Form 1040 instructions. Cat. No. 17145C **Schedule A (Form 1040) 2012**

SCHEDULE B (Form 1040A or 1040)

Department of the Treasury Internal Revenue Service (99)

Interest and Ordinary Dividends

▶ Attach to Form 1040A or 1040.

▶ Information about Schedule B (Form 1040A or 1040) and its instructions is at *www.irs.gov/form1040*.

OMB No. 1545-0074

2012

Attachment Sequence No. 08

Name(s) shown on return | Your social security number

Part I Interest

(See instructions on back and the instructions for Form 1040A, or Form 1040, line 8a.)

Note. If you received a Form 1099-INT, Form 1099-OID, or substitute statement from a brokerage firm, list the firm's name as the payer and enter the total interest shown on that form.

			Amount
1	List name of payer. If any interest is from a seller-financed mortgage and the buyer used the property as a personal residence, see instructions on back and list this interest first. Also, show that buyer's social security number and address ▶	1	
2	Add the amounts on line 1	2	
3	Excludable interest on series EE and I U.S. savings bonds issued after 1989. Attach Form 8815	3	
4	Subtract line 3 from line 2. Enter the result here and on Form 1040A, or Form 1040, line 8a ▶	4	

Note. If line 4 is over $1,500, you must complete Part III.

Part II Ordinary Dividends

(See instructions on back and the instructions for Form 1040A, or Form 1040, line 9a.)

Note. If you received a Form 1099-DIV or substitute statement from a brokerage firm, list the firm's name as the payer and enter the ordinary dividends shown on that form.

			Amount
5	List name of payer ▶	5	
6	Add the amounts on line 5. Enter the total here and on Form 1040A, or Form 1040, line 9a ▶	6	

Note. If line 6 is over $1,500, you must complete Part III.

Part III Foreign Accounts and Trusts

(See instructions on back.)

You must complete this part if you **(a)** had over $1,500 of taxable interest or ordinary dividends; **(b)** had a foreign account; or **(c)** received a distribution from, or were a grantor of, or a transferor to, a foreign trust.

		Yes	No
7a	At any time during 2012, did you have a financial interest in or signature authority over a financial account (such as a bank account, securities account, or brokerage account) located in a foreign country? See instructions		
	If "Yes," are you required to file Form TD F 90-22.1 to report that financial interest or signature authority? See Form TD F 90-22.1 and its instructions for filing requirements and exceptions to those requirements		
b	If you are required to file Form TD F 90-22.1, enter the name of the foreign country where the financial account is located ▶		
8	During 2012, did you receive a distribution from, or were you the grantor of, or transferor to, a foreign trust? If "Yes," you may have to file Form 3520. See instructions on back		

For Paperwork Reduction Act Notice, see your tax return instructions. Cat. No. 17146N **Schedule B (Form 1040A or 1040) 2012**

SCHEDULE D (Form 1040)

Department of the Treasury Internal Revenue Service (99)

Capital Gains and Losses

▶ Attach to Form 1040 or Form 1040NR.
▶ Information about Schedule D and its separate instructions is at *www.irs.gov/form1040*.
▶ Use Form 8949 to list your transactions for lines 1, 2, 3, 8, 9, and 10.

OMB No. 1545-0074

2012

Attachment Sequence No. **12**

Name(s) shown on return | **Your social security number**

Part I Short-Term Capital Gains and Losses—Assets Held One Year or Less

Complete Form 8949 before completing line 1, 2, or 3. This form may be easier to complete if you round off cents to whole dollars.	**(d)** Proceeds (sales price) from Form(s) 8949, Part I, line 2, column (d)	**(e)** Cost or other basis from Form(s) 8949, Part I, line 2, column (e)	**(g)** Adjustments to gain or loss from Form(s) 8949, Part I, line 2, column (g)	**(h) Gain or (loss)** Subtract column (e) from column (d) and combine the result with column (g)
1 Short-term totals from all Forms 8949 with **box A** checked in **Part I**				
2 Short-term totals from all Forms 8949 with **box B** checked in **Part I**				
3 Short-term totals from all Forms 8949 with **box C** checked in **Part I**				

4 Short-term gain from Form 6252 and short-term gain or (loss) from Forms 4684, 6781, and 8824 .	**4**	
5 Net short-term gain or (loss) from partnerships, S corporations, estates, and trusts from Schedule(s) K-1	**5**	
6 Short-term capital loss carryover. Enter the amount, if any, from line 8 of your **Capital Loss Carryover Worksheet** in the instructions	**6**	( )
7 **Net short-term capital gain or (loss).** Combine lines 1 through 6 in column (h). If you have any long-term capital gains or losses, go to Part II below. Otherwise, go to Part III on the back	**7**	

Part II Long-Term Capital Gains and Losses—Assets Held More Than One Year

Complete Form 8949 before completing line 8, 9, or 10. This form may be easier to complete if you round off cents to whole dollars.	**(d)** Proceeds (sales price) from Form(s) 8949, Part II, line 4, column (d)	**(e)** Cost or other basis from Form(s) 8949, Part II, line 4, column (e)	**(g)** Adjustments to gain or loss from Form(s) 8949, Part II, line 4, column (g)	**(h) Gain or (loss)** Subtract column (e) from column (d) and combine the result with column (g)
8 Long-term totals from all Forms 8949 with **box A** checked in **Part II**				
9 Long-term totals from all Forms 8949 with **box B** checked in **Part II**				
10 Long-term totals from all Forms 8949 with **box C** checked in **Part II**				

11 Gain from Form 4797, Part I; long-term gain from Forms 2439 and 6252; and long-term gain or (loss) from Forms 4684, 6781, and 8824	**11**	
12 Net long-term gain or (loss) from partnerships, S corporations, estates, and trusts from Schedule(s) K-1	**12**	
13 Capital gain distributions. See the instructions	**13**	
14 Long-term capital loss carryover. Enter the amount, if any, from line 13 of your **Capital Loss Carryover Worksheet** in the instructions	**14**	( )
15 **Net long-term capital gain or (loss).** Combine lines 8 through 14 in column (h). Then go to Part III on the back	**15**	

For Paperwork Reduction Act Notice, see your tax return instructions. Cat. No. 11338H **Schedule D (Form 1040) 2012**

Schedule D (Form 1040) 2012 Page **2**

Part III **Summary**

16 Combine lines 7 and 15 and enter the result . . . . **16** ______

- If line 16 is a **gain**, enter the amount from line 16 on Form 1040, line 13, or Form 1040NR, line 14. Then go to line 17 below.
- If line 16 is a **loss**, skip lines 17 through 20 below. Then go to line 21. Also be sure to complete line 22.
- If line 16 is **zero**, skip lines 17 through 21 below and enter -0- on Form 1040, line 13, or Form 1040NR, line 14. Then go to line 22.

17 Are lines 15 and 16 **both** gains?

☐ **Yes.** Go to line 18.

☐ **No.** Skip lines 18 through 21, and go to line 22.

18 Enter the amount, if any, from line 7 of the **28% Rate Gain Worksheet** in the instructions . . ▶ **18** ______

19 Enter the amount, if any, from line 18 of the **Unrecaptured Section 1250 Gain Worksheet** in the instructions . . . . ▶ **19** ______

20 Are lines 18 and 19 **both** zero or blank?

☐ **Yes.** Complete the **Qualified Dividends and Capital Gain Tax Worksheet** in the instructions for Form 1040, line 44 (or in the instructions for Form 1040NR, line 42). **Do not** complete lines 21 and 22 below.

☐ **No.** Complete the **Schedule D Tax Worksheet** in the instructions. **Do not** complete lines 21 and 22 below.

21 If line 16 is a loss, enter here and on Form 1040, line 13, or Form 1040NR, line 14, the **smaller** of:

- The loss on line 16 or
- ($3,000), or if married filing separately, ($1,500)

. . . . **21** (   )

Note. When figuring which amount is smaller, treat both amounts as positive numbers.

22 Do you have qualified dividends on Form 1040, line 9b, or Form 1040NR, line 10b?

☐ **Yes.** Complete the **Qualified Dividends and Capital Gain Tax Worksheet** in the instructions for Form 1040, line 44 (or in the instructions for Form 1040NR, line 42).

☐ **No.** Complete the rest of Form 1040 or Form 1040NR.

Schedule D (Form 1040) 2012

SCHEDULE E (Form 1040)

Department of the Treasury
Internal Revenue Service (99)

Supplemental Income and Loss

(From rental real estate, royalties, partnerships, S corporations, estates, trusts, REMICs, etc.)

▶ Attach to Form 1040, 1040NR, or Form 1041.

▶ Information about Schedule E and its separate instructions is at *www.irs.gov/form1040*.

OMB No. 1545-0074

2012

Attachment Sequence No. **13**

Name(s) shown on return | **Your social security number**

Part I **Income or Loss From Rental Real Estate and Royalties** **Note.** If you are in the business of renting personal property, use **Schedule C** or **C-EZ** (see instructions). If you are an individual, report farm rental income or loss from **Form 4835** on page 2, line 40.

A Did you make any payments in 2012 that would require you to file Form(s) 1099? (see instructions) ☐ Yes ☐ No

B If "Yes," did you or will you file required Forms 1099? ☐ Yes ☐ No

1a	Physical address of each property (street, city, state, ZIP code)
A	
B	
C	

1b	Type of Property (from list below)	**2** For each rental real estate property listed above, report the number of fair rental and personal use days. Check the **QJV** box only if you meet the requirements to file as a qualified joint venture. See instructions.		**Fair Rental Days**	**Personal Use Days**	**QJV**
A			**A**			
B			**B**			
C			**C**			

Type of Property:

1 Single Family Residence
2 Multi-Family Residence
3 Vacation/Short-Term Rental
4 Commercial
5 Land
6 Royalties
7 Self-Rental
8 Other (describe)

Income:	**Properties:**	**A**	**B**	**C**
3 Rents received	**3**			
4 Royalties received	**4**			
Expenses:				
5 Advertising	**5**			
6 Auto and travel (see instructions)	**6**			
7 Cleaning and maintenance	**7**			
8 Commissions	**8**			
9 Insurance	**9**			
10 Legal and other professional fees	**10**			
11 Management fees	**11**			
12 Mortgage interest paid to banks, etc. (see instructions)	**12**			
13 Other interest	**13**			
14 Repairs	**14**			
15 Supplies	**15**			
16 Taxes	**16**			
17 Utilities	**17**			
18 Depreciation expense or depletion	**18**			
19 Other (list) ▶	**19**			
20 Total expenses. Add lines 5 through 19	**20**			
21 Subtract line 20 from line 3 (rents) and/or 4 (royalties). If result is a (loss), see instructions to find out if you must file **Form 6198**	**21**			
22 Deductible rental real estate loss after limitation, if any, on **Form 8582** (see instructions)	**22**	( )	( )	( )

23a Total of all amounts reported on line 3 for all rental properties	**23a**	
b Total of all amounts reported on line 4 for all royalty properties	**23b**	
c Total of all amounts reported on line 12 for all properties	**23c**	
d Total of all amounts reported on line 18 for all properties	**23d**	
e Total of all amounts reported on line 20 for all properties	**23e**	
24 **Income.** Add positive amounts shown on line 21. **Do not** include any losses	**24**	
25 **Losses.** Add royalty losses from line 21 and rental real estate losses from line 22. Enter total losses here	**25**	( )
26 **Total rental real estate and royalty income or (loss).** Combine lines 24 and 25. Enter the result here. If Parts II, III, IV, and line 40 on page 2 do not apply to you, also enter this amount on Form 1040, line 17, or Form 1040NR, line 18. Otherwise, include this amount in the total on line 41 on page 2	**26**	

For Paperwork Reduction Act Notice, see your tax return instructions. Cat. No. 11344L **Schedule E (Form 1040) 2012**

Schedule E (Form 1040) 2012 Attachment Sequence No. **13** Page **2**

Name(s) shown on return. Do not enter name and social security number if shown on other side. | **Your social security number**

Caution. The IRS compares amounts reported on your tax return with amounts shown on Schedule(s) K-1.

Part II Income or Loss From Partnerships and S Corporations

Note. If you report a loss from an at-risk activity for which **any** amount is **not** at risk, you **must** check the box in column **(e)** on line 28 and attach **Form 6198.** See instructions.

27 Are you reporting any loss not allowed in a prior year due to the at-risk or basis limitations, a prior year unallowed loss from a passive activity (if that loss was not reported on Form 8582), or unreimbursed partnership expenses? If you answered "Yes," see instructions before completing this section. ☐ **Yes** ☐ **No**

28	**(a)** Name	**(b)** Enter **P** for partnership; **S** for S corporation	**(c)** Check if foreign partnership	**(d)** Employer identification number	**(e)** Check if any amount is not at risk
A			☐		☐
B			☐		☐
C			☐		☐
D			☐		☐

	Passive Income and Loss		Nonpassive Income and Loss		
	(f) Passive loss allowed (attach **Form 8582** if required)	**(g)** Passive income from **Schedule K-1**	**(h)** Nonpassive loss from **Schedule K-1**	**(i)** Section 179 expense deduction from **Form 4562**	**(j)** Nonpassive income from **Schedule K-1**
A					
B					
C					
D					
29a Totals					
b Totals					

30	Add columns (g) and (j) of line 29a	30	
31	Add columns (f), (h), and (i) of line 29b	31	( )
32	**Total partnership and S corporation income or (loss).** Combine lines 30 and 31. Enter the result here and include in the total on line 41 below	32	

Part III Income or Loss From Estates and Trusts

33	**(a)** Name	**(b)** Employer identification number
A		
B		

	Passive Income and Loss		Nonpassive Income and Loss	
	(c) Passive deduction or loss allowed (attach Form 8582 if required)	**(d)** Passive income from **Schedule K-1**	**(e)** Deduction or loss from **Schedule K-1**	**(f)** Other income from **Schedule K-1**
A				
B				
34a Totals				
b Totals				

35	Add columns (d) and (f) of line 34a	35	
36	Add columns (c) and (e) of line 34b	36	( )
37	**Total estate and trust income or (loss).** Combine lines 35 and 36. Enter the result here and include in the total on line 41 below	37	

Part IV Income or Loss From Real Estate Mortgage Investment Conduits (REMICs)—Residual Holder

38	**(a)** Name	**(b)** Employer identification number	**(c)** Excess inclusion from **Schedules Q,** line 2c (see instructions)	**(d)** Taxable income (net loss) from **Schedules Q,** line 1b	**(e)** Income from **Schedules Q,** line 3b

39	Combine columns (d) and (e) only. Enter the result here and include in the total on line 41 below	39	

Part V Summary

40	Net farm rental income or (loss) from **Form 4835**. Also, complete line 42 below	40	
41	**Total income or (loss).** Combine lines 26, 32, 37, 39, and 40. Enter the result here and on Form 1040, line 17, or Form 1040NR, line 18 ▶	41	
42	**Reconciliation of farming and fishing income.** Enter your **gross** farming and fishing income reported on Form 4835, line 7; Schedule K-1 (Form 1065), box 14, code B; Schedule K-1 (Form 1120S), box 17, code U; and Schedule K-1 (Form 1041), box 14, code F (see instructions)	42	
43	**Reconciliation for real estate professionals.** If you were a real estate professional (see instructions), enter the net income or (loss) you reported anywhere on Form 1040 or Form 1040NR from all rental real estate activities in which you materially participated under the passive activity loss rules	43	

Schedule E (Form 1040) 2012

Schedule R (Form 1040A or 1040)

Department of the Treasury
Internal Revenue Service (99)

Credit for the Elderly or the Disabled

▶ Complete and attach to Form 1040A or 1040.
▶ **Information about Schedule R and its separate instructions is at *www.irs.gov/form1040*.**

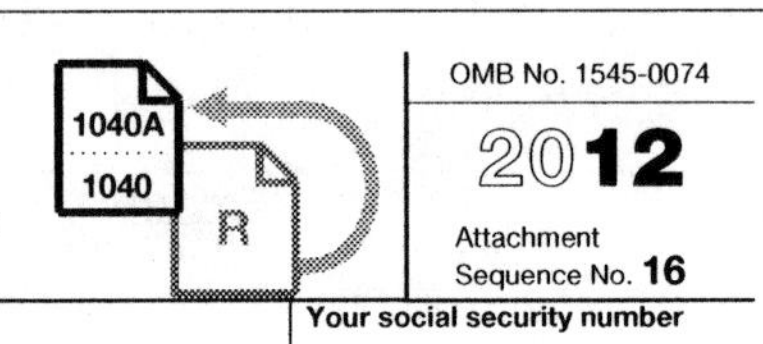

OMB No. 1545-0074

2012

Attachment Sequence No. **16**

Name(s) shown on Form 1040A or 1040 | **Your social security number**

You may be able to take this credit and reduce your tax if by the end of 2012:
- You were age 65 or older **or** • You were under age 65, you retired on **permanent and total** disability, and you received taxable disability income.

But you must also meet other tests. See instructions.

TIP In most cases, the IRS can figure the credit for you. See instructions.

Part I Check the Box for Your Filing Status and Age

If your filing status is:	And by the end of 2012:		Check only one box:
Single, Head of household, or Qualifying widow(er)	**1** You were 65 or older	**1**	☐
	2 You were under 65 and you retired on permanent and total disability	**2**	☐
Married filing jointly	**3** Both spouses were 65 or older	**3**	☐
	4 Both spouses were under 65, but only one spouse retired on permanent and total disability	**4**	☐
	5 Both spouses were under 65, and both retired on permanent and total disability	**5**	☐
	6 One spouse was 65 or older, and the other spouse was under 65 and retired on permanent and total disability	**6**	☐
	7 One spouse was 65 or older, and the other spouse was under 65 and **not** retired on permanent and total disability	**7**	☐
Married filing separately	**8** You were 65 or older and you lived apart from your spouse for all of 2012	**8**	☐
	9 You were under 65, you retired on permanent and total disability, and you lived apart from your spouse for all of 2012	**9**	☐

Did you check box 1, 3, 7, or 8?
- **Yes** ▶ Skip Part II and complete Part III on the back.
- **No** ▶ Complete Parts II and III.

Part II Statement of Permanent and Total Disability (Complete **only** if you checked box 2, 4, 5, 6, or 9 above.)

If: 1 You filed a physician's statement for this disability for 1983 or an earlier year, or you filed or got a statement for tax years after 1983 and your physician signed line B on the statement, **and**

2 Due to your continued disabled condition, you were unable to engage in any substantial gainful activity in 2012, check this box . . . ▶ ☐

- If you checked this box, you do not have to get another statement for 2012.
- If you **did not** check this box, have your physician complete the statement in the instructions. You **must** keep the statement for your records.

For Paperwork Reduction Act Notice, see your tax return instructions. Cat. No. 11359K **Schedule R (Form 1040A or 1040) 2012**

Form **8949**

Department of the Treasury
Internal Revenue Service

Sales and Other Dispositions of Capital Assets

▶ **Information about Form 8949 and its separate instructions is at *www.irs.gov/form8949*.**

▶ **File with your Schedule D to list your transactions for lines 1, 2, 3, 8, 9, and 10 of Schedule D.**

OMB No. 1545-0074

2012

Attachment Sequence No. **12A**

Name(s) shown on return | **Social security number or taxpayer identification number**

Most brokers issue their own substitute statement instead of using Form 1099-B. They also may provide basis information (usually your cost) to you on the statement even if it is not reported to the IRS. Before you check Box A, B, or C below, determine whether you received any statement(s) and, if so, the transactions for which basis was reported to the IRS. Brokers are required to report basis to the IRS for most stock you bought in 2011 or later.

Part I **Short-Term.** Transactions involving capital assets you held one year or less are short term. For long-term transactions, see page 2.

You *must* check Box A, B, *or* C below. Check only one box. If more than one box applies for your short-term transactions, complete a separate Form 8949, page 1, for each applicable box. If you have more short-term transactions than will fit on this page for one or more of the boxes, complete as many forms with the same box checked as you need.

☐ **(A)** Short-term transactions reported on Form(s) 1099-B showing basis **was** reported to the IRS
☐ **(B)** Short-term transactions reported on Form(s) 1099-B showing basis was **not** reported to the IRS
☐ **(C)** Short-term transactions not reported to you on Form 1099-B

1 **(a)** Description of property (Example: 100 sh. XYZ Co.)	**(b)** Date acquired (Mo., day, yr.)	**(c)** Date sold or disposed (Mo., day, yr.)	**(d)** Proceeds (sales price) (see instructions)	**(e)** Cost or other basis. See the **Note** below and see *Column (e)* in the separate instructions	**Adjustment, if any, to gain or loss.** If you enter an amount in column (g), enter a code in column (f). **See the separate instructions.** **(f)** Code(s) from instructions	**(g)** Amount of adjustment	**(h)** **Gain or (loss).** Subtract column (e) from column (d) and combine the result with column (g)
2 Totals. Add the amounts in columns (d), (e), (g), and (h) (subtract negative amounts). Enter each total here and include on your Schedule D, **line 1** (if **Box A** above is checked), **line 2** (if **Box B** above is checked), or **line 3** (if **Box C** above is checked) . ▶							

Note. If you checked Box A above but the basis reported to the IRS was incorrect, enter in column (e) the basis as reported to the IRS, and enter an adjustment in column (g) to correct the basis. See *Column (g)* in the separate instructions for how to figure the amount of the adjustment.

For Paperwork Reduction Act Notice, see your tax return instructions. Cat. No. 37768Z Form **8949** (2012)

Form 8949 (2012) Attachment Sequence No. **12A** Page **2**

Name(s) shown on return. (Name and SSN or taxpayer identification no. not required if shown on other side.) | **Social security number or taxpayer identification number**

Most brokers issue their own substitute statement instead of using Form 1099-B. They also may provide basis information (usually your cost) to you on the statement even if it is not reported to the IRS. Before you check Box A, B, or C below, determine whether you received any statement(s) and, if so, the transactions for which basis was reported to the IRS. Brokers are required to report basis to the IRS for most stock you bought in 2011 or later.

Part II **Long-Term.** Transactions involving capital assets you held more than one year are long term. For short-term transactions, see page 1.

You *must* check Box A, B, *or* C below. Check only one box. If more than one box applies for your long-term transactions, complete a separate Form 8949, page 2, for each applicable box. If you have more long-term transactions than will fit on this page for one or more of the boxes, complete as many forms with the same box checked as you need.

☐ **(A)** Long-term transactions reported on Form(s) 1099-B showing basis **was** reported to the IRS
☐ **(B)** Long-term transactions reported on Form(s) 1099-B showing basis was **not** reported to the IRS
☐ **(C)** Long-term transactions not reported to you on Form 1099-B

3 (a) Description of property (Example: 100 sh. XYZ Co.)	(b) Date acquired (Mo., day, yr.)	(c) Date sold or disposed (Mo., day, yr.)	(d) Proceeds (sales price) (see instructions)	(e) Cost or other basis. See the **Note** below and see *Column (e)* in the separate instructions	**Adjustment, if any, to gain or loss.** If you enter an amount in column (g), enter a code in column (f). **See the separate instructions.** (f) Code(s) from instructions	(g) Amount of adjustment	(h) **Gain or (loss).** Subtract column (e) from column (d) and combine the result with column (g)
4 Totals. Add the amounts in columns (d), (e), (g), and (h) (subtract negative amounts). Enter each total here and include on your Schedule D, **line 8** (if **Box A** above is checked), **line 9** (if **Box B** above is checked), or **line 10** (if **Box C** above is checked) ▶							

Note. If you checked Box A above but the basis reported to the IRS was incorrect, enter in column (e) the basis as reported to the IRS, and enter an adjustment in column (g) to correct the basis. See *Column (g)* in the separate instructions for how to figure the amount of the adjustment.

Form **8949** (2012)

Form **4868**

Department of the Treasury
Internal Revenue Service (99)

Application for Automatic Extension of Time To File U.S. Individual Income Tax Return

► **Information about Form 4868 and its instructions is available at *www.irs.gov/form4868*.**

OMB No. 1545-0074

2012

There are three ways to request an automatic extension of time to file a U.S. individual income tax return.

1. You can file Form 4868 electronically by accessing IRS *e-file* using your home computer or by using a tax professional who uses *e-file*.
2. You can pay all or part of your estimate of income tax due using a credit or debit card or by using the Electronic Federal Tax Payment System (EFTPS).
3. You can file a paper Form 4868.

It's Convenient, Safe, and Secure

IRS *e-file* is the IRS's electronic filing program. You can get an automatic extension of time to file your tax return by filing Form 4868 electronically. You will receive an electronic acknowledgment once you complete the transaction. Keep it with your records. Do not send in Form 4868 if you file electronically, unless you are making a payment with a check or money order (see page 3).

Complete Form 4868 to use as a worksheet. If you think you may owe tax when you file your return, you will need to estimate your total tax liability and subtract how much you have already paid (lines 4, 5, and 6 below).

Several companies offer free e-filing of Form 4868 through the Free File program. For more details, go to IRS.gov and click on *freefile*.

E-file Using Your Personal Computer or Through a Tax Professional

Refer to your tax software package or tax preparer for ways to file electronically. Be sure to have a copy of your 2011 tax return—you will be asked to provide information from the return for taxpayer verification. If you wish to make a payment, you can pay by electronic funds withdrawal or send your check or money order to the address shown in the middle column under *Where To File a Paper Form 4868* (see page 4).

Pay by Credit or Debit Card or EFTPS

You can get an extension if you pay part or all of your estimate of income tax due by using a credit or debit card. Your payment must be at least $1. You can also get an extension when you pay part or all of your estimate of income tax due using EFTPS. You can pay by phone or over the Internet (see page 3).

File a Paper Form 4868

If you wish to file on paper instead of electronically, fill in the Form 4868 below and mail it to the address shown on page 4.

For information on using a private delivery service, see page 4.

Note. If you are a fiscal year taxpayer, you must file a paper Form 4868.

General Instructions

Purpose of Form

Use Form 4868 to apply for 6 more months (4 if "out of the country" (defined on page 2) and a U.S. citizen or resident) to file Form 1040, 1040A, 1040EZ, 1040NR, 1040NR-EZ, 1040-PR, or 1040-SS.

Gift and generation-skipping transfer (GST) tax return (Form 709). An extension of time to file your 2012 calendar year income tax return also extends the time to file Form 709 for 2012. However, it does not extend the time to pay any gift and GST tax you may owe for 2012. To make a payment of gift and GST tax, see Form 8892. If you do not pay the amount due by the regular due date for Form 709, you will owe interest and may also be charged penalties. If the donor died during 2012, see the instructions for Forms 709 and 8892.

Qualifying for the Extension

To get the extra time you must:

1. Properly estimate your 2012 tax liability using the information available to you,
2. Enter your total tax liability on line 4 of Form 4868, and
3. File Form 4868 by the regular due date of your return.

CAUTION *Although you are not required to make a payment of the tax you estimate as due, Form 4868 does not extend the time to pay taxes. If you do not pay the amount due by the regular due date, you will owe interest. You may also be charged penalties. For more details, see* Interest *and* Late Payment Penalty *on page 2. Any remittance you make with your application for extension will be treated as a payment of tax.*

You do not have to explain why you are asking for the extension. We will contact you only if your request is denied.

Do not file Form 4868 if you want the IRS to figure your tax or you are under a court order to file your return by the regular due date.

▼ DETACH HERE ▼

Form **4868**

Department of the Treasury
Internal Revenue Service (99)

Application for Automatic Extension of Time To File U.S. Individual Income Tax Return

OMB No. 1545-0074

2012

For calendar year 2012, or other tax year beginning , 2012, ending , 20 .

Part I Identification

1 Your name(s) (see instructions)

Address (see instructions)

City, town, or post office	State	ZIP Code

2 Your social security number	3 Spouse's social security number

Part II Individual Income Tax

4	Estimate of total tax liability for 2012 . .	$
5	Total 2012 payments	
6	**Balance due.** Subtract line 5 from line 4 (see instructions)	
7	Amount you are paying (see instructions) ►	
8	Check here if you are "out of the country" and a U.S. citizen or resident (see instructions) . . . . . . ►	☐
9	Check here if you file Form 1040NR or 1040NR-EZ and did not receive wages as an employee subject to U.S. income tax withholding. . . . . ►	☐

For Privacy Act and Paperwork Reduction Act Notice, see page 4. Cat. No. 13141W Form **4868** (2012)

Form **4562**

Department of the Treasury
Internal Revenue Service (99)

Depreciation and Amortization
(Including Information on Listed Property)

▶ See separate instructions. ▶ Attach to your tax return.

OMB No. 1545-0172

2012

Attachment Sequence No. **179**

Name(s) shown on return	Business or activity to which this form relates	Identifying number

Part I Election To Expense Certain Property Under Section 179
Note: *If you have any listed property, complete Part V before you complete Part I.*

1	Maximum amount (see instructions)	1	
2	Total cost of section 179 property placed in service (see instructions)	2	
3	Threshold cost of section 179 property before reduction in limitation (see instructions)	3	
4	Reduction in limitation. Subtract line 3 from line 2. If zero or less, enter -0-	4	
5	Dollar limitation for tax year. Subtract line 4 from line 1. If zero or less, enter -0-. If married filing separately, see instructions	5	

6	(a) Description of property	(b) Cost (business use only)	(c) Elected cost
7	Listed property. Enter the amount from line 29	7	

8	Total elected cost of section 179 property. Add amounts in column (c), lines 6 and 7	8	
9	Tentative deduction. Enter the **smaller** of line 5 or line 8	9	
10	Carryover of disallowed deduction from line 13 of your 2011 Form 4562	10	
11	Business income limitation. Enter the smaller of business income (not less than zero) or line 5 (see instructions)	11	
12	Section 179 expense deduction. Add lines 9 and 10, but do not enter more than line 11	12	
13	Carryover of disallowed deduction to 2013. Add lines 9 and 10, less line 12 ▶	13	

Note: *Do not use Part II or Part III below for listed property. Instead, use Part V.*

Part II Special Depreciation Allowance and Other Depreciation (Do not include listed property.) (See instructions.)

14	Special depreciation allowance for qualified property (other than listed property) placed in service during the tax year (see instructions)	14	
15	Property subject to section 168(f)(1) election	15	
16	Other depreciation (including ACRS)	16	

Part III MACRS Depreciation (Do not include listed property.) (See instructions.)

Section A

17	MACRS deductions for assets placed in service in tax years beginning before 2012	17	
18	If you are electing to group any assets placed in service during the tax year into one or more general asset accounts, check here ▶ ☐		

Section B—Assets Placed in Service During 2012 Tax Year Using the General Depreciation System

(a) Classification of property	(b) Month and year placed in service	(c) Basis for depreciation (business/investment use only—see instructions)	(d) Recovery period	(e) Convention	(f) Method	(g) Depreciation deduction
19a 3-year property						
b 5-year property						
c 7-year property						
d 10-year property						
e 15-year property						
f 20-year property						
g 25-year property			25 yrs.		S/L	
h Residential rental			27.5 yrs.	MM	S/L	
property			27.5 yrs.	MM	S/L	
i Nonresidential real			39 yrs.	MM	S/L	
property				MM	S/L	

Section C—Assets Placed in Service During 2012 Tax Year Using the Alternative Depreciation System

20a Class life					S/L	
b 12-year			12 yrs.		S/L	
c 40-year			40 yrs.	MM	S/L	

Part IV Summary (See instructions.)

21	Listed property. Enter amount from line 28	21	
22	**Total.** Add amounts from line 12, lines 14 through 17, lines 19 and 20 in column (g), and line 21. Enter here and on the appropriate lines of your return. Partnerships and S corporations—see instructions	22	
23	For assets shown above and placed in service during the current year, enter the portion of the basis attributable to section 263A costs	23	

For Paperwork Reduction Act Notice, see separate instructions. Cat. No. 12906N Form **4562** (2012)

Form 4562 (2012) Page **2**

Part V **Listed Property** (Include automobiles, certain other vehicles, certain computers, and property used for entertainment, recreation, or amusement.)

Note: *For any vehicle for which you are using the standard mileage rate or deducting lease expense, complete* ***only*** *24a, 24b, columns (a) through (c) of Section A, all of Section B, and Section C if applicable.*

Section A—Depreciation and Other Information (Caution: *See the instructions for limits for passenger automobiles.***)**

24a Do you have evidence to support the business/investment use claimed? ☐ **Yes** ☐ **No** | **24b** If "Yes," is the evidence written? ☐ **Yes** ☐ **No**

(a) Type of property (list vehicles first)	(b) Date placed in service	(c) Business/ investment use percentage	(d) Cost or other basis	(e) Basis for depreciation (business/investment use only)	(f) Recovery period	(g) Method/ Convention	(h) Depreciation deduction	(i) Elected section 179 cost
25 Special depreciation allowance for qualified listed property placed in service during the tax year and used more than 50% in a qualified business use (see instructions) .						**25**		
26 Property used more than 50% in a qualified business use:								
		%						
		%						
		%						
27 Property used 50% or less in a qualified business use:								
		%				S/L –		
		%				S/L –		
		%				S/L –		
28 Add amounts in column (h), lines 25 through 27. Enter here and on line 21, page 1 .						**28**		
29 Add amounts in column (i), line 26. Enter here and on line 7, page 1							**29**	

Section B—Information on Use of Vehicles

Complete this section for vehicles used by a sole proprietor, partner, or other "more than 5% owner," or related person. If you provided vehicles to your employees, first answer the questions in Section C to see if you meet an exception to completing this section for those vehicles.

	(a) Vehicle 1		(b) Vehicle 2		(c) Vehicle 3		(d) Vehicle 4		(e) Vehicle 5		(f) Vehicle 6	
30 Total business/investment miles driven during the year (**do not** include commuting miles) .												
31 Total commuting miles driven during the year												
32 Total other personal (noncommuting) miles driven												
33 Total miles driven during the year. Add lines 30 through 32												
	Yes	**No**	**Yes**	**No**	**Yes**	**No**	**Yes**	**No**	**Yes**	**No**	**Yes**	**No**
34 Was the vehicle available for personal use during off-duty hours?												
35 Was the vehicle used primarily by a more than 5% owner or related person? . .												
36 Is another vehicle available for personal use?												

Section C—Questions for Employers Who Provide Vehicles for Use by Their Employees

Answer these questions to determine if you meet an exception to completing Section B for vehicles used by employees who **are not** more than 5% owners or related persons (see instructions).

	Yes	**No**
37 Do you maintain a written policy statement that prohibits all personal use of vehicles, including commuting, by your employees?		
38 Do you maintain a written policy statement that prohibits personal use of vehicles, except commuting, by your employees? See the instructions for vehicles used by corporate officers, directors, or 1% or more owners . .		
39 Do you treat all use of vehicles by employees as personal use?		
40 Do you provide more than five vehicles to your employees, obtain information from your employees about the use of the vehicles, and retain the information received?		
41 Do you meet the requirements concerning qualified automobile demonstration use? (See instructions.) . . .		
Note: *If your answer to 37, 38, 39, 40, or 41 is "Yes," do not complete Section B for the covered vehicles.*		

Part VI **Amortization**

(a) Description of costs	(b) Date amortization begins	(c) Amortizable amount	(d) Code section	(e) Amortization period or percentage	(f) Amortization for this year
42 Amortization of costs that begins during your 2012 tax year (see instructions):					
43 Amortization of costs that began before your 2012 tax year				**43**	
44 Total. Add amounts in column (f). See the instructions for where to report				**44**	

Form **4562** (2012)

Form **2555**

Department of the Treasury
Internal Revenue Service

Foreign Earned Income

▶ Attach to Form 1040.

▶ Information about Form 2555 and its separate instructions is at *www.irs.gov/form2555*.

OMB No. 1545-0074

2012

Attachment Sequence No. **34**

For Use by U.S. Citizens and Resident Aliens Only

Name shown on Form 1040 | **Your social security number**

Part I General Information

1 Your foreign address (including country) | **2** Your occupation

3 Employer's name ▶

4a Employer's U.S. address ▶

b Employer's foreign address ▶

5 Employer is (check any that apply): **a** ☐ A foreign entity **b** ☐ A U.S. company **c** ☐ Self **d** ☐ A foreign affiliate of a U.S. company **e** ☐ Other (specify) ▶

6a If you previously filed Form 2555 or Form 2555-EZ, enter the last year you filed the form. ▶

b If you did not previously file Form 2555 or 2555-EZ to claim either of the exclusions, check here ▶ ☐ and go to line 7.

c Have you ever revoked either of the exclusions? . . . ☐ **Yes** ☐ **No**

d If you answered "Yes," enter the type of exclusion and the tax year for which the revocation was effective. ▶

7 Of what country are you a citizen/national? ▶

8a Did you maintain a separate foreign residence for your family because of adverse living conditions at your tax home? See **Second foreign household** in the instructions . . . ☐ **Yes** ☐ **No**

b If "Yes," enter city and country of the separate foreign residence. Also, enter the number of days during your tax year that you maintained a second household at that address. ▶

9 List your tax home(s) during your tax year and date(s) established. ▶

Next, complete either Part II or Part III. If an item does not apply, enter "NA." If you do not give the information asked for, any exclusion or deduction you claim may be disallowed.

Part II Taxpayers Qualifying Under Bona Fide Residence Test (see instructions)

10 Date bona fide residence began ▶ , and ended ▶

11 Kind of living quarters in foreign country ▶ **a** ☐ Purchased house **b** ☐ Rented house or apartment **c** ☐ Rented room **d** ☐ Quarters furnished by employer

12a Did any of your family live with you abroad during any part of the tax year? . . . ☐ **Yes** ☐ **No**

b If "Yes," who and for what period? ▶

13a Have you submitted a statement to the authorities of the foreign country where you claim bona fide residence that you are not a resident of that country? See instructions . . . ☐ **Yes** ☐ **No**

b Are you required to pay income tax to the country where you claim bona fide residence? See instructions . ☐ **Yes** ☐ **No**

If you answered "Yes" to 13a and "No" to 13b, you do not qualify as a bona fide resident. Do not complete the rest of this part.

14 If you were present in the United States or its possessions during the tax year, complete columns **(a)–(d)** below. **Do not** include the income from column **(d)** in Part IV, but report it on Form 1040.

(a) Date arrived in U.S.	**(b)** Date left U.S.	**(c)** Number of days in U.S. on business	**(d)** Income earned in U.S. on business (attach computation)	**(a)** Date arrived in U.S.	**(b)** Date left U.S.	**(c)** Number of days in U.S. on business	**(d)** Income earned in U.S. on business (attach computation)

15a List any contractual terms or other conditions relating to the length of your employment abroad. ▶

b Enter the type of visa under which you entered the foreign country. ▶

c Did your visa limit the length of your stay or employment in a foreign country? If "Yes," attach explanation . ☐ **Yes** ☐ **No**

d Did you maintain a home in the United States while living abroad? . . . ☐ **Yes** ☐ **No**

e If "Yes," enter address of your home, whether it was rented, the names of the occupants, and their relationship to you. ▶

For Paperwork Reduction Act Notice, see the Form 1040 instructions. Cat. No. 11900P Form **2555** (2012)

Part III Taxpayers Qualifying Under Physical Presence Test (see instructions)

16 The physical presence test is based on the 12-month period from ▶ ________ through ▶ ________

17 Enter your principal country of employment during your tax year. ▶ ________

18 If you traveled abroad during the 12-month period entered on line 16, complete columns **(a)–(f)** below. Exclude travel between foreign countries that did not involve travel on or over international waters, or in or over the United States, for 24 hours or more. If you have no travel to report during the period, enter "Physically present in a foreign country or countries for the entire 12-month period." **Do not** include the income from column **(f)** below in Part IV, but report it on Form 1040.

(a) Name of country (including U.S.)	**(b)** Date arrived	**(c)** Date left	**(d)** Full days present in country	**(e)** Number of days in U.S. on business	**(f)** Income earned in U.S. on business (attach computation)

Part IV All Taxpayers

Note: *Enter on lines 19 through 23 all income, including noncash income, you earned and actually or constructively received during your 2012 tax year for services you performed in a foreign country. If any of the foreign earned income received this tax year was earned in a prior tax year, or will be earned in a later tax year (such as a bonus), see the instructions.* ***Do not*** *include income from line 14, column* ***(d),*** *or line 18, column* ***(f).*** *Report amounts in U.S. dollars, using the exchange rates in effect when you actually or constructively received the income.*

If you are a cash basis taxpayer, report on Form 1040 all income you received in 2012, no matter when you performed the service.

	2012 Foreign Earned Income				**Amount (in U.S. dollars)**
19	Total wages, salaries, bonuses, commissions, etc.			**19**	
20	Allowable share of income for personal services performed (see instructions):				
a	In a business (including farming) or profession			**20a**	
b	In a partnership. List partnership's name and address and type of income. ▶			**20b**	
21	Noncash income (market value of property or facilities furnished by employer—attach statement showing how it was determined):				
a	Home (lodging)			**21a**	
b	Meals			**21b**	
c	Car			**21c**	
d	Other property or facilities. List type and amount. ▶			**21d**	
22	Allowances, reimbursements, or expenses paid on your behalf for services you performed:				
a	Cost of living and overseas differential	**22a**			
b	Family	**22b**			
c	Education	**22c**			
d	Home leave	**22d**			
e	Quarters	**22e**			
f	For any other purpose. List type and amount. ▶	**22f**			
g	Add lines 22a through 22f			**22g**	
23	Other foreign earned income. List type and amount. ▶			**23**	
24	Add lines 19 through 21d, line 22g, and line 23			**24**	
25	Total amount of meals and lodging included on line 24 that is excludable (see instructions)			**25**	
26	Subtract line 25 from line 24. Enter the result here and on line 27 on page 3. This is your **2012 foreign earned income** ▶			**26**	

Form 2555 (2012) Page 3

Part V **All Taxpayers**

27	Enter the amount from line 26	27	
	Are you claiming the housing exclusion or housing deduction? ☐ **Yes.** Complete Part VI. ☐ **No.** Go to Part VII.		

Part VI **Taxpayers Claiming the Housing Exclusion and/or Deduction**

28	Qualified housing expenses for the tax year (see instructions)	28	
29a	Enter location where housing expenses incurred (see instructions) ▶		
b	Enter limit on housing expenses (see instructions)	29b	
30	Enter the **smaller** of line 28 or line 29b	30	
31	Number of days in your qualifying period that fall within your 2012 tax year (see instructions) . . . . **31** **days**		
32	Multiply $41.57 by the number of days on line 31. If 366 is entered on line 31, enter $15,216.00 here	32	
33	Subtract line 32 from line 30. If the result is zero or less, do not complete the rest of this part or any of Part IX	33	
34	Enter employer-provided amounts (see instructions) **34**		
35	Divide line 34 by line 27. Enter the result as a decimal (rounded to at least three places), but do not enter more than "1.000"	35	× .
36	**Housing exclusion.** Multiply line 33 by line 35. Enter the result but do not enter more than the amount on line 34. Also, complete Part VIII . . . . ▶	36	
	Note: *The housing deduction is figured in Part IX. If you choose to claim the foreign earned income exclusion, complete Parts VII and VIII before Part IX.*		

Part VII **Taxpayers Claiming the Foreign Earned Income Exclusion**

37	Maximum foreign earned income exclusion	37	$95,100 00
38	• If you completed Part VI, enter the number from line 31. • All others, enter the number of days in your qualifying period that fall within your 2012 tax year (see the instructions for line 31). **38** **days**		
39	• If line 38 and the number of days in your 2012 tax year (usually 366) are the same, enter "1.000." • Otherwise, divide line 38 by the number of days in your 2012 tax year and enter the result as a decimal (rounded to at least three places).	39	× .
40	Multiply line 37 by line 39	40	
41	Subtract line 36 from line 27	41	
42	**Foreign earned income exclusion.** Enter the **smaller** of line 40 or line 41. Also, complete Part VIII ▶	42	

Part VIII **Taxpayers Claiming the Housing Exclusion, Foreign Earned Income Exclusion, or Both**

43	Add lines 36 and 42	43	
44	Deductions allowed in figuring your adjusted gross income (Form 1040, line 37) that are allocable to the excluded income. See instructions and attach computation	44	
45	Subtract line 44 from line 43. Enter the result here and in parentheses on **Form 1040, line 21.** Next to the amount enter "Form 2555." On Form 1040, subtract this amount from your income to arrive at total income on Form 1040, line 22	45	

Part IX **Taxpayers Claiming the Housing Deduction**—Complete this part only if **(a)** line 33 is more than line 36 and **(b)** line 27 is more than line 43.

46	Subtract line 36 from line 33	46	
47	Subtract line 43 from line 27	47	
48	Enter the **smaller** of line 46 or line 47	48	
	Note: *If line 47 is **more than** line 48 and you could not deduct all of your 2011 housing deduction because of the 2011 limit, use the housing deduction carryover worksheet in the instructions to figure the amount to enter on line 49. Otherwise, go to line 50.*		
49	Housing deduction carryover from 2011 (from housing deduction carryover worksheet in the instructions)	49	
50	**Housing deduction.** Add lines 48 and 49. Enter the total here and on Form 1040 to the left of line 36. Next to the amount on Form 1040, enter "Form 2555." Add it to the total adjustments reported on that line . . . . ▶	50	

Form **2555** (2012)

Form **2555-EZ**

Department of the Treasury
Internal Revenue Service (99)

Foreign Earned Income Exclusion

▶ **Attach to Form 1040.**

▶ **Information about Form 2555-EZ and its separate instructions is at *www.irs.gov/form2555*.**

OMB No. 1545-0074

2012

Attachment Sequence No. **34A**

Name shown on Form 1040 | **Your social security number**

You May Use This Form If You:

- Are a U.S. citizen or a resident alien.
- Earned wages/salaries in a foreign country.
- Had total foreign earned income of $95,100 or less.
- Are filing a calendar year return that covers a 12-month period.

And You:

- Do not have self-employment income.
- Do not have business/moving expenses.
- Do not claim the foreign housing exclusion or deduction.

Part I Tests To See If You Can Take the Foreign Earned Income Exclusion

1 Bona Fide Residence Test

a Were you a bona fide resident of a foreign country or countries for a period that includes an entire tax year (see page 2 of the instructions)? . . . ☐ **Yes** ☐ **No**

- If you answered "Yes," you meet this test. Fill in line 1b and then go to line 3.
- If you answered "No," you **do not** meet this test. Go to line 2 to see if you meet the Physical Presence Test.

b Enter the date your bona fide residence began ▶ ____________, and ended (see instructions) ▶ ____________.

2 Physical Presence Test

a Were you physically present in a foreign country or countries for at least 330 full days during—
{ 2012 **or** any other period of 12 months in a row starting or ending in 2012? } . . . ☐ **Yes** ☐ **No**

- If you answered "Yes," you meet this test. Fill in line 2b and then go to line 3.
- If you answered "No," you **do not** meet this test. You **cannot** take the exclusion unless you meet the Bona Fide Residence Test above.

b The physical presence test is based on the 12-month period from ▶ ____________ through ▶ ____________.

3 Tax Home Test. Was your tax home in a foreign country or countries throughout your period of bona fide residence or physical presence, whichever applies? . . . ☐ **Yes** ☐ **No**

- If you answered "Yes," you can take the exclusion. Complete Part II below and then go to page 2.
- If you answered "No," you **cannot** take the exclusion. **Do not** file this form.

Part II General Information

4 Your foreign address (including country)		5 Your occupation
6 Employer's name	7 Employer's U.S. address (including ZIP code)	8 Employer's foreign address

9 Employer is (check any that apply):

a A U.S. business . . . ☐

b A foreign business . . . ☐

c Other (specify) ▶ ____________ ☐

10a If you previously filed Form 2555 or 2555-EZ, enter the last year you filed the form. ▶ ____________

b If you did not previously file Form 2555 or 2555-EZ, check here ▶ ☐ and go to line 11a now.

c Have you ever revoked the foreign earned income exclusion? . . . ☐ **Yes** ☐ **No**

d If you answered "Yes," enter the tax year for which the revocation was effective. ▶ ____________

11a List your tax home(s) during 2012 and date(s) established. ▶ ____________

b Of what country are you a citizen/national? ▶ ____________

For Paperwork Reduction Act Notice, see the Form 1040 instructions. Cat. No. 13272W Form **2555-EZ** (2012)

Form 2555-EZ (2012) Page **2**

Part III **Days Present in the United States—** Complete this part if you were in the United States or its possessions during 2012.

12 **(a)** Date arrived in U.S.	**(b)** Date left U.S.	**(c)** Number of days in U.S. on business	**(d)** Income earned in U.S. on business (attach computation)

Part IV **Figure Your Foreign Earned Income Exclusion**

13	Maximum foreign earned income exclusion	13	$95,100 00
14	Enter the number of days in your qualifying period that fall within 2012 . 14 ______ days		
15	Did you enter 366 on line 14? ☐ **Yes.** Enter "1.000." ☐ **No.** Divide line 14 by 366 and enter the result as a decimal (rounded to at least three places).	15	× .
16	Multiply line 13 by line 15	16	
17	Enter, in U.S. dollars, the total foreign earned income you earned and received in 2012 (see instructions). Be sure to include this amount on Form 1040, line 7	17	
18	**Foreign earned income exclusion.** Enter the **smaller** of line 16 or line 17 here and in parentheses on **Form 1040, line 21.** Next to the amount enter "2555-EZ." On Form 1040, subtract this amount from your income to arrive at total income on Form 1040, line 22 . . . . ▶	18	

Form **2555-EZ** (2012)

Form **3903**

Department of the Treasury
Internal Revenue Service (99)

Moving Expenses

▶ Information about Form 3903 and its instructions is available at *www.irs.gov/form3903.*
▶ Attach to Form 1040 or Form 1040NR.

OMB No. 1545-0074

2012

Attachment Sequence No. **170**

Name(s) shown on return | **Your social security number**

Before you begin: ✓ See the **Distance Test** and **Time Test** in the instructions to find out if you can deduct your moving expenses.
✓ See **Members of the Armed Forces** in the instructions, if applicable.

1	Transportation and storage of household goods and personal effects (see instructions) . . .	1	
2	Travel (including lodging) from your old home to your new home (see instructions). **Do not** include the cost of meals	2	
3	Add lines 1 and 2	3	
4	Enter the total amount your employer paid you for the expenses listed on lines 1 and 2 that is **not** included in box 1 of your Form W-2 (wages). This amount should be shown in box 12 of your Form W-2 with code **P**	4	
5	Is line 3 **more than** line 4? ☐ **No.** You **cannot** deduct your moving expenses. If line 3 is less than line 4, subtract line 3 from line 4 and include the result on Form 1040, line 7, or Form 1040NR, line 8. ☐ **Yes.** Subtract line 4 from line 3. Enter the result here and on Form 1040, line 26, or Form 1040NR, line 26. This is your **moving expense deduction**	5	

For Paperwork Reduction Act Notice, see your tax return instructions. Cat. No. 12490K Form **3903** (2012)

THIS PAGE INTENTIONALLY LEFT BLANK

Form **8917**

Department of the Treasury
Internal Revenue Service

Tuition and Fees Deduction

See Instructions.
Attach to Form 1040 or Form 1040A.
Instructions and more are at *www.IRS.gov/form8917*

OMB No. 1545-0074
2012
Attachment Sequence No. **60**

Name(s) shown on return | **Your social security number**

CAUTION: *You **cannot** take both an education credit from Form 8863 and the tuition and fees deduction from this form for the **same student** for the same tax year.*

Before you begin:
- ✔ To see if you qualify for this deduction, see *Who Can Take the Deduction* in the instructions below.
- ✔ If you file Form 1040, figure any write-in adjustments to be entered on the dotted line next to Form 1040, line 36. See the 2012 Form 1040 instructions for line 36.

1	**(a)** Student's name (as shown on page 1 of your tax return) First name / Last name	**(b)** Student's social security number (as shown on page 1 of your tax return)	**(c)** Adjusted qualified expenses (see instructions)

2	Add the amounts on line 1, column (c), and enter the total	2	
3	Enter the amount from Form 1040, line 22, or Form 1040A, line 15 — 3		
4	Enter the total from either: • Form 1040, lines 23 through 33, plus any write-in adjustments entered on the dotted line next to Form 1040, line 36, **or** • Form 1040A, lines 16 through 18 — 4		
5	Subtract line 4 from line 3.* If the result is more than $80,000 ($160,000 if married filing jointly), **stop**; you cannot take the deduction for tuition and fees	5	
	*If you are filing Form 2555, 2555-EZ, or 4563, or you are excluding income from Puerto Rico, see *Effect of the Amount of Your Income on the Amount of Your Deduction* in Pub. 970, chapter 6, to figure the amount to enter on line 5.		
6	**Tuition and fees deduction.** Is the amount on line 5 more than $65,000 ($130,000 if married filing jointly)? ☐ **Yes.** Enter the smaller of line 2, or $2,000. ☐ **No.** Enter the smaller of line 2, or $4,000. **Also enter** this amount on Form 1040, line 34, or Form 1040A, line 19.	6	

Section references are to the Internal Revenue Code unless otherwise noted.

What's New

Future developments. The IRS has created a page on IRS.gov for information about Form 8917, at *www.irs.gov/form8917*. Information about any future developments affecting Form 8917 (such as legislation enacted after we release it) will be posted on that page.

General Instructions

Purpose of Form

Use Form 8917 to figure and take the deduction for tuition and fees expenses **paid in 2012.**

This deduction is based on adjusted qualified education expenses paid to an eligible postsecondary educational institution. See *Qualified Education Expenses,* later, for more information.

You may be able to take the American opportunity credit or lifetime learning credit for your education expenses instead of the tuition and fees deduction. See Form 8863, Education Credits, and Pub. 970, Tax Benefits for Education, for more information about these credits.

Who Can Take the Deduction

You may be able to take the deduction if you, your spouse, or a dependent you claim on your tax return was a student enrolled at or attending an eligible educational institution. The deduction is based on the amount of qualified education expenses you paid for the student in 2012 for academic periods beginning in 2012 and those beginning in the first 3 months of 2013.

Generally, in order to claim the deduction for education expenses for a dependent, you must have paid the expenses in 2012 and must claim an exemption for the student as a dependent on your 2012 tax return (line 6c of Form 1040 or 1040A). For additional information, see chapter 6 of Pub. 970.

You **cannot** claim the tuition and fees deduction if any of the following apply.

- Your filing status is married filing separately.
- Another person can claim an exemption for you as a dependent on his or her tax return. You cannot take the deduction even if the other person does not actually claim that exemption.
- Your modified adjusted gross income (MAGI), as figured on line 5, is more than $80,000 ($160,000 if filing a joint return).
- You were a nonresident alien for any part of the year and did not elect to be treated as a resident alien for tax purposes. More information on nonresident aliens can be found in Pub. 519, U.S. Tax Guide for Aliens.

You **cannot** claim a tuition and fees deduction for any student if you or anyone else claims an American opportunity or lifetime learning credit (Form 8863) in 2012 with respect to expenses of the student for whom the qualified education expenses were paid. However, a state tax credit will not disqualify you from claiming a tuition and fees deduction.

Qualified Education Expenses

Generally, qualified education expenses are amounts you paid in 2012 for tuition and fees required for the student's enrollment or attendance at an eligible educational institution. Required fees include amounts for books, supplies, and equipment used in a course of study if required to be paid to the institution as a condition of enrollment or attendance. It does not matter whether the expenses were paid in cash, by check, by credit card, or with borrowed funds.

Qualified education expenses include nonacademic fees, such as student activity fees, athletic fees, or other expenses unrelated to the academic course of instruction, **only if** the fee must be paid to the institution as a condition of enrollment or attendance. However, fees for personal expenses (described below) are never qualified education expenses.

Qualified education expenses **do not** include amounts paid for:

- Personal expenses. This means room and board, insurance, medical expenses (including student health fees), transportation, and other similar personal, living, or family expenses.

For Paperwork Reduction Act Notice, see your tax return instructions. Cat. No. 37728P Form **8917** (2012)

• Any course or other education involving sports, games, or hobbies, or any noncredit course, unless such course or other education is part of the student's degree program or helps the student acquire or improve job skills.

Qualified education expenses do not include any expenses for which you take any other deduction, such as on Schedule A (Form 1040) or Schedule C (Form 1040).

You should receive Form 1098-T, Tuition Statement, from the institution reporting either payments received in 2012 (box 1) or amounts billed in 2012 (box 2). However, the amount in box 1 or 2 of Form 1098-T may be different from the amount you paid (or are treated as having paid). In completing Form 8917, use only the amounts you actually paid (plus any amounts you are treated as having paid) in 2012 (reduced, as necessary, as described in *Adjusted Qualified Education Expenses,* later). See chapter 6 of Pub. 970 for more information on Form 1098-T.

Qualified education expenses paid directly to the institution by someone other than you or the student are treated as paid to the student and then paid by the student to the institution.

Academic Period

An academic period is any quarter, semester, trimester, or any other period of study as reasonably determined by an eligible educational institution. If an eligible educational institution uses credit hours or clock hours and does not have academic terms, each payment period may be treated as an academic period.

Prepaid Expenses

Qualified education expenses paid in 2012 for an academic period that begins in the first 3 months of 2013 can be used in figuring the tuition and fees deduction for 2012 only. See *Academic Period,* earlier. For example, if you pay $2,000 in December 2012 for qualified tuition for the 2013 winter quarter that begins in January 2013, you can use that $2,000 in figuring the tuition and fees deduction for 2012 only (if you meet all the other requirements).

You cannot use any amount you paid in 2011 or 2013 to figure the qualified education expenses you use to figure your 2012 tuition and fees deduction.

Adjusted Qualified Education Expenses

For each student, reduce the qualified education expenses paid by or on behalf of that student under the following rules. The result is the amount of adjusted qualified education expenses for each student.

Tax-free educational assistance. For tax-free educational assistance you received in 2012, reduce the qualified education expenses for each academic period by the amount of tax-free educational assistance allocable to that academic period. See *Academic Period,* earlier.

Tax-free educational assistance includes:

1. The tax-free part of any scholarship or fellowship (including Pell grants),
2. The tax-free part of any employer-provided educational assistance,
3. Veterans' educational assistance, and
4. Any other educational assistance that is excludable from gross income (tax free), other than as a gift, bequest, devise, or inheritance.

Generally, any scholarship or fellowship you receive is treated as tax-free educational assistance. However, a scholarship or fellowship is not treated as tax-free educational assistance to the extent you include it in gross income (if you are required to file a tax return) for the year the scholarship or fellowship is received and either:

• The scholarship or fellowship (or any part of it) **must** be applied (by its terms) to expenses (such as room and board) other than qualified education expenses as defined in *Qualified education expenses* in Pub. 970, chapter 1; or

• The scholarship or fellowship (or any part of it) **may** be applied (by its terms) to expenses (such as room and board) other than qualified education expenses as defined in *Qualified education expenses* in Pub. 970, chapter 1.

You may be able to increase the combined value of your tuition and fees deduction and certain educational assistance if you include some or all of the educational assistance in income in the year it is received. For details, see Adjustments to Qualified Education Expenses, *in chapter 6 of Pub. 970.*

Some tax-free educational assistance received after 2012 may be treated as a refund of qualified education expenses paid in 2012. This tax-free educational assistance is any tax-free educational assistance received by you or anyone else after 2012 for qualified education expenses paid on behalf of a student in 2012 (or attributable to enrollment at an eligible educational institution during 2012).

If this tax-free educational assistance is received after 2012 but before you file your 2012 income tax return, see *Refunds received after 2012 but before your income tax return is filed,* later. If this tax-free educational assistance is received after 2012 and after you file your 2012 income tax return, see *Refunds received after 2012 and after your income tax return is filed,* later.

Refunds. A refund of qualified education expenses may reduce adjusted qualified education expenses for the tax year or may require you to include some or all of the refund in your gross income for the year the refund is received. See chapter 6 of Pub. 970 for more information. Some tax-free educational assistance received after 2012 may be treated as a refund. See *Tax-free educational assistance,* earlier.

Refunds received in 2012. For each student, figure the adjusted qualified education expenses for 2012 by adding all the qualified education expenses paid in 2012 and subtracting any refunds of those expenses received from the eligible educational institution during 2012.

Refunds received after 2012 but before your income tax return is filed. If you receive a refund after 2012 of qualified education expenses you paid in 2012 and the refund is received before you file your 2012 income tax return, reduce the amount of qualified education expenses for 2012 by the amount of the refund.

Refunds received after 2012 and after your income tax return is filed. If you receive a refund after 2012 of qualified education expenses you paid in 2012 and the refund is received after you file your 2012 income tax return, you may need to include some or all of the refund in your gross income for the year the refund is received. See chapter 6 of Pub. 970 for more information.

Coordination with Coverdell education savings accounts and qualified tuition programs. Reduce your qualified education expenses by any qualified education expenses used to figure the exclusion from gross income of (a) interest received under an education savings bond program, or (b) any distribution from a Coverdell education savings account or qualified tuition program (QTP). For a QTP, this applies only to the amount of tax-free earnings that were distributed, not to the recovery of contributions to the program.

Eligible Educational Institution

An eligible educational institution is generally any accredited public, nonprofit, or proprietary (private) college, university, vocational school, or other postsecondary institution. Also, the institution must be eligible to participate in a student aid program administered by the Department of Education. Virtually all accredited postsecondary institutions meet this definition.

Additional Information

See Pub. 970, chapter 6, for more information about the tuition and fees deduction.

Specific Instructions

Line 1

Complete columns (a) through (c) on line 1 for each student for whom you elect to take the tuition and fees deduction.

Note. If you have more than three students who qualify for the tuition and fees deduction, enter "See attached" next to line 1 and attach a statement with the required information for each additional student. Include the amounts from line 1, column (c), for all students in the total you enter on line 2.

Column (c)

For each student, enter the amount of adjusted qualified education expenses. The expenses must have been paid for the student in 2012 for academic periods beginning after 2011 but before April 1, 2013.

Form **4952**

Department of the Treasury
Internal Revenue Service (99)

Investment Interest Expense Deduction

▶ Information about Form 4952 and its instructions is at *www.irs.gov/form4952.*

▶ Attach to your tax return.

OMB No. 1545-0191

2012

Attachment Sequence No. 51

Name(s) shown on return	Identifying number

Part I Total Investment Interest Expense

1	Investment interest expense paid or accrued in 2012 (see instructions)		1	
2	Disallowed investment interest expense from 2011 Form 4952, line 7		2	
3	**Total investment interest expense.** Add lines 1 and 2		3	

Part II Net Investment Income

4a	Gross income from property held for investment (excluding any net gain from the disposition of property held for investment)	4a			
b	Qualified dividends included on line 4a	4b			
c	Subtract line 4b from line 4a			4c	
d	Net gain from the disposition of property held for investment	4d			
e	Enter the **smaller** of line 4d or your net capital gain from the disposition of property held for investment (see instructions)	4e			
f	Subtract line 4e from line 4d			4f	
g	Enter the amount from lines 4b and 4e that you elect to include in investment income (see instructions)			4g	
h	Investment income. Add lines 4c, 4f, and 4g			4h	
5	Investment expenses (see instructions)			5	
6	**Net investment income.** Subtract line 5 from line 4h. If zero or less, enter -0-			6	

Part III Investment Interest Expense Deduction

7	Disallowed investment interest expense to be carried forward to 2013. Subtract line 6 from line 3. If zero or less, enter -0-	7	
8	**Investment interest expense deduction.** Enter the **smaller** of line 3 or 6. See instructions	8	

For Paperwork Reduction Act Notice, see page 4. Cat. No. 13177Y Form **4952** (2012)

THIS PAGE INTENTIONALLY LEFT BLANK

Form **4684**

Department of the Treasury
Internal Revenue Service

Casualties and Thefts

▶ Information about Form 4684 and its separate instructions is at *www.irs.gov/form4684*.
▶ Attach to your tax return.
▶ Use a separate Form 4684 for each casualty or theft.

OMB No. 1545-0177

2012

Attachment Sequence No. 26

Name(s) shown on tax return | Identifying number

SECTION A—Personal Use Property (Use this section to report casualties and thefts of property **not** used in a trade or business or for income-producing purposes.)

1 Description of properties (show type, location, and date acquired for each property). Use a separate line for each property lost or damaged from the same casualty or theft.

Property **A** ______
Property **B** ______
Property **C** ______
Property **D** ______

		Properties			
		A	B	C	D
2 Cost or other basis of each property	2				
3 Insurance or other reimbursement (whether or not you filed a claim) (see instructions)	3				
Note: *If line 2 is* ***more*** *than line 3, skip line 4.*					
4 Gain from casualty or theft. If line 3 is **more** than line 2, enter the difference here and skip lines 5 through 9 for that column. See instructions if line 3 includes insurance or other reimbursement you did not claim, or you received payment for your loss in a later tax year	4				
5 Fair market value **before** casualty or theft	5				
6 Fair market value **after** casualty or theft	6				
7 Subtract line 6 from line 5	7				
8 Enter the **smaller** of line 2 or line 7	8				
9 Subtract line 3 from line 8. If zero or less, enter -0-	9				

10 Casualty or theft loss. Add the amounts on line 9 in columns A through D	10	
11 Enter the **smaller** of line 10 or $100	11	
12 Subtract line 11 from line 10	12	
Caution: *Use only one Form 4684 for lines 13 through 18.*		
13 Add the amounts on line 12 of all Forms 4684	13	
14 Add the amounts on line 4 of all Forms 4684.	14	
15 • If line 14 is **more** than line 13, enter the difference here and on Schedule D. **Do not** complete the rest of this section (see instructions).	15	
• If line 14 is **less** than line 13, enter -0- here and go to line 16.		
• If line 14 is **equal** to line 13, enter -0- here. **Do not** complete the rest of this section.		
16 If line 14 is **less** than line 13, enter the difference	16	
17 Enter 10% of your adjusted gross income from Form 1040, line 38, or Form 1040NR, line 37. Estates and trusts, see instructions	17	
18 Subtract line 17 from line 16. If zero or less, enter -0-. Also enter the result on Schedule A (Form 1040), line 20, or Form 1040NR, Schedule A, line 6. Estates and trusts, enter the result on the "Other deductions" line of your tax return	18	

For Paperwork Reduction Act Notice, see instructions. Cat. No. 12997O Form **4684** (2012)

Form 4684 (2012) Attachment Sequence No. **26** Page **2**

Name(s) shown on tax return. Do not enter name and identifying number if shown on other side. | **Identifying number**

SECTION B—Business and Income-Producing Property

Part I Casualty or Theft Gain or Loss (Use a separate Part I for each casualty or theft.)

19 Description of properties (show type, location, and date acquired for each property). Use a separate line for each property lost or damaged from the same casualty or theft.

Property **A** ________________

Property **B** ________________

Property **C** ________________

Property **D** ________________

Line	Description		Properties A	B	C	D
20	Cost or adjusted basis of each property	20				
21	Insurance or other reimbursement (whether or not you filed a claim). See the instructions for line 3	21				
	Note: *If line 20 is **more** than line 21, skip line 22.*					
22	Gain from casualty or theft. If line 21 is **more** than line 20, enter the difference here and on line 29 or line 34, column (c), except as provided in the instructions for line 33. Also, skip lines 23 through 27 for that column. See the instructions for line 4 if line 21 includes insurance or other reimbursement you did not claim, or you received payment for your loss in a later tax year	22				
23	Fair market value **before** casualty or theft	23				
24	Fair market value **after** casualty or theft	24				
25	Subtract line 24 from line 23	25				
26	Enter the **smaller** of line 20 or line 25	26				
	Note: *If the property was totally destroyed by casualty or lost from theft, enter on line 26 the amount from line 20.*					
27	Subtract line 21 from line 26. If zero or less, enter -0-	27				
28	Casualty or theft loss. Add the amounts on line 27. Enter the total here and on line 29 **or** line 34 (see instructions)				28	

Part II Summary of Gains and Losses (from separate Parts I)

Line	(a) Identify casualty or theft		(b) Losses from casualties or thefts: (i) Trade, business, rental or royalty property	(b) (ii) Income-producing and employee property	(c) Gains from casualties or thefts includible in income
	Casualty or Theft of Property Held One Year or Less				
29			( )	( )	
			( )	( )	
30	Totals. Add the amounts on line 29	30	( )	( )	
31	Combine line 30, columns (b)(i) and (c). Enter the net gain or (loss) here and on Form 4797, line 14. If Form 4797 is not otherwise required, see instructions			31	
32	Enter the amount from line 30, column (b)(ii) here. Individuals, enter the amount from income-producing property on Schedule A (Form 1040), line 28, or Form 1040NR, Schedule A, line 14, and enter the amount from property used as an employee on Schedule A (Form 1040), line 23, or Form 1040NR, Schedule A, line 9. Estates and trusts, partnerships, and S corporations, see instructions			32	
	Casualty or Theft of Property Held More Than One Year				
33	Casualty or theft gains from Form 4797, line 32			33	
34			( )	( )	
			( )	( )	
35	Total losses. Add amounts on line 34, columns (b)(i) and (b)(ii)	35	( )	( )	
36	Total gains. Add lines 33 and 34, column (c)			36	
37	Add amounts on line 35, columns (b)(i) and (b)(ii)			37	
38	If the loss on line 37 is **more** than the gain on line 36:				
a	Combine line 35, column (b)(i) and line 36, and enter the net gain or (loss) here. Partnerships (except electing large partnerships) and S corporations, see the note below. All others, enter this amount on Form 4797, line 14. If Form 4797 is not otherwise required, see instructions			38a	
b	Enter the amount from line 35, column (b)(ii) here. Individuals, enter the amount from income-producing property on Schedule A (Form 1040), line 28, or Form 1040NR, Schedule A, line 14, and enter the amount from property used as an employee on Schedule A (Form 1040), line 23, or Form 1040NR, Schedule A, line 9. Estates and trusts, enter on the "Other deductions" line of your tax return. Partnerships (except electing large partnerships) and S corporations, see the note below. Electing large partnerships, enter on Form 1065-B, Part II, line 11			38b	
39	If the loss on line 37 is **less** than or **equal** to the gain on line 36, combine lines 36 and 37 and enter here. Partnerships (except electing large partnerships), see the note below. All others, enter this amount on Form 4797, line 3			39	

Note: *Partnerships, enter the amount from line 38a, 38b, or line 39 on Form 1065, Schedule K, line 11. S corporations, enter the amount from line 38a or 38b on Form 1120S, Schedule K, line 10.*

Form **4684** (2012)

Form **2106**

Department of the Treasury
Internal Revenue Service (99)

Employee Business Expenses

▶ Attach to Form 1040 or Form 1040NR.
▶ Information about Form 2106 and its separate instructions is available at *www.irs.gov/form2106*.

OMB No. 1545-0074
2012
Attachment Sequence No. 129

Your name	Occupation in which you incurred expenses	Social security number

Part I **Employee Business Expenses and Reimbursements**

Step 1 Enter Your Expenses		**Column A** Other Than Meals and Entertainment	**Column B** Meals and Entertainment
1 Vehicle expense from line 22 or line 29. (Rural mail carriers: See instructions.)	1		
2 Parking fees, tolls, and transportation, including train, bus, etc., that **did not** involve overnight travel or commuting to and from work	2		
3 Travel expense while away from home overnight, including lodging, airplane, car rental, etc. **Do not** include meals and entertainment	3		
4 Business expenses not included on lines 1 through 3. **Do not** include meals and entertainment	4		
5 Meals and entertainment expenses (see instructions)	5		
6 **Total expenses.** In Column A, add lines 1 through 4 and enter the result. In Column B, enter the amount from line 5	6		

Note: *If you were not reimbursed for any expenses in Step 1, skip line 7 and enter the amount from line 6 on line 8.*

Step 2 Enter Reimbursements Received From Your Employer for Expenses Listed in Step 1

7 Enter reimbursements received from your employer that were **not** reported to you in box 1 of Form W-2. Include any reimbursements reported under code "L" in box 12 of your Form W-2 (see instructions)	7		

Step 3 Figure Expenses To Deduct on Schedule A (Form 1040 or Form 1040NR)

8 Subtract line 7 from line 6. If zero or less, enter -0-. However, if line 7 is greater than line 6 in Column A, report the excess as income on Form 1040, line 7 (or on Form 1040NR, line 8)	8		
Note: *If **both columns** of line 8 are zero, you cannot deduct employee business expenses. Stop here and attach Form 2106 to your return.*			
9 In Column A, enter the amount from line 8. In Column B, multiply line 8 by 50% (.50). (Employees subject to Department of Transportation (DOT) hours of service limits: Multiply meal expenses incurred while away from home on business by 80% (.80) instead of 50%. For details, see instructions.)	9		
10 Add the amounts on line 9 of both columns and enter the total here. **Also, enter the total on Schedule A (Form 1040), line 21** (or on **Schedule A (Form 1040NR), line 7**). (Armed Forces reservists, qualified performing artists, fee-basis state or local government officials, and individuals with disabilities: See the instructions for special rules on where to enter the total.) ▶	10		

For Paperwork Reduction Act Notice, see your tax return instructions. Cat. No. 11700N Form **2106** (2012)

Form 2106 (2012) Page **2**

Part II Vehicle Expenses

Section A—General Information (You must complete this section if you are claiming vehicle expenses.)

			(a) Vehicle 1	(b) Vehicle 2
11	Enter the date the vehicle was placed in service	11	/ /	/ /
12	Total miles the vehicle was driven during 2012	12	miles	miles
13	Business miles included on line 12	13	miles	miles
14	Percent of business use. Divide line 13 by line 12	14	%	%
15	Average daily roundtrip commuting distance	15	miles	miles
16	Commuting miles included on line 12	16	miles	miles
17	Other miles. Add lines 13 and 16 and subtract the total from line 12	17	miles	miles

18	Was your vehicle available for personal use during off-duty hours?	☐ **Yes**	☐ **No**
19	Do you (or your spouse) have another vehicle available for personal use?	☐ **Yes**	☐ **No**
20	Do you have evidence to support your deduction?	☐ **Yes**	☐ **No**
21	If "Yes," is the evidence written?	☐ **Yes**	☐ **No**

Section B—Standard Mileage Rate (See the instructions for Part II to find out whether to complete this section or Section C.)

22	Multiply line 13 by 55.5¢ (.555). Enter the result here and on line 1	22	

Section C—Actual Expenses

			(a) Vehicle 1	(b) Vehicle 2
23	Gasoline, oil, repairs, vehicle insurance, etc.	23		
24a	Vehicle rentals	24a		
b	Inclusion amount (see instructions)	24b		
c	Subtract line 24b from line 24a	24c		
25	Value of employer-provided vehicle (applies only if 100% of annual lease value was included on Form W-2—see instructions)	25		
26	Add lines 23, 24c, and 25.	26		
27	Multiply line 26 by the percentage on line 14	27		
28	Depreciation (see instructions)	28		
29	Add lines 27 and 28. Enter total here and on line 1	29		

Section D—Depreciation of Vehicles (Use this section only if you owned the vehicle and are completing Section C for the vehicle.)

			(a) Vehicle 1	(b) Vehicle 2
30	Enter cost or other basis (see instructions)	30		
31	Enter section 179 deduction and special allowance (see instructions)	31		
32	Multiply line 30 by line 14 (see instructions if you claimed the section 179 deduction or special allowance).	32		
33	Enter depreciation method and percentage (see instructions)	33		
34	Multiply line 32 by the percentage on line 33 (see instructions)	34		
35	Add lines 31 and 34	35		
36	Enter the applicable limit explained in the line 36 instructions	36		
37	Multiply line 36 by the percentage on line 14	37		
38	Enter the **smaller** of line 35 or line 37. If you skipped lines 36 and 37, enter the amount from line 35. Also enter this amount on line 28 above	38		

Form **2106** (2012)

Form **2106-EZ**

Department of the Treasury
Internal Revenue Service (99)

Unreimbursed Employee Business Expenses

▶ Attach to Form 1040 or Form 1040NR.

▶ Information about Form 2106 and its separate instructions is available at *www.irs.gov/form2106*.

OMB No. 1545-0074

2012

Attachment
Sequence No. **129A**

Your name	Occupation in which you incurred expenses	Social security number

You Can Use This Form Only if All of the Following Apply.

- You are an employee deducting ordinary and necessary expenses attributable to your job. An ordinary expense is one that is common and accepted in your field of trade, business, or profession. A necessary expense is one that is helpful and appropriate for your business. An expense does not have to be required to be considered necessary.
- You **do not** get reimbursed by your employer for any expenses (amounts your employer included in box 1 of your Form W-2 are not considered reimbursements for this purpose).
- If you are claiming vehicle expense, you are using the standard mileage rate for 2012.

Caution: *You can use the standard mileage rate for 2012* ***only if: (a)*** *you owned the vehicle and used the standard mileage rate for the first year you placed the vehicle in service,* ***or (b)*** *you leased the vehicle and used the standard mileage rate for the portion of the lease period after 1997.*

Part I Figure Your Expenses

1	Complete Part II. Multiply line 8a by 55.5¢ (.555). Enter the result here	1	
2	Parking fees, tolls, and transportation, including train, bus, etc., that **did not** involve overnight travel or commuting to and from work	2	
3	Travel expense while away from home overnight, including lodging, airplane, car rental, etc. **Do not** include meals and entertainment	3	
4	Business expenses not included on lines 1 through 3. **Do not** include meals and entertainment	4	
5	Meals and entertainment expenses: $ __________ × 50% (.50). (Employees subject to Department of Transportation (DOT) hours of service limits: Multiply meal expenses incurred while away from home on business by 80% (.80) instead of 50%. For details, see instructions.)	5	
6	**Total expenses.** Add lines 1 through 5. Enter here and on **Schedule A (Form 1040), line 21** (or on **Schedule A (Form 1040NR), line 7**). (Armed Forces reservists, fee-basis state or local government officials, qualified performing artists, and individuals with disabilities: See the instructions for special rules on where to enter this amount.)	6	

Part II Information on Your Vehicle. Complete this part **only** if you are claiming vehicle expense on line 1.

7 When did you place your vehicle in service for business use? (month, day, year) ▶ ______ / ______ / ______

8 Of the total number of miles you drove your vehicle during 2012, enter the number of miles you used your vehicle for:

a Business ______________ **b** Commuting (see instructions) ______________ **c** Other ______________

9 Was your vehicle available for personal use during off-duty hours? . . . . ☐ **Yes** ☐ **No**

10 Do you (or your spouse) have another vehicle available for personal use? . . . . ☐ **Yes** ☐ **No**

11a Do you have evidence to support your deduction? . . . . ☐ **Yes** ☐ **No**

b If "Yes," is the evidence written? . . . . ☐ **Yes** ☐ **No**

For Paperwork Reduction Act Notice, see your tax return instructions. Cat. No. 20604Q Form **2106-EZ** (2012)

Form **1116**

Department of the Treasury
Internal Revenue Service (99)

Foreign Tax Credit

(Individual, Estate, or Trust)

▶ Attach to Form 1040, 1040NR, 1041, or 990-T.

▶ Information about Form 1116 and its separate instructions is at *www.irs.gov/form1116*.

OMB No. 1545-0121

2012

Attachment Sequence No. **19**

Name | **Identifying number** as shown on page 1 of your tax return

Use a separate Form 1116 for each category of income listed below. See **Categories of Income** in the instructions. Check only one box on each Form 1116. Report all amounts in U.S. dollars except where specified in Part II below.

a ☐ Passive category income
b ☐ General category income
c ☐ Section 901(j) income
d ☐ Certain income re-sourced by treaty
e ☐ Lump-sum distributions

f Resident of (name of country) ▶

Note: *If you paid taxes to only one foreign country or U.S. possession, use column A in Part I and line A in Part II. If you paid taxes to* ***more than one*** *foreign country or U.S. possession, use a separate column and line for each country or possession.*

Part I Taxable Income or Loss From Sources Outside the United States (for Category Checked Above)

	Foreign Country or U.S. Possession			Total
	A	B	C	(Add cols. A, B, and C.)
g **Enter the name of the foreign country or U.S. possession** ▶				
1a Gross income from sources within country shown above and of the type checked above (see instructions):				**1a**
b Check if line 1a is compensation for personal services as an employee, your total compensation from all sources is $250,000 or more, and you used an alternative basis to determine its source (see instructions) ▶ ☐				
Deductions and losses (*Caution:* *See instructions*):				
2 Expenses **definitely related** to the income on line 1a (attach statement)				
3 Pro rata share of other deductions **not definitely related:**				
a Certain itemized deductions or standard deduction (see instructions)				
b Other deductions (attach statement)				
c Add lines 3a and 3b				
d Gross foreign source income (see instructions)				
e Gross income from all sources (see instructions)				
f Divide line 3d by line 3e (see instructions)				
g Multiply line 3c by line 3f				
4 Pro rata share of interest expense (see instructions):				
a Home mortgage interest (use the Worksheet for Home Mortgage Interest in the instructions)				
b Other interest expense				
5 Losses from foreign sources				
6 Add lines 2, 3g, 4a, 4b, and 5				**6**
7 Subtract line 6 from line 1a. Enter the result here and on line 15, page 2 ▶				**7**

Part II Foreign Taxes Paid or Accrued (see instructions)

Country	Credit is claimed for taxes (you must check one) (h) ☐ Paid (i) ☐ Accrued	Foreign taxes paid or accrued								
		In foreign currency				In U.S. dollars				
		Taxes withheld at source on:				Taxes withheld at source on:				
	(j) Date paid or accrued	**(k)** Dividends	**(l)** Rents and royalties	**(m)** Interest	**(n)** Other foreign taxes paid or accrued	**(o)** Dividends	**(p)** Rents and royalties	**(q)** Interest	**(r)** Other foreign taxes paid or accrued	**(s)** Total foreign taxes paid or accrued (add cols. (o) through (r))
A										
B										
C										

8 **Add lines A through C, column (s). Enter the total here and on line 9, page 2** ▶ **8**

For Paperwork Reduction Act Notice, see instructions. Cat. No. 11440U Form **1116** (2012)

Form 1116 (2012) Page **2**

Part III Figuring the Credit

Line	Description	Box	Amount	Box	Amount
9	Enter the amount from line 8. These are your total foreign taxes paid or accrued for the category of income checked above Part I . .	9			
10	Carryback or carryover (attach detailed computation)	10			
11	Add lines 9 and 10	11			
12	Reduction in foreign taxes (see instructions)	12	( )		
13	Taxes reclassified under high tax kickout (see instructions) . .	13			
14	Combine lines 11, 12, and 13. This is the total amount of foreign taxes available for credit . . .			14	
15	Enter the amount from line 7. This is your taxable income or (loss) from sources outside the United States (before adjustments) for the category of income checked above Part I (see instructions)	15			
16	Adjustments to line 15 (see instructions)	16			
17	Combine the amounts on lines 15 and 16. This is your net foreign source taxable income. (If the result is zero or less, you have no foreign tax credit for the category of income you checked above Part I. Skip lines 18 through 22. However, if you are filing more than one Form 1116, you must complete line 20.)	17			
18	**Individuals:** Enter the amount from Form 1040, line 41, or Form 1040NR, line 39. **Estates and trusts:** Enter your taxable income without the deduction for your exemption	18			
	Caution: *If you figured your tax using the lower rates on qualified dividends or capital gains, see instructions.*				
19	Divide line 17 by line 18. If line 17 is more than line 18, enter "1"			19	
20	**Individuals:** Enter the amount from Form 1040, line 44. If you are a nonresident alien, enter the amount from Form 1040NR, line 42. **Estates and trusts:** Enter the amount from Form 1041, Schedule G, line 1a, or the total of Form 990-T, lines 36 and 37			20	
	Caution: *If you are completing line 20 for separate category* **e** *(lump-sum distributions), see instructions.*				
21	Multiply line 20 by line 19 (maximum amount of credit)			21	
22	Enter the **smaller** of line 14 or line 21. If this is the only Form 1116 you are filing, skip lines 23 through 27 and enter this amount on line 28. Otherwise, complete the appropriate line in Part IV (see instructions) . . . . ▶			22	

Part IV Summary of Credits From Separate Parts III (see instructions)

Line	Description	Box	Amount	Box	Amount
23	Credit for taxes on passive category income	23			
24	Credit for taxes on general category income	24			
25	Credit for taxes on certain income re-sourced by treaty	25			
26	Credit for taxes on lump-sum distributions	26			
27	Add lines 23 through 26			27	
28	Enter the **smaller** of line 20 or line 27			28	
29	Reduction of credit for international boycott operations. See instructions for line 12			29	
30	Subtract line 29 from line 28. This is your **foreign tax credit.** Enter here and on Form 1040, line 47; Form 1040NR, line 45; Form 1041, Schedule G, line 2a; or Form 990-T, line 40a . . . . . . ▶			30	

Form **1116** (2012)

Form **2441**

Department of the Treasury
Internal Revenue Service (99)

Child and Dependent Care Expenses

► Attach to Form 1040, Form 1040A, or Form 1040NR.

► Information about Form 2441 and its separate instructions is at *www.irs.gov/form2441*.

1040 / 1040A / 1040NR / 2441

OMB No. 1545-0074

2012

Attachment Sequence No. 21

Name(s) shown on return | Your social security number

Part I **Persons or Organizations Who Provided the Care**—You **must** complete this part. (If you have more than two care providers, see the instructions.)

1 (a) Care provider's name	(b) Address (number, street, apt. no., city, state, and ZIP code)	(c) Identifying number (SSN or EIN)	(d) Amount paid (see instructions)

Did you receive **dependent care benefits?** — **No** → Complete only Part II below.
Yes → Complete Part III on the back next.

Caution. If the care was provided in your home, you may owe employment taxes. If you do, you cannot file Form 1040A. For details, see the instructions for Form 1040, line 59a, or Form 1040NR, line 58a.

Part II **Credit for Child and Dependent Care Expenses**

2 Information about your **qualifying person(s).** If you have more than two qualifying persons, see the instructions.

(a) Qualifying person's name — First	Last	(b) Qualifying person's social security number	(c) **Qualified expenses** you incurred and paid in 2012 for the person listed in column (a)

3 Add the amounts in column (c) of line 2. **Do not** enter more than $3,000 for one qualifying person or $6,000 for two or more persons. If you completed Part III, enter the amount from line 31 3

4 Enter your **earned income.** See instructions 4

5 If married filing jointly, enter your spouse's earned income (if your spouse was a student or was disabled, see the instructions); **all others,** enter the amount from line 4 5

6 Enter the **smallest** of line 3, 4, or 5 6

7 Enter the amount from Form 1040, line 38; Form 1040A, line 22; or Form 1040NR, line 37. 7

8 Enter on line 8 the decimal amount shown below that applies to the amount on line 7

If line 7 is: Over	But not over	Decimal amount is	If line 7 is: Over	But not over	Decimal amount is
$0	15,000	.35	$29,000	31,000	.27
15,000	17,000	.34	31,000	33,000	.26
17,000	19,000	.33	33,000	35,000	.25
19,000	21,000	.32	35,000	37,000	.24
21,000	23,000	.31	37,000	39,000	.23
23,000	25,000	.30	39,000	41,000	.22
25,000	27,000	.29	41,000	43,000	.21
27,000	29,000	.28	43,000	No limit	.20

8 X.

9 Multiply line 6 by the decimal amount on line 8. If you paid 2011 expenses in 2012, see the instructions 9

10 Tax liability limit. Enter the amount from the Credit Limit Worksheet in the instructions. 10

11 **Credit for child and dependent care expenses.** Enter the **smaller** of line 9 or line 10 here and on Form 1040, line 48; Form 1040A, line 29; or Form 1040NR, line 46 11

For Paperwork Reduction Act Notice, see your tax return instructions. Cat. No. 11862M Form **2441** (2012)

Form 2441 (2012) Page 2

Part III Dependent Care Benefits

12	Enter the total amount of **dependent care benefits** you received in 2012. Amounts you received as an employee should be shown in box 10 of your Form(s) W-2. **Do not** include amounts reported as wages in box 1 of Form(s) W-2. If you were self-employed or a partner, include amounts you received under a dependent care assistance program from your sole proprietorship or partnership . . .	12	
13	Enter the amount, if any, you carried over from 2011 and used in 2012 during the grace period. See instructions . . .	13	
14	Enter the amount, if any, you forfeited or carried forward to 2013. See instructions . . .	14	( )
15	Combine lines 12 through 14. See instructions . . .	15	
16	Enter the total amount of **qualified expenses** incurred in 2012 for the care of the **qualifying person(s)** . . . 16		
17	Enter the **smaller** of line 15 or 16 . . . 17		
18	Enter your **earned income.** See instructions . . . 18		
19	Enter the amount shown below that applies to you. • If married filing jointly, enter your spouse's earned income (if your spouse was a student or was disabled, see the instructions for line 5). • If married filing separately, see instructions. • All others, enter the amount from line 18. . . . 19		
20	Enter the **smallest** of line 17, 18, or 19 . . . 20		
21	Enter $5,000 ($2,500 if married filing separately **and** you were required to enter your spouse's earned income on line 19) . . . 21		
22	Is any amount on line 12 from your sole proprietorship or partnership? (Form 1040A filers go to line 25.) ☐ **No.** Enter -0-. ☐ **Yes.** Enter the amount here . . .	22	
23	Subtract line 22 from line 15 . . . 23		
24	**Deductible benefits.** Enter the **smallest** of line 20, 21, or 22. Also, include this amount on the appropriate line(s) of your return. See instructions . . .	24	
25	**Excluded benefits. Form 1040 and 1040NR filers:** If you checked "No" on line 22, enter the smaller of line 20 or 21. Otherwise, subtract line 24 from the smaller of line 20 or line 21. If zero or less, enter -0-. **Form 1040A filers:** Enter the **smaller** of line 20 or line 21 . .	25	
26	**Taxable benefits. Form 1040 and 1040NR filers:** Subtract line 25 from line 23. If zero or less, enter -0-. Also, include this amount on Form 1040, line 7; or Form 1040NR, line 8. On the dotted line next to Form 1040, line 7; or Form 1040NR, line 8, enter "DCB." **Form 1040A filers:** Subtract line 25 from line 15. Also, include this amount on Form 1040A, line 7. In the space to the left of line 7, enter "DCB" . . .	26	

To claim the child and dependent care credit, complete lines 27 through 31 below.

27	Enter $3,000 ($6,000 if two or more qualifying persons) . . .	27	
28	**Form 1040 and 1040NR filers:** Add lines 24 and 25. **Form 1040A filers:** Enter the amount from line 25 . . .	28	
29	Subtract line 28 from line 27. If zero or less, **stop.** You cannot take the credit. **Exception.** If you paid 2011 expenses in 2012, see the instructions for line 9 . . .	29	
30	Complete line 2 on the front of this form. **Do not** include in column (c) any benefits shown on line 28 above. Then, add the amounts in column (c) and enter the total here. . . .	30	
31	Enter the **smaller** of line 29 or 30. Also, enter this amount on line 3 on the front of this form and complete lines 4 through 11 . . .	31	

Form **2441** (2012)

Form **8863**

Department of the Treasury
Internal Revenue Service (99)

Education Credits
(American Opportunity and Lifetime Learning Credits)

► See separate instructions to find out if you are eligible to take the credits.
► Instructions and more are at *www.irs.gov/form8863*. Attach to Form 1040 or Form 1040A.

OMB No. 1545-0074
2012
Attachment Sequence No. 50

Name(s) shown on return | Your social security number

CAUTION *Complete a separate Part III on page 2 for each student for whom you are claiming either credit before you complete Parts I and II.*

Part I Refundable American Opportunity Credit

1	After completing Part III for each student, enter the total of all amounts from all Parts III, line 30	1	
2	Enter: $180,000 if married filing jointly; $90,000 if single, head of household, or qualifying widow(er)	2	
3	Enter the amount from Form 1040, line 38, or Form 1040A, line 22. If you are filing Form 2555, 2555-EZ, or 4563, or you are excluding income from Puerto Rico, see Pub. 970 for the amount to enter	3	
4	Subtract line 3 from line 2. If zero or less, **stop**; you cannot take any education credit	4	
5	Enter: $20,000 if married filing jointly; $10,000 if single, head of household, or qualifying widow(er)	5	
6	If line 4 is: • Equal to or more than line 5, enter 1.000 on line 6 . . . . • Less than line 5, divide line 4 by line 5. Enter the result as a decimal (rounded to at least three places)	6	.
7	Multiply line 1 by line 6. **Caution:** If you were under age 24 at the end of the year **and** meet the conditions described in the instructions, you **cannot** take the refundable American opportunity credit; skip line 8, enter the amount from line 7 on line 9, and check this box . . . . ► ☐	7	
8	**Refundable American opportunity credit.** Multiply line 7 by 40% (.40). Enter the amount here and on Form 1040, line 66, or Form 1040A, line 40. Then go to line 9 below.	8	

Part II Nonrefundable Education Credits

9	Subtract line 8 from line 7. Enter here and on line 8 of the Credit Limit Worksheet (see instructions)	9	
10	After completing Part III for each student, enter the total of all amounts from all Parts III, line 31. If zero skip lines 11 through 17, enter -0- on line 18, and go to line 19	10	
11	Enter the smaller of line 10 or $10,000	11	
12	Multiply line 11 by 20% (.20)	12	
13	Enter: $124,000 if married filing jointly; $62,000 if single, head of household, or qualifying widow(er)	13	
14	Enter the amount from Form 1040, line 38, or Form 1040A, line 22. If you are filing Form 2555, 2555-EZ, or 4563, or you are excluding income from Puerto Rico, see Pub. 970 for the amount to enter	14	
15	Subtract line 14 from line 13. If zero or less, skip lines 16 and 17, enter -0- on line 18, and go to line 19	15	
16	Enter: $20,000 if married filing jointly; $10,000 if single, head of household, or qualifying widow(er)	16	
17	If line 15 is: • Equal to or more than line 16, enter 1.000 on line 17 and go to line 18 • Less than line 16, divide line 15 by line 16. Enter the result as a decimal (rounded to at least three places)	17	.
18	Multiply line 12 by line 17. Enter here and on line 1 of the Credit Limit Worksheet (see instructions) ►	18	
19	**Nonrefundable education credits.** Enter the amount from line 13 of the Credit Limit Worksheet (see instructions) here and on Form 1040, line 49, or Form 1040A, line 31	19	

For Paperwork Reduction Act Notice, see your tax return instructions. IRS.gov/form8863 Cat. No. 25379M Form **8863** (2012)

Form 8863 (2012) Page **2**

Name(s) shown on return | **Your social security number**

CAUTION ***Complete Part III for each student for whom you are claiming either the American opportunity credit or lifetime learning credit. Use additional copies of Page 2 as needed for each student.***

Part III **Student and Educational Institution Information**
See instructions.

20 Student name (as shown on page 1 of your tax return)	**21** Student social security number (as shown on page 1 of your tax return)
22 Educational institution information (see instructions)	
a. Name of first educational institution	**b.** Name of second educational institution (if any)
(1) Address. Number and street (or P.O. box). City, town or post office, state, and ZIP code. If a foreign address, see instructions.	**(1)** Address. Number and street (or P.O. box). City, town or post office, state, and ZIP code. If a foreign address, see instructions.
(2) Did the student receive Form 1098-T from this institution for 2012? ☐ Yes ☐ No	**(2)** Did the student receive Form 1098-T from this institution for 2012? ☐ Yes ☐ No
(3) Did the student receive Form 1098-T from this institution for 2011 with Box 2 filled in and Box 7 checked? ☐ Yes ☐ No	**(3)** Did the student receive Form 1098-T from this institution for 2011 with Box 2 filled in and Box 7 checked? ☐ Yes ☐ No
If you checked "No" in **both (2) and (3)**, skip **(4)**.	If you checked "No" in **both (2) and (3)**, skip **(4)**.
(4) If you checked "Yes" in **(2) or (3)**, enter the institution's federal identification number (from Form 1098-T). __ __ - __ __ __ __ __ __ __	**(4)** If you checked "Yes" in **(2) or (3)**, enter the institution's federal identification number (from Form 1098-T). __ __ - __ __ __ __ __ __ __

23	Has the Hope Scholarship Credit or American opportunity credit been claimed for this student for any 4 prior tax years?	☐ Yes — **Stop!** Go to line 31 for this student.	☐ No — Go to line 24.
24	Was the student enrolled at least half-time for at least one academic period that began in 2012 at an eligible educational institution in a program leading towards a postsecondary degree, certificate, or other recognized postsecondary educational credential? (see instructions)	☐ Yes — Go to line 25.	☐ No — **Stop!** Go to line 31 for this student.
25	Did the student complete the first 4 years of post-secondary education before 2012?	☐ Yes — **Stop!** Go to line 31 for this student.	☐ No — Go to line 26.
26	Was the student convicted, before the end of 2012, of a felony for possession or distribution of a controlled substance?	☐ Yes — **Stop!** Go to line 31 for this student.	☐ No — See *Tip* below and complete **either** lines 27-30 **or** line 31 for this student.

TIP *When you figure your taxes, you may want to compare the American opportunity credit and lifetime learning credits, and choose the credit for each student that gives you the lower tax liability. You **cannot** take the American opportunity credit and the lifetime learning credit for the **same student** in the same year. If you complete lines 27 through 30 for this student, do not complete line 31.*

American Opportunity Credit

27	Adjusted qualified education expenses (see instructions). **Do not enter more than $4,000**	**27**	
28	Subtract $2,000 from line 27. If zero or less enter -0-	**28**	
29	Multiply line 28 by 25% (.25)	**29**	
30	If line 28 is zero, enter the amount from line 27. Otherwise, add $2,000 to the amount on line 29 and enter the result. Skip line 31. Include the total of all amounts from all Parts III, line 30 on Part I, line 1 .	**30**	

Lifetime Learning Credit

31	Adjusted qualified education expenses (see instructions). Include the total of all amounts from all Parts III, line 31, on Part II, line 10	**31**	

Form **8863** (2012)

Form **8854**

Department of the Treasury
Internal Revenue Service

Initial and Annual Expatriation Statement

For calendar year 2012 or other tax year beginning ______, 2012, and ending ______, 20__

► Information about Form 8854 and its separate instructions is at *www.irs.gov/form8854.*

► Please print or type.

OMB No. 1545-0074

2012

Attachment Sequence No. **112**

Name | Identifying number (see instructions)

Part I General Information. For all filers.

1 Mailing address and telephone number where you can be reached after expatriation ______

2 Address of principal foreign residence (if different from line 1) ______

3 Country of tax residence (if different from line 2) ______

4 **Expatriation date.** Check the box that applies (see instructions).

☐ June 4, 2004 – June 16, 2008. Complete Parts II and V

☐ June 17, 2008 – December 31, 2011. Complete Part III if:
- You made an election to defer the payment of tax on a prior year Form 8854,
- You have an item of eligible deferred compensation, or
- You have an interest in a nongrantor trust.

Otherwise, you do not need to file Form 8854.

☐ January 1, 2012 – December 31, 2012. Complete Parts IV and V

5 Date of notification of expatriating act, termination of residency, or claim of treaty benefits (see instructions).

☐ Citizen. Date notification given to Department of State ______

☐ Long-term resident. Date notification given to Department of Homeland Security ______

☐ Long-term resident with dual residency in a treaty country. Date commencing to be treated, for tax purposes, as a resident of the treaty country ______

6 Number of days you were physically present in the United States in the current year ______

7 List all countries (other than the United States) of which you are a citizen.

a Name of country ______

b Date you became a citizen of each country listed in line 7a ______

8 How you became a U.S. citizen ☐ By birth ☐ By naturalization

Part II For Persons Who Expatriated After June 3, 2004, and Before June 17, 2008

1 Did you complete Form 8854 for any period after June 3, 2004, and before June 17, 2008?

☐ **No. STOP.** You must complete Form 8854 for the year in which you expatriated for immigration purposes before filing this form (see instructions).

☐ **Yes.** Tax year for which Form 8854 first filed ______. Go to line 2.

2 Were you physically present in the United States for more than 30 days but not more than 60 days during the tax year? . . . . . ☐ **Yes** ☐ **No**

a If you checked "**Yes**" to line 2, were you performing services for an unrelated employer? . . . . ☐ **Yes** ☐ **No**

b If you checked "**Yes**" to line 2a, are you a citizen or resident, fully liable for income tax, in the country in which you were born, your spouse was born, or either of your parents was born? . . . . ☐ **Yes** ☐ **No**

Next: Go to Part V.

For Paperwork Reduction Act Notice, see the separate instructions. Cat. No. 24126N Form **8854** (2012)

Form 8854 (2012) Page 2

Part III For Persons Who Expatriated After June 16, 2008, and Before January 1, 2012

- If you made an election to defer the payment of tax, complete line 1.
- If you have an item of eligible deferred compensation, complete line 2.
- If you have an interest in a nongrantor trust, complete line 3.

1 Complete columns (a), (b), and (c) for all property on which you deferred tax on a prior year Form 8854. Complete column (d) for any property you disposed of in 2012 and see the instructions for Part III.

(a) Description of property	(b) Amount of mark-to-market gain or (loss) reported on prior year Form 8854	(c) Amount of tax deferred on prior year Form 8854	(d) Date of disposition (if any)

2 Did you receive any distributions of eligible deferred compensation items for 2012? ☐ Yes ☐ No
If "Yes," Amount of distribution: ______ Amount withheld at source, if any: ______

3 Did you receive any distributions from a nongrantor trust for 2012? ☐ Yes ☐ No
If "Yes," Amount of distribution: ______ Amount withheld at source, if any: ______

Part IV For Persons Who Expatriated During 2012

Section A Expatriation Information

1 Enter your U.S. income tax liability (after foreign tax credits) for the 5 tax years ending before the date of expatriation.

1st Year Before Expatriation	2nd Year Before Expatriation	3rd Year Before Expatriation	4th Year Before Expatriation	5th Year Before Expatriation
$	$	$	$	$

2 Enter your net worth on the date of your expatriation for tax purposes . . . . $______

3 Did you become at birth a U.S. citizen and a citizen of another country, and do you continue to be a citizen of, and taxed as a resident of, that other country? . . . . ☐ Yes ☐ No

4 If you answered "Yes" to question 3, have you been a resident of the United States for not more than 10 of the last 15 tax years? . . . . ☐ Yes ☐ No

5 Were you under age 18½ on the date you expatriated and have you been a U.S. resident for not more than 10 years? . . . . ☐ Yes ☐ No

6 Do you certify under penalties of perjury that you have complied with all of your tax obligations for the 5 preceding tax years (see instructions)? . . . . ☐ Yes ☐ No

Form **8854** (2012)

Form 8854 (2012) Page **3**

Section B | **Property Owned on Date of Expatriation**

Do not complete Section B if:

- Your average net income tax liability for the 5 tax years immediately before expatriation (see line 1 in Section A) was not more than $151,000, your net worth (see line 2 in Section A) was under $2 million, and you checked "**Yes**" on line 6 in Section A;
- In Section A, you checked "**Yes**" on lines 3, 4, and 6; or
- In Section A, you checked "**Yes**" on lines 5 and 6.

7a Do you have any **eligible deferred compensation items?** Checking the "Yes" box is an irrevocable waiver of any right to claim any reduction in withholding for such eligible deferred compensation item under any treaty with the United States . . . . ☐ **Yes** ☐ **No**

b Do you have any **ineligible deferred compensation items?** If "Yes," you must include in income the present value of your account on the day before your expatriation date . . . . ☐ **Yes** ☐ **No**

c Do you have any **specified tax deferred accounts?** If "Yes," you must include in income the entire account balance on the day before your expatriation date . . . . ☐ **Yes** ☐ **No**

d Do you have an interest in a **nongrantor trust?** Checking the "Yes" box is a waiver of any right to claim any reduction in withholding on any distribution from such trust under any treaty with the United States unless you make the election below . . . . ☐ **Yes** ☐ **No**

☐ Check this box to elect under section 877A(f)(4)(B) to be treated as having received the value of your entire interest in the trust (as determined for purposes of section 877A) as of the day before your expatriation date. Attach a copy of your valuation letter ruling issued by the IRS (see instructions).

8 Recognition of gain or loss on the deemed sale of mark-to-market property. **Caution**. Do not include in column (a) any property described on line 7a, 7b, 7c, or 7d.

Complete column (g) only if you are deferring tax on gain from any property listed in column (a).

(a) Description of property	(b) Fair market value on day before date of expatriation	(c) Cost or other basis*	(d) **Gain or (loss).** Subtract (c) from (b)	(e) Gain after allocation of the exclusion amount (see instructions)	(f) Form or Schedule on which gain or loss is reported	(g) Amount of tax deferred (attach computations)
9 Total. Add the amounts in column (d) and column (e) . . .						
10 Total tax deferred. Add the amounts in column (g). Enter here and on line 15						

*You must designate any property for which you are electing to figure basis without regard to section 877A(h)(2). Identify as "(h)(2)." This election is irrevocable.

Form **8854** (2012)

Form 8854 (2012) Page **4**

Section C **Deferral of Tax**

Election to defer tax. *You can defer tax only if you have provided adequate security.* Adequate security is described in the instructions.

11 Are you electing to defer tax under section 877A(b)?
Checking the "Yes" box is an irrevocable waiver of any right under any treaty of the United States that would prevent assessment or collection of any tax imposed because of section 877A. ☐ **Yes** ☐ **No**

If you checked the "Yes" box, continue to line 12. Otherwise, do not complete lines 12 through 15.

12	Enter the total tax you would have reported on Form 1040, line 61, for the part of the year including the day before the expatriation date absent the deferral election	**12**	
13	Enter the total tax for the same part of the tax year determined without regard to the amounts attributable to section 877A(a). Attach computation	**13**	
14	Subtract line 13 from line 12. **This is the amount of tax eligible for deferral**	**14**	
15	Enter the total tax deferred from line 10, column (g)	**15**	
	• If you are filing Form 1040, enter this amount in brackets to the left of the entry space for line 61. Identify as "EXP."		
	• If you are filing Form 1040NR, enter this amount in brackets to the left of the entry space for line 60. Identify as "EXP."		

Form **8854** (2012)

Form 8854 (2012) Page 5

Part V Balance Sheet and Income Statement

Schedule A Balance Sheet

List in U.S. dollars the fair market value (column (a)) and the U.S. adjusted basis (column (b)) of your assets and liabilities as of the following date.

- Part II filers - the end of the tax year for which you are filing the form
- Part IV filers - your expatriation date

For more details, see the separate instructions.

	Assets	(a) Fair market value (FMV)	(b) U.S. adjusted basis	(c) Gain or (loss). Subtract column (b) from column (a)	(d) FMV on beginning date of U.S. residency (optional, for long-term residents only)
1	Cash, including bank deposits				
2	Marketable stock and securities issued by U.S. companies				
3	Marketable stock and securities issued by foreign companies				
4	Nonmarketable stock and securities issued by U.S. companies				
5	Nonmarketable stock and securities issued by foreign companies				
a	Separately state stock issued by foreign companies that would be controlled foreign corporations if you were still a U.S. citizen or permanent resident (see instructions)				
b	Provide the name, address, and EIN, if any, of any such company ______				
6	Pensions from services performed in the United States				
7	Pensions from services performed outside the United States				
8	Partnership interests (see instructions)				
9	Assets held by trusts you own under sections 671 through 679 (see instructions)				
10	Beneficial interests in nongrantor trusts (see instructions)				
11	Intangibles used in the United States				
12	Intangibles used outside the United States				
13	Loans to U.S. persons				
14	Loans to foreign persons				
15	Real property located in the United States				
16	Real property located outside the United States				
17	Business property located in the United States				
18	Business property located outside the United States				
19	Other assets (see instructions)				
20	Total assets. Add lines 1 through 5 and lines 6 through 19. Do not include amounts on line 5a in this total				

	Liabilities	Amount
21	Installment obligations	
22	Mortgages, etc.	
23	Other liabilities (see instructions)	
24	Total liabilities. Add lines 21 through 23	
25	**Net worth.** Subtract line 24 from line 20, column (a)	

Form **8854** (2012)

Form 8854 (2012) Page **6**

Schedule B **Income Statement**

Provide income information for the following period.

- Part II filers - the tax year for which you are filing the form
- Part IV filers - the part of the tax year that ends with the day before your expatriation date; but enter -0- for lines 5 through 7.

1	U.S. source gross income not effectively connected with the conduct of a U.S. trade or business.				
a	Interest	**1a**			
b	Dividends	**1b**			
c	Royalties	**1c**			
d	Pension distributions	**1d**			
e	Other	**1e**			
f	**Total.** Add lines a through e			**1f**	
2	Gross income that is effectively connected with the conduct of a U.S. trade or business			**2**	
3	Income from the performance of services in the United States			**3**	
4	Gains from the sale or exchange of:				
a	Property (other than stock or debt obligations) located in the United States	**4a**			
b	Stock issued by a U.S. domestic corporation	**4b**			
c	Debt obligations of U.S. persons or of the United States, a state or political subdivision thereof, or the District of Columbia	**4c**			
d	**Total.** Add lines a through c			**4d**	
5	Income or gain derived from certain foreign corporations to the extent of your share of earnings and profits earned or accumulated before the date of expatriation (see instructions)			**5**	
6	Gains on certain exchanges of property that ordinarily would not be recognized (see instructions)			**6**	
7	Income received or accrued by certain foreign corporations (see instructions)			**7**	
8	Add lines 1f, 2, 3, 4d, 5, 6, and 7			**8**	
9	Gross income from all other sources			**9**	
10	**Total.** Add lines 8 and 9			**10**	

Sign Here

Under penalties of perjury, I declare that I have examined this form, including accompanying schedules and statements, and to the best of my knowledge and belief, it is true, correct, and complete. Declaration of preparer (other than filer) is based on all information of which preparer has any knowledge.

Your signature	Date

Paid Preparer Use Only

Print/Type preparer's name	Preparer's signature	Date	Check ☐ if self-employed	PTIN
Firm's name ▶			Firm's EIN ▶	
Firm's address ▶			Phone no.	

Form **8854** (2012)

Form **8891**
(Rev. December 2012)
Department of the Treasury
Internal Revenue Service

U.S. Information Return for Beneficiaries of Certain Canadian Registered Retirement Plans

▶ Attach to Form 1040.

For calendar year 20 , or tax year beginning , 20 , and ending , 20 .

▶ **Information about Form 8891 and its instructions is at *www.irs.gov/form8891*.**

OMB No. 1545-0074

Attachment Sequence No. **139**

Name as shown on Form 1040 | **Identifying number** (see instructions)

Address

1	Name of plan custodian	2	Account number of plan
3	Address of plan custodian	4	Type of plan (check one box): ☐ Registered Retirement Savings Plan (RRSP) ☐ Registered Retirement Income Fund (RRIF)

5 Check the applicable box for your status in the plan (see *Definitions* in the instructions):
☐ Beneficiary
☐ Annuitant (Complete only lines 7a, 7b, and 8.)

6a Have you previously made an election under Article XVIII(7) of the U.S.-Canada income tax treaty to defer U.S. income tax on the undistributed earnings of the plan? . . . . ▶ ☐ **Yes** ☐ **No**

b If "Yes," enter the first year the election came into effect ____________ and go to line 7a. If "No," go to line 6c.

c If you have not previously made the election described on line 6a above, you can make an irrevocable election for this year and subsequent years by checking this box . . . . ▶ ☐

7a	Distributions received from the plan during the year. Enter here and include on Form 1040, line 16a	**7a**		
b	Taxable distributions received from the plan during the year. Enter here and include on Form 1040, line 16b	**7b**		
8	Plan balance at the end of the year. If you checked the "Annuitant" box on line 5, the "Yes" box on line 6a, or the box on line 6c, **stop here. Do not** complete the rest of the form	**8**		
9	Contributions to the plan during the year	**9**		
10	**Undistributed earnings of the plan during the year:**			
a	Interest income. Enter here and include on Form 1040, line 8a	**10a**		
b	Total ordinary dividends. Enter here and include on Form 1040, line 9a	**10b**		
c	Qualified dividends. Enter here and include on Form 1040, line 9b	**10c**		
d	Capital gains. Enter here and include on Form 1040, line 13	**10d**		
e	Other income. Enter here and include on Form 1040, line 21. List type and amount ▶ ------------	**10e**		

For Paperwork Reduction Act Notice, see instructions. Cat. No. 37699X Form **8891** (Rev. 12-2012)

Section references are to the Internal Revenue Code.

Future Developments

For the latest information about developments related to Form 8891 and its instructions, such as legislation enacted after they were published, go to *www.irs.gov/form8891*.

General Instructions

Purpose of Form

Form 8891 is used by U.S. citizens or residents (a) to report contributions to Canadian registered retirement savings plans (RRSPs) and registered retirement income funds (RRIFs), (b) to report undistributed earnings in RRSPs and RRIFs, and (c) to report distributions received from RRSPs and RRIFs. See Notice 2003-75, which is available at IRS.gov.

Form 8891 also can be used to make an election pursuant to Article XVIII(7) of the U.S.-Canada income tax treaty to defer U.S. income tax on income earned by an RRSP or an RRIF that has been accrued, but not distributed. Taxpayers who have not previously made the election can make it on this form by checking the box on line 6c.

Who Must File

Form 8891 must be completed and attached to Form 1040 by any U.S. citizen or resident who is a beneficiary of an RRSP or RRIF. Do **not** file Form 8891 by itself.

A U.S. citizen or resident who is an annuitant of an RRSP or RRIF must file the form for any year in which he or she receives a distribution from the RRSP or RRIF.

A separate Form 8891 must be filed for each RRSP or RRIF for which there is a filing requirement. If you and your spouse are both required to file Form 8891, each of you must complete and attach a separate Form 8891 to Form 1040, even if you file a joint return.

Definitions

Beneficiary. A beneficiary of an RRSP or RRIF is an individual who is subject to current U.S. income taxation on income accrued in the RRSP or RRIF or would be subject to current income taxation had the individual not made the election under Article XVIII(7) of the U.S.-Canada income tax treaty to defer U.S. income taxation of income accrued in the RRSP or RRIF.

Annuitant. For purposes of this form, an annuitant of an RRSP or RRIF is an individual who is designated pursuant to the RRSP or RRIF as an annuitant and is not also a beneficiary as defined above.

Record Retention

Taxpayers must retain supporting documentation relating to the information reported on Form 8891, including Canadian forms T4RSP, T4RIF, or NR4, and periodic or annual statements issued by the custodian of the RRSP or RRIF.

Other Reporting Requirements

Pursuant to section 6048(d)(4), annuitants and beneficiaries who are required to file Form 8891 will not be required to file Form 3520 and will not be subject to the associated penalties described in section 6677 on such RRSPs or RRIFs.

You may be required to file Form TD F 90-22.1, Report of Foreign Bank and Financial Accounts. You may also be required to file Form 8938, Statement of Specified Foreign Financial Assets, for other Canadian assets not reported on this Form 8891. For more information, see the instructions for Schedule B (Form 1040A or 1040) at *www.irs.gov/form1040,* and the instructions for Form 8938 at *www.irs.gov/form8938.*

Specific Instructions

All amounts listed must be in U.S. dollars.

Name and Address

Enter your name and address as shown on Form 1040. Even if you are filing a joint Form 1040 with your spouse, enter only your name.

Identifying number

Enter your U.S. social security number (SSN) or individual taxpayer identification number (ITIN). Do not enter a Canadian identifying number.

Beneficiaries

A beneficiary who previously made the election to defer income on the plan or is making it initially by checking the box on line 6c must only complete lines 1 through 8 of the form.

Annuitants

If you are treated as an annuitant for purposes of this form (see *Definitions*), you should complete only lines 1 through 5, 7a, 7b, and 8.

Line 6(a)

If the election you made previously was made under Rev. Proc. 89-45, check the "No" box. If an election (other than an election under Rev. Proc. 89-45) was made for an RRSP, and amounts from the RRSP were rolled over tax-free to an RRIF or another RRSP, the election is considered to have been made for the plan which received the tax-free rollover.

Line 6(c)

If you did not make the election under Article XVIII to defer income tax on income earned by an RRSP or an RRIF in a previous year, you cannot make a late election on Form 8891. However, you may be able to seek relief from the IRS for failure to timely elect the deferral of income on Form 8891 in an earlier year.

Line 7(b)

For information on figuring taxable distributions, see section 72 and Pub. 939, General Rule for Pensions and Annuities.

Paperwork Reduction Act Notice

We ask for the information on this form to carry out the Internal Revenue laws of the United States. You are required to give us the information. We need it to ensure that you are complying with these laws and to allow us to figure and collect the right amount of tax.

You are not required to provide the information requested on a form that is subject to the Paperwork Reduction Act unless the form displays a valid OMB control number. Books or records relating to a form or its instructions must be retained as long as their contents may become material in the administration of any Internal Revenue law. Generally, tax returns and return information are confidential, as required by Internal Revenue Code section 6103.

The average time and expenses required to complete and file this form will vary depending on individual circumstances. For the estimated averages, see the instructions for your income tax return.

If you have suggestions for making this form simpler, we would be happy to hear from you. See the instructions for your income tax return.

Form **8833** (Rev. December 2012) Department of the Treasury Internal Revenue Service

Treaty-Based Return Position Disclosure Under Section 6114 or 7701(b)

▶ Attach to your tax return.

▶ Information about Form 8833 and its instructions is at *www.irs.gov/form8833*.

OMB No. 1545-1354

Attach a separate Form 8833 for each treaty-based return position taken. Failure to disclose a treaty-based return position may result in a penalty of $1,000 ($10,000 in the case of a C corporation) (see section 6712).

Name	**U.S. taxpayer identifying number**
Address in country of residence	Address in the United States

Check one or both of the following boxes as applicable:

- The taxpayer is disclosing a treaty-based return position as required by section 6114 . . . . ▶ ☐
- The taxpayer is a dual-resident taxpayer and is disclosing a treaty-based return position as required by Regulations section 301.7701(b)-7 . . . . ▶ ☐

Note. If the taxpayer is a dual-resident taxpayer and a long-term resident, by electing to be treated as a resident of a foreign country for purposes of claiming benefits under an applicable income tax treaty, the taxpayer will be deemed to have expatriated pursuant to section 877A. For more information, see the instructions.

Check this box if the taxpayer is a U.S. citizen or resident or is incorporated in the United States . . . . ▶ ☐

1 Enter the specific treaty position relied on:

a Treaty country

b Article(s)

2 List the Internal Revenue Code provision(s) overruled or modified by the treaty-based return position

3 Name, identifying number (if available to the taxpayer), and address in the United States of the payor of the income (if fixed or determinable annual or periodical). See instructions.

4 List the provision(s) of the limitation on benefits article (if any) in the treaty that the taxpayer relies on to prevent application of that article ▶

5 Explain the treaty-based return position taken. Include a brief summary of the facts on which it is based. Also, list the nature and amount (or a reasonable estimate) of gross receipts, each separate gross payment, each separate gross income item, or other item (as applicable) for which the treaty benefit is claimed

For Paperwork Reduction Act Notice, see the instructions. Cat. No. 14895L Form **8833** (Rev. 12-2012)

THIS PAGE INTENTIONALLY LEFT BLANK

Form **8621** (Rev. December 2011) Department of the Treasury Internal Revenue Service

Information Return by a Shareholder of a Passive Foreign Investment Company or Qualified Electing Fund

▶ **See separate instructions.**

OMB No. 1545-1002

Attachment Sequence No. **69**

Name of shareholder | **Identifying number** (see instructions)

Number, street, and room or suite no. (If a P.O. box, see instructions.) | Shareholder tax year: calendar year 20 or other tax year beginning , 20 and ending , 20 .

City or town, state, and ZIP code or country

Check type of shareholder filing the return: ☐ Individual ☐ Corporation ☐ Partnership ☐ S Corporation ☐ Nongrantor Trust ☐ Estate

Name of passive foreign investment company (PFIC) or qualified electing fund (QEF) | **Employer identification number** (if any)

Address (Enter number, street, city or town, and country.) | Tax year of company or fund: calendar year 20 or other tax year beginning , 20 and ending , 20 .

Part I Elections (See instructions.)

A ☐ **Election To Treat the PFIC as a QEF.** I, a shareholder of a PFIC, elect to treat the PFIC as a QEF. *Complete lines 1a through 2c of Part II.*

B ☐ **Deemed Sale Election.** I, a shareholder on the first day of a PFIC's first tax year as a QEF, elect to recognize gain on the deemed sale of my interest in the PFIC. *Enter gain or loss on line 10f of Part IV.*

C ☐ **Deemed Dividend Election.** I, a shareholder on the first day of a PFIC's first tax year as a QEF that is a controlled foreign corporation (CFC), elect to treat an amount equal to my share of the post-1986 earnings and profits of the CFC as an excess distribution. *Enter this amount on line 10e of Part IV.*

D ☐ **Election To Extend Time For Payment of Tax.** I, a shareholder of a QEF, elect to extend the time for payment of tax on the undistributed earnings and profits of the QEF until this election is terminated. *Complete lines 3a through 4c of Part II to calculate the tax that may be deferred.*

Note: *If any portion of line 1a or line 2a of Part II is includible under section 951, you may* **not** *make this election. Also, see sections 1294(c) and 1294(f) and the related regulations for events that terminate this election.*

E ☐ **Election To Recognize Gain on Deemed Sale of PFIC.** I, a shareholder of a former PFIC or a PFIC to which section 1297(d) applies, elect to treat as an excess distribution the gain recognized on the deemed sale of my interest in the PFIC, or, if I qualify, my share of the PFIC's post-1986 earnings and profits deemed distributed, on the last day of its last tax year as a PFIC under section 1297(a). *Enter gain on line 10f of Part IV.*

F ☐ **Election To Mark-to-Market PFIC Stock.** I, a shareholder of a PFIC, elect to mark-to-market the PFIC stock that is marketable within the meaning of section 1296(e). *Complete Part III.*

G ☐ **Deemed Dividend Election With Respect to a Section 1297(e) PFIC.** I, a shareholder of a section 1297(e) PFIC, within the meaning of Regulations section 1.1291-9(j)(2)(v), elect to make a deemed dividend election with respect to the Section 1297(e) PFIC. My holding period in the stock of the Section 1297(e) PFIC includes the CFC qualification date, as defined in Regulations section 1.1297-3(d).

H ☐ **Deemed Dividend Election With Respect to a Former PFIC.** I, a shareholder of a former PFIC, within the meaning of Regulations section 1.1291-9(j)(2)(iv), elect to make a deemed dividend election with respect to the former PFIC. My holding period in the stock of the former PFIC includes the termination date, as defined in Regulations section 1.1298-3(d).

Part II Income From a Qualified Electing Fund (QEF).

All QEF shareholders complete lines 1a through 2c. If you are making Election D, also complete lines 3a through 4c. (See instructions.)

Line	Description				
1a	Enter your pro rata share of the ordinary earnings of the QEF	1a			
b	Enter the portion of line 1a that is included in income under section 951 or that may be excluded under section 1293(g)	1b			
c	Subtract line 1b from line 1a. Enter this amount on your tax return as ordinary income			1c	
2a	Enter your pro rata share of the total net capital gain of the QEF	2a			
b	Enter the portion of line 2a that is included in income under section 951 or that may be excluded under section 1293(g)	2b			
c	Subtract line 2b from line 2a. This amount is a net long-term capital gain. Enter this amount in Part II of the Schedule D used for your income tax return. (See instructions.)			2c	
3a	Add lines 1c and 2c			3a	
b	Enter the total amount of cash and the fair market value of other property distributed or deemed distributed to you during the tax year of the QEF. (See instructions.)	3b			
c	Enter the portion of line 3a not already included in line 3b that is attributable to shares in the QEF that you disposed of, pledged, or otherwise transferred during the tax year	3c			
d	Add lines 3b and 3c			3d	
e	Subtract line 3d from line 3a, and enter the difference (if zero or less, enter amount in brackets)			3e	
	Important: *If line 3e is greater than zero, and no portion of line 1a or 2a is includible in income under section 951, you may make Election D with respect to the amount on line 3e.*				
4a	Enter the total tax for the tax year (See instructions.)	4a			
b	Enter the total tax for the tax year determined without regard to the amount entered on line 3e	4b			
c	Subtract line 4b from line 4a. **This is the deferred tax, the time for payment of which is extended by making Election D. See instructions**			4c	

For Disclosure, Privacy Act, and Paperwork Reduction Act Notice, see separate instructions. Cat. No. 64174H Form **8621** (Rev. 12-2011)

Form 8621 (Rev. 12-2011) Page **2**

Part III Gain or (Loss) From Mark-to-Market Election (See instructions.)

5a	Enter the fair market value of your PFIC stock at the end of the tax year	**5a**	
b	Enter your adjusted basis in the stock at the end of the tax year	**5b**	
c	Subtract line 5b from line 5a. If a gain, do not complete lines 6 and 7. Include this amount as ordinary income on your tax return. If a loss, go to line 6	**5c**	
6	Enter any unreversed inclusions (as defined in section 1296(d))	**6**	
7	Enter the loss from line 5c, but only to the extent of unreversed inclusions on line 6. Include this amount as an ordinary loss on your tax return	**7**	
8	**If you sold or otherwise disposed of any section 1296 stock (see instructions) during the tax year:**		
a	Enter the fair market value of the stock on the date of sale or disposition	**8a**	
b	Enter the adjusted basis of the stock on the date of sale or disposition	**8b**	
c	Subtract line 8b from line 8a. If a gain, do not complete line 9. Include this amount as ordinary income on your tax return. If a loss, go to line 9	**8c**	
9a	Enter any unreversed inclusions (as defined in section 1296(d))	**9a**	
b	Enter the loss from line 8c, but only to the extent of unreversed inclusions on line 9a. Include this amount as an ordinary loss on your tax return. If the loss on line 8c exceeds unreversed inclusions on line 9a, complete line 9c	**9b**	
c	Enter the amount by which the loss on line 8c exceeds unreversed inclusions on line 9a. Include this amount on your tax return according to the rules generally applicable for losses provided elsewhere in the Code and regulations	**9c**	

Note. See instructions in case of multiple dispositions.

Part IV Distributions From and Dispositions of Stock of a Section 1291 Fund (See instructions.)

*Complete a **separate** Part IV for each excess distribution (see instructions).*

10a	Enter your total distributions from the section 1291 fund during the current tax year with respect to the applicable stock. If the holding period of the stock began in the current tax year, see instructions	**10a**	
b	Enter the total distributions (reduced by the portions of such distributions that were excess distributions but not included in income under section 1291(a)(1)(B)) made by the fund with respect to the applicable stock for each of the 3 years preceding the current tax year (or if shorter, the portion of the shareholder's holding period before the current tax year)	**10b**	
c	Divide line 10b by 3. (See instructions if the number of preceding tax years is less than 3.)	**10c**	
d	Multiply line 10c by 125% (1.25)	**10d**	
e	Subtract line 10d from line 10a. This amount, if more than zero, is the excess distribution with respect to the applicable stock. If zero or less and you did not dispose of stock during the tax year, **do not** complete the rest of Part IV. See instructions if you received more than one distribution during the current tax year. Also, see instructions for rules for reporting a nonexcess distribution on your income tax return	**10e**	
f	Enter gain or loss from the disposition of stock of a section 1291 fund or former section 1291 fund. If a gain, complete line 11. If a loss, show it in brackets and **do not** complete line 11.	**10f**	
11a	Attach a statement for each distribution and disposition. Show your holding period for each share of stock or block of shares held. Allocate the excess distribution to each day in your holding period. Add all amounts that are allocated to days in each tax year.		
b	Enter the total of the amounts determined in line 11a that are allocable to the current tax year and tax years before the foreign corporation became a PFIC (pre-PFIC tax years). Enter these amounts on your income tax return as other income	**11b**	
c	Enter the aggregate increases in tax (before credits) for each tax year in your holding period (other than the current tax year and pre-PFIC years). (See instructions.)	**11c**	
d	Foreign tax credit. (See instructions.)	**11d**	
e	Subtract line 11d from line 11c. Enter this amount on your income tax return as "additional tax." (See instructions.)	**11e**	
f	Determine interest on each net increase in tax determined on line 11e using the rates and methods of section 6621. Enter the aggregate amount of interest here. (See instructions.)	**11f**	

Form **8621** (Rev. 12-2011)

Form 8621 (Rev. 12-2011) Page 3

Part V **Status of Prior Year Section 1294 Elections and Termination of Section 1294 Elections**

Complete a separate column for each outstanding election. Complete lines 9 and 10 only if there is a partial termination of the section 1294 election.

		(i)	(ii)	(iii)	(iv)	(v)	(vi)
1	Tax year of outstanding election						
2	Undistributed earnings to which the election relates						
3	Deferred tax						
4	Interest accrued on deferred tax (line 3) as of the filing date						
5	Event terminating election						
6	Earnings distributed or deemed distributed during the tax year						
7	Deferred tax due with this return						
8	Accrued interest due with this return						
9	Deferred tax outstanding after partial termination of election						
10	Interest accrued after partial termination of election						

Form **8621** (Rev. 12-2011)

Form **8938** (November 2012)
Department of the Treasury Internal Revenue Service

Statement of Specified Foreign Financial Assets

► Information about Form 8938 and its separate instructions is at *www.irs.gov/form8938*.
► Attach to your tax return

OMB No. 1545-2195
Attachment Sequence No. **175**

If you have attached additional sheets, check here ☐

Name(s) shown on return | Identifying number

Number, street, and room or suite no. (if a P.O. box, see instructions)

City or town, province or state, and country (including postal code)

For tax year beginning , 20 , and ending , 20

Note. All information must be in English. Show all amounts in U.S. dollars. Show currency conversion rates in Part I, line 6(2), or Part II, line 6(2).

Type of filer
a Specified individual **(1)** ☐ Married filing a joint return **(2)** ☐ Married filing a separate return **(3)** ☐ Other individual
b Specified domestic entity **(1)** ☐ Partnership **(2)** ☐ Corporation **(3)** ☐ Trust

Check this box if this is an amended or supplemental Form 8938 for the tax year . . . . ☐

Part I Foreign Deposit and Custodial Accounts (see instructions)

If you have more than one account to report, attach a continuation sheet with the same information for each additional account (see instructions).

1 Type of account ☐ Deposit ☐ Custodial | 2 Account number or other designation

3 Check all that apply **a** ☐ Account opened during tax year **b** ☐ Account closed during tax year
c ☐ Account jointly owned with spouse **d** ☐ No tax item reported in Part III with respect to this account

4 Maximum value of account during tax year . . . . $

5 Did you use a foreign currency exchange rate to convert the value of the account into U.S. dollars? . . ☐ Yes ☐ No

6 If you answered "Yes" to line 5, complete all that apply.

(1) Foreign currency in which account is maintained	**(2)** Foreign currency exchange rate used to convert to U.S. dollars	**(3)** Source of exchange rate used if not from U.S. Treasury Financial Management Service

7 Name of financial institution in which account is maintained

8 Mailing address of financial institution in which account is maintained. Number, street, and room or suite no.

9 City or town, province or state, and country (including postal code)

Part II Other Foreign Assets (see instructions)

Note. *If you reported specified foreign financial assets on Forms 3520, 3520-A, 5471, 8621, 8865, or 8891 you do not have to include the assets on Form 8938. You must complete Part IV. See instructions.*

If you have more than one asset to report, attach a continuation sheet with the same information for each additional asset (see instructions).

1 Description of asset | 2 Identifying number or other designation

3 Complete all that apply. See instructions for reporting of multiple acquisition or disposition dates.
a Date asset acquired during tax year, if applicable . . . .
b Date asset disposed of during tax year, if applicable . . . .
c ☐ Check if asset jointly owned with spouse **d** ☐ Check if no tax item reported in Part III with respect to this asset

4 Maximum value of asset during tax year (check box that applies)
a ☐ $0 - $50,000 **b** ☐ $50,001 - $100,000 **c** ☐ $100,001 - $150,000 **d** ☐ $150,001 - $200,000
e If more than $200,000, list value . . . . $

5 Did you use a foreign currency exchange rate to convert the value of the asset into U.S. dollars? . . . ☐ Yes ☐ No

For Paperwork Reduction Act Notice, see the separate instructions. Cat. No. 37753A Form **8938** (11-2012)

Form 8938 (11-2012) Page **2**

Part II Other Foreign Assets *(continued)*

6 If you answered "Yes" to line 5, complete all that apply.

(1) Foreign currency in which asset is denominated	(2) Foreign currency exchange rate used to convert to U.S. dollars	(3) Source of exchange rate used if not from U.S. Treasury Financial Management Service

7 If asset reported in Part II, line 1, is stock of a foreign entity or an interest in a foreign entity, report the following information.

a Name of foreign entity

b Type of foreign entity **(1)** ☐ Partnership **(2)** ☐ Corporation **(3)** ☐ Trust **(4)** ☐ Estate

c Mailing address of foreign entity. Number, street, and room or suite no.

d City or town, province or state, and country (including postal code)

8 If asset reported in Part II, line 1, is not stock of a foreign entity or an interest in a foreign entity, report the following information for the asset.

Note. If this asset has more than one issuer or counterparty, attach a continuation sheet with the same information for each additional issuer or counterparty (see instructions).

a Name of issuer or counterparty

Check if information is for ☐ Issuer ☐ Counterparty

b Type of issuer or counterparty

(1) ☐ Individual **(2)** ☐ Partnership **(3)** ☐ Corporation **(4)** ☐ Trust **(5)** ☐ Estate

c Check if issuer or counterparty is a ☐ U.S. person ☐ Foreign person

d Mailing address of issuer or counterparty. Number, street, and room or suite no.

e City or town, province or state, and country (including postal code)

Part III Summary of Tax Items Attributable to Specified Foreign Financial Assets (see instructions)

Asset Category	Tax item	Amount reported on form or schedule	Where reported	
			Form and line	Schedule and line
I. Foreign Deposit and Custodial Accounts	**a** Interest	$		
	b Dividends	$		
	c Royalties	$		
	d Other income	$		
	e Gains (losses)	$		
	f Deductions	$		
	g Credits	$		
II. Other Foreign Assets	**a** Interest	$		
	b Dividends	$		
	c Royalties	$		
	d Other income	$		
	e Gains (losses)	$		
	f Deductions	$		
	g Credits	$		

Part IV Excepted Specified Foreign Financial Assets (see instructions)

If you reported specified foreign financial assets on the following forms, check the appropriate box(es). Indicate number of forms filed. You do not need to include these assets on Form 8938 for the tax year.

☐ 3520 Number of forms ________ ☐ 3520-A Number of forms ________ ☐ 5471 Number of forms ________

☐ 8621 Number of forms ________ ☐ 8865 Number of forms ________ ☐ 8891 Number of forms ________

Form **8938** (11-2012)

TD F 90-22.1
(Rev. January 2012)
Department of the Treasury

Do not use previous editions of this form

REPORT OF FOREIGN BANK AND FINANCIAL ACCOUNTS

Do NOT file with your Federal Tax Return

OMB No. 1545-2038

1 This Report is for Calendar Year Ended 12/31

___ ___ ___ ___

Amended ☐

Part I Filer Information

2 Type of Filer
a ☐ Individual b ☐ Partnership c ☐ Corporation d ☐ Consolidated e ☐ Fiduciary or Other—Enter type ________

3 U.S. Taxpayer Identification Number **If filer has no U.S. Identification Number complete Item 4.**	4 Foreign identification (Complete only if item 3 is not applicable.) a Type: ☐ Passport ☐ Other ________ b Number c Country of Issue	5 Individual's Date of Birth MM/DD/YYYY
6 Last Name or Organization Name	7 First Name	8 Middle Initial

9 Address (Number, Street, and Apt. or Suite No.)

10 City	11 State	12 Zip/Postal Code	13 Country

14 Does the filer have a financial interest in 25 or more financial accounts?
☐ Yes If "Yes" enter total number of accounts ________
(If "Yes" is checked, do not complete Part II or Part III, but retain records of this information)

☐ No

Part II Information on Financial Account(s) Owned Separately

15 Maximum value of account during calendar year reported	16 Type of account a ☐ Bank b ☐ Securities c ☐ Other—Enter type below

17 Name of Financial Institution in which account is held

18 Account number or other designation	19 Mailing Address (Number, Street, Suite Number) of financial institution in which account is held

20 City	21 State, if known	22 Zip/Postal Code, if known	23 Country

Signature

44 Filer Signature	45 Filer Title, if not reporting a personal account	46 Date (MM/DD/YYYY)

File this form with: U.S. Department of the Treasury, P.O. Box 32621, Detroit, MI 48232-0621

This form should be used to report a financial interest in, signature authority, or other authority over one or more financial accounts in foreign countries, as required by the Department of the Treasury Regulations 31 CFR 1010.350 (formerly 31 CFR 103.24). No report is required if the aggregate value of the accounts did not exceed $10,000. **See Instructions For Definitions.**

PRIVACY ACT AND PAPERWORK REDUCTION ACT NOTICE

Pursuant to the requirements of Public Law 93-579 (Privacy Act of 1974), notice is hereby given that the authority to collect information on TD F 90-22.1 in accordance with 5 USC 552a (e) is Public Law 91-508; 31 USC 5314; 5 USC 301; 31 CFR 1010.350 (formerly 31 CFR 103.24).

The principal purpose for collecting the information is to assure maintenance of reports where such reports or records have a high degree of usefulness in criminal, tax, or regulatory investigations or proceedings. The information collected may be provided to those officers and employees of any constituent unit of the Department of the Treasury who have a need for the records in the performance of their duties. The records may be referred to any other department or agency of the United States upon the request of the head of such department or agency for use in a criminal, tax, or regulatory investigation or proceeding. The information collected may also be provided to appropriate state, local, and foreign law enforcement and regulatory personnel in the performance of their official duties. Disclosure of this information is mandatory. Civil and criminal penalties, including in certain circumstances a fine of not more than $500,000 and imprisonment of not more than five years, are provided for failure to file a report, supply information, and for filing a false or fraudulent report. Disclosure of the Social Security number is mandatory. The authority to collect is 31 CFR 1010.350 (formerly 31 CFR 103.24) . The Social Security number will be used as a means to identify the individual who files the report.

The estimated average burden associated with this collection of information is 75 minutes per respondent or record keeper, depending on individual circumstances. Comments regarding the accuracy of this burden estimate, and suggestions for reducing the burden should be directed to the Internal Revenue Service, Bank Secrecy Act Policy, 5000 Ellin Road C-3-242, Lanham MD 20706.

Cat. No. 12996D Form **TD F 90-22.1** (Rev. 1-2012)

Streamlined Filing Compliance Procedures for Non-Resident, Non-Filer Taxpayers Questionnaire

NAME			
ADDRESS			
TIN			
TAX YEARS	YEAR:	YEAR:	YEAR:

Please respond to the following questions by checking YES or NO or providing the requested information.

ELIGIBILTY	**YES**	**NO**
1. Have you resided in the U.S. for any period of time since January 1, 2009?		
2. Have you filed a U.S. tax return for tax year 2009 or later?		
3. Do you owe more than $1,500 in U.S. tax on any of the tax returns you are submitting through this program?		
4. If you are submitting an amended return (Form 1040X) solely for the purpose of requesting a retroactive deferral of income on Form 8891, are there any adjustments reported on the amended return to income, deductions, credits or tax?		
If you answered yes to questions 1, 2 (except for taxpayers submitting amended returns solely for the purpose of requesting a retroactive deferral of income on Form 8891), 3, or 4, any returns submitted through this program will not be eligible for the streamlined processing procedures and will be treated as high risk returns subject to an examination. If your answer is yes to any of these questions, you may want to consider a submission through the Offshore Voluntary Disclosure Program.		
FINANCIAL ACCOUNTS/ENTITIES		
5. Since January 1, 2006, have you had a financial interest in or signature or other authority over any financial accounts located outside your country of residence?		
a. If yes, are the accounts held in your name?		
b. If yes, list the countries where the accounts were/are held.		
6. Since January 1, 2006, did you have a financial interest in any entities located outside your country of residence?		
a. If yes, do these entities control U.S. investments?		
b. If yes, list the countries where the entities were/are located.		
7. Do you have a retirement account located in your country of residence?		

a. If yes, are earnings from the retirement account non-taxable in the U.S. under current treaty provisions?		
b. If yes, is the retirement account located in Canada and are you filing a delinquent Form 8891 for each year?		
TAX ADVISORS		
8. Did you rely on the advice of a tax professional for not filing required U.S. tax returns?		
a. If yes, is your tax advisor located in the U.S.?		
9. During the above-listed tax years for this submission did you know that you were a U.S. citizen or resident alien?		
a. If yes, did you disclose to your tax professional that you were a U.S. citizen or resident alien?		
10. During the above-listed tax years for this submission, have you declared all of your income in your country of residence?		
11. If you used a tax professional, did you disclose the existence of the accounts/entities you hold outside your country of residence to your tax professional?		
12. Did you know you had a Report of Foreign Bank and Financial Accounts (FBAR), Form TD F 90-22.1, filing requirement when you failed to file an FBAR?		
TAX POSITION		
13. Have you ever filed a U.S. tax return?		
14. Are you currently under audit or investigation by the IRS?		
15. Have you ever filed an FBAR?		
16. Have you received an FBAR warning letter for any of the above-listed tax years for failing to file an FBAR?		
17. Do you have a treaty-based position for your country of residence that reduces your U.S. tax liability?		
18. Were you employed by a U.S. company or entity during any of the above-listed tax years?		
19. During any of the above-listed tax years, did you receive income from any of the following income sources in your country of residence: rental income, sales of property, inheritance?		
20. Are you claiming a refund on any of the returns you are submitting through this program?		

Under penalties of perjury, I declare that I have examined the facts stated in this Questionnaire and to the best of my knowledge and belief, they are true, correct and complete.

Taxpayer(s) Signature(s)	**Date**

U. S. Department of State

BUREAU OF CONSULAR AFFAIRS

OMB NO. 1405-0178
EXPIRES: 12/31/2013
Estimated Burden -15 minutes

REQUEST FOR DETERMINATION OF POSSIBLE LOSS OF UNITED STATES CITIZENSHIP

The following information is needed to determine your present citizenship status and possible loss of U.S. citizenship. You cannot lose U.S. citizenship unless you VOLUNTARILY perform an act designated by U.S. statute and do so with the intent to relinquish U.S. citizenship. You are advised to consult an attorney before completing this form. If you have any questions about the form, you should discuss them with a member of our consular staff before completing the form. You are requested to complete this form carefully. Use extra paper as needed and attach any supporting documents to this form.

PART I

1. Name *(Last, First, MI)*	2. Date of Birth *(mm-dd-yyyy)*	3. Place of Birth

4. (a) Last U.S. Passport Number	(b) Issued at *(Place)*	(c) Issued on *(Date)* *(mm-dd-yyyy)*

5. If not born in the United States, did you acquire citizenship by birth outside the United States to U.S. citizen parent(s): ☐ Yes ☐ No;
or Naturalization? *(Naturalization petitions prior to 11/29/1990 were submitted to and adjudicated by a court. After that date they were submitted to and adjudicated by INS/USCIS.)* ☐ Yes ☐ No

(a) Name of Naturalizing Court/Office ______________ (b) Date of Naturalization *(mm-dd-yyyy)* ______

Dates and Countries of Residence Outside the United States Since Birth

Date *(From) (mm-dd-yyyy)*	Date *(To) (mm-dd-yyyy)*	Country

6. When did you first become aware that you might be a United States citizen *(Give Approximate Date)*?

7. How did you find out that you are a citizen of the United States? *(For example, did you always know you were a U.S. citizen? If not, when did you learn about your citizenship? Did someone tell you that you are a U.S. citizen?)*

8. Are you a national or citizen of any other country other than the United States? ☐ Yes ☐ No

(a) If yes, of what country? ______________

(b) If yes, did you acquire that citizenship in the foreign country by:

(i) Birth? ☐ Yes ☐ No

(ii) Marriage? ☐ Yes ☐ No

(iii) Naturalization or registration; if yes, please provide a date *(mm-dd-yyyy)* ______ ☐ Yes ☐ No

(c) If other, explain.

(d) If you checked YES to question 8 (B) part (iii) by what means, or in what kind of proceeding, were you naturalized as a citizen of a foreign state?

9. Have you taken an oath or made an affirmation or other formal declaration of allegiance to a foreign state? ☐ Yes ☐ No

If yes, please provide a date *(mm-dd-yyyy)* and country __________ ____________________

(a) If you checked YES to question 8 or 9 or both, what was the nature of the oath you took? What were the words used? If you have a copy of the oath please attach it.

10. Have you served in the armed forces of a foreign state? ☐ Yes ☐ No

(a) If so, what country? ____________________

(b) In which branch of the armed forces did you serve? ____________________

(c) Dates of Service *(mm-dd-yyyy)* __________ __________

(d) What ranks did you hold? ____________________

(e) What was your highest rank? ____________________

(f) What responsibilities did you have and what functions and activities were you engaged in?

(g) Did you take an oath? If so, describe the oath. ☐ Yes ☐ No

11. Have you accepted, served in, or performed the duties of any office, post or employment with the government of a foreign state? ☐ Yes ☐ No

(a) If yes, please provide dates of service, country and the job title

__________ ____________________ ____________________

__________ ____________________ ____________________

__________ ____________________ ____________________

__________ ____________________ ____________________

(b) What were your duties and responsibilities for each of the foreign government jobs you held?

(c) Did you take an oath, affirmation, declaration or allegiance in connection with the job? If yes, describe the oath, affirmation, declaration or allegiance. ☐ Yes ☐ No

12. What ties did you have to the country where you performed the act or acts indicated in Questions 8-11? For example:

(a) Did you maintain a residence? If yes, please explain. ☐ Yes ☐ No

(b) Did you own property? If yes, please explain. ☐ Yes ☐ No

(c) Do you have family or social ties? If yes, please explain. ☐ Yes ☐ No

(d) Do you vote? If yes, please explain. ☐ Yes ☐ No

(e) What other ties did you have to the country where you performed the act or acts indicated in Questions 8-11?

13. What ties do you retain with the United States? For example:

(a) Do you maintain a residence? If yes, please explain. ☐ Yes ☐ No

(b) Do you own property? If yes, please explain. ☐ Yes ☐ No

(c) Do you have family or social ties? If yes, please explain. ☐ Yes ☐ No

(d) Do you vote? If yes, please explain. ☐ Yes ☐ No

(e) Do you file U.S. income or other tax returns? If yes, please explain. ☐ Yes ☐ No

(f) Do you maintain a profession, occupation, or license in the United States? If yes, please explain. ☐ Yes ☐ No

(g) Have you registered your children as citizens of the United States? ☐ Yes ☐ No

14. What passport do you use to travel to and from the United States?

15. What passport do you use to travel to and from other countries?

16. Have you renounced your U.S. nationality at a U.S. Consulate or Embassy? If yes, provide a date and place. ☐ Yes ☐ No

_______________ ____

17. Describe in detail the circumstances under which you performed the act or acts indicated in Questions 8-16.

18. Did you perform the act or acts voluntarily? ☐ Yes ☐ No

(a) If not, in what sense was your performance of the act or acts involuntary?

(b) Did you perform the acts with the intent to relinquish U.S. citizenship? If so, please explain your answer. ☐ Yes ☐ No

19. Did you know that by performing the act described in Questions 8-18 you might lose U.S. citizenship? Please explain your answer.

20. Your answers on this form will become part of the official record in your case. Before signing this form, you are advised to consider consulting with an attorney, and to read over your answers to make certain that they are as complete and accurate as possible. If you would like to provide additional information you believe relevant to a determination of your citizenship status, and in particular to your intention or lack of intention to relinquish U.S. citizenship, you may attach separate sheets with that information.

If your answer to each of the questions above is "No," please sign below before a Consular Officer at a U.S. Embassy or Consulate. If you answered "Yes", to one or more of questions 8(b)(iii)-11 and your action was completely VOLUNTARY, please continue with PART II.

Subscribed and Sworn

[SEAL]

____
Signature

____
Signature of Consular Officer

21. You should be aware that under United States law, a citizen may lose U.S. citizenship if he/she voluntarily performs any of the acts specified above in questions 8(b)(iii)-11 with the intent of relinquishing United States citizenship. If you voluntarily performed an act stated above with the intent to relinquish United States citizenship, you may sign Part II of this statement before a Consular Officer at a U.S. Embassy or Consulate. The U.S. Consulate or Embassy will prepare the forms necessary to document your loss of U.S. citizenship.

PART II

STATEMENT OF VOLUNTARY RELINQUISHMENT OF U.S. CITIZENSHIP

Subscribed and Sworn

I, ______________________________, performed the act of expatriation indicated in Questions 8-19, voluntarily and with the intent to relinquish my U.S. citizenship.

	______________________ Signature	______________________ Date *(mm-dd-yyyy)*
[SEAL]		
	______________________ Signature of Consular Officer	______________________ Date *(mm-dd-yyyy)*

PRIVACY ACT STATEMENT

AUTHORITIES: The information on this form is requested under the authority of 8 U.S.C. 1104, 1481, 1483, 1488, and 1501, and 22 U.S.C. 212. Although furnishing the information is voluntary, applicants may not be eligible for a U.S. passport or for relinquishment or renunciation of U.S. nationality if they do not provide the required information.

PURPOSE: The principal purpose of gathering this information is to determine if the individual performed a potentially expatriating act as defined in 8 U.S.C. 1481 voluntarily and with the intention of relinquishing U.S. nationality.

ROUTINE USES: The information solicited on this form may be made available to foreign government agencies to fulfill passport control and immigration duties, to investigate or prosecute violations of law, or when a request for information is made pursuant to customary international practice. In the event a finding of loss of nationality is made, the information solicited on this form may be made available to other federal entities with law enforcement responsibilities relating to or affected by nationality, including but not limited to the U.S. Citizenship and Immigration Service, the Internal Revenue Service, and the Federal Bureau of Investigation. The information provided also may be released to federal, state or local agencies for law enforcement, counter-terrorism and homeland security purposes; to Congress and courts within their sphere of jurisdiction; and to other federal agencies for certain personnel and records management matters.

Paperwork Reduction Act (PRA) Statement

Public reporting burden for this collection of information is estimated to average 15 minutes per response, including time required for searching existing data sources, gathering the necessary documentation, providing the information and/or documents required, and reviewing the final collection. You do not have to supply this information unless this collection displays a currently valid OMB control number. If you have comments on the accuracy of this burden estimate and/or recommendations for reducing it, please send them to: A/GIS/DIR, Room 2400 SA-22, U.S. Department of State, Washington, DC 20522-2202.

Appendix 2

2012 TAX TABLES

2012 Tax Table

See the instructions for line 44 to see if you must use the Tax Table below to figure your tax.

Example. Mr. and Mrs. Brown are filing a joint return. Their taxable income on Form 1040, line 43, is $25,300. First, they find the $25,300–25,350 taxable income line. Next, they find the column for married filing jointly and read down the column. The amount shown where the taxable income line and filing status column meet is $2,929. This is the tax amount they should enter on Form 1040, line 44.

Sample Table

At Least	But Less Than	Single	Married filing jointly *	Married filing sepa-rately	Head of a house-hold
		Your tax is—			
25,200	**25,250**	3,349	2,914	3,349	3,164
25,250	**25,300**	3,356	2,921	3,356	3,171
25,300	**25,350**	3,364	(2,929)	3,364	3,179
25,350	**25,400**	3,371	2,936	3,371	3,186

If line 43 (taxable income) is—		And you are—			
At least	But less than	Single	Married filing jointly *	Married filing sepa-rately	Head of a house-hold
		Your tax is—			
0	**5**	0	0	0	0
5	**15**	1	1	1	1
15	**25**	2	2	2	2
25	**50**	4	4	4	4
50	**75**	6	6	6	6
75	**100**	9	9	9	9
100	**125**	11	11	11	11
125	**150**	14	14	14	14
150	**175**	16	16	16	16
175	**200**	19	19	19	19
200	**225**	21	21	21	21
225	**250**	24	24	24	24
250	**275**	26	26	26	26
275	**300**	29	29	29	29
300	**325**	31	31	31	31
325	**350**	34	34	34	34
350	**375**	36	36	36	36
375	**400**	39	39	39	39
400	**425**	41	41	41	41
425	**450**	44	44	44	44
450	**475**	46	46	46	46
475	**500**	49	49	49	49
500	**525**	51	51	51	51
525	**550**	54	54	54	54
550	**575**	56	56	56	56
575	**600**	59	59	59	59
600	**625**	61	61	61	61
625	**650**	64	64	64	64
650	**675**	66	66	66	66
675	**700**	69	69	69	69
700	**725**	71	71	71	71
725	**750**	74	74	74	74
750	**775**	76	76	76	76
775	**800**	79	79	79	79
800	**825**	81	81	81	81
825	**850**	84	84	84	84
850	**875**	86	86	86	86
875	**900**	89	89	89	89
900	**925**	91	91	91	91
925	**950**	94	94	94	94
950	**975**	96	96	96	96
975	**1,000**	99	99	99	99

If line 43 (taxable income) is—		And you are—			
At least	But less than	Single	Married filing jointly *	Married filing sepa-rately	Head of a house-hold
		Your tax is—			
1,000					
1,000	**1,025**	101	101	101	101
1,025	**1,050**	104	104	104	104
1,050	**1,075**	106	106	106	106
1,075	**1,100**	109	109	109	109
1,100	**1,125**	111	111	111	111
1,125	**1,150**	114	114	114	114
1,150	**1,175**	116	116	116	116
1,175	**1,200**	119	119	119	119
1,200	**1,225**	121	121	121	121
1,225	**1,250**	124	124	124	124
1,250	**1,275**	126	126	126	126
1,275	**1,300**	129	129	129	129
1,300	**1,325**	131	131	131	131
1,325	**1,350**	134	134	134	134
1,350	**1,375**	136	136	136	136
1,375	**1,400**	139	139	139	139
1,400	**1,425**	141	141	141	141
1,425	**1,450**	144	144	144	144
1,450	**1,475**	146	146	146	146
1,475	**1,500**	149	149	149	149
1,500	**1,525**	151	151	151	151
1,525	**1,550**	154	154	154	154
1,550	**1,575**	156	156	156	156
1,575	**1,600**	159	159	159	159
1,600	**1,625**	161	161	161	161
1,625	**1,650**	164	164	164	164
1,650	**1,675**	166	166	166	166
1,675	**1,700**	169	169	169	169
1,700	**1,725**	171	171	171	171
1,725	**1,750**	174	174	174	174
1,750	**1,775**	176	176	176	176
1,775	**1,800**	179	179	179	179
1,800	**1,825**	181	181	181	181
1,825	**1,850**	184	184	184	184
1,850	**1,875**	186	186	186	186
1,875	**1,900**	189	189	189	189
1,900	**1,925**	191	191	191	191
1,925	**1,950**	194	194	194	194
1,950	**1,975**	196	196	196	196
1,975	**2,000**	199	199	199	199

If line 43 (taxable income) is—		And you are—			
At least	But less than	Single	Married filing jointly *	Married filing sepa-rately	Head of a house-hold
		Your tax is—			
2,000					
2,000	**2,025**	201	201	201	201
2,025	**2,050**	204	204	204	204
2,050	**2,075**	206	206	206	206
2,075	**2,100**	209	209	209	209
2,100	**2,125**	211	211	211	211
2,125	**2,150**	214	214	214	214
2,150	**2,175**	216	216	216	216
2,175	**2,200**	219	219	219	219
2,200	**2,225**	221	221	221	221
2,225	**2,250**	224	224	224	224
2,250	**2,275**	226	226	226	226
2,275	**2,300**	229	229	229	229
2,300	**2,325**	231	231	231	231
2,325	**2,350**	234	234	234	234
2,350	**2,375**	236	236	236	236
2,375	**2,400**	239	239	239	239
2,400	**2,425**	241	241	241	241
2,425	**2,450**	244	244	244	244
2,450	**2,475**	246	246	246	246
2,475	**2,500**	249	249	249	249
2,500	**2,525**	251	251	251	251
2,525	**2,550**	254	254	254	254
2,550	**2,575**	256	256	256	256
2,575	**2,600**	259	259	259	259
2,600	**2,625**	261	261	261	261
2,625	**2,650**	264	264	264	264
2,650	**2,675**	266	266	266	266
2,675	**2,700**	269	269	269	269
2,700	**2,725**	271	271	271	271
2,725	**2,750**	274	274	274	274
2,750	**2,775**	276	276	276	276
2,775	**2,800**	279	279	279	279
2,800	**2,825**	281	281	281	281
2,825	**2,850**	284	284	284	284
2,850	**2,875**	286	286	286	286
2,875	**2,900**	289	289	289	289
2,900	**2,925**	291	291	291	291
2,925	**2,950**	294	294	294	294
2,950	**2,975**	296	296	296	296
2,975	**3,000**	299	299	299	299

(Continued)

2012 Tax Table—*Continued*

If line 43 (taxable income) is—		And you are—			
At least	But less than	Single	Married filing jointly *	Married filing sepa-rately	Head of a house-hold
		Your tax is—			
3,000					
3,000	3,050	303	303	303	303
3,050	3,100	308	308	308	308
3,100	3,150	313	313	313	313
3,150	3,200	318	318	318	318
3,200	3,250	323	323	323	323
3,250	3,300	328	328	328	328
3,300	3,350	333	333	333	333
3,350	3,400	338	338	338	338
3,400	3,450	343	343	343	343
3,450	3,500	348	348	348	348
3,500	3,550	353	353	353	353
3,550	3,600	358	358	358	358
3,600	3,650	363	363	363	363
3,650	3,700	368	368	368	368
3,700	3,750	373	373	373	373
3,750	3,800	378	378	378	378
3,800	3,850	383	383	383	383
3,850	3,900	388	388	388	388
3,900	3,950	393	393	393	393
3,950	4,000	398	398	398	398
4,000					
4,000	4,050	403	403	403	403
4,050	4,100	408	408	408	408
4,100	4,150	413	413	413	413
4,150	4,200	418	418	418	418
4,200	4,250	423	423	423	423
4,250	4,300	428	428	428	428
4,300	4,350	433	433	433	433
4,350	4,400	438	438	438	438
4,400	4,450	443	443	443	443
4,450	4,500	448	448	448	448
4,500	4,550	453	453	453	453
4,550	4,600	458	458	458	458
4,600	4,650	463	463	463	463
4,650	4,700	468	468	468	468
4,700	4,750	473	473	473	473
4,750	4,800	478	478	478	478
4,800	4,850	483	483	483	483
4,850	4,900	488	488	488	488
4,900	4,950	493	493	493	493
4,950	5,000	498	498	498	498
5,000					
5,000	5,050	503	503	503	503
5,050	5,100	508	508	508	508
5,100	5,150	513	513	513	513
5,150	5,200	518	518	518	518
5,200	5,250	523	523	523	523
5,250	5,300	528	528	528	528
5,300	5,350	533	533	533	533
5,350	5,400	538	538	538	538
5,400	5,450	543	543	543	543
5,450	5,500	548	548	548	548
5,500	5,550	553	553	553	553
5,550	5,600	558	558	558	558
5,600	5,650	563	563	563	563
5,650	5,700	568	568	568	568
5,700	5,750	573	573	573	573
5,750	5,800	578	578	578	578
5,800	5,850	583	583	583	583
5,850	5,900	588	588	588	588
5,900	5,950	593	593	593	593
5,950	6,000	598	598	598	598

If line 43 (taxable income) is—		And you are—			
At least	But less than	Single	Married filing jointly *	Married filing sepa-rately	Head of a house-hold
		Your tax is—			
6,000					
6,000	6,050	603	603	603	603
6,050	6,100	608	608	608	608
6,100	6,150	613	613	613	613
6,150	6,200	618	618	618	618
6,200	6,250	623	623	623	623
6,250	6,300	628	628	628	628
6,300	6,350	633	633	633	633
6,350	6,400	638	638	638	638
6,400	6,450	643	643	643	643
6,450	6,500	648	648	648	648
6,500	6,550	653	653	653	653
6,550	6,600	658	658	658	658
6,600	6,650	663	663	663	663
6,650	6,700	668	668	668	668
6,700	6,750	673	673	673	673
6,750	6,800	678	678	678	678
6,800	6,850	683	683	683	683
6,850	6,900	688	688	688	688
6,900	6,950	693	693	693	693
6,950	7,000	698	698	698	698
7,000					
7,000	7,050	703	703	703	703
7,050	7,100	708	708	708	708
7,100	7,150	713	713	713	713
7,150	7,200	718	718	718	718
7,200	7,250	723	723	723	723
7,250	7,300	728	728	728	728
7,300	7,350	733	733	733	733
7,350	7,400	738	738	738	738
7,400	7,450	743	743	743	743
7,450	7,500	748	748	748	748
7,500	7,550	753	753	753	753
7,550	7,600	758	758	758	758
7,600	7,650	763	763	763	763
7,650	7,700	768	768	768	768
7,700	7,750	773	773	773	773
7,750	7,800	778	778	778	778
7,800	7,850	783	783	783	783
7,850	7,900	788	788	788	788
7,900	7,950	793	793	793	793
7,950	8,000	798	798	798	798
8,000					
8,000	8,050	803	803	803	803
8,050	8,100	808	808	808	808
8,100	8,150	813	813	813	813
8,150	8,200	818	818	818	818
8,200	8,250	823	823	823	823
8,250	8,300	828	828	828	828
8,300	8,350	833	833	833	833
8,350	8,400	838	838	838	838
8,400	8,450	843	843	843	843
8,450	8,500	848	848	848	848
8,500	8,550	853	853	853	853
8,550	8,600	858	858	858	858
8,600	8,650	863	863	863	863
8,650	8,700	868	868	868	868
8,700	8,750	874	873	874	873
8,750	8,800	881	878	881	878
8,800	8,850	889	883	889	883
8,850	8,900	896	888	896	888
8,900	8,950	904	893	904	893
8,950	9,000	911	898	911	898

If line 43 (taxable income) is—		And you are—			
At least	But less than	Single	Married filing jointly *	Married filing sepa-rately	Head of a house-hold
		Your tax is—			
9,000					
9,000	9,050	919	903	919	903
9,050	9,100	926	908	926	908
9,100	9,150	934	913	934	913
9,150	9,200	941	918	941	918
9,200	9,250	949	923	949	923
9,250	9,300	956	928	956	928
9,300	9,350	964	933	964	933
9,350	9,400	971	938	971	938
9,400	9,450	979	943	979	943
9,450	9,500	986	948	986	948
9,500	9,550	994	953	994	953
9,550	9,600	1,001	958	1,001	958
9,600	9,650	1,009	963	1,009	963
9,650	9,700	1,016	968	1,016	968
9,700	9,750	1,024	973	1,024	973
9,750	9,800	1,031	978	1,031	978
9,800	9,850	1,039	983	1,039	983
9,850	9,900	1,046	988	1,046	988
9,900	9,950	1,054	993	1,054	993
9,950	10,000	1,061	998	1,061	998
10,000					
10,000	10,050	1,069	1,003	1,069	1,003
10,050	10,100	1,076	1,008	1,076	1,008
10,100	10,150	1,084	1,013	1,084	1,013
10,150	10,200	1,091	1,018	1,091	1,018
10,200	10,250	1,099	1,023	1,099	1,023
10,250	10,300	1,106	1,028	1,106	1,028
10,300	10,350	1,114	1,033	1,114	1,033
10,350	10,400	1,121	1,038	1,121	1,038
10,400	10,450	1,129	1,043	1,129	1,043
10,450	10,500	1,136	1,048	1,136	1,048
10,500	10,550	1,144	1,053	1,144	1,053
10,550	10,600	1,151	1,058	1,151	1,058
10,600	10,650	1,159	1,063	1,159	1,063
10,650	10,700	1,166	1,068	1,166	1,068
10,700	10,750	1,174	1,073	1,174	1,073
10,750	10,800	1,181	1,078	1,181	1,078
10,800	10,850	1,189	1,083	1,189	1,083
10,850	10,900	1,196	1,088	1,196	1,088
10,900	10,950	1,204	1,093	1,204	1,093
10,950	11,000	1,211	1,098	1,211	1,098
11,000					
11,000	11,050	1,219	1,103	1,219	1,103
11,050	11,100	1,226	1,108	1,226	1,108
11,100	11,150	1,234	1,113	1,234	1,113
11,150	11,200	1,241	1,118	1,241	1,118
11,200	11,250	1,249	1,123	1,249	1,123
11,250	11,300	1,256	1,128	1,256	1,128
11,300	11,350	1,264	1,133	1,264	1,133
11,350	11,400	1,271	1,138	1,271	1,138
11,400	11,450	1,279	1,143	1,279	1,143
11,450	11,500	1,286	1,148	1,286	1,148
11,500	11,550	1,294	1,153	1,294	1,153
11,550	11,600	1,301	1,158	1,301	1,158
11,600	11,650	1,309	1,163	1,309	1,163
11,650	11,700	1,316	1,168	1,316	1,168
11,700	11,750	1,324	1,173	1,324	1,173
11,750	11,800	1,331	1,178	1,331	1,178
11,800	11,850	1,339	1,183	1,339	1,183
11,850	11,900	1,346	1,188	1,346	1,188
11,900	11,950	1,354	1,193	1,354	1,193
11,950	12,000	1,361	1,198	1,361	1,198

(Continued)

2012 Tax Table—*Continued*

If line 43 (taxable income) is—		And you are—			
At least	But less than	Single	Married filing jointly *	Married filing separately	Head of a household
		Your tax is—			
12,000					
12,000	12,050	1,369	1,203	1,369	1,203
12,050	12,100	1,376	1,208	1,376	1,208
12,100	12,150	1,384	1,213	1,384	1,213
12,150	12,200	1,391	1,218	1,391	1,218
12,200	12,250	1,399	1,223	1,399	1,223
12,250	12,300	1,406	1,228	1,406	1,228
12,300	12,350	1,414	1,233	1,414	1,233
12,350	12,400	1,421	1,238	1,421	1,238
12,400	12,450	1,429	1,243	1,429	1,244
12,450	12,500	1,436	1,248	1,436	1,251
12,500	12,550	1,444	1,253	1,444	1,259
12,550	12,600	1,451	1,258	1,451	1,266
12,600	12,650	1,459	1,263	1,459	1,274
12,650	12,700	1,466	1,268	1,466	1,281
12,700	12,750	1,474	1,273	1,474	1,289
12,750	12,800	1,481	1,278	1,481	1,296
12,800	12,850	1,489	1,283	1,489	1,304
12,850	12,900	1,496	1,288	1,496	1,311
12,900	12,950	1,504	1,293	1,504	1,319
12,950	13,000	1,511	1,298	1,511	1,326
13,000					
13,000	13,050	1,519	1,303	1,519	1,334
13,050	13,100	1,526	1,308	1,526	1,341
13,100	13,150	1,534	1,313	1,534	1,349
13,150	13,200	1,541	1,318	1,541	1,356
13,200	13,250	1,549	1,323	1,549	1,364
13,250	13,300	1,556	1,328	1,556	1,371
13,300	13,350	1,564	1,333	1,564	1,379
13,350	13,400	1,571	1,338	1,571	1,386
13,400	13,450	1,579	1,343	1,579	1,394
13,450	13,500	1,586	1,348	1,586	1,401
13,500	13,550	1,594	1,353	1,594	1,409
13,550	13,600	1,601	1,358	1,601	1,416
13,600	13,650	1,609	1,363	1,609	1,424
13,650	13,700	1,616	1,368	1,616	1,431
13,700	13,750	1,624	1,373	1,624	1,439
13,750	13,800	1,631	1,378	1,631	1,446
13,800	13,850	1,639	1,383	1,639	1,454
13,850	13,900	1,646	1,388	1,646	1,461
13,900	13,950	1,654	1,393	1,654	1,469
13,950	14,000	1,661	1,398	1,661	1,476
14,000					
14,000	14,050	1,669	1,403	1,669	1,484
14,050	14,100	1,676	1,408	1,676	1,491
14,100	14,150	1,684	1,413	1,684	1,499
14,150	14,200	1,691	1,418	1,691	1,506
14,200	14,250	1,699	1,423	1,699	1,514
14,250	14,300	1,706	1,428	1,706	1,521
14,300	14,350	1,714	1,433	1,714	1,529
14,350	14,400	1,721	1,438	1,721	1,536
14,400	14,450	1,729	1,443	1,729	1,544
14,450	14,500	1,736	1,448	1,736	1,551
14,500	14,550	1,744	1,453	1,744	1,559
14,550	14,600	1,751	1,458	1,751	1,566
14,600	14,650	1,759	1,463	1,759	1,574
14,650	14,700	1,766	1,468	1,766	1,581
14,700	14,750	1,774	1,473	1,774	1,589
14,750	14,800	1,781	1,478	1,781	1,596
14,800	14,850	1,789	1,483	1,789	1,604
14,850	14,900	1,796	1,488	1,796	1,611
14,900	14,950	1,804	1,493	1,804	1,619
14,950	15,000	1,811	1,498	1,811	1,626

If line 43 (taxable income) is—		And you are—			
At least	But less than	Single	Married filing jointly *	Married filing separately	Head of a household
		Your tax is—			
15,000					
15,000	15,050	1,819	1,503	1,819	1,634
15,050	15,100	1,826	1,508	1,826	1,641
15,100	15,150	1,834	1,513	1,834	1,649
15,150	15,200	1,841	1,518	1,841	1,656
15,200	15,250	1,849	1,523	1,849	1,664
15,250	15,300	1,856	1,528	1,856	1,671
15,300	15,350	1,864	1,533	1,864	1,679
15,350	15,400	1,871	1,538	1,871	1,686
15,400	15,450	1,879	1,543	1,879	1,694
15,450	15,500	1,886	1,548	1,886	1,701
15,500	15,550	1,894	1,553	1,894	1,709
15,550	15,600	1,901	1,558	1,901	1,716
15,600	15,650	1,909	1,563	1,909	1,724
15,650	15,700	1,916	1,568	1,916	1,731
15,700	15,750	1,924	1,573	1,924	1,739
15,750	15,800	1,931	1,578	1,931	1,746
15,800	15,850	1,939	1,583	1,939	1,754
15,850	15,900	1,946	1,588	1,946	1,761
15,900	15,950	1,954	1,593	1,954	1,769
15,950	16,000	1,961	1,598	1,961	1,776
16,000					
16,000	16,050	1,969	1,603	1,969	1,784
16,050	16,100	1,976	1,608	1,976	1,791
16,100	16,150	1,984	1,613	1,984	1,799
16,150	16,200	1,991	1,618	1,991	1,806
16,200	16,250	1,999	1,623	1,999	1,814
16,250	16,300	2,006	1,628	2,006	1,821
16,300	16,350	2,014	1,633	2,014	1,829
16,350	16,400	2,021	1,638	2,021	1,836
16,400	16,450	2,029	1,643	2,029	1,844
16,450	16,500	2,036	1,648	2,036	1,851
16,500	16,550	2,044	1,653	2,044	1,859
16,550	16,600	2,051	1,658	2,051	1,866
16,600	16,650	2,059	1,663	2,059	1,874
16,650	16,700	2,066	1,668	2,066	1,881
16,700	16,750	2,074	1,673	2,074	1,889
16,750	16,800	2,081	1,678	2,081	1,896
16,800	16,850	2,089	1,683	2,089	1,904
16,850	16,900	2,096	1,688	2,096	1,911
16,900	16,950	2,104	1,693	2,104	1,919
16,950	17,000	2,111	1,698	2,111	1,926
17,000					
17,000	17,050	2,119	1,703	2,119	1,934
17,050	17,100	2,126	1,708	2,126	1,941
17,100	17,150	2,134	1,713	2,134	1,949
17,150	17,200	2,141	1,718	2,141	1,956
17,200	17,250	2,149	1,723	2,149	1,964
17,250	17,300	2,156	1,728	2,156	1,971
17,300	17,350	2,164	1,733	2,164	1,979
17,350	17,400	2,171	1,738	2,171	1,986
17,400	17,450	2,179	1,744	2,179	1,994
17,450	17,500	2,186	1,751	2,186	2,001
17,500	17,550	2,194	1,759	2,194	2,009
17,550	17,600	2,201	1,766	2,201	2,016
17,600	17,650	2,209	1,774	2,209	2,024
17,650	17,700	2,216	1,781	2,216	2,031
17,700	17,750	2,224	1,789	2,224	2,039
17,750	17,800	2,231	1,796	2,231	2,046
17,800	17,850	2,239	1,804	2,239	2,054
17,850	17,900	2,246	1,811	2,246	2,061
17,900	17,950	2,254	1,819	2,254	2,069
17,950	18,000	2,261	1,826	2,261	2,076

If line 43 (taxable income) is—		And you are—			
At least	But less than	Single	Married filing jointly *	Married filing separately	Head of a household
		Your tax is—			
18,000					
18,000	18,050	2,269	1,834	2,269	2,084
18,050	18,100	2,276	1,841	2,276	2,091
18,100	18,150	2,284	1,849	2,284	2,099
18,150	18,200	2,291	1,856	2,291	2,106
18,200	18,250	2,299	1,864	2,299	2,114
18,250	18,300	2,306	1,871	2,306	2,121
18,300	18,350	2,314	1,879	2,314	2,129
18,350	18,400	2,321	1,886	2,321	2,136
18,400	18,450	2,329	1,894	2,329	2,144
18,450	18,500	2,336	1,901	2,336	2,151
18,500	18,550	2,344	1,909	2,344	2,159
18,550	18,600	2,351	1,916	2,351	2,166
18,600	18,650	2,359	1,924	2,359	2,174
18,650	18,700	2,366	1,931	2,366	2,181
18,700	18,750	2,374	1,939	2,374	2,189
18,750	18,800	2,381	1,946	2,381	2,196
18,800	18,850	2,389	1,954	2,389	2,204
18,850	18,900	2,396	1,961	2,396	2,211
18,900	18,950	2,404	1,969	2,404	2,219
18,950	19,000	2,411	1,976	2,411	2,226
19,000					
19,000	19,050	2,419	1,984	2,419	2,234
19,050	19,100	2,426	1,991	2,426	2,241
19,100	19,150	2,434	1,999	2,434	2,249
19,150	19,200	2,441	2,006	2,441	2,256
19,200	19,250	2,449	2,014	2,449	2,264
19,250	19,300	2,456	2,021	2,456	2,271
19,300	19,350	2,464	2,029	2,464	2,279
19,350	19,400	2,471	2,036	2,471	2,286
19,400	19,450	2,479	2,044	2,479	2,294
19,450	19,500	2,486	2,051	2,486	2,301
19,500	19,550	2,494	2,059	2,494	2,309
19,550	19,600	2,501	2,066	2,501	2,316
19,600	19,650	2,509	2,074	2,509	2,324
19,650	19,700	2,516	2,081	2,516	2,331
19,700	19,750	2,524	2,089	2,524	2,339
19,750	19,800	2,531	2,096	2,531	2,346
19,800	19,850	2,539	2,104	2,539	2,354
19,850	19,900	2,546	2,111	2,546	2,361
19,900	19,950	2,554	2,119	2,554	2,369
19,950	20,000	2,561	2,126	2,561	2,376
20,000					
20,000	20,050	2,569	2,134	2,569	2,384
20,050	20,100	2,576	2,141	2,576	2,391
20,100	20,150	2,584	2,149	2,584	2,399
20,150	20,200	2,591	2,156	2,591	2,406
20,200	20,250	2,599	2,164	2,599	2,414
20,250	20,300	2,606	2,171	2,606	2,421
20,300	20,350	2,614	2,179	2,614	2,429
20,350	20,400	2,621	2,186	2,621	2,436
20,400	20,450	2,629	2,194	2,629	2,444
20,450	20,500	2,636	2,201	2,636	2,451
20,500	20,550	2,644	2,209	2,644	2,459
20,550	20,600	2,651	2,216	2,651	2,466
20,600	20,650	2,659	2,224	2,659	2,474
20,650	20,700	2,666	2,231	2,666	2,481
20,700	20,750	2,674	2,239	2,674	2,489
20,750	20,800	2,681	2,246	2,681	2,496
20,800	20,850	2,689	2,254	2,689	2,504
20,850	20,900	2,696	2,261	2,696	2,511
20,900	20,950	2,704	2,269	2,704	2,519
20,950	21,000	2,711	2,276	2,711	2,526

(Continued)

2012 Tax Table—*Continued*

If line 43 (taxable income) is—		And you are—			
At least	But less than	Single	Married filing jointly *	Married filing sepa-rately	Head of a house-hold
		Your tax is—			
21,000					
21,000	21,050	2,719	2,284	2,719	2,534
21,050	21,100	2,726	2,291	2,726	2,541
21,100	21,150	2,734	2,299	2,734	2,549
21,150	21,200	2,741	2,306	2,741	2,556
21,200	21,250	2,749	2,314	2,749	2,564
21,250	21,300	2,756	2,321	2,756	2,571
21,300	21,350	2,764	2,329	2,764	2,579
21,350	21,400	2,771	2,336	2,771	2,586
21,400	21,450	2,779	2,344	2,779	2,594
21,450	21,500	2,786	2,351	2,786	2,601
21,500	21,550	2,794	2,359	2,794	2,609
21,550	21,600	2,801	2,366	2,801	2,616
21,600	21,650	2,809	2,374	2,809	2,624
21,650	21,700	2,816	2,381	2,816	2,631
21,700	21,750	2,824	2,389	2,824	2,639
21,750	21,800	2,831	2,396	2,831	2,646
21,800	21,850	2,839	2,404	2,839	2,654
21,850	21,900	2,846	2,411	2,846	2,661
21,900	21,950	2,854	2,419	2,854	2,669
21,950	22,000	2,861	2,426	2,861	2,676
22,000					
22,000	22,050	2,869	2,434	2,869	2,684
22,050	22,100	2,876	2,441	2,876	2,691
22,100	22,150	2,884	2,449	2,884	2,699
22,150	22,200	2,891	2,456	2,891	2,706
22,200	22,250	2,899	2,464	2,899	2,714
22,250	22,300	2,906	2,471	2,906	2,721
22,300	22,350	2,914	2,479	2,914	2,729
22,350	22,400	2,921	2,486	2,921	2,736
22,400	22,450	2,929	2,494	2,929	2,744
22,450	22,500	2,936	2,501	2,936	2,751
22,500	22,550	2,944	2,509	2,944	2,759
22,550	22,600	2,951	2,516	2,951	2,766
22,600	22,650	2,959	2,524	2,959	2,774
22,650	22,700	2,966	2,531	2,966	2,781
22,700	22,750	2,974	2,539	2,974	2,789
22,750	22,800	2,981	2,546	2,981	2,796
22,800	22,850	2,989	2,554	2,989	2,804
22,850	22,900	2,996	2,561	2,996	2,811
22,900	22,950	3,004	2,569	3,004	2,819
22,950	23,000	3,011	2,576	3,011	2,826
23,000					
23,000	23,050	3,019	2,584	3,019	2,834
23,050	23,100	3,026	2,591	3,026	2,841
23,100	23,150	3,034	2,599	3,034	2,849
23,150	23,200	3,041	2,606	3,041	2,856
23,200	23,250	3,049	2,614	3,049	2,864
23,250	23,300	3,056	2,621	3,056	2,871
23,300	23,350	3,064	2,629	3,064	2,879
23,350	23,400	3,071	2,636	3,071	2,886
23,400	23,450	3,079	2,644	3,079	2,894
23,450	23,500	3,086	2,651	3,086	2,901
23,500	23,550	3,094	2,659	3,094	2,909
23,550	23,600	3,101	2,666	3,101	2,916
23,600	23,650	3,109	2,674	3,109	2,924
23,650	23,700	3,116	2,681	3,116	2,931
23,700	23,750	3,124	2,689	3,124	2,939
23,750	23,800	3,131	2,696	3,131	2,946
23,800	23,850	3,139	2,704	3,139	2,954
23,850	23,900	3,146	2,711	3,146	2,961
23,900	23,950	3,154	2,719	3,154	2,969
23,950	24,000	3,161	2,726	3,161	2,976

If line 43 (taxable income) is—		And you are—			
At least	But less than	Single	Married filing jointly *	Married filing sepa-rately	Head of a house-hold
		Your tax is—			
24,000					
24,000	24,050	3,169	2,734	3,169	2,984
24,050	24,100	3,176	2,741	3,176	2,991
24,100	24,150	3,184	2,749	3,184	2,999
24,150	24,200	3,191	2,756	3,191	3,006
24,200	24,250	3,199	2,764	3,199	3,014
24,250	24,300	3,206	2,771	3,206	3,021
24,300	24,350	3,214	2,779	3,214	3,029
24,350	24,400	3,221	2,786	3,221	3,036
24,400	24,450	3,229	2,794	3,229	3,044
24,450	24,500	3,236	2,801	3,236	3,051
24,500	24,550	3,244	2,809	3,244	3,059
24,550	24,600	3,251	2,816	3,251	3,066
24,600	24,650	3,259	2,824	3,259	3,074
24,650	24,700	3,266	2,831	3,266	3,081
24,700	24,750	3,274	2,839	3,274	3,089
24,750	24,800	3,281	2,846	3,281	3,096
24,800	24,850	3,289	2,854	3,289	3,104
24,850	24,900	3,296	2,861	3,296	3,111
24,900	24,950	3,304	2,869	3,304	3,119
24,950	25,000	3,311	2,876	3,311	3,126
25,000					
25,000	25,050	3,319	2,884	3,319	3,134
25,050	25,100	3,326	2,891	3,326	3,141
25,100	25,150	3,334	2,899	3,334	3,149
25,150	25,200	3,341	2,906	3,341	3,156
25,200	25,250	3,349	2,914	3,349	3,164
25,250	25,300	3,356	2,921	3,356	3,171
25,300	25,350	3,364	2,929	3,364	3,179
25,350	25,400	3,371	2,936	3,371	3,186
25,400	25,450	3,379	2,944	3,379	3,194
25,450	25,500	3,386	2,951	3,386	3,201
25,500	25,550	3,394	2,959	3,394	3,209
25,550	25,600	3,401	2,966	3,401	3,216
25,600	25,650	3,409	2,974	3,409	3,224
25,650	25,700	3,416	2,981	3,416	3,231
25,700	25,750	3,424	2,989	3,424	3,239
25,750	25,800	3,431	2,996	3,431	3,246
25,800	25,850	3,439	3,004	3,439	3,254
25,850	25,900	3,446	3,011	3,446	3,261
25,900	25,950	3,454	3,019	3,454	3,269
25,950	26,000	3,461	3,026	3,461	3,276
26,000					
26,000	26,050	3,469	3,034	3,469	3,284
26,050	26,100	3,476	3,041	3,476	3,291
26,100	26,150	3,484	3,049	3,484	3,299
26,150	26,200	3,491	3,056	3,491	3,306
26,200	26,250	3,499	3,064	3,499	3,314
26,250	26,300	3,506	3,071	3,506	3,321
26,300	26,350	3,514	3,079	3,514	3,329
26,350	26,400	3,521	3,086	3,521	3,336
26,400	26,450	3,529	3,094	3,529	3,344
26,450	26,500	3,536	3,101	3,536	3,351
26,500	26,550	3,544	3,109	3,544	3,359
26,550	26,600	3,551	3,116	3,551	3,366
26,600	26,650	3,559	3,124	3,559	3,374
26,650	26,700	3,566	3,131	3,566	3,381
26,700	26,750	3,574	3,139	3,574	3,389
26,750	26,800	3,581	3,146	3,581	3,396
26,800	26,850	3,589	3,154	3,589	3,404
26,850	26,900	3,596	3,161	3,596	3,411
26,900	26,950	3,604	3,169	3,604	3,419
26,950	27,000	3,611	3,176	3,611	3,426

If line 43 (taxable income) is—		And you are—			
At least	But less than	Single	Married filing jointly *	Married filing sepa-rately	Head of a house-hold
		Your tax is—			
27,000					
27,000	27,050	3,619	3,184	3,619	3,434
27,050	27,100	3,626	3,191	3,626	3,441
27,100	27,150	3,634	3,199	3,634	3,449
27,150	27,200	3,641	3,206	3,641	3,456
27,200	27,250	3,649	3,214	3,649	3,464
27,250	27,300	3,656	3,221	3,656	3,471
27,300	27,350	3,664	3,229	3,664	3,479
27,350	27,400	3,671	3,236	3,671	3,486
27,400	27,450	3,679	3,244	3,679	3,494
27,450	27,500	3,686	3,251	3,686	3,501
27,500	27,550	3,694	3,259	3,694	3,509
27,550	27,600	3,701	3,266	3,701	3,516
27,600	27,650	3,709	3,274	3,709	3,524
27,650	27,700	3,716	3,281	3,716	3,531
27,700	27,750	3,724	3,289	3,724	3,539
27,750	27,800	3,731	3,296	3,731	3,546
27,800	27,850	3,739	3,304	3,739	3,554
27,850	27,900	3,746	3,311	3,746	3,561
27,900	27,950	3,754	3,319	3,754	3,569
27,950	28,000	3,761	3,326	3,761	3,576
28,000					
28,000	28,050	3,769	3,334	3,769	3,584
28,050	28,100	3,776	3,341	3,776	3,591
28,100	28,150	3,784	3,349	3,784	3,599
28,150	28,200	3,791	3,356	3,791	3,606
28,200	28,250	3,799	3,364	3,799	3,614
28,250	28,300	3,806	3,371	3,806	3,621
28,300	28,350	3,814	3,379	3,814	3,629
28,350	28,400	3,821	3,386	3,821	3,636
28,400	28,450	3,829	3,394	3,829	3,644
28,450	28,500	3,836	3,401	3,836	3,651
28,500	28,550	3,844	3,409	3,844	3,659
28,550	28,600	3,851	3,416	3,851	3,666
28,600	28,650	3,859	3,424	3,859	3,674
28,650	28,700	3,866	3,431	3,866	3,681
28,700	28,750	3,874	3,439	3,874	3,689
28,750	28,800	3,881	3,446	3,881	3,696
28,800	28,850	3,889	3,454	3,889	3,704
28,850	28,900	3,896	3,461	3,896	3,711
28,900	28,950	3,904	3,469	3,904	3,719
28,950	29,000	3,911	3,476	3,911	3,726
29,000					
29,000	29,050	3,919	3,484	3,919	3,734
29,050	29,100	3,926	3,491	3,926	3,741
29,100	29,150	3,934	3,499	3,934	3,749
29,150	29,200	3,941	3,506	3,941	3,756
29,200	29,250	3,949	3,514	3,949	3,764
29,250	29,300	3,956	3,521	3,956	3,771
29,300	29,350	3,964	3,529	3,964	3,779
29,350	29,400	3,971	3,536	3,971	3,786
29,400	29,450	3,979	3,544	3,979	3,794
29,450	29,500	3,986	3,551	3,986	3,801
29,500	29,550	3,994	3,559	3,994	3,809
29,550	29,600	4,001	3,566	4,001	3,816
29,600	29,650	4,009	3,574	4,009	3,824
29,650	29,700	4,016	3,581	4,016	3,831
29,700	29,750	4,024	3,589	4,024	3,839
29,750	29,800	4,031	3,596	4,031	3,846
29,800	29,850	4,039	3,604	4,039	3,854
29,850	29,900	4,046	3,611	4,046	3,861
29,900	29,950	4,054	3,619	4,054	3,869
29,950	30,000	4,061	3,626	4,061	3,876

(Continued)

2012 Tax Table—*Continued*

If line 43 (taxable income) is—		And you are—			
At least	But less than	Single	Married filing jointly *	Married filing sepa-rately	Head of a house-hold
		Your tax is—			
30,000					
30,000	30,050	4,069	3,634	4,069	3,884
30,050	30,100	4,076	3,641	4,076	3,891
30,100	30,150	4,084	3,649	4,084	3,899
30,150	30,200	4,091	3,656	4,091	3,906
30,200	30,250	4,099	3,664	4,099	3,914
30,250	30,300	4,106	3,671	4,106	3,921
30,300	30,350	4,114	3,679	4,114	3,929
30,350	30,400	4,121	3,686	4,121	3,936
30,400	30,450	4,129	3,694	4,129	3,944
30,450	30,500	4,136	3,701	4,136	3,951
30,500	30,550	4,144	3,709	4,144	3,959
30,550	30,600	4,151	3,716	4,151	3,966
30,600	30,650	4,159	3,724	4,159	3,974
30,650	30,700	4,166	3,731	4,166	3,981
30,700	30,750	4,174	3,739	4,174	3,989
30,750	30,800	4,181	3,746	4,181	3,996
30,800	30,850	4,189	3,754	4,189	4,004
30,850	30,900	4,196	3,761	4,196	4,011
30,900	30,950	4,204	3,769	4,204	4,019
30,950	31,000	4,211	3,776	4,211	4,026
31,000					
31,000	31,050	4,219	3,784	4,219	4,034
31,050	31,100	4,226	3,791	4,226	4,041
31,100	31,150	4,234	3,799	4,234	4,049
31,150	31,200	4,241	3,806	4,241	4,056
31,200	31,250	4,249	3,814	4,249	4,064
31,250	31,300	4,256	3,821	4,256	4,071
31,300	31,350	4,264	3,829	4,264	4,079
31,350	31,400	4,271	3,836	4,271	4,086
31,400	31,450	4,279	3,844	4,279	4,094
31,450	31,500	4,286	3,851	4,286	4,101
31,500	31,550	4,294	3,859	4,294	4,109
31,550	31,600	4,301	3,866	4,301	4,116
31,600	31,650	4,309	3,874	4,309	4,124
31,650	31,700	4,316	3,881	4,316	4,131
31,700	31,750	4,324	3,889	4,324	4,139
31,750	31,800	4,331	3,896	4,331	4,146
31,800	31,850	4,339	3,904	4,339	4,154
31,850	31,900	4,346	3,911	4,346	4,161
31,900	31,950	4,354	3,919	4,354	4,169
31,950	32,000	4,361	3,926	4,361	4,176
32,000					
32,000	32,050	4,369	3,934	4,369	4,184
32,050	32,100	4,376	3,941	4,376	4,191
32,100	32,150	4,384	3,949	4,384	4,199
32,150	32,200	4,391	3,956	4,391	4,206
32,200	32,250	4,399	3,964	4,399	4,214
32,250	32,300	4,406	3,971	4,406	4,221
32,300	32,350	4,414	3,979	4,414	4,229
32,350	32,400	4,421	3,986	4,421	4,236
32,400	32,450	4,429	3,994	4,429	4,244
32,450	32,500	4,436	4,001	4,436	4,251
32,500	32,550	4,444	4,009	4,444	4,259
32,550	32,600	4,451	4,016	4,451	4,266
32,600	32,650	4,459	4,024	4,459	4,274
32,650	32,700	4,466	4,031	4,466	4,281
32,700	32,750	4,474	4,039	4,474	4,289
32,750	32,800	4,481	4,046	4,481	4,296
32,800	32,850	4,489	4,054	4,489	4,304
32,850	32,900	4,496	4,061	4,496	4,311
32,900	32,950	4,504	4,069	4,504	4,319
32,950	33,000	4,511	4,076	4,511	4,326

If line 43 (taxable income) is—		And you are—			
At least	But less than	Single	Married filing jointly *	Married filing sepa-rately	Head of a house-hold
		Your tax is—			
33,000					
33,000	33,050	4,519	4,084	4,519	4,334
33,050	33,100	4,526	4,091	4,526	4,341
33,100	33,150	4,534	4,099	4,534	4,349
33,150	33,200	4,541	4,106	4,541	4,356
33,200	33,250	4,549	4,114	4,549	4,364
33,250	33,300	4,556	4,121	4,556	4,371
33,300	33,350	4,564	4,129	4,564	4,379
33,350	33,400	4,571	4,136	4,571	4,386
33,400	33,450	4,579	4,144	4,579	4,394
33,450	33,500	4,586	4,151	4,586	4,401
33,500	33,550	4,594	4,159	4,594	4,409
33,550	33,600	4,601	4,166	4,601	4,416
33,600	33,650	4,609	4,174	4,609	4,424
33,650	33,700	4,616	4,181	4,616	4,431
33,700	33,750	4,624	4,189	4,624	4,439
33,750	33,800	4,631	4,196	4,631	4,446
33,800	33,850	4,639	4,204	4,639	4,454
33,850	33,900	4,646	4,211	4,646	4,461
33,900	33,950	4,654	4,219	4,654	4,469
33,950	34,000	4,661	4,226	4,661	4,476
34,000					
34,000	34,050	4,669	4,234	4,669	4,484
34,050	34,100	4,676	4,241	4,676	4,491
34,100	34,150	4,684	4,249	4,684	4,499
34,150	34,200	4,691	4,256	4,691	4,506
34,200	34,250	4,699	4,264	4,699	4,514
34,250	34,300	4,706	4,271	4,706	4,521
34,300	34,350	4,714	4,279	4,714	4,529
34,350	34,400	4,721	4,286	4,721	4,536
34,400	34,450	4,729	4,294	4,729	4,544
34,450	34,500	4,736	4,301	4,736	4,551
34,500	34,550	4,744	4,309	4,744	4,559
34,550	34,600	4,751	4,316	4,751	4,566
34,600	34,650	4,759	4,324	4,759	4,574
34,650	34,700	4,766	4,331	4,766	4,581
34,700	34,750	4,774	4,339	4,774	4,589
34,750	34,800	4,781	4,346	4,781	4,596
34,800	34,850	4,789	4,354	4,789	4,604
34,850	34,900	4,796	4,361	4,796	4,611
34,900	34,950	4,804	4,369	4,804	4,619
34,950	35,000	4,811	4,376	4,811	4,626
35,000					
35,000	35,050	4,819	4,384	4,819	4,634
35,050	35,100	4,826	4,391	4,826	4,641
35,100	35,150	4,834	4,399	4,834	4,649
35,150	35,200	4,841	4,406	4,841	4,656
35,200	35,250	4,849	4,414	4,849	4,664
35,250	35,300	4,856	4,421	4,856	4,671
35,300	35,350	4,864	4,429	4,864	4,679
35,350	35,400	4,874	4,436	4,874	4,686
35,400	35,450	4,886	4,444	4,886	4,694
35,450	35,500	4,899	4,451	4,899	4,701
35,500	35,550	4,911	4,459	4,911	4,709
35,550	35,600	4,924	4,466	4,924	4,716
35,600	35,650	4,936	4,474	4,936	4,724
35,650	35,700	4,949	4,481	4,949	4,731
35,700	35,750	4,961	4,489	4,961	4,739
35,750	35,800	4,974	4,496	4,974	4,746
35,800	35,850	4,986	4,504	4,986	4,754
35,850	35,900	4,999	4,511	4,999	4,761
35,900	35,950	5,011	4,519	5,011	4,769
35,950	36,000	5,024	4,526	5,024	4,776

If line 43 (taxable income) is—		And you are—			
At least	But less than	Single	Married filing jointly *	Married filing sepa-rately	Head of a house-hold
		Your tax is—			
36,000					
36,000	36,050	5,036	4,534	5,036	4,784
36,050	36,100	5,049	4,541	5,049	4,791
36,100	36,150	5,061	4,549	5,061	4,799
36,150	36,200	5,074	4,556	5,074	4,806
36,200	36,250	5,086	4,564	5,086	4,814
36,250	36,300	5,099	4,571	5,099	4,821
36,300	36,350	5,111	4,579	5,111	4,829
36,350	36,400	5,124	4,586	5,124	4,836
36,400	36,450	5,136	4,594	5,136	4,844
36,450	36,500	5,149	4,601	5,149	4,851
36,500	36,550	5,161	4,609	5,161	4,859
36,550	36,600	5,174	4,616	5,174	4,866
36,600	36,650	5,186	4,624	5,186	4,874
36,650	36,700	5,199	4,631	5,199	4,881
36,700	36,750	5,211	4,639	5,211	4,889
36,750	36,800	5,224	4,646	5,224	4,896
36,800	36,850	5,236	4,654	5,236	4,904
36,850	36,900	5,249	4,661	5,249	4,911
36,900	36,950	5,261	4,669	5,261	4,919
36,950	37,000	5,274	4,676	5,274	4,926
37,000					
37,000	37,050	5,286	4,684	5,286	4,934
37,050	37,100	5,299	4,691	5,299	4,941
37,100	37,150	5,311	4,699	5,311	4,949
37,150	37,200	5,324	4,706	5,324	4,956
37,200	37,250	5,336	4,714	5,336	4,964
37,250	37,300	5,349	4,721	5,349	4,971
37,300	37,350	5,361	4,729	5,361	4,979
37,350	37,400	5,374	4,736	5,374	4,986
37,400	37,450	5,386	4,744	5,386	4,994
37,450	37,500	5,399	4,751	5,399	5,001
37,500	37,550	5,411	4,759	5,411	5,009
37,550	37,600	5,424	4,766	5,424	5,016
37,600	37,650	5,436	4,774	5,436	5,024
37,650	37,700	5,449	4,781	5,449	5,031
37,700	37,750	5,461	4,789	5,461	5,039
37,750	37,800	5,474	4,796	5,474	5,046
37,800	37,850	5,486	4,804	5,486	5,054
37,850	37,900	5,499	4,811	5,499	5,061
37,900	37,950	5,511	4,819	5,511	5,069
37,950	38,000	5,524	4,826	5,524	5,076
38,000					
38,000	38,050	5,536	4,834	5,536	5,084
38,050	38,100	5,549	4,841	5,549	5,091
38,100	38,150	5,561	4,849	5,561	5,099
38,150	38,200	5,574	4,856	5,574	5,106
38,200	38,250	5,586	4,864	5,586	5,114
38,250	38,300	5,599	4,871	5,599	5,121
38,300	38,350	5,611	4,879	5,611	5,129
38,350	38,400	5,624	4,886	5,624	5,136
38,400	38,450	5,636	4,894	5,636	5,144
38,450	38,500	5,649	4,901	5,649	5,151
38,500	38,550	5,661	4,909	5,661	5,159
38,550	38,600	5,674	4,916	5,674	5,166
38,600	38,650	5,686	4,924	5,686	5,174
38,650	38,700	5,699	4,931	5,699	5,181
38,700	38,750	5,711	4,939	5,711	5,189
38,750	38,800	5,724	4,946	5,724	5,196
38,800	38,850	5,736	4,954	5,736	5,204
38,850	38,900	5,749	4,961	5,749	5,211
38,900	38,950	5,761	4,969	5,761	5,219
38,950	39,000	5,774	4,976	5,774	5,226

(Continued)

2012 Tax Table—*Continued*

If line 43 (taxable income) is—		And you are—			
At least	But less than	Single	Married filing jointly *	Married filing separately	Head of a household
		Your tax is—			
39,000					
39,000	39,050	5,786	4,984	5,786	5,234
39,050	39,100	5,799	4,991	5,799	5,241
39,100	39,150	5,811	4,999	5,811	5,249
39,150	39,200	5,824	5,006	5,824	5,256
39,200	39,250	5,836	5,014	5,836	5,264
39,250	39,300	5,849	5,021	5,849	5,271
39,300	39,350	5,861	5,029	5,861	5,279
39,350	39,400	5,874	5,036	5,874	5,286
39,400	39,450	5,886	5,044	5,886	5,294
39,450	39,500	5,899	5,051	5,899	5,301
39,500	39,550	5,911	5,059	5,911	5,309
39,550	39,600	5,924	5,066	5,924	5,316
39,600	39,650	5,936	5,074	5,936	5,324
39,650	39,700	5,949	5,081	5,949	5,331
39,700	39,750	5,961	5,089	5,961	5,339
39,750	39,800	5,974	5,096	5,974	5,346
39,800	39,850	5,986	5,104	5,986	5,354
39,850	39,900	5,999	5,111	5,999	5,361
39,900	39,950	6,011	5,119	6,011	5,369
39,950	40,000	6,024	5,126	6,024	5,376

At least	But less than	Single	Married filing jointly *	Married filing separately	Head of a household
40,000					
40,000	40,050	6,036	5,134	6,036	5,384
40,050	40,100	6,049	5,141	6,049	5,391
40,100	40,150	6,061	5,149	6,061	5,399
40,150	40,200	6,074	5,156	6,074	5,406
40,200	40,250	6,086	5,164	6,086	5,414
40,250	40,300	6,099	5,171	6,099	5,421
40,300	40,350	6,111	5,179	6,111	5,429
40,350	40,400	6,124	5,186	6,124	5,436
40,400	40,450	6,136	5,194	6,136	5,444
40,450	40,500	6,149	5,201	6,149	5,451
40,500	40,550	6,161	5,209	6,161	5,459
40,550	40,600	6,174	5,216	6,174	5,466
40,600	40,650	6,186	5,224	6,186	5,474
40,650	40,700	6,199	5,231	6,199	5,481
40,700	40,750	6,211	5,239	6,211	5,489
40,750	40,800	6,224	5,246	6,224	5,496
40,800	40,850	6,236	5,254	6,236	5,504
40,850	40,900	6,249	5,261	6,249	5,511
40,900	40,950	6,261	5,269	6,261	5,519
40,950	41,000	6,274	5,276	6,274	5,526

At least	But less than	Single	Married filing jointly *	Married filing separately	Head of a household
41,000					
41,000	41,050	6,286	5,284	6,286	5,534
41,050	41,100	6,299	5,291	6,299	5,541
41,100	41,150	6,311	5,299	6,311	5,549
41,150	41,200	6,324	5,306	6,324	5,556
41,200	41,250	6,336	5,314	6,336	5,564
41,250	41,300	6,349	5,321	6,349	5,571
41,300	41,350	6,361	5,329	6,361	5,579
41,350	41,400	6,374	5,336	6,374	5,586
41,400	41,450	6,386	5,344	6,386	5,594
41,450	41,500	6,399	5,351	6,399	5,601
41,500	41,550	6,411	5,359	6,411	5,609
41,550	41,600	6,424	5,366	6,424	5,616
41,600	41,650	6,436	5,374	6,436	5,624
41,650	41,700	6,449	5,381	6,449	5,631
41,700	41,750	6,461	5,389	6,461	5,639
41,750	41,800	6,474	5,396	6,474	5,646
41,800	41,850	6,486	5,404	6,486	5,654
41,850	41,900	6,499	5,411	6,499	5,661
41,900	41,950	6,511	5,419	6,511	5,669
41,950	42,000	6,524	5,426	6,524	5,676

At least	But less than	Single	Married filing jointly *	Married filing separately	Head of a household
42,000					
42,000	42,050	6,536	5,434	6,536	5,684
42,050	42,100	6,549	5,441	6,549	5,691
42,100	42,150	6,561	5,449	6,561	5,699
42,150	42,200	6,574	5,456	6,574	5,706
42,200	42,250	6,586	5,464	6,586	5,714
42,250	42,300	6,599	5,471	6,599	5,721
42,300	42,350	6,611	5,479	6,611	5,729
42,350	42,400	6,624	5,486	6,624	5,736
42,400	42,450	6,636	5,494	6,636	5,744
42,450	42,500	6,649	5,501	6,649	5,751
42,500	42,550	6,661	5,509	6,661	5,759
42,550	42,600	6,674	5,516	6,674	5,766
42,600	42,650	6,686	5,524	6,686	5,774
42,650	42,700	6,699	5,531	6,699	5,781
42,700	42,750	6,711	5,539	6,711	5,789
42,750	42,800	6,724	5,546	6,724	5,796
42,800	42,850	6,736	5,554	6,736	5,804
42,850	42,900	6,749	5,561	6,749	5,811
42,900	42,950	6,761	5,569	6,761	5,819
42,950	43,000	6,774	5,576	6,774	5,826

At least	But less than	Single	Married filing jointly *	Married filing separately	Head of a household
43,000					
43,000	43,050	6,786	5,584	6,786	5,834
43,050	43,100	6,799	5,591	6,799	5,841
43,100	43,150	6,811	5,599	6,811	5,849
43,150	43,200	6,824	5,606	6,824	5,856
43,200	43,250	6,836	5,614	6,836	5,864
43,250	43,300	6,849	5,621	6,849	5,871
43,300	43,350	6,861	5,629	6,861	5,879
43,350	43,400	6,874	5,636	6,874	5,886
43,400	43,450	6,886	5,644	6,886	5,894
43,450	43,500	6,899	5,651	6,899	5,901
43,500	43,550	6,911	5,659	6,911	5,909
43,550	43,600	6,924	5,666	6,924	5,916
43,600	43,650	6,936	5,674	6,936	5,924
43,650	43,700	6,949	5,681	6,949	5,931
43,700	43,750	6,961	5,689	6,961	5,939
43,750	43,800	6,974	5,696	6,974	5,946
43,800	43,850	6,986	5,704	6,986	5,954
43,850	43,900	6,999	5,711	6,999	5,961
43,900	43,950	7,011	5,719	7,011	5,969
43,950	44,000	7,024	5,726	7,024	5,976

At least	But less than	Single	Married filing jointly *	Married filing separately	Head of a household
44,000					
44,000	44,050	7,036	5,734	7,036	5,984
44,050	44,100	7,049	5,741	7,049	5,991
44,100	44,150	7,061	5,749	7,061	5,999
44,150	44,200	7,074	5,756	7,074	6,006
44,200	44,250	7,086	5,764	7,086	6,014
44,250	44,300	7,099	5,771	7,099	6,021
44,300	44,350	7,111	5,779	7,111	6,029
44,350	44,400	7,124	5,786	7,124	6,036
44,400	44,450	7,136	5,794	7,136	6,044
44,450	44,500	7,149	5,801	7,149	6,051
44,500	44,550	7,161	5,809	7,161	6,059
44,550	44,600	7,174	5,816	7,174	6,066
44,600	44,650	7,186	5,824	7,186	6,074
44,650	44,700	7,199	5,831	7,199	6,081
44,700	44,750	7,211	5,839	7,211	6,089
44,750	44,800	7,224	5,846	7,224	6,096
44,800	44,850	7,236	5,854	7,236	6,104
44,850	44,900	7,249	5,861	7,249	6,111
44,900	44,950	7,261	5,869	7,261	6,119
44,950	45,000	7,274	5,876	7,274	6,126

At least	But less than	Single	Married filing jointly *	Married filing separately	Head of a household
45,000					
45,000	45,050	7,286	5,884	7,286	6,134
45,050	45,100	7,299	5,891	7,299	6,141
45,100	45,150	7,311	5,899	7,311	6,149
45,150	45,200	7,324	5,906	7,324	6,156
45,200	45,250	7,336	5,914	7,336	6,164
45,250	45,300	7,349	5,921	7,349	6,171
45,300	45,350	7,361	5,929	7,361	6,179
45,350	45,400	7,374	5,936	7,374	6,186
45,400	45,450	7,386	5,944	7,386	6,194
45,450	45,500	7,399	5,951	7,399	6,201
45,500	45,550	7,411	5,959	7,411	6,209
45,550	45,600	7,424	5,966	7,424	6,216
45,600	45,650	7,436	5,974	7,436	6,224
45,650	45,700	7,449	5,981	7,449	6,231
45,700	45,750	7,461	5,989	7,461	6,239
45,750	45,800	7,474	5,996	7,474	6,246
45,800	45,850	7,486	6,004	7,486	6,254
45,850	45,900	7,499	6,011	7,499	6,261
45,900	45,950	7,511	6,019	7,511	6,269
45,950	46,000	7,524	6,026	7,524	6,276

At least	But less than	Single	Married filing jointly *	Married filing separately	Head of a household
46,000					
46,000	46,050	7,536	6,034	7,536	6,284
46,050	46,100	7,549	6,041	7,549	6,291
46,100	46,150	7,561	6,049	7,561	6,299
46,150	46,200	7,574	6,056	7,574	6,306
46,200	46,250	7,586	6,064	7,586	6,314
46,250	46,300	7,599	6,071	7,599	6,321
46,300	46,350	7,611	6,079	7,611	6,329
46,350	46,400	7,624	6,086	7,624	6,336
46,400	46,450	7,636	6,094	7,636	6,344
46,450	46,500	7,649	6,101	7,649	6,351
46,500	46,550	7,661	6,109	7,661	6,359
46,550	46,600	7,674	6,116	7,674	6,366
46,600	46,650	7,686	6,124	7,686	6,374
46,650	46,700	7,699	6,131	7,699	6,381
46,700	46,750	7,711	6,139	7,711	6,389
46,750	46,800	7,724	6,146	7,724	6,396
46,800	46,850	7,736	6,154	7,736	6,404
46,850	46,900	7,749	6,161	7,749	6,411
46,900	46,950	7,761	6,169	7,761	6,419
46,950	47,000	7,774	6,176	7,774	6,426

At least	But less than	Single	Married filing jointly *	Married filing separately	Head of a household
47,000					
47,000	47,050	7,786	6,184	7,786	6,434
47,050	47,100	7,799	6,191	7,799	6,441
47,100	47,150	7,811	6,199	7,811	6,449
47,150	47,200	7,824	6,206	7,824	6,456
47,200	47,250	7,836	6,214	7,836	6,464
47,250	47,300	7,849	6,221	7,849	6,471
47,300	47,350	7,861	6,229	7,861	6,479
47,350	47,400	7,874	6,236	7,874	6,489
47,400	47,450	7,886	6,244	7,886	6,501
47,450	47,500	7,899	6,251	7,899	6,514
47,500	47,550	7,911	6,259	7,911	6,526
47,550	47,600	7,924	6,266	7,924	6,539
47,600	47,650	7,936	6,274	7,936	6,551
47,650	47,700	7,949	6,281	7,949	6,564
47,700	47,750	7,961	6,289	7,961	6,576
47,750	47,800	7,974	6,296	7,974	6,589
47,800	47,850	7,986	6,304	7,986	6,601
47,850	47,900	7,999	6,311	7,999	6,614
47,900	47,950	8,011	6,319	8,011	6,626
47,950	48,000	8,024	6,326	8,024	6,639

(Continued)

2012 Tax Table—*Continued*

If line 43 (taxable income) is— At least	But less than	And you are— Single	Married filing jointly *	Married filing separately	Head of a household
		Your tax is—			
48,000					
48,000	48,050	8,036	6,334	8,036	6,651
48,050	48,100	8,049	6,341	8,049	6,664
48,100	48,150	8,061	6,349	8,061	6,676
48,150	48,200	8,074	6,356	8,074	6,689
48,200	48,250	8,086	6,364	8,086	6,701
48,250	48,300	8,099	6,371	8,099	6,714
48,300	48,350	8,111	6,379	8,111	6,726
48,350	48,400	8,124	6,386	8,124	6,739
48,400	48,450	8,136	6,394	8,136	6,751
48,450	48,500	8,149	6,401	8,149	6,764
48,500	48,550	8,161	6,409	8,161	6,776
48,550	48,600	8,174	6,416	8,174	6,789
48,600	48,650	8,186	6,424	8,186	6,801
48,650	48,700	8,199	6,431	8,199	6,814
48,700	48,750	8,211	6,439	8,211	6,826
48,750	48,800	8,224	6,446	8,224	6,839
48,800	48,850	8,236	6,454	8,236	6,851
48,850	48,900	8,249	6,461	8,249	6,864
48,900	48,950	8,261	6,469	8,261	6,876
48,950	49,000	8,274	6,476	8,274	6,889
49,000					
49,000	49,050	8,286	6,484	8,286	6,901
49,050	49,100	8,299	6,491	8,299	6,914
49,100	49,150	8,311	6,499	8,311	6,926
49,150	49,200	8,324	6,506	8,324	6,939
49,200	49,250	8,336	6,514	8,336	6,951
49,250	49,300	8,349	6,521	8,349	6,964
49,300	49,350	8,361	6,529	8,361	6,976
49,350	49,400	8,374	6,536	8,374	6,989
49,400	49,450	8,386	6,544	8,386	7,001
49,450	49,500	8,399	6,551	8,399	7,014
49,500	49,550	8,411	6,559	8,411	7,026
49,550	49,600	8,424	6,566	8,424	7,039
49,600	49,650	8,436	6,574	8,436	7,051
49,650	49,700	8,449	6,581	8,449	7,064
49,700	49,750	8,461	6,589	8,461	7,076
49,750	49,800	8,474	6,596	8,474	7,089
49,800	49,850	8,486	6,604	8,486	7,101
49,850	49,900	8,499	6,611	8,499	7,114
49,900	49,950	8,511	6,619	8,511	7,126
49,950	50,000	8,524	6,626	8,524	7,139
50,000					
50,000	50,050	8,536	6,634	8,536	7,151
50,050	50,100	8,549	6,641	8,549	7,164
50,100	50,150	8,561	6,649	8,561	7,176
50,150	50,200	8,574	6,656	8,574	7,189
50,200	50,250	8,586	6,664	8,586	7,201
50,250	50,300	8,599	6,671	8,599	7,214
50,300	50,350	8,611	6,679	8,611	7,226
50,350	50,400	8,624	6,686	8,624	7,239
50,400	50,450	8,636	6,694	8,636	7,251
50,450	50,500	8,649	6,701	8,649	7,264
50,500	50,550	8,661	6,709	8,661	7,276
50,550	50,600	8,674	6,716	8,674	7,289
50,600	50,650	8,686	6,724	8,686	7,301
50,650	50,700	8,699	6,731	8,699	7,314
50,700	50,750	8,711	6,739	8,711	7,326
50,750	50,800	8,724	6,746	8,724	7,339
50,800	50,850	8,736	6,754	8,736	7,351
50,850	50,900	8,749	6,761	8,749	7,364
50,900	50,950	8,761	6,769	8,761	7,376
50,950	51,000	8,774	6,776	8,774	7,389
51,000					
51,000	51,050	8,786	6,784	8,786	7,401
51,050	51,100	8,799	6,791	8,799	7,414
51,100	51,150	8,811	6,799	8,811	7,426
51,150	51,200	8,824	6,806	8,824	7,439
51,200	51,250	8,836	6,814	8,836	7,451
51,250	51,300	8,849	6,821	8,849	7,464
51,300	51,350	8,861	6,829	8,861	7,476
51,350	51,400	8,874	6,836	8,874	7,489
51,400	51,450	8,886	6,844	8,886	7,501
51,450	51,500	8,899	6,851	8,899	7,514
51,500	51,550	8,911	6,859	8,911	7,526
51,550	51,600	8,924	6,866	8,924	7,539
51,600	51,650	8,936	6,874	8,936	7,551
51,650	51,700	8,949	6,881	8,949	7,564
51,700	51,750	8,961	6,889	8,961	7,576
51,750	51,800	8,974	6,896	8,974	7,589
51,800	51,850	8,986	6,904	8,986	7,601
51,850	51,900	8,999	6,911	8,999	7,614
51,900	51,950	9,011	6,919	9,011	7,626
51,950	52,000	9,024	6,926	9,024	7,639
52,000					
52,000	52,050	9,036	6,934	9,036	7,651
52,050	52,100	9,049	6,941	9,049	7,664
52,100	52,150	9,061	6,949	9,061	7,676
52,150	52,200	9,074	6,956	9,074	7,689
52,200	52,250	9,086	6,964	9,086	7,701
52,250	52,300	9,099	6,971	9,099	7,714
52,300	52,350	9,111	6,979	9,111	7,726
52,350	52,400	9,124	6,986	9,124	7,739
52,400	52,450	9,136	6,994	9,136	7,751
52,450	52,500	9,149	7,001	9,149	7,764
52,500	52,550	9,161	7,009	9,161	7,776
52,550	52,600	9,174	7,016	9,174	7,789
52,600	52,650	9,186	7,024	9,186	7,801
52,650	52,700	9,199	7,031	9,199	7,814
52,700	52,750	9,211	7,039	9,211	7,826
52,750	52,800	9,224	7,046	9,224	7,839
52,800	52,850	9,236	7,054	9,236	7,851
52,850	52,900	9,249	7,061	9,249	7,864
52,900	52,950	9,261	7,069	9,261	7,876
52,950	53,000	9,274	7,076	9,274	7,889
53,000					
53,000	53,050	9,286	7,084	9,286	7,901
53,050	53,100	9,299	7,091	9,299	7,914
53,100	53,150	9,311	7,099	9,311	7,926
53,150	53,200	9,324	7,106	9,324	7,939
53,200	53,250	9,336	7,114	9,336	7,951
53,250	53,300	9,349	7,121	9,349	7,964
53,300	53,350	9,361	7,129	9,361	7,976
53,350	53,400	9,374	7,136	9,374	7,989
53,400	53,450	9,386	7,144	9,386	8,001
53,450	53,500	9,399	7,151	9,399	8,014
53,500	53,550	9,411	7,159	9,411	8,026
53,550	53,600	9,424	7,166	9,424	8,039
53,600	53,650	9,436	7,174	9,436	8,051
53,650	53,700	9,449	7,181	9,449	8,064
53,700	53,750	9,461	7,189	9,461	8,076
53,750	53,800	9,474	7,196	9,474	8,089
53,800	53,850	9,486	7,204	9,486	8,101
53,850	53,900	9,499	7,211	9,499	8,114
53,900	53,950	9,511	7,219	9,511	8,126
53,950	54,000	9,524	7,226	9,524	8,139
54,000					
54,000	54,050	9,536	7,234	9,536	8,151
54,050	54,100	9,549	7,241	9,549	8,164
54,100	54,150	9,561	7,249	9,561	8,176
54,150	54,200	9,574	7,256	9,574	8,189
54,200	54,250	9,586	7,264	9,586	8,201
54,250	54,300	9,599	7,271	9,599	8,214
54,300	54,350	9,611	7,279	9,611	8,226
54,350	54,400	9,624	7,286	9,624	8,239
54,400	54,450	9,636	7,294	9,636	8,251
54,450	54,500	9,649	7,301	9,649	8,264
54,500	54,550	9,661	7,309	9,661	8,276
54,550	54,600	9,674	7,316	9,674	8,289
54,600	54,650	9,686	7,324	9,686	8,301
54,650	54,700	9,699	7,331	9,699	8,314
54,700	54,750	9,711	7,339	9,711	8,326
54,750	54,800	9,724	7,346	9,724	8,339
54,800	54,850	9,736	7,354	9,736	8,351
54,850	54,900	9,749	7,361	9,749	8,364
54,900	54,950	9,761	7,369	9,761	8,376
54,950	55,000	9,774	7,376	9,774	8,389
55,000					
55,000	55,050	9,786	7,384	9,786	8,401
55,050	55,100	9,799	7,391	9,799	8,414
55,100	55,150	9,811	7,399	9,811	8,426
55,150	55,200	9,824	7,406	9,824	8,439
55,200	55,250	9,836	7,414	9,836	8,451
55,250	55,300	9,849	7,421	9,849	8,464
55,300	55,350	9,861	7,429	9,861	8,476
55,350	55,400	9,874	7,436	9,874	8,489
55,400	55,450	9,886	7,444	9,886	8,501
55,450	55,500	9,899	7,451	9,899	8,514
55,500	55,550	9,911	7,459	9,911	8,526
55,550	55,600	9,924	7,466	9,924	8,539
55,600	55,650	9,936	7,474	9,936	8,551
55,650	55,700	9,949	7,481	9,949	8,564
55,700	55,750	9,961	7,489	9,961	8,576
55,750	55,800	9,974	7,496	9,974	8,589
55,800	55,850	9,986	7,504	9,986	8,601
55,850	55,900	9,999	7,511	9,999	8,614
55,900	55,950	10,011	7,519	10,011	8,626
55,950	56,000	10,024	7,526	10,024	8,639
56,000					
56,000	56,050	10,036	7,534	10,036	8,651
56,050	56,100	10,049	7,541	10,049	8,664
56,100	56,150	10,061	7,549	10,061	8,676
56,150	56,200	10,074	7,556	10,074	8,689
56,200	56,250	10,086	7,564	10,086	8,701
56,250	56,300	10,099	7,571	10,099	8,714
56,300	56,350	10,111	7,579	10,111	8,726
56,350	56,400	10,124	7,586	10,124	8,739
56,400	56,450	10,136	7,594	10,136	8,751
56,450	56,500	10,149	7,601	10,149	8,764
56,500	56,550	10,161	7,609	10,161	8,776
56,550	56,600	10,174	7,616	10,174	8,789
56,600	56,650	10,186	7,624	10,186	8,801
56,650	56,700	10,199	7,631	10,199	8,814
56,700	56,750	10,211	7,639	10,211	8,826
56,750	56,800	10,224	7,646	10,224	8,839
56,800	56,850	10,236	7,654	10,236	8,851
56,850	56,900	10,249	7,661	10,249	8,864
56,900	56,950	10,261	7,669	10,261	8,876
56,950	57,000	10,274	7,676	10,274	8,889

(Continued)

2012 Tax Table—*Continued*

If line 43 (taxable income) is—		And you are—			
At least	But less than	Single	Married filing jointly *	Married filing sepa-rately	Head of a house-hold
		Your tax is—			
57,000					
57,000	57,050	10,286	7,684	10,286	8,901
57,050	57,100	10,299	7,691	10,299	8,914
57,100	57,150	10,311	7,699	10,311	8,926
57,150	57,200	10,324	7,706	10,324	8,939
57,200	57,250	10,336	7,714	10,336	8,951
57,250	57,300	10,349	7,721	10,349	8,964
57,300	57,350	10,361	7,729	10,361	8,976
57,350	57,400	10,374	7,736	10,374	8,989
57,400	57,450	10,386	7,744	10,386	9,001
57,450	57,500	10,399	7,751	10,399	9,014
57,500	57,550	10,411	7,759	10,411	9,026
57,550	57,600	10,424	7,766	10,424	9,039
57,600	57,650	10,436	7,774	10,436	9,051
57,650	57,700	10,449	7,781	10,449	9,064
57,700	57,750	10,461	7,789	10,461	9,076
57,750	57,800	10,474	7,796	10,474	9,089
57,800	57,850	10,486	7,804	10,486	9,101
57,850	57,900	10,499	7,811	10,499	9,114
57,900	57,950	10,511	7,819	10,511	9,126
57,950	58,000	10,524	7,826	10,524	9,139
58,000					
58,000	58,050	10,536	7,834	10,536	9,151
58,050	58,100	10,549	7,841	10,549	9,164
58,100	58,150	10,561	7,849	10,561	9,176
58,150	58,200	10,574	7,856	10,574	9,189
58,200	58,250	10,586	7,864	10,586	9,201
58,250	58,300	10,599	7,871	10,599	9,214
58,300	58,350	10,611	7,879	10,611	9,226
58,350	58,400	10,624	7,886	10,624	9,239
58,400	58,450	10,636	7,894	10,636	9,251
58,450	58,500	10,649	7,901	10,649	9,264
58,500	58,550	10,661	7,909	10,661	9,276
58,550	58,600	10,674	7,916	10,674	9,289
58,600	58,650	10,686	7,924	10,686	9,301
58,650	58,700	10,699	7,931	10,699	9,314
58,700	58,750	10,711	7,939	10,711	9,326
58,750	58,800	10,724	7,946	10,724	9,339
58,800	58,850	10,736	7,954	10,736	9,351
58,850	58,900	10,749	7,961	10,749	9,364
58,900	58,950	10,761	7,969	10,761	9,376
58,950	59,000	10,774	7,976	10,774	9,389
59,000					
59,000	59,050	10,786	7,984	10,786	9,401
59,050	59,100	10,799	7,991	10,799	9,414
59,100	59,150	10,811	7,999	10,811	9,426
59,150	59,200	10,824	8,006	10,824	9,439
59,200	59,250	10,836	8,014	10,836	9,451
59,250	59,300	10,849	8,021	10,849	9,464
59,300	59,350	10,861	8,029	10,861	9,476
59,350	59,400	10,874	8,036	10,874	9,489
59,400	59,450	10,886	8,044	10,886	9,501
59,450	59,500	10,899	8,051	10,899	9,514
59,500	59,550	10,911	8,059	10,911	9,526
59,550	59,600	10,924	8,066	10,924	9,539
59,600	59,650	10,936	8,074	10,936	9,551
59,650	59,700	10,949	8,081	10,949	9,564
59,700	59,750	10,961	8,089	10,961	9,576
59,750	59,800	10,974	8,096	10,974	9,589
59,800	59,850	10,986	8,104	10,986	9,601
59,850	59,900	10,999	8,111	10,999	9,614
59,900	59,950	11,011	8,119	11,011	9,626
59,950	60,000	11,024	8,126	11,024	9,639

If line 43 (taxable income) is—		And you are—			
At least	But less than	Single	Married filing jointly *	Married filing sepa-rately	Head of a house-hold
		Your tax is—			
60,000					
60,000	60,050	11,036	8,134	11,036	9,651
60,050	60,100	11,049	8,141	11,049	9,664
60,100	60,150	11,061	8,149	11,061	9,676
60,150	60,200	11,074	8,156	11,074	9,689
60,200	60,250	11,086	8,164	11,086	9,701
60,250	60,300	11,099	8,171	11,099	9,714
60,300	60,350	11,111	8,179	11,111	9,726
60,350	60,400	11,124	8,186	11,124	9,739
60,400	60,450	11,136	8,194	11,136	9,751
60,450	60,500	11,149	8,201	11,149	9,764
60,500	60,550	11,161	8,209	11,161	9,776
60,550	60,600	11,174	8,216	11,174	9,789
60,600	60,650	11,186	8,224	11,186	9,801
60,650	60,700	11,199	8,231	11,199	9,814
60,700	60,750	11,211	8,239	11,211	9,826
60,750	60,800	11,224	8,246	11,224	9,839
60,800	60,850	11,236	8,254	11,236	9,851
60,850	60,900	11,249	8,261	11,249	9,864
60,900	60,950	11,261	8,269	11,261	9,876
60,950	61,000	11,274	8,276	11,274	9,889
61,000					
61,000	61,050	11,286	8,284	11,286	9,901
61,050	61,100	11,299	8,291	11,299	9,914
61,100	61,150	11,311	8,299	11,311	9,926
61,150	61,200	11,324	8,306	11,324	9,939
61,200	61,250	11,336	8,314	11,336	9,951
61,250	61,300	11,349	8,321	11,349	9,964
61,300	61,350	11,361	8,329	11,361	9,976
61,350	61,400	11,374	8,336	11,374	9,989
61,400	61,450	11,386	8,344	11,386	10,001
61,450	61,500	11,399	8,351	11,399	10,014
61,500	61,550	11,411	8,359	11,411	10,026
61,550	61,600	11,424	8,366	11,424	10,039
61,600	61,650	11,436	8,374	11,436	10,051
61,650	61,700	11,449	8,381	11,449	10,064
61,700	61,750	11,461	8,389	11,461	10,076
61,750	61,800	11,474	8,396	11,474	10,089
61,800	61,850	11,486	8,404	11,486	10,101
61,850	61,900	11,499	8,411	11,499	10,114
61,900	61,950	11,511	8,419	11,511	10,126
61,950	62,000	11,524	8,426	11,524	10,139
62,000					
62,000	62,050	11,536	8,434	11,536	10,151
62,050	62,100	11,549	8,441	11,549	10,164
62,100	62,150	11,561	8,449	11,561	10,176
62,150	62,200	11,574	8,456	11,574	10,189
62,200	62,250	11,586	8,464	11,586	10,201
62,250	62,300	11,599	8,471	11,599	10,214
62,300	62,350	11,611	8,479	11,611	10,226
62,350	62,400	11,624	8,486	11,624	10,239
62,400	62,450	11,636	8,494	11,636	10,251
62,450	62,500	11,649	8,501	11,649	10,264
62,500	62,550	11,661	8,509	11,661	10,276
62,550	62,600	11,674	8,516	11,674	10,289
62,600	62,650	11,686	8,524	11,686	10,301
62,650	62,700	11,699	8,531	11,699	10,314
62,700	62,750	11,711	8,539	11,711	10,326
62,750	62,800	11,724	8,546	11,724	10,339
62,800	62,850	11,736	8,554	11,736	10,351
62,850	62,900	11,749	8,561	11,749	10,364
62,900	62,950	11,761	8,569	11,761	10,376
62,950	63,000	11,774	8,576	11,774	10,389

If line 43 (taxable income) is—		And you are—			
At least	But less than	Single	Married filing jointly *	Married filing sepa-rately	Head of a house-hold
		Your tax is—			
63,000					
63,000	63,050	11,786	8,584	11,786	10,401
63,050	63,100	11,799	8,591	11,799	10,414
63,100	63,150	11,811	8,599	11,811	10,426
63,150	63,200	11,824	8,606	11,824	10,439
63,200	63,250	11,836	8,614	11,836	10,451
63,250	63,300	11,849	8,621	11,849	10,464
63,300	63,350	11,861	8,629	11,861	10,476
63,350	63,400	11,874	8,636	11,874	10,489
63,400	63,450	11,886	8,644	11,886	10,501
63,450	63,500	11,899	8,651	11,899	10,514
63,500	63,550	11,911	8,659	11,911	10,526
63,550	63,600	11,924	8,666	11,924	10,539
63,600	63,650	11,936	8,674	11,936	10,551
63,650	63,700	11,949	8,681	11,949	10,564
63,700	63,750	11,961	8,689	11,961	10,576
63,750	63,800	11,974	8,696	11,974	10,589
63,800	63,850	11,986	8,704	11,986	10,601
63,850	63,900	11,999	8,711	11,999	10,614
63,900	63,950	12,011	8,719	12,011	10,626
63,950	64,000	12,024	8,726	12,024	10,639
64,000					
64,000	64,050	12,036	8,734	12,036	10,651
64,050	64,100	12,049	8,741	12,049	10,664
64,100	64,150	12,061	8,749	12,061	10,676
64,150	64,200	12,074	8,756	12,074	10,689
64,200	64,250	12,086	8,764	12,086	10,701
64,250	64,300	12,099	8,771	12,099	10,714
64,300	64,350	12,111	8,779	12,111	10,726
64,350	64,400	12,124	8,786	12,124	10,739
64,400	64,450	12,136	8,794	12,136	10,751
64,450	64,500	12,149	8,801	12,149	10,764
64,500	64,550	12,161	8,809	12,161	10,776
64,550	64,600	12,174	8,816	12,174	10,789
64,600	64,650	12,186	8,824	12,186	10,801
64,650	64,700	12,199	8,831	12,199	10,814
64,700	64,750	12,211	8,839	12,211	10,826
64,750	64,800	12,224	8,846	12,224	10,839
64,800	64,850	12,236	8,854	12,236	10,851
64,850	64,900	12,249	8,861	12,249	10,864
64,900	64,950	12,261	8,869	12,261	10,876
64,950	65,000	12,274	8,876	12,274	10,889
65,000					
65,000	65,050	12,286	8,884	12,286	10,901
65,050	65,100	12,299	8,891	12,299	10,914
65,100	65,150	12,311	8,899	12,311	10,926
65,150	65,200	12,324	8,906	12,324	10,939
65,200	65,250	12,336	8,914	12,336	10,951
65,250	65,300	12,349	8,921	12,349	10,964
65,300	65,350	12,361	8,929	12,361	10,976
65,350	65,400	12,374	8,936	12,374	10,989
65,400	65,450	12,386	8,944	12,386	11,001
65,450	65,500	12,399	8,951	12,399	11,014
65,500	65,550	12,411	8,959	12,411	11,026
65,550	65,600	12,424	8,966	12,424	11,039
65,600	65,650	12,436	8,974	12,436	11,051
65,650	65,700	12,449	8,981	12,449	11,064
65,700	65,750	12,461	8,989	12,461	11,076
65,750	65,800	12,474	8,996	12,474	11,089
65,800	65,850	12,486	9,004	12,486	11,101
65,850	65,900	12,499	9,011	12,499	11,114
65,900	65,950	12,511	9,019	12,511	11,126
65,950	66,000	12,524	9,026	12,524	11,139

(Continued)

2012 Tax Table—*Continued*

If line 43 (taxable income) is—		And you are—			
At least	But less than	Single	Married filing jointly *	Married filing sepa-rately	Head of a house-hold
		Your tax is—			
66,000					
66,000	66,050	12,536	9,034	12,536	11,151
66,050	66,100	12,549	9,041	12,549	11,164
66,100	66,150	12,561	9,049	12,561	11,176
66,150	66,200	12,574	9,056	12,574	11,189
66,200	66,250	12,586	9,064	12,586	11,201
66,250	66,300	12,599	9,071	12,599	11,214
66,300	66,350	12,611	9,079	12,611	11,226
66,350	66,400	12,624	9,086	12,624	11,239
66,400	66,450	12,636	9,094	12,636	11,251
66,450	66,500	12,649	9,101	12,649	11,264
66,500	66,550	12,661	9,109	12,661	11,276
66,550	66,600	12,674	9,116	12,674	11,289
66,600	66,650	12,686	9,124	12,686	11,301
66,650	66,700	12,699	9,131	12,699	11,314
66,700	66,750	12,711	9,139	12,711	11,326
66,750	66,800	12,724	9,146	12,724	11,339
66,800	66,850	12,736	9,154	12,736	11,351
66,850	66,900	12,749	9,161	12,749	11,364
66,900	66,950	12,761	9,169	12,761	11,376
66,950	67,000	12,774	9,176	12,774	11,389
67,000					
67,000	67,050	12,786	9,184	12,786	11,401
67,050	67,100	12,799	9,191	12,799	11,414
67,100	67,150	12,811	9,199	12,811	11,426
67,150	67,200	12,824	9,206	12,824	11,439
67,200	67,250	12,836	9,214	12,836	11,451
67,250	67,300	12,849	9,221	12,849	11,464
67,300	67,350	12,861	9,229	12,861	11,476
67,350	67,400	12,874	9,236	12,874	11,489
67,400	67,450	12,886	9,244	12,886	11,501
67,450	67,500	12,899	9,251	12,899	11,514
67,500	67,550	12,911	9,259	12,911	11,526
67,550	67,600	12,924	9,266	12,924	11,539
67,600	67,650	12,936	9,274	12,936	11,551
67,650	67,700	12,949	9,281	12,949	11,564
67,700	67,750	12,961	9,289	12,961	11,576
67,750	67,800	12,974	9,296	12,974	11,589
67,800	67,850	12,986	9,304	12,986	11,601
67,850	67,900	12,999	9,311	12,999	11,614
67,900	67,950	13,011	9,319	13,011	11,626
67,950	68,000	13,024	9,326	13,024	11,639
68,000					
68,000	68,050	13,036	9,334	13,036	11,651
68,050	68,100	13,049	9,341	13,049	11,664
68,100	68,150	13,061	9,349	13,061	11,676
68,150	68,200	13,074	9,356	13,074	11,689
68,200	68,250	13,086	9,364	13,086	11,701
68,250	68,300	13,099	9,371	13,099	11,714
68,300	68,350	13,111	9,379	13,111	11,726
68,350	68,400	13,124	9,386	13,124	11,739
68,400	68,450	13,136	9,394	13,136	11,751
68,450	68,500	13,149	9,401	13,149	11,764
68,500	68,550	13,161	9,409	13,161	11,776
68,550	68,600	13,174	9,416	13,174	11,789
68,600	68,650	13,186	9,424	13,186	11,801
68,650	68,700	13,199	9,431	13,199	11,814
68,700	68,750	13,211	9,439	13,211	11,826
68,750	68,800	13,224	9,446	13,224	11,839
68,800	68,850	13,236	9,454	13,236	11,851
68,850	68,900	13,249	9,461	13,249	11,864
68,900	68,950	13,261	9,469	13,261	11,876
68,950	69,000	13,274	9,476	13,274	11,889
69,000					
69,000	69,050	13,286	9,484	13,286	11,901
69,050	69,100	13,299	9,491	13,299	11,914
69,100	69,150	13,311	9,499	13,311	11,926
69,150	69,200	13,324	9,506	13,324	11,939
69,200	69,250	13,336	9,514	13,336	11,951
69,250	69,300	13,349	9,521	13,349	11,964
69,300	69,350	13,361	9,529	13,361	11,976
69,350	69,400	13,374	9,536	13,374	11,989
69,400	69,450	13,386	9,544	13,386	12,001
69,450	69,500	13,399	9,551	13,399	12,014
69,500	69,550	13,411	9,559	13,411	12,026
69,550	69,600	13,424	9,566	13,424	12,039
69,600	69,650	13,436	9,574	13,436	12,051
69,650	69,700	13,449	9,581	13,449	12,064
69,700	69,750	13,461	9,589	13,461	12,076
69,750	69,800	13,474	9,596	13,474	12,089
69,800	69,850	13,486	9,604	13,486	12,101
69,850	69,900	13,499	9,611	13,499	12,114
69,900	69,950	13,511	9,619	13,511	12,126
69,950	70,000	13,524	9,626	13,524	12,139
70,000					
70,000	70,050	13,536	9,634	13,536	12,151
70,050	70,100	13,549	9,641	13,549	12,164
70,100	70,150	13,561	9,649	13,561	12,176
70,150	70,200	13,574	9,656	13,574	12,189
70,200	70,250	13,586	9,664	13,586	12,201
70,250	70,300	13,599	9,671	13,599	12,214
70,300	70,350	13,611	9,679	13,611	12,226
70,350	70,400	13,624	9,686	13,624	12,239
70,400	70,450	13,636	9,694	13,636	12,251
70,450	70,500	13,649	9,701	13,649	12,264
70,500	70,550	13,661	9,709	13,661	12,276
70,550	70,600	13,674	9,716	13,674	12,289
70,600	70,650	13,686	9,724	13,686	12,301
70,650	70,700	13,699	9,731	13,699	12,314
70,700	70,750	13,711	9,741	13,711	12,326
70,750	70,800	13,724	9,754	13,724	12,339
70,800	70,850	13,736	9,766	13,736	12,351
70,850	70,900	13,749	9,779	13,749	12,364
70,900	70,950	13,761	9,791	13,761	12,376
70,950	71,000	13,774	9,804	13,774	12,389
71,000					
71,000	71,050	13,786	9,816	13,786	12,401
71,050	71,100	13,799	9,829	13,799	12,414
71,100	71,150	13,811	9,841	13,811	12,426
71,150	71,200	13,824	9,854	13,824	12,439
71,200	71,250	13,836	9,866	13,836	12,451
71,250	71,300	13,849	9,879	13,849	12,464
71,300	71,350	13,861	9,891	13,861	12,476
71,350	71,400	13,874	9,904	13,875	12,489
71,400	71,450	13,886	9,916	13,889	12,501
71,450	71,500	13,899	9,929	13,903	12,514
71,500	71,550	13,911	9,941	13,917	12,526
71,550	71,600	13,924	9,954	13,931	12,539
71,600	71,650	13,936	9,966	13,945	12,551
71,650	71,700	13,949	9,979	13,959	12,564
71,700	71,750	13,961	9,991	13,973	12,576
71,750	71,800	13,974	10,004	13,987	12,589
71,800	71,850	13,986	10,016	14,001	12,601
71,850	71,900	13,999	10,029	14,015	12,614
71,900	71,950	14,011	10,041	14,029	12,626
71,950	72,000	14,024	10,054	14,043	12,639
72,000					
72,000	72,050	14,036	10,066	14,057	12,651
72,050	72,100	14,049	10,079	14,071	12,664
72,100	72,150	14,061	10,091	14,085	12,676
72,150	72,200	14,074	10,104	14,099	12,689
72,200	72,250	14,086	10,116	14,113	12,701
72,250	72,300	14,099	10,129	14,127	12,714
72,300	72,350	14,111	10,141	14,141	12,726
72,350	72,400	14,124	10,154	14,155	12,739
72,400	72,450	14,136	10,166	14,169	12,751
72,450	72,500	14,149	10,179	14,183	12,764
72,500	72,550	14,161	10,191	14,197	12,776
72,550	72,600	14,174	10,204	14,211	12,789
72,600	72,650	14,186	10,216	14,225	12,801
72,650	72,700	14,199	10,229	14,239	12,814
72,700	72,750	14,211	10,241	14,253	12,826
72,750	72,800	14,224	10,254	14,267	12,839
72,800	72,850	14,236	10,266	14,281	12,851
72,850	72,900	14,249	10,279	14,295	12,864
72,900	72,950	14,261	10,291	14,309	12,876
72,950	73,000	14,274	10,304	14,323	12,889
73,000					
73,000	73,050	14,286	10,316	14,337	12,901
73,050	73,100	14,299	10,329	14,351	12,914
73,100	73,150	14,311	10,341	14,365	12,926
73,150	73,200	14,324	10,354	14,379	12,939
73,200	73,250	14,336	10,366	14,393	12,951
73,250	73,300	14,349	10,379	14,407	12,964
73,300	73,350	14,361	10,391	14,421	12,976
73,350	73,400	14,374	10,404	14,435	12,989
73,400	73,450	14,386	10,416	14,449	13,001
73,450	73,500	14,399	10,429	14,463	13,014
73,500	73,550	14,411	10,441	14,477	13,026
73,550	73,600	14,424	10,454	14,491	13,039
73,600	73,650	14,436	10,466	14,505	13,051
73,650	73,700	14,449	10,479	14,519	13,064
73,700	73,750	14,461	10,491	14,533	13,076
73,750	73,800	14,474	10,504	14,547	13,089
73,800	73,850	14,486	10,516	14,561	13,101
73,850	73,900	14,499	10,529	14,575	13,114
73,900	73,950	14,511	10,541	14,589	13,126
73,950	74,000	14,524	10,554	14,603	13,139
74,000					
74,000	74,050	14,536	10,566	14,617	13,151
74,050	74,100	14,549	10,579	14,631	13,164
74,100	74,150	14,561	10,591	14,645	13,176
74,150	74,200	14,574	10,604	14,659	13,189
74,200	74,250	14,586	10,616	14,673	13,201
74,250	74,300	14,599	10,629	14,687	13,214
74,300	74,350	14,611	10,641	14,701	13,226
74,350	74,400	14,624	10,654	14,715	13,239
74,400	74,450	14,636	10,666	14,729	13,251
74,450	74,500	14,649	10,679	14,743	13,264
74,500	74,550	14,661	10,691	14,757	13,276
74,550	74,600	14,674	10,704	14,771	13,289
74,600	74,650	14,686	10,716	14,785	13,301
74,650	74,700	14,699	10,729	14,799	13,314
74,700	74,750	14,711	10,741	14,813	13,326
74,750	74,800	14,724	10,754	14,827	13,339
74,800	74,850	14,736	10,766	14,841	13,351
74,850	74,900	14,749	10,779	14,855	13,364
74,900	74,950	14,761	10,791	14,869	13,376
74,950	75,000	14,774	10,804	14,883	13,389

(Continued)

2012 Tax Table—*Continued*

75,000

If line 43 (taxable income) is— At least	But less than	And you are— Single	Married filing jointly *	Married filing separately	Head of a household
		Your tax is—			
75,000	75,050	14,786	10,816	14,897	13,401
75,050	75,100	14,799	10,829	14,911	13,414
75,100	75,150	14,811	10,841	14,925	13,426
75,150	75,200	14,824	10,854	14,939	13,439
75,200	75,250	14,836	10,866	14,953	13,451
75,250	75,300	14,849	10,879	14,967	13,464
75,300	75,350	14,861	10,891	14,981	13,476
75,350	75,400	14,874	10,904	14,995	13,489
75,400	75,450	14,886	10,916	15,009	13,501
75,450	75,500	14,899	10,929	15,023	13,514
75,500	75,550	14,911	10,941	15,037	13,526
75,550	75,600	14,924	10,954	15,051	13,539
75,600	75,650	14,936	10,966	15,065	13,551
75,650	75,700	14,949	10,979	15,079	13,564
75,700	75,750	14,961	10,991	15,093	13,576
75,750	75,800	14,974	11,004	15,107	13,589
75,800	75,850	14,986	11,016	15,121	13,601
75,850	75,900	14,999	11,029	15,135	13,614
75,900	75,950	15,011	11,041	15,149	13,626
75,950	76,000	15,024	11,054	15,163	13,639

76,000

At least	But less than	Single	Married filing jointly *	Married filing separately	Head of a household
76,000	76,050	15,036	11,066	15,177	13,651
76,050	76,100	15,049	11,079	15,191	13,664
76,100	76,150	15,061	11,091	15,205	13,676
76,150	76,200	15,074	11,104	15,219	13,689
76,200	76,250	15,086	11,116	15,233	13,701
76,250	76,300	15,099	11,129	15,247	13,714
76,300	76,350	15,111	11,141	15,261	13,726
76,350	76,400	15,124	11,154	15,275	13,739
76,400	76,450	15,136	11,166	15,289	13,751
76,450	76,500	15,149	11,179	15,303	13,764
76,500	76,550	15,161	11,191	15,317	13,776
76,550	76,600	15,174	11,204	15,331	13,789
76,600	76,650	15,186	11,216	15,345	13,801
76,650	76,700	15,199	11,229	15,359	13,814
76,700	76,750	15,211	11,241	15,373	13,826
76,750	76,800	15,224	11,254	15,387	13,839
76,800	76,850	15,236	11,266	15,401	13,851
76,850	76,900	15,249	11,279	15,415	13,864
76,900	76,950	15,261	11,291	15,429	13,876
76,950	77,000	15,274	11,304	15,443	13,889

77,000

At least	But less than	Single	Married filing jointly *	Married filing separately	Head of a household
77,000	77,050	15,286	11,316	15,457	13,901
77,050	77,100	15,299	11,329	15,471	13,914
77,100	77,150	15,311	11,341	15,485	13,926
77,150	77,200	15,324	11,354	15,499	13,939
77,200	77,250	15,336	11,366	15,513	13,951
77,250	77,300	15,349	11,379	15,527	13,964
77,300	77,350	15,361	11,391	15,541	13,976
77,350	77,400	15,374	11,404	15,555	13,989
77,400	77,450	15,386	11,416	15,569	14,001
77,450	77,500	15,399	11,429	15,583	14,014
77,500	77,550	15,411	11,441	15,597	14,026
77,550	77,600	15,424	11,454	15,611	14,039
77,600	77,650	15,436	11,466	15,625	14,051
77,650	77,700	15,449	11,479	15,639	14,064
77,700	77,750	15,461	11,491	15,653	14,076
77,750	77,800	15,474	11,504	15,667	14,089
77,800	77,850	15,486	11,516	15,681	14,101
77,850	77,900	15,499	11,529	15,695	14,114
77,900	77,950	15,511	11,541	15,709	14,126
77,950	78,000	15,524	11,554	15,723	14,139

78,000

At least	But less than	Single	Married filing jointly *	Married filing separately	Head of a household
78,000	78,050	15,536	11,566	15,737	14,151
78,050	78,100	15,549	11,579	15,751	14,164
78,100	78,150	15,561	11,591	15,765	14,176
78,150	78,200	15,574	11,604	15,779	14,189
78,200	78,250	15,586	11,616	15,793	14,201
78,250	78,300	15,599	11,629	15,807	14,214
78,300	78,350	15,611	11,641	15,821	14,226
78,350	78,400	15,624	11,654	15,835	14,239
78,400	78,450	15,636	11,666	15,849	14,251
78,450	78,500	15,649	11,679	15,863	14,264
78,500	78,550	15,661	11,691	15,877	14,276
78,550	78,600	15,674	11,704	15,891	14,289
78,600	78,650	15,686	11,716	15,905	14,301
78,650	78,700	15,699	11,729	15,919	14,314
78,700	78,750	15,711	11,741	15,933	14,326
78,750	78,800	15,724	11,754	15,947	14,339
78,800	78,850	15,736	11,766	15,961	14,351
78,850	78,900	15,749	11,779	15,975	14,364
78,900	78,950	15,761	11,791	15,989	14,376
78,950	79,000	15,774	11,804	16,003	14,389

79,000

At least	But less than	Single	Married filing jointly *	Married filing separately	Head of a household
79,000	79,050	15,786	11,816	16,017	14,401
79,050	79,100	15,799	11,829	16,031	14,414
79,100	79,150	15,811	11,841	16,045	14,426
79,150	79,200	15,824	11,854	16,059	14,439
79,200	79,250	15,836	11,866	16,073	14,451
79,250	79,300	15,849	11,879	16,087	14,464
79,300	79,350	15,861	11,891	16,101	14,476
79,350	79,400	15,874	11,904	16,115	14,489
79,400	79,450	15,886	11,916	16,129	14,501
79,450	79,500	15,899	11,929	16,143	14,514
79,500	79,550	15,911	11,941	16,157	14,526
79,550	79,600	15,924	11,954	16,171	14,539
79,600	79,650	15,936	11,966	16,185	14,551
79,650	79,700	15,949	11,979	16,199	14,564
79,700	79,750	15,961	11,991	16,213	14,576
79,750	79,800	15,974	12,004	16,227	14,589
79,800	79,850	15,986	12,016	16,241	14,601
79,850	79,900	15,999	12,029	16,255	14,614
79,900	79,950	16,011	12,041	16,269	14,626
79,950	80,000	16,024	12,054	16,283	14,639

80,000

At least	But less than	Single	Married filing jointly *	Married filing separately	Head of a household
80,000	80,050	16,036	12,066	16,297	14,651
80,050	80,100	16,049	12,079	16,311	14,664
80,100	80,150	16,061	12,091	16,325	14,676
80,150	80,200	16,074	12,104	16,339	14,689
80,200	80,250	16,086	12,116	16,353	14,701
80,250	80,300	16,099	12,129	16,367	14,714
80,300	80,350	16,111	12,141	16,381	14,726
80,350	80,400	16,124	12,154	16,395	14,739
80,400	80,450	16,136	12,166	16,409	14,751
80,450	80,500	16,149	12,179	16,423	14,764
80,500	80,550	16,161	12,191	16,437	14,776
80,550	80,600	16,174	12,204	16,451	14,789
80,600	80,650	16,186	12,216	16,465	14,801
80,650	80,700	16,199	12,229	16,479	14,814
80,700	80,750	16,211	12,241	16,493	14,826
80,750	80,800	16,224	12,254	16,507	14,839
80,800	80,850	16,236	12,266	16,521	14,851
80,850	80,900	16,249	12,279	16,535	14,864
80,900	80,950	16,261	12,291	16,549	14,876
80,950	81,000	16,274	12,304	16,563	14,889

81,000

At least	But less than	Single	Married filing jointly *	Married filing separately	Head of a household
81,000	81,050	16,286	12,316	16,577	14,901
81,050	81,100	16,299	12,329	16,591	14,914
81,100	81,150	16,311	12,341	16,605	14,926
81,150	81,200	16,324	12,354	16,619	14,939
81,200	81,250	16,336	12,366	16,633	14,951
81,250	81,300	16,349	12,379	16,647	14,964
81,300	81,350	16,361	12,391	16,661	14,976
81,350	81,400	16,374	12,404	16,675	14,989
81,400	81,450	16,386	12,416	16,689	15,001
81,450	81,500	16,399	12,429	16,703	15,014
81,500	81,550	16,411	12,441	16,717	15,026
81,550	81,600	16,424	12,454	16,731	15,039
81,600	81,650	16,436	12,466	16,745	15,051
81,650	81,700	16,449	12,479	16,759	15,064
81,700	81,750	16,461	12,491	16,773	15,076
81,750	81,800	16,474	12,504	16,787	15,089
81,800	81,850	16,486	12,516	16,801	15,101
81,850	81,900	16,499	12,529	16,815	15,114
81,900	81,950	16,511	12,541	16,829	15,126
81,950	82,000	16,524	12,554	16,843	15,139

82,000

At least	But less than	Single	Married filing jointly *	Married filing separately	Head of a household
82,000	82,050	16,536	12,566	16,857	15,151
82,050	82,100	16,549	12,579	16,871	15,164
82,100	82,150	16,561	12,591	16,885	15,176
82,150	82,200	16,574	12,604	16,899	15,189
82,200	82,250	16,586	12,616	16,913	15,201
82,250	82,300	16,599	12,629	16,927	15,214
82,300	82,350	16,611	12,641	16,941	15,226
82,350	82,400	16,624	12,654	16,955	15,239
82,400	82,450	16,636	12,666	16,969	15,251
82,450	82,500	16,649	12,679	16,983	15,264
82,500	82,550	16,661	12,691	16,997	15,276
82,550	82,600	16,674	12,704	17,011	15,289
82,600	82,650	16,686	12,716	17,025	15,301
82,650	82,700	16,699	12,729	17,039	15,314
82,700	82,750	16,711	12,741	17,053	15,326
82,750	82,800	16,724	12,754	17,067	15,339
82,800	82,850	16,736	12,766	17,081	15,351
82,850	82,900	16,749	12,779	17,095	15,364
82,900	82,950	16,761	12,791	17,109	15,376
82,950	83,000	16,774	12,804	17,123	15,389

83,000

At least	But less than	Single	Married filing jointly *	Married filing separately	Head of a household
83,000	83,050	16,786	12,816	17,137	15,401
83,050	83,100	16,799	12,829	17,151	15,414
83,100	83,150	16,811	12,841	17,165	15,426
83,150	83,200	16,824	12,854	17,179	15,439
83,200	83,250	16,836	12,866	17,193	15,451
83,250	83,300	16,849	12,879	17,207	15,464
83,300	83,350	16,861	12,891	17,221	15,476
83,350	83,400	16,874	12,904	17,235	15,489
83,400	83,450	16,886	12,916	17,249	15,501
83,450	83,500	16,899	12,929	17,263	15,514
83,500	83,550	16,911	12,941	17,277	15,526
83,550	83,600	16,924	12,954	17,291	15,539
83,600	83,650	16,936	12,966	17,305	15,551
83,650	83,700	16,949	12,979	17,319	15,564
83,700	83,750	16,961	12,991	17,333	15,576
83,750	83,800	16,974	13,004	17,347	15,589
83,800	83,850	16,986	13,016	17,361	15,601
83,850	83,900	16,999	13,029	17,375	15,614
83,900	83,950	17,011	13,041	17,389	15,626
83,950	84,000	17,024	13,054	17,403	15,639

(Continued)

2012 Tax Table—*Continued*

If line 43 (taxable income) is—		And you are—			
At least	But less than	Single	Married filing jointly *	Married filing separately	Head of a household
		Your tax is—			
84,000					
84,000	84,050	17,036	13,066	17,417	15,651
84,050	84,100	17,049	13,079	17,431	15,664
84,100	84,150	17,061	13,091	17,445	15,676
84,150	84,200	17,074	13,104	17,459	15,689
84,200	84,250	17,086	13,116	17,473	15,701
84,250	84,300	17,099	13,129	17,487	15,714
84,300	84,350	17,111	13,141	17,501	15,726
84,350	84,400	17,124	13,154	17,515	15,739
84,400	84,450	17,136	13,166	17,529	15,751
84,450	84,500	17,149	13,179	17,543	15,764
84,500	84,550	17,161	13,191	17,557	15,776
84,550	84,600	17,174	13,204	17,571	15,789
84,600	84,650	17,186	13,216	17,585	15,801
84,650	84,700	17,199	13,229	17,599	15,814
84,700	84,750	17,211	13,241	17,613	15,826
84,750	84,800	17,224	13,254	17,627	15,839
84,800	84,850	17,236	13,266	17,641	15,851
84,850	84,900	17,249	13,279	17,655	15,864
84,900	84,950	17,261	13,291	17,669	15,876
84,950	85,000	17,274	13,304	17,683	15,889
85,000					
85,000	85,050	17,286	13,316	17,697	15,901
85,050	85,100	17,299	13,329	17,711	15,914
85,100	85,150	17,311	13,341	17,725	15,926
85,150	85,200	17,324	13,354	17,739	15,939
85,200	85,250	17,336	13,366	17,753	15,951
85,250	85,300	17,349	13,379	17,767	15,964
85,300	85,350	17,361	13,391	17,781	15,976
85,350	85,400	17,374	13,404	17,795	15,989
85,400	85,450	17,386	13,416	17,809	16,001
85,450	85,500	17,399	13,429	17,823	16,014
85,500	85,550	17,411	13,441	17,837	16,026
85,550	85,600	17,424	13,454	17,851	16,039
85,600	85,650	17,436	13,466	17,865	16,051
85,650	85,700	17,450	13,479	17,879	16,064
85,700	85,750	17,464	13,491	17,893	16,076
85,750	85,800	17,478	13,504	17,907	16,089
85,800	85,850	17,492	13,516	17,921	16,101
85,850	85,900	17,506	13,529	17,935	16,114
85,900	85,950	17,520	13,541	17,949	16,126
85,950	86,000	17,534	13,554	17,963	16,139
86,000					
86,000	86,050	17,548	13,566	17,977	16,151
86,050	86,100	17,562	13,579	17,991	16,164
86,100	86,150	17,576	13,591	18,005	16,176
86,150	86,200	17,590	13,604	18,019	16,189
86,200	86,250	17,604	13,616	18,033	16,201
86,250	86,300	17,618	13,629	18,047	16,214
86,300	86,350	17,632	13,641	18,061	16,226
86,350	86,400	17,646	13,654	18,075	16,239
86,400	86,450	17,660	13,666	18,089	16,251
86,450	86,500	17,674	13,679	18,103	16,264
86,500	86,550	17,688	13,691	18,117	16,276
86,550	86,600	17,702	13,704	18,131	16,289
86,600	86,650	17,716	13,716	18,145	16,301
86,650	86,700	17,730	13,729	18,159	16,314
86,700	86,750	17,744	13,741	18,173	16,326
86,750	86,800	17,758	13,754	18,187	16,339
86,800	86,850	17,772	13,766	18,201	16,351
86,850	86,900	17,786	13,779	18,215	16,364
86,900	86,950	17,800	13,791	18,229	16,376
86,950	87,000	17,814	13,804	18,243	16,389

If line 43 (taxable income) is—		And you are—			
At least	But less than	Single	Married filing jointly *	Married filing separately	Head of a household
		Your tax is—			
87,000					
87,000	87,050	17,828	13,816	18,257	16,401
87,050	87,100	17,842	13,829	18,271	16,414
87,100	87,150	17,856	13,841	18,285	16,426
87,150	87,200	17,870	13,854	18,299	16,439
87,200	87,250	17,884	13,866	18,313	16,451
87,250	87,300	17,898	13,879	18,327	16,464
87,300	87,350	17,912	13,891	18,341	16,476
87,350	87,400	17,926	13,904	18,355	16,489
87,400	87,450	17,940	13,916	18,369	16,501
87,450	87,500	17,954	13,929	18,383	16,514
87,500	87,550	17,968	13,941	18,397	16,526
87,550	87,600	17,982	13,954	18,411	16,539
87,600	87,650	17,996	13,966	18,425	16,551
87,650	87,700	18,010	13,979	18,439	16,564
87,700	87,750	18,024	13,991	18,453	16,576
87,750	87,800	18,038	14,004	18,467	16,589
87,800	87,850	18,052	14,016	18,481	16,601
87,850	87,900	18,066	14,029	18,495	16,614
87,900	87,950	18,080	14,041	18,509	16,626
87,950	88,000	18,094	14,054	18,523	16,639
88,000					
88,000	88,050	18,108	14,066	18,537	16,651
88,050	88,100	18,122	14,079	18,551	16,664
88,100	88,150	18,136	14,091	18,565	16,676
88,150	88,200	18,150	14,104	18,579	16,689
88,200	88,250	18,164	14,116	18,593	16,701
88,250	88,300	18,178	14,129	18,607	16,714
88,300	88,350	18,192	14,141	18,621	16,726
88,350	88,400	18,206	14,154	18,635	16,739
88,400	88,450	18,220	14,166	18,649	16,751
88,450	88,500	18,234	14,179	18,663	16,764
88,500	88,550	18,248	14,191	18,677	16,776
88,550	88,600	18,262	14,204	18,691	16,789
88,600	88,650	18,276	14,216	18,705	16,801
88,650	88,700	18,290	14,229	18,719	16,814
88,700	88,750	18,304	14,241	18,733	16,826
88,750	88,800	18,318	14,254	18,747	16,839
88,800	88,850	18,332	14,266	18,761	16,851
88,850	88,900	18,346	14,279	18,775	16,864
88,900	88,950	18,360	14,291	18,789	16,876
88,950	89,000	18,374	14,304	18,803	16,889
89,000					
89,000	89,050	18,388	14,316	18,817	16,901
89,050	89,100	18,402	14,329	18,831	16,914
89,100	89,150	18,416	14,341	18,845	16,926
89,150	89,200	18,430	14,354	18,859	16,939
89,200	89,250	18,444	14,366	18,873	16,951
89,250	89,300	18,458	14,379	18,887	16,964
89,300	89,350	18,472	14,391	18,901	16,976
89,350	89,400	18,486	14,404	18,915	16,989
89,400	89,450	18,500	14,416	18,929	17,001
89,450	89,500	18,514	14,429	18,943	17,014
89,500	89,550	18,528	14,441	18,957	17,026
89,550	89,600	18,542	14,454	18,971	17,039
89,600	89,650	18,556	14,466	18,985	17,051
89,650	89,700	18,570	14,479	18,999	17,064
89,700	89,750	18,584	14,491	19,013	17,076
89,750	89,800	18,598	14,504	19,027	17,089
89,800	89,850	18,612	14,516	19,041	17,101
89,850	89,900	18,626	14,529	19,055	17,114
89,900	89,950	18,640	14,541	19,069	17,126
89,950	90,000	18,654	14,554	19,083	17,139

If line 43 (taxable income) is—		And you are—			
At least	But less than	Single	Married filing jointly *	Married filing separately	Head of a household
		Your tax is—			
90,000					
90,000	90,050	18,668	14,566	19,097	17,151
90,050	90,100	18,682	14,579	19,111	17,164
90,100	90,150	18,696	14,591	19,125	17,176
90,150	90,200	18,710	14,604	19,139	17,189
90,200	90,250	18,724	14,616	19,153	17,201
90,250	90,300	18,738	14,629	19,167	17,214
90,300	90,350	18,752	14,641	19,181	17,226
90,350	90,400	18,766	14,654	19,195	17,239
90,400	90,450	18,780	14,666	19,209	17,251
90,450	90,500	18,794	14,679	19,223	17,264
90,500	90,550	18,808	14,691	19,237	17,276
90,550	90,600	18,822	14,704	19,251	17,289
90,600	90,650	18,836	14,716	19,265	17,301
90,650	90,700	18,850	14,729	19,279	17,314
90,700	90,750	18,864	14,741	19,293	17,326
90,750	90,800	18,878	14,754	19,307	17,339
90,800	90,850	18,892	14,766	19,321	17,351
90,850	90,900	18,906	14,779	19,335	17,364
90,900	90,950	18,920	14,791	19,349	17,376
90,950	91,000	18,934	14,804	19,363	17,389
91,000					
91,000	91,050	18,948	14,816	19,377	17,401
91,050	91,100	18,962	14,829	19,391	17,414
91,100	91,150	18,976	14,841	19,405	17,426
91,150	91,200	18,990	14,854	19,419	17,439
91,200	91,250	19,004	14,866	19,433	17,451
91,250	91,300	19,018	14,879	19,447	17,464
91,300	91,350	19,032	14,891	19,461	17,476
91,350	91,400	19,046	14,904	19,475	17,489
91,400	91,450	19,060	14,916	19,489	17,501
91,450	91,500	19,074	14,929	19,503	17,514
91,500	91,550	19,088	14,941	19,517	17,526
91,550	91,600	19,102	14,954	19,531	17,539
91,600	91,650	19,116	14,966	19,545	17,551
91,650	91,700	19,130	14,979	19,559	17,564
91,700	91,750	19,144	14,991	19,573	17,576
91,750	91,800	19,158	15,004	19,587	17,589
91,800	91,850	19,172	15,016	19,601	17,601
91,850	91,900	19,186	15,029	19,615	17,614
91,900	91,950	19,200	15,041	19,629	17,626
91,950	92,000	19,214	15,054	19,643	17,639
92,000					
92,000	92,050	19,228	15,066	19,657	17,651
92,050	92,100	19,242	15,079	19,671	17,664
92,100	92,150	19,256	15,091	19,685	17,676
92,150	92,200	19,270	15,104	19,699	17,689
92,200	92,250	19,284	15,116	19,713	17,701
92,250	92,300	19,298	15,129	19,727	17,714
92,300	92,350	19,312	15,141	19,741	17,726
92,350	92,400	19,326	15,154	19,755	17,739
92,400	92,450	19,340	15,166	19,769	17,751
92,450	92,500	19,354	15,179	19,783	17,764
92,500	92,550	19,368	15,191	19,797	17,776
92,550	92,600	19,382	15,204	19,811	17,789
92,600	92,650	19,396	15,216	19,825	17,801
92,650	92,700	19,410	15,229	19,839	17,814
92,700	92,750	19,424	15,241	19,853	17,826
92,750	92,800	19,438	15,254	19,867	17,839
92,800	92,850	19,452	15,266	19,881	17,851
92,850	92,900	19,466	15,279	19,895	17,864
92,900	92,950	19,480	15,291	19,909	17,876
92,950	93,000	19,494	15,304	19,923	17,889

(Continued)

2012 Tax Table—*Continued*

If line 43 (taxable income) is—		And you are—			
At least	But less than	Single	Married filing jointly *	Married filing sepa- rately	Head of a house- hold
		Your tax is—			
93,000					
93,000	93,050	19,508	15,316	19,937	17,901
93,050	93,100	19,522	15,329	19,951	17,914
93,100	93,150	19,536	15,341	19,965	17,926
93,150	93,200	19,550	15,354	19,979	17,939
93,200	93,250	19,564	15,366	19,993	17,951
93,250	93,300	19,578	15,379	20,007	17,964
93,300	93,350	19,592	15,391	20,021	17,976
93,350	93,400	19,606	15,404	20,035	17,989
93,400	93,450	19,620	15,416	20,049	18,001
93,450	93,500	19,634	15,429	20,063	18,014
93,500	93,550	19,648	15,441	20,077	18,026
93,550	93,600	19,662	15,454	20,091	18,039
93,600	93,650	19,676	15,466	20,105	18,051
93,650	93,700	19,690	15,479	20,119	18,064
93,700	93,750	19,704	15,491	20,133	18,076
93,750	93,800	19,718	15,504	20,147	18,089
93,800	93,850	19,732	15,516	20,161	18,101
93,850	93,900	19,746	15,529	20,175	18,114
93,900	93,950	19,760	15,541	20,189	18,126
93,950	94,000	19,774	15,554	20,203	18,139
94,000					
94,000	94,050	19,788	15,566	20,217	18,151
94,050	94,100	19,802	15,579	20,231	18,164
94,100	94,150	19,816	15,591	20,245	18,176
94,150	94,200	19,830	15,604	20,259	18,189
94,200	94,250	19,844	15,616	20,273	18,201
94,250	94,300	19,858	15,629	20,287	18,214
94,300	94,350	19,872	15,641	20,301	18,226
94,350	94,400	19,886	15,654	20,315	18,239
94,400	94,450	19,900	15,666	20,329	18,251
94,450	94,500	19,914	15,679	20,343	18,264
94,500	94,550	19,928	15,691	20,357	18,276
94,550	94,600	19,942	15,704	20,371	18,289
94,600	94,650	19,956	15,716	20,385	18,301
94,650	94,700	19,970	15,729	20,399	18,314
94,700	94,750	19,984	15,741	20,413	18,326
94,750	94,800	19,998	15,754	20,427	18,339
94,800	94,850	20,012	15,766	20,441	18,351
94,850	94,900	20,026	15,779	20,455	18,364
94,900	94,950	20,040	15,791	20,469	18,376
94,950	95,000	20,054	15,804	20,483	18,389
95,000					
95,000	95,050	20,068	15,816	20,497	18,401
95,050	95,100	20,082	15,829	20,511	18,414
95,100	95,150	20,096	15,841	20,525	18,426
95,150	95,200	20,110	15,854	20,539	18,439
95,200	95,250	20,124	15,866	20,553	18,451
95,250	95,300	20,138	15,879	20,567	18,464
95,300	95,350	20,152	15,891	20,581	18,476
95,350	95,400	20,166	15,904	20,595	18,489
95,400	95,450	20,180	15,916	20,609	18,501
95,450	95,500	20,194	15,929	20,623	18,514
95,500	95,550	20,208	15,941	20,637	18,526
95,550	95,600	20,222	15,954	20,651	18,539
95,600	95,650	20,236	15,966	20,665	18,551
95,650	95,700	20,250	15,979	20,679	18,564
95,700	95,750	20,264	15,991	20,693	18,576
95,750	95,800	20,278	16,004	20,707	18,589
95,800	95,850	20,292	16,016	20,721	18,601
95,850	95,900	20,306	16,029	20,735	18,614
95,900	95,950	20,320	16,041	20,749	18,626
95,950	96,000	20,334	16,054	20,763	18,639
96,000					
96,000	96,050	20,348	16,066	20,777	18,651
96,050	96,100	20,362	16,079	20,791	18,664
96,100	96,150	20,376	16,091	20,805	18,676
96,150	96,200	20,390	16,104	20,819	18,689
96,200	96,250	20,404	16,116	20,833	18,701
96,250	96,300	20,418	16,129	20,847	18,714
96,300	96,350	20,432	16,141	20,861	18,726
96,350	96,400	20,446	16,154	20,875	18,739
96,400	96,450	20,460	16,166	20,889	18,751
96,450	96,500	20,474	16,179	20,903	18,764
96,500	96,550	20,488	16,191	20,917	18,776
96,550	96,600	20,502	16,204	20,931	18,789
96,600	96,650	20,516	16,216	20,945	18,801
96,650	96,700	20,530	16,229	20,959	18,814
96,700	96,750	20,544	16,241	20,973	18,826
96,750	96,800	20,558	16,254	20,987	18,839
96,800	96,850	20,572	16,266	21,001	18,851
96,850	96,900	20,586	16,279	21,015	18,864
96,900	96,950	20,600	16,291	21,029	18,876
96,950	97,000	20,614	16,304	21,043	18,889
97,000					
97,000	97,050	20,628	16,316	21,057	18,901
97,050	97,100	20,642	16,329	21,071	18,914
97,100	97,150	20,656	16,341	21,085	18,926
97,150	97,200	20,670	16,354	21,099	18,939
97,200	97,250	20,684	16,366	21,113	18,951
97,250	97,300	20,698	16,379	21,127	18,964
97,300	97,350	20,712	16,391	21,141	18,976
97,350	97,400	20,726	16,404	21,155	18,989
97,400	97,450	20,740	16,416	21,169	19,001
97,450	97,500	20,754	16,429	21,183	19,014
97,500	97,550	20,768	16,441	21,197	19,026
97,550	97,600	20,782	16,454	21,211	19,039
97,600	97,650	20,796	16,466	21,225	19,051
97,650	97,700	20,810	16,479	21,239	19,064
97,700	97,750	20,824	16,491	21,253	19,076
97,750	97,800	20,838	16,504	21,267	19,089
97,800	97,850	20,852	16,516	21,281	19,101
97,850	97,900	20,866	16,529	21,295	19,114
97,900	97,950	20,880	16,541	21,309	19,126
97,950	98,000	20,894	16,554	21,323	19,139
98,000					
98,000	98,050	20,908	16,566	21,337	19,151
98,050	98,100	20,922	16,579	21,351	19,164
98,100	98,150	20,936	16,591	21,365	19,176
98,150	98,200	20,950	16,604	21,379	19,189
98,200	98,250	20,964	16,616	21,393	19,201
98,250	98,300	20,978	16,629	21,407	19,214
98,300	98,350	20,992	16,641	21,421	19,226
98,350	98,400	21,006	16,654	21,435	19,239
98,400	98,450	21,020	16,666	21,449	19,251
98,450	98,500	21,034	16,679	21,463	19,264
98,500	98,550	21,048	16,691	21,477	19,276
98,550	98,600	21,062	16,704	21,491	19,289
98,600	98,650	21,076	16,716	21,505	19,301
98,650	98,700	21,090	16,729	21,519	19,314
98,700	98,750	21,104	16,741	21,533	19,326
98,750	98,800	21,118	16,754	21,547	19,339
98,800	98,850	21,132	16,766	21,561	19,351
98,850	98,900	21,146	16,779	21,575	19,364
98,900	98,950	21,160	16,791	21,589	19,376
98,950	99,000	21,174	16,804	21,603	19,389
99,000					
99,000	99,050	21,188	16,816	21,617	19,401
99,050	99,100	21,202	16,829	21,631	19,414
99,100	99,150	21,216	16,841	21,645	19,426
99,150	99,200	21,230	16,854	21,659	19,439
99,200	99,250	21,244	16,866	21,673	19,451
99,250	99,300	21,258	16,879	21,687	19,464
99,300	99,350	21,272	16,891	21,701	19,476
99,350	99,400	21,286	16,904	21,715	19,489
99,400	99,450	21,300	16,916	21,729	19,501
99,450	99,500	21,314	16,929	21,743	19,514
99,500	99,550	21,328	16,941	21,757	19,526
99,550	99,600	21,342	16,954	21,771	19,539
99,600	99,650	21,356	16,966	21,785	19,551
99,650	99,700	21,370	16,979	21,799	19,564
99,700	99,750	21,384	16,991	21,813	19,576
99,750	99,800	21,398	17,004	21,827	19,589
99,800	99,850	21,412	17,016	21,841	19,601
99,850	99,900	21,426	17,029	21,855	19,614
99,900	99,950	21,440	17,041	21,869	19,626
99,950	100,000	21,454	17,054	21,883	19,639

$100,000 or over — use the Tax Computation Worksheet

Appendix 3

HISTORICAL IRS UNDERPAYMENT RATES

The following table was taken from http://www.taxalmanac.org/index.php/Federal_Underpayment_Interest_Rates. For greater certainty, please consult the following IRS website– http://www.irs.gov/irb/2012-13_IRB/ar07.html.

Year	Qtr 1 1/01–3/31	Qtr 2 4/01–6/30	Qtr 3 7/01–9/30	Qtr 4 10/01–12/31
2012	3%	3%	3%	3%
2011	3%	4%	4%	3%
2010	4%	4%	4%	4%
2009	5%	4%	4%	4%
2008	7%	6%	5%	6%
2007	8%	8%	8%	8%
2006	7%	7%	8%	8%
2005	5%	6%	6%	7%
2004	4%	5%	4%	5%
2003	5%	5%	5%	4%
2002	6%	6%	6%	6%
2001	9%	8%	7%	7%
2000	8%	9%	9%	9%
1999	7%	8%	8%	8%
1998	9%	8%	8%	8%
1997	9%	9%	9%	9%
1996	9%	8%	9%	9%
1995	9%	10%	9%	9%
1994	7%	7%	8%	9%
1993	7%	7%	7%	7%
1992	9%	8%	8%	7%
1991	11%	10%	10%	10%
1990	11%	11%	11%	11%
1989	11%	12%	12%	11%
1988	11%	10%	10%	11%
1987	9%	9%	9%	10%
1986	10%	10%	9%	9%
1985	13%	13%	11%	11%
1984	11%	11%	11%	11%
1983	16%	16%	11%	11%

INDEX

A

AMT, *see* Alternative minimum tax
Adjusted cost basis calculation, 62–63, 81–83
Adjusted gross income, 123
Alternative minimum tax (AMT), 192–193
American opportunity credit, 218, 257–258, 259–264
Assets, selling
  capital gains/losses, 61
  ordinary gains/losses, 61
Audit by IRS, 323–324

B

Bonds, *see* Stocks, bonds, and US mutual funds
Business expenses for certain employees, *see* Employee expenses/business deductions

C

Canadian banks
  IRS information sharing, 3
Canadian mutual funds, 291
  Form 8621, 292–293
  mark-to-market election, 296–299
  passive foreign investment corporation tests, 292
  QEF election, 293–295
  reporting, 291–292
  section 1291 fund, 300–304
Capital gains or losses, 49, 61
  adjusted cost basis, calculating, 62–63
  calculating, 61–62, 83–84
  Form 8949, 64
  loss carryovers, 68–69
  reporting, 63–68, 83–89
Casualty and theft losses deduction, 169
  casualty loss defined, 169
  computing value of a loss, 170–173
  deduction limits, 173–174
  proving a loss, 170
  reporting of, 174–175
  theft defined, 170
Charitable contributions deduction, 165
  deduction limits, 167
  eligible contributions, 166
  qualified organizations, 165–166
  reporting of, 167–168
Child and dependent care expenses credit, 215, 241
  amount of credit, 243
  eligibility for, 241–242
  eligible expenses, 242
  Form 2441, 243–245
  limitations on expenses, 242
Child tax credit, 216, 218, 247
  credit amount, 248
  qualifying child, 247
Currency conversion, 11–12

D

Deductions, *see also* Medical and dental expenses deduction, Taxes paid deduction, Mortgage interest deduction, Investment interest deduction, Charitable contributions deduction, Casualty and theft losses deduction, Employee expenses/business deductions, Miscellaneous deductions
  amount of standard, 142–143
  itemized deductions, 143–144
    limits on, 145
    reporting of, 144–145
  itemized or standard choice, 141
Dependents, 41–43
  children, 41–42
  relatives, 42–43
Dividend income, 48
  more than $1500, 59–60
  ordinary dividends, 55–56
  qualified dividends, 57–59
  reporting, 57, 59

E

Earned income tax credit, 218
Education tax credit, 215–216, 257
- American opportunity credit, 218, 257–258, 259–264
- ineligibility to claim, 258
- lifetime learning credit, 257–258, 264–267

Educator expenses, 123
Elderly or disabled tax credit, 251
- claiming, 252–255
- credit limit, 252
- qualifying for, 251–252

Employee expenses/business deductions, 123–124, 177
- deduction limited, 184–185
- entertainment expenses, 178–179
- gift expenses, 180
- record keeping, 181–183
- reporting of, 183–184
- transportation expenses, 180–181
- travel expenses, 177–178

Employment insurance benefits, 50
Estate and gift tax
- estate tax, 279–280
- gift tax, 280

Estimated tax, 209, 217
- calculation of, 210, 211
- payment mechanisms, 211
- penalties, 211–212
- when to pay, 210
- who owes, 209–210

Exclusions, *see* Foreign earned income exclusion, *see* Foreign housing income exclusion

F

FBAR, *see* Foreign bank and financial accounts
Farm income, 50
Filing due dates of returns, 9–10
- extensions, 10

Filing status, 18–19, 40–41
First-time home buyer credit, 218
Foreign bank and financial accounts (FBAR), 309
- FBAR form, 310
- how and when to file FBAR, 309
- penalties, 311
- who must file FBAR form, 309

Foreign earned income exclusion, 21, 109
- amount to exclude, 112
- consequences of taking, 120
- eligibility for, 21–23
- Forms 2555-EZ and 1040, 23–27
- moving expenses and, 129–130
- qualifying for, tests, 110–112
  - *bona fide* residence test, 111
  - physical presence test, 111
  - tax home, 110
- reporting of, 112–114
- types of income to exclude, 109–110

Foreign financial interests exceeding $200,000, 313
- Form 8938, 314–317
- penalties, 319–320
- reporting threshold, 313–314

Foreign housing income exclusion, 109
- calculation of, 115–116
- consequences of taking, 120
- qualifying for, 114
- reporting of, 116–119
- types of income to exclude, 109–110

Foreign tax credit, 215, 221
- eligible taxes, 222
- Form 1116, 224–230
- income by categories, 223
- income by source, 222

Form 1040
- introduction to, 15–16, 31
- reproduced, 32–33

Forms and publications, IRS, 7

G

Gambling income, 51

H

Health savings account deduction, 124
Home, sale of
- amount realized (sale price), 83
- calculating adjusted cost base, 81–83
- calculating basis (cost), 79–81
- calculating capital gain/loss, 83–84
  - gain larger than exclusion, 87
- main home (principal residence), 79, 84
- not main home real estate sale, 90
- reporting capital gain/loss, 84–89

I

IRA, *see* Investment retirement account
Income
alimony, 49
business income, self-employed, 49
capital gains or losses, 49
dividend, 48, *see also* Dividend income
employment insurance benefits, 50
farm, 50
interest, 48, *see also* Interest income
IRA distributions, 50
ordinary gains and losses, 49, 61
other income, 51
pension and annuities, 50
rental real estate, 95, *see also* Rental property income
retirement, *see* Retirement income
social security benefits, 50
state and local tax refunds, 48–49
wages and salary, 47–48
Individual taxpayer identification number (ITIN), 17–18
acquisition of, 39
Interest income, 48, 53–55
more than $1500, 59–60
tax-exempt, 55
tax free savings account, 48
Investment interest deduction, 161
deductible, 161
limitations on, 162
non-deductible, 161–162
reporting of, 162–163
Investment retirement account (IRA)
deduction, 125
distributions, 50

L

Lifetime learning credit, 257–258, 264–267

M

MAGI, *see* Modified annual gross income
Main home (principal residence), 79, 84
Medical and dental expenses deduction, 147
deductible expenses, 147–149
deduction limitations, 151
non-deductible expenses, 149
reimbursements of expenses, 150
reporting of, 151–152
whose can be deducted, 147
Miscellaneous deductions, 187–188
tax preparation fees, 187
Modified annual gross income (MAGI), 136–137
Mortgage interest deduction, 157
fully deductible, 157–158
partially deductible, 158–159
reporting of, 159–160
Moving expenses, 124, 127
criteria to claim, 127
deductible expenses, 128
foreign earned income exclusion, and, 129–130
non-deductible expenses, 128
reporting of, 129
Mutual funds, Canadian, *see* Canadian mutual funds
Mutual funds, US, *see* Stocks, bonds, and US mutual funds

O

Ordinary gains and losses, 49, 61
Overdue tax returns, 285
amnesty eligibility, 285–286

P

Pension and annuities income, 50
non-taxable pension income, 94
Publications and forms, IRS, 7

R

RDSP, see Registered disability savings plan
RESP, *see* Registered education savings plan
RRSP, *see* Registered retirement savings plan
Refundable tax credits, 219
Registered disability savings plan (RDSP), 305–307
Registered education savings plan (RESP), 305–307

Registered retirement savings plan (RRSP), 287
 deduction of RRSP contributions on US return, 288–289
 Form 8833, 288
 Form 8891, 287
 how to defer tax payable, 287–288
Rental property income
 classification of rental property, 95–96
 depreciation, 98, 100–101, 105
 for profit rental property, 96–104
  calculating basis (cost), 98–100
  calculating expenses, 96–97
  calculating income, 96
  reporting of, 102–104
 losses from rental real estate, 100–102
 personal use rental property, 105–107
  calculating expenses, 105
  calculating income, 105
  reporting income and expenses, 106–107
Residential energy tax credit, 216
Retirement income
 non-taxable pension income, 94
 reporting of, 93–94
 social security benefits, 94
 types of, 91–93
Retirement savings contribution tax credit, 216

S

Self-employment deductions, 124
Self-employment income, 49
Selling assets, *see* Assets, selling
Social security benefits, 50
Social security number, 16–17
 acquisition of, 37–39
 individual taxpayer identification number (ITIN), 17–18
Software, tax, 6–7
Spouse, non-US citizen
 election to treat as US citizen, 19–20
State and local taxes, 271
 domicile defined, 272–273
 refunds, 48–49
 residency determination, 271–272
 rules for each state, chart, 273–276
Stocks, bonds, and US mutual funds
 calculating basis (cost), 71–72
 gains/losses from sale, 71
  calculation of, 72–73
  reporting of, 73–78
 length of ownership, 73
Student loan interest deduction, 125, 131
 eligible education institution, 132
 foreign earned income and housing exclusions, and, 132–133
 qualified higher education expenses, 131–132
 qualified student loan, 131
 reporting of, 133

T

TFSA, *see* Tax free savings account
Tax credits, *see* Child and dependent care expenses credit, Child tax credit, Earned income tax credit, Education tax credit, Elderly or disabled tax credit, Foreign tax credit, Residential energy tax credit, Retirement savings contribution tax credit
 other credits, 216
Tax, estimated, *see* Estimated tax
Taxes owed calculation, 191–207
 did not take foreign earned income exclusion, 197–202
 took foreign earned income exclusion, 202–207
Taxes paid deduction, 153
 deductible taxes, 153–154
 foreign earned income and/or housing exclusions, and, 154–155
 non-deductible taxes, 154
 reporting of, 155–156
Tax free savings account (TFSA), 48, 305–307
Tax returns, *see also* Overdue tax returns
 how to file, 10–11
 who must file, 9
Tuition fees deduction, 125, 135
 eligible education institution, 136
 eligible expenses, 136
 eligible student, 136
 income cut-off, 136–137
 reporting of, 137–138
 who can claim, 135
 who cannot claim, 135–136

U

US citizen defined, 9
US citizenship renunciation, 327
    appointment with US consulate, 327–328
    final US tax return, 329–331
    Form 8854, 329–335

W

Wages and salary, 47–48
Who must file US return, 9
W-2 form, 21